WITHDRAWN

Clinton Heylin

SUMMIT BOOKS

New York   London   Toronto
Sydney   Tokyo   Singapore

A Biography

BOB DYLAN

Behind the Shades

Summit Books
Simon & Schuster Building
Rockefeller Center
1230 Avenue of the Americas
New York, New York 10020

SUMMIT BOOKS and colophon are trademarks
of Simon & Schuster Inc.

Designed by Nina D'Amario / Levavi & Levavi
Manufactured in the United States of America

10 9 8 7 6 5 4 3 2 1

Library of Congress Cataloging in Publication Data

Heylin, Clinton.
    Bob Dylan : behind the shades : a biography / Clinton Heylin,
        p.   cm.
    "A Bob Dylan sessionography, 1961–90": p.
    Includes bibliographical references and index.
    1. Dylan, Bob, 1941–   .   2. Singers—United States—Biography,
I. Title.
ML420.D98H49   1991
782.42162′0092—dc20
[B]   91-8858
                                                                    CIP
                                                                    MN

ISBN 0-671-73894-1

Contents

Contents

For Jill, "the girl with me behind the shades," and pretty Penny-O

Acknowledgments

I would like to thank first the editor of *The Telegraph*, John Bauldie, for his generosity with the resources of *Wanted Man* and for the use of the many important interviews he has undertaken on behalf of *Wanted Man*.

I would also like to thank all my fellow *Wanted Man* subscribers who have carried out interviews on the behalf of the *Telegraph* and other Dylan-related publications and have thus provided such an impressive archive of Dylan's career. They are: Jonathan Morley, Chris Cooper, Reid Kopel, Marcus Whitman, Jorgen Lindstrom, Ake Johnson, Arne Hartelius, Patrick Humphries, Jacques Van Son, Val Lawlan, Spencer Leigh, Brian Wells, Roger Gibbons, Chris Hockenhull, Graham Barrett, Miles, John Hinchey, Stephen Pickering, Wes Stace, Andy Bell and Adrian Deevoy.

Thanks to all those who have given gladly of their time to discuss their association with Dylan, whether to myself or to the people noted above. Especial thanks to Kenny Aaronson, Ira Ingber, Markus Innocenti and Eddie Arno, Al Kooper, Farida McFree, Scarlet Rivera, Rob Stoner, Anthea Joseph, Howie Wyeth and Pete Seeger.

Thanks for general help in putting me in touch with important people in this story and/or for generosity with their archives and hospitality: Mitch Blank, Glen Dundas, Dalton Deelan, Susan and Mike Decapite, Raymond Foye, Pete Howard, Bruce Gary, Harvey Kornhaber, Larry Hansen, Steve Keene, Pete Vincent, Rob Whitehouse, Ian Woodward and Paul Williams.

Finally thanks to my friends Pete Vincent, John Lindley and Steve Shepard, to Dominick Anfuso at Summit and to my enthusiastic editor at Penguin, Tony Lacey, for their comments, opinions and brickbats about the various manuscripts this book has passed through. Whatever the finished version may offer, it would have been an inferior book indeed without them.

Permissions

Preface

In the beginning was Scaduto. It was 1971. For five long years Bob Dylan had maintained a public profile that Howard Hughes would have been proud of. Anthony Scaduto's was the first serious biography of the man, at a time when there was little information about his roots, his early life and his dreams of fame. It dutifully recorded his small-town youth in Hibbing, Minnesota, his year in Minneapolis and his early days in New York. By 1965 Dylan had outgrown the former friends Scaduto had talked to, and in its final section Scaduto's previously racy book, bereft of any major sources except Dylan's own rewriting of his history in cagey interviews with the author, dissipated into song analysis and speculation.

It was another fifteen years before the publication of the second serious Dylan biography. In that time Dylan had reached the peak of his commercial success, released perhaps his most perfect album, converted to born-again Christianity and embarked on a series of tours all exceeding in scope his mid-sixties touring activities. On September 29, 1986—the twenty-fifth anniversary of his famous original endorsement of Dylan in *The New York Times*—Robert Shelton published his own long-awaited biography of his old friend.

Shelton's plans for a book had been first mentioned in the summer of 1966. The volume had been two decades in the making. Not surprisingly, given the level of expectation, it was a profound disappointment. He barely advanced the story beyond Dylan's fabled 1966 motorcycle accident, and much of the chunky tome was filled with pat song analysis and clippings-file outtakes. Though he filled important gaps in Scaduto's narrative of the early years, Shelton did Dylan a great disservice by interring him in the period he had already spent twenty years trying to live down.

Since Shelton there has been one pretender to the title of serious Dylan biographer. In the fall of 1988 Bob Spitz, author of a previous book on the 1969

Woodstock festival, published a biography as expansive as Shelton's and as racy as Scaduto's. Yet, despite conducting many original interviews, Spitz did not advance Dylan's story. His interviewees were mostly the familiar names used by Scaduto and Shelton, and his Albert Goldman approach, excruciating prose style, dubious sense of Dylan's history and—yet again—virtual exclusion of Dylan's postaccident career resulted in what one reviewer described appositely as "a thick, petrified, one-pound hunk of wood-fiber."

Now Bob Dylan is fifty. It is twenty-five years since he fell off his motorcycle in Woodstock, yet the history of those twenty-five years remains untold. Two thirds of this book is devoted to Dylan's postaccident career. It is my intention to show the full sweep of his life to date, and his postaccident years actually represent five sixths of his entire recording career.

Of course, Bob Dylan's rise to fame is an important part of his story, and the first section of *Bob Dylan: Behind the Shades* deals with the well-documented preaccident years. Though Scaduto and Shelton have provided good coverage of this period, I have tried to follow a particular thread that I find weaving in and out of their books, but rarely overtly: What made Dylan so different from his contemporaries in Hibbing, in Minneapolis, in Greenwich Village and among the pop music icons of the mid-sixties? Why did he continue to grow when others, equally regarded, stagnated? The ability constantly to reinvent who Bob Dylan was, and is, remains the primary characteristic of his art. It is the way he unleashes new works. The process may be subtler now, but it remains apparent. In the early and mid-sixties the reinventions proceeded at such a frantic pace it actually seemed as if Dylan had no control over his chameleon changes. It is likely that Dylan never really knew in those days how close he was to the precipice.

How Dylan has coped with the legacy of those "amphetamine years" is an equally remarkable story. Like another "would-be genius," Orson Welles, he is generally thought to have created his masterpiece before he was even twenty-five, and then spent the next twenty-five years twisting in the wind determined to assert himself as an abidingly creative artist. But unlike Welles, he did manage to surpass his youthful masterpiece, the *Blonde on Blonde* album, with the remarkable *Blood on the Tracks*, and came close twice more during his so-called religious period.

If the motorcycle accident represents an obvious demarcation point in Dylan's career, his religious conversion has been the other major break with his past. That his postconversion career has been detailed in less than thirty pages by both Spitz and Shelton does a grave injustice to a major period of Dylan's ever-changing career. Though the last decade reads as a catalog of missed chances and poor judgment, it is the story of a very personal battle to construct a worldview that retains his faith in both God and humanity. The struggle has led to its fair share of great Dylan songs. Yet if the story in Part Two of *Bob Dylan: Behind the Shades* in no way parallels Orson Welles's post–*Citizen Kane* career, the Part Three narrative is rather similar in its repeated hints of revival and in the promise of masterpieces often unfulfilled or rendered minor by lack of discipline, poor judgment or the neophobic impulses of others, though the release of *Oh Mercy* and *Under the Red Sky* enables a tinge of optimism to color the final pages of my book.

How much do the works reflect the man? That was the question I constantly asked myself while writing this book. Of course, if the works do not reflect the man, then the story still needed to be told but from a different viewpoint: Why are the works so different from the man? In Dylan's case, though, his works reflect his state of mind.

Dylan's perennial reinventions of himself led me to structure this book around each new guise that he has taken upon himself. In most cases a chapter revolves around a major work or tour introducing a new Dylan (e.g., *Another Side of Bob Dylan, Blood on the Tracks, Tarantula, Renaldo and Clara*, the Rolling Thunder tours). It is a convenient form to use, but it is only a convenience.

Dylan's career could as easily be divided by where he lived. Certain chapters fit neatly into the geographic notion, coinciding with artistic periods as well. Thus, his 1960 apprenticeship in Minneapolis marks an obvious divide. His fleeing New York for Durango, and finally settling in Malibu, again marked an important change, while his "retreat" (1966–69) is often referred to as his Woodstock Period (a slight misnomer, given that he had been spending most of his free time there since 1964). Certain albums have been the product of Dylan's geography: Most of *Another Side* was written in Greece in May 1964; *The Basement Tapes* was written and recorded in Woodstock; *New Morning* was the first product of his return to New York City at the end of 1969; *Blood on the Tracks* was largely composed during a summer on his Minnesota farm, as was *Street-Legal*. Yet ultimately the locale is only a part of what inspires Dylan to his finest moments, certainly not the *raison d'être* of his work.

A credible biography is a bringing together of such strands. It draws from all and distills down to a point of view. With a living artist the picture can never be complete. Dylan surely has many years of creativity left in him, so this book can only be a signpost along the way. Dylan also is a difficult subject because he has trusted people and they have repaid him accordingly. Many of the most important people in his life have refused to talk about their relationship with him. Largely absent from this book are the voices of his wife, Sara; his ex-manager, the late Albert Grossman; and his confidants Victor Maimudes and Bobby Neuwirth. Fortunately, most of his important musical collaborators have been less recalcitrant.

Dylan himself cooperated with both Scaduto and Shelton in the composition of their books, freely giving interviews and, in Shelton's case, suggesting people he should contact. Yet in both cases there was a price to pay. Though neither book could be described as authorized, Dylan exerted his influence upon both. Inevitably this led to a slightly sanitized portrait of the man, particularly in Shelton's book. Spitz, predictably, went to the other extreme and chronicled each and every tale of anyone who had a chip on his shoulder and a grudge to bear. Dylan, like most biographical subjects, is not looking for an accurate portrayal but a favorable one. To quote Orson Welles, "I don't want any description of me to be accurate, I want it to be flattering. I don't think people who have to sing for their supper ever like to be described truthfully—not in print anyway."

Dylan's voice, though freely represented in this book, is not the voice of a man presenting an authorized portrait of himself, save perhaps in the few instances where I have drawn from his comments in the *Biograph* booklet. His words have been selected from over two hundred interviews he has given in the last thirty years, from raps he gave at concerts in his more gregarious days, from bio-poems he has written. It is one of the great myths of Dylan lore that his interviews are invariably a stream of put-ons and put-downs. In fact, at certain points in his life, notably in 1978 and 1985, he has been very eager to talk about his past in a surprisingly frank and honest manner. Readers will find Dylan's voice represented here on a far greater scale than in previous biographies, but without a concomitant personal influence upon the finished product.

Many of those who offer their version of Dylan here did not do so for this book, though certainly they were aware they were contributing to a detailed chronicling of his career. Most of the original interviews quoted were conducted over the last nine years, intended for and published in *The Telegraph,*the journal of Wanted Man, the Bob Dylan Information Office. The majority of these were conducted by myself or John Bauldie, cofounder with me of *Wanted Man* and editor of *The Telegraph.* I consider the use of this archive of exclusive interviews to be one of the book's strengths. People do not talk to a biographer the way they talk to someone from what could be referred to as a cross between a very high-quality fanzine and a critical quarterly.

The use of this impressive archive of interviews, I believe, enables a far more accurate portrait than the one that would have resulted from the guarded interviews I might have obtained in the guise of biographer. I trust I have performed no disservice to those who freely gave of their time for the purpose of being interviewed about Dylan, and I hope they will share my belief that the result is considerably fairer and more accurate than previous Dylan biographies have been.

I have tried to give each commentator his own voice, rather than provide a secondhand paraphrase of what has been said. I trust the reader will feel a sense of Dylan's many-sided self through his verbatim recollections and the recollections of those around him, a feeling that for me rarely comes through in other accounts of him. Needless to say, I have tried to document what I believe really happened, but the reader must be aware that there is much myth-building at stake here and that Dylan's friends and collaborators revel in that process as much as the man himself does. For each brick I pull down, there may well be another put in its place.

Finally, I should like to comment on the viewpoint from which this book was written. I hope that readers will find *Bob Dylan: Behind the Shades* an invigorating mixture of original research, cutting-file hopping and skeptical but informed commentary. What will readily be apparent from the book is that I believe that Dylan is (not "was") an artistic genius. Though popular art forms have produced few such geniuses, scarcely a handful in the sixty years of mass communication introduced by the talkie era (my own selection, in case you may be curious, totals only four: Fred Astaire, Orson Welles, Bob Dylan and Jimi Hendrix), the notion that popular art cannot by its nature produce them is absurd.

Though a reader who does not share my appraisal of Dylan will still find his story a fascinating one, he will find it hard not to notice an abiding faith in the quality of Dylan's work. This does not mean that I am wholly, or indeed largely, uncritical of Dylan. Indeed, the way that he has (mis)used his talents at points in his career is dealt with at length in *Bob Dylan: Behind the Shades*. Still, those who are looking for an exposé of a fraudulent sixties icon will be sadly disappointed. After all, "to live outside the law you must be honest."

Clinton Heylin, August 1990

Part
1

Busy Being Born...

1 | 1941–59: In My Younger Days

Bob Dylan: My country is the Minnesota–North Dakota territory / that's where I was born an learned how t walk / an it's where I was raised an went to school . . . my youth was spent wildly among the snowy hills an sky blue lakes, willow fields an abandoned open pit mines / contrary t rumors, I am very proud of where I'm from an also of the many blood streams that run in my roots. [1963]

At a 1986 press conference a middle-aged, prematurely wizened old rock and roller insisted, "I'm only Bob Dylan when I have to be." Asked who he was the rest of the time, he replied, "Myself." In 1986 Bob Dylan was twenty-six years old. His creator, Robert Allen Zimmerman, was forty-five. An inevitable fascination with the roots of this creator of his own mythology has meant that the path of Bob Dylan's youth has become a well-worn one, though Robert Zimmerman's search for a new identity was only belatedly apparent in his final two years in high school.

Each biographer has filled in progressively more detail, but in essence the story remains the one told by Anthony Scaduto in his 1971 biography, indeed by Toby Thompson in his 1969 articles on Dylan's youth in *The Village Voice*. That story is: Dylan was born a Jew named Robert Allen Zimmerman on May 24, 1941, in Duluth, Minnesota; he moved with his family to Hibbing, seventy miles away, when not yet seven; by adolescence he had rejected his heritage, formed several rock and roll bands and was seeking an escape from the suffocating conformity of his hometown, Hibbing; meanwhile he met Echo Helstrom, his original Girl from the North Country, with whom he shared many of his later days at high school, waiting to bust the chains and head down Highway 61, to Minneapolis.

That standard biography tends to deal with Robert Zimmerman's sense of rebellion primarily in terms of a rejection of his Jewish identity rather than a rebuttal of the limits placed on imagination by the bulk of the citizens of Hibbing (he has often talked about the visions he had as a youth and how they sustained him).

This conventional "bio" underestimates the sense of community he felt as a Jew, at least until well into adolescence. It also fails to emphasize how eclectic he was in his selection of early heroes, musical and celluloid (his catholic influences would be a key factor in his subsequent success), and his own uncertainty about how and when to leave the confines of small-town America.

Most of all, though, it fails to explain why Robert Zimmerman should desire a new identity, should wish to reinvent himself—an integral part of his rejection of Hibbing. When Robert Zimmerman became Bob Dylan, or indeed Elston Gunn or any of his other unknown new identities, it was an attempt to disavow his small-town background.

The Jewish community in Hibbing in the late forties and fifties was small; the Jews were a minority in an essentially Catholic infrastructure. From an early age Jews were aware of an undercurrent of anti-Semitism, which led them to form a close-knit group. The Jews of Hibbing looked to the larger town of Duluth for cultural activities and religious guidance.

Robert Zimmerman's mother, the former Beattie Stone, came from a solid middle-class family, and it was mostly her relatives who resided in Hibbing. His father, Abraham Zimmerman, was himself from Duluth, but had moved to Hibbing at Beattie's bidding in 1947, shortly after she gave birth to Robert's younger brother, David.

Beattie Zimmerman: My grandfather owned the theaters, that would be Bob's great-grandfather. His grandfather on his father's side had a shoe store in Duluth. Then we had an appliance store in Hibbing. We moved back because that was my hometown. I was born and raised in Hibbing.

According to Dylan, there was another important reason why the family moved back to Hibbing:

Bob Dylan: My grandfather had come over from Russia in the 1920s. He was a peddler and made shoes. . . . My father was a very active man, but he was stricken very early by an attack of polio. The illness put and end to all his dreams. . . . When we moved from the North of the country two of his brothers, who were electrical fitters, opened a shop and they took him with them so that he could mind the shop. [1978]

His father's electrical-goods store gave Robert Zimmerman a secure, stable environment to grow up in, unlike many on the Minnesota Range. Hibbing's primary source of income was the huge open-pit mine that provided America with much of its iron ore up to the end of the Second World War. After the war, Hibbing slipped into a steady decline, something that obviously affected the impressionable young Zimmerman, who would store his memories up until a time when they could come out in song.* He later told Chris Welles of *Life* magazine:

Bob Dylan: I was born with death around me. I was raised in a town that was dying. There weren't no need for that town to die. It was a perfectly valid town. [1964]

Not surprisingly in such a small community, Robert Zimmerman was related to most of the Jews in Hibbing. In his own words, "My grandmother had about seventeen kids on the one side, and on the other side about thirteen kids. So there was always a lot of family-type people around."

Bob Dylan: When I was young, my life was built around the family. We got together all the time. There weren't many Jews around. [1978]

According to Dylan, at about the time Robert Zimmerman was due to be bar mitzvahed the Jews in Hibbing needed to find a new rabbi.

Bob Dylan: The town didn't have a rabbi, and it was time for me to be bar mitzvahed. Suddenly a rabbi showed up under strange circumstances for only a year. He and his wife got off the bus in the middle of winter. He showed up just in time for me to learn this stuff. He was an old man from Brooklyn who had a white beard and wore a black hat and black clothes. They put him upstairs above the café, which was the local hangout. It was a rock and roll café where I used to hang out, too. I used to go up there every day to learn this stuff, either after school or after dinner. After studying with him an hour or so, I'd come down and boogie. [1985]

Like most Dylan anecdotes, this tale contains its share of inaccuracies. Robert's bar mitzvah was in the spring of 1954. He could hardly have been playing or listening to rock and roll. Nevertheless, it indicates the sense of isolation the Jews in Hibbing felt that they should have only a temporary rabbi residing above a local café.

---

* The composition most overtly derived from these childhood memories would be "North Country Blues," released on his January 1964 album, *The Times They Are a-Changin'*.

The only hint of things to come evinced by young Robert before his bar mitzvah was an early proclivity for writing poetry. Shelton's biography details two poems written at the age of ten to his mother and father, and he was, according to his mother, a prodigious writer of poetry throughout his youth. When talking to TV host Les Crane in 1965, Dylan was at pains to separate his early scribblings from his later songwriting impulses.

Bob Dylan: Well, I started writing a long time ago. You know how you write, you write these insane things down when you really don't know what else to do. That's when I started writing. When I started writing songs—that's a different story. I started writing songs after I heard Hank Williams. [1965]

If rock and roll is generally perceived as having been Robert Zimmerman's first love, it was country music that first inspired him. Early in 1955 he discovered "all sorts of Hanks," as he would later put it.

Bob Dylan: You know, where I'm from I only heard country music from Hank Williams, Hank Snow, Hank Payne. [1980]

His first real idol was Hank Williams. Like many of his later role models— James Dean, Woody Guthrie (whose crippling disease lingered but who was creatively dead by the mid-fifties), Robert Johnson, Arthur Rimbaud—Williams died young, his legacy possibly the most impressive corpus of songs in country music. He was found dead in the back of a car on the way to a gig, on New Year's Day 1953, at the age of twenty-nine.

Bob Dylan: I started singing . . . when I was about ten—ten or eleven—and started out just country and western—Hank Williams, Lefty Frizzell kind of things. [1966]

In September 1955, Robert's second idol, James Dean, was killed in an automobile accident near Paso Robles in California, at the age of twenty-four. If Hank Williams gave the young Zimmerman a sound, Dean gave him an image. A composite of the characters Dean played in *Rebel without a Cause* and *East of Eden* became the first adopted image of Robert Zimmerman. The teenage angst of Dean seemed to mirror directly the sense of isolation of Robert Zimmerman and a hundred thousand other teenagers.

Bob Dylan: [I liked James Dean for the] same reason you liked anybody, I guess. You see somethin' of yourself in them. [1987]

Bill Marinac: The two of us went to *Rebel without a Cause* a couple of times. And he kept going—I think he went at least four times. He was one of the first to get a red jacket like James Dean. That was a good film. It made a really big impact on us. I think it was the times. Maybe you had to be there, in a small town in the fifties.

There is nothing profound or revelatory about a teenager searching for identity. Robert Zimmerman in 1955 was fourteen, the archetypal age of rebellion. What made this individual different was that his quest for an identity would be unceasing, going far beyond the simple expedient of finding a comfortable niche in society. Robert Zimmerman aka Bob Dylan would constantly reinvent himself, year in, year out.

In 1956 Zimmerman, along with much of teenage America, discovered rock and roll. Like many of his contemporaries in small-town America, young Robert's connection with this new music was mainly through the radio stations that late at night beamed to outposts of civilization like Hibbing. Much has been written about the sociological impact of rock and roll. Suffice to say that Robert Zimmerman found a new purpose in the music. The lyrics crystallized all his feelings of ambition, rebellion and individual identity while the music made his body move from the groin out. Hibbing no longer represented a frontier to his aspirations.

Bob Dylan: I was never gonna be anything else, never. I was playing when I was twelve years old, and that was all I wanted to do—play my guitar. [1984]

Young Robert would have to wait one more year before he could get his first motorcycle and be mobile enough to attend gigs, taking off on weekends either in his father's car or on his bike. Duluth was the closest any live rock and roll act was likely to play.

Yet if he was unable to see live rock and roll, young Robert could always make his own. At the age of fifteen, as rock and roll music was making its first serious assault on American consciousness, Zimmerman started playing with the Hibbing high school band which consisted of Chuck Nara, Tony Connors, Bill Marinac, Larry Fabbro, John Shepard and now himself, though he quickly aspired to form his own band.

Though Dylan claimed to have played guitar from the age of twelve and piano at some point shortly afterward, Monte Edwardson, with whom he formed his own first band, said Robert Zimmerman in 1956 played the piano, and came to learn the guitar only when Edwardson showed him the basics some time in 1957.

This makes some kind of sense. The Zimmermans had a piano, which Robert's younger brother, David, had begun to play at a young age, becoming an accomplished musician in his own right. Robert never had the necessary discipline for formal training, but between the ages of twelve and fourteen he started to pound out a rudimentary rhythm on the keys. Even at this stage the rhythm was the thing, melody just a minor incursion.

Val Petersen (Hibbing High music teacher): When Bobby played the piano he would stand and really pound it. But when David played, he sat and played very nicely.

The chronology of Robert Zimmerman's many teenage bands is a confusing one. It would appear that the first of his own bands was with Bill Marinac, Larry Fabbro and Chuck Nara and was probably called the Shadow Blasters.

Bill Marinac: I had a big old Zenith radio in my basement. My dad had an antenna hooked up to the TV antenna. We'd sit there with our instruments and try to copy the music lines right off the radio. His dad had a hookup like that in their house. Our parents were very understanding.

The Shadow Blasters' only gig of note came in the summer or fall of 1956 when they auditioned for College Capers, a talent contest organized by Hibbing Junior College. The quartet ran through their one Little Richard tune (probably "Long Tall Sally"), though Robert was barely audible. Hibbing was not attuned to such hollerin' and the Shadow Blasters did not make the College Capers. Unlike Zimmerman, Nara, Fabbro and Marinac had no serious musical intentions, and the band disbanded shortly after the College Capers debacle. By the end of 1956, Robert had formed his second and most famous Hibbing band, the Golden Chords, with Leroy Hoikkala and Monte Edwardson. This band would last until the spring of 1958, debuting at the high school Jacket Jamboree Festival early in 1957, at which they were by far the loudest and most raucous band to play. They then began to play regularly at Van Feldt's snack bar and a small barbecue joint called Collier's on Sunday afternoons; these were more like jam sessions with an audience present than full-blown gigs. Nevertheless, by this point rock and roll had assumed bona fide teenage revolution status, and though Hibbing's teenagers may have realized the Golden Chords were no great shakes, they were still the only rock and roll combo they had.

Leroy Hoikkala: He was improvising quite a lot, and he was really good at it. . . . He'd hear a song and make up his own version of it.

Their most talked-about show was in February 1958 when they played the Winter Frolic Talent Contest and supposedly received an enthusiastic response from the 250 kids packed into the little theater of the Hibbing Memorial Building, though their brand of music was never going to win the actual talent contest, which was decided by parents and teachers. Even at this point Zimmerman seems to have realized he was doing something different, and somehow threatening.

Bob Dylan: We were just the loudest band around. . . . What we were doing, there wasn't anyone else around doing. [The music scene] was mostly horn kind of stuff, jazz—there was one other band in town with trumpet, bass, guitar and drums. Mostly that type of stuff. And you had to play polkas. [1986]

"Success," however limited, inevitably meant a degree of notoriety at school. After the Chords' debut at the Jacket Jamboree Festival, Robert Zimmerman's fellow pupils noted the contrast between his performing self and his introverted nature in class.

George Haben: He would get up [at school] and do songs, imitating Elvis and so on, and it was hilarious! To hear this wild singing coming out of a boy who kept to himself, [who] was really very quiet.

By the summer of 1958, Zimmerman had formed his last Hibbing band, Elston Gunn and the Rock Boppers. According to his then-girlfiend, Echo Helstrom, it was during that summer Bob Zimmerman ran around to her place and informed her that he had found a stage name, and it was Bob Dillon. In fact, this is extremely unlikely. Since he had formed a band called Elston Gunn and the Rock Boppers, and later, according to Bobby Vee, asked to be called Elston Gunn when he joined Vee's band, it is likely that Helstrom's memory is faulty. Robert Zimmerman may well have chosen his first pseudonym at this time, but it was in all likelihood Elston Gunn. It was probably this band that Helstrom remembers being booed at the St. Louis County Fair in Hibbing that summer.

Echo Helstrom: Bob was pretty serious about his band and they practiced a lot. It was all a blues sound then. . . . Bob sang and played the piano, and he used to practice with the band in garages around the neighborhood. Nobody liked their music much, least of all Bob's voice. . . . He and the band played around town fairly often, at school assemblies, at the youth club and at Collier's Barbecue. At Collier's it wasn't so bad . . . but in the big auditoriums people would laugh and hoot at Bob.

Robert Zimmerman seemed oblivious to such hostile reactions. He was able to play his beloved rock and roll music and that was all he asked. In the fall of 1958 he formed a band with his cousin, based in Duluth. Now that he was mobile, with his own motorcycle, he could regularly make the seventy-mile trek to Duluth. The Satin Tones became something of a local success, playing one song on a local TV station in Superior, Wisconsin, just over the border from Duluth, recording a session on Hibbing radio and playing at least one show at the relatively prestigious Hibbing Armory. However, they disbanded in the spring of 1959, as Robert began to consider his academic and personal future.

At the same time that Robert discovered rock and roll, he seems to have discovered girls. According to Robert Shelton, most of his early girlfriends were "plump and large-breasted." Undoubtedly Echo Helstrom, a young blond-haired woman whom he dated throughout the late summer and fall of 1957 and most of 1958, was the best known and probably the most long-standing of his Hibbing girlfriends. The initial connection was rock and roll, which probably explains why the relationship was not quite as ephemeral as others.

Echo Helstrom: I met him . . . at the L & B Café in Hibbing. That was back at the beginning of our eleventh-grade year, 1957. . . . He was always so well dressed and quiet, I had him pegged for a goody-goody. . . . I mentioned [the song] "Maybellene.". . . " 'Maybellene,' " he screamed. " 'Maybellene' by Chuck Berry? You bet I've heard it! . . ." And on and on about Chuck Berry, Fats Domino, Little Richard, Jimmy Reed—Bob thought he was fabulous, the best!

By the time Robert met Echo Helstrom he was already looking for an escape from Hibbing, and now rode a motorbike—the image required it. This was, after all, the post–*Wild One* era, when Brando became the quintessential rebel, surpassing even Dean in the moodiness stakes. While Robert rode around Minnesota and Wisconsin, he felt sure the smitten Echo would be there when he returned. He spent part of the summer of 1958 at a coed camp in Wisconsin, working on ways of impressing the girls. It was here that he first met Judy Rubin, who would later be an important woman in his life, though at this time theirs was an innocent enough friendship. He seemed to perceive camp as just another audience to impress.

Steve Friedman: We went to Camp Herzl together. Louis Kemp also went. It's somewhere about a hundred miles south [of Duluth], a coed Jewish summer camp. We were all about fourteen, fifteen, sixteen. . . . He was the star of the camp. He used to sing just like Jerry Lee Lewis, a dazzling imitation. He'd play a piano while standing up and everything.

Zimmerman was also taking every opportunity through 1958 and 1959 to hitchhike or ride down to Minneapolis and St. Paul to check out the action there. Minneapolis and St. Paul were where he wanted to be, and it was to the Twin Cities that he was looking to escape when the opportunities arose. It was there that Dylan first was able to experience live rock and roll, and he began to realize how parochial Hibbing truly was, though he would later tell a rather different and somewhat embroidered version of his first exposure to rhythm and blues.

Bob Dylan: I happened to go to Detroit once when I was about twelve or so, with a friend of mine. We had relatives there. I can't remember how it happened, but I found myself in a pool-hall parlor, where people were comin' to eat all day and play bingo all night, and there was a dance band in the back. . . . Anyway, this was my first time face to face with rhythm and blues. [1980]

Steve Friedman: Sometimes we'd hitchhike down to St. Paul, stay in a lousy hotel and look for live music . . . rock, rhythm and blues—Bob was very into black music.

However, if young Robert felt that he could continue to have his fun and still return to Echo in Hibbing, he finally pushed his luck too far. In the first semester of his final year at high school, Echo gave him his first rejection slip.

Echo Helstrom: He began taking off every weekend, going down to Minneapolis or St. Paul to listen to music he said, but I knew he was seeing other girls as well.

Echo's beliefs were not unfounded. Robert Zimmerman was developing a roving eye, and was hanging out around the university, which he perhaps already envisioned attending after high school. At a coffeehouse on the university campus, the Ten O'Clock Scholar, he met Bonnie Beecher, though they would not develop a lasting friendship until they attended college together that fall.

They struck up a conversation when Beecher overheard Zimmerman talking to a friend about blues singers. Just as Helstrom had endeared herself to him by sharing a mutual interest in rock and roll, Bonnie first attracted Zimmerman through her interest in blues music.

It is impossible now to do more than surmise what led Robert Zimmerman to start to abandon rock and roll in favor of other forms of music. Possibly his regular trips to bohemian Minneapolis made him realize that rock and roll was not entirely the hip form of music he had thought it was back in Hibbing. It was juvenile. Kids' stuff. According to fellow Hibbing musician Bill Marinac, the change came some time early in 1959.

Bill Marinac: In '59 he started dabbling in folk very seriously. We had a jam together, just the two of us, in his house. At that time, he did it on electric guitar. We were talking about . . . [what it would be like] if somebody could write lyrics with some social meaning, and could do that in a rock vein. He was already into it.

It should be remembered that the young Zimmerman had always maintained eclectic tastes in music. His first love had not been rock and roll but country music. And his love of rock and roll soon extended beyond the white man's sanitized version back to its precursor—rhythm and blues. Jimmy Reed was an early hero. Jim Dandy, a disc jockey from Virginia, Minnesota, who had befriended Zimmerman in the first flush of his enthusiasm for rock and roll in 1957–58, and who was the object of regular pilgrimages by Robert Zimmerman and John Bucklen, Bob's best friend in Hibbing, introduced them not only to the rhythm and blues artists from whose sound Presley and Little Richard derived theirs, but also to country blues singers such as Son House, Bukka White and Leadbelly. As he was developing a purist's feel for the blues, Robert was turning away from the band mentality required for rock and roll. He was also developing a preference for the guitar over the piano.

Late June of 1959 Robert Zimmerman joined his last rock and roll band. He was staying with some relatives in Fargo, North Dakota, working at the Red Apple Café, when he was offered an opportunity to join Bobby Vee's band. Vee, a Fargo native, had already recorded a single for the Minneapolis-based Soma label and was looking to expand his backing band to include a piano player.

Bobby Vee: There was just a rhythm section at that time, and [we thought that if we added a piano] we would probably have the ultimate rock and roll band. So we sort of asked around the Fargo area and a friend of ours suggested a guy that had been staying at his house and working at a café as a busboy, the Red Apple Café in Fargo. So my brother met with him and they went over to the radio station to use the piano. He sort of plonked around a bit and played "Whole Lot of Shakin' " in the key of C. . . . He told my brother that he'd played with Conway Twitty, so he didn't even want to audition the guy and he got the job.

Bobby Vee: He was kind of a scruffy little guy, but he was really into it, loved to rock and roll. He was pretty limited by what he could play. . . . He liked to do handclaps, like Gene Vincent and the Blue Caps, who had two guys who were handclappers. He would come up [to my mike] and do that every now and then and then scurry back to the piano. He wanted us to use the stage name of Elston Gunn for him.

Bobby Vee: We went out and played a couple of small jobs in North Fargo, then . . . since we didn't have a piano and weren't in a position where we wanted to buy one and lug a piano around with us . . . we decided to work as a four-piece band again. We told him that we'd decided not to use a piano. And he was a bit disappointed at the time and eventually left Fargo . . . and went down to Minneapolis [and] went to school.

Possibly his experience with Vee was the death knell of his rock and roll dreams, and the beginning of a different kind of dream. Whatever the case, it would seem that Elston Gunn died when Vee decided he could do without a piano player. Robert Zimmerman would have to reinvent himself again.

Aside from his brief sojourn in Fargo in June, where was Robert Zimmerman in the three months before he started at the university in Minneapolis? He was rarely in Hibbing and, unlike previous years, he was not at Camp Herzl for much of the summer. Rather this seems to be the summer that Bob's parents sent him to a somewhat different school from Hibbing High (from which he graduated on June 5).

Though Robert was a member of a large and closely knit Jewish family unit, there is no doubt that as his teens progressed and he channeled his rebellious feelings into rock and roll (and its attendant "Wild One" image), he and his father became estranged.

Much has been made of Dylan's rejection of his family name. Indeed it has been interpreted as a deliberate rejection of his religious identity, though he would have been hard pressed to disguise his Jewish physicality. It is far more likely that he saw it as a denial of his father. Bonnie Beecher specifically recalls that in the early months of 1960 "there was some conflict about his father wanting him to use the name Zimmerman and Dylan refusing to use the name." Scaduto cites several sources who knew Dylan in 1960–61 and recall Dylan implying that his father was simply "too hard to get along with" and that "he couldn't stand his father."

The first documented alias Robert adopted was in the summer of 1958, which Echo Helstrom clearly indicates was a period of considerable strife between Robert and his father, Abraham. Indeed, Robert was spending much of his time at the Helstrom's, where he felt more comfortable.

By seventeen his search for a new identity was no longer just a rejection of small-town myopia but increasingly a repudiation of his father's values. His father was a great believer in the work ethic and placed great store upon the respect of his fellow citizens. Robert was already separating the world into the square and the hip. Never a great respecter of authority figures, Robert found it increasingly hard to relate to his father's solid middle-class virtues and mores.

At some point his father decided that strict discipline was needed to bring

Robert back in line. He was clearly disturbed by Robert's rebellious ways and appears to have genuinely believed his son had some psychological problems. He had learned of a school in Pennsylvania that specialized in dealing with difficult adolescents and, at considerable expense, Robert was sent there in 1959. It is not known how long Robert was in Pennsylvania, but it is likely that he drew upon his experiences there when writing about the somewhat stricter regime of a reform school in his 1963 composition, "Walls of Redwing."

After his time in Pennsylvania, Robert was to continue his education at the University of Minneapolis (Dylan would later suggest he attended there on "a phony scholarship" though his grades were just about adequate to secure him a place on merit). To Robert, Minneapolis represented freedom from small (town)-mindedness and paternal authority figures. In Minneapolis he could be beyond his parents' command.

Bob Dylan: I left where I'm from because there's nothing there. . . . When I left there, I knew one thing: I had to get out of there and not come back. Just from my senses I knew there was something more than Walt Disney movies. [1965]

Bob Dylan: I'm not the only one that left there and traveled around . . . everybody left there. I don't know really of anybody that stayed there. [1965]

2 1960: SAMmy Bound for Glory

Minneapolis was excitingly new yet oddly familiar. Having spent many weekends in his final high school year visiting the city, Zimmerman knew a small coterie of fellow Hibbing-Duluth Jews, some of whom were also freshmen at UMinn, including Larry Keegan, one of his longest-standing friends. He also knew at least two women whom he liked and got along with, both of whom were due to attend the University of Minnesota that fall.

Virtually his first act after setting himself up at the Sigma Alpha Mu fraternity house was to go to the Ten O'Clock Scholar coffeehouse to try for a gig. Its owner, David Lee, had recently started using folksingers to entertain the customers, though payment was not one of the perks—Lee simply offered them the opportunity to play to people. According to Lee, when he asked the kid his name, Robert Allen Zimmerman replied, "Bob Dylan." Though Echo Helstrom later claimed that young Robert had first thought up the Dylan alias in Hibbing, Dylan himself said in 1971, "It just came to me as I was standing there in the Scholar." It seems more likely that he would have thought of the name before entering the Scholar. He had, after all, displayed an early penchant for aliases, and Elston Gunn was hardly the name of a folksinger. Dylan, though, has continued to insist that it was only in the Scholar that he adopted the name.

Whatever the immediate significance of his new name was, the metamorphosis into Bob Dylan had begun. This process was aided greatly by the people he came to know in Minneapolis, of whom three women were crucial to his development—Judy Rubin, Bonnie Beecher and Gretel Hoffman.

Judy Rubin was probably the woman he had known the longest—they regularly met up each summer at Camp Herzl. Indeed, young Bob had a considerable crush on Judy, and throughout his first autumn and winter in Minneapolis he sustained an attempt to become "serious" with her. In a remarkable unpublished poem he would write nearly four years later, in December 1963, Dylan recalled his first Christmas in Minneapolis and how much he missed Judy. This poem corresponds very closely with the events of that Christmas as related to Bob Spitz by Judy Rubin herself, notably her family's hostility toward Dylan and their refusal to treat him as a serious suitor for their daughter's affections:

Bob Dylan: "ring ring her ma answers her ma hates me snobby sort . . . wants the best for her daughter society bitch bitch of a mother . . . talks down at me when she knows it's me callin' " [1963]

Though Judy attended his gigs at the Scholar, shouting requests and generally encouraging him, she was never in love with him.

Judy Rubin: My parents didn't like him, neither did a lot of my friends, and there were too many things, including drugs, that separated us.

By the beginning of 1960, she finally realized that Dylan was not content to be "just a friend," and, as she had fallen in love with someone else, their friendship ended. Many years later Dylan would jokingly suggest that Judy Rubin's rejection of him set his ethnic awareness back many years; certainly the fact that he still recalled the breakup suggests the degree of turmoil it produced.

More important to Dylan's development during his early days in Minneapolis was Bonnie Beecher. According to Shelton, Beecher was Dylan's "real" Girl from the North Country, and his relationship with Beecher appears to have been the most intimate and long-standing of all his relationships in Minneapolis.

Dylan had met Bonnie, like Judy, before arriving at the university, though in this case they had met on campus, at the Ten O'Clock Scholar. Bonnie was then in her final year at high school, due to attend the university the following academic year. By the time she met Dylan he was already immersing himself in folk and blues music, discussing such matters with a fellow student named Harvey Abrams.

Bonnie Beecher: I didn't know anybody else who knew who Cat Iron was, or Sleepy John Estes, so I perked up my ears and turned around and I started to join the conversation.

Unlike Judy Rubin, Bonnie did not respond to peer-group pressure to disassociate herself from such a "deadbeat." Bonnie has described one incident in which, after Dylan passed out from drink the night before an important exam, she cleaned him up and got him to the exam on time. As well as illustrating a Dylan who, having loosened the bonds around him in Minneapolis, was experimenting with too much drink, occasional marijuana and a lot of late nights, it shows a remarkably self-assured young woman.

Bonnie Beecher: I was walking to the building where I had [a] final and I noticed a crowd standing around. Sure enough, Dylan was lying in the middle of the street and [he was] just a mess, you know. He had thrown up and he was passed out on the street. . . . And I remember thinking, "I could just keep walking . . . I don't have to go in there and say I know this person. . . ." But I took a big sigh, knew I was going to be late for my test and dammit, I went in and picked him up. He was barely conscious. I had this ludicrous drunk hanging on me, covered in vomit! I walked him to the ladies' room, cleaned him up. I wanted to take him home, but he said, "Naw! I have to be at the Music Building!"

Bonnie Beecher ended up being kicked out of her sorority house for associating with such dubious company. Certainly she took him under her wing, clearly feeling a need to mother him, a common emotion among those women who sought Dylan's interest at this time.

Bonnie Beecher: No one would let him even play for dinner. I ended up shoplifting for him, stealing food from my sorority house.

The amount of mothering that Dylan inspired became something of a running joke among his male friends in Minneapolis. He seemed to have no problem endearing himself to most women, even those somewhat older. Clearly Judy Rubin's mother was in the minority. According to Ellen Baker, another girlfriend from his Minneapolis days, Dylan's charm worked on both her and her mother, and he stayed at the Bakers' house regularly. As a useful adjunct to this accommodation, Dylan learned that Ellen's father had an unsurpassed collection of folk-music literature and records, which he had open access to.

Ellen Baker: He hardly ever seemed to have a place to live, but he liked our house just fine. . . . Besides having both my mother and me charmed and a free place to stay, he had my father's huge collection of bound folk music to peruse. . . . My father was quite a collector. He had old manuscripts, sheet music and folk magazines. . . . We'd harmonize old tunes from my father's old records, and songs that were the type Bob was doing then. Not the bluesy stuff he picked up later, but traditional things, sort of A-minorish folky.

For a nineteen-year-old, Dylan seemed remarkably aware of his ability to charm women, and he was not unduly selective when it came to satisfying his more basic urges.

Ellen Baker: Bob was funny about his women. At first he seemed very shy, sort of scared . . . but it didn't take long before you found out a good deal of that was an act. Bob was surprisingly amorous, and undiscriminating! He'd see a girl on the street or at a party, and it didn't matter what she looked like or who she was with, if he was in that mood.

He was clearly interested in experiencing as much as life could show a nineteen-year-old would-be beatnik fresh from Hibbing. He did not restrict his sexual adventures to the equally inexperienced women he came across while playing at coffeehouses or parties, as illustrated by an incident from Dylan's brief stay in Chicago in December 1960.

Bob Dylan: I met this woman in a bar. She picked me up. It was horrible. I felt used. I was about nineteen and she was, well, she was old. Really old. God, it's all coming back to me. I'll never forget her red hair. . . . She was big. I thought she had a lot of experience. I'm not going to tell you her name. Even if I could remember it. . . . She was wearing a print dress. And a girdle. She made love to me, did it all. I just walked into her room and stood there with my eyes hanging out. She lived in just one room, with a closet, a sink and a window which looked out over the street. She had a dresser with a mirror on top that you can tilt whichever way you want, and a bed with a mattress that sagged clear to the floor in the middle. . . . That woman was sixty years old and she had filed down her teeth! [1978]

Apart from acts of immediate gratification, Dylan did manage to establish friendships with women, but only with those who were interested in his type of music. Both Bonnie Beecher and Ellen Baker were very supportive of Dylan in his music-making, and both shared an abiding interest in folk and blues. Bonnie in particular was witness to Dylan's almost pathological interest in getting back to the source of each recording he heard.

Bonnie Beecher: I would go off and find a record—a collection of old blues stuff with a bunch of different artists on—bring it back to Minnesota and we would play it through.

Harvey Abrams: Dylan was the purest of the pure. He had to get the oldest record and, if possible, the Library of Congress record.

A sorority sister of Beecher's, Cynthia Fincher, was equally intrigued by Dylan. She played banjo, and in the fall of 1960 they would often play together at the Purple Onion pizza parlor. It is her voice that can be heard on the (so-called) First Minneapolis Tape from September 1960, berating him for not playing what she wanted him to.

The other woman Dylan met soon after arriving in Minneapolis was Gretel Hoffman. Dave Whitaker, who would marry her that May, much to Dylan's initial chagrin, and who would himself become a vital influence on Dylan, said it was Gretel who introduced Dylan to the music of Odetta, who became Dylan's first folk hero.

Bob Dylan: The first thing that turned me on to folksinging was Odetta. I heard a record of hers in a record store, back when you could listen to records there in the store. That was in '58 or something like that. Right then and there, I went out and traded my electric guitar and amplifier for an acoustical guitar, a flat-top Gibson. . . . Anyway, from Odetta I went to Harry Belafonte, the Kingston Trio, little by little uncovering more as I went along. Finally, I was doing nothing but Carter Family and Jesse Fuller songs. [1978]

It sounds here as if Dylan went from playing Little Richard to playing Odetta.

In fact, the change was considerably more gradual. It was more an uncovering of the layers that formed the basis of the music he loved—rock and roll. The first layer was rhythm and blues. The second was blues. His interest in Odetta, whose music formed a bridge between the blues singers he already knew and the myriad forms of "white" folk music, was a logical development by which he started discovering the ballad tradition, which was the primary element in white man's folk music, and then more topical songwriters such as Pete Seeger and Woody Guthrie.

Bob Dylan: I was singing stuff like "Ruby Lee" by the Sunny Mountain Boys, and "Jack o' Diamonds" by Odetta. . . . [Sometimes I was] part of a duo with Spider John Koerner, who played mostly ballads and Josh White–type blues. He knew more songs than I did. "Whoa, Boys, Can't Ya Line 'M," "John Hardy," "Golden Vanity," I learned all those from him. [1985]

Sadly, there is no documentary evidence—recordings or reliable reports—relating what material Dylan was playing when he first started appearing at the Ten O'Clock Scholar in October 1959. However, it seems likely that he was playing songs by Odetta and Leadbelly plus some popular traditional folk and blues tunes. At this point he was relatively inexperienced with the acoustic guitar, which he had only begun to play early in 1959, he was playing no harmonica and he was singing in a sweet, rich voice that sounded like a cross between the country twang of Hank Williams and the more saccharine kind of folk popularized by the Kingston Trio.

Everyone who knew Dylan at this time comments on his voice, and how different it was from what it later became. Spider John Koerner, with whom he started playing in January 1960, says it was "a pretty voice." It was this sweet voice that first impressed Terri Wallace. Terry Wallace was one of Dylan's earliest fans and regularly attended Dylan's gigs at the Ten O'Clock Scholar in the spring of 1960. Her sister Karen would make the first known recording of Bob Dylan when she saw him playing at the Scholar.

Terri Wallace: He had . . . the most beautiful voice, which I was really impressed with. I really thought he had a good singing voice—which I might add was something of a disappointment after he became well known and I heard the voice that made him famous. It was really disappointing to me because it was so different from the voice that I had first heard coming out of him.

It was not just his friends who witnessed his not-so-gradual development. Also regularly attending his shows at the Scholar was his first small coterie of devotees. It was Terri Wallace who suggested in early spring that Dylan consider playing at the Purple Onion as well as, or perhaps in preference to, the Ten O'Clock Scholar. He had asked for a raise at the latter, where he was now bringing some business in, and was promptly refused. The Purple Onion duly benefited.

Terri Wallace: I met Bob Dylan at the Ten O'Clock Scholar when some friends and I decided that we wanted to try something different . . . this was during the days when Expresso coffee places were the big rage. . . . He just reminded me of a little choirboy, he had such a cute little cherub face and the most beautiful voice, which I was really impressed with. . . . I remember a pair of brown corduroy pants that he wore almost all the time and I know that he wasn't real concerned with his appearance. . . . He had worn them so often he had a rip in the crotch. . . . If I remember correctly, the Purple Onion had more or less just opened, and he was looking for other places to sing.

The first known Dylan recording—indeed the only recording definitely extant from the period before his summer 1960 trip to Denver, Colorado—was made some time around May 1960 at the apartment of Terri Wallace's sister, Karen. On it Dylan's voice matches his contemporaries' description. On "The Two Sisters," a traditional song collected that year in Alan Lomax's *Folk Songs of North America*, he can be heard singing, "I'll be true to my luuurve." The unfamiliarity of this voice even led one major Dylan collector to make the unfounded, and subsequently disproved, allegation that the tape was a fake.

The twenty-seven-song St. Paul Tape (as it is generally known) is a useful document for indicating the sort of material Dylan was performing by spring 1960. By this point he had met and played with Spider John Koerner. He had also met Dave Whitaker, who would be a trenchant and galvanizing influence on him. Along with Bonnie Beecher, Harvey Abrams, Gretel Hoffman and Hugh Brown (who would later become Dylan's roommate), Whitaker began to reshape Dylan's worldview. He and Gretel Hoffman taught Dylan a lot of traditional folk material. Beecher and Abrams stayed more interested in the blues. When Dylan himself came to write his first "original" composition, it was the blues he turned to. The song was called "One Eyed Jacks" and it appears on the St. Paul Tape. In it he affected a world-weariness that a fifty-year-old bluesman would have been proud of.

Dylan would write in the fall of 1963 that meeting people like Whitaker, Hugh Brown, Harvey Abrams and later Tony Glover was responsible for a key transformation:

Bob Dylan: I'd fell in with a new kind a people there in Minneapolis. I was going t new kinds a parties an thinkin new kinds a things. . . . I read into what I was doing an saw myself romantically breakin off all ties with all things of the established order although I'd never really been accepted by that order anyway . . . what I saw connected with the fraternity house summed up the whole established world. [1963]

By the spring of 1960, Dylan had begun to feel extremely uncomfortable with his brothers in the Sigma Alpha Mu fraternity house. He had never really fit in with this rather conventional Jewish lodge. He was reluctant to contribute to fraternity life and did not enjoy being ridiculed by those brothers who knew of his nighttime activities down at the Scholar. His departure from the fraternity house was really the end of his formal education. Though he continued to attend lectures intermittently, he was immersing himself more and more in the bohemian life-style of his new, "hipper" friends.

Ellen Baker: Bob was serious about his schoolwork for a while. At the very start. He tried very hard, but it wasn't him. He finally decided he just wanted to play the guitar and party.

Dylan was drinking a lot in those days, usually cheap but drinkable wine. Though the milder drugs—pills and dope—were around in 1960, and though Dylan was certainly smoking marijuana in Minneapolis, it was drinking that gave him the bravado to come on with women, and to conquer his stage fright. He also seemed to have an ability to perform when substantially the worse for wear.

Dave Whitaker: One thing I do remember about Dylan was that he always had his guitar in his hands. He'd drink and go on—he used to get really fucking drunk, we all did. But he could always play that guitar when he couldn't even stand up.

Dave Whitaker was the primary influence in the transformation of Dylan into a hip individual. Dylan later said that meeting Whitaker was the most direct reason for his change of life-style. He was "on this side," met Whitaker, "and suddenly I was on that side." Dylan started staying up all night, reading books Whitaker recommended and rap-talking over a bottle of wine till dawn.

Dave Whitaker: There was a black club we used to go to, and all of these prostitutes were sitting there and you'd come in and there'd be these guys playing the blues. And using drugs. Drugs were coming in. The truckers were

using bennies [amphetamines] and we used to take four or five and we'd go on
for two or three days at a time, drinking beer, playing guitar, and going from
scene to scene.

In May 1960, Dylan met Dave "Tony" Glover, the second important male
influence on him in Minneapolis. It was at a party given by the now-married
Gretel Whitaker. Though it would be late summer before he and Glover became close, Glover noticed Dylan, who was playing and refused to continue
because certain people were not listening to him. Like others, Glover noticed
Dylan's insatiable thirst to learn at this time, an incredible way he had of
soaking up influences, styles, tunes, though he didn't impress him musically.
Glover recalls that Dylan was playing songs by Odetta and Josh White and the
occasional Guthrie cover.

Bob Dylan: I can remember . . . if somebody played the guitar, that's who
you went to see. You didn't necessarily go to meet them, you just went . . . to
watch them, listen to them, and, if possible, learn how to do something. . . .
And usually at that time it was quite a selfish type of thing. . . . It wasn't
necessarily a song; it was technique and style. . . . I certainly spent a lot of
hours just trying to do what other people had been doing. [1968]

The speed at which he was metamorphosing may not have been apparent to
his Minneapolis friends when he was around every day. Then he seemingly
vanished during the summer of 1960, and by the time he returned he seemed
a different singer. This time his development was remarked on by just about all
his friends.
He had spent a large portion of the summer in Denver, Colorado. Why
Dylan went to Denver that summer will in all likelihood remain a mystery. It
was hardly a local excursion from Minnesota, being 920 miles from home.

Bob Dylan: [When] I hitchhiked to Denver I think I went there because I
knew a girl whose floor I could sleep on. . . . I stayed around Denver for a
while, but there was only one coffeehouse, and they wouldn't give me a job. But
then I met a stripper who worked at a bar called the Gilded Garter, and she
bought me some clothes and got me a job playing "Mule Skinner Blues"
between strip acts. [1978]

He did not find the woman he intended to stay with. Walt Conley was then
playing at the Satire, one of two Denver night spots Dylan was interested in

playing at. In Conley's account in Bob Spitz's biography, Dylan arrived at the Satire telling Conley that an ex-girlfriend from Minneapolis had suggested he look him up. Again according to Conley, Dylan auditioned unsuccessfully at the Satire, and subsequently crashed at Conley's house for three weeks, until Conley managed to get rid of him by getting him a gig at an out-of-town place called the Gilded Garter, in Central City. Within a week Dylan had apparently left the Gilded Garter, having stolen twenty dollars from the owner, and returned to Denver.

This does not accord with Dylan's own version, that he met a stripper who worked there and she got him the job. It also does not explain how Conley would have known that Dylan was a perfectly competent piano player. That was what the Gilded Garter actually required, it being a touristy honky-tonk joint. Dylan had played guitar and sung at the Satire, but had evidently not played piano. In fact, the only matter Dylan and Conley seem to agree on was that the Gilded Garter gig did not last long. In October 1961 Dylan told Izzy Young, an acquaintance in the New York folk-music community, that he lasted a week and a half (though in 1966 he told Robert Shelton, more plausibly, that it lasted "a few weeks").

Bob Dylan: I played for twenty minutes, strippers worked for forty minutes with a rock and roll band, I'd play for twenty minutes again. Never stopped. One night I was about ready to strip myself. [1961]

Corroboration for at least part of Dylan's story comes from Kevin Krown, a local folksinger he met in Denver. Krown later told Scaduto that he met Dylan while Dylan "was playing piano in this Central City joint" (the Gilded Garter) and that "he was living with this stripper down the road." If he was living with a stripper, which both Dylan and Krown say he was, it seems surprising that he played the burlesque house for only ten days, particularly as his Minneapolis friends say he was gone most of the summer. Also, despite Conley's insistence that Dylan stayed at his house for three weeks, it is difficult to see how Dylan could have survived for that long without a job. According to Krown, Dylan came to Denver having been offered a job at the Gilded Garter, and his portrait of Dylan contrasts dramatically with Conley's.

Kevin Krown: In those days he had the money, he was the one doing the buying. He had a job and a few dollars and I was broke. He actually gave me a couple of bucks when I was ready to start hitching again.

Quite probably Conley's portrait of Dylan was colored by the fact that Dylan attempted to run off with Conley's record collection before leaving Denver.

According to Shelton, they had already fallen out over a woman they were both chasing. Whatever the truth, of the three Dylan biographies to date only Scaduto's 1971 study correctly places Dylan in Denver in the summer of 1960; Shelton places him there, totally implausibly, in the summer of 1959, and Spitz places him there in the fall of 1960 just before he headed for New York.

Krown met Dylan at the Exodus, the coffeehouse where, according to Dylan, "they wouldn't give me a job." The Exodus was a prestigious gig, and it would have been a considerable surprise if Dylan had been allowed to play there. However, he did see at least two singers perform at the venue, Jesse Fuller and Judy Collins. The more important at this point in his career would be Jesse Fuller.

Jesse Fuller played guitar and harmonica; his harmonica was placed in a metal neck brace and he blew into the instrument between verses. This style of playing was, in the summer of 1960, considered unorthodox, and it clearly intrigued Dylan. Though a couple of uncorroborated sources have suggested that Dylan played harmonica from his early days in Minneapolis, there is no evidence he played it until after his return from Denver. Indeed, close friends comment on Dylan learning to play harmonica at this point. The connection with Fuller is no mere coincidence. Dylan told Izzy Young in October 1961 that he "met Jesse Fuller in Denver at the Exodus. . . ." He later told Robert Shelton that he had "quizzed Fuller" about playing harmonica using the rack.

After Dylan had spent most of the summer in Denver, it was time to return to Minneapolis. The Dylan who came back surprised his friends. He had been out on the road, and he had returned to tell his friends about his adventures, suitably embroidered by his soaring imagination. Dave Whitaker was one of the first to notice a change.

Dave Whitaker: The difference had actually happened before . . . going to New York. He came back [from Denver] with a difference in accent. He spoke differently. He was more sure of himself really. He had gone to Denver to the Exodus, and he came back with one song that he used to play, that was entirely a new level in show business, called "The Clan.". . . It was a surrealistic poem. . . . Someone wrote it and gave it to him.

That someone was Walt Conley (it was his one direct influence on Dylan). Before the more profound influence Fuller had wrought upon him could fully flower, Whitaker introduced him to a new guru, one who would finally provide him with the impetus to abandon Minneapolis and head for New York's Greenwich Village.

The story of Whitaker introducing Dylan to Woody Guthrie's romanticized autobiography *Bound for Glory* is well known. It is important to remember that Whitaker had regularly recommended books for him to read, books that never appeared as part of any university curriculum. One book Dylan read in 1960 was Jack Kerouac's *Mexico City Blues*, and in all likelihood Whitaker encouraged Dylan to read the other beats, Ginsberg and Ferlinghetti in particular. But it was Guthrie who gave Dylan the requisite new persona.

Dave Whitaker: My role, as far as Bob was concerned, is that I taught him to read, turning him on to the world of books. . . . For him reading had always been a painful process outside of his existence. He told me in Oakland, in 1978, . . . "I never thought of reading books until I met you." I'd say, "Bob, you've got to read this," and he'd read it, run around with it. And I gave him *Bound for Glory*, which is the story of these folksingers and how you could earn your living going from place to place, he and Cisco Houston, playing these songs and taking a collection. . . . And for days Bob carried it around, and he read it, and he came to me and said, "Come on, Dave, I want to show you something." And he went and picked up his guitar and he had memorized "Tom Joad." . . . It's a twenty-minute song! . . . Bob did have this marvelous ability to hear a song once and commit it totally to memory.

The chronology of Dylan's development is very important here. Within a matter of weeks of returning from Denver, already having developed dramatically as a performer, he would become a Guthrie disciple, and shortly afterward begin to play the harmonica, which within six months would become his trademark. Indeed, Dylan's adoption of the Guthrie persona seems to have come so soon after his return that some old friends thought it was an affectation he had developed while away.

Bonnie Beecher: He came back talking with a real thick Oklahoma accent and wearing a cowboy hat and boots. He was into Woody Guthrie in a big, big way. . . . At the time it seemed ludicrous and pretentious and foolish, but now I see it as allowing a greater Bob Dylan to come out.

What is often not considered by those who refer disparagingly to Dylan's adoption of the Guthrie character is that it was a very specific version of Guthrie that he adopted. Dylan was already perfectly conversant with Guthrie. What really appealed to Dylan was the figure Guthrie painted of himself in *Bound for Glory*, a mythological figure. As Whitaker himself said, the story of *Bound for Glory* is "the story of these folksingers and how you could earn your living going from place to place."

Many of Dylan's friends had respectable collections of Guthrie's work, and on the May 1960 St. Paul Tape he had performed four songs credited to Guthrie: "This Land Is Your Land," "Who's Gonna Shoe Your Pretty Little Feet," "The Great Historical Bum" and "Columbus Stockade Blues." What he had not yet been performing—and could not have with the sweet style of singing he was using—were Guthrie's talking blues, loose, almost free-verse songs with very easy, cascading tunes and an extended line at the end of every verse to allow a suitably weighted verbal riposte. It was the talking blues that gave Dylan the perfect opportunity to affect an Oklahoma twang. And that twang became more and more pronounced as he immersed himself totally in Guthrie's oeuvre and character.

The second-earliest recording of Dylan—normally referred to as the First Minneapolis Tape—shows a unique version of the Dylan persona. Recorded probably at the beginning of September, it features a Dylan who had discovered the *Bound for Glory* Guthrie and the talking blues form—there are four talking blues on the tape, three by Guthrie, one improvised by Dylan about his indolent roommate, Hugh Brown—but who had yet to fuse it with his harmonica sound. It was this fusion that transformed Dylan from just another Guthrie impersonator. As Harvey Abrams has observed, "He was the first white performer to combine the Sonny Terry harmonica with the Woody Guthrie guitar."

On his return to Minneapolis, Dylan had begun to spend a lot of time at Ellen Baker's, playing along to Guthrie records on guitar and/or harmonica:

Ellen Baker: We'd sing Woody's songs all afternoon, play my father's old records . . . and I think it was just about that time that Bob got a harmonica.

Throughout the fall of 1960 he worked at his harmonica playing. Though he still played the Purple Onion, he had another regular gig in St. Paul, at the Bastille, a more prestigious locale than the pizza parlor. Sometimes he would play with Cynthia Fincher, who played the banjo; sometimes he would play with Tony Glover. Though Dylan had first met Glover in May 1960, only in the fall did they become close friends. Possibly only at this point did Glover consider Dylan a worthy enough musical companion. Glover and his partner, Dave Ray, were highly respected musicians on the local scene. It was Glover who provided Dylan some much-needed tutoring on the mouth harp, though he chooses to underplay his role in Dylan's development. Glover recollects that Dylan originally had a chord harmonica—that is, one that can play different keys. Though suitable for certain types of traditional music, this type of harmonica was not of much use when playing the blues, where you were required to bend notes. It also required a degree of musical expertise somewhat greater than the conventional "blues" harmonica. Glover suggested a mouth harp tuned to a particular key and showed Dylan the cross-harp approach, where the harp player plays in a different key than the one the harmonica is tuned to, a style of playing that Dylan quickly adopted.

The remarkable thing is the pace of Dylan's development as a harmonica player. When he reached New York in January 1961 he was a competent player—indeed, most of his early gigs there were as a mouth-harp accompanist. Dylan was an avaricious learner and he had a quality few others have—he genuinely didn't give a shit. Back in Hibbing he had pounded on the piano so loud he broke a pedal. Some hooted, but he was oblivious. Likewise, his harmonica playing early on was a subject of considerable ridicule.

Bonnie Beecher: I got him his first harmonica holder at Schmidt's Music Shop. He would come over to the sorority house . . . and he'd play this harmonica, which he didn't know how to play! And my friends would come in and they would just go, "Uurgh! Who is this geek?" I wanted him to play guitar, which he could play well and which I knew would impress them, but he just wasn't having any of it. He was saying, "Naw, I wanna get this"—hwang! WHwaongg! . . . I was mortified, but he didn't give a shit.

When his old friend from Hibbing, Bill Marinac, visited him that fall in Minneapolis he was surprised how far his ex–rock and roller friend had come.

Bob Marinac: After he went down to the university, he had an acoustic and his harmonica. We got together and jammed again. He'd started to write some music. It was really tender, a lot of very good blues, a lot of things about growing up.

Marinac was not the only one to be impressed by Dylan's development. In the fall of 1960 Rolf Cahn came to Minneapolis. A renowned guitarist with his own recordings on the Folkways label, Cahn apparently informed a few friends on his departure that Dylan was "the most talented guy around." The singer Cynthia Gooding also came to town, and when Dylan played to her at a postgig party she was duly amazed.* Gooding would later become friendly with Dylan in New York. So would Odetta, who also came to Minneapolis that fall. Again Dylan played to her and received a favorable response.

Bonnie Beecher: I remember Cynthia Fincher coming running over to my house saying, "She said that Dylan has real talent and he can make it!"

---

* Shelton credits this to 1959 but the 1959 Dylan would hardly have impressed a recognized figure like Gooding.

Such plaudits no doubt reinforced Dylan's consummate faith in the value of what he was doing. Certainly some on the Minneapolis folk scene would be very bitter about Dylan after his departure, finding it hard to believe that the untalented runt they had heard in Minneapolis was now the hottest young talent on the New York scene and signed to a contract with Columbia Records. An indication of the way he perceived his own importance can be gleaned from a remark made when he was being taped by Beecher. He informed her that he considered the recording she was making (subsequently lost) to be worth the considerable sum of two hundred dollars.

Bonnie Beecher: He sits down to make a tape, and he says to me, "I don't want you ever to let anyone make a copy of these tapes, so that when someone from the Library of Congress asks you for them, I want you to sell them for two hundred dollars."

When Dylan finally did decide to head for New York that December, there was a degree of incredulity from certain contemporaries.

Stanley Gottlieb: When he told us he was going to New York, we thought he was crazy. We said, "You can't make it here; how the fuck are you gonna make it there?"

In fact, Dylan *had* made it in Minneapolis, at least in terms of his ascendancy on the local music scene. He was now considered by many of his peers a noteworthy performer, even if his love for Guthrie covers could be a little wearing at times. He could make no further progress in a Midwest town. Many who would later disparage the 1960 Dylan had seen a lot of him in the spring and early summer, and far less of him in the fall, as he worked more frequently in St. Paul, away from the college campus. They had not seen the startling pace at which Dylan had developed as a performer. Dylan himself knew instinctively that it was time to move on. He had talked about going to New York for so long. The time for indecision had passed.

Bob Dylan: I'd learned as much as I could and used up all my options. . . . When I arrived in Minneapolis it had seemed like a big city or a big town. When I left it was like some rural outpost. [1985]

Yet it would appear that—despite the independent self he considered himself to be—he actually returned to Hibbing to tell his parents of his intention to go to New York, a remarkable gesture that debunks the notion that he had wholly cut himself off from his family.

Maurice Zimmerman: Bobby was . . . independent—like when he quit school. Came home from Minneapolis and told his parents he wanted to go to New York, to try and make it on his own. Didn't want any help, just took enough money from his father to get east.

It was almost certainly this occasion that prompted Dylan to ask Bonnie Beecher to crop his now-long hair. His concern in avoiding upsetting his parents, while presumably partially motivated by his desire to ensure he obtained the necessary funds to reach New York, also perhaps suggests a suitably respectful son.

Bonnie Beecher: It was an unexpected trip he had to make up to Hibbing and he wanted me to cut his hair "real short, real short so that she won't know that I wear long hair." He kept saying, "Shorter! Shorter! Get rid of the sideburns!" Then in the door come Dave Morton, Johnny Koerner and Harvey Abrams. They looked at him and said,"Oh my God, you look terrible! What did you do?" And then he went and wrote that song, "Bonnie, why'd you cut my hair? Now I can't go nowhere!"

Maurice Zimmerman's remarks do not agree with Whitaker's later account, given to both Scaduto and Shelton, that Dylan set out for New York on a whim to visit Guthrie, after being up all night and phoning Guthrie at Greystone Hospital, where he was confined while his hereditary Huntington's chorea slowly wasted his body away. Though Dylan clearly realized that going to New York would provide an opportunity to visit Guthrie, it would have been an uncharacteristic display of naïveté on his part if he had really traveled to New York specifically or mainly to see Guthrie. It seems more likely that Greenwich Village was his primary destination.

Scaduto is the only biographer to chronicle Dylan's trip from Minneapolis to New York accurately. Both Shelton and Spitz are wildly inaccurate. Spitz claims that Dylan headed straight from Denver to New York, an astonishing claim denied by a mountain of evidence to the contrary. Shelton claims, even more implausibly, that Dylan arrived in New York in December 1960 and spent two months in Times Square hustling as a male prostitute. Shelton bases his tall tale on one of Dylan's "recollections" in 1966 during an all-night flight out of Lincoln, Nebraska. Dylan told a similar story to a journalist named Adrian Rawlins in Australia a month later. At least it proves that Dylan continued to distort and reinvent his past long after his stories of running away as a child to join the circus had been revealed as a sham. In fact, Dylan's convoluted journey to New York is well documented, and took in both Chicago and Madison, Wisconsin.

Bob Dylan: I went to Chicago first and stayed there. Then I went up to Wisconsin, which was more or less the same general scene as it was at the school in Minnesota. And from there I went to New York. That was quite a trip. Another guitar player and myself got a ride with a young couple from the campus whose parents were from Brooklyn. They were going there and wanted some more drivers, so we just drove. [1978]

Though Madison lies between Chicago and Minneapolis, not between Chicago and New York, neither Dylan nor Scaduto is mistaken. Having arrived in Chicago around Christmas and having crashed at Kevin Krown's place for a couple of days before moving in with a woman (who may be the sixty-year-old red-haired woman he later claimed he briefly lived with in Chicago), Dylan decided to give up the idea of New York and return to Minneapolis. Stopping in Madison, whose campus had an active folk scene akin to Minneapolis's, Dylan wrote to the Whitakers informing them of his change of mind.

Marshall Brickman: When I was going to school in Wisconsin, Eric Weissberg and I roomed together. Our apartment was the place where all the folksingers wound up. We were the underground railroad. One day this guy, Bob Zimmerman, came through town on his way from Minnesota [sic]. He had a brown suit and tie and played sort of blues on the piano.

Though he failed to impress Brickman and Weissberg, Dylan did find a new friend, Danny Kalb, a superb blues guitarist, with whom he played at a local coffeehouse. Perhaps surprisingly, he accompanied Kalb on harmonica. He stayed in Madison only a few days, intending to find a ride to Minneapolis. Instead, as luck would have it, he was offered a lift to New York as relief driver for another folksinger, Fred Underhill. So he now found himself completing the journey he had set out on, and Fred proved an invaluable companion. He "was from Williamstown . . . and he knew New York." So long, Madison, howdy, Hudson River.

3 | 1961: Hard Times in New York Town

B ob Dylan arrived in a freezing cold Manhattan on January 24, 1961, and was dropped off uptown with Fred Underhill. They quite probably walked the fifty blocks to the Village—after all, this was New York, money was tight and Dylan had a lot to take in—though he would later claim he took "a rockin', reelin', rollin' ride" on the subway. They eventually arrived at Greenwich Village and the Cafe Wha?, a fairly seedy "basket house," where acts played without payment from the venue and relied upon donations derived from "passing the basket" at the end of each set. It was Tuesday—hootenanny night—and anyone was allowed to get up on stage and sing a couple of songs. Dylan would later claim that the audience "flipped," though it seems unlikely that there was a large crowd on a bitterly cold January night. However, the Wha's owner, Manny Roth, must have been vaguely impressed because Dylan soon began playing there in the afternoons. After his brief set that night, Roth told the few Village stalwarts in attendance that Bob and Fred were looking for a place to crash for the night. The new arrivals did not make the best selection from the few volunteers.

Bob Dylan: My buddy and I . . . picked out this fellow who was with a girl. Then my buddy says to me, "He doesn't look so hot. . . . He looks pretty gay." And I said, "He looks OK"—and anyway, he was with a girl. And so we went up with him. And the girl got off at Thirty-fourth Street, and we got off at Forty-second Street! Well, we went in a bar before we went to find this place to stay, and we met his [gentleman] friend "Dora." "Dora" was his friend who stayed with him. And both of us looked, and ran out of the bar. [1961]

It seems unlikely that they really took off at this point. They needed a place to stay and the alternatives were not good. They barely had enough money to eat, let alone stay in a hotel, and they had arrived smack in the middle of what Dylan called the "coldest winter in seventeen years" (it was actually the worst in twenty-eight years). So they probably took their chances and spent a warm if worrying night with Dora and his friend.

That first week in New York, Dylan did the rounds of the many folk joints in the Village. He traveled out to New Jersey to the daunting Greystone Hospital to visit Guthrie; he even made it to Howard Beach to visit Guthrie's family. The first weekend, he turned up at Izzy Young's Folklore Center, a small shop that sold an impressive assortment of folk fare on both vinyl and paper, plus assorted acoustic instruments. It also had a back room in which folkies regularly congregated, talked and sang. The first Sunday, Dylan was to be heard at the back of the shop running through "Mule Skinner Blues" on Autoharp. J. R. Goddard of *The Village Voice* would later comment on the general reaction.

J. R. Goddard: People looked on in amusement as he began hopping around a bit. He was funny to watch, and anybody with half an ear could tell he had a unique style.

His regular trips to Greystone Hospital were not as important as the weekends at Sid and Bob Gleason's (friends of Guthrie's) in East Orange, New Jersey. Woody Guthrie was allowed by the hospital to spend each Sunday there in the company of old friends. Congregated there would be figures like Alan Lomax, the noted musicologist, and Ramblin' Jack Elliot, a well-known folksinger. Though Dylan was initially daunted by such notable company, his exuberant self-confidence soon flowered and within a couple of weeks he was unselfconsciously playing and talking and laughing, often staying over at the Gleasons' for several days at a time.

Dylan soon scouted out those places in the Village where he could get up and play. Initially his only real opportunities were at the basket houses. There were numerous such establishments in the Village at this time, including the Figaro, the Commons and the Wha. After all, America was undergoing something of a folk revival, albeit inspired by the saccharine style of the Kingston Trio, and Greenwich Village was perceived as the center of a buzzing new scene.

By the beginning of February, Dylan was playing regularly at the Commons, the Cafe Wha? and even the Gaslight. More upmarket establishments such as the Limelight, the Village Gate and Gerdes' Folk City remained as yet inaccessible, except on hootenanny nights when amateur talent could attempt to impress a club owner enough to secure a playing gig. At the Cafe Wha?, Dylan's first stop in the Village that cold January evening, he was mostly employed as a harmonica player rather than as a singer.

Bob Dylan: I worked for Manny [Roth] all afternoons, from twelve till eight. I worked the day shift back then. . . . It stayed open from eleven in the morning until four in the morning and there was constantly something happening on the stage. . . . You never really did get popular there 'cause people never knew who you were. Nobody was billed on the outside. . . . You passed the basket. . . . That's why I started wearing hats. [1984]

Bob Dylan: It was just a nonstop flow of people—usually they were tourists who were looking for beatniks in the Village. There'd be maybe five groups that played there. I used to play with a guy called Fred Neil. . . . He would play mostly these types of songs that Josh White might sing. I would play harmonica for him, and then once in a while get to sing a song . . . when he was taking a break or something. It was his show, he would be on for about half an hour, then a conga player would get on. . . . And then this girl . . . used to play sweet Southern Mountain Appalachian ballads, with electric guitar and a small amplifier. And then another guy . . . a sort of crooner. Then there'd be a comedian, then an impersonator. And that'd be the whole show, and this whole unit would go around nonstop. And you got fed there, which was actually the best thing about the place. [1984]

Dylan would later suggest, somewhat caustically, that he was "blowin' his lungs out for a dollar a day." Certainly it was hard work for little pay—but it was experience and it allowed him to join the band of young authentic troubadours who wandered the streets of the Village. He was a folk musician! When he wrote to the Whitakers at the beginning of February he told them he was playing the Commons, where "people clap for me." However, his Minneapolis friends might have had trouble recognizing the man singing at the Wha as their old buddy. His Okie accent had become even more pronounced, and in the Village he was considered first and foremost a harmonica player—the man who had made that awful racket learning to play the harmonica barely five months earlier had quickly discovered a natural aptitude for the instrument. He had also—seemingly unconsciously—developed an unusual way of playing it, a style that was unique among his Village contemporaries.

Bob Dylan: This sounds a little vague, but sometimes, like most of the time, I would blow out on the harmonica because everybody sucks in. The proper way to play is like Little Walter or Sonny Boy Williamson would play—which would be to cross it—and I found myself blowing out more because nobody was doing that in that area. And that's what defined that harmonica and guitar sound which I hadn't heard until that point. I just stumbled on it one day. [1978]

Dylan himself readily admits that there were some conscious influences involved in his style of playing. If it was Jesse Fuller who had first impressed him when he saw him in performance in Denver, he did not forget the music he had heard in Hibbing and Minneapolis, and the sound that most impressed him when he listened to his blues records was the sound of Jimmy Reed playing his mouth harp. Dylan was synthesizing existing styles, combining Reed's style of harmonica playing with his own new Guthriesque drawl and the country-tinged way he had of holding his notes, a throwback to Jimmie Rodgers, the prewar country singer who invented the blues yodel.

Bob Dylan: Jimmy Reed blew out instead of sucking in on [the harmonica]. He had his own style of playing—he'd play like three notes, sometimes the whole solo would be like three notes. [1989]

In those first few months Dylan was developing at such a pace that the chronology has become twisted by inconsistent and unreliable recollections. Some ex–Village folkies have Dylan writing prodigiously long before he did. Others omit his days as a harmonica accompanist or forget the occasions when he played piano at Gerdes' hootenannies.

The furious pace Dylan kept up during those first few months in New York means that events have become compressed in contemporaries' minds. Certainly between February and September 1961 he steadily rose through the echelons of the small Village folk community. The landmarks around which accounts of Dylan's early Village career are usually hung are his two residencies at Gerdes' Folk City. In April he supported John Lee Hooker, his first sustained paying gig (he had in fact played at the University of New York Folk Society six days earlier). That first Gerdes' residency moved him off the bottom rung of the ladder. His September residency, during which he received a rave review in *The New York Times* and secured a recording contract with CBS, would signify the end of the first phase of his career. By then he was considered to be *the* rising star among the new breed of Village folksingers.

In fact, there are several other important dates on Dylan's 1961 calendar. In May he finally had the opportunity to gauge how far he had come in those six months: He returned to Minneapolis. Those who had envisaged a humbled Dylan coming home after weeks of being treated as an unskilled country hick by New York folkies were in for a shock.

Paul Davies: When he came back . . . and played at Kaufman Union on campus . . . he sounded like an Okie. You could hardly understand what he was saying.

The two "party tapes" that exist from Dylan's May stay in Minneapolis show an artist who has grown beyond the comprehension of those who once knew him. A mythology surrounding that quantum leap was inevitable. How he changed so quickly from the Guthrie clone to a genuine interpreter, capable of powerful harmonica playing and marvelously expressive singing, will never be definitely understood. Even Dylan himself was mystified by the process. Indeed, when he attempted to write his first book two years later, his initial intention was to base it on his arrival in New York, that point where one road ended and another began.

Of course, Dylan himself would greatly enjoy the growth of a romantic myth regarding the "change" in him—something like selling his soul to the devil, just as Robert Johnson allegedly did. Perhaps, as Paris unleashed Rimbaud's muse, it was New York itself that released Dylan's.

In May, Dylan also played at an obscure folk festival at a hotel in Branford, Connecticut. He met Bobby Neuwirth there, who would be a regular sidekick for many years to come, and Robert L. Jones, a Boston folksinger. In June he went to Cambridge, Massachusetts, home of the famous Club 47, where he again met Jones, who introduced him to a folksinger named Eric von Schmidt. He would return in August, again hooking up with von Schmidt, and this time he would meet folksinger Carolyn Hester and her husband, Richard Fariña, get to play at the Club 47 at Hester's invitation and be invited to play harp on the forthcoming sessions for her debut album for CBS. Dylan's Cambridge affiliations were the vital connection that resulted in his meeting the fabled CBS producer John Hammond.

Such simple twists of fate made all the difference, though Dylan was also prepared to work at securing his "lucky break." Starting in June, he began to work on coaxing Robert Shelton, *The New York Times* folk critic, to review one of his gigs. In July he phoned Shelton to tell him he was playing a week at the Gaslight, but Shelton considered that strictly small-time. At the end of July he received a small but favorable mention by Shelton in his review of a twelve-hour concert at Riverside Church, at which he had performed a four-song set. WRVR-FM had broadcast the entire day's proceedings; this was Dylan's first radio broadcast since his Hibbing days. Finally, Dylan convinced Shelton to come down to see the first night of a second Gerdes' Folk City residency at the end of September, at which he was the opening act for the Greenbriar Boys.

How was Dylan viewed by his contemporaries during his first six months in New York? The one thing that comes across from all the firsthand accounts of his performances at this time was that he sounded different, in fact unique. Whether you found him interesting depended in part upon how "purist" your tastes were. Looking back, it is easy to forget how divided the early-sixties folk scene in New York was. There was a traditional purist side and there was a more "progressive" side, composed of those more interested in whether a song was good than in its origins on a chicken farm in Alabama.

Bob Dylan: Folk music was very split up—there was a purist side to it. You know, many people didn't want to hear it if you couldn't play the song exactly the way that Aunt Molly Jackson played it. I just kind of blazed my way through all that kind of stuff. [1984]

Even among the more enlightened folksingers there was a purism in the type of music they would allow themselves to assimilate. Folk was good. Blues was fine. The less mawkish kind of traditional country music was just about acceptable. Dylan, though, was considerably more eclectic. In Hibbing and Minneapolis he had assimilated a hugely diverse amount of music, from polkas and country and western through country blues, rock and roll, rhythm and blues, Mississippi Delta blues to Kingston Trio–type folk music, traditional Appalachian music and the politically motivated folk music of Guthrie, Sarah Ogan Gunning and Joe Hill.

In December 1961 Dylan told Robert Shelton, "I really couldn't decide which I liked the best, country or blues. So I suppose I ended up by becoming a mixture of Hank Williams and Woody Guthrie." But these were only two figures in Dylan's synthesis. He would later admit to other major influences, observing that "I combined other people's styles unconsciously. . . . I crossed Sonny Terry with the Stanley Brothers with Roscoe Holscomb with Big Bill Broonzy with Woody Guthrie." Others would notice that his synthesis was not wholly derived from such traditional music forms.

Peter Stampfel: He was doing all traditional songs, but it was his approach! His singing style and phrasing were stone rhythm and blues—he fitted the two styles together perfectly, clear as a bell.

By the end of 1961 Dylan was not trying to become either Woody Guthrie or Hank Williams, but rather himself. By this time the Guthrie phase was fast receding. In December he recorded his third Minneapolis Tape. The only Guthrie songs among the twenty-six titles were "Ramblin' Blues"; his own adaptation of "Sally Don't You Grieve," entitled "Sally Gal"; and Guthrie's obscure quartet of songs about venereal disease.

The other major aspect of Dylan's development during those early months in New York was his increasing confidence as a performer. He began to tell long, rambling monologues to his audience, often hilariously disjointed but combining the beat poet's form of rap with his down-home style. Indeed, at this point he worked up an astonishing version of Lord Buckley's "Black Cross," a spoken monologue that told the story of a poor black farmer, Hezekiah Jones, who was hung by white racists for being well read.

Jack Nissenson: He was always an incredible storyteller. He was distant . . . onstage, very into his own thing, but he could do these long, long monologues, with no point, and no punch line—except they kept you in hysterics. Same when you talked to him. He either told you a story, or he said, "Yeah? Is that right?" as if what you were telling him was the most amazing thing he'd ever heard.

Arthur Kretchmer: Onstage he was essentially a funny character. Maybe that isn't what he intended to be, but the audience reaction was one of laughing, not at but with Dylan. I recall him standing up there looking behind the curtains for the words to his next song, or cracking up about something which he was mumbling to himself. He was natural and loose, a real country character, and that is what everybody loved about him. . . . Sometimes he would play piano, or tell a funny story, or just clown around for a few minutes.

But it would be inaccurate to portray Dylan as being universally accepted by those on the Village scene, or by the numerous tourists turning up in the Village to hear a Kingston Trio style of folk music. Indeed, friends recall that Dylan proved an extremely adept "house-clearer" whenever the club owners wanted to shift those last few recalcitrant customers.

Happy Traum: Before he made his first album he was even rougher sounding and more off pitch, and he didn't tune his guitar. . . . We used to play in a place called Gerdes' Folk City . . . we would let him come in and do some songs for the late show. . . . He'd start playing and if there were ten people in the audience five people would get up and walk out.

Dylan also found it hard to secure gigs out of town, where his unique style of performing was an unknown quantity. Club 47 in Cambridge repeatedly refused to book him, preferring the dulcet tones of Joan Baez or Carolyn Hester's restrained musings. Dylan seemed to engender wildly contrasting opinions wherever people heard him. Some club owners seemed prepared to book him for the sheer joy of seeing him play; others would go to any lengths to keep him out. Terri Thal, folksinger Dave Van Ronk's girlfriend (and later his wife), took on the part-time responsibility of managing Dylan, and succeeded in obtaining bookings at the Café Lena in Saratoga Springs, New York, where Lena Spencer, the owner, loved his performance and asked him to come back despite much heckling from the audience; and also at a club in Springfield,

Massachusetts. But generally he was confined to consolidating his reputation in New York City.

Terry Thal: We made a tape of Bob and I took it up to Springfield, Massachusetts, where Carolyn Hester and Richard Fariña were playing. The guy who ran the club flipped. We really did a selling job. We went to Boston and I tried to get Joan Baez's manager Manny Greenhill to do a concert with Dave and Bobby, and he turned me down. I went to Cambridge's top folk club, Club 47, and a couple of other places, and they all turned me down. Nobody wanted him.

The tape Thal is referring to here was a recording made one night at the beginning of September by Victor Maimudes at the Gaslight Café. It featured performances of some six songs by Dylan, including three of his own titles, "Man on the Street," "Song to Woody" and "Talkin' Bear Mountain Picnic Massacre Blues." The tape, apart from generating out-of-town gigs, was intended to engender interest from record companies. Indeed, two of Dylan's friends, Carla Rotolo and Sybil Weinberger, tried to interest John Hammond at CBS in the tape, without success.

Dylan had begun writing his own songs, or, more accurately, his own words to "traditional" tunes—at this point all of his tunes were wholly derivative. Inevitably, most of the songs he had written by September were talking blues in the Guthrie vein. It was a form that allowed full rein to his mordant wit and clever turns of phrase. His talking blues were more extensions of his storytelling monologues than full-blown songs, but they proved extremely popular. "Talkin' New York," written in May 1961 as he headed for Minnesota, was a sardonic depiction of his early weeks in the Village. "Talkin' Hava Negeilah Blues" mercilessly parodied the type of folk song repeatedly requested by the weekend tourists. "Talkin' Bear Mountain Picnic Massacre Blues," perhaps the finest of this early trilogy, was a hilarious résumé of a boat trip to Bear Mountain that had been oversold because of counterfeit tickets.

The most notable of his early compositions, though, was "Song to Woody," his affecting tribute to his last idol. Dylan actually had the impertinence to lift the tune from one of Guthrie's own efforts, "1913 Massacre," but there can be little doubting the sincerity of the singer's paean. The song was written in February 1961.

Even at this early stage Dylan was aware enough of the need for his own identity to conclude the song with a degree of equivocation. After glorifying those who "come with the dust," Dylan states he would rather not admit to a desire for "some hard travelin' too." He had his own trail of troubles to stride down.

Friends in the Village were not always sure if any song he introduced into his set was an obscure traditional tune he had uncovered or one of his adaptations. In the summer he incorporated a couple of impressive new adaptations, a plaintive ballad called "He Was a Friend of Mine" and the more conventional blues of "Baby, Let Me Follow You Down" (also known as "Baby, Let Me Lay It on You"). He had in fact just returned from Cambridge, where he had spent a rewarding afternoon with the talented Eric von Schmidt.

Eric von Schmidt: Dylan came up once. It was Huck Finn hat time, before his first record. . . . When we got to my apartment he wasn't much interested in playing; he wanted to listen. So I played "He Was a Friend of Mine," "Wasn't That a Mighty Storm," "Baby Let Me Lay It on You," "Acne" and a couple of others. It was something the way he was soaking up material in those days.

Dylan was particularly impressed by "He Was a Friend of Mine," which eulogizes a recently departed friend.

Eric von Schmidt: He was very impressed by that concept of being able to take the black expression in that kind of song and being able to sing it. He wasn't at that time quite able to handle material that related to the blues, and he was still feeling around for a way to do that.

At this stage in his development Dylan was prepared to learn material from anybody. He soaked up an enormous amount just by listening to contemporaries like von Schmidt, Mark Spoelstra, Dave Van Ronk and Carolyn Hester. But his attempts to assimilate all forms of acoustic music did not end there. From the summer of 1961 he had access to two very important archives, and he was also able to rely on the expertise of the archives' owners. The first important archive was owned by Robert Shelton, whom Dylan was careful to cultivate as a friend. Sometimes Shelton would even take him along to concerts.

Liam Clancy: Shelton used to bring him to our concerts and tell him, "Now this is how you have to put a show together!" . . . Do you know what Dylan was when he came to the Village? . . . The only thing I can compare him with was blotting paper. He soaked everything up. He had this immense curiosity; he was totally blank, and ready to suck up everything that came within his range.

Pete Seeger: He didn't have to hear [a song] five times, he'd hear it once and latch right onto it. . . . This is the folk process.

More often Shelton would provide him with a place to rehearse and open access to his impressive folk-music collection. Shelton also acted as a useful barometer to indicate whether Dylan was working up something truly original or simply regurgitating old values already reiterated a thousand times by somewhat more authentic troubadours than a middle-class white boy from Minnesota.

Robert Shelton: We used to knock around listening to music together, and that period was interesting because Dylan was listening to every bit of music he could hear. He walked around with his ears hanging out, eager to follow whatever was going on in folk music. He'd come over to my house and play piano and listen to records.

The other important archive belonged to Carla Rotolo. Carla was the dark-haired older sister of a seventeen-year-old golden-haired beauty named Suze. Suze had become a regular attendee at Dylan's gigs during his first spring in New York, a companion for the love-struck Sue Zuckerman, though when Suze herself met Dylan at a party after the Riverside Church gig it was she who interested Dylan. Soon Suze and Dylan began to be seen together regularly in the Village. Dylan found himself flung into his first serious romance since Minneapolis.

Carla was, if anything, more of a fan of Dylan's music than her sister. It was she who regularly sang his praises to Shelton and, with Sybil Weinberger, tried to take Dylan's crude audition tape around to the record labels. Carla also had another major attraction: She worked for Alan Lomax, the premier living folklorist in America, whose definitive *Folk Songs of North America* had been published the previous year, after he had worked for years on similar folk-song anthologies with his father, John. Dylan could regularly go around to Carla's and listen to records from her collection, browse through printed material or even call upon Lomax himself (whom he had met at the Gleasons'). Thus he was able to dig out obscure songs like a heartbreaking blues Lomax's father had learned from a lady called Dink, known simply as "Dink's Blues." It would become one of the highlights of Dylan's fall sets.

His association with Suze also temporarily provided some much-needed stability, though their romance was accelerating at a frightening pace. During his first few months in New York, Dylan had made considerable use of the maternal instincts that he seemed to engender in otherwise sane women and that he had utilized so successfully in Minneapolis.

Liam Clancy: Dylan had this image of the lost waif, and all the girls wanted to mother him—he made out like a bandit because he was a lost waif!

Dylan's already noted lack of discrimination, his penchant for "plump, large-breasted" women and a mock shyness that concealed a considerable libido was a successful combination in the Village, where the more bohemian women could find a previously unsuspected deep desire to mother someone being brought out by this chubby, boyish Huck Finn from Minnesota. He delighted in showing off his prowess to his male friends, most of whom were more bashful (or maybe just more discriminating) than Dylan.

Mark Spoelstra: He had a lot of nerve with girls. More than I did. Chasing them, coming on to them, not being intimidated—man, Dylan was remarkable.

Suze temporarily subdued his polygamous instincts, and he finally prevailed upon her to move into his West Fourth Street apartment in December, a major commitment for both of them. With a steady relationship, the respect of his peers and an increasing repertoire of songs, both original and traditional, Dylan's career in the summer of 1961 seemed to be heading in only one direction and that was up. Actually, as indicated by Terri Thal, he was not readily accepted outside the Village. He was also initially unsuccessful in his attempts to secure a recording contract with the well-known folk labels (even his profound ambition did not extend to trying to attract the interest of a major label).

Izzy Young: I took him to Moe Asch of Folkways Records, who turned him down immediately. Then I took him to Jac Holzman at Elektra Records. When I asked Jac Holzman about that years later, he said that he doesn't remember me bringing him. . . . Then I took him to Vanguard Records. [The owner of Vanguard,] Manny Solomon . . . [later] said, "Listen, Izzy, I'm glad I didn't put him out on a record, because I don't want a freak on my label."

Dylan would later say that when he went up to Folkways Records, he thought he'd gone to the wrong address, such was the nature of his reception. Izzy Young was one of his important supporters that first summer in New York. Young even arranged for him to make his first studio radio appearance, on Oscar Brand's WNYC show, "Folksong Festival." Dylan apparently performed his two or three songs at the piano, which would have made a unique recording if the appearances had been preserved.

Izzy Young: I had a reputation in New York that I didn't call up people every day to say, "Hey, this guy's great." It was very few times. So I called up Oscar Brand, "Listen, there's this guy in my store, he writes really good songs, you should really listen to him." He said, "OK, send him over." So I went over to his studio, which was in the Village at the time, and he sang two songs . . . his own songs, and he was mumbling. You couldn't understand 'em. I was very embarrassed and Oscar was embarrassed. But anyway, he put him on the radio.

Young's other venture to boost Dylan's career was a concert uptown at the small two-hundred-seat Carnegie Recital Hall, which was part of the Carnegie Hall complex. Young arranged to book the hall, printed up the programs and attempted to sell the hundred tickets required to break even. Unfortunately, according to Young only fifty-three people attended the November 4 concert, and many of them were friends of Young's and Dylan's and so had not even paid for their tickets. The performance—the first half of which has been circulating for many years among collectors—seems a trifle hesitant, though Dylan still managed to deliver sensitive versions of Leadbelly's "In the Pines" and the traditional "Young but Daily Growin'." Interestingly enough, as Paul Cable has observed in his book, the latter performance proves that Dylan's pre-Guthrie voice had not been wholly lost, and at times he comes eerily close to crossing the years between Minneapolis and Woodstock. Young was bitter when the show was not even reviewed.

Izzy Young: The [Carnegie Recital] concert was never written up, which I could never figure out why, 'cause he [had been] written up in Gerdes'. But the write-up in Gerdes' was arranged between Al Grossman and Mike Porco [owner of Gerdes'], [and] *The New York Times*'s Bob Shelton.

According to Young, Shelton's September 29, 1961, review of Dylan in *The New York Times* had been no whim on his part. Shelton had been musing upon how best to introduce Dylan for some weeks before his review. If Shelton had been originally reluctant to listen to the kid who was so highly thought of by the Van Ronks and Carla Rotolo, when he finally heard him, in June, "Boom! He went nuts for him," according to Carla Rotolo. The other Village folkies soon became aware of how much Shelton thought of him, and Shelton, as *The New York Times* folk critic, was a figure of considerable influence. His support caused some animosity toward Dylan in the Village.

Liam Clancy: [Shelton], more than anyone, was responsible for Bob Dylan. He pushed and pushed and pushed. He thought Bobby Dylan was a tremendous poet. He had made a very folkie record at that time with John Hammond that wasn't doing anything, but Shelton kept pushing.

Shelton's first and most famous review certainly provided Dylan with much-needed credibility. Indeed, Suze Rotolo recollects that Dylan, who had been told by Shelton of the review, raced down to the corner store to buy a stack of copies, one of which he surely sent back to his family in Hibbing, proof that he was making something of himself in the Big Apple. Subsequently, Shelton virtually became Dylan's unpaid press officer, writing the liner notes for his first album [under the pseudonym Stacy Williams], giving him glowing reviews for his October 1962 appearance at the Town Hall with the Travelin' Hootenanny, his solo performance there in April 1963, his guest appearance with Baez at Forest Hills in August of the same year and his triumphant Carnegie Hall gig in October. Izzy Young even suggests that Shelton's articles were approved by a small coterie of advisers before he ran them.

Izzy Young: At the time, [Dylan] was living at Dave Van Ronk's house, and playing at Bob Shelton's house a lot. That's when I got to know him and that's when I became part of the little mafia around Bob Dylan. . . . Bob Shelton was the main mafia. [*sic*] He'd write an article in the *Times* about him being in Mike Porco's place and I'd read the article beforehand and Dave Van Ronk would read the article beforehand, and we would approve it. And then it would be put in the paper.

Even Dylan was caught out by the enthusiastic tone of that first review in September 1961. He had been trying to secure a contract with CBS, and Shelton's review seemed to provide a final endorsement. Though John Hammond subsequently claimed that he signed Dylan to CBS the day before Shelton's review, Shelton recollects Dylan telling him the night of the review that he had seen John Hammond that afternoon and that Hammond had offered Dylan a five-year contract with CBS. The standard story, which Shelton reiterates in his own biography, goes like this: Dylan attends Columbia session (held the day of Shelton's *New York Times* review) for Carolyn Hester's first CBS album, Hammond is impressed by Dylan's authentic look and his harp playing and offers to sign him without even hearing him sing.

There are very few plausible aspects about this version of events. It would appear that Hammond's decision was largely unaffected by Shelton's review— though the review certainly made it easier for Hammond to get his whim endorsed by the upper echelons of CBS. Hammond had already been told about Dylan by his son, John Hammond, Jr., who it seemed recognized an authentic talent as well as his father. Hammond senior first met Dylan in mid-September at a rehearsal session for Hester's album (on which Dylan was to provide harmonica accompaniment), which she held at her friend Ned O'Gorman's apartment on West Tenth Street (Spitz says this rehearsal took place on September 14, though he provides no specific evidence).

Carolyn Hester: We began to play and John Hammond just plain liked Bob Dylan. It wasn't that Dylan had written stuff then. He just felt this charisma that Bob had, and I certainly agreed with that.

Throughout the rehearsal Dylan showed his mastery of the harmonica. Hammond was impressed enough to want to hear more. Despite the many repeated stories that he offered him a contract on the spot, Hammond would subsequently insist that he did audition Dylan, asking at the rehearsal if Dylan could come up to Columbia and perform some of his songs for him. It would certainly have been not only unorthodox but profoundly imprudent for Hammond not to have asked Dylan to provide evidence of his ability as a singer.

John Hammond: When I first saw Bob Dylan, it was at a rehearsal of Carolyn Hester's down on West Tenth Street and he had on his cap . . . this was before he opened at Gerdes' Folk City. . . . I liked what I heard of him there so much I asked him to come up to the studio. I didn't know that he did much singing, but I knew that he wrote. So I asked him to come up and I heard some of the things that he did and I signed him on the spot.

This fits in with Shelton's assertion that Dylan had already signed with CBS the night of September 29 (though his signing required the rubber stamp from upstairs), and logic suggests that this was a more likely scenario for Dylan's signing than the notion that he was signed up on the evidence of his session work for Hester's unstartling debut CBS album the very same day. Hammond can only have signed Dylan as a performer. Despite Hammond's comment that he "knew that he wrote," apart from "Song to Woody" and a couple of amusing talking blues that would not translate easily to vinyl, Dylan at this point had no really strong original material.

When Hammond and Dylan began to record his debut album, simply called *Bob Dylan*, in November 1961, Dylan offered only "Song to Woody," "Man on the Street," which was not on the final album, and "Talkin' New York" as examples of his own compositions. Dylan would later claim that he "was still learning language then" and what he was writing he "was still scared to sing." He would soon disavow the album as unrepresentative of his work, which by the time it was released—a mere four months after he recorded it—it was.

The album was recorded in a mere two days, with Dylan recording some twenty songs over both sessions. Though Dylan often popped the mike and was occasionally overzealous in a vocal performance, the fact that he managed to record an album in two days suggests remarkable discipline on his part, even if both Hammond and Dylan were later unhappy with the results.

Evidence of how fast Dylan was moving was provided a month to the day after his final session for the first album. Having selected some thirteen songs for his recorded debut, he proceeded to perform twice as many at Bonnie Beecher's apartment in Minneapolis on December 22. Tony Glover recorded them on a reel-to-reel tape recorder. The legendary so-called Minneapolis Hotel Tape was a far more diverse selection of songs, and illustrated Dylan's harmonica and guitar work to much greater effect, than the bulk of his debut album.

As an illustration of how quickly he outgrew the hastily assembled material chosen for his commercial debut, there are only four songs from his month-old album on the Hotel tape. Dylan also premiered for his friends two new songs he had written during the previous month, "I Was Young When I Left Home" and "Hard Times in New York Town." "Hard Times in New York Town" was based on the traditional "Down on Penney's Farm" and was really no more than "Talkin' New York" revisited. "I Was Young When I Left Home," though, was a superb adaptation of "Nine Hundred Miles." Its portrayal of a young man who, having made his home "out in the wind," is needed back home but feels he "can't go home this way" remains one of Dylan's rare attempts to write a song that sounds authentically traditional yet bears the stamp of his personality. It also proved that von Schmidt's assessment back in June that Dylan "wasn't at that time quite able to handle material that related to the blues" no longer applied.

Tony Glover was certainly impressed, particularly with Dylan's new-found ability to pick the guitar rather than strum it but also by his convincing performances of bottleneck blues and his harmonica playing. * He was not the only one impressed. Little Sandy Review editors Jon Pankake and Paul Nelson later recalled: "The change in Bob was, to say the least, incredible. . . . He had learned to churn up exciting, bluesy hard-driving harmonica-and-guitar music. †

On the Hotel Tape Dylan was interpolating lines into songs that had never previously included them. Thus his "Wade in the Water" is not the simple spiritual tale that the traditional song told. Rather it was a reworking that resembled more Robert Johnson's hellbound-on-my-trail form of the blues than a gospel song basking in the promise of eternal salvation. "Cocaine Blues" blends lines from both "Cocaine Blues" and "Cocaine Bill and Morphine Sue" into a cogent whole, in the style of the Reverend Gary Davis.

* Dylan polished off a bottle of Jim Beam and the recording session in just over two-and-a-half hours, one track after another. Dylan was so happy with his performance that he asked for half-a-dozen dubs of the tape to give to friends.

† Pankake and Nelson say they are describing Dylan's return in May 1961. However, their recollection does not accord with the May 1961 Dylan and seems appropriate only in relation to his December "Hotel" tape.

"Stealin' " lifts verses wholesale from well-known blues tunes, but Dylan delivers the lines with such verve that he carries it off. If only Hammond could have brought a CBS recording machine to Beecher's apartment that night! Dylan proved he was the master interpreter his friends in New York knew him to be. In the new year he would prove that he could interpret his own words just as well as those of others.

4 | 1962–63: I Am My Words

Bob Dylan: I just wanted a song to sing, and there came a certain point where I couldn't sing anything. So I had to write what I wanted to sing 'cause nobody else was writing what I wanted to sing. I couldn't find it anywhere. If I could I probably would have never started writing. [1984]

If, by the end of 1961, Dylan had established himself as a unique and compelling performer, he was not as yet considered a songwriter of note by his Village contemporaries. Only "Song to Woody" had drawn any plaudits from his peers.

At the beginning of 1962, though, Dylan started writing at a furious rate. In January he was once again recording songs. This time, though, he was recording seven of his own songs. John Hammond, in an attempt to raise some funds for him between the recording and release of his debut album, had arranged a music publishing deal with Leeds Music. The seven originals were to be included in Dylan's first songbook, along with five arrangements of traditional songs recorded for the first album. Though the tape of these demos includes two nondescript blues and three less notable 1961 compositions, there were also two new and important originals.

The more remarkable song was originally called "Reminiscence Blues" (it would be copyrighted as "Ballad for a Friend"). It shared its theme with the traditional "He Was a Friend of Mine," recorded at the sessions for his first album, and showed that Dylan had mastered the blues form with remarkable ease. In six three-line verses he had written his first song about the North Country, in this case a eulogy to a friend whom he heard later had been left dead "on a Utah road" by a diesel truck. It is by no means a conventional blues: The three-line verses are understated and leave appropriate gaps in the story for the listener to use his own imagination—a common Dylan technique, but one rarely used by fellow "topical" singers, who seemed bent on describing every minute detail.

The lesser song, both in terms of the writing and the performance, was "Ramblin' Gamblin' Willie." It was the first in an extensive catalog of outlaw songs by Dylan. Willie is the supreme Robin Hood figure, spreading "his money far and wide, to help the sick and poor." He meets his death when he is gunned down after being dealt the dead man's hand—aces and eights. The song ends, as did most of Dylan's songs at this time, with a moralistic verse. In this case he informs us "the moral of the story is very plain to see": gamble and you'll end up like Willie—a strange moral after the earlier portrayals of Willie's glorious exploits.

What is perhaps surprising and pertinent to observe is that Dylan had not as yet written about political issues such as civil rights, racism and nuclear holocaust. His songs of "protest" to date, if they could be considered as such, were about little men in the grip of an uncaring system—"Man on the Street," "Hard Times in New York Town"—or straightforward tales of man's exploitation of man, like "Talkin' Bear Mountain Picnic Massacre Blues."

This would soon change. At the end of January, Dylan wrote the first of what for two years would be a steady flow of contemporary protest songs. Despite her subsequent protestations, it can be no coincidence that such songs started to flow from Dylan's pen shortly after he moved into his West Fourth Street apartment with Suze Rotolo. Suze came from a family with a strong left-wing bias, and at the age of seventeen she was stuffing envelopes at the headquarters of the Congress of Racial Equality (CORE). On February 23, 1962, Dylan was due to appear as part of a benefit for CORE. On February 1 he walked into Izzy Young's Folklore Center and told him he had written a song especially for that benefit. It was called "The Death of Emmett Till," and it was hardly a topical song, given that Till was murdered for whistling at a white woman in 1955, but it was appropriate to the CORE cause.

Possibly Dylan was not consciously aware at this point of the profound influence Suze was having on him, though he would later tell Shelton that Suze "was into this equality-freedom thing long before I was. I checked the songs out with her." After all, she was considerably better read, her sister had access to the most impressive archive of American folk music anywhere in the world and her views on the authentic expressions of protest provided him with valuable feedback. Others worried about Suze's influence.

Eve MacKenzie: Suze . . . wanted him to go Pete Seeger's way. She wanted Bobby to be involved in civil rights and all the radical causes Seeger was involved in. Suze was very much with the cause. . . . She influenced Bobby considerably that way.

Certainly Dylan was going through a major change. Within four weeks of writing "Emmett Till," he had written an uproariously funny skit on the John Birch Society, "Talkin' John Birch Society Blues," a song about the building of fallout shelters, "Let Me Die in My Footsteps," the best of his early protest songs; and a song about a murderer who had never known life outside prison, "The Ballad of Donald White." It seemed as if Dylan was now prepared to assume Guthrie's mantle, and he quickly realized that the songs were being well received.

Indeed, one of Dylan's early champions was Woody's long-standing friend, Pete Seeger. That winter Seeger, along with Sis Cunningham, founded a new magazine that would publish nothing but new songs. It was to be called *Broadside*. Not surprisingly, the emphasis in the magazine was not just new songs, but topical songs. In the very first issue, Cunningham stated, "*Broadside* may never publish a song that could be called a 'folk song.' But many of our best folk songs were topical songs at their inception."

According to Seeger, he had heard about Dylan from his fellow folksingers, but it was a broadsheet of a talking blues Dylan had written especially for Izzy Young's Folklore Center that first made him take note of Dylan as a songwriter.

Pete Seeger: He had made up a song called "Talkin' Folklore Center." . . . I took him up to *Broadside* magazine and introduced him to Sis Cunningham and *Broadside* was the first magazine that published Bob. *

At his first meeting with Cunningham, Dylan played her his brand-new talking blues about the John Birch Society, and its wry humor and scathing portrayal of the right-wingers made it ideal fodder for *Broadside*. "Talkin' John Birch" appeared in the very first issue of the magazine late in February 1962. For the remainder of 1962 and through 1963, Dylan would be *Broadside's* most regular contributor (it would be the first to carry such important Dylan songs as "Blowin' in the Wind" and "Masters of War"). It became a further medium for his outpouring of songs, which he seemed to be writing just about any time he was not walking, sleeping or singing.

---

* The song was almost certainly "Talkin' John Birch," "Talkin' Folklore Center" was not written until March.

Bob Dylan: I wrote wherever I happened to be. Sometimes I'd spend a whole day sitting at a corner table in a coffeehouse just writing whatever came into my head . . . just anything. I'd look at people for hours and I'd make up things about them, or I'd think, "What kind of song would they like to hear?" and I'd make one up. [1965]

Dylan was happy to feed the rapidly growing myth of his fecundity. In one instance, Pete Seeger asked him about all the songs he was writing during a radio show being recorded for WBAI in May 1962 (it was apparently never broadcast).

Bob Dylan: Sometimes I go for about two weeks without making up a song—well, the songs I sing. I might go for two weeks without writing those songs. I write a lot of stuff, in fact I wrote five songs last night, but I gave all the papers away. It was in a place called the Bitter End. . . . But I don't sit around with the newspapers like a lot of people do and pick out something to write a song about. [1962]

To put Dylan's newly discovered skills as a songwriter in context, he was only providing his own words to existing tunes, generally using not only the tune but the same structure as his original source. Often where his tunes seemed to be adaptations rather than straight copies, it was only because Dylan never heard a song the same way everyone else did. He couldn't help but make it sound different. Much has been made of his appropriation of traditional melodies, but in fact this has always been an aspect of the folk tradition, Guthrie being perhaps the master at reworking existing tunes for his own purposes, and Dylan was happy to acknowledge his influences. Talking about "The Ballad of Emmett Till," he admitted to Gil Turner that he "stole" the tune.

Bob Dylan: When [Len Chandler] plays and sings he uses a lot of chords but he's really good . . . and he's been always trying to tell me to use more chords and sing a couple of songs in minor keys. . . . He taught me these chords. . . . He was singing a song to these chords and I saw him do the chords and stole it from him. [1962]

Initially, Dylan was reluctant to assume the title of "protest singer." He recognized it as limiting, an early attempt to categorize him. In April, at a performance at Gerdes' Folk City, Dylan prefaced a new song he had just written by saying, "This here ain't a protest song or anything like that, 'cause I don't write protest songs. . . . I'm just writing it as something to be said for somebody, by somebody." The song was "Blowin' in the Wind."

At this stage the song only had two verses (the first and third—the inferior second published verse came later), but its impact was fairly spectacular. It was the first song Dylan had written that had such a wide-ranging and intangible theme, and this time he wisely refrained from ending it with a "the moral of this song" verse. This inventory of unanswerable questions was a far more effective approach.

It would be some months before Dylan would write another protest song of such note. Perhaps he was indeed considering how to reinvent the topical song form to suit his purposes, having already progressed beyond its existing form. This did not mean that Dylan backpedaled on his newfound political consciousness. When Gil Turner interviewed him for the folk-music magazine *Sing Out!* that summer, Dylan was happy to admit to his credentials as a singer of topical songs.

Bob Dylan: I don't have to be anybody like those guys up on Broadway that're always writin' about "I'm hot for you and you're hot for me—ooka dooka dicka dee." There's other things in the world besides love and sex that're important too. People shouldn't turn their backs on 'em just because they ain't pretty to look at. How is the world ever gonna get any better if we're afraid to look at these things? [1962]

Likewise, Dylan still seemed happy to talk about his songs. Though a song like "Blowin' in the Wind" was difficult to describe (with admirable obtuseness he informed one inquirer at the time, "There ain't too much I can say about this song except that the answer is blowing in the wind"), he was less guarded when discussing more obvious songs like "Let Me Die in My Footsteps," "Donald White" and "Emmett Till." He talked to journalist Nat Hentoff at great length about the genesis of "Let Me Die in My Footsteps," one of his great unreleased gems from this period:

Bob Dylan: I was going through some town . . . and they were making this bomb shelter right outside of town, one of these sort of Coliseum-type things, and there were construction workers and everything. I was there for about an hour, just looking at them build, and I just wrote the song in my head back then, but I carried it with me for two years until I finally wrote it down. As I watched them building, it struck me sort of funny that they would concentrate so much on digging a hole underground when there were so many other things they should do in life. If nothing else, they could look at the sky, and walk around and live a little bit instead of doing this immoral thing. [1963]

After writing "Blowin' in the Wind," which was published on the front page of *Broadside* number 6 in May, Dylan had personal concerns about which to write: Suze was leaving him. She was going to Italy to work on her art—Suze was a talented painter—and would be away for several months. She left on June 8. Dylan was pining by the ninth.

A month and a day after Suze had "sailed away in the morning," Dylan was in Columbia's New York studios recording material for his second album. Though the first session for the album had taken place back in April, it was with this session that he began the album in earnest. The original working title for the album was *Bob Dylan's Blues*, and Dylan stuck to this theme—having already recorded four blues "adaptations" at the April session—for most of this second session, recording versions of "Corrina, Corrina" and "Rocks and Gravel," songs that illustrated the increasing inventiveness of his arrangements. In the case of "Corrina, Corrina" he used very little of the traditional song, abandoning its conventional four-line ballad form in favor of the more suitable six-line blues mode, and liberally borrowing most of the song's imagery from Robert Johnson, the great Delta blues singer who had begun to fascinate him in the early months of 1962. Of course, a major part of Johnson's appeal was the mystique surrounding his life and early death, at the age of twenty-seven (or twenty-six), when he was poisoned (or was it stabbed?) by a jealous woman (or her husband), having made just twenty-nine of the greatest blues recordings ever. Indeed, in February Dylan had informed Izzy Young he was writing a song called "The Death of Robert Johnson."

"Rocks and Gravel" likewise used very little of Brownie McGhee's "Solid Road," the song it appeared to be based on, and little more of Big Joe Williams's own version of the same song.

Bob Dylan: I learned one verse of "Rocks and Gravel" from Big Joe Williams and the rest I put together out of lines that seemed to go with the story. [1963]

Dylan also recorded two of his own blues, both inventive uses of the medium. "Quit Your Lowdown Ways," which did not appear on his second album, castigates a fallen woman in the tone of a righteous preacher seeking her repentance, though the person the singer is trying to save her for is himself. "Down the Highway," which did appear on the second album, is a straightforward blues akin to "Standing on the Highway," an earlier Leeds Music demo, which itself was based heavily on Robert Johnson's "Crossroads Blues." However, Dylan's performance is anything but standard—a real lonesome tone drives this song, which is about his love taking his heart in a suitcase all the way to Italy.

At this session he also recorded "Blowin' in the Wind" and an adaptation of Henry Thomas's "Honey, Just Allow Me One More Chance," which demonstrated that he could perform exuberant blues tunes as readily as he could the more plaintive. Under John Hammond's guidance, Dylan was clearly determined to show how far he had come since November 1961. If Dylan was affected by talk at CBS that his signing was "Hammond's folly," it only hardened his determination to succeed. The first album, released in March 1962, had sold poorly—supposedly five thousand copies in the first year. Hammond's reputation and his commitment to Dylan ensured he would get a second chance. He knew that a third opportunity would be asking too much. So he worked long and hard on album number two, harder than on any other album he would make over the next twenty years. There were sessions in April, July, October, November and December 1962 and finally a last session in April 1963 before he was happy with the results. Not surprisingly, *The Freewheelin' Bob Dylan* comes across as a real *tour de force*, a milestone in Dylan's development as a performer and as a writer.

Throughout September and October Dylan was writing at a furious pace. Now that his pain and sorrow at Suze's departure had eased a little, he turned his pen to each of the genres he knew. Of course, the love songs of a lonely man still predominated. Indeed, only now did he approach his anguish with sufficient perspective to write two of his greatest love songs, "Tomorrow Is a Long Time" and "Don't Think Twice, It's All Right." The first of these was a late-night "tomorrow may never come" song, with the singer unable to face sleeping in an empty bed, preferring to hark back to better days. "Don't Think Twice" is a different kind of song altogether, and could be considered the first of his "make me feel better" songs. Though the tone could be considered light, lines that on the surface seem just wry putdowns also suggest a real hurt—"she wanted my soul," an absurd request if he had not already given his heart.

Dylan was also writing songs about broader concerns. In September, with the Cuban missile crisis imminent and tension-filled talk in all the coffeehouses, he wrote a song that cataloged a world gone mad, full of worried souls, a world where "black is the color and none is the number." According to some, he wrote "A Hard Rain's a-Gonna Fall" as a poem and only later put it to music. However, the fact that it was loosely based on the Child ballad "Lord Randall" suggests he had a song in mind all along—particularly as the last verse insists, "I'll know my song well before I start singin'."

Within a matter of days of "Hard Rain's" composition, Dylan was part of a hootenanny organized by Pete Seeger at Carnegie Hall. He decided he would premiere his new song to the largest audience of his career as part of his twenty-minute set. It would be the first time that Seeger—whose own version of the long song became a concert favorite in the following twelve months—heard the song.

Pete Seeger: We had a Carnegie Hall hootenanny. I think it was '61 or '62. . . . Once again they had too many people on the program and I had to announce to all the singers, "Folks, you're gonna be limited to three songs. No more. 'Cause we each have ten minutes apiece and no more." And Bob raised his hand, and said, "What am I supposed to do? One of my songs is ten minutes long."

Inevitably the hard rain that Dylan referred to in this song was taken to be nuclear fallout, but he was at pains to point out that the song had a broader sweep, a wider meaning, one appropriate before, during and after the Cuban missile crisis. This hard rain had more in common with a biblical apocalypse than with bombs falling through the air.

Bob Dylan: It's not atomic rain, it's not fallout rain. . . . I mean some sort of end that's just got to happen. [1963]

Bob Dylan: I wrote it at the time of the Cuban crisis. I was in Bleecker Street in New York. We just hung around at night—people sat around wondering if it was the end, and so did I. Would ten o'clock the next day ever come? . . . It was a song of desperation. What could we do? Could we control men on the verge of wiping us out? The words came fast—very fast. It was a song of terror. Line after line after line, trying to capture the feeling of nothingness. [1965]

At almost the same time Dylan also wrote his first antiwar song, the crass "John Brown"—proving that he was still unable to apply rigid quality control to the songs he was writing—as well as a song about the civil rights struggle down in Mississippi, the jaunty "Oxford Town," and a grim tale of a father killing his starving family, "Ballad of Hollis Brown," introduced by him at a Canadian concert many years later as "a tragic tale of independence and free will." By now it seemed as if these types of songs were expected of him. "John Brown" in particular reads like a song written to form.

In the months after Suze's departure, Dylan seemed more conscious of his commercial goals. Though always motivated to achieve fame via his music, Dylan in 1962 seemed to be approaching his career for the first time in a businesslike way. Through 1961 he had lacked the guidance of a truly motivated entrepreneur working on his behalf. It had been sufficient for Terri Thal to arrange a few out-of-town gigs; he could always play the Village clubs. Now Albert Grossman, a well-known entrepreneur on the folk scene, had made moves to assume control of Dylan's career. He immediately extricated Dylan from the Leeds Music contract and signed him to Witmark, a higher profile publisher with which Grossman could do business. In August 1962 Robert Zimmerman legally changed his name to Bob Dylan, and in November 1962 Grossman began his campaign against John Hammond, aiming to remove

Dylan from his field of influence. Hammond was, after all, the other music business figure in whom Dylan had placed his trust. During an experimental session with a studio band, Grossman's partner, John Court, was ordered out of the studio by Hammond. Hammond's association with Dylan was unlikely to last much longer, and Hammond knew it.

John Hammond: While he was doing his second album for us, he came up to me and asked me about Albert Grossman. He said that Albert Grossman . . . wanted to sign him and what did I think. I said we'd been on the board of the Newport [Folk] Festival together and I thought I could work with him. I found out later I couldn't. . . . Grossman's first idea was to combine Dylan with a Dixieland band and that didn't work very well.

Albert Grossman was a man about whom everyone had an opinion. Dylan's association with Grossman was seen by some as tainting him; others saw it as incontrovertible proof that Dylan's aim all along was to succeed. Not surprisingly, it was primarily Dylan's contemporaries who resented Grossman. They knew that Dylan was being groomed for success and both envied and feared him.

Izzy Young: Al Grossman, he was smarter than Bob Dylan was, 'cause he was managing Bob Dylan, then he was managing Peter, Paul and Mary, then he was owning the company that had the copyrights to the songs that Bob Dylan was writing and Peter, Paul and Mary were singing, then he owned a recording company that was recording everybody. . . . Every time there was a move, he was getting a slice out of it. He probably ended up making more money out of Bob Dylan at that point than Bob Dylan was.

Though many believe that Grossman was the main reason that Dylan grew into the national phenomenon he became, Dylan's career had a momentum of its own in this period. Nevertheless, Grossman's influence was a stabilizing factor during the increasingly frenetic rise to fame.

Peter Yarrow: Albert was a man of unusual tastes and a different kind of insight into music. He was concerned first and foremost with authenticity. Did the music have real substance, value and honesty? But he was also concerned with having impact and influence in the larger world, the heartland. It was a very rare combination. . . . There never would have been a Peter, Paul and Mary, there never would have been a Bob Dylan who could have survived and made it, without Albert Grossman. Personally, artistically and in a business sense, Albert Grossman was the sole reason Bob Dylan made it.

D. A. Pennebaker: I think Albert was one of the few people that saw Dylan's worth very early on, and played it absolutely without equivocation or any kind of compromise. He refused to let him go on any rinky-dink TV shows, refused to let Columbia do bullshit things with him. . . . And Dylan in his early stages required that kind of handling—'cause Dylan himself would go off at spurious tangents.

The "spurious tangents" Dylan liked to indulge in manifested themselves in November 1962, when he recorded and released his first single. "Mixed Up Confusion" would later be seen as indubitable evidence of his undiminished love of rock and roll during his folk period. Sounding like an outtake from one of those fabled mid-fifties Sun sessions (he recorded a version of "That's All Right, Mama" at the same session), "Mixed Up Confusion" sank without a trace and was quickly deleted.

Despite such diversions, on December 6, 1962, Dylan completed his second album—or so he believed. An album featuring "Blowin' in the Wind," "A Hard Rain's a-Gonna Fall," "Oxford Town" and "Let Me Die in My Footsteps" seemed destined to be well received by a politically conscious audience. He was already a major figure in the Village, and perhaps considered the most talented of the "young 'uns."

In December, Dylan also completed a major part of his not-so-formal education in folk music: He made his first trip to England, home of the folk-ballad tradition. Albert Grossman had somehow managed to convince the BBC to pay his airfare to fly to London simply to play a small part in a BBC drama called "Madhouse on Castle Street." Why the BBC would pay for someone with no acting experience to fly all the way across the Atlantic to play a minor part in an unexceptional television play has never been adequately explained.

Dylan flew to London Airport in mid-December, a couple of weeks early (filming was scheduled for December 30), planning to explore London and immerse himself in its folk scene. Grossman and Odetta, another talent on Grossman's roster, were both already in London when Dylan arrived. Ironically, as he headed for Europe, Suze was returning home. She set sail from Italy on December 13, arriving home five days later. Dylan, meanwhile, arrived in London on or around Tuesday, the eighteenth.

Tuesday nights were Troubadour nights. Perhaps the most renowned English folk club at the time, the Troubadour was an obvious starting point for Dylan's sojourn through the London folk scene that winter. Having abandoned the Mayfair Hotel, into which he had been booked by the BBC, for the Cumberland, a more homely locale near Marble Arch, Dylan headed for Soho, where most of the London folk clubs lay. Pete Seeger had suggested Dylan look up Anthea Joseph, who ran the Troubadour on Tuesday nights.

Anthea Joseph: The day before he turned up I had been in Collet's record shop. . . . And I got the latest copy of *Sing Out!* that they had, in which was the first Shelton interview [*sic*] with Dylan and I read it and thought, This sounds interesting. . . . The following day, which was the Tuesday, there I was [at the Troubadour]. . . . So I'm sitting there being bored stiff by the Strawbs [*sic*] and these feet came down the stairs—cowboy boots, which in those days were rather unusual, and jeans, which were also fairly unusual. Then the jacket. Then this face. Then the hat. He had the hat on. . . . He trundled up to my cubbyhole and started shoving money at me and said, "I'm looking for Anthea. Can I come in please?" And I said, "Well, I'm Anthea"—and the penny dropped—and I said, "You're Bob Dylan, aren't you?" And he said, "Yes." I said, "Right, well you can have your money back provided you sing for us."

Having made his first important contact on the English folk scene, he soon made his second. At some point in the evening Martin Carthy arrived at the Troubadour. Carthy was a talented English singer, about the same age as Dylan, not a member of the old guard, and willing to recognize and accept a new face on the scene. Carthy soon struck up a strong friendship with Dylan, and over the next four weeks Dylan would often crash on Martin and Dorothy Carthy's floor.

Martin Carthy: He was in England for about three months [*sic*]. . . . We'd see each other at the various clubs there were. There was the King & Queen, there was the Troubadour, there was the Ballads & Blues on a Saturday night at the Roundhouse pub down on Wardour Street. . . . I've read a lot of books about him and not one of them talks in any detail about his time in England. As far as I can hear, by listening to his records, his time in England was actually crucial to his development. If you listen to *Freewheelin'*, most of which was made before he came to England, and you listen to the next album after that, which is *Times They Are a-Changin'*, there's an enormous difference in the way he's singing, in the sort of tunes he's singing, the way he's putting words together. . . . Bob Dylan's a piece of blotting paper when it comes to listening to tunes. If he doesn't learn the tune he learns the idea of the tune and he can do something like it. It had a colossal effect on him.

Carthy himself was a strong influence on Dylan. He introduced Dylan to traditional English songs that Dylan was unaware of or only knew from Appalachian derivatives. By the end of 1962 Dylan had become something of a walking encyclopedia of American folk music, but his knowledge of English folk music was minimal. Of course, there were considerable similarities, and for nearly three years Dylan had been singing English ballads which had been transposed to America. Indeed, recordings from two months prior to this visit have him performing songs such as "Barbara Allen," "Handsome Molly" and "The Cuckoo Is a Pretty Bird."

Soon after Carthy played him songs from his own repertoire, Dylan, ever the sponge, was working on his first adaptations of authentic English folk songs. Two of the songs certainly introduced to him by Carthy were "Scarborough Fair" and "Lord Franklin." "Lord Franklin" was rewritten as "Bob Dylan's Dream"; "Scarborough Fair" provided him with the basic melody for two of his most beautiful love songs, "Girl from the North Country" and "Boots of Spanish Leather," both started during a five-day vacation in Italy at the beginning of January.

Bob Dylan: I ran into some people in England who really knew those [traditional English] songs—Martin Carthy, another guy named Nigel Davenport [sic]. Martin Carthy's incredible. I learned a lot of stuff from Martin. "Girl from the North Country" is based on a song I heard him sing. [1984]

Carthy was not the only English folksinger from whom Dylan learned something of the English folk tradition. A good friend of Carthy's, Bob Davenport, was considerably more knowledgeable than Carthy at this time, and he also befriended Dylan. Though Davenport's influence is less apparent than Carthy's, Dylan certainly wrote at least half a dozen songs based directly on English folk songs, either during his stay in England or shortly after his return to America, and two of these may well have been based on versions played by Davenport. "Masters of War," his scathing attack on warmongers, and "Only a Hobo," a superior reworking of the earlier "Man on the Street," took as their sources "Nottamun Town" and "Poor Miner's Lament" respectively. Both Dylan songs were composed in January or February 1963.

Also written at the time was "Fare Thee Well" (or "Farewell," to use its published title), a straightforward reworking of "The Leaving of Liverpool." The Clancy Brothers claim that Dylan lifted the song directly from their arrangement of the tune, but this appears to be incorrect. All evidence indicates that Dylan learned the song from Scottish folksinger Nigel Denver, another important influence on Dylan at this time. Indeed, he would often ask Denver to play the song.

Martin Carthy: He would always ask me to sing "Scarborough Fair" or "Lord Franklin." If Nigel was on, he would ask him for "Kieshmul's Galley" or "The Leaving of Liverpool."

"The Leaving of Liverpool" was not the only song in Denver's repertoire that intrigued Dylan. According to another English folksinger, Jim McLean, there was one song Denver sang, Dominic Behan's "The Patriot Game," that Dylan took a particular interest in. He asked McLean about the song and within three months had adapted the tune, and indeed the theme of the song. It became Dylan's most brilliant debunking of the God-and-Country ethos, "With God on Our Side."

Jim McLean: [Dylan asked me], "What does it mean, 'Patriot Game'?" . . . I explained—probably lectured him—about Dr. [Samuel] Johnson, who's one of Dominic [Behan]'s favorite writers, and that's where Dominic picked it up, saying, "Patriotism is the last refuge of a scoundrel." I explained the song to Dylan at the time.

However, unlike Carthy and Davenport, Denver never became Dylan's friend. Indeed, after an incident in late December they became rather estranged.

Anthea Joseph: They had a row. It was [over] the fact he considered Bob couldn't sing his way out of a paper bag, couldn't play a guitar and couldn't play a harp, and that Nigel was infinitely better.

Needless to say, Dylan did not appreciate Denver's opinions, and on New Year's Day 1963 he proceeded to show what he thought of Mr. Denver at the King & Queen pub, a venue where, according to Carthy, Dylan had previously met with an extremely good reception.

Ron Gould: The featured guest that night was a Scottish singer called Nigel Denver—a Scottish nationalist, fiercely patriotic. He was singing an unaccompanied Scottish ballad, nice and quiet, when Dylan came in and stood at the back of the audience. Straightaway he began to create a disturbance, talking very, very loudly, saying, "What's all this fuckin' shit?" or something of that nature, really nasty. "What's going on? Where's the drinks? How do you get a drink here?" And this went on all through the song, with people in the audience telling him to be quiet. Nobody knew who he was. Then Nigel said, "I don't know if you realize it but we allow the performers to perform, during which time the audience keeps quiet." And Dylan looked up and said, "I don't fuckin' have to keep quiet. I'm Bob Dylan." Which really enamored him with the audience!

According to Anthea Joseph, who was present, Dylan had good reason to heckle Denver that night.

Anthea Joseph: He was drunk . . . and so was Nigel—again. . . . And he was awfully bad that night.

In London, Dylan himself generally seemed to be consuming more than enough drink. In the final week of his stay, he was providing some harmonica accompaniment for an album Richard Fariña and Eric von Schmidt were recording at Dobell's. Fariña and von Schmidt had hooked up with Dylan at the beginning of January, and again after his return from Rome, where he had gone for five days with Odetta.* Fariña and von Schmidt proved serious drinking companions. On the first day at Dobell's, Dylan arrived with a bag full of beer. A loose session was planned. Offered a bottle of Guinness, he took a swig, exclaimed, "My God, what's this?" and emptied the remainder of the bottle on the floor. By the second day Dylan, von Schmidt and Fariña were well juiced. Having completed the session, they headed down to the Troubadour one last time (Dylan and von Schmidt were going home the following day).

Anthea Joseph: They all turned up about eleven o'clock absolutely out of their gourds except for Ethan Signer, the fiddle player. Ethan was straight as a die and very embarrassed by this collection of bozos that he was looking after. . . . The Troubadour has—you can't call it a stage—a platform. [It's] less than a foot. [Dylan] was falling off it. And finally I supplied him with a stool and said, "You'd better sing sitting down 'cause otherwise you're gonna hurt yourself."

In the middle of Dylan's impromptu set Nigel Denver arrived at the club, fully expecting to sing with Judy Silvers, the scheduled act that night, who had already performed her first (and, as it turned out, last) set. Denver began heckling Dylan from the floor, but Dylan was too drunk to care, and no matter how much Denver taunted Dylan, he refused to admit to Denver's existence. Denver finally stormed out of the club. As von Schmidt later commented, "Dylan [just] wouldn't let him exist."

Perhaps Dylan's most legendary performance in London, though, had been shortly before Christmas, when he went to the Singers' Club with Anthea Joseph. Part of Denver's fierce resentment of Dylan was because he wrote his own songs, and Denver had the purist's view that all folk songs must be exclusively traditional. Carthy and Davenport were prepared to accept Dylan as a valid troubadour who utilized but was not mired in the folk tradition. Of course, the Village had its fair share of purists. But in London there were the

---

*Scaduto's story that he went to Italy to find Suze is wholly apocryphal. Dylan was fully aware that she was back in New York.

purest of the pure, those for whom even Appalachian ballads were a trifle sullied, and their home was the Singers' Club, run by Ewan MacColl and Peggy Seeger.

Anthea Joseph: I took him to the Singers' Club. Folklorist Bert Lloyd was there and I walked into the bar with Bob, clutching guitar, and we went up to the bar, bought a drink, and Bert knew about Dylan and I introduced them. So Bert then introduced him to Ewan and Ewan sort of looked at the guitar and we all trailed upstairs. The first half of the Singers' Club was deadly serious—no floor singers in the first half, not ever—and the audience by this time had begun to recognize [Dylan]—not because of any publicity, but because the word had got out. So the muttering was "Bob Dylan's here, Bob Dylan's here." They kept on sort of looking at him and Bob was getting the giggles. . . . And we went downstairs at halftime, had another jar, went back upstairs and it was getting people off the floor, and there was no way they could say no. He had to be got up! . . . [Of course] he wasn't trad. And it was distinctly traditional. . . . He did "Masters of War" [sic] and "Ballad of Hollis Brown," which goes on forever with the chorus and many extra verses. When you got up off the floor your maximum was five minutes really. [Dylan did] twenty! And he did it on purpose. I'm sure of it. Absolutely sure of it. And brought the house down.

MacColl never forgave this young Yankee upstart and would later write several vitriolic articles dismissing Dylan's work, but by then Dylan had long progressed beyond the limits set by the MacColls of this world. His English visit gave a new dimension to his writing. He returned to New York at last prepared to concentrate on reworking the traditional forms rather than perpetuating them. From now on it would be exclusively Bob Dylan songs that his audiences would hear, even if some of the melodies to which he put his chains of flashing images still sounded mighty familiar.

5 | 1963: From Town Hall to Carnegie Hall

If the change in Dylan after his trip to London was not as dramatic as on his return from Denver in 1960, his friends noticed a new dynamism in him. Part of this was the gradually increasing influence of Al Grossman. But Dylan no longer seemed content to just write songs and sing them. He required a reason.

In 1965, when he was the king of folk-rock and required to be dismissive of his past, he would repeatedly insist that he had jumped into a scene he saw happening when he began writing protest songs. Many commentators have dismissed this as the rewriting of history by Dylan, arguing that the sincerity evident in songs such as "Only a Pawn in Their Game" and "Masters of War" belies his later claims. Such commentators mistake sincerity for zeal. The "finger-pointing" songs Dylan had written in 1962 and would write in 1963 were unquestionably sincere expressions of frustration and anger at neophobes who attempted to subvert the process of change. However, they represented only one facet of his songwriting skills. It was a conscious decision on his part to suppress the other genres he had mastered in order to emphasize the finger-pointing aspect of his songwriting.

He made that decision on returning from England in the winter of 1962–63. Part of the reason for his choice was that the times were indeed a-changin', and Dylan was shrewd enough to recognize the first signs. The starting point, though, for the emergence of the Protest Singer was the fall of 1962. He had gradually become more active in making contributions to *Broadside*, Sis Cunningham's mimeographed publication of topical songs. In November 1962, he recorded the first of several sessions for *Broadside*, intended to provide material for the magazine. The first session included three songs in the finger-pointing vein. "Oxford Town" was the best of the bunch. The other two were "Ye Playboys and Playgirls," an innocuous little ditty about the sort of people who shouldn't run this world, and "Paths of Victory," the second of Dylan's "exhortation" songs. The first such song in his repertoire, "Ain't Gonna Grieve," had been published by *Broadside* the previous August, his first contribution since "Blowin' in the Wind."

Though inconsequential songs in themselves, "Ain't Gonna Grieve" and "Paths of Victory" were the direct antecedents of "The Times They Are a-Changin' " and "When the Ship Comes In," Dylan's two most famous "exhortation" songs. They were simple reworkings of the hand-clapping, foot-stomping form of gospel song, but the promise was of an egalitarian emancipation rather than of some postlapsarian Eden. Indeed, "Ain't Gonna Grieve" was a straight rewrite of the traditional spiritual, "Ain't Gonna Grieve My Lord No More."

In the final two months of 1962 *Broadside* published three of Dylan's finger-pointing songs, two resulting from this session (the other being "Death of Emmett Till"). Returning to New York in January, Dylan worked up perhaps his most vengeful song of this kind, "Masters of War." Delighted with the result, he made a rare appearance at a Gerdes' hootenanny the Monday after his return and premiered the song to the by now usual plaudits from his friends, who recognized how quickly he was outstripping their own efforts. Within a couple of days he was recording the song for *Broadside*. In attendance at that session were Sis Cunningham, Happy Traum, Suze Rotolo and Phil Ochs. Ochs, the new kid on the block, was in awe of Dylan's mastery of the protest genre yet was soon attempting to emulate his efforts, the first of a tidal wave of Dylan copyists.

Dylan's new direction that winter led him to reconsider the songs he had already selected for *Freewheelin'*. There is a common belief that Dylan was forced by CBS to replace "Talkin' John Birch Society Blues" and three other songs that were finally deemed unsuitable for his second album. The chronology of the events surrounding the album's release, though, tends to contradict this assumption. The story presupposes that such an instruction followed Dylan's last-minute refusal to appear on "The Ed Sullivan Show" on May 12, 1963. However, the four replacement songs were recorded at the end of April (the twenty-fourth). According to official files, *Freewheelin'* was released on May 27, 1963. This would hardly allow time to recut the album, reprint the liner notes and issue the new version, all within two weeks of the Ed Sullivan debacle.

The decision to replace four of the songs on *Freewheelin'* must have come before "The Ed Sullivan Show." It was probably Dylan who made the decision, and thus it seems that the purpose of the April 24 session was specifically to record replacement songs for "Let Me Die in My Footsteps," "Ramblin' Gamblin' Willie," "Rocks and Gravel" and "Talkin' John Birch Society Blues," all written (or, in the case of "Rocks and Gravel," adapted) in the first three months of 1962. Dylan simply felt he had outgrown these songs. The four new songs included two new finger-pointing songs, "Masters of War" and his last and wittiest talking blues, "Talkin' World War III Blues." Dylan himself told a friend in April 1963, the month of this session, that he was unhappy with *Freewheelin'* as it then stood.

Bob Dylan: There's too many old-fashioned songs in there, stuff I tried to write like Woody. I'm goin' through changes. Need some more finger-pointin' songs in it, 'cause that's where my head's at right now. [1963]

Dylan was outgrowing his old songs. He also seemed to be outgrowing a few old friends. In April, John Hammond was finally ousted as his producer due to pressure from Al Grossman, who still nursed a grudge against Hammond for ordering his partner, John Court, out of a Columbia studio. For his April session, Dylan had a new young black producer, Tom Wilson, at the console. Wilson had a superb ear for the innovative, though he had no knowledge of folk music. He quickly recognized that Dylan was not "merely folk."

Tom Wilson: I was introduced to Dylan by [producer] David Kapralik at a time when I was not properly working for Columbia. I was being used by them, shall we say. He said, "Why don't you guys stick around and do a coupla things?" I said, "What do you mean? I don't even work for Columbia." What's more, I didn't even particularly like folk music. I'd been recording Sun Ra and Coltrane and I thought folk music was for the dumb guys. This guy played like the dumb guys, but then these words came out. I was flabbergasted.

If the April session tilted the balance on *Freewheelin'* in favor of Dylan's more recent work (only two songs would date from sessions prior to October 1962), he had already presented an even more updated Dylan model to an appreciative audience at New York's Town Hall on April 12. That Dylan could play Town Hall was a remarkable achievement, even though he failed to sell out the nine-hundred-seat venue. (According to folksinger Tom Paxton, "There were entire rows that were empty," though it was in fact three quarters full.) His ground-breaking second album had yet to be released, his first album had bombed and less than eighteen months earlier he could hardly find fifty people who would turn up at the Carnegie Recital Hall to hear him perform. The Town Hall gig was a notable performance, and when the show was enthusiastically reviewed by both *Billboard* and *The New York Times*, executives at CBS were beaming.

Never one to give the audience what they expected, Dylan played no songs from his one and only released album, and for the first time he played a set wholly composed of original compositions. His perversity was such that he did not include "Blowin' in the Wind," at this point his best-known song. Indeed, he played only three songs that would appear on his forthcoming album, and two of those he had yet to record.

The remainder of the set consisted of what can only be described as a wave of new finger-pointing songs. Wisely mixing the lightweight with the topical, Dylan combined rag tunes such as "New Orleans Rag" and "All Over You" with the social commentaries he was becoming known for. Along with earlier songs such as "John Brown," "Ballad of Hollis Brown" and "A Hard Rain's a-Gonna Fall," he included four brand-new finger-pointing songs, "Masters of War," "Walls of Redwing," "Who Killed Davey Moore" (boxer Davey Moore had died only eighteen days earlier from wounds sustained in a title fight) and the impressive "With God on Our Side." Dylan even had the remarkable self-assurance to encore by reading an eight-minute poem he had written, entitled "Last Thoughts on Woody Guthrie." CBS recorded the show, ever mindful of the advantages of some live material in the vaults should it require "product" during a fallow period from one of its artists.

With emphasis on jocularity or social commentary, by far the most moving moment came midway through the show when Dylan performed an achingly lovely rendition of a song he had written for Suze during her absence in Italy, "Tomorrow Is a Long Time." Dylan and Suze had in fact had a terrible argument before the show, which could not have helped to steady his nerves. "Tomorrow Is a Long Time" sounds like the most beautiful apology possible.

Suze and Dylan had become reconciled on his return from England in January. Despite Suze's soon-rekindled doubt about the nature of their relationship, Dylan himself seemed happy enough to be back with her. He even convinced her to move back into his Fourth Street apartment within days of his return, despite her original intention to keep the relationship on a more manageable basis than before her departure. Dylan's spurt of songs about love and loneliness temporarily dried up with Suze's return, and the flood of finger-pointing songs he wrote that spring and early summer seemed a replacement for his songs of sorrow.

Meanwhile, Grossman was working on building Dylan's career on a solid bedrock of mystery. Thus, he encouraged Dylan to stop playing New York club gigs, despite his inability to sell out larger venues. He also encouraged Dylan to play fewer gigs altogether. Obscure local radio appearances, such as he had made in 1962 on the shows of Cynthia Gooding, Billy Faier and Henrietta Yurchenco, were strictly out. TV was the medium on which to get Dylan across, preferably national TV.

Late in April, Dylan did play an important club date, but many miles from New York, at a place in Chicago called the Bear. He was booked to play this small gig because Grossman had a part interest in the club, and because he was scheduled to appear on Studs Terkel's radio show while in Chicago. Terkel was a renowned social commentator and his show had a large following; in the Midwest, Dylan needed the exposure appearing on Terkel's popular show would provide. While playing the Bear, Dylan also met up and jammed with a talented local guitarist named Michael Bloomfield. Bloomfield's original intention in turning up had been somewhat different.

Michael Bloomfield: I had heard the first Bob Dylan album. I thought it was just terrible. I couldn't believe that this guy was so well touted. So I went down [to the Bear in Chicago] to see him, y'know, to meet him, to get up there and blow him off the stage. But to my surprise, he was enchanting. He couldn't really sing, y'know, but he could get it over . . . better than any guy I've met.

Through the spring and summer of 1963 Grossman ensured that Dylan's profile was kept at an optimum and that the phrase "spokesman for a generation" accompanied each report. In May, Grossman arranged for Dylan to make his first national TV appearance on "The Ed Sullivan Show," but during rehearsals Dylan was informed by the man in charge of program practices that his talking blues about the John Birch Society would upset upstanding American citizens.

Bob Dylan: After they told me I couldn't sing "Talkin' John Birch Society Blues" I walked out. I could have sung a substitute song, something like "East Virginia Blues," but I just couldn't do it after coming so close to the John Birch talkin' thing. [1963]

Ironically, the uproar about this blatant act of censorship did Dylan considerably more good, by portraying him as a rebel and counterculture hero, than if he had appeared on the show and performed a couple of his tunes to an uncaring national TV audience. As it was, *The New York Times* and *The Village Voice* both ran major stories on the furor, and *Time* and *Playboy* mentioned the incident in articles on the folk-music revival, both emphasizing Dylan as the most promising of all the up-and-coming folksingers. Nat Hentoff's profile in *Playboy* even included a story about Dylan's original audition for "The Ed Sullivan Show" at the time of the release of his first album. His friends then told him that the show's producers would eventually call and Dylan replied, "Well, they won't tell me what to sing."

In the summer of 1963, after the Sullivan debacle, Dylan did appear on two TV folk-music specials broadcast in New York, performing two songs on WNBC-TV and three on WNEW-TV. More importantly, in July, Peter, Paul and Mary released their own version of "Blowin' in the Wind," and within two weeks it was number two on the national charts. Thus when Dylan played the

Newport Folk Festival during the last week in July he was the rising member of
the folk pantheon. As if recognized as the heir apparent, that weekend he would
perform with both the current king and queen of folk, Pete Seeger and Joan
Baez, as well as playing his own set. On the Sunday evening he received the
ultimate endorsement when as a finale the ensemble sang not just the traditional "We Shall Overcome" but also his "Blowin' in the Wind."

He had already sung with Joan Baez prior to Newport. She had joined him
to duet on the recently written "With God on Our Side" during his set at the
Monterey Folk Festival in May. Baez had first met Dylan when he was playing
at Gerdes' Folk City in 1961, but had been unimpressed by his urchin look. At
a later meeting Dylan was too busy trying to impress her attractive younger sister
Mimi to take undue notice of Joan. According to Eric von Schmidt, she first
took note of his music when her manager, Manny Greenhill, gave her an
acetate of his songs (probably a test pressing of the original *Freewheelin'*). At this
point she apparently "began to realize the power of the lyric content."

Their next meeting was in Cambridge, Massachusetts, in April 1963 when,
after a show at the Cafe Yana one Saturday, he appeared at a Sunday hoot at
Cambridge's Club 47. Baez was at the Club 47, and when everyone adjourned
to Sally Schoenfeld's apartment after the hoot, Baez managed to spend some
time with him. Presumably she also got to hear "With God on Our Side,"
which he had only premiered nine days earlier. When they met at Monterey
three weeks later, they picked up where they had left off and Dylan ended up
spending several days after Monterey at Baez's home in Carmel, California.
Their "romance" had begun.

When Dylan turned up at Newport with Suze, Baez showed that she could
be slightly temperamental by introducing her version of "Don't Think Twice"
as a song about a love affair that has lasted too long. Suze, who suspected Dylan
of having an affair with Baez, was furious, and her demeanor did not improve
when Dylan informed her that he was going on a brief tour with Baez that
August. Suze, tired of Dylan's infidelities and his possessiveness, moved in with
her sister Carla. This only resulted in Dylan becoming a virtual resident at
Carla's apartment, where Dylan and Carla had a series of arguments about
Suze, her needs and how each knew what was really in her best interests.

Respite came only when Dylan chose to play out-of-town shows. In August
he played as Baez's guest, singing a couple of songs on his own and then
duetting with her on three or four more of his own tunes. The minitour
culminated in a show at Forest Hills Stadium in front of twelve thousand fans,
and gave him much-needed exposure.

Joan Baez: I was getting audiences of up to ten thousand at that point, and
dragging my little vagabond out onto the stage was a grand experiment. . . .

The people who had not heard of Bob were often infuriated and sometimes even booed him.

Because of the self-evident commercial gains Dylan stood to make through his intimate relationship with Baez, some have doubted the sincerity of his feelings for her at this point. Certainly his cavalier attitude toward her through-out most of 1964 and 1965 suggests that he felt none of the emotional extremes that his relationship with Suze engendered. He did not seem unduly perturbed to be away from Baez for long periods of time. After September 1963, they had only limited opportunities to spend time together. In 1964 they managed to spend days rather than hours in each other's company only in February, late July, August and November.

However, in the summer of 1963 they spent a great deal of time together, and Dylan was perhaps at his most susceptible to Baez's charm. After their August tour, Dylan spent little time in New York trying to repair relations with Suze before he headed to Carmel for a couple of weeks' vacation and some necessary solitude in order that he could get on with writing songs for his third album. In early October, Dylan joined Baez at a prestigious gig at the Hollywood Bowl in Los Angeles, though the Californians were unable to accept Dylan and re-sponded by heckling and booing him, and complaining about his interrupting pure Baez.

Dylan finally returned to New York to complete his third album and play a crucial gig at the three-thousand seat Carnegie Hall, an acid test of whether he had "arrived" as a performer. It would be four months of disquiet and personal doubt before he saw Baez again.

If Dylan had been avoiding playing headlining gigs throughout the sum-mer, presumably in accordance with Grossman's master plan, he did make a major solo appearance in addition to his sets at Newport, and it was an im-portant one. The location was the Hotel Americana in San Juan, Puerto Rico. This was not an obvious locale for an important gig, but it was the CBS sales convention he was singing at, and, uncompromising as ever in his art if not in his private life, Dylan took the opportunity to remind the reps that here was the man censored by the CBS TV network and he was still singing a few home truths.

Tom Wilson: In the first Columbia convention, in '63, I had two acts, Dylan and Terry Thornton. I'd just joined the company. I was brand new. Dylan had just written that song about Emmett Till and another one called "With God on Our Side." . . . He sang it and half the cats in the convention got up and split. All the Columbia guys just started to walk out. They didn't want to hear this. Those were his two strongest songs at the time and he didn't spare them.

Despite the reps' distaste for him, Dylan was now recognized as an up-and-coming artist on the roster. Less than two months later, *Freewheelin'* finally cracked the *Billboard* album charts, where it would remain for some thirty-two weeks. The song Dylan sang that so offended the southern reps was almost certainly not "Emmett Till" (or indeed "Oxford Town," another 1962 composition, as Bob Spitz claims), which he had dropped from his set twelve months earlier, but another song about the unjust murder of a black man, Medgar Evers. The song was called "Only a Pawn in Their Game," and he had premiered it less than two weeks earlier at a voter-registration rally in Greenwood, Mississippi, where he had flown to provide some moral support to those fighting the civil rights battle on the front lines and to sing a few of his own finger-pointing songs. Medgar Evers had been the Mississippi leader of the National Association for the Advancement of Colored People. Dylan's song portrayed the murderer as just a poor dumb white bigot manipulated by powerful racist forces.

A month later Dylan was motivated to write another song about the death of a black person at the hands of a white man. "The Lonesome Death of Hattie Carroll" was written in Carmel during his September idyll there. The finger-pointing songs seemed to be pouring out of him, despite the troubled relationship with Suze. That summer he wrote not just "Only a Pawn in Their Game" and "The Lonesome Death of Hattie Carroll," but also his clarion calls "The Times They Are a-Changin' " and "When the Ship Comes In," and two songs that portrayed evil judges, one who used his position to seduce a poor girl trying to save her father from the gallows ("Seven Curses"), the other refusing to reprieve a man unjustly imprisoned for life ("Percy's Song").

These latter two songs would not be included on Dylan's third album, though both were recorded at the sessions. Both showed a new sophistication in Dylan's handling of traditional ballad forms. In an open letter to Tony Glover that July, he had written that he could no longer sing "Red Apple Juice," he had to sing "Masters of War," and he could not sing "Little Maggie," he had to sing "Seven Curses." Yet he made it clear what a debt he owed to the traditional songs that taught him how to express himself: "The folk songs showed me . . . that songs can say somethin human."

In the case of "Seven Curses" and "Percy's Song" he seemed to be attempting to write new songs that were self-consciously traditional in form, style and imagery. The melodies, of course, were authentically traditional (based on "Anthea" and "The Wind and the Rain," respectively). It was as if he wished to prove he could write in the traditional ballad forms and yet make them "say somethin' human." Dylan would later return to such an approach to songwriting for much of the *John Wesley Harding* album.

Of these half a dozen topical songs, perhaps the two anthems, "The Times

They Are a-Changin' " and "When the Ship Comes In," would be the most important. "The Times They Are a-Changin' ," next to "Blowin' in the Wind," remains the best known of Dylan's songs from his "folk" period, yet it seems a far more conscious effort than the half-realized "Blowin' in the Wind." Indeed, according to Tony Glover, Dylan's sidekick from his Minneapolis days and the man to whom he wrote the open letter, it was not only a conscious communication of a feeling, it was a deliberate attempt to write a song that would fuse the anthemic nature of "Blowin' in the Wind" with the apocalyptic conceit of "A Hard Rain's a-Gonna Fall."

Dylan's old friend Tony Glover had flown into New York early in October to record for Elektra and went up to Dylan's apartment on Fourth Street to see his old cohort. The place was, as usual, strewn with lyrics and typescripts. Picking one up at random, he read the line, "Come senators, congressmen, please heed the call." When he asked Dylan what the hell it was, Dylan replied, "Well, you know, it seems to be what the people like to hear."

Glover, along with most of his fellow Minneapolis folkies, was reluctant to see Dylan adopting the mantle of prophet of the civil rights movement. As early as 1962, when they reviewed his first album, Paul Nelson and Jon Pankake, editors of Minneapolis's *Little Sandy Review*, were exhorting Dylan to avoid the topical song vein: "We sincerely hope that Dylan will steer clear of the Protesty people, continue to write songs near the traditional manner, and continue to develop his mastery of his difficult, delicate, highly personal style."
When Dylan returned to Minneapolis in late June 1963, Dylan and Nelson got into a friendly but heated discussion at Glover's apartment about the role of politics in folk music. Nelson once again attempted to convince Dylan to abandon the topical song genre, which subverted the music to the cause. Dylan insisted that politics—in the widest sense—were an integral element of his songs' lyrics, and that social issues "are more important than music."
"The Times They Are a-Changin' " was rapidly adopted by wider causes than the civil rights activists. The rebellious young considered it a song as much about the generation gap as about that between the liberal and conservative forces in the country. Dylan would once again be forced to emphasize its wider meaning.

Bob Dylan: It happened that maybe those were the only words I could find to separate aliveness from deadness. It had nothing to do with age. [1964]

Bob Dylan: I can't really say that adults don't understand young people any more than you can say big fishes don't understand little fishes. I didn't mean it as a statement. . . . It's a feeling. [1965]

"When the Ship Comes In" was a landmark composition for different reasons. The song itself is a vengefully joyous paean to an apocalypse that will sweep away the fools the author does not suffer gladly: the neophobes, the masters of war, the playboys who run his world. It was written that August in a fit of pique in a hotel room, after he had been refused admission by an impertinent hotel clerk until his companion, Joan Baez, vouched for his good character.

The song, like most of Dylan's at the time, was based on another, older song. However, this time it was not a traditional folk song that he was creating from. "When the Ship Comes In" is based on "Pirate Jenny" from Brecht and Weill's *Threepenny Opera*, an equally vengeful song in which Jenny dreams of the destruction of all her enemies by a mysterious ship. It was Suze who first introduced Dylan to Brecht.

Suze Rotolo: My interest in Brecht was certainly an influence on him. I was working for the Circle in the Square Theater and he came to listen all the time. He was very affected by the song that Lotte Lenya's known for, "Pirate Jenny."

The influence of Brecht was the first indication that Dylan was applying a new sophistication to the sources from which he was drawing inspiration. With Suze's encouragement and hints from Van Ronk, both voracious readers, Dylan was expanding his intellectual frontiers. While in Britain at the beginning of the year he had been reading Robert Graves's *The White Goddess*, a "historical grammar of poetic myth." He also began reading the French symbolists Rimbaud, Baudelaire and Verlaine, as well as Villon and Apollinaire.

"The Times They Are a-Changin' " and "When the Ship Comes In" also showed a considerable knowledge of the Bible. Allusions to the apocalyptic tracts of the Old Testament abound in both songs, but perhaps the most overt allusion in "The Times They Are a-Changin' " is to the New Testament Gospel according to Matthew, in which Jesus says of the Last Judgment, "But many that are first will be last, and the last first." As the symbolism in Dylan's songs became more sophisticated, the restrictions of the finger-pointing genre he had been committing himself to throughout 1963 became apparent. In September he composed the most hymnal of his acoustic songs, "Lay Down Your Weary Tune." With this song he proved that he was capable of writing something other than my-baby-left-me and/or topical songs, and that he could handle more abstract themes and feelings with considerable skill.

If he needed warning about the image he was developing as a civil rights activist, an interview published in the left-wing *National Guardian* (conducted by editor Jack Smith) provided it. The Dylan that comes across in the interview seems wholly committed to "the Cause," yet apparently he was very unhappy with the way he was portrayed in the article. He seemed to misunderstand the workings of the press, not realizing that if he talked for twenty minutes about his youth and twenty minutes about the civil rights struggle, an activist paper like the *National Guardian* would concentrate heavily on pronouncements such as:

Bob Dylan: I don't think when I write. I just react and put it down on paper. I'm serious about everything I write. For instance, I get mad when I see friends of mine sitting in southern jails, getting their heads beat in. What comes out in my music is a call to action. [1963]

Dylan's mishandling of the press did not cause just such relatively minor difficulties as the *National Guardian* article. In October he reluctantly agreed to be interviewed by a *Newsweek* reporter, Andrea Svedburg, after she had dug up something of his Minnesota past and threatened to use the material if he did not agree to an interview. However, their conversation apparently soon deteriorated into a slanging match and Svedburg went ahead and published a vicious hatchet job on Dylan. Though the unveiling of his Hibbing past was nothing but a minor inconvenience, Svedburg brought up an old story that a high school student named Lorre Wyatt had written "Blowin' in the Wind" and sold it to Dylan for a thousand dollars and, while carefully avoiding saying Wyatt *had* written the song, she managed to sow a large seed of doubt by implication.

Coming hard on the heels of the completion of his third album and a triumphant concert at Carnegie Hall, the Svedburg story brought Dylan down to earth. As it was on the streets by October 29, he barely had time to savor his Carnegie Hall success three nights earlier. As in his Town Hall concert in April, he used his Carnegie Hall show to present a new Dylan. This time he did perform "Blowin' in the Wind." More important, he performed eight of the songs scheduled for his third album, and four songs recorded for but not eventually chosen to be on *The Times They Are a-Changin'*. The fans who attended the show must have been very disappointed when the *Times They Are a-Changin'* album appeared without "Lay Down Your Weary Tune," "Percy's Song" and "Seven Curses," all of which he performed superbly that night. They made for a more rounded portrait than the album would offer on its release in January. He had his parents flown in from Hibbing to see his triumph.

Beattie Zimmerman: We knew he was gifted when we went to Carnegie

Hall. . . . We flew in for the concert and we stayed for a few days and we knew that he was really enjoying what he was doing and that was important to us.

Recording for the third album had gone far more smoothly than for *Freewheelin'*, which was now riding high on the *Billboard* chart. In fact, *The Times They Are a-Changin'* album was recorded in just three August sessions and three October sessions. The emphasis, though, was very different from that of *Freewheelin'*. Though *The Times They Are a-Changin'* is a far more intense album, it is less richly diverse. There is an unrelentedness to the tales of hard times and moral outrages. An album containing "Ballad of Hollis Brown," "North Country Blues," "Only a Pawn in Their Game," "With God on Our Side" and "The Lonesome Death of Hattie Carroll" could hardly be said to paint an overwhelmingly optimistic view of the world.

Dylan even seemed to emphasize the unrelenting nature of the material with the droning melodies he utilized and the monotony of his vocal delivery. Though he recorded the beautiful "Lay Down Your Weary Tune" and "Eternal Circle" at the later sessions, he refrained from including them, presumably because he felt they would break the mood of the album. The stark black-and-white cover also reinforced the album's monochrome feel. Only the two love songs seek to break the mood, and both "Boots of Spanish Leather" and "One Too Many Mornings" tell heartbreaking tales of love gone wrong.

Although *The Times They Are a-Changin'* was well received by Dylan's politically conscious audience, it is an album that has not worn well. Despite containing a couple of songs of great beauty, the manner of delivery and the length of some of the more turgid finger-pointing songs make it a grueling listening experience. However, it was what Dylan fans had wanted—the last album for a very long time about which that could be said. The next album would show another side altogether. Meanwhile, Dylan had one more song to record to complete the album, and he recorded it two days after Svedburg's story hit the stands.

6 | 1963: Troubled and I Don't Know Why

The *Newsweek* story had an immediate consequence. Though he had seemingly finished his third album at the two sessions before the Carnegie Hall show, Dylan returned to Columbia's New York studios on the final day in October to record the concluding song, one he had written in response to the "dust of rumors" that Svedburg had conjured up in her *Newsweek* article. The song was based on a traditional "bid-you-adieu" tune called "The Parting Glass," and was called "Restless Farewell." What it was a restless farewell to remained as yet unclear. However, it gave fair warning that he was not content to remain the Woody Guthrie of his generation.

Possibly Dylan envisaged a restless farewell to song. In the next three months he would write a profusion of poems, but the only new song that he appears to have recorded during this period (and he may have written it earlier) was the ironic "Guess I'm Doing Fine," for which he made a publisher's demo. It seems he was temporarily uncertain of his direction. The occasional live performances he gave were presentations of *The Times They Are a-Changin'* persona, an identity with which he seemed increasingly uncomfortable.

Dylan's move away from protest, though it would not be discernible for some months, is generally credited to two events that occurred in the fall of 1963—the assassination of President John F. Kennedy and the Emergency Civil Liberties Committee award ceremony at which he received the Tom Paine award. Certainly both events affected him considerably. But while they—along with the *Newsweek* story—precipitated his next change in direction, he had in fact already tired of his newly assumed mantle.

Two of the songs left off his third album celebrated the nature of song itself—"Lay Down Your Weary Tune" and "Eternal Circle"—but Dylan seemed temporarily reluctant to follow the direction in which his muse was steering him. Instead, he withdrew from public gaze for three weeks at the end of October, hanging out with Terri Thal and Dave Van Ronk, who were now married, and with the folksinger Barry Kornfeld, and also writing a lot of poetry. It seemed at this point as if he could best express his own thoughts and feelings without the restrictions that song imposed.

Part of Dylan's problem was that his new songs were becoming increasingly difficult to fit into the rigid patterns of the long-established folk melodies he had been using. Thus, though "Lay Down Your Weary Tune" was based on a traditional Scottish melody, it required a particularly inventive reworking to allow the words to flow freely within their new context. Yet the songs on *The Times They Are a-Changin'* in most cases still had ascertainable antecedents— "Hollis Brown" was loosely based on "Pretty Polly," "With God on Our Side" on "The Patriot Game," "Boots of Spanish Leather" on "Scarborough Fair," "When the Ship Comes In" on "Pirate Jenny," "Lonesome Death of Hattie Carroll" on "Mary Hamilton" and "Restless Farewell" on "The Parting Glass."

Later, on the day he recorded his next album, he discussed the constrictions songs imposed with Nat Hentoff:

Bob Dylan: It's hard being free in a song—getting it all in. Songs are so confining. Woody Guthrie told me once that songs don't have to do anything like that. But it's not true. A song has to have some kind of form to fit into the music. You can bend the words and the meter, but it still has to fit somehow. I've been getting freer in the songs I write, but I still feel confined. That's why I write a lot of poetry, if that's the word. Poetry can make its own form. [1964]

The apex of Dylan's poetry writing would be in these last two months of 1963, though throughout 1963 and the first part of 1964 he regularly turned to free verse forms to expound his thoughts. In April he had presented two of his first free-verse poems to the audience at his Town Hall show. One, the bio-poem "My Life in a Stolen Moment," was included in the concert program. The second, called "Last Thoughts on Woody Guthrie," was performed as an encore at the show, the only known example of Dylan actually reading his poetry aloud.

"My Life in a Stolen Moment" would later be regularly reprinted in concert programs and bootleg productions, until it finally formed part of his *Writings and Drawings* anthology. It is a surprisingly straightforward account of his past. Though embroidered to include the myth of running away as a child and the typically anti-intellectual stance of attending university "on a phony scholarship that I never had," most of the poem rings true, save for the outrageous travel-ogue in which Dylan, between Minneapolis and New York, manages to take in Texas, California, Oregon, Washington, New Mexico and Louisiana. He refers to learning to play guitar, to sing and to write—"but I never ever did take the time to find out why." Again Dylan refuses to admit to being anything but the unconsciously inspired troubadour, a persona that Guthrie, a well-read and informed man himself, adopted long before him.

"My Life in a Stolen Moment" was the start of a yearlong flirtation with free verse, before Dylan's nonlyric writings coalesced into the prose-poem form adopted for his first book, *Tarantula*. In that time Dylan contributed to concert programs, album sleeves—whether his own or friends'—and magazines published by friends.

Bob Dylan: I used to get scared that I wouldn't be around much longer, so I'd write my poems down on anything I could find—the backs of my albums, the backs of Joan's albums, anywhere I could find. [1965]

He also wrote a number of unpublished works that hint at a couple of long-term projects—to write a play and to work on some form of biography. The biography initially seems to have been intended to take the form of a series of bio-poems like "My Life in a Stolen Moment." In a statement to Studs Terkel on a Chicago radio show in late April 1963, Dylan suggested that he had begun work on such a biography:

Bob Dylan: It's about my first week in New York. . . . It's about somebody who has come to the end of one road, knows there's another road there but doesn't exactly know where it is, and knows he can't go back on this one road. . . . It's got all kinds of . . . thoughts in my head, all about teachers in school, all about hitchhikers around the country. . . . I'd never been to New York before, and I'm still carrying these memories with me so I decided to write it all down. [1963]

In a recently emerged set of manuscripts, the so-called Margolis and Moss manuscripts, which date from the end of 1963, there is what appears to be a two-page excerpt from a Dylan "autobiography." The 120-line typescript takes the form of college recollections. More specifically, it is about spending the 1959 Christmas vacation wishing he were with Judy Rubin, his girlfriend at that time. It is a surprisingly frank account of remembered feelings: "I love Judy. Judy says she loves me but she also says she's busy. I told her I love her. . . . I hate her cause I sence she don't love me. . . . I wish I didn't love her I wish she'd invite me for christmas for christ's sake."

The poem ends with Dylan phoning Judy, losing his cool, insulting her and having her hang up on him: "girls have hung up on me an have hung me up as far back as I remember . . . each one promises t be the last." As a coda to his musings upon that Christmas, he rejects what he experienced of university life with one of his many anti-intellectual tirades: "what I saw connected with the fraternity house summed up the whole established world. . . . underpants . . . cats standin in underpants being inspected by others with serious looks in their eyes . . . jive wide smiles in hairy sweaters. . . . what the fuck thats got t do with learnin I never will know . . . never hope to either."

This remarkable excerpt is part of a sheaf of papers that all appear to date from the week or weeks following President Kennedy's assassination in Dallas, Texas, on November 22, 1963. Indeed, on the back of the second sheet featuring Dylan's Minneapolis recollection is a poem about his own response to the assassination, along with a brief six-line poem with a somewhat familiar ring to it: "the colors of friday were dull as cathedral bells were gently burnin strikin for the gentle strikin for the kind strikin for the crippled ones an strikin for the blind."

The seed of Dylan's new form of song—the chains of flashing images that would, when bound together, form "Chimes of Freedom" (and later "Mr. Tambourine Man," "Gates of Eden" and "It's Alright, Ma")—were being sown while he worked through his inner turmoil. If the *Newsweek* story, his continued doubts about his relationships with Suze Rotolo and Joan Baez and a general fear of his steadily increasing fame all contributed to this turmoil, it would be unwise to underestimate the effect of Kennedy's assassination on Dylan.

Dylan later told Anthony Scaduto that when he played a show in upstate New York the day after the assassination he began, as always, with "The Times They Are a-Changin'." At this point he felt "that song was just too much for the day after the assassination. . . . I couldn't understand . . . why I wrote that song, even." Perhaps Dylan realized that, with the song not even commercially released, it was already redundant. Events had overtaken him, and that would always be the way if he continued to write so-called topical songs. It would take Dylan eighteen months wholly to disavow that song and its sentiments.

The Margolis and Moss manuscripts include several unfinished poems about the assassination, clearly written as immediate responses to the events in Dallas. In one he admits it is useless to "recall the day once more." In another he uses an image he would later reuse to dismiss the validity of party politics, though this time he uses it to rail against the bullet and assassin: "there is no right or left there is only up and down."

At the same time that Dylan was struggling to find ways of expressing his anger, frustration and sorrow, he was working on eleven poems that would later form the liner notes to his third album. These "11 Outlined Epitaphs" would not fit on the album's back cover and were continued on an insert.

In epitaph two, Dylan again recalls his youth in Hibbing, which was clearly something he was coming to terms with in the wake of *Newsweek* uncovering his background for the benefit of (as he put it in epitaph nine) "unknowin eyes." In epitaph four, he questions Jim (presumably Jim Forman) about the validity of party politics. Quite possibly this was written after the ECLC dinner. In epitaph six he ponders the question of why Woody Guthrie was his last idol. In epitaph eight he makes his famous confession of plagiarism—"Yes, I am a thief of thoughts / not, I pray, a stealer of souls." Epitaph nine is a further attack upon Svedburg and her ilk, refuting the notion that these hacks could somehow expose him. After all he exposed himself "every time I step out / on the stage."

The final two epitaphs seem more conciliatory, as if they were continuations of "Restless Farewell," expositions indeed on that song. For here, as there, he seeks to recall the wrongs he may have done, the causes he may have fought and the battles he may have lost. Three albums into his career, Dylan was already trying to live down his past. In the tenth epitaph he muses on whether the cockroaches "still crawl" around Dave and Terri Van Ronk's apartment. But his autobiographical musings at this time were not restricted to his "Outlined Epitaphs" or his unpublished bio-poems. Liner notes he wrote for Peter, Paul and Mary's second album were recollections of his first New York winter—once again reminiscent of his remark to Studs Terkel: "Snow was piled up the stairs an onto the street / that first winter when i laid around New York City / it was a different street then."

Earlier in the fall, he had composed the most ambitious of his bio-poems, quite probably written in September, while staying with Joan Baez in Carmel. The poem appeared in October on the jacket of Baez's second *In Concert* album. The poem commences in Hibbing with a young Dylan crouching on the grass watching the trains roll by. Passing through the time when he adopted idols as role models—choosing his idols "T be my voice an tell my tale"—he finally rejects them ("I learned that they were only men / An had reasons for their deeds"). Then he begins to define terms such as *beauty* for himself—"the only beauty's ugly man"—finally learning to recognize beauty in the voice of a lady singer he knows.

Dylan's "Poem to Joannie" proved that his free-form poems could retain their own structure and move to their own rhythm. It almost certainly gave him new confidence to work harder and more exclusively at his free-verse poetry that fall. He also enjoyed using even freer forms in prose-poem letters to friends.

Interestingly enough, Baez has suggested that much of the material he wrote at her house but never reclaimed was more akin to the bio-poems than to the sort of material eventually used in his book *Tarantula*.

Joan Baez: He wrote some beautiful things about running up to his own house and trying to get in. He had to pee, something about his mother behind the screen door and he was jumping up and down—he had to pee. . . . He never edited anything. He couldn't bear to take anything out of the sentence he'd written.

The prose-poem letters would prove the most readable part of *Tarantula*. Prose poetry was a form he adopted fairly early on, both in private and public correspondence. The first such letter published was one to Dave "Tony" Glover, which Dylan allowed to be included in the program for the 1963 Newport Folk Festival. The letter starts with him admitting he hasn't written lately and that Glover has hinted "in a quiet way if I changed my ways so hard that I don remember old friends." The remainder of the letter deals with all the reasons why he has not written. Among his musings he hints that he is trying to learn to do unconsciously what he used to do consciously: "now I really aint thinkin / about what I'm doing no more."

The poem concludes by saying, "I don know why I aint written t yuh / Maybe cause I never write letters t m'self." The other two "open letters" from this period are considerably more troubled affairs. Both were written in December 1963, some six months after his contribution to the Newport program. The first was written within days of Dylan's attending a dinner at the Hotel Americana in New York, at which he received the annual Tom Paine award given by the Emergency Civil Liberties Committee (ECLC).

The dinner was a complete fiasco. Dylan was a poor choice for such an award, unschooled as he was in the art of public speaking, and a chronically nervous performer at the best of times. In an environment peopled by middle-aged liberals beneficently donating money for their chosen cause, he was immediately uptight and began drinking heavily. According to Edith Tiger, when it came his turn to speak, she found him vomiting in the men's toilet. Led to the dais, he announced, "I haven't got any guitar—I can talk, though." His subsequent speech, wholly devoid of diplomacy and finesse, proved that this was not the case: He informed all bald and aging people they should be on the beach soaking up the sun, not fighting causes in this "young man's world." He then revealed that he saw something of Lee Harvey Oswald, Kennedy's alleged assassin, in himself. Not for the first or last time in his life he was subject to a volley of boos. Since the dinner was primarily an excuse for raising funds for the ECLC, his ill-considered speech cost the committee a considerable sum of money.

Afterward he penned "A Message to the ECLC," an open letter that sets out with the intention of apologizing for his actions but ends up recalcitrant. Forced to speak publicly, he wrote the ECLC, "I tore everything loose from my mind / an said 'just be honest, dylan, just be honest.' " He defended his comments about Oswald, insisting he was "speaking of the times." Eventually he stated that he was no speaker and that he should remember to stay what he was: "I am a writer an a singer of the words I write I am no speaker nor any politician an my songs speak for me because I write them in the confinement of my own mind an have t cope with no one except my own self." This is an open admission that he does not wish to be a spokesman, but will stay true to his songs. Finally he offers to make up the shortfall in donations, a generous offer but one that he did not in fact fulfill.

In an open letter to *Broadside* magazine, to which he was providing fewer and fewer songs, published within four weeks of the ECLC debacle, he still showed a troubled mind. He admitted, "I am now famous," and the notion clearly scared him. He wrote that people asked him "why do I write the way I do" and it infuriated him.

Dylan also made references to both his novel and his play in the *Broadside* letter. The novel was frustrating him: "it dont even tell a story / it's about a million scenes long / an takes place on a billion scraps / of paper." Before it would be finished it would frustrate him considerably more. The play that Dylan was writing, though, he now seemed fully committed to: "an I'm up to my belly button in it / quite involved / yes I've discovered the power of playwritin means as opposed t song writing means / altho both are equal, I'm wrapped in playwritin for the minute / my songs tell only about me an how I feel."

Dylan's ambitions as a poet and prose writer, rather than as a songwriter, may have been further fed at the end of December when he met the renowned beat poet Allen Ginsberg. Dylan had first been introduced to Ginsberg's writings back in Minneapolis and, along with the French symbolists, the beats were a primary influence on his development as a songwriter in 1964.

Bob Dylan: I didn't start writing poetry until I was out of high school. I was eighteen or so when I discovered Ginsberg, Gary Snyder, Philip Whalen, Frank O'Hara and those guys. Then I went back and started reading the French guys, Rimbaud and François Villon. [1985]

The play that occupied Dylan at this point was presumably the untitled, unfinished fifteen-page play that recently emerged as part of the Margolis and Moss manuscripts. If so, the play, which concerns a number of characters with names like John B. Pimp, Mrs. Agnas McBroad and Eeny Weeny, who meet in a combination church/barroom/hotel because they have been told they must do so or they will die, shows only that he was no playwright. The dialogue is forced and unconvincing, plot development minimal and pacing nonexistent. Possibly this was one of several plays Dylan attempted at this time—in May 1964 he informed Max Jones he was working on two plays. Fortunately such projects came to naught.

At the end of January and beginning of February 1964, Dylan was in Canada filming a half-hour TV special for the Canadian Broadcasting Company. While there he talked to two Canadian journalists about his work. He informed both that he was working on a novel and a play, and told a journalist from *Gargoyle* magazine that the play would be finished before the novel and that he wanted to see it performed. He also made his most unequivocal statement about his abandonment of topical song, even though at this point he seemed unclear what form of songwriting would replace the genre he had made his own.

Bob Dylan: I used to write songs, like I'd say, "Yeah, what's bad, pick out something bad, like segregation, OK, here we go," and I'd pick one of the thousand million little points I can pick and explode it, some of them which I didn't know about. I wrote a song about Emmett Till, which in all honesty was a bullshit song. . . . I realize now that my reasons and motives behind it were phony. I didn't have to write it. [1964]

In the true tradition of the beats, he had decided to go On the Road, to explore America and find a way to bring out those chains of flashing images. He had been away from song too long.

7   1964:   On the Heels of Rimbaud

Dylan's trip through the United States in February 1964 has been very well documented by Scaduto, Shelton and, to a lesser extent, Spitz. All have devoted a respectful chunk of pages to Dylan's On the Road Revisited trek. In all instances their primary sources have been the notes and recollections of Dylan's traveling companion Pete Karman, though Karman seemed a strange choice for a companion in the first place. He was, after all, a close friend of Suze's, and a journalist. Thus, when Dylan spent the night with a female student after his Emory University concert, Karman was there to chronicle it. Finally, when they reached San Francisco and Dylan's presumably long-awaited liaison with Baez, Karman was told to pack his bags. Dylan later told Shelton, "We had to kick Pete out and send him home on a plane." In fact, Karman has said that he actually had to pay for his own way back. The other two companions on Dylan's trek, Paul Clayton and Victor Maimudes, were old friends, trustworthy and above all "cool." They knew how to play Dylan's moods.

The twenty-day trek to California from New York by station wagon weaved its way through Virginia, North Carolina (where they stopped off to meet Carl Sandburg in Hendersonville, finding him unimpressed by Dylan's hard sell of his credentials as a poet), South Carolina, Georgia (where Dylan played at Emory University), Mississippi and Louisiana (where they were intent on experiencing the New Orleans Mardi Gras, which took place on the eleventh). Setting out from New Orleans on the twelfth for the second leg of their journey, Dylan and his trio of companions took turns driving and roared through Texas, Oklahoma, Kansas, Colorado (where Dylan premiered a new song at a concert at the Denver Civic Auditorium) and finally on through Utah and Nevada to California.

Dylan's own version of the three-week journey through America was typically fanciful. In his version, "We hit forty-six halls from Augusta, Georgia, to Berkeley, California. We talked to people in bars, miners. Talking to people—that's where it's at, man." In fact, on the one occasion he came into direct contact with "the common people," when he stopped in a record shop in Charlottesville, Virginia, and was recognized by fans, he apparently said, "Man, there's a lot of people in here. Let's split." He was better able to deal with his admirers when expecting public attention, as when he stopped at the Denver Folklore Center on the day of his Denver concert. He had to accept that he was now a famous figure and three-week trips in search of the "common man" were becoming increasingly impracticable.

However, there is another important factor in Dylan's motives for the trip. He hoped that it would be inspirational. Dylan regularly sat in the back of the station wagon tapping away at his typewriter, working on songs and probably poems. The song he spent most of his time working on as they drove down to New Orleans was "Chimes of Freedom." The refrain "strikin for the gentle / strikin for the kind / strikin for the crippled ones / an strikin for the blind . . . ," which appeared in one of the December 1963 Margolis and Moss poems, had obviously been haunting him. While his three companions alternated at the wheel—they generally dissuaded Dylan from taking his turn, as he was a notoriously bad driver—he completed the song.

In many ways the antecedents of "Chimes of Freedom" are to be found in the material he recorded for his third album. Its sense of the power of nature—the song is set during a storm as two friends or lovers huddle in a church doorway to see "the chimes of freedom flashing"—closely mirrors "Lay Down Your Weary Tune." It is also unashamedly apocalyptic, as both "The Times They

Are a-Changin' " and "When the Ship Comes In" were. It is closer to "When the Ship Comes In." The difference is in the promise of universal emancipation (or even redemption?). The song is sung "for every hung-up person in the whole wide universe," rather than for just the chosen few. Ironically, if the final verse of "When the Ship Comes In" had been dropped, the effect would have been largely the same. After all, the power of nature is a central part of that song too, and only in the final verse are the foes identified.

"Chimes of Freedom" is similar to "When the Ship Comes In" in the way that the lyrics detail a coherent vision perceived by the singer. As his life became more chaotic, he seemed to take upon himself the visionary mantle that Rimbaud required of the true poet:* In February 1964 Dylan told his companions, "Rimbaud's where it's at. That's the kind of stuff that means something. That's the kind of writing I'm gonna do."

The composition of "Chimes of Freedom" reflected an important shift in Dylan's perception, a move toward the intensely poetic songs he would write later in the year. Apart from "Chimes of Freedom," Dylan worked on scraps of other songs in the back of the station wagon. He mentioned to Karman the rather trite line from "Ballad in Plain D," "Are birds free from the chains of the skyway?" though it would take a very personal trauma to engender the remainder of the song.

According to Dylan, in his *Biograph* notes, he also began another song while in New Orleans, entitled "Mr. Tambourine Man." This certainly makes sense logically and historically. "Mr. Tambourine Man" seems stylistically very close to "Chimes of Freedom," more so than later visionary songs such as "Gates of Eden." "Mr. Tambourine Man" was definitely completed before the June 1964 CBS session, when he made his first attempt to record it. According to Al Aronowitz, a New York journalist who was a friend of Dylan's, Dylan was working on the song in New York, which would tend to place it in March/April (Dylan was in Europe for the four weeks immediately before the CBS session). According to one recollection, Dylan even performed it at London's Royal Festival Hall in May. "Mr. Tambourine Man" also seems to tie in with the idea of Mardi Gras. As Mardi Gras stretches through the night and into the early hours of the morning the "skippin' reels of rhyme" continue to haunt the streets, until the partying souls collapse into sweet dreams. At such times visions would surely come with relative ease. Dylan later said he got some amazing projections after staying up all night.

---

* "The poet makes himself a seer by a long, prodigious and rational disordering of the senses. . . . He reaches [for] the unknown and even if, crazed, he ends up by losing the understanding of his visions, at least he has seen them."—Arthur Rimbaud to Georges Izambard, May 13, 1871

In "Mr. Tambourine Man" the singer certainly seems to crave that *dérèg-lement de tous les sens* that Rimbaud wrote about. It is this disordering of the senses that will open him up to the unknown and through which he must follow the Rimbaudian seer onto his "magic swirlin' ship" (or is it really just a drunken boat?). With "Mr. Tambourine Man," Dylan leapt beyond the boundaries of folk song once and for all. Some would follow him, others would not. Dylan himself had just begun the most prolific two years of his life.

Of course, "Mr. Tambourine Man" is also a celebration song. The choice of a musician as the seer is no whim. Dylan was looking to advance his music. Having assimilated the traditional modes of expression that envelop folk and blues, perhaps he felt like bringing it all back home. If he did, time had turned his way. In January 1964, America was shaken by a new wave of popular music from the other side of "the pond," the vanguard led by the Beatles. According to Eric Burdon of the Animals, Dylan's awareness of the possibilities of fusing rock with folk was first realized when he heard the Animals' version of "House of the Rising Sun," a song he had recorded on his first album.

Eric Burdon: Well, it seems that one day Dylan was drivin' up to San Francisco from New Orleans or somewhere, when our record came over his radio. When it was announced he said to Joan Baez—who was with him at the time—"This'll be the first time I've heard this version," although it was at that time number one in the States. So he listened to it, stopped the car, ran around the car five times, banged his head on the bumper and began leapin' about shouting, "It's great! it's great!"

In fact, "House of the Rising Sun" did not chart until August 1964 and it was September before it reached the number-one spot. His evocative description of Dylan getting out of a car while traveling from New Orleans to San Francisco places the event in February 1964, and the record that was number one at the time, indeed throughout the month, was the Beatles' first U.S. number one, "I Want to Hold Your Hand." Though Dylan would later be impressed by "House of the Rising Sun," it was the Beatles' incursion into American culture that finally redefined rock and roll. If evidence of the sorry state of American pop music at this time is required, the five number one acts before the Beatles were Jimmy Gilmer and the Fireballs, Nino Tempo and April Stevens, Dale and Grace, the Singing Nun and Bobby Vinton. No wonder the folkies held pop music in such contempt! Dylan was one of the first to realize that everything had changed.

Bob Dylan: All you heard [back in the late fifties] was rock and roll and country and western and rhythm and blues music. Now, at a certain time the whole field got taken over into some milk, you know—into Frankie Avalon, Fabian and this kind of thing. . . . So everybody got out of it. And I remember when everybody got out of it. But nobody really lost that whole thing. And then folk music came in as some kind of substitute for a while, but it was only a substitute. . . . Now it's different again, because of the English thing. . . . What the English thing did was, they proved that you could make money at playing the same old kind of music that you used to play. [1966]

On February 22, 1964, Dylan and his traveling crew reached San Francisco for a sellout concert at the Berkeley Community Theater. Apart from his appearance at the Monterey Folk Festival the previous May, and his brief guest appearance at Baez's Hollywood Bowl show, he had not played in California, and the level of anticipation for the concert was unnaturally high. As Richard Fariña wrote, it was as if the students "seemed, occasionally, to believe he might not actually come, that some malevolent force or organization would get in the way." In fact, Dylan's performance was a stunning *tour de force* that even convinced San Francisco *Chronicle* reviewer Ralph J. Gleason to recant his previous view that Dylan was overrated, and he wrote up the concert with the zeal of a new convert.

Dylan gave his hip West Coast audience a foretaste of his new direction by performing "Chimes of Freedom" and "Eternal Circle," the latter his first song to deal with the nature of song itself. Inevitably, Baez insisted on lending her dulcet tones to a few duets of old favorites, but Dylan no longer needed her endorsement. Though he dedicated a song to her in Los Angeles, he did not join her onstage at any of her shows that winter. However, he did return to Carmel for a few days after completing his brief West Coast tour at the end of February, and he was still prepared to continue—or perhaps unwilling to discontinue—their romance.

Yet if he felt he could return to the increasingly distraught Suze in New York that March, he was displaying a surprising naïveté. Suze could not take his double standard anymore. He was happy to gallivant around the States, living a life of sex, drugs and folk music,* but he was fiercely possessive and jealous whenever she tried to maintain her own independence. The argument that finally ended their stormy relationship was interrupted by Carla Rotolo's return to her apartment, where Suze was now living. As Dylan accused Carla of setting Suze against him, Suze finally "freaked out." Carla ordered Dylan out of the apartment and, though he later returned in a desperate attempt to achieve a reconciliation, the romance was over.

Barry Kornfeld: [Clayton and I] walked in and there was Carla practically foaming at the mouth, Dylan practically foaming at the mouth and Suze sitting

---

* Karman relates the profuse amounts of marijuana consumed by all the passengers in his account.

in bed, literally in shock. Suze had just sort of tuned out. Bob and Carla were still going at it—they were both totally incoherent.

Looking back on their relationship now, Suze is remarkably forgiving of Dylan. She recognizes that the nature of his ever-increasing fame—and his own hunger for mass status—altered their relationship irrevocably, and made it impossible for them to work out their problems by themselves.

Suze Rotolo: We were young and vulnerable. A lot of crazy things happened. It is strange to think that so much is made of us together in those years. It could have run its course naturally, but it was shaded and formed by all these outside influences, because of his growing fame. . . . He began snubbing his old friends. But it was all so understandable in an odd way. He could see these things happening to him and he wanted to make sure they would happen, so at the same time he didn't have time to just hang out anymore. He was working on his image and his career. . . . There was a period when I was part of his possessions. I don't think he wanted me to do anything separate from him. He wanted me to be completely one hundred percent a part of what he was. He was tied up with his own development, and it was just his world that became concentrated in just music.

Dylan was distraught. However badly he had behaved toward Suze, he still loved her and found it hard to accept her loss. In late March he went back on the road playing a series of dates on the East Coast, up from New York. He was continuing his On the Road Revisited phase, traveling with Maimudes and enjoying wine, women and song. He needed something to keep his mind off the grief he was feeling.

John Cooke: Sixty-four was the year of the greatest Dylan concerts. It was just Bob and Victor Maimudes in a blue Ford station wagon with perpetual bottles of Beaujolais.

As previously, when Suze had run off to Italy for six months, he found himself writing "makin' me feel better" songs. The first one he performed that spring was "It Ain't Me Babe." It seemed a blunt disavowal of whatever roles his ex-lover had tried to foist upon him. In perhaps a fantasy of wish fulfillment he refuses to take her back, and tells her bluntly that he's "not alone." However, "It Ain't Me Babe" was much more than a neat update of "Don't Think Twice, It's All Right." It is difficult not to see the song as directed at the false expectations of certain sections of his audience as well as the hopes of a disappointed lover. When he informs "her," "I will only let you down," he was recognizing that he could never live up to the myth, whether imposed by a lover or an audience.

In May 1964 he returned to England. Grossman had arranged a show at the three-thousand-seat Royal Festival Hall in London. Dylan was in demand. The week of his arrival, *Freewheelin'* finally cracked the U.K. top twenty, and his show was a sellout. It was a very different situation from sixteen months earlier, when he could wander anonymously around London. After his two-hour performance on a sunny Sunday afternoon, he went to make his exit from the hall.

Anthea Joseph: We were walking out of the stage door—now this tells you that nobody realized what a star he was—we were going out to get a taxi to go to an Indian restaurant for supper. I mean, CBS hadn't laid on anything. I don't think there was anyone from CBS there, even. And Bob was going out in front of me, and I was walking along with Albert, and Bob disappeared under this wave of humanity who were sort of grabbing at his clothes and his hair. He was terrified! And Albert and I dived in and hoisted him out, the two of us being the tallest and the largest people about, and got him back inside. . . . It wasn't something you expected. I mean, that happened to pop stars. You knew it happened to pop stars—but not singer-songwriters.

Clearly Beatlemania had other consequences besides revolutionizing American pop music. One of these consequences was increased media interest in pop stars for interviews and radio and TV appearances. Since Dylan was playing only one show in London, in order to extract maximum mileage out of his visit he had to be accessible to the media. After all, it had taken a year to get *Freewheelin'* onto the charts. Grossman intended to keep it there.

Thus, Dylan was ferried up to Manchester to record three songs for a Sunday TV entertainment program called "Halleluiah." He also recorded a song for the BBC's "Tonight" program, though an appearance on the popular "Saturday Club" radio show was canceled because of a two-day delay in his arrival. He was interviewed by several journalists, including Max Jones from *Melody Maker,* whom Dylan responded to very well, having met him on his previous trip. Other interviewers he treated far more cavalierly, in particular Maureen Cleave from the London *Evening Standard.* Dylan did not take to the uninterested and ill-informed Cleave, while she was not used to such an uncooperative subject.

Anthea Joseph: He didn't like her but he flirted with her unmercifully. That's when he started [the games], having this posey young woman coming up and asking stupid questions and really beginning to get the hang of how to handle these idiots.

Dylan was learning to handle the press his way. If the *Newsweek* story had taught him anything, it was to recognize an adversary in the media. Cleave would later suggest that Dylan rocked back and forth in the motion of masturbating himself while she talked to him, though the published article did not show her displeasure at this bohemian urchin. However, Dylan remained determined to ridicule the "straight" press at every opportunity.

Four days after his triumphant Festival Hall concert—the reviews of which were ecstatic, *The Times*'s reviewer comparing Dylan with Segovia—he flew to Paris with Ben Carruthers, another regular sidekick. While in Paris he looked up Hugues Aufray, who had translated some of his songs into French. Dylan initially stayed with Aufray, but was soon introduced by Carruthers to an intriguing chanteuse named Nico. After going to Nico's studio apartment for a meal, Dylan ended up staying with her, playing her his newly composed "It Ain't Me Babe" and writing a new song for her, "I'll Keep It with Mine." Leaving Paris a week later, Dylan looked up Aufray's cousin in Berlin. After a couple of days in Berlin he finally set out for Vernilya, a small village just outside Athens, where he stayed for a week, writing the bulk of the songs for his fourth album, which he was due to record on his return to New York.

Among the songs presumably composed in Vernilya was "Ballad in Plain D." Based upon an old English folksong, "Once I Had a Sweetheart" (aka "The False Bride"), the song graphically detailed the night of his breakup with Suze. His portrayal of Carla as the "parasite sister" remains a cruel and inaccurate portrait of a woman who had started out as one of his biggest fans and who changed as she saw the emotional blackmail he continually wrought upon her younger sister. A critic once described listening to the song as like reading somebody else's mail, and certainly it still sounds that way today. When Dylan was asked in 1985 whether there were any songs he regretted writing, "Ballad in Plain D" was the one song he singled out.

Bob Dylan: That one I look back at and say, "I must have been a real schmuck to write that." I look back at that particular one and say . . . maybe I could have left that alone. [1985]

Other songs that he worked on in Greece were more sympathetic studies of a broken relationship, though pain and sorrow sometimes clouded his artistic vision. "To Ramona" was a particularly beautiful portrait of a woman whose friends betray her with their words of advice. It is probably the reason why "I'll Keep It with Mine," an equally moving song, did not make the album, dealing as it does with a similar idea. Though Baez would later claim "Mama You Bin on My Mind" for herself, if it was "about" anybody it was surely "about" Suze. It too failed to make the album. The songs he wrote that week were a catharsis for him, designed to expunge all his feelings of sorrow, remorse, loneliness and desire.

Suze Rotolo: People have asked how I felt about those songs that were bitter, like "Ballad in Plain D," since I inspired some of those, too, yet I never felt hurt by them. I understood what he was doing. It was the end of something and we both were hurt and bitter. His art was his outlet, his exorcism. It was healthy. That was the way he wrote out his life . . . the loving songs, the cynical songs, the political songs.

Now that his records were selling—*The Times They Are a-Changin'* had made it to the top twenty—CBS was pressuring him to keep up the flow of albums. After all, this was an era when the Beatles and the Rolling Stones regularly issued two (or, once their respective American labels had bastardized the U.K. albums, three) albums a year. By the time Dylan returned to New York at the beginning of June it had been more than eight months since he had been in a Columbia studio, and the powers that be wanted a new album in time for the fall sales convention. Dylan allowed himself to record his new album quickly and without due consideration. Indeed, when he arrived at the New York studios on June 9 he informed Nat Hentoff, who was writing a profile on him for *The New Yorker*, that he would be trying to record the entire album in that one night. He also informed Hentoff that he was attempting to record an album very different from his previous efforts.

Bob Dylan: There aren't any finger-pointing songs in here. . . . Those records I've made, I'll stand behind them, but some of that was jumping into the scene to be heard and a lot of it was because I didn't see anybody else doing that kind of thing. . . . You know—pointing to all the things that are wrong. Me, I don't want to write for people anymore. You know—be a spokesman. . . . From now on, I want to write from inside me, and to do that I'm going to have to get back to writing like I used to when I was ten—having everything come out naturally. The way I like to write is for it to come out the way I walk or talk. [1964]

While putting away a bottle or two of Beaujolais, Dylan did indeed record his fourth album, plus half a dozen outtakes, in one night. By the time he recorded the official take of "My Back Pages" at one thirty in the morning, the album was finished. The *Another Side of Bob Dylan* session was a prodigious effort even for a man used to recording quickly and with a minimum of fuss. It also turned out to be his last entirely acoustic session. Perhaps he had so mastered recording solo that he felt he had no option but to record with a studio band. It seems more likely that songs like "Black Crow Blues"—his first piano-backed song on record—signified a leaning toward his former rhythm and blues roots.

The album was not well received even in his established market, though its flaws were not the reasons why it came in for such flak from former supporters. It did not lack social comment as they said, but when it dealt with large issues, as on "My Back Pages," it was embarrassingly self-conscious. When it dealt with the breakup with Suze literally, as on "Ballad in Plain D," it was just plain embarrassing. When it attempted humorous romps like "All I Really Want to Do," "I Shall Be Free No. 10" and "Motorpsycho Nitemare," the results sounded forced and unconvincing. Only the familiar terrain of cynical love songs such as "I Don't Believe You" and "It Ain't Me Babe" proved he could be as incisive as ever, and "Chimes of Freedom" was bound to be the standout track on the album. "Mr. Tambourine Man" was attempted at the session but was left off the album; Dylan later claimed he felt too close to it.

The inconsistency in the material on *Another Side* was precisely because Dylan was too close to the experiences he was drawing upon. He was also still experimenting with the style of language found on "Chimes of Freedom" and "Mr. Tambourine Man." "My Back Pages" was the least successful, with its bizarre images of "corpse evangelists" and "confusion boats." If it had been written two months later, it would have been a superior song. The album was recorded less than two weeks after most of the songs were written, and little editing seems to have taken place. Inevitably, Dylan was forced to defend the album on its release.

Bob Dylan: The songs are insanely honest, not meanin t twist any heads an written only for the reason that i myself me alone wanted and needed t write them. i've conceded the fact there is no understanding of anything, at best, just winks of the eye an that is all i'm lookin for now i guess. [1964]

Matters were not helped by the title of the album, which seemed a declaration of intent. Dylan clearly wanted to present a different side of himself from the dogmatic tones of the third album, but the title seemed to invite resistance even before the results were heard. It seemed as if he did not wish to let his listeners down gently.

Bob Dylan: I didn't want them to call [my fourth album] *Another Side of Bob Dylan* . . . because I thought it was just too corny. . . . I just felt trouble coming when they titled it that. I figured if they could have titled it something else, I wouldn't have had the resistance to it. [1978]

Another Side fared considerably worse than Dylan's previous two albums: Its failure to make even the top forty indicated that his existing audience was no longer listening and that he was not attracting new fans in sufficient numbers. If he was reluctant to admit that *Another Side* was a mistake at the time, within a year he would recognize its evident faults. He would then tell a university student that the 1964 songs were lacking in substance.

Bob Dylan: The big difference is that the songs I was writing last year, songs like "Ballad in Plain D," they were what I call one-dimensional songs, but my new songs I'm trying to make more three-dimensional, you know. There's more symbolism, they're written on more than one level. [1965]

By the fall of 1964, with the album barely out, Dylan had already excised songs like "Ballad in Plain D" and "My Back Pages" from his repertoire. He was more interested in performing the songs he had been writing in upstate New York that summer. Of the songs from *Another Side*, by November 1964 he was performing just "To Ramona," "I Don't Believe You" and "All I Really Want to Do" (plus "It Ain't Me Babe" if Baez emerged from the wings) in his regular set. Even "Chimes of Freedom" had been excluded so that his more recent visions could take center stage.

8 | 1964–65: The Ghost Of Electricity

On July 24, 1964, Dylan "premiered" his new songs (he had in fact already played them at a couple of warm-up shows in Michigan) at the Newport Folk Festival, scene of his greatest triumph twelve months earlier and of his greatest controversy twelve months later. Surrounded by these two pillars of Dylan iconography, his 1964 appearance has been largely ignored. In fact, it was very important, his two sets generating their fair share of controversy. *Another Side* had yet to be released and it had been nine months since his triumphant show at Carnegie Hall.

Dylan's first appearance that weekend, at a Friday topical-song workshop, was brief. In an ironic gesture, lost on the crowd, he opened with "It Ain't Me Babe." He then performed "Mr. Tambourine Man," and the crowd responded enthusiastically to the instantly memorable melody and lilting refrain. Indeed, the crowd stood to acclaim another work of genius from their authentic troubadour. The positive response to "Mr. Tambourine Man" presumably encouraged Dylan to include it in his Sunday set, along with three songs from *Another Side*. Though "All I Really Want to Do" was a poor opener to the set, "To Ramona" and "Chimes of Freedom" were probably the two most impressive songs on his forthcoming album and had "the audience frantically calling for more when [he] at last had to leave," according to the Providence *Journal*. He returned to perform a duet with Baez, the inevitable "With God on Our Side."

If the audience enjoyed the performance, his previous supporters in the media did not. Robert Shelton felt that he was stoned and that the performance had suffered accordingly. Irwin Sibler wrote an open letter to Dylan in the next edition of *Sing Out!* accusing him of writing maudlin songs and generally letting down his old friends, concluding that the old Dylan "never wasted our precious time." In *Broadside* Dylan was also subject to criticism: Paul Wolfe recognized that his performance represented "the renunciation of topical music by its major prophet," an astute enough observation undermined by his then-stated opinion that the new songs "degenerated into confusion and innocuousness." Of course, having heard—and hated—the best of Dylan's new songs, the old guard had a field day when they finally heard the entire fourth album.

If the criticism had an effect on Dylan, he did not let it show (though he would provide a sarcastic rebuttal to his critics in the program notes to his October New York concert, "Advice to Geraldine on Her Miscellaneous Birthday"). Instead, he retired to Woodstock to spend a quiet August in the company of Joan Baez, her sister Mimi and his old buddy (and Mimi's new husband) Richard Fariña.

Joan Baez: Bobby invited me, Mimi, and her husband, Dick Fariña, to house-sit Albert Grossman's, in Woodstock, New York. . . . Bob had a 350 Triumph motorcycle which I rode around in the woods and on the back roads, sometimes with him on the back. Most of the month or so we were there, Bob stood at the typewriter in the corner of his room, drinking red wine and smoking and tapping away relentlessly for hours. And in the dead of night, he would wake up, grunt, grab a cigarette, and stumble over to the typewriter again. He was turning out songs like ticker tape, and I was stealing them as fast as he wrote them.

Woodstock in upstate New York, two hours from Manhattan, had become a regular haven for Dylan since the previous summer, when he had spent a happy month with Suze at a cabin owned by Pete Yarrow of Peter, Paul and Mary. Grossman gave him free rein of his house, and in 1964–65 he spent nearly as much time there as he did in New York. Another incentive to visit was a woman by the name of Sara Lowndes, a regular guest at the Grossmans' and one of the oldest friends of Grossman's wife, Sally. Baez later discovered that, having outlasted Suze, she was not immune from a little two-timing herself.

Joan Baez: [In 1975,] when I finally met and became friends with Sara, we talked for hours about those days when the Original Vagabond was two-timing us. I told Sara that I'd never found Bob to be much at giving gifts, but that he had once bought me a green corduroy coat, and had told me to keep a lovely blue nightgown from the Woodstock house. "Oh!" said Sara, "that's where it went!"

In fact, despite Baez's recollections of Dylan "turning out songs like ticker tape," it is not clear what songs he was working on that August. Only two songs seem to date from this lull, and "If You Gotta Go, Go Now," though amusing enough, would hardly have taxed him for long. Clearly most of the time he was working on his book, which lay somewhere between Walk Down Crooked Highway and Tarantula. The other new song he would premiere in September was called "It's Alright, Ma (I'm Only Bleeding)." He was probably also working on "Gates of Eden," which he premiered in October.

Though introduced later, "Gates of Eden" seems more closely related to "Chimes of Freedom" and "Mr. Tambourine Man" than to "It's Alright, Ma." Like these, it is a visionary song, once again constructed in the form of a dream, though he makes it deliberately unclear whether it is his dream or that of his lover, who comes to him at dawn "and tells me of her dreams." The turns of phrase he was searching for on "My Back Pages" are now in place. Lines like "motorcycle black madonna two-wheeled gypsy queen" no longer sound forced, but are powerful and suggestive.

"It's Alright, Ma" is an epic that dwarfs even "Gates of Eden." If, as seems likely, he wrote it that August in Woodstock, he must have worked long and hard on the structure of the song. Its fifteen verses and five slightly different refrains provide an impressive catalog of social ills. For "It's Alright, Ma" was far more of a finger-pointing song than anything on *The Times They Are a-Changin'*. Adopting the apocalyptic tradition he so skillfully used on "The Times They Are a-Changin' " and "A Hard Rain's a-Gonna Fall," he produced a damning roster of American society's malaises, including perhaps more memorable aphorisms than in any other popular song—"Money doesn't talk it swears," "He not busy being born is busy dying," and so on. If fans felt that Dylan had abandoned the realms of social relevance, "It's Alright, Ma" reminded them that the topical song was only one way of writing about contemporary America, and that his new, more surreal approach might be a more appropriate way of dealing with the kaleidoscopic nature of the mid-sixties.

Throughout the fall of 1964 Dylan toured extensively, playing far more one-night stands than he had ever attempted before. After Pennsylvania, Michigan, Minnesota, New York, Connecticut and Ontario, the tour culminated in California, where Baez was again waiting for the return of her wandering minstrel. However, he appeared to be tiring of his old songs. The set had become rigid and predictable, as had the audiences' response. Dylan was now screening himself from friends and fans with an entourage of hipsters like Bobby Neuwirth and Victor Maimudes, who would provide both verbal and physical intimidation where necessary. One interviewer who talked to him that December in Santa Barbara wrote to *Sing Out!* berating him for his newly found isolation:

Bob Blackamar: I met and talked with Bob Dylan a few weeks ago. He really has lost contact with his audiences and much of reality. . . . I met part of Mr. Dylan's clique as well, and it is true that Bob is only interested in singing for their enjoyment as well as his.

Evidently he no longer entertained notions of meeting "the common people." He restricted his companions to those who could withstand his word games, the verbal numbers he ran on the unhip simply for the mutual gratification and entertainment of the Hip. Ironically, Baez, with whom Dylan continued to involve himself on a sporadic basis, was one of the butts of his verbal jousting, as was any journalist—except those who had received honorary membership of the inner circle during his rise to fame. Thus Robert Shelton, Nat Hentoff, Al Aronowitz, Ralph J. Gleason and J. R. Goddard may have been immune from most of his games, but any new interviewer was tested by his wit. In February 1965 he appeared on Les Crane's popular TV show and duly demolished Crane on the air. Seemingly content to refer to his host as Less, he neatly ducked each and every question. When, predictably, he was asked what his main message might be, he replied, "Eat." Asked what a movie he was planning to make would be about, he informed Crane it would be a horror cowboy movie. Asked if he played the horror cowboy, he said, "No. I play my mother."

His baiting of the press even extended that winter of 1965 to concocting a script for a Dylan press conference with J. R. Goddard of *The Village Voice*, who had reviewed his first album back in 1962. Published in the *Voice* in March 1965, the article, entitled "Dylan Meets the Press," was the supposed result of a press conference in Woodstock, where "Dylan had consented to answer all those deep, meaningful, searching questions he's been bombarded with by reporters and TV interviews through the years." When asked who he thought could save the world, he replied Al Aronowitz. It was his first such flirtation with parody. It would not be his last.

In rapid succession he also conducted a one-page interview wholly about wearing a tie when writing his songs (for the men's magazine *Cavalier*) and a brief absurdist interview with a relatively hip West Coast journalist named Paul Jay Robbins from the underground paper the *Los Angeles Free Press*. He would have ample opportunity to sharpen his verbal barbs on the U.K. press when he toured England in May.

Meanwhile, he had an album to make. He had finally decided that the time had come to record with a band. After the end of his West Coast tour he had three or four weeks in Woodstock to write enough songs to fill out his fifth album. In a burst of creativity he came up with a dozen new songs.

The eighteen "new" songs he brought to the first session included the four songs he had been playing on the road, "It's Alright, Ma," "Mr. Tambourine Man," "Gates of Eden" and "If You Gotta Go, Go Now" plus "I'll Keep It with Mine," which he had yet to record for CBS. If none of these songs, save "If You Gotta Go, Go Now," seemed to lend themselves to an "electric" arrangement, the new songs he had written clearly did. One song in particular, "Subterranean Homesick Blues," seemed inconceivable without some suitable backing. As Dylan described the problem later that year:

Bob Dylan: I had this thing called "Subterranean Homesick Blues." It just didn't sound right by myself. . . . But it fit right in with the band. [1965]

He had written another three songs, "Maggie's Farm," "On the Road Again" and "Outlaw Blues," that all lent themselves to some good ol' rhythm and blues. The major problem was whom to recruit to play them.

Daniel Kramer: Tom Wilson, his recording producer, started a search for musicians who could work with him. It was crucial to use musicians who could really play, who could really accommodate Dylan's needs. . . . [They] would have to adjust to his unorthodox style and method of delivery.

Dylan insisted on picking the guitarist. His choice was Bruce Langhorne, whom he had worked with back in 1962 during the *Freewheelin'* electric sessions and who had provided second guitar on a couple of acoustic recordings at that time. The remainder of the musicians were chosen by Tom Wilson. They were an experienced bunch of session men, including John Sebastian, soon to form the Lovin' Spoonful, on bass, and Bobby Gregg, who would tour with

Dylan later in the year, on drums. John Hammond, Jr., son of Dylan's old producer, provided some acoustic guitar accompaniment.

The sessions progressed remarkably smoothly. Working through the day and into the night, Dylan completed the album in three sessions over a period of two days. It was astonishing progress considering that he had no real experience of working with bands in the studio. He also showed that he relied heavily on instinct when working up the best version of a song. This aspect of Dylan's work on *Bringing It All Back Home* would remain a consistent feature of his studio recordings. He used multiple takes as excuses to try different arrangements, different approaches, different tempos, often improvising lyrics on the spot. He did not attempt to perfect an existing version that had not come out quite right. The air of spontaneity is suggested at the beginning of "Bob Dylan's 115th Dream" when he starts the song and the band fails to come in on time. Dylan and Wilson begin laughing and Wilson's voice can be heard saying, "Start again," and sure enough Dylan and the band tumble in—right on time—on what sounds like a first complete take.

Daniel Kramer: It was obvious from the very beginning that something exciting was happening, and much of it happened spontaneously. When the playback of "Maggie's Farm" was heard over the studio speakers, we were all elated. There was no question about it—it swung, it was happy, it was good music and, most of all, it was Dylan. The musicians were enthusiastic. They conferred with one another to work out the problems as they arose. Dylan bounced around from one man to another, explaining what he wanted, often showing them on the piano what was needed until, like a giant puzzle, the pieces would fit and the picture emerged whole. Dylan worked like a painter covering a huge canvas with the colors that the different musicians could supply him, adding depth and dimension to the total work. All in all, most of the songs went down easily and needed only three or four takes before they were accepted. In some cases, the first take sounded entirely different from the final one because the material was played at a different tempo, perhaps, or a different chord was chosen, or solos may have been rearranged. . . . His method of working, the certainty of what he wanted, kept things moving. He would listen to the playbacks in the control booth, discuss what was happening with Tom Wilson and move on to the next number. If he tried something that didn't go well, he would put it off for another session. In this way, he never bogged down—he just kept on going.

In fact, Dylan did not intend to issue a wholly "electric" album. Since the songs he had been performing at his acoustic shows did not self-evidently lend themselves to electric arrangements, he chose to record an acoustic side to the album to counterbalance the side of electric music. Langhorne accompanied Dylan on "Mr. Tambourine Man" and bassist William E. Lee on a new song called "It's All Over Now, Baby Blue," but these were the only embellishments on side two of the album. "It's All Over Now, Baby Blue" was another of his "go out in the real world" songs, like "To Ramona," though less conciliatory—the tone crueler and more demanding. The three songs he had already been performing live, which would make up the bulk of the acoustic side of the album, he had the audacity to record in one continuous take, with barely a pause between each song.

The completion of *Bringing It All Back Home* in a mere three sessions must have surprised even Dylan. That the album is one of the most enduring (he plays more songs from this album in 1990 than from any subsequent album) says a lot for the quality of the songwriting. Though the folkies would not agree, it was Dylan's most rounded album to date. Whimsical romps such as "115th Dream" and "Outlaw Blues" counterbalanced the beautiful "Love Minus Zero/ No Limit" and "She Belongs to Me"; the social commentaries of "Subterranean Homesick Blues" and "Maggie's Farm" were now set to amphetamine riffs and the visionary poems made up a cogent second side.

While CBS set about releasing Dylan's first "folk-rock" album and his second "folk-rock" single ("Subterranean Homesick Blues")—some two and a half years after "Mixed Up Confusion"—he made his American farewell to acoustic shows with a brief tour with Joan Baez. A joint tour had been discussed previously, and now that Dylan's commercial stock was as great as Baez's it seemed practicable. Of course, the difference was that Dylan's star was in the ascendant and Baez's was not. Grossman made sure that his client's interests were protected.

Bobby Neuwirth: The feeling around that [Dylan/Baez] tour was pretty good. The only one who was in a sweat about it was Manny [Greenhill]. As far as Bob was concerned, Albert was the guy who took care of all that shit. . . . Albert would ask him if he wanted to do something, and he'd say yes or no. There was never any of the evil shit that a lot of people imagined.

Despite the seeming camaraderie on the tour, Dylan was tiring of his relationship with Baez. It seems strangely bizarre yet oddly typical that he should play such a tour with her and even stay with her in Carmel when playing a few solo shows on the West Coast at the beginning of April, yet treat her so harshly a month later. However, there remains serious doubts about how committed Dylan had been to their relationship in the previous six months. Though flattered by her, and despite their "romance" having lasted nearly two and a half years after his breakup with Suze, Dylan never seems to have deepened their relationship, and their assignations every couple of months remained set to suit his convenience. Meanwhile, he was spending more and more time with Sara Lowndes.

Dylan was increasingly at odds with Baez's commitment to the causes of civil rights and nonviolence and her holier-than-thou attitude. Songs like "Maggie's Farm" and "It's All Over Now, Baby Blue" were individualistic expressions of rebellion, without any of the sense of community that was important to Baez. Whatever the reasons for their drifting apart, it seems clear he did not want her to come with him to England. Yet when she was unable to take the hint, he was unable to say no, she could not come. It was to make his first English tour an extremely fraught affair.

9 | 1965: Over Your Shoulder

If the brief Dylan/Baez East Coast tour is something of a black hole in the record of Dylan's career, the equally brief English tour he undertook at the beginning of May 1965 is generally well documented and fondly remembered. The main reason is Don (D. A.) Pennebaker's primitive *cinéma vérité* study *Don't Look Back*, a ninety-minute monochrome documentary of the tour. The portrait of Dylan he composed in that movie has become fixed in people's minds as Dylan 1965. Certainly the film is a remarkable study of the pressures of fame as they affected a self-assured and talented young singer. Dylan, though, has never been entirely comfortable with the portrait Pennebaker presented. Indeed, when Pennebaker completed the movie and showed it to him, Dylan said they would have to make a lot of changes. Yet having stated that he would detail these changes at a subsequent screening, at this second preview the Gemini Dylan decided to let the film stand.

Bob Dylan: *Don't Look Back* was . . . somebody else's movie. . . . I don't think it was accurate at all in terms of showing my formative years. It showed only one side. He made it seem like I wasn't doing anything but living in hotel rooms, playing the typewriter and holding press conferences for journalists. All that is true, you know. Throwing some bottles, there's something about it in the movie. Joan Baez is in it. But it's one-sided. [1978]

Dylan's original intentions in making the film remain unclear. Clearly his hiring of Pennebaker suggested that he had a documentary movie in mind. Sara Lowndes had recommended Pennebaker. When Dylan, accompanied by Bobby Neuwirth, met Pennebaker at the Cedar Tavern in New York he tested Pennebaker's suitability in the usual way by playing a few verbal games, the test of coolness being to avoid reacting to them. Pennebaker wisely played along.

D. A. Pennebaker: [Grossman] and Dylan had approached us because Sara had worked with us at *Life*. She was working there for about a year and a half, so I knew Sara quite well. Then I came back, and Albert said, "My client's going to England. Would you like to make a film about it?" I said, "Sure.". . . I think that Dylan had a very parochial sense about his operation. He was going to do things totally different from the way they'd been done; he was gonna revamp network schedules; he was gonna revamp movies; he was gonna make everything in a new way—without being quite sure how he'd do it.

Pennebaker was taking something of a risk, and with his money as well. He did not really know Dylan's work, nor indeed what filming him would be like, though his meeting with Dylan and Neuwirth gave him something of a fore-taste, and Grossman's deal with Pennebaker was that Leacock-Pennebaker, Inc., would put up the costs of making the film and any profits would be divided equally. So Pennebaker was taking a lot on faith. Yet, as soon as he arrived in London on April 26, he could see that some fascinating process was taking place.

D. A. Pennebaker: There was the problem of sticking with Dylan, who was under a number of pressures, including those from Joan Baez (personal) and the concerts (public). I had to take it on faith the film would not be a series of press conferences and getting in and out of concert halls. . . . It became clear that Dylan was going through some kind of change, and I knew that if I could stick with him I'd see something of it.

The first indication of the pressures that Dylan faced came the minute he landed at London Airport. How aware he was of the scale of his popularity in England we do not know. Clearly Grossman would have been kept fully informed, and Dylan would have known his records were selling in England. But the commercial snowball that had been rolling since he appeared at the Festival Hall in May 1964 had reached critical mass that April. His first U.K. single had just entered the charts. It was, rather incongruously, "The Times They Are a-Changin'," a song he had spent eighteen months running away from. Two weeks later the steady-selling *Freewheelin'* finally made it to number one on the album charts, having been a regular feature on the charts for nearly a year. This achievement needs to be placed in context. Since March 9, 1963, when the album *Please Please Me* first made it to number one, only albums by the Beatles and the Rolling Stones had been at the top spot. This, after all, was the era that marked the hegemony of English pop.

Not only did *Freewheelin'* create the first fissure in the Beatles/Stones edifice, but Dylan's entire catalog—*Bringing It All Back Home* was just about to be released—had gone top twenty in the last six months, and *The Times They Are a-Changin'* and *Another Side* were in the top ten. So Dylan was not merely some well-known folksinger, he was a *star*. Since England had a well-established, tabloid-dominated national press, events that in America might have warranted a mention in the *New York Post* were national news in England.

Dylan almost certainly did not appreciate how famous he now was in England. However, he knew the press would be awaiting his arrival, and he entered his first (genuine) press conference, held in the VIP lounge of London Airport, carrying a large industrial light bulb. Knowing that he would inevitably be asked what his main message was—after all, no American journalist had resisted asking the question in the last two years—he responded with what seemed a remarkably quick-witted reply, "Keep a good head and always carry a light bulb." If his stunt with the light bulb was an in-joke at the press's expense (Dylan would repeat his use of props in later press conferences, bringing a doll, which he christened Finian, to his 1966 Paris conference), he actually seemed happy to talk and was surprisingly cooperative.

A press conference the following day at the Savoy Hotel found him less cooperative and, as the round of interviews filled up the three days before his first concert in Sheffield, he grew tired of the endless questions, always obvious, often demeaning of his work (witness Cleave's question in *Don't Look Back*: "Do your fans understand a word you sing?"). Subsequent interviews with the "straight" press would be scathing affairs, with Dylan mercilessly putting on his interviewers. Yet when in the company of the hipper members of the music press, like Ray Coleman of *Melody Maker* or the amateur student journalists occasionally encountered along the way, he played few games and gave straight answers to honest questions. Interviewed in Sheffield for the university paper, Dylan gave a surprisingly frank response as to why he played his games with the "straight" press.

Bob Dylan: They ask the wrong questions, like, What did you have for breakfast, What's your favorite color, stuff like that. Newspaper reporters, man, they're just hung-up writers, frustrated novelists, they don't hurt me none by putting fancy labels on me. They got all these preconceived ideas about me, so I just play up to them. [1965]

The most famous of Dylan's verbal batterings must be the interview by the *Time* reporter Horace Judson. In *Don't Look Back* the editing of the interview is such that Dylan is already working on Judson when the scene starts, and the camera cuts away when Dylan informs Judson he can sing as well as Caruso "and I can hold my breath three times as long." According to Anthea Joseph, who can sometimes be seen in the background of *Don't Look Back*, Judson did not just crawl away meekly after Dylan's verbal onslaught.

Anthea Joseph: The man was such a prat. And Bob was being absolutely appalling, but so brilliant. By this time I'd learnt that he could pull strips of skin off people, verbally. . . . [Judson] was quite abusive as well. He was extremely upset, he really was; and in a way I suppose it was not really his fault, not properly briefed, treating Bob as some sort of curiosity, not as a serious artist.

But Judson was just one of a series of victims fed to Dylan by uncomprehending editors. Not all were as offended as Judson. Laurie Henshaw of *Disc and Music Echo* encountered a Dylan who was, if anything, even ruder than he was to Judson. However, his stream of put-ons delighted Henshaw, who published the interview as it was, claiming he had secured Dylan's most outrageous interview to date. And indeed he probably had. Terry Ellis, a naive science student who spoke to Dylan backstage at Newcastle City Hall, also survived a verbal battering; he went on to found Chrysalis Records and manage the band Jethro Tull.

Terry Ellis: I remember he had a wicked glint in his eye—I couldn't tell you if that was chemically induced. In retrospect, I don't think he was actually being cruel to me, he was being quite pleasant—but in his own caustic way.

If Dylan's toying with the press makes up a major part of *Don't Look Back*, the film certainly features an "on" Dylan all the time. He seems always onstage, meeting fans, entertaining friends and hangers-on or putting the press on. Even the hotel jam with Baez is a performance, albeit for a chosen few: Neuwirth, Baez, Grossman and Pennebaker. Even when he is having a party in his room, Donovan asks him to play. The portrait that Pennebaker paints is deliberately one of the public Dylan. In private he was a very different man, able to revert to the self he had shown more easily on his previous trips to England—but only when he was comfortable in the company he was in. And this was becoming increasingly rare.

Anthea Joseph: I think he was being overpeopled. . . . It was quite extraordinary the difference. . . . When it was just us he was perfectly comfortable, perfectly relaxed and perfectly easy. But once the place was full of people there was a little gear change in a way and he became the public person. But every now and then he'd go and disappear and start bashing away at the typewriter which was on the desk.

The need to be permanently "on" was draining Dylan. During a day off before two shows at the Royal Albert Hall, he was enjoying hanging out with assorted friends in Soho when he heard that his whereabouts had become known to some of his fans and they were heading for the club. For the first timed he was having to come to terms with being a teenybopper idol. When he hotfooted it to the Savoy he found he was expected to party.

Anthea Joseph: There was Donovan, the Pretty Things, assorted other odds and sods. . . . We take over a table downstairs [at Les Cousins]. . . . Baez wasn't there. She was still in the hotel in a sulk. . . . And then we got word—a friend of mine came into the pub—and said, "Did you know they've heard that Dylan's in here and they're beginning to come up the road?" So I said to him we leave. So Dorothy and me hoiked him out and this taxi came round the corner into Wardour Street with his light on. I stopped him and got in and there was this blond person in it and we do not know where she came from. However, she paid the fare. We were halfway to the Savoy and realized that none of us had enough money for the fare. . . . [So we managed to reach the Savoy], the three of us planning to just have a really nice chat, and Bob invited this girl to come up. She didn't say no. And so we were sort of milling around talking about old times and that sort of nonsense and the phone rang. It was the porter, saying, "There's an awful lot of people downstairs saying you're having a party." I said, "Are you having a party?" [Dylan] said, "No." I said, "Well, they seem to think you're having a party." He said, "Well, I suppose we ought to have a party." So I said, "OK, you get onto room service and order the booze, I'm not taking responsibility for this," and they all turned up. . . . There's this perfectly good party going on. All sorts of people turned up. Allen [Ginsberg] was there. I mean everybody was there. And I was going around dishing out the drinks. And then this row broke out. . . . These two bozos had locked themselves in the bathroom, where it had beautiful glass shelves. Those wonderful sort of thirties bathrooms! Vast marble bath. They were just chucking them out. . . .

Daryll Adams was trying to smooth everybody down, as I was. And Bob was sort of jumping [up and down]. I'd never seen him lose his temper before. It was really quite frightening. He went up like a little torch and rightfully so, too.

The culmination of this tense evening is captured in *Don't Look Back* as Dylan explodes, "WHO THREW THAT FUCKING GLASS?!?"

The evening described by Joseph was not an isolated example. The suite at the Savoy was constantly overrun with people. If it was not cocktail parties arranged by Grossman, it was journalists wanting one-to-one interviews; if not journalists, it was Allen Ginsberg and his beat friends; if not them, it was assorted members of England's thriving beat-group scene come to pay their respects.

The Beatles were in regular attendance. An article in *Melody Maker* announcing that "The Beatles Dig Dylan," published that January, had been a major fillip to his commercial standing in the U.K. He had met them the previous August in New York, when he was introduced to them by Al Aronowitz, and they spent two nights talking at the Delmonico Hotel. Dylan and Aronowitz apparently suggested they all unwind with a little grass. The Beatles had not previously indulged. Yet when Dylan met up with them again in May 1965 he found their experiments with mind-expanding chemicals had progressed somewhat.

John Lennon: I just remember . . . that we were both in shades and both on fucking junk and all these freaks around us and Ginsberg and all those people. I was anxious as shit.

Despite their own status, the Beatles were very much in awe of Dylan. Lennon had already begun to be heavily influenced by him, though their songs had only just begun to explore themes beyond the well-worn young love idiom. The Rolling Stones also regularly attended Dylan's Savoy Hotel suite, though it was Brian Jones who was most taken by Dylan.

Dana Gillespie: Every night the Stones and the Beatles used to come to the Savoy Hotel and they would play each other their latest recordings and you could see them vying for the top spot as the top British band, but . . . [Dylan] was the one person that both the Stones and the Beatles had great admiration for, so when he held court in one of the hotel rooms, everyone sat and listened.

In *Don't Look Back* there is an indication of the constant mayhem that filled the suite when Neuwirth, Dylan and Baez were finally left alone (save for Pennebaker, "the eye") in Dylan's room, and Neuwirth says, "Welcome home.

It's the first time that this room hasn't been full of a bunch of insane lunatics, man, that I can remember. . . . It's the first time it's been cool around here." However, Baez's presence was hardly conducive to Dylan relaxing at this point. Indeed, in this scene in the film Neuwirth seems to be picking on Baez, telling her, "Sister, you fagged out long ago," while Dylan looks on impassively. In fact, according to Baez, Neuwirth was one of the reasons she kept relatively sane during all the games that were being played around her on that tour.

Joan Baez: One night I went to Neuwirth's room crying. He put his arms around me and mopped a pint of tears off my cheeks and chin, and begged me to pack up my bags and leave the tour. "But Bob asked me to come. He *asked* me," I protested. "I know, but he don't know what's happening anymore, can't you see? He's just out there spinnin' and he wants to do it by himself."

Whatever Baez's expectations about the tour, Dylan clearly had no intention of introducing her at his concerts. Baez was planning to play her own concerts in England that summer, but she was considerably less well known there than in America and performing with Dylan would have been a considerable endorsement. The implied rejection hurt, but it was in fact only the beginning of Dylan's somewhat ruthless deflating of Baez's considerable ego. Marianne Faithfull, talking at the time, provided a journalist with an example of the way he would demean her in the company of friends.

Marianne Faithfull: [Baez] insisted on singing her high vibrato version of "Here Comes the Night" and "Go Now," which Dylan complained about. He hates her voice and tells her so. At one point he held up a bottle as she sang a high note, and drawled, "Break that!" She just laughed.

Dylan was also happy to seduce other women during his English tour, seemingly unaffected by the heartbreak such activities must have caused Baez, who was by this point overwhelmingly in love with him. Thus when he met up with the amply endowed Dana Gillespie at an official welcoming party on the first day of his visit, Baez discovered firsthand the sort of philandering that had tortured Suze before her.

Dana Gillespie: Dylan and I started talking almost as soon as I walked in. I guess he fancied me. He was fairly blatant about it and made some remark about my forty-four-inch bust.

If Baez could dismiss Dylan's relationship with Gillespie as purely sexual, she found it harder to deal with the presence of Sara Lowndes, a mysterious dark-haired American beauty who appeared in his company after a brief vacation in Portugal. After the English tour, Lowndes had joined him in Paris and they had then traveled together to Portugal and back to London. Lowndes answered the door of Dylan's hotel suite when Baez called to see if Dylan was OK after a bout of food poisoning. At this point Baez realized their relationship was indeed over, and she headed for France. They would not sing together again for a further ten years, though Baez would continue to address Dylan in song, and continue to believe that he addressed her in song.

D. A. Pennebaker: Well, you've got to understand a peculiar situation around royal entourages, palaces, courts in general, politics, and that is that you can be number four or five, but if you're used to being number one or two it's a big jolt—and that's kind of what that was about. There were other people in Dylan's life—there was Sara—and Baez kind of knew it.

Most viewers of *Don't Look Back* don't realize how short the time span covered by the film is. Dylan spent more time in England, France and Portugal after the end of his tour than he did on it. *Don't Look Back* covers only two weeks in his life, and during that time he played only eight concerts, hardly the most rigorous schedule ever devised. The concerts themselves were well received, though Dylan's performances were beginning to sound a little stale. Indeed, Pennebaker has said that he didn't feel that playing live was the most important part of what was happening to Dylan in 1965, but that it was in 1966. The tapes bear this opinion out. Though the performances are not exactly lackluster, a certain vibrancy is lacking.

Of course, part of the problem with the tour was that in England Dylan was still seen as the man who had made *Freewheelin'* and three other acoustic albums. Only at the end of the tour did *Bringing It All Back Home* get released and "Subterranean Homesick Blues" begin to climb the charts. In fact, *Bringing It All Back Home* would make number one on the album charts at the end of May, signaling considerable commercial acceptance for his new sound. Irrespective of the sales reaction to his new sound, he was no longer comfortable in his acoustic guise. In *Don't Look Back* he can be seen talking to a band that plays electric versions of his songs, and he is eager to hear how they sound. When a fan tells him she does not like his new single, he mutters, "Oh, you're one of those. I understand now." Two days after the conclusion of his brief tour, Dylan went into the studio with perhaps the finest of the British rhythm and blues bands, John Mayall's Bluesbreakers. Tom Wilson had flown over from New York to produce the session.

Eric Clapton: He was interested in John Mayall. John had recorded a song called "Life Is Like a Slow Train Going up a Hill" and that interested Bob. Bob came in, looked for John Mayall. I was just the guitar player on the session. He had a friend called Bobby Neuwirth who was a fantastic player. Bobby Neuwirth was his kind of court jester at the time. [He] kept coming up to me and saying, "You're playing too much blues, man. He needs to be more country!"

Hughie Flint: Dylan wanted to try something out with a British R & B band, which was the vogue at the time. It could've been anyone . . . but we were available. . . . We thought we were going to accompany Dylan because we all knew that he was a guitar player and so John Mayall was going to play keyboards and we were going to play along with whatever he did. But when he came in, Dylan immediately sat down at the piano and started playing.

Evidently Dylan at this stage was looking to record some material for his next album, and this time it would be an all-out rhythm & blues sound. The session was a disaster, primarily because both Dylan and Wilson were consuming vast quantities of wine and, as he became the worse for drink, Dylan started taking an inordinate interest in Nadia Catouse, a singer who was attending the session. Soon he and Wilson departed arm in arm, presumably intending to search out further wine and entertainment.

Hughie Flint: All through the session it was just messing around. I don't think we played a complete number. It was a real mess. There was a lot of booze there, crates and crates of wine—I'd never seen so much wine, and everybody got very pissed, very quickly, no one more so than Dylan.

On June 1, 1965, Dylan recorded two thirty-five-minute TV specials for the BBC. He had been due to record them the previous week but had been laid up in bed in the Savoy, and later in St Mary's Hospital in Paddington, suffering from a severe bout of food poisoning contracted in Portugal. The BBC broadcasts would be Dylan's last entirely acoustic performances for many years, and briefly threatened to be his final performance ever. He had decided to quit.

10 1964–65: A Book of Words

Dylan's most talked-about project during his rise to fame was a book he was supposedly writing. He had referred to it first in April 1963, then repeatedly in interviews and press conferences during 1964 and 1965—all the while becoming increasingly imprecise about its contents. By the time of his accident in July 1966 it had still not appeared.* Dylan arrived at the approach adopted in *Tarantula* only after going through several unsuccessful projects.

Though there have been several attempts to evaluate *Tarantula*'s literary merits, the history of the book's composition has never really been fully explored. Dylan himself has always given the impression that he was cajoled into producing a book after the success of John Lennon's two collections of whimsical prose and verse.

Bob Dylan: I was doing interviews before and after concerts, and reporters would say things like "What else do you write?" And I would say, "Well, I don't write much of anything else." And they would say, "Oh, come on. You must write other things. Tell us something else. Do you write books?" And I'd say, "Sure, I write books." After the publishers saw that I wrote books, they began to send me contracts . . . we took the biggest one, and then owed them a book. [1969]

The reality is that he freely confessed that he was writing at least one book, and one or two plays, in several interviews in 1964—by which point he was already signed up with Macmillan. According to Bob Markel, the editor at Macmillan who supervised the publication of *Tarantula*, it was not a hard-and-fast commitment Dylan had made, and he was as uncertain as Dylan as to what Macmillan might eventually get.

---

*It would be 1970 before *Tarantula* saw the light of day at least officially.

Bob Markel: I met Albert Grossman before I met Bob Dylan. . . . Bob was just beginning to make an impression as a singer and writer. Albert explained to me that he thought Dylan was a very hot property who might want to do a book one day, and that if I were interested, we might be able to work out a contract for a book. . . . We gave him an advance for an untitled book of writings. . . . The publisher was taking a risk on a young, untested potential phenomenon. In time we'd figure out a book, but it was worth having a contract. He was uncertain what the book would be.

Uncertainty about the exact nature of the book would last some time. Dylan had first suggested he was working on a book back in April 1963, when he mentioned it to Studs Terkel. The book he discussed then, though, was no surreal voyage through language. It was supposed to be loosely historical, at least in the way that "My Life in a Stolen Moment" and "Last Thoughts on Woody Guthrie," two contemporary bio-poems, were "historical," that is, it was supposed to look back upon the genesis of Bob Dylan, New York folksinger.

In the fall of 1963, Dylan met the poet Lawrence Ferlinghetti and discussed the possibility of producing a book for his firm, City Lights, publisher of the beat poets and therefore an excellent choice in terms of Dylan's credibility. However, by April 1964 he still had not forwarded any manuscript, and he wrote to Ferlinghetti that he kept changing his approach to the project: "I do got things of songs an stories for you. my hangup is tho that I know there will be more. I want t send the more more then I want t send the got. yes I guess that's it."

By the time that Macmillan expressed an interest in spring 1964, the project was still undefined. According to Markel, the original contract drawn up by Macmillan was for a book of photographs on Hollywood. The photos were to be by Barry Feinstein, husband of Mary Travers of Peter, Paul and Mary and the man responsible for the stark portrait of Dylan that graced the cover of *The Times They Are a-Changin'*. Text would be provided by Dylan. Dylan discussed this book with *Melody Maker's* Max Jones when he talked to him in London in May 1964.

Bob Dylan: It's just pictures and the words I'm going to write that [not so much] coincide with the photographer's, but somehow fall into the same direction or mood. All the pictures were shot in Hollywood: shots of everything, a whole picture of Hollywood from the beautiful sign on the hill to Marlon Brando speaking while someone holds up a sign saying "Nigger Lover.". . . . I dig this photographer, and I dig taking pictures myself. [1964]

Dylan also informed Max Jones that he had at least one more book in mind, and that he was working on a play or two as well—indeed, three months earlier he had told a Canadian reporter that the play "is going to be done sooner than the novel." Meanwhile he was still working on the free-verse form of poetry he had developed in "11 Outlined Epitaphs." As he completed his fourth album, *Another Side*, in June 1964, he once again wished to include his own notes on the album jacket. The problem—as with *The Times They Are a-Changin'*—was that he had too many poems to fit on a single album jacket. As a result, the *Another Side* poems—which were ironically entitled "Some Other Kinds of Songs," an admission that despite his best endeavors these free-form poems were something different from his recorded words—were crammed onto the album sleeve in microscopic type. Despite this, only five of these "kinds of songs" could be included on the back cover. Six further examples were eventually published as a surprise bonus in Dylan's 1973 omnibus, *Writings and Drawings*.

"Some Other Kinds of Songs" are unlike "11 Outlined Epitaphs" and the other poems he had been writing in the fall of 1963. The principal difference is the line breaks. In the "Outlined Epitaphs" the line breaks seem to puncture the text at points where one thought ends and another begins. In "Some Other Kinds of Songs" it seems as if any kind of line break is an encumbrance. They now either directly anticipate the amphetamine jolts of rhythm later adopted on songs like "Subterranean Homesick Blues" or seem random intrusions into free-rolling prose poems. And indeed, such prose poems seemed to be what Dylan was now steering toward.

Macmillan's Bob Markel had met Dylan by the time he was writing "Some Other Kinds of Songs," and clearly Dylan's concept of the book had already moved toward a *Tarantula*esque form. The initial working title was apparently *Side One*.

Bob Markel: Our first meeting took place in the great big marvelous old downtown Macmillan offices. It was probably the winter of 1964. When I spoke to Bob on the telephone he asked that the meeting take place after dark, as he felt he couldn't travel in broad daylight. He was driving a motorcycle around New York in those days. . . . There was no book at the time. . . . The first title I ever saw on it was *Side One*. . . . The material at that point was hazy, sketchy. The poetry editor called it "inaccessible." The symbolism was not easily understood, but on the other hand it was earthy, filled with obscure but marvelous imagery. . . . I felt it had a lot of value and was very different from Dylan's output till then. It was not a book.

The best evidence of Dylan's increasingly surreal approach to his prose poems comes in four remarkable letters he wrote to Tami Dean, a student at Oklahoma State University, through 1964. The letters—not published until 1984, sixteen years after Dean's death in a car accident—detail a clear development in his style. The first letter—from early March 1964 on the evidence of his reference to visiting Dallas three weeks earlier—shows a style of writing similar to the free-verse letters to Tony Glover, Sis Cunningham and the Emergency Civil Liberties Committee from the previous year, albeit in straight prose form: "I'll see you sometime . . . on a strange nite. when the leaves're blowin. an it's close t shiverin. when the headlights pass above the bluff . . . yes I'll meet you by the crossing. . . . on the edge of town. in the brown dust." The second letter, which probably dates from spring 1964, continues in the same style—though it includes perhaps an oblique reference to "Chimes of Freedom": "i gaze out of cathedral windows when I can. at other times I gaze up at them from the rainy street."

Letters three and four, though, are a world apart from these chains of thought. Apparently dating from the late summer or, more likely, the fall of 1964, both are more explicitly surreal; they slip easily into a stream-of-consciousness style that piles the incongruous upon the absurd. Neither directly addresses Tami Dean—save for a momentary incursion in letter three in which "doctor zen" says hi to her—but are rather expositions of Dylan's state of mind. The third letter is the more coherent, and is a hilarious parody of a "Dear Ma, everyone's fine" letter, which he had previously ridiculed in a letter to Baez's mother from August 1964 (the letter is reproduced in Baez's autobiography *And a Voice to Sing With*). The character of doctor zen is in exactly the same tradition as syd dangerous, Silly Eyes and herold the professor in *Tarantula*, or the family of lunatics portrayed in "On the Road Again": "nothin new is happenin. doctor zen says hello. i told him you were off in oklahoma. he says no she's not. i say ok i dig. there is no oklahoma. he says you asshole there is no she. i say ok ok he says say hi to her. doc gets weird sometimes. he stuffs lsd in his turban most everyday."

The fourth letter has even fewer stylistic antecedents in his previous poetry. A direct precursor of *Tarantula*'s mixture of prose poems and free-verse "epistles," the letter reads like a Dadaist chronicle. It opens with "so there i was. riding on this umbrella" and progresses through a travelogue that closely parallels the insane world of songs like "Bob Dylan's 115th Dream": watch for cave ins an dont be too good t nobody. they might get wrong idea. sneer at graveyard. make patty cake thank you mam good gawd son is 'at london bridge about t go? i mix up crazy phantoms. exchange their eyes bust into plate glass predictions. get in two timed position. try to make it with the manacans."

The letter concludes with twenty-nine lines of free verse. The advisory tone in lines such as "watch for cave ins an dont be too good t nobody" can be found more fully flowered in "It's Alright Ma" and in what can perhaps be seen as the first of his fully fledged prose poems, which was published at the end of October

1964. In the program for his first New York concert in a year, the Halloween 1964 show, he included a piece called "Advice for Geraldine on Her Miscellaneous Birthday." In a hilarious romp about staying in line and conformity in general, he advises the mysterious Geraldine never to create anything as "it will be misinterpreted" and will haunt her the remainder of her life. Though more extended than any of the "letters" in *Tarantula*, the way in which it directly addresses some abstract friend/critic/member of his audience—and attempts to undermine some of the critical flak he had started to pick up since the fall of 1963—ties it thematically and stylistically to the letters of the butter sculptor and herold the professor (in *Tarantula*).

In the first few months of 1965, Dylan's published writings began wholly to adopt the prose style found in *Tarantula*. Indeed, two prose poems published in the winter of 1964–65 were credited as being from his forthcoming book. The first such "excerpt" was included as an introduction for "All I Really Want to Do" in *Sing Out!* The excerpt was apparently condensed from *Walk Down Crooked Highway*, clearly a working title for *Tarantula*, and its stream-of-consciousness prose makes it likely that at one time it was indeed intended for inclusion in *Tarantula*, given lines like "laura speaks of God almighty dragon up avenue B cut throat lyer in long pants."

The next "excerpt" from his (on this occasion untitled) forthcoming book was published in the Chicago-based magazine *Pageant*, along with a photographic portfolio by Daniel Kramer. Brief "commentaries"—for example, "i would like to do something worthwhile / like perhaps plant some daisies on the desert / but i'm just a guitar player"—were printed alongside each photo and had in fact been created in a spare couple of hours in Woodstock at Kramer's request, though they could just have easily been part of the book. The final prose poem published by Dylan in the winter of 1964–65 was in the form of liner notes for his forthcoming album, *Bringing It All Back Home*. In fact, this prose poem was his most unorthodox to date—and was perhaps the closest he ever came to using William Burroughs's cutup technique in his writings. When talking about his forthcoming book to Paul Jay Robbins in early April, he suggested that cutups had some part to play in the way the book—now supposedly called *Bob Dylan off the Record*—would be constructed.

Bob Dylan: [The working title is,] tentatively, *Bob Dylan off the Record*. But they tell me there's already books out with that *Off the Record* title. The book can't really be titled, that's the kind of book it is. I'm also going to write the reviews for it. . . . I've written some songs which are kind of far out, a long continuation of verses, stuff like that. . . . I haven't really gotten into writing a completely free song. You dig something like cutups? . . . I wrote the book because there's a lot of stuff in there I can't possibly sing. . . . Something that had no rhyme, all cut up, no nothing except something happening which is words. [1965]

It would appear that he was here describing a finished form for the book. The vast bulk of *Tarantula* was written in the last weeks of 1964 and the first few months of 1965. Dylan seemed to be working flat out on the book, despite not having found a title he was happy with. Staying with Baez in Carmel, as winter turned to spring he wrote and wrote. According to Baez, he left a huge wad of drafts for the book at her house and never reclaimed them.

By the time he arrived in England at the end of April, he had also finally come up with a title, which he revealed to Michael Hellicar of the *Daily Sketch* before embarking on his English tour. The choice of *Tarantula* as the title has rarely been convincingly explained. Only he knows the real reason for the choice, just as only he knows why he chose the name Dylan. However, there can be little doubt that he had by now read a particular chapter from a classic of nineteenth-century philosophy, entitled "On Tarantulas": "Behold, this is the hole of the tarantula. Do you want to see the tarantula itself? Here hangs its web; touch it, that it tremble! There it comes willingly; welcome tarantula! Your triangle and symbol sits black on your back; and I know also what sits in your soul. Revenge sits in your soul: whenever you bite, black scabs grow. Your poison makes the soul whirl with revenge . . . therefore I tear at your webs that your rage may lure you out of your lie-holes and your revenge may leap out from behind your word justice. For that man be delivered from revenge, that is for me the bridge to the highest hope, and a rainbow after long storms."

Thus spoke Nietzsche, via Zarathustra. Nietzsche would get a name-check in the liner notes to the *Highway 61 Revisited* album; and though the style of *Thus Spoke Zarathustra* bears little similarity to that of *Tarantula*, as a book of prose poems portraying the visions of a traveling seer, it may well have provided some kind of model. Another book of prose poems, again with little stylistic similarity, but the visions of a seer whose memory served him well, was probably also inspirational: Rimbaud's *A Season in Hell*.

Yet whatever *Tarantula*'s antecedents—and there is clearly a healthy dose of the beats there, in among its Symbolist overtones—its symbolism is uniquely Dylan, so uniquely his that he soon began to believe that his book of private jokes would be lost on his fans and those literary critics who were waiting for an excuse to denigrate the so-called bard of the airwaves. In his own words, he realized that "the folks back home just aren't going to understand this at all." He was right, of course. Perhaps only *Finnegans Wake* among works of modern literature is as sustainedly unreadable as the prose sections of *Tarantula*.

His problem now was that everyone expected a book called *Tarantula*. Journalists wanted him to talk about the book. Dylan accordingly developed a potpourri of descriptions for it: vague, obtuse, generic hints of some hidden theme. Thus, "It's about spiders. . . . It's an insect book. . . . My next book is a collection of epitaphs"; alternatively it was "a book of confusion, tiny little sayings. It's like a splash on the wall"; or, more honestly, "I can't really say what it's about. It's not a narrative or anything like that."

He began to doubt the worth of what he had written. He carried the galleys with him from show to show, from state to state, all the while reading it to friends and other strangers, seeking their honest opinions. In October 1965 he hinted to Allen Stone that he had very real doubts about the book's merits.

Bob Dylan: I have a lot of words written for it but I can't use anything I've written . . . before a year ago. . . . I can't really use the ideas. They're so deformed and just not really right ideas. Stuff which has been expressed a million times in the past. . . . I don't write now unless it just happens. [1965]

Later that fall, when speaking to Nat Hentoff, he was even more up front about his serious doubts concerning the book's merits. Though he delivers a virtual parable to Hentoff about a novel he was working on "one time," it seems self-evident that he is really talking about *Tarantula*:

Bob Dylan: One time I wanted to write a novel, and so I was putting a lot of time in. It must have been about six months, off and on . . . and finally I just came to the conclusion. . . . Is this gonna be THE novel, THE statement? Is this my message? My thing? And no matter how many pages—I had about five hundred pages of it—I said, "No, of course not." That's bullshit. This is nothing. If I finish this novel, it's not gonna come out until at least a year and a half to two years from now. It's gonna be a completely different thing by the time it does come out. . . . Meantime, I'm not even gonna be there any more. . . . It won't even be me that wrote that novel. And from then on I have to live up to that novel. . . . People are gonna ask me what I'm doing. . . . I'm gonna HAVE to say I'm writing another novel! [1965]

Yet by the beginning of 1966 he had seemingly committed himself to the book's publication. In January 1966 he assured a bookseller, "It will be out within two months. . . . I've just got to go over it one more time, through the galleys." Sure enough, the galleys joined him on the world tour. The publicity machine was geared up for a major fall 1966 campaign on its release. It was not to be. He had enough expectations he was unwilling to live up to without adding one more.

Tarantula was the culmination of Dylan's desire to step outside the confines of song. After "Like a Rolling Stone," he realized he could fit everything he wanted to say into song, even if he had to redefine song in the process. His last prose poems (save for his 1974 sleeve notes to *Planet Waves*) would be included on the rear sleeve of *Highway 61 Revisited* and in the program for the Newport Folk Festival of 1965. The events of that fateful weekend would lead him toward a new direction. And there would be no spiders tempted to tarantella after him.

Bob Dylan: All my writing goes into the songs now. Other forms don't interest me anymore. [1966]

11 1965: I Accept Chaos

Bob Dylan: If you're talking about what [the] breakthrough [was] for me, I would have to say . . . "Like a Rolling Stone" because I wrote that after I'd quit, I'd literally quit singing and playing, and I found myself writing this song, this story, this long piece of vomit about twenty pages long, and out of it I took "Like a Rolling Stone" and made it as a single. . . . After writing that, I wasn't interested in writing a novel, or a play. [1966]

Bob Dylan: Everything is changed now from before. Last spring, I guess I was going to quit singing. I was very drained. I was playing a lot of songs I didn't want to play. I was singing words I didn't really want to sing. But "Like a Rolling Stone" changed it all. It was something that I myself could dig. It's very tiring having other people tell you how much they dig you if you yourself don't dig you. [1965]

As Dylan left London Airport the day after his session for the BBC, he found that not only had he just flown away from a storm of publicity but he was now flying back to one in America. He had been away just over a month, but in that time he had secured his first U.S. top forty single with "Subterranean Homesick Blues," and *Bringing It All Back Home* was making its way toward the top ten.

Meanwhile, the Byrds, another CBS act, were heading for the number-one spot with their instantly memorable version of "Mr. Tambourine Man."

His final days in London had been troubled ones. A week in bed had given him a lot of time to think. In that time it seems that he had made up his mind that he could go no further with his music and he should quit. He would later talk at length about this briefly maintained decision to journalists who interviewed him on his 1965–66 tour with the Hawks.

His decision to quit, however brief a time it lasted, was no frivolous whim. He had previously considered abandoning music back in the fall of 1963. With the chart information that was presumably being relayed from the States, he realized that the media mayhem he had just been subjected to in the U.K. could be duplicated on the other side of the pond. For most acts in pop music, the process of impending fame happens so rapidly that there is little time to perceive the phenomenon. The process in Dylan's case had taken three years, since "Blowin' in the Wind" had been a huge hit for Peter, Paul and Mary. At the end of May he had the choice. He could commit himself to his boyhood dreams and become a rock and roll star, or he could walk away from it all. It would be unwise to underestimate how seriously he considered the latter option. He would later tell Nat Hentoff, "People have one great blessing—obscurity."

One of the reasons for his dilemma was simply artistic restlessness. In the fall of 1963 he had considered moving away from song into plays and poems. In the spring of 1965 he was hard at work on his first book. Such diversions were part of a thirst for something more than the acoustic music he was making. If *Bringing It All Back Home* found him back on terra firma, it also seemed to Dylan at the time to represent the limits of where he could see himself going. And his attempts to record with a rhythm and blues band in England had been a disaster.

"Like a Rolling Stone" provided him with the new approach he was seeking. Though he had been impressed by the sound that the Beatles, the Animals and the Byrds had succeeded in getting, he wanted something that was more soulful, that truly brought it all back home—a rhythm and blues sound but with a folk sensibility. When "Like a Rolling Stone" introduced it to the world it would be called folk-rock, though Dylan always justifiably hated that expression.

Bob Dylan: I was doing fine, you know, singing and playing my guitar. It was a sure thing. . . . I was getting very bored with that. I couldn't go out and play like that. I was thinking of quitting. Out front it was a sure thing. I knew what the audience was going to do, how they would react. It was very automatic. . . . What I'm doing now, it's a whole other thing. We're not playing rock music. It's not a hard sound. These people call it folk-rock—if they want to call it that, something that simple, it's good for selling the records. As far as it being what it is, I don't know what it is. I can't call it folk-rock. It's a whole way of doing things. [1965]

Though the birth of folk-rock has been attributed by some to the Byrds and their cover of "Mr. Tambourine Man," the sound of that record was too twee and hid the meaning of the song. Dylan required a harder sound that lent meaning to the words. The song he wrote on his return from America—indeed, according to him it was started on the airplane home—had such a sound. Originally, "Like a Rolling Stone" was an ill-formed mass of words whose purpose and direction were uncertain, a long screed directing all the anger inside him at some abstract point.

Bob Dylan: [When] it was ten pages long, it wasn't called anything, just a rhythm thing on paper all about my steady hatred directed at some point that was honest. [1966]

But he condensed it down and down and down until what was left was the essence, which formed perhaps his most memorable song. Writing "Like a Rolling Stone" removed all desire to experiment with his "other" writings, which had distracted him throughout the last two years of his so-called folk period. It was the death knell for *Tarantula*, though he would not yet admit it. All the evidence suggests that the vast bulk of the published *Tarantula* was finished by this point, though small tinkerings and a few additions would occupy a further twelve months of indecision. But it documented a period of uncertainty for Dylan. If there seems little connection between "aretha / crystal jukebox queen of hymn and him diffused in drunk transfusion" and "Once upon a time you dressed so fine," it is surely feasible to envisage "Like a Rolling Stone" emerging out of ten pages of such "vomitific" prose.

Of course, by writing "Like a Rolling Stone," he did not "invent" or even produce the synthesis labeled folk-rock. The nature of recorded song required that he perform it in order to complete it. At times in his career he has shown an almost deliberate lack of discipline when approaching this final process in the production of his works. His desire for spontaneity and improvisation has not always been fruitful. In June 1965 he needed to consider *how* he wanted to record "Like a Rolling Stone."

As with the songs on *Bringing It All Back Home*, the first step in his equation was the guitar sound. Then it had been Bruce Langhorne who had provided the solution. This time Dylan remembered Michael Bloomfield, the great white blues guitarist he had jammed with in Chicago back in April 1963. He had run into Bloomfield again at an after-gig party when he was playing Chicago's

Orchestra Hall in December 1963. Though they talked, he had his mind on other matters:

Michael Bloomfield: He was trying to get pussy and, believe me, he got a lot of pussy, [but] we hung out at that party and we talked.

However, it was really reports coming from Chicago in the winter of 1965 that Bloomfield was whipping up a storm in a foot-to-the-floor howl of rhythm and blues called the Paul Butterfield Blues Band that reminded Dylan to renew contact. After all, Butterfield's blues band was as close to England's Bluesbreakers as America could provide in 1965. So Bloomfield was summoned to Woodstock in the second week of June.

Michael Bloomfield: I didn't even have a guitar case. I just had my Telecaster. And Bob picked me up at the bus station and took me to this house where he lived . . . and Sara was there . . . and she made very strange food, tuna fish salad with peanuts in it, toasted, and he taught me these songs, "Like a Rolling Stone," and all those songs from that album and he said, "I don't want you to play any of that B. B. King shit, none of that fucking blues, I want you to play something else," so we fooled around and finally played something he liked, it was very weird, he was playing in weird keys which he always does, all on the black keys of the piano. . . . We fucked around there for a few days and then we went to New York to cut the record and I started seeing that this guy Dylan was really a famous guy.

The session at CBS Studios in New York on June 15, 1965, has now passed into pop lore. The main source of the lore is Al Kooper's version of events in his autobiography, *Backstage Passes.* Kooper had secured an invitation to the session from Tom Wilson, the producer, harboring hopes of convincing Dylan to let him play guitar. When Dylan arrived he was accompanied by Bloomfield, who, Kooper soon realized, was out of Kooper's own league as a guitar player. When Dylan started recording his new song, though, he decided he wanted both piano and organ and Kooper volunteered his services at the organ. As Kooper tells it, he felt his "way through the changes like a little kid fumbling in the dark for a light switch." Dylan, though, liked the sound and halfway through the playback asked Wilson to turn the organ up. Thus was born that unique mixture of organ and guitar that identified Dylan's 1965–66 sound.

The fluke that resulted in Kooper's unique style of organ playing making its mark on "Like a Rolling Stone" was, according to most witnesses, one of many accidents occurring at these sessions, not all of them so serendipitous. The first two sessions for what would become the *Highway 61 Revisited* album took place on June 15 and 16. According to Kooper, versions of "Tombstone Blues" and

"Queen Jane Approximately" were attempted on the sixteenth. If so, they ended up unused. Certainly no further songs seem to have resulted from the session on the fifteenth, and the two released songs that seem most likely to date from the sixteenth, "Jet Pilot" and the original version of "From a Buick 6" (which remains to this day the take available on the Japanese version of *Highway 61 Revisited*), sound like half-formed ideas looking for a sound. Dylan certainly spent much of his time at these sessions improvising, as evidenced by these two songs, as if the process of reproducing the sound of "Like a Rolling Stone" was temporarily eluding him. According to Bloomfield, a large part of the problem was the producer.

Michael Bloomfield: They had a great bass player named Russ Savakus, a terrific guy. It was his first date playing electric bass. He was scared about that. And they had the best studio drummer. But no one understood nothing. The producer was a nonproducer . . . I think it was a black guy named Tom Wilson. He didn't know what was happening, man! . . . We did twenty alternate takes of every song, and it got ridiculous because they were long songs. . . . It was never like: Here's one of the tunes, we're gonna learn it, work out the arrangement. That just wasn't done. The thing just sort of fell together in this haphazard, half-assed way. . . . It was just like a jam session, it really was.

Though Savakus played on the June sessions, he would be replaced after the first of the post-Newport sessions, when his nerves got the better of him and he "freaked out a bit" during a take of "Tombstone Blues." Kooper assured Dylan that he knew a suitable replacement, and secured the gig for his friend Harvey Brooks. Dylan clearly loved Brooks's bass playing and would ask him to play in his first live band, while Bloomfield would later recruit him for the Electric Flag. However, if Kooper and Brooks were relative rookies, Dylan also utilized Bobby Gregg and Paul Griffin at the sessions, both of whom had contributed so much on *Bringing It All Back Home*, and Bloomfield was at the peak of his playing powers. When Dylan returned to the studio after Newport, all these musicians would be recalled. Tom Wilson, though, would not be. He was replaced by Bob Johnston.

Why Wilson was replaced still remains something of a mystery. Despite the assessments of Bloomfield and of Paul Rothchild, who sat in on several of Dylan's acoustic sessions and considered that Wilson was wont to try to move sessions along at the expense of good takes, the results that Wilson produced testify to some empathy with Dylan.

Wilson himself would have been the first to admit that he had never previously recorded folk music and was ill suited to producing acoustic artists. However, once Dylan made the move to electric sounds, Wilson was in his element.

It was he who chose most of the band that recorded *Bringing It All Back Home* and, as is well known, it was he who had the idea of using the same musicians to overdub some electric accompaniment for an acoustic duo called Simon and Garfunkel. He would also go on the following year to produce three of the most important and innovative albums of the sixties, the first Mothers of Invention album and the bulk of the first two Velvet Underground albums, all for MGM. Al Kooper certainly did not share Bloomfield and Rothchild's assessment.

Al Kooper: I don't think it was a good idea [replacing Wilson] because I think Tom Wilson was more something than Bob Johnston . . . more soulful. Plus he was a real experimenter.

Dylan and Wilson had seemed to be on rather good terms when they departed arm in arm from the May London session; the fact that he asked Wilson to fly to London to produce it suggests that he held Wilson in high esteem. In 1969, when specifically asked by Jann Wenner of *Rolling Stone* why Wilson was replaced after producing the masterful "Like a Rolling Stone," Dylan avoided answering. Wilson also remained oblique about the reason for his removal, though he did make it clear in a later interview with Chris Charlesworth of *Melody Maker* that he and Dylan had had a major disagreement, and Dylan had said to him, "Maybe we should try Phil Spector." Of course, Spector's obsession with perfection via endless takes was completely anathema to Dylan's own way of working.

If Wilson was replaced because Dylan was unhappy with his work, Bob Johnston, who produced the subsequent sessions for the album, was hardly an inspired choice.

Al Kooper: Bob Johnston, I would say, is the kinda guy that just pats you on the back and says you're fantastic and just keeps you going.

As Johnston would later comment, his "attitude was if Dylan wanted to record under a palm tree in Hawaii with a ukulele, I'd be there with a tape machine." Hardly an inspired, creative partnership! While Dylan's instinctive genius was working overtime, Johnston's lack of creative input was not a major issue. As Bloomfield later observed, it was really Dylan who was responsible for selecting the mix on *Highway 61 Revisited* and "it was astutely mixed. . . . He knew he had a sound in mind."

Before he could start work in earnest on *Highway 61 Revisited*, Dylan had some songs to write. If he had written several songs in the interim between completing *Bringing It All Back Home* and writing "Like a Rolling Stone"—in an interview with Max Jones in March he said he had "about four or five songs" ready for the next album—his new approach resulted in their remaining unused. New songs that suited his new sound were required. Thus began a month of intense writing in Woodstock, where he had just bought a house of his own near Grossman's in Byrdcliffe. It seems that his relationship with Sara had been intensifying in the last couple of months, and this may have been a motive for purchasing his own property. Before resuming work on his third album in a year, he had a major commitment to undertake. He was due to appear at the Newport Folk Festival the weekend of July 24 and 25.

Dylan's set at the 1965 Newport Festival may well be the most written-about performance in the history of rock and roll. Even at the time it was recognized as the point when Dylan went one way and the purists in the folk field went another. There are as many opinions about the events of that weekend as there were witnesses. Most of the major protagonists have axes to grind, particularly in hindsight, having seen that Dylan was right to go his own way, and they generally feel obliged to defend their initial resistance to change.

Dylan himself, talking about those events twenty years later, remarked, "I had a hit record out so I don't know how people expected me to do anything different." It is important to recall that not only had he already released *Bringing It All Back Home* with its electric side, but he had had a hit single with "Subterranean Homesick Blues," which—utilizing as it did Chuck Berry's "Too Much Monkey Business" riff—should have convinced anybody with two ears that Dylan had been a latent rocker all along. More importantly, "Like a Rolling Stone" was issued the week before Newport, a mere month after it was recorded, as Dylan and his label attempted to capitalize upon the new interest in his work. Within four days of its release the single was on the charts and on the radio, just in time to remind the fifteen thousand fans who made it to Freebody Park of the direction he was heading in. It is thus pertinent to recall the level of expectation that July weekend.

Joe Boyd: There was a tremendous anticipation at Newport about Dylan—"Is he here yet? Has he arrived?"—and instead of this blue-jeaned, work-shirted guy who'd arrived in 1964 to be the Pied Piper, he arrived rather secretively; he was staying in a luxurious hotel just on the outside of town and he arrived with Bob Neuwirth and Al Kooper—that was the entourage, Neuwirth, Kooper and Dylan. And they were all wearing puff-sleeved dueling shirts—one of them was polka dot—and they were not wearing blue jeans. . . . They wore sunglasses. The whole image was very, very different. They were very clannish, very secretive.

What Dylan's intentions were on arriving at Newport has never been adequately resolved. He surely had no intention of performing a wholly acoustic set after his thoughts on retirement two months earlier. Yet nobody there seemed aware of any intention regarding a backing band, and on the Saturday afternoon he was scheduled to appear at a songwriters' workshop, akin to the topical song workshop the previous year where he had premiered "Mr. Tambourine Man." He would certainly have to play acoustic on this occasion. The workshop, which was on one of the side stages set up for such events, was in fact absolute bedlam, and Dylan's set had to be abbreviated because of the chaos his presence was causing. The tension was mounting, and inevitably the resultant fury was directed at Dylan and his high-and-mighty manager, Albert Grossman.

Joe Boyd: The crowd around the songwriters' workshop was so immense that it was swamping the other workshops. People were complaining: "Turn up the Dylan one because we're getting bleed from the banjo one on the other side!" This was very much against the spirit of what the festival was supposed to be about. . . . Grossman became a focus of hostility for a lot of [the officials]. He'd never been popular amongst these people. He'd always been seen as one of the money changers at the gate of the temple and not a priest, y'know. And Grossman was arrogant, particularly with Dylan now being so big. Grossman was being very cool, but Grossman's way of being cool got up people's noses.

The tide of resentment did not spill over until later that afternoon, during another workshop. It is often forgotten that the Newport Folk Festival was in fact intended to be—and was billed as—a folk and blues festival. Anyone watching *Festival*, the Howard Alk documentary film, can gain an idea of the mixture of folk and blues that really made up the Newport festivals. There was to be a blues workshop that afternoon, but it was not just folk that was getting an electric shock that weekend. Scheduled to play at the blues workshop were Paul Butterfield's blues band, with Bloomfield on lead guitar, and they had added two words in front—"rhythm and." The band's appearance on the bill had already been a source of some contention when respected musicologist Alan Lomax stepped up to introduce them.

Joe Boyd: There had been a lot of pressure from Peter Yarrow on adding the Paul Butterfield band to the lineup of the festival—he really put a lot of pressure on the other members of the board to get the invitation, and Lomax was really against it. Against Butterfield. Against white boys doing the blues really. . . . Lomax was forced to introduce the Butterfield band at the blues workshop, and he gave them an introduction which was very condescending. . . . As the group started to take the stage Lomax came offstage to be confronted by Grossman, who basically said unkind words about the introduction that Lomax had just given. . . . Next thing you know . . . these two men, both rather oversized, were rolling around in the dirt throwing punches. They had to be pulled apart. Lomax then called an emergency meeting of the board of the festival that night . . . the board actually voted in favor of banning Grossman from the grounds of the festival. George Wein, who was a nonvoting adviser to the board, had to step in and say, "Look, I don't have a vote, it's up to you, but I tell you right now that if you do bar Grossman you have to prepare yourselves for the walkout of Bob Dylan, Peter, Paul and Mary and Buffy Sainte-Marie!" . . . So the board reconsidered and dropped the action against Grossman, but there was obviously a tremendous simmering of feeling.

The important point to consider here is that acts who appeared at Newport were not paid anything more than nominal fees, certainly not the sort of fees people like Dylan, Peter, Paul and Mary and Baez now commanded. They appeared for the exposure and for the sense of community. The threat of a walkout by Grossman's acts was no exaggeration; it was a likelihood.

At this point the chronicling becomes a little unclear. The primary issue is whether Dylan arrived at Newport with any specific intention of playing with a band, particularly the Paul Butterfield Blues Band. According to Al Kooper, he did not meet up with Dylan until he arrived and Grossman informed him that Dylan had been looking for him. According to Eric von Schmidt, Dylan "heard Butterfield in the blues workshop a couple of days earlier [sic] and realized they were a great blues band, and he said, 'Wanna do "Maggie's Farm?'"

In fact, this reliance on serendipity sounds a shade unconvincing, not to say implausible. First of all, it assumes that Dylan was unaware of the Paul Butterfield Blues Band up to this point. This does not seem likely. Paul Rothchild, a good friend of both Dylan's and Neuwirth's who regularly attended Dylan studio sessions, had "discovered" the Butterfield band early in January 1965 and signed them to his label, Elektra. He had also suggested the recruitment of Mike Bloomfield for the band. Bloomfield was then playing in another blues outfit on the same Chicago scene. The band were brought to New York, where they made several attempts to record a debut album. In the meantime, Rothchild had phoned Grossman and asked him if he would be interested in managing the band. Grossman, a Chicago native, came and saw the band play at the Cafe Au Go-Go and apparently told Rothchild, "I'll see them at Newport."

Meanwhile, Dylan had recruited Bloomfield for his studio sessions that June, at least partly because of what he had heard about his playing with Butterfield, and on completing the "Like a Rolling Stone" single had invited Rothchild over to his apartment in New York to play him the results. This all suggests an awareness of each other's activities which makes it unlikely that Dylan had not already considered using the Butterfield Blues Band for his brief appearance at the festival. The fact that, on meeting Kooper at Newport, he told him he had been phoning him trying to get hold of him clearly suggests that he wanted Kooper to play with him at Newport *before* the event. Indeed, Joe Boyd recalls, "We had known that Dylan was going to do something with more than just himself."

Whatever the truth, Grossman apparently told the Butterfield band that Saturday that he wanted to manage them; and Bloomfield, possibly as a result of that decision, told Dylan that he could not go on the road with him. Clearly at this stage Dylan wanted Bloomfield and Kooper to tour with him as integral elements in his new sound. (Even though he did not tour with Dylan, Kooper was later called up for the *Blonde on Blonde* sessions.)

Dylan, along with Bloomfield, Sam Lay and Jerome Arnold—all from Butterfield's band—plus Al Kooper and, at Bloomfield's suggestion, Barry Goldberg, rehearsed through the night at a big house near the festival site for what threatened to be a stormy Sunday, in all senses of the word.

According to Nick Gravenites, a friend of Bloomfield's, this ensemble was selected only after several auditions. If Gravenites's memory is reliable, which is open to doubt, the "auditions" must have involved very few musicians, as Dylan's options were extremely limited. According to Kooper, "We rehearsed until dawn." According to Bloomfield, the rehearsals did not go that well, with Arnold constantly throwing the rest of the musicians out.

Michael Bloomfield: We were all at Newport, Kooper, me, Barry [Goldberg] and this *schwartze* Jerome from the Butterfield band playing bass, and he can't play and he's fucking up everything, and we're practicing there in a room and Odetta's staring at us and Mary Travers is there and we're playing and it's sounding horrible and finally it's time for the gig and Barry and me are throwing up in these outhouses.

They worked up only three songs, two of which were fairly standard blues tunes—"Maggie's Farm" and the equally up-tempo "Phantom Engineer" (which later evolved into "It Takes a Lot to Laugh, It Takes a Train to Cry")—but Dylan was happy enough by dawn to proceed with the unveiling. Both of his recent biographers, Robert Shelton and Bob Spitz, have claimed that there was no soundcheck for Dylan and the band. Spitz does this despite including a photo from the soundcheck in his biography. There is no question that they had a soundcheck. Indeed, filmed footage from the soundcheck that afternoon is included in Alk's festival documentary, and Joe Boyd, perhaps the most reliable of the eyewitnesses to events both backstage and onstage that weekend, recalls the soundcheck in considerable detail.

Joe Boyd: By the time the concert had finished that [Sunday] afternoon, and before the start of the Butterfield set that evening, we had two hours . . . so the whole area was cleared and we got to do our soundchecks. Now, we had known that Dylan was going to do something with more than just himself, and that he was going to need a soundcheck. . . . We had taken the precaution of doing soundchecks on almost all the other performers for Sunday night earlier that morning. . . . We hadn't heard Dylan, but we had kept this time clear. . . . Anyway, so on came Dylan with the Butterfield band and Al Kooper on keyboards. We set up the stage the way they wanted it set up. It was set up anyway for Butterfield in the first set. They started playing. Obviously this was great. We all knew that this was significant. . . . I said, "How many songs are you going to do?" And they—Butterfield, Bloomfield and Dylan—looked at each other and said, "Well, we only know three, so that's what we're going to do."

The soundcheck provided the organizers with their first intimation of what Dylan had in mind for Sunday evening, and it was evidently a cause for concern.

Pete Seeger: It wasn't a real soundcheck. They were tinkering around with it and all they knew was, "Turn the sound up! Turn the sound up!" They wanted to get volume.

Throughout the remainder of the afternoon and early evening, Dylan stayed backstage. During the first half of the evening concert the Paul Butterfield Blues Band played their own set. Then, after a short break, the penultimate act in the first half was Dylan. When he came onstage he was dressed all in black.

Liam Clancy: I was actually filming at the Newport festival that year. I was up a twelve-foot platform, filming with a telephoto lens so I could zoom in close. And Dylan came out, and it was obvious that he was stoned, bobbing around the stage, very Chaplinesque actually.

There have been a lot of accounts of the twenty-five minutes that Dylan was onstage that evening. According to the account in Spitz's biography, Pete Seeger was attempting to wrest the mixing board from Paul Rothchild throughout Dylan's set. There have also been several suggestions that the sound was bad and that fans were shouting because Dylan was inaudible. The mix on the soundboard tape certainly does not lend credence to this theory. Of all the accounts of Dylan's set by those intimately involved with the organization of the event, Joe Boyd's account—from an interview conducted for *The Telegraph*—rings truest.

Joe Boyd: Dylan wasn't on, even, at the end of the concert, he was on in the middle. He was on one act before the interval, at around nine fifteen. So out comes Dylan and I'm out there onstage before he comes out, setting up all the amps to exactly the right levels, and Rothchild's got everything cranked up, and when that first note of "Maggie's Farm" hit, I mean, by today's standards it wasn't very loud, but by those standards of the day it was the loudest thing anybody had ever heard. The volume. That was the thing, the volume. It wasn't just the music, it wasn't just the fact that he came out and played with an electric band. . . . Care was taken to get Paul Rothchild to mix the sound. Because you had Paul Rothchild on the sound, you didn't have some square sound guy fumbling with the dials and having the thing creep up to where it should have been. You would have had just badly mixed rock and roll. It wasn't. It was powerfully, ballsy-mixed, expertly done rock and roll. . . . As soon as I had gotten the stage set, I ran around to the press enclosure, which was the front section, press and friends and people, and stood sort of at the door of the gates, and watched at the side of the stage, and I thought, "This is great!" I was lapping it all up. Somebody pulled at my elbow and said, "You'd better go backstage, they want to talk to you." So I went backstage and there I was confronted by Seeger and Lomax and, I think, Theodore Bikel or somebody, saying, "It's too loud! You've got to turn it down! It's far too loud! We can't have it like this. It's just unbearably loud!" And they were really upset. Very, very upset. I said, "Well, I don't control the sound, the sound is out there in the middle of the audience." And so Lomax said, "How do you get there? Tell me how to get there, I'll go out there." I said, "Well, Alan, you walk right to the back—it's only about half a mile—and then you walk around to the center thing, show your badge and just come down the center aisle." And he said, "There must be a quicker way." So I said, "Well, you can climb over the fence." I was looking at his girth, you know! And he said, "Now, look, you go out there. You can get there, I know you know how to get there. Go out there and tell them that the board orders them to turn the sound down." I said, "OK." So I went out—there was a place where anyone could climb on top of a box and get over the fence from backstage. By this time I think it was the beginning of the second number, and there was Grossman and Neuwirth and Yarrow and Rothchild all sitting at the sound desk, grinning, very, very pleased with themselves, and meanwhile the audience was going nuts. . . . There were arguments between people sitting next to each other! Some people were booing, some people were cheering. . . . I relayed Lomax's message and Peter Yarrow said, "Tell Alan Lomax," and extended his middle finger, and I said, "C'mon, Peter, gimme a break!" He said, "Well, just tell Alan that the board of the festival are adequately represented on the sound console and that we have things fully under control and we think that the sound is at the correct level." So I went back, climbed over the fence, and by this time all I could see of Pete Seeger was the back of Pete Seeger disappearing down the road past the car park. . . . I was confronted by Lomax and Bikel again, frothing at the mouth, and I relayed Yarrow's message and they just cursed and gnashed their teeth. By this time the thing was almost over.

Seeger himself admits that he was furious with Dylan, but only because he considered the sound so distorted that nobody could understand the words. Unlike Lomax, he saw nothing fundamentally heretical about playing with electric instruments: "It's all how you use it." However, this does not explain why he got so worked up that, in his own words, "I was ready to chop the microphone cord." Clearly the raucousness of the performance also upset him.

Al Kooper, up on stage, knew better than anybody that there were problems with the sound, but they were not related to the mix or volume but to the band's own lack of confidence about what they were doing.

Al Kooper: What happened was in "Maggie's Farm" the beat got turned around so instead of playing on two and four, [the drummer, Sam Lay,] was playing on one and three. That's an accident that can happen and it happened so it was sort of a disaster. . . . I got lost myself.

Yet Kooper was unaware of the pandemonium that the performance was generating until they finished the three songs, at which point he finally heard the boos.

Al Kooper: They were definitely booing, but they were booing . . . 'cause he only played three songs. . . . These people paid a lot of money. . . . And I don't think anybody cared who else was on the show. They came to see Dylan and then he played three songs, when someone like Son House played for forty-five minutes. . . . "Like a Rolling Stone" was number one or very close to it at the time of Newport. So what did they expect to hear, "Who Killed Davey Moore?" . . . But at the festival there definitely was a dispute about electric people playing so I think they got meshed together in the booing legend.

Kooper's belief that the majority of fans were booing at the brevity of the set—though certainly there must have been some very upset people who began booing only when they realized that that was it—does not explain the reaction during the set itself.

According to some accounts, Dylan left the stage tearful and was cajoled into returning with acoustic guitar in hand. The reaction from the audience had certainly been mixed, but as Kooper himself observes, a large part of the 1965 audience was composed of new Dylan fans who had been only dimly aware of him up to *Bringing It All Back Home*. They must have wondered what the fuss was all about. Dylan had rehearsed only three songs with the band, but the fans were shouting for more. Eventually Yarrow came out and told them Dylan would be coming back—he was just getting an acoustic guitar. In fact, he must have been composing himself. The reaction had been more vehement than perhaps even he had expected.

Bob Dylan: I did this very crazy thing. I didn't know what was going to happen, but they certainly booed, I'll tell you that. You could hear it all over the place. [1965]

According to Bloomfield "he looked real shook up," but, ever the crowd-pleaser, he obliged with two songs solo. However, the two songs were both from his first electric album, and "Mr. Tambourine Man" and "It's All Over Now, Baby Blue" could hardly be considered in the topical song genre. After the intermission, Seeger and Lomax got their wish and had a set composed of all the things they held dear, but the drama of what had happened could not help but cast a shadow over the remaining proceedings.

Joe Boyd: After the interval, for some reason, the scheduling misfired and every washed-up, boring, old, folky, left-wing fart you could imagine in a row, leading up to Peter, Paul and Mary in the final thing—Ronnie Gilbert, Oscar Brand, Josh White, who was very much beyond his powers at that point, Theodore Bikel—they all went on, one after another. It was like an object lesson in what was going on here. Like, you guys are all washed up. This is all finished. There's something else now that we're dealing with. . . . You knew, as it was happening, that paths were parting.

Meanwhile, there was the traditional after-Newport party for the organizers, the performers and their guests to attend. Maria Muldaur in *Baby, Let Me Follow You Down* implies that Dylan was still badly shaken by the events, perhaps racked with worry about the consequences of what he had done.

Maria Muldaur: Dylan was off in a corner buried, and Fariña told me to go over and ask Dylan to dance. . . . So I went over to him and said, "Do you want to dance?" and he looked up at me and said, "I would, but my hands are on fire."

Bloomfield suggests that the aftereffects of Newport wore off rather quickly and that Dylan was soon indulging in his old games:

Michael Bloomfield: When I saw him afterward, he looked real shook up and I didn't know the nature of what made him all shook up but the next night he was at this party and he's sitting next to this girl and her husband and he's got his hand right up her pussy, right next to her husband, and she's letting him do this and her husband's going crazy, so Dylan seemed quite untouched by it the next day.

If this was indeed the following day or days, then Dylan had had enough time to assimilate the press reaction and speak to friends about their responses and those of others around them. Clearly what he heard steeled him for the next stage in his transformation into the "King of Folk-Rock."

Bob Dylan: There were a lot of people there who were very pleased that I got booed. I saw them afterward. I do resent somewhat, though, that everybody that booed said they did it because they were old fans. [1966]

He was back in the studio within four days of Newport, and in the interim he had written his own personal message to those who had been so vitriolic in their response, those who "said they did it because they were old fans." The song was called "Positively 4th Street." It would make "Like a Rolling Stone" sound like "I Want to Hold Your Hand," and it would be this third hit single of 1965 when issued the first week in September, following "Like a Rolling Stone" into the top ten.

One of the other songs from this first July session illustrates the success of Dylan's approach to recording in 1965. Having performed a new song at Newport, the blasting blues "Phantom Engineer," he recorded a version for his new album. However, after laying down a satisfactory take, while the group took a lunch break he reworked the tune alone at the piano and came back with a somewhat slower, more soulful approach to the song. The final result was the beautiful album cut of "It Takes a Lot to Laugh, It Takes a Train to Cry."

The remaining sessions seemed to progress smoothly enough. Dylan worked on songs but was careful not to work them into the ground. For the final session Johnston had suggested flying Charlie McCoy, a respected Nashville musician, to New York to accompany Dylan in recording an eleven-minute Kafkaesque parade of freaks entitled "Desolation Row." The song had been attempted with bass and electric guitar accompaniment (provided by Kooper and Brooks), but Dylan was unhappy with the results and decided not to attempt a further take until McCoy's arrival, when it was recorded with just two acoustic guitars.

Charlie McCoy: They called me up to New York City to play on Dylan's album. . . . They just told me to go out and pick up a guitar and play what I felt like playing. I finished and I went in and asked Dylan if it suited him. And he said, "Yeah, that's fine." . . . We just did one song. The only one I played on was eleven minutes long. . . . We just did two takes and . . . [I] left.

Of course, Dylan's approach was prone to the occasional disaster, but the spontaneity of the situation seemed adequate compensation for those times when nothing came out right. Thus, at least a couple of the sessions produced only minimal results (unlike the three sessions at which the entire *Bringing It All Back Home* album was recorded), and Bob Johnston was hardly an improvement on Tom Wilson, who at least was hip to how rock and roll should sound.

Michael Bloomfield: There were chord charts for these songs but no one had any idea what the music was supposed to sound like. . . . It all sort of went around Dylan. I mean, he didn't direct the music, he just sang the songs and played piano and guitar and it just sort of went on around him. . . . But the sound was a matter of pure chance . . . the producer did not tell people what to play or have a sound in mind, nor did Bob. . . . I was there, man, I'm telling you it was a result of chuckle-fucking, of people stepping on each other's dicks until it came out right.

Dylan clearly loved playing with the band and trying out ideas on the spur of the moment. At the July 29 session, he tried to work up another of largely improvised blues called "Sitting on a Barbed Wire Fence." The two known takes illustrate the way Dylan would rework songs from take to take. The second features some nice vamped organ and bluesy guitar flourishes, indicative of the indefinable chemistry the band was finding. The first was loose and more honky-tonk, with piano and harmonica at the heart of the performance.

However, the notion that everything that happened was purely spontaneous and relied entirely on serendipity is nonsense. After the first two July sessions, there was a weekend break, with sessions resuming on Monday morning. Dylan, Al Kooper, Tony Glover and a lady friend all drove to Woodstock, where Dylan spent most of Saturday writing out chord charts with Kooper. It would be a role Kooper would also adopt for the *Blonde on Blonde* sessions.

The album was completed in five July/August sessions—along with the two June sessions, it took a week of recording. But taking seven days to produce an album of this quality could hardly be considered to be wrenching the music out of Dylan note by note.

Highway 61 Revisited reinvented rock and roll in a way perhaps only half a dozen albums have done in the forty-year history of the art. Next to *Highway 61 Revisited*, side one of *Bringing It All Back Home* sounds like no more than a demo. No one had ever written lyrics like these for a rock and roll album. But there was no mistaking the fact that this was a rock and roll album, from that snare drum kicking everyone in on "Like a Rolling Stone" to the exuberant guitar playing on "Highway 61 Revisited" to the stately sound of "Ballad of a Thin Man" or the bluesiness of Dylan's singing on "Just Like Tom Thumb's Blues." Clearly he was tapping the same roots as the first Rolling Stones album or Mayall's Bluesbreakers with Eric Clapton or even the debut album by the Paul Butterfield Blues Band. If Bloomfield was committing himself to playing with Butterfield, Dylan was going to have to find a new guitarist if he was going to do justice to these songs live. His chances of finding an adequate replacement seemed slim.

12   1965–66:   Just Like a Freeze Out

Allen Ginsberg: Dylan has sold out to God. That is to say, his command was to spread his beauty as wide as possible. It was an artistic challenge to see if great art can be done on a jukebox. And he proved it can. [1966]

Whatever really happened at the Newport Folk Festival, it was immediately written up as Dylan playing his new brand of folk-rock and the folkies roundly booing him for his arrogance. The controversy only heightened media interest in Dylan, who was rapidly turning into the pop music phenomenon of 1965. He was also providing a welcome American antidote to the British invasion.

Having completed his follow-up to *Bringing It All Back Home*, though, he needed to take his new sound out on the road, which meant that he had to form a touring band. The two main ingredients he needed had been provided in the studio by Al Kooper and Michael Bloomfield. Kooper was willing to play a couple of prestigious shows lined up for the end of August, and Harvey Brooks, who had been so outstanding on the album sessions, was prepared to take bass duties, but Dylan needed a replacement for Bloomfield.

It seems remarkable now to consider that not only did Dylan record two albums long recognized as classics and two equally notable nonalbum singles in 1965, but that he used three different but equally talented guitarists in his 1965 studio activities. Bruce Langhorne and Michael Bloomfield, though, did not face the ultimate test of playing live night after night with the man. Robbie Robertson would.

Dylan actually required both a drummer and a guitarist to complete his band. Bobby Gregg, his first choice as a drummer, was too busy with his session work, so Levon Helm, the drummer in Robertson's band, the Hawks, was recruited as well. Robertson and Helm had been playing in the Hawks for five years, mainly on their home turf around Toronto. The band was named after the man they regularly provided support for, the imposing rock and rolling hulk Ronnie Hawkins. Recently, though, Helm, Robertson and organist Garth Hudson had provided backup on sessions for an album by John Hammond, Jr., entitled *So Many Roads* and had been gigging around New York and New Jersey. As with Butterfield, it was Robertson and Helm's work on an album by an old friend of Dylan's that provided the initial contact.

Robbie Robertson: He'd heard of us somehow, maybe through Ian and Sylvia, maybe through John Hammond [Jr.], I'm not really sure . . . we were lolling in the sand when he phoned us and said, "You wanna play Hollywood Bowl?" So we asked him who else was gonna be on the show. "Just us," he said.

In fact, the first of two major gigs, one on the East Coast, one on the West, was not at the Hollywood Bowl, where Dylan was scheduled to play on September 3. It was August 28, when Dylan was due to play the fifteen-thousand-capacity Forest Hills Stadium in New York, and this time he intended to be prepared. His new four-piece ensemble rehearsed with him at Carroll's Rehearsal Hall for two weeks, working up a forty-five-minute electric set.

The day of the Forest Hills show the sky was overcast and black and the wind was cold and rainy, whipping through the open-air stadium, as Dylan ran through the band set one more time during an afternoon soundcheck. Yet when it came time for Dylan to go onstage that evening, fans were delighted to see he was alone, armed with just a harmonica and a guitar. For forty-five minutes he mystified his new fans and delighted his folk-loving audience with a version of the old Dylan. In fact, it was no such thing. Only "To Ramona" was drawn from his pre-1965 albums, and for ten minutes he weaved a spell with a new, and on first hearing incomprehensible, song called "Desolation Row." The incongruous images brought titters and occasional laughs from the audience, but aside from such moments the mood was deadly serious among the freezing fans.

Al Kooper: [Of course,] anybody else 'cept Bob Dylan would have said, "Well, I'm gonna take a break and then we're gonna come out and play a few electric songs."

After a short intermission, Dylan was set to return and it occurred to the more perceptive members of the audience that he probably had a reason for all those imposing speakers and amps enfolding the stage. The second set was going to be a little noisier than the first. Dylan and the band were fully rehearsed and suspected that a rocky ride was in store.

Al Kooper: He knew something was gonna happen because he gave us like a pep talk before the show. He said, "Now, there's gonna be some kinda circus out there. Just ignore whatever happens and play the show." He knew something was gonna happen.

In a preconcert telephone interview with Shelton to provide quotes for a write-up in *The New York Times*, Dylan had told him that if his so-called fans "can't understand green clocks, wet chairs, purple lamps or hostile statues, they're missing something." There were a lot of uncomprehending individuals out there that night. This time there was no mistaking the reaction. If "catastrophe and confusion are the basis of my songs," they were also the basis of his concerts throughout the momentous ten months of touring inaugurated by Forest Hills.

Al Kooper: They booed at Forest Hills because they'd read that they were supposed to. . . . They booed us when we came out and they never really stopped booing us.

Dylan did not make it easy on his audience by playing the light, skiffling form of electric music found on the first side of *Bringing It All Back Home*. The sound that the band was making that night was intense and immense, rich and rhythmic. Meanwhile, he dismissed talk of rock and roll and folk rot, yet refused to define what it was he and the band were playing.

Bob Dylan: It's easy for people to classify it as rock and roll, to put it down. Rock and roll is a straight twelve-bar blues progression. My new songs aren't. I used to play rock and roll a long time ago, before I even started playing old-fashioned folk. [1965]

The forty-five-minute set at Forest Hills was also largely composed of new songs, songs that would seem initially oblique even in ideal listening conditions with a modern PA system. On a chilly night, with a furious wind roaring around the stadium and a primitive PA, opening a set with "The sweet pretty things are in bed now of course . . ." was not conducive to enlightenment. Of the new songs, "Ballad of a Thin Man" was the only one remotely intelligible that night, and that was performed by Dylan at the piano. A story that has gained much currency has Dylan instructing the band to play the introduction to this song over and over again until the crowd quieted down. In fact, there is no evidence of this on the audience tape of the show, though his desire for a little quiet would be understandable when playing a piano to fifteen thousand fans in an open-air stadium. He may indeed have wanted the so-called fans to hear the immortal refrain: "Something is happening and you don't know what it is."

Though the ever-optimistic Dylan had worked up two possible encores with the band, the virulence of the response was enough for him to abandon the stage after "Like a Rolling Stone." A week later in Los Angeles's Hollywood Bowl the response—though still mixed—was more than positive enough to warrant that encore. Perhaps he was beginning to win them over.

If everyone thought he was putting his fans on, by this point he was certainly putting the press on. Throughout the fall of 1965 and into 1966 Dylan would become the enfant terrible any journalist feared to interview. His moods were wildly unpredictable. Thus in December two press conferences in San Francisco and Los Angeles, conducted a mere two weeks apart, were worlds apart in mood. In San Francisco his fifty-minute press conference—broadcast on local TV—showed him being witty, sharp, playful. When asked if he wrote some of his songs to show some people the error of their ways, he replied, "I just want to needle them," but the way he put it across belied any real sense of hostility. In Los Angeles thirteen days later he looked tired, his answers seemed more than a little tinged with bile and there was a cynical air to his words.

The day after his September Hollywood Bowl show, Dylan had given his first bona fide American press conference, at the Beverly Hills Hotel. He was in a good mood—far better than at his second LA press conference three months later—though this did not restrain him from playing word games designed to be unrevelatory. When asked how he felt about the power grabbers, Dylan launched into one of his outrageous surreal screeds:

Bob Dylan: They can't hurt me. Sure they can crush you and kill you. They can lay you out on Forty-second and Broadway and put the hoses on you and flush you in the sewers and put you on the subway and carry you out to Coney Island and bury you on the Ferris wheel. But I refuse to sit here and worry about dying. [1965]

Whenever questions threatened to delve seriously into his success, Dylan would become flippant (when asked if his songs now had more urban imagery than previously, Dylan replied, "Well, I watch too much TV, I guess"); whenever those he was putting on became antagonistic he would ridicule them ("Hey, well, I don't wanna disappoint anybody. I mean, tell me what I should say"). The press conferences gave him the best opportunity for such games, because they did not allow journalists the opportunity to nail him down and say, "I'm sorry, but what exactly did you mean by that?"

Dylan's games did not end with such ribaldry at the expense of the unhip. As he had constructed a press conference with J. R. Goddard back in March, so in the fall of 1965 he "rewrote" two major articles about him to provide two of his funniest comedy scripts. The first such piece was published in the *New York Herald Tribune* in December 1965 accompanying a portfolio of Daniel Kramer's photographs of Dylan. It was called "A Night with Bob Dylan." Jointly composed by Al Aronowitz and Dylan himself, the article debunked the very notion of prying into his personal life by putting the reader through a surreal journey of New York nightclubs and hotel rooms peopled by characters such as Soupy Sales and Mr. Egg.

His second and more famous rewrite was the well-known *Playboy* interview conducted by Nat Hentoff in the fall of 1965. For years, fans found it hard to believe that even Dylan could be as sustainedly and spontaneously funny as the 1966 *Playboy* interview implied. Anthony Scaduto then suggested that Dylan had recomposed the whole interview after having a surprisingly straight interview hacked up by a *Playboy* editor, but that Hentoff was reluctant to discuss it. In fact, Hentoff seemed perfectly happy to discuss the saga when interviewed by Brian Stibal of *Zimmerman Blues* some years later:

Nat Hentoff: There were two [*Playboy*] interviews. The first was really an almost unusually straight interview. As I recall it was a quite sober, almost historical, biographical account, a lot of opinion, a certain amount of his—you know, he can't avoid being sardonically funny, but just a straight interview. The galleys were sent to him and I don't recall him making more than two changes of no significance. Then the final set came to him after they messed with it in Chicago. I don't know what they did but I think they put some words in his mouth. They fooled around with it. I got a call and he was furious. I said, "Look, tell them to go to hell. Tell them you don't want it to run." And he said, "No, I got a better idea. I'm gonna make one up." I said it probably will work if they very much want to have a Dylan interview. We were on the phone and I did not have a tape recorder then. This was all by hand. I'll never forget, I could hardly move the damn thing for a day. He made up an interview. I helped, I must say. Some of the good straight lines in there are mine, but all the really funny stuff . . . is his. It was run as was with absolutely no indication it was a put-on. I remember I saw him two or three times in the month or two after and he'd say, "Hey, when's it coming out, when's it coming out?" because he thought it was a very funny caper, which it was.

Dylan's games did not even begin and end with toying with the media. Throughout the summer and fall of 1965 he became increasingly difficult to communicate with. Both his friends and other strangers were repeatedly subjected to verbal put-ons—straight answers became wholly a thing of the past. The small coterie of the hip that Dylan seemed prepared to associate with became an exclusive club delighting in ridiculing each and every combatant foolish enough to confront them. Even those who genuinely liked Dylan found an unmistakable glee to the cruel games he played.

Michael Bloomfield: He changed. . . . I would see him consciously be that cruel, man, I didn't understand the game they played, that constant insane sort of sadistic put-down game. Who's king of the hill? Who's on top? To me it seemed like much ado about nothing but to David Blue and Phil Ochs it was real serious.

Folksinger Phil Ochs in particular was the subject of Dylan's "bayonet," to use Carla Rotolo's word. The increasing pressures of fame seemed to increase his cruelty with each notch up the *Billboard* charts. In one incident that fall, Ochs was ordered from Dylan's car after daring to criticize his new single, "Can You Please Crawl Out Your Window?"

Phil Ochs: I had a fight with Dylan. He used to come around to the Kettle of Fish, and he was . . . superarrogant then. He used to try to categorize all the other writers in terms of how good he was. He used to say, "Well, Eric Andersen, you're not really a writer," or he'd say, "Phil, you're not really a writer, you're a journalist, you shouldn't try to write." And he went through this whole fantastic riff of how we shouldn't try to write, and that he was really the writer. Which, on straight aesthetics, I would admit was true. Y'know, he was the best writer. Anyway, one day he was being photographed by Jerry Schatzberg and he was playing one of his new singles. And he was asking everybody what they thought. And he asked me what I thought, and I said I didn't like it. And he said, "What do you mean you don't like it?" I said, "Well, it's not as good as your old stuff, and speaking commercially I don't think it'll sell." We were all in a limousine, David Blue was there . . . and Dylan had gotten furious. He said, "Get out of the car." So I got out of the car.

Clearly Dylan was finding it hard to accept opinions that contradicted the ones he was getting from ingratiating sycophants. Though he would constantly invite comment, his response to Ochs suggests that he did not take criticism well. The irony was that, despite the unmistakable quality of "Can You Please Crawl Out Your Window?" Ochs was right on both counts. It was not "as good" as "Like a Rolling Stone" and "Positively 4th Street." It trod the same ground as both singles with its vengeful put-downs of the (male) subject; and the chorus was but a marginal rewrite of ideas more successfully explored in "To Ramona" and "It's All Over Now, Baby Blue." And after two top ten singles, "Can You Please Crawl Out Your Window?" peaked at a mightily disappointing fifty-eight. When the more masterful follow-up single, "One of Us Must Know," failed to chart at all, it seemed as if Dylan's commercial credibility was in tatters.

If most of Dylan's games seemed harmless enough to him and his friends, his so-called truth attacks were very hurtful and vindictive. As we have seen, Dylan was something of a womanizer. He seemed capable of bewitching a lot of women into believing they were more important to him than they were. In the fall of 1965 he had been skirting the edges of Andy Warhol's coterie, befriended by Barbara Rubin (who is the lady seen massaging his hair on the back cover of *Bringing It All Back Home*) and Edie Sedgwick, two women with strong Warhol associations. Sedgwick, who had become a minor starlet-in-the-ascendant after appearing in Warhol's films, was looking for new frontiers. She latched onto Dylan and Neuwirth, who were both patently attracted to her, and set about extricating herself from Warhol's influence.

Paul Morrissey: The Dylan relationship came up one night when we saw Edie at the Ginger Man.. She told us that she didn't want Andy to show her films anymore. . . . She told us that she had signed a contract with Bob Dylan's manager, Albert Grossman. . . . Dylan was calling her up and inviting her out, telling her not to tell Andy or anyone that she was seeing him. He invited her up to Woodstock and told her that Grossman hoped to put her together with him. She could be his leading lady. . . . She signed with Grossman at Dylan's urging. . . . She said, "They're going to make a film and I'm supposed to star in it with Bobby." Suddenly it was Bobby this and Bobby that, and we realized that she had a crush on him. . . . So Andy couldn't resist asking, "Did you know, Edie, that Bob Dylan had gotten married?" She just went pale. "What? I don't believe it."

Edie took the revelation of Dylan's recent, secret marriage badly. It has been suggested that his "rejection" of Edie was the beginning of her decline into drug dependency. According to Nico, it was Edie who was the subject of "Leopard-skin Pill-box Hat," a rather ironic look at a woman and her affectations.

Gerard Malanga: It was after Edie left Andy and got involved with Dylan and then she started being passed around hand to hand, so to speak, that she got involved with heavy drugs. . . . It's not true that the Dylan group were responsible for Edie's demise, though they probably helped it along.

Edie Sedgwick was not the only one amazed by the revelation that Dylan had married in November 1965. Sara Lowndes was largely unknown to the habitual attendees of Dylan's nightly gatherings at the Kettle of Fish or other Village hangouts. Dylan seemed to feel unhindered by his marriage vows when it came to restricting his infidelities, or indeed his whole frenetic pill-popping life-style.

Since Sara was a friend of Sally Grossman's, she had always been a regular visitor at Grossman's Woodstock residence. Dylan clearly felt especially comfortable in her presence. When Daniel Kramer took some photographs in Woodstock in the spring of 1965 for a possible cover for *Tarantula*, it was the then unknown Sara who was seen peering around doors and holding enigmatic items alongside Dylan. When Dylan took a relaxing vacation at the end of his English tour, it was with Sara that he chose to do it, and when Bloomfield arrived in Woodstock that June, it was Sara who seemed to be his constant companion. Clearly the relationship had progressed steadily, and his increasing attachment to Sara may have been an important motive in the brutal way that Dylan intimidated Baez into realizing that it was over between them.

Part of Sara's appeal to Dylan was that she did not seem after a piece of the legend. Indeed, initially she did not even know who he was.

Sally Grossman: I remember the first time Bobby was ever on television. I watched the program with Sara. I probably shouldn't say this, but she thought we were going to watch Bobby Darin!

Yet despite their increasing closeness and her Zenlike detachment from the paraphernalia of fame that surrounded Dylan, his marriage seemed a surprising move, particularly when he was due to spend most of the next six months on the road, away from her. Shortly after his divorce in 1978, he himself hinted rather obliquely of some underlying motive for his timing in marrying Sara on November 22, 1965.

Bob Dylan: I'd rather not tell the world why I got married. Even though my ex-wife and I don't have a relationship now, she is still the mother of my children and I see fit to protect her. [1978]

Given the birth of their first child in the early months of 1966, it is clear that Sara was by now pregnant with Dylan's child. However, if Dylan had persuaded Suze to have an abortion as Spitz contends in his biography, he would not necessarily have seen the fact that Sara was pregnant as requiring the ultimate commitment from him. Perhaps he just felt the time had come to put at least some of his life in order.

After all, he was increasingly spinning out of control. The pressures were such that he seemed to need stronger and stronger stimulants to maintain his ability to perform, both on and off stage. Dylan's "official" position on drugs, as stated in the published *Playboy* interview in 1966, was that grass was fine but hard drugs were not.

Bob Dylan: I wouldn't advise anybody to use drugs—certainly not the hard drugs; drugs are medicine. But opium and hash and pot—now, those things aren't drugs; they just bend your mind a little. I think everybody's mind should be bent once in a while. [1966]

This somewhat contradicts his actual statement to Hentoff during the original interview intended for *Playboy* magazine, conducted back in the fall of 1965.

Bob Dylan: It's fine if they use pot and LSD and heroin and sex and every-thing. I mean, that's groovy. . . . To know pot—or to know any drug—is fine, and it's not gonna fuck you up. . . . I mean, LSD is a medicine. You take it and you know . . . you don't really have to keep taking it all the time. [1965]

Dylan would later dismiss the influence of drugs on his songs, saying that they just helped him keep pumping new songs out. He would also later dismiss the psychedelics that came into vogue in the mid-sixties, suggesting that their use made people abandon reality in favor of some unreal dreamscape.

Bob Dylan: Grass was everywhere in the clubs. It was always there in the jazz clubs, and in the folk-music clubs. There was just grass and it was available to musicians. . . . When psychedelics happened, everything became irrelevant. Because that had nothing to do with making music, or writing poems. . . . People were deluded into thinking they were something that they weren't: birds, fire hydrants, whatever. [1978]

However, by 1965 he was clearly indulging in a lot more than grass or Beaujolais, his two traditional stimulants from 1960 to 1964. What he would refer to as "powerful medicine" certainly included the regular use of amphet-amines, particularly Methedrine and Benzedrine. He also seemed to be experimenting with harder, more dangerous drugs, including LSD, and possibly cocaine. The drugs certainly were a major contributory factor in sending his worldview askew, spiraling downward into dark paranoia.

Yet as the saying goes: Just 'cause you're paranoid does not mean they are not out to get you! Dylan and his touring band were playing night after night to largely hostile crowds and the wave of critical indignation was not letting up. Izzy Young, Irwin Sibler, Tom Paxton and Ewan MacColl all wrote articles critical of Dylan's new stance in *Sing Out!*, the bimonthly bastion of folkdom (though MacColl had never been impressed by Dylan, even when his fellow folksingers were).

Ironically, after their mildly successful performance at the Hollywood Bowl, Kooper finally plucked up the courage to tell Dylan he was not looking forward to the prospect of converting the heartland of America to this new music, starting with two dates in Texas. As Kooper observed in *Backstage Passes*, "Look at what they did to J.F.K. down there, and he was the leading symbol of the establishment." Not surprisingly, the news of Kooper's decision to quit was greeted enthusiastically by Robertson and Helm, who badly wanted to be re-united with their fellow Hawks, and who had been working on Dylan to convince him to dispense with the services of Kooper and Brooks and use the entire band.

Al Kooper: I think my call was probably like a day before his call would have come to me . . . Garth and Richard and them really wanted to get the band back together.

Dylan duly went to Toronto a week before the fall tour was scheduled to start rehearsing in earnest with the newly reconstituted Hawks, who were back in their hometown playing at Friars. Though Robertson and Helm had already fully briefed the band, Dylan insisted on two all-night rehearsals before being convinced that here was a band that could play with sufficient invention and flair to be suitable support for America's premier folk-rocker.

Of course, he would have been well and truly stuck if the Hawks had not worked out. A week was barely time enough to rehearse other musicians. Fortunately, Dylan and the Hawks jelled immediately and there were two warm-up shows in Texas to iron out any problems before they played an important gig at Carnegie Hall on October 1. The shows in Austin and Dallas proved surprisingly successful, and Dylan and the Hawks managed a few days' rehearsals in Woodstock prior to Carnegie Hall. The New York show was equally well received, and this time Dylan rewarded his fickle New York fans with an encore.

But Dylan was in for a shock if he felt that the tide had irrevocably turned.

The out-of-town shows he played most weekends in October still attracted a fair number of hecklers suggesting he "Go back to England!" or "Get rid of the band!" If he was upset by the renewed hostility, he was delighted with his new band. The Hawks were a superb outfit who were determined to make great music, leaving the waxing poetic to Dylan—though his primary opportunity to do so came in the forty-five-minute acoustic set that preceded the set with the Hawks.

Robbie Robertson: We never remarked, "Oh, that third line in that fourth verse is such a whammy," I mean nobody cared about the third line in the fourth verse, we cared about how it phrased and connected and slid into that fourth line much more. If it said anything really incredible at the same time, terrific, that was a bonus.

Surprisingly the first person to want to bail out of the most controversial tour in rock's brief history was not one of the new boys but Levon Helm, who soon tired of the barracking, and felt that perhaps there was a genuine fault with the band that he was unable to hear. By the end of November, just before a two-week tour of the West Coast, Helm had left the Hawks. He was replaced for the West Coast leg by Bobby Gregg, who had performed such an outstanding job on both of Dylan's 1965 albums but who normally preferred session work to the rigors of nationwide gigging.

Levon Helm: Back in those days when you played for some of the folk-purist crowds, the electrical portion, which was us, would get all the booing and hissing and stuff. After a while it wasn't a whole lot of fun. . . . I figured maybe we should practice or something.

Robbie Robertson: I don't think Levon could handle people just booing every night. He said, "I don't want to do this anymore." . . . To me it was like, "Yeah, but the experience equals this music in the making. We will find the music. It will take some time but we will find it and eventually we'll make it something that we need to get out of it." In the beginning, it was a little too much bashing.

The drummer's stool would actually have two more residents before the conclusion of the world tour in May 1966. When Dylan resumed touring the States in February 1966, Sandy Konikoff took up the sticks. On the world tour, and thus the legendary so-called Royal Albert Hall bootleg, it would be (Mickey Jones).

While *Highway 61 Revisited* entered the charts the day after the Carnegie Hall show and remained there until Dylan completed his world tour, he had to give serious thought to recording his follow-up. Once again—despite insisting he had nothing more to live up to—he was the victim of increased expectations. Talking in the fall of 1965, he would tell reporters that he thought *Highway 61 Revisited* represented the best that he could do. In fact, he was having serious problems coming up with a successor that would have equal, or even greater, impact. Never one to tread the same old ground, he was again looking for a breakthrough.

There were several attempts to record material for the next album before he actually got anything down for *Highway 61 Revisited*'s successor. The first post–*Highway 61* studio session was in New York on October 20. The results are unknown, though it was apparently at this session that Dylan and the Hawks recorded the single version of "Can You Please Crawl Out Your Window?" (A version of the song had in fact been recorded during the *Highway 61* sessions.) A few early mispressings of the "Positively 4th Street" single contained the *Highway 61* version of "Can You Please Crawl Out Your Window?" by mistake, which presumably explains the haste with which the newly recorded version was released in December, as disc jockeys were playing the mistaken version as if it were his new single.

A further session was scheduled for the beginning of November in Nashville but was canceled at the last minute. Later that month, Dylan and the Hawks did make it into a Los Angeles studio for an all-night session to work on a major new song that he had just written. The song was called "Freeze Out." It would later be slightly rewritten and renamed "Visions of Johanna." The November version features a wholly different arrangement, though the words are pretty much all in place. Once again Dylan had achieved a quantum leap for the popular song form. "Freeze Out" (aka "Visions of Johanna") may well be his most perfect song. The imagery is bone-chillingly precise, conveying an ominous if indefinable sense of apocalypse that surrounds the seemingly omnipresent yet physically absent Johanna, while the Hawks lend a verve to the performance missing from the *Blonde on Blonde* version (which in its own stately way is perfect as well).

Despite the presence that the Hawks stamped on their studio recordings with Dylan, the sessions in the fall of 1965 did not produce the results he wanted. Dylan persevered with the Hawks in the studio, setting up three full days of sessions in New York in January 1966. However, the only positive result from the sessions was a new single, "One of Us Must Know." Another attempt at "Freeze Out" still did not satisfy him. A further seven-minute-plus masterpiece, "She's Your Lover Now," was never completed in any satisfactory way and remains one of his greatest unreleased songs. On Bob Fass's radio show the night after the final session, Dylan admitted "going [in] to make an album" but coming out with only one song.

By the time he took a break from his U. S. tour in mid-February to make another attempt to record a new album in Nashville, Tennessee, "One of Us Must Know" was already failing to generate sufficient airplay to suggest a chart contender. If he was serious about establishing himself as a credible challenger to the Beatles' and Stones' domination of pop music, he needed to consolidate the earlier successes of "Like a Rolling Stone," "Positively 4th Street" and the *Highway 61 Revisited* album. A five-day respite in his tour schedule meant he had precious little time to achieve this goal, particularly as he had only scraps of songs to take to Nashville with him.

His producer, Bob Johnston, has said that he had been trying to convince Dylan to record in Nashville for some time. The aborted session in November came after months of cajoling. Dylan himself had been greatly impressed by Charlie McCoy's work on the version of "Desolation Row" on *Highway 61 Revisited*.

Dylan, though, still had very specific ideas about how he wanted to sound and insisted on sticking to the twin-engined organ-guitar sound that had worked so well on *Highway 61*. The change in the equation was Robbie Robertson's guitar sound, which was very different from Bloomfield's. Despite three months of playing live with Garth Hudson, Dylan recalled Al Kooper to provide the organ sound once again. The Robertson/Kooper combination, ably supported by crack Nashville musicians such as Charlie McCoy, Kenneth Buttrey and Joe South, was the culmination of "that wild mercury sound" Dylan was seeking, with the Nashville musicians adding a full, rich warmth only hinted at on the previous album.

Bob Dylan: The closest I ever got to the sound I hear in my mind was on individual bands in the *Blonde on Blonde* album. It's that thin, that wild mercury sound. It's metallic and bright gold, with whatever that conjures up. That's my particular sound. I haven't been able to succeed in getting it all the time. Mostly I've been driving at a combination of guitar, harmonica and organ. [1978]

Al Kooper: They didn't know who [Dylan] was, but everybody gets treated the same way down there, with a lot of respect and a lot of room. They knew he was somebody. . . . There were some incredible people on those sessions. I was just knocked out to play with Joe South.

However, on day one of the sessions Dylan found that Nashville musicians were not used to someone with his love for spontaneity and improvisation.

Whereas Dylan had improvised a lot at the *Highway 61* sessions, he barely had the time, and the Nashville musicians barely had the inclination, to allow him to lay down a set of half-formed songs in the hope that they would come together in the studio.

Allen Ginsberg: Dylan always did improvise quite a bit. . . . 'Round '65 he told me that . . . he used to go into a studio and chat up the musicians and babble into the microphone, then rush into the control room and listen to what he said, and write it down, and then maybe arrange it a little bit, and then maybe rush back out in front and sing it!

Dylan therefore had to spend large chunks of the booked studio time finishing the lyrics to songs he had only partially completed before the sessions. One song in particular seems to have been all but wholly written during the first session, while the baffled Nashville session musicians played cards. Thankfully, the twelve-minute "Sad Eyed Lady of the Lowlands" was then recorded in one take, the musicians falling easily into a groove and Johnston duly setting the tape machine rolling.

Pete Rowan: People weren't going over licks and saying, "Yeah, we'll use this lick," and stuff like that. . . . Everyone was just sitting around, the drums were going and pretty soon everyone would fall in with the drums and play.

As during the *Highway 61* sessions, Dylan worked overtime in his hotel room to hone the material he wanted to record. Kooper was present during these hotel writing sessions and learned the songs well enough to be able to run through them later with the Nashville musicians, so in most cases they were not as unprepared as the legends tend to indicate.

Al Kooper: He had a piano in his room at the hotel and during the day I would go up there and he would teach me the song. I would be like a cassette machine. I would play the song over and over on the piano for him. This served a double purpose. One, he could concentrate on writing lyrics and didn't have to mess with playing the piano; two, I could go to the studio early that night and teach it to the band before he even got there so they could be playing the song before he even walked through the door.

Aside from "Sad Eyed Lady of the Lowlands," these four days of sessions resulted in two eight-minute masterpieces: a version of "Visions of Johanna" that Dylan was finally happy with; and the kaleidoscopic "Stuck Inside of Mobile with the Memphis Blues Again." There were also two more lightweight pieces recorded at these Nashville sessions, "Leopard-skin Pill-box Hat" and "4th Time Around," two of Dylan's wittiest parodies, the latter of which was his second pastiche of the Beatles in six months, the butt of this one being their own piece of whimsy, "Norwegian Wood" (the other, "I Wanna Be Your Lover," would not be released until 1985 on *Biograph*).

Along with "One of Us Must Know," the Nashville songs gave Dylan enough material for an album, including three of his longest and most intense slabs of surrealism. These six songs would certainly have made a remarkable follow-up to *Highway 61 Revisited*, but he still had something left to say and arranged for further sessions in Nashville in three weeks' time, during a further week-long break from the road.

The March sessions would introduce some pop sensibility to the double album he now seemed bent on recording. Among the eight titles recorded at the two March Nashville sessions were three of his most enduring songs: "Rainy Day Women #12 & 35," "I Want You" and "Just Like a Woman," which between them would return him to the status of important singles artist and provide him with three top forty singles before the end of 1966. "Rainy Day Women" in particular would duplicate the success of "Like a Rolling Stone," reaching number two on the American charts and generating considerable controversy regarding what exactly he meant by the word *stoned*—as if it were not self-evident. Though "Rainy Day Women" would open the *Blonde on Blonde* album, it was in fact the last song to be cut.

Charlie McCoy: Dylan said he wanted to get kind of a Salvation Army sound so they asked me if I could find a slide trombone player. I got one named Wayne Butler and after he arrived at the studio we cut "Rainy Day Women" in about seventeen minutes . . . in one [complete] take.

Dylan later expressed his delight with the results of his two sojourns in Nashville. Indeed, it would be 1970 before he would return to New York to record an album.

Bob Dylan: You've more space in Nashville than you do in New York. . . . In Nashville people sit around if they want to. If they want to make good records they just sit around and wait all night till you're ready. But they won't do that in New York. [1966]

On April 7, 1966, having stayed an extra day in Los Angeles to complete the task of supervising the final mix of *Blonde on Blonde*, Dylan packed four one-sided acetates of his new album with a few belongings he required and flew to Hawaii. He was not flying to Honolulu for a vacation. Honolulu was gig number one on a two-month world tour, his first suck trek. It represented two months away from Sara. She had been with him as he completed the final leg of an exhausting winter tour of the States less than two weeks earlier.

He was once again facing the unknown, playing before unknowing eyes in Hawaii, Australia, Sweden, Denmark, Ireland, England, Wales, Scotland, France and then England again. Perhaps at some point he recalled Rimbaud's thoughts about confronting the unknown: "[When] the poet makes himself a seer . . . he reaches [into] the unknown and even if, crazed, he ends up by losing the understanding of his visions, at least he has seen them!" How prophetic Rimbaud's words would seem in the light of the events on that famous world tour.

13   1966:   A Curious Way to Make a Living

S uze Rotolo: People live with hope for green trees and beautiful flowers, but Dylan seems to lack that sort of simple hope—at least he did from 1964 to 1966. This darkness wasn't new to me. [But] it became stronger as the years passed by.

Dylan's world tour of 1966 seems very small-scale these days, in terms of both the size of venues which he was playing (virtually without exception these were theaters of three to four thousand capacity) and the breadth of the tour itself, which consisted of one show in Hawaii, seven in Australia, three in mainland Europe and thirteen in Britain and Ireland—a mere twenty-four shows. On the face of it, it was hardly a punishing schedule, particularly as the tour lasted from April 7 to May 27.

However, Dylan's life-style and the nature of his newfound fame made these 24 dates seem like 124 dates. The first problem was that, ever since Newport, the folk-rock controversy had steadily been casting a shadow over his work. His own moods had become very dark and his temper unstable.

D. A. Pennebaker: I don't know what kind of chemicals he and Robbie were putting down, but I'm telling you, it made him very irascible and very peculiar. He never slept—and I just couldn't take it after a while.

When Pennebaker suggested that he never slept, this barely qualifies as an exaggeration. Dylan himself has admitted that they were constantly "on" during this tour, if not playing concerts, then filming, or being interviewed, or giving press conferences (he gave a press conference for every single concert in Australia and mainland Europe, though only one in Britain).

Bob Dylan: We were going all the time, even when we weren't going. We were always doing something else, which is just as draining as performing. We were looking for Loch Ness monsters, staying up for four days running—and making all those eight o'clock curtains besides. [1974]

Required to be "on" all the time, Dylan became imperious toward outsiders and conspiratorial in relation to members of the inner sanctum. In Melbourne, Australian journalist Adrian Rawlins was temporarily admitted to that inner sanctum, showing Dylan, Robertson and Victor Maimudes around Fitzroy, Melbourne's slum district, and hanging out with Dylan after his Melbourne shows.

Adrian Rawlins: Bob Dylan came into the [hotel] room. His entrances at that time were very choreographed, athletic events. He danced everywhere and couldn't keep still—head moving, feet shuffling. . . . He said he and Robbie Robertson had been driving around Melbourne looking for me. "Where have you been? . . . Come up and talk." Then he twirled around and said: "You, you, you and you can come too." It was very much a power situation. . . . We went up to his suite, ordered Cokes and pots of tea and sat there talking from two A.M. till about seven thirty the next morning.

The all-night session Rawlins describes was typical of many nights on the world tour. Shelton details a similar session in Denver in March, as does another Australian temporarily befriended by Dylan, an actress named Rosemary Gerrette. He had met Gerrette at his final Australian press conference in Perth, and she hung out with him for the remaining three days in Australia.

Rosemary Gerrette: I sat up with the group until dawn. . . . They were leaving for Stockholm for concerts. They were trying to get tired so they could sleep through the twenty-seven-hour flight and I was able to listen to a composing session. Countless cups of tea; none of the group drinks. Things happened, and six new songs were born. The poetry seemed already to have been written. Dylan says, "Picture one of these cats with a horn, coming over the hill at daybreak. Very Elizabethan, you dig? Wearing garters." And out of the imagery, he and the lead guitarist work on a tune and Dylan's leg beats time with the rhythm, continuously, even when the rhythm is in his own mind. Six A.M. and he asks me am I tired? Later he plays a melody to us, a very special one. "I'll never have it published, recorded. I wrote it for this way-out moon chick. We just sat on the floor on these mattresses . . . and like for two hours I spoke to her with my guitar. And she understood . . . of course, this isn't quite like I played it, because it meant something to me at the time, but now it doesn't."

Gerrette, though, was one who suffered from Dylan's wildly oscillating moods, and he ordered her out of the hotel room later that morning. Like many who came across Dylan on the tour, Gerrette was convinced that he was on some kind of death trip. Certainly his dark moods, the apocalyptic conceit in his new songs and in his utterances to the press, his copious consumption of chemicals, his refusal to sleep and the intensity of his performances onstage all seemed to support that theory. If Dylan himself never thought he was on a death trip, he certainly felt the pressures of expectation and they were slowly crushing him. He would later tell Scaduto:

Bob Dylan: The pressures were unbelievable. They were just something you can't imagine unless you go through them yourself. Man, they hurt so much. [1971]

Anthea Joseph: I don't think he was on a death trip. I just think he was working unbelievably hard. He was constantly working. I mean, if he wasn't actually on the stage he was traveling, he was writing. He just never ever stopped. . . . You get so wired on adrenaline and you daren't stop 'cause you know if you do you'll be in bed for a week.

The booing had not ceased. In fact, it was more intense. By the early months of 1966, when Dylan was touring the States, his fans knew what to expect. But in England his old fans had seen him less than a year ago performing acoustic, indeed topical, songs such as "Lonesome Death of Hattie Carroll" and "Talking World War III Blues." Perhaps this partially explains why the reception in the English-speaking countries now was the most hostile. Dylan seemed oblivious to the booing. He was reveling in the sheer majesty of the sound that he and the Hawks were making.

D. A. Pennebaker: In Ireland, I recall there was a lot of reaction when he did the electric. But in general, he was having so much a better time with the band than he was by himself that you could see right away that the difference was night and day in terms of his performance. . . . Dylan was so happy, he was jumping around like a cricket in the middle of the thing. . . . Oh, there was a lot of weird behavior on that trip, [but] I don't think it was a death trip. The pressures were enormous. . . . Albert Hall was the wildest . . . people were really shouting at him and he was screaming back. He was very wild at Albert Hall.

If Dylan was relishing the experience, neither did the Hawks seem unduly fazed by the reception they were getting night after night. They had played many an authentic redneck joint with Ronnie Hawkins. They had paid their dues.

Robbie Robertson: We didn't mind the booing so much. After all, we'd played in joints where they'd thrown beer bottles. Our main thought was that it was a strange way to make a living. You get in this private plane, they fly you to a town, we got to this place, we play our music and people boo us. Then we get back on the plane, we go to another town, we play our music and they boo us.

By this point, though, Dylan and Robertson knew instinctively that what they were doing was right, in every sense of the word. If the Hawks had been a little hesitant in their playing back in the fall of 1965, the sound they were producing now was stately, immense, compelling.

Robbie Robertson: By the time we did the Australia and Europe tours we had discovered whatever this thing was. It was not light, it was not folky. It was very dynamic, very explosive and very violent.

Listening to live recordings of the Rolling Stones and the Beatles from 1966, it is clear just how far behind Dylan both bands were in producing their music onstage. Ironically, according to Robertson the reason that we can compare the live 1966 sound of Dylan with those of his contemporaries is that Dylan and he wanted to analyze why the response was so fierce.

Robbie Robertson: The only reason tapes of those [1966] shows exist today is because we wanted to know, "Are we crazy?" We'd go back to the hotel room, listen to a tape of the show and think, "Shit, that's not bad. Why is everybody so upset?"

Of course, the reality is that the response was wholly unconnected to the music or its majesty. Indeed, the more powerful the sound, the less authentic Dylan's ex-fans considered his new music to be. Perhaps in the power of his performances Dylan was perversely feeding upon the anger of the audiences, as if determined to hurl back their fury at them.

Robertson's explanation for the preservation of the concerts is partially true. However, the tapes in common circulation among collectors (and there are parts of nearly half the shows on the world tour) cannot be accounted for simply because the Hawks were curious about how they sounded. In fact, many of the shows were recorded to provide a musical sound track for the documentary that Pennebaker was filming of the European leg of the tour. A nightly ritual, which involved Dylan in further late-night sessions, was the process of preliminary selections for the sound track, which generally took place after each show.

French reporter: The entire group meets in a suite. Five musicians, four filmmakers and sound technicians, one sound man, Tom (the driver of the Rolls who is also acting as Dylan's bodyguard), Henri (who looks after the guitars), Al Grossman, Bob Neuwirth, Fred Perry (. . . the tour manager), Bob Dylan and myself, plus a few girls picked up at the end of the show. . . . They have to listen and choose the recordings made of the concert. It's a daily routine. Sitting on the floor, on cushions, everyone listens in silence. . . . The music is played very loudly, and apprehensive waiters come and go with trays full of cups of tea and beer. The night will go on for a long time yet. Bob is having a film made of the tour for American television and these recordings have to be synchronized later with the pictures. Gradually people begin to leave; one by one they go to bed. At six A.M. there are only three or four people left: Bob, myself and a couple of musicians.

The documentary, which would later become "Eat the Document," a one-hour TV special broadcast only once, on a local New York TV station in 1979, had been commissioned by ABC for a series to be called "Stage 67." Dylan insisted on complete control of the finished product and was duly allowed full artistic rein. Pennebaker was thus enlisted by Dylan not as a film producer/director, as in 1965, but simply on a filming assignment, for which he would be paid a flat fee. Yet Dylan seems to have had very few specific ideas about what kind of film it should be. He certainly did not seem intent on adopting a *cinéma vérité* approach akin to the 1965 documentary.

D. A. Pennebaker: He'd put little scenes together. I believe there was one up in my room in the hotel. We were at the Georges V. There was this huge mirrored clothes cabinet. And he had people going in, closing the doors and coming out. There would be a succession of people—I don't know where they came from. . . . There would be strange women and guys and I would just film these little scenes.

Pennebaker felt that Dylan was missing a remarkable opportunity, failing to exploit the real-life drama taking place every time he stepped on stage. Indeed, he felt that Dylan was deliberately avoiding documenting the events happening onstage, preferring the types of scenes described above. So one night in Glasgow, Pennebaker actually filmed Dylan with the Hawks, right under his nose.

D. A. Pennebaker: When I came back [from Cannes], that's when I shot that thing on stage with him. We didn't tell Dylan I was going to do it or anything—Robbie and I cooked it up. And so when he came out on stage and I was out there with a camera alongside Robbie and everybody else with the band, Dylan really cracked up. . . . I filmed the whole thing by just walking around on stage with him.

In fact, Glasgow was one of the less well-received shows, with fans shouting "Rubbish" and "Shut up" and slow-handclapping him before "Leopard-skin Pill-box Hat" (a similar occurrence is immortalized on the Albert Hall bootleg). Dylan, though, saved most of his interest for scenes like the one that later appeared in "Eat the Document" in which he and Richard Manuel of the Hawks attempted to buy a Swedish boy's girlfriend from him. Pennebaker himself had business at the Cannes Film Festival that year and missed two or three shows during the British leg of the tour, giving his assistant Howard Alk the ideal opportunity to film his type of footage, which more closely accorded with Dylan's own ideas.

D. A. Pennebaker: Making home movies . . . simply doesn't interest me very much. . . . I'm not sure how to . . . make other people's home movies for them. . . . Let them shoot whatever they want. And in a way, we were doing that. Howard [Alk] was doing some of that himself.

Alk did capture some immediate postconcert interviews with disgruntled fans coming out of Dylan's Manchester show on May 17. Their angry responses are cleverly cut up in "Eat the Document" with parts of a particularly fierce version of "Ballad of a Thin Man," Dylan's portrayal of Mr. C. W. Jones adrift in a world wholly peopled by freaks. It makes a pleasing counterpoint to the fury of the ex-fans. One in particular seems as likely a candidate for the man who shouted "Judas" as any. In "Eat the Document" the earnest young man spouts,

"Any pop group could produce better rubbish than that. It was a bloody disgrace, it was. He wants shooting. He's a traitor."

Manchester constituted the most notorious battleground on the tour, and the show there forms the bulk of the legendary Albert Hall bootleg. Though there are many eyewitnesses who attended the Albert Hall show, Anthea Joseph and D. A. Pennebaker among them, who swear it was there that a fan shouted "Judas" at Dylan, it was at Manchester that he was slow-handclapped before "One Too Many Mornings," then he burbled nonsense into the microphone until the clapping stopped, at which point he said, "If only you just wouldn't clap so hard." Before the final song of the show, immortalized on the bootleg album, a disaffected fan shouted, "Judas," to which Dylan retorted, "I don't believe you, you're a liar." Then he turned to the Hawks, as Mickey Jones held his drumsticks aloft, and instructed them, "Play FUCKING LOUD!!!"

Dylan had presumably decided that CBS should record the final shows on his world tour to prove, to posterity at least, that he was right and the heckling fans wrong. At Manchester, Dylan and the Hawks rehearsed in the afternoon (the rehearsal was filmed by Alk) in preparation for another stormy evening. Both his seductive and extremely stoned solo set and the set with the Hawks were recorded. Columbia also recorded the final two shows of the tour, at the Albert Hall in London.

Before that, though, he was to play his first concert in Rimbaud country. The hype surrounding his Paris concert was considerable. L'Olympia had been sold out for weeks, even though the ticket prices were set at an unprecedented forty and sixty francs. *France-Soir* announced Dylan's arrival with typical sourness, calling him "Champion of the Singing Beatniks." On the plane, he interrogated the journalist from *Salut les Copains* who had accompanied the entourage on much of the second part of his English leg, concerned as to what exactly might be the response of the French fans and media:

French reporter: [Dylan said,] "Can you tell me what I'm doing in a country where nobody understands a word I say? Do you think they'll boo at the Olympia?" As we assured him that this wouldn't happen, he went on: "What questions are they going to ask at the press conference?" Nothing important, don't worry—what you think about the war in Vietnam, why you changed your style, what you think of long hair—that kind of stuff. "Good. In that case I'll say the first thing that comes to mind."

He certainly said whatever he felt like saying at the press conference, conducted at the deluxe Hôtel Georges V the day after his arrival. Carrying an old puppet, which he introduced as Finian, he informed the press, "It's a religious symbol." If not prepared to state what he *did* believe in, he did deign to provide a clear statement of what he *did not* believe in: "I don't belong to any movement. I've only got some ideas in my head and I tell them. I don't support anybody's cause. No revolution ever came about because of songs."

The following day, Dylan was twenty-five. In just five years he had transformed popular music beyond recognition, making rock and roll capable of saying a great deal more than just "Awopbopaloobop," and had been vilified, glorified, even deified for his trouble. If he never produced another album—or indeed if he died on top of the hill—he could rest assured that he would be considered one of the most important artists of his era.

The final three shows of the world tour replicated previous hostilities. The Paris show was unique in that Dylan managed to antagonize the audience even before bringing on the band. He had genuine difficulty tuning his guitar, which was one he had been forced to use after his favorite guitar "got broke" in Australia, and his usual forty-five-minute acoustic set extended that night to somewhere between sixty and sixty-five minutes. When fans expressed dissatisfaction, he told them to read their newspapers or maybe go down to a bowling alley until he had finished.

Having not endeared himself to the bemused Parisians, he appeared for the "electric" half of the show with a large American flag draped across the rear of the stage—a highly provocative act in the light of America's unpopular involvement in Vietnam—prompting shouts of "Get rid of the flag!" and "U.S. go home!" The Paris headlines were suitably brusque in their assessment of the show: *Paris-Jour* suggested, "Bob Dylan Go Home!"; *24 Heures* insisted, "Mr. Dylan's Reputation Is Too Flattering"; *France-Soir* remarked that "Bob Dylan Disappointed the Most Loyal Audience of the Season."

The Albert Hall shows were no less traumatic. At the final show, Dylan finally lost his cool and suggested to one fan, "Come up here and say that!" If he had previously restrained himself from making more than the occasional passing comment about the furor he was creating, the Albert Hall shows saw Dylan finally talking back. In fact, he had made a few comments previously. In Liverpool, when someone suggested the (still-living) Guthrie would turn in his grave, Dylan informed everyone, "There's someone down here looking for a saint."

He told the London audience before "Visions of Johanna" that this was what the English press would call a "drurg song." He then told them he didn't write "drurg" songs, "It's just vulgar to think so." If he was not writing about drugs, he was certainly using them just to keep going. Mainly he confined himself to popping pills.

Anthea Joseph: I was the only one that drank. They were all dropping pills and eating acid and generally misbehaving. . . . Anything that was going to tear my mind to pieces I had no interest in whatsoever. So I was happy smoking dope in a corner while they ate things.

Bob Dylan: We were taking a lot of chemicals which doctors had prescribed for entertainers and athletes. [1978]

One strange aspect of the shows, though, was that Dylan's demeanor onstage during the acoustic sets seemed indicative of someone stoned on marijuana; yet by the time he returned with the Hawks he had seemingly metamorphosed into a speed freak. Thus, from the slurred diction in his lengthy acoustic renditions of "4th Time Around" or "Just Like a Woman" in the first half, he emerged for the second half spitting his words like a demon bastard child of Verlaine and Rimbaud. The three songs extant from that final electric set are, if anything, even more furious than the more famous Manchester recordings. Dylan, though, seemed at breaking point. The *Daily Telegraph* reviewer of that final London show pertinently observed, "He is beginning to show the signs of a man who does not care whether he communicates or not."

If Dylan was asking himself, "Can this really be the end?" it was despite the knowledge that Grossman was already in the throes of organizing a fall tour of the States that would dwarf his previous tours. Perhaps at this point he recalled a pointed warning made by Phil Ochs in an article defending Dylan published in *Broadside* in October 1965, before their falling out. In it Ochs wrote that he could not conceive of Dylan touring even a year hence because of the danger of an attack by a mad assailant.

Phil Ochs: There's something very dangerous, something very frightening about this whole thing now. Dylan is very disturbing. Dylan gets up there and sings great thoughts and great poetry to everybody, and when you say everybody you mean also to neurotics, to immature people, to the lumpen proletariat, to people not in control of themselves. Dylan is forcing everybody to listen to him, the quality of his work is so good and so communicative. . . . I wonder what's going to happen. I don't know if Dylan can get on the stage a year from now. I don't think so. I mean the phenomenon of Dylan will be so much that it will be dangerous. . . . He's gotten inside so many people's heads—Dylan has become part of so many people's psyches—and there're so many screwed-up people in America, and death is such a part of the American scene now.

The difference between Ochs's prophecy and Dylan's actual retirement was that there would be no externalized threat. It would take an altogether different flirtation with death itself to bring him around and make him realize it was his own dark self that he had to come to terms with.

Part
2

Learning to Do Consciously . . .

1966–67: Evening Things Up

After the rigors of the world tour, Dylan and Sara took a brief vacation in Spain, where Dylan must have mused upon the unrelenting pressure of the cauldron he had allowed himself to be placed in. A daunting fall schedule of concerts in America to publicize the imminent release of *Blonde on Blonde* was being finalized.* This tour promised to be even more daunting than his fall 1965 schedule. Meanwhile, *Tarantula* was just about ready for publication and an hour-long special on the 1966 tour was also expected for the fall, composed from the footage Pennebaker had shot throughout May.

Dylan's two immediate concerns, then, were to approve the final galleys of *Tarantula* and to compose a rough cut of the documentary he intended to present to ABC. Having returned to Woodstock in June 1966, he needed time to recuperate from the tour. Above all, he had to consider more personal matters now that he had returned from gallivanting around the world. Sara, his bride of seven months, had given him a son, Jesse.

Obviously pleased to escape from the pressures of the outside world, he remained in Woodstock throughout most of July. † When Dylan's Macmillan editor, Bob Markel, needed final approval of the galleys for *Tarantula* before going to press, he had to travel up to Woodstock, where he found Dylan attempting to unravel the footage Pennebaker had shot in Europe.

Bob Markel: We brought a set of galleys to him so he could take one last good

---

*According to official records, the album was released on May 16, but since it did not enter the U.S. charts until the day after his motorcycle accident, in late July, this would appear to be incorrect.

†According to Spitz, Dylan attended a party in the last week of July at the Chelsea Hotel, with both Brian Jones and Mick Jagger also present. However, Jones and Jagger were not in New York at this point, they were in California. If Dylan attended such a party it was on or around the second of July, when the Stones played Forest Hills.

look at it before we printed it and bound it and started to fill all the orders that had come in. Bob took a break from some film editing he was doing. We talked a little about the book and about Rameau and Rimbaud and Bob promised to finish "making a few changes" in two weeks. A few days after that, Bob stopped working.

The editing of "Eat the Document," as the 1966 documentary would later be called, was not initially undertaken by Dylan and Howard Alk, who would end up making the finished movie. Dylan asked Pennebaker to put together a version with the help of Neuwirth, after which Dylan would look at the results. It seemed he was already disenchanted with the footage that Pennebaker had shown him and did not really want to be involved in producing the film. Yet Pennebaker had never been employed to edit the film—he still had to organize the release of *Don't Look Back*. He had simply been hired to shoot the necessary footage. Pennebaker was clearly as unhappy as Dylan to be placed in the position he now found himself in.

D. A. Pennebaker: He came some time in July. He drove down and looked at stuff—we spent two or three days looking at stuff in the studio—and then he said, "Well I want you guys to go ahead and make some sort of rough edit to get an idea of what you did because ABC is coming after it." . . . So Neuwirth and I started to edit something together . . . a twenty- or thirty-minute thing. . . . Then Dylan had his accident and Albert got pissed at me 'cause he said I wasn't helping him edit enough and I explained to him that I was never supposed to be editing it.

A cut of that film still exists in Pennebaker's private collection. It is, needless to say, very different from, and far more straightforward than, the film Dylan and Alk would produce.

On July 29, 1966, the whole wheel on which Dylan was bound came crashing down, bringing him with it: He had a motorcycle accident. Dylan himself has been asked about his motorcycle accident on many occasions, part of the attempt to unravel why he "changed" afterward, as if there were some cathartic point as he sailed over the handlebars when he realized all is phony (Ray Lowry, the cartoonist, would later parody such notions with a drawing in which Dylan flies over the bike and a lightbulb saying "Country Rock" comes on over his head). His most extensive answer was given to Sam Shepard in an "interview" for *Esquire* in 1987.

Bob Dylan: It was real early in the morning on top of a hill near Woodstock. I can't even remember how it happened. I was blinded by the sun. . . . I was drivin' right straight into the sun, and I looked up into it even though I re-member someone telling me a long time ago when I was a kid never to look straight at the sun. . . . I went blind for a second and I kind of panicked or something. I stomped down on the brake and the rear wheel locked up on me and I went flyin'. . . . [Sara] was followin' me in a car. She picked me up. Spent a week in the hospital, then they moved me to this doctor's house in town. In his attic. Had a bed up there in the attic with a window lookin' out. Sara stayed there with me. [1987]

If a shade metaphorical, Dylan's account here rings reasonably true. He told Robert Shelton that "it happened one morning after I'd been up for three days," clearly suggesting he had not entirely abandoned his punishing life-style during his break from the road. The extent of the damage from the accident seems to have been cracked vertebrae and a mild concussion. He was taken to the hospital, though in little more than a week he was back in Woodstock, where he may have temporarily recuperated at a doctor's house.* He was in a neck brace when Don Pennebaker arrived in Woodstock a few days after the accident, but he was fully functioning.

D. A. Pennebaker: I heard about the accident when I was in California and then I came and I saw him a couple of days later, walking around with a brace. He didn't appear very knocked out by the accident so I never quite knew what happened. . . . But he was very pissed at everybody and I don't know whether it was because they were putting pressure on him to get the film ready for TV.

Another visitor who called on Dylan was Allen Ginsberg. On August 19, exactly three weeks after the accident, Ginsberg brought him a pile of books to read while recuperating. According to Ginsberg, contradicting Pennebaker, it would be another two weeks before Dylan was really up and about.

Allen Ginsberg: I brought him a box full of books of all kinds. All the modern poets I knew. Some ancient poets like Sir Thomas Wyatt, Campion, Dickin-son, Rimbaud, Lorca, Apollinaire, Blake, Whitman and so forth.

The motorcycle accident was the axial event around which Dylan's career is still perceived to revolve. This neat fracture in the chronology of his career has been seized on ever since as evidence that Dylan lost "it" the day he fell off his motorcycle. In recent years there has been considerable speculation as to

---

* According to Spitz, the stay at the doctor's house came some time later, which accords with the accounts of Pennebaker and Ginsberg.

whether Dylan ever had an accident at all, though such suggestions have never been based on any sound evidence. However, there is considerable evidence that the accident was nowhere near as serious as Dylan and Grossman made it appear as 1966 wore on and Dylan evidently decided that he was no longer interested in honoring contractual obligations at the expense of his health and sanity.

His full recuperation from the crash was undoubtedly hindered by the poor physical shape he was in. The punishment his body had undergone in the last year was more than enough to tax a healthy man, but the chemicals he had been liberally taking in 1966 cannot have improved his constitution. The stories in the press at the time seemed determined to portray the accident as a near-death trauma. *Time* magazine claimed in its August 12 edition that Dylan was not wearing a crash helmet and had sustained "severe face and back cuts." The *New York Daily News* hinted that Dylan might never perform again, so disfigured had the accident made him. Though the reports were all wildly off the mark, they provided Dylan with an opportunity to avoid fulfilling his obligations. The men from Macmillan, ABC and CBS (to whom he owed one more album under his existing contract) were hardly likely to trek up to Woodstock to remind a badly injured man of his legal duties.

Thus in the latter months of 1966 Dylan had the opportunity to reevaluate where he had come to at the age of twenty-five. It was not the accident but the breathing space it gave him that afforded him an opportunity to change his life-style, and made him realize that he could not carry on living as he had been doing. He quickly realized he no longer had the will to play live. Yet the accident had only compounded the Dylan myth. With his decision to retire came an awareness of his new responsibilities. He now had a baby boy as well as a wife to consider. The last people he wanted to think of were the agents and managers who wanted him back out in the marketplace.

Bob Dylan: I had that motorcycle accident. . . . When I woke up and caught my senses, I realized I was just workin' for all these leeches. And I didn't want to do that. Plus, I had a family, and I just wanted to see my kids. [1984]

Talking about the weeks after the accident as he was returning to the stage in 1974, he recalled one particular night in Woodstock. He hinted at a bitterness, a desire for revenge, a sense that he had been taken in by the "leeches."

Bob Dylan: The turning point was back in Woodstock. A little after the accident. Sitting around one night under a full moon, I looked out in the bleak woods and I said, "Something's gotta change." There was some business that had to be taken care of. [1974]

He made a similar reference to taking care of some business—his phrase was "evening things up"—when he was interviewed by Michael Iachetta in May 1967. Iachetta, who had interviewed him back in 1963, tracked him down to his house in Woodstock to obtain his first public pronouncements in a year. Dylan told Iachetta of the self-analysis his rest had allowed.

Bob Dylan: What I've been doin' mostly is seein' only a few close friends, readin' little 'bout the outside world, porin' over books by people you never heard of, thinkin' about where I'm goin', and why am I runnin', and am I mixed up too much, and what am I knowin', and what I am givin' and what am I takin'. . . . Songs are in my head like they always are. And they're not goin' to get written down until some things are evened up. Not until some people come forth and make up for some of the things that happened. [1967]

It seems likely that a part of Dylan's therapy was simply sitting down and viewing again the footage Pennebaker had shot on the 1966 tour. The man he saw, at center stage even in the offstage scenes, must have seemed a crazed individual to him. He was also profoundly unimpressed by the quality of the footage that had been shot.

Bob Dylan: They had made another *Don't Look Back*, only this time it was for television. I had nothing better to do than to see the film. All of it, including unused footage. And it was obvious from looking at the film that it was garbage. It was miles and miles of garbage. That was my introduction to film. [1978]

The chance to run through that footage also made Dylan realize that Pennebaker's and Neuwirth's ideas for the film were not the same as his own, and he decided to set about reediting an entirely new movie from the footage, with the help of two friends, Howard Alk—who had shot much of the footage in both *Don't Look Back* and *Eat the Document* and was an old friend of both Grossman's and Dylan's—and Robbie Robertson, whom Dylan now encouraged to come up to Woodstock with the remainder of the Hawks.

Robbie Robertson: The first reason I went to Woodstock was that he was working on *Eat the Document* and he asked me to help on the film, and that's what I did, I went up and lived at his house and worked on the film for a while, and Bobby Neuwirth was kind of in and out . . . and it seemed like a nice scene.

At this point in the project Pennebaker was happy to bow out. He had never considered Alk's ideas about movies to be compatible with his own, and was clearly annoyed that Dylan was going to produce a movie that did not really represent what he thought had happened on the tour, in the way that his *cinéma vérité* study of the 1965 tour, *Don't Look Back*, would.

D. A. Pennebaker: I've always felt that he made *Eat the Document* out of our outs . . . he set out to make his own film. How much of it is his film and how much was Howard Alk's film I don't know. . . . I think he was very influenced by Howard's film ideas, which didn't interest me much. . . . I think they tend to be sort of intellectual ideas but they're not visual ideas.

As his first creative activity since the accident, Dylan wanted to produce more than just a conventional one-hour TV documentary. The *cinéma vérité* approach did not particularly appeal to him. Both Alk and Dylan had specific ideas about setting scenes up and letting people act out certain ideas. A small number of such scenes do appear to have been filmed in England during a brief period when Pennebaker was in Cannes and Alk was able to film footage unsupervised and unhindered. Alk and Dylan were also eager to use a lot of cuts in the film to achieve a sense of the amphetamine pace of the tour. With *Eat the Document* they found that "the eye" (Pennebaker) had limited the scope of their more ambitious ideas.*

Bob Dylan: What we had to work with was not what you would conceive of if you were going shooting a film. What we were trying to do was to make a logical story out of this newsreel-type footage . . . to make a story which consisted of stars and starlets who were taking the roles of other people, just like a normal movie would do. We were trying to do the same thing with this footage. That's not what anyone else had in mind, but this is what myself and Mr. Alk had in mind. And we were very limited because the film was not shot by us, but by the eye, and we had come upon this decision to do this only after everything else had failed. . . . What we tried to do was to construct a stage and an environment, taking it out and putting it together like a puzzle. And we did, that's the strange part about it. Now if we had the opportunity to reshoot the camera under this procedure, we could really make a wonderful film. [1968]

Robertson, clearly more than happy with the approach adopted by Dylan and Alk, also contributed his own suggestions.

Robbie Robertson: It's an incredible film. It's very far out. It's very strange.

---

*Their ideas would not be fully realized until nine years later, when they began work on *Renaldo and Clara*.

It's not a documentary. It was hard to make it so it wouldn't be a documentary. But it was done and we liked it. Then after the film, we started to make some more music together.

Apart from viewing the footage from the European tour, Dylan once again read through the galleys for *Tarantula*. He decided he could not proceed with the book as it stood, and informed Macmillan that he was going to work on a new book. He had always been uncertain about the merits of *Tarantula*. The book's lack of any coherent thread had made him feel that it would not be understood by his fans and would be lambasted by literary critics.

Though the book had changed little in the previous twelve months, it seemed that before the accident Dylan had decided it would be too much effort to rework the book and had finally prepared himself for its publication. The accident allowed him to change his mind again and halt publication. In 1968, talking to Happy Traum and John Cohen, he dismissed the book. It would take some time for him to revise that opinion.

Bob Dylan: I just put down all these words and sent them off to my publishers and they'd send back the galleys, and I'd be so embarrassed at the nonsense I'd written I'd change the whole thing. And all the time they had a hundred thousand orders. . . . The trouble with it, it had no story. I'd been reading all these trash books, works suffering from sex and excitement and foolish things. [1968]

While Dylan was hard at work editing *Eat the Document* and preparing to start making music again, Pennebaker had finally arranged for *Don't Look Back* to be released. With Dylan's sudden disappearance from public gaze, Pennebaker's film, which premiered in San Francisco on May 17, 1967, allowed fans a glimpse of the "real" Dylan, in turn warm, funny, abusive, gentle, sarcastic, up, down, onstage and backstage, all in ninety grainy minutes of black-and-white celluloid. The film reinforced a public perception of Dylan that was already outdated.

The first hint that Dylan was preparing to emerge from his self-imposed hiatus in music-making came in an article by an old friend of his, Al Aronowitz, published in *Cheetah* in 1967. Aronowitz visited Dylan in Woodstock in the spring of that year and sat listening to him jam on some new songs with the Hawks (minus Levon Helm, who had yet to return to the ranks).

Al Aronowitz: "Dylan had been doing nothing, absolutely nothing," said Jamie [Robbie] Robertson, Dylan's guitarist, to an inquiring reporter. . . . But that was just a contribution to the Dylan mystery. Actually, Dylan was writing ten new songs a week, rehearsing them in his living room with Robertson's group, the Hawks, and trying to complete a one-hour film TV special for ABC, which said it couldn't use the program because it was seven months late.

There seems to be some doubt about when the sessions that would result in *The Basement Tapes* started. Some credit April as the starting point, but according to the album's liner notes it was June. Whatever the case, in the spring of 1967 Dylan was hanging out every day with the Hawks, who had all recently settled in Woodstock at a rented house in West Saugerties that, with its distinctive bright pink exterior, was known locally as Big Pink. According to Robertson, their daily sessions would commence early in the afternoon.

Robbie Robertson: We used to get together every day at one o'clock in the basement of Big Pink. And it was just a routine. We would get there and to keep [every] one of us from going crazy, we would play music every day. And he wrote a bunch of songs out of that.

The informal sessions served to unlock Dylan's muse. Once he was writing again, the flood of new songs was, if anything, even greater than during his days in New York City. In less than six months Dylan and the Hawks recorded at least thirty new Dylan compositions, including some of his best (and best-known) songs, gems of the quality of "I Shall Be Released," "This Wheel's on Fire," "The Mighty Quinn," "Million Dollar Bash," "Tears of Rage" and "You Ain't Goin' Nowhere."

Songs of equal worth were recorded but remain considerably less well known, and in many cases unreleased, even after the 1975 issue of the *Basement Tapes* double album. Several songs of real quality were largely improvised on the spot, notably "Apple Suckling Tree," "I'm Not There (1956)" and "Sign on the Cross." Of course, Dylan had always improvised in the studio. The *Highway 61 Revisited* sessions in particular had seen Dylan and the band often playing purely on intuition. In 1967 Dylan returned to such an approach, working in the intimate surroundings of the Big Pink basement, often almost extemporizing while the band played around him. He was once again spontaneously experimenting with country and blues forms, mouthing line upon line of oblique but dazzling images. On "Sign on the Cross" he delivers a lengthy monologue in the style of a fundamentalist preacher that is both inspired and inspirational. On "I'm Not There (1956)" he seems to be free-forming words around only a rudimentary outline, and indeed a typescript of the song confirms this impression.

Garth Hudson: We were doing seven, eight, ten, sometimes fifteen songs a day. Some were old ballads and traditional songs, some were already written by

Bob and Richard [Manuel of the Hawks], but others Bob would make up as he went along. . . . ["Sign on the Cross"] would have been a real good one, but Bob never finished it. We'd play the melody, he'd sing a few words he'd written, and then make up some more, or else just mouth the words or even syllables as he went along. It's a pretty good way to write songs.

The monologue style used in the bridge of "Sign on the Cross" was repeated on several of the other recordings Dylan made that spring and summer. "Clothes Line Saga" was delivered in its entirety in that "hi, 'm gonna tell y'all a story" voice. One of the takes of "Nothing Was Delivered" features an animated middle section in which Dylan seems to be exhorting a congregation to accept the fact that nothing was indeed delivered. The verses of "Million Dollar Bash" and "Lo and Behold!" also feature a half-spoken, half-sung intonation unique to these sessions. The original source of the persona Dylan was adopting here can be found on one of the many country covers they also recorded that summer, "(Be Careful of the) Stones That You Throw," a song about gossip originally written and performed by Hank Williams in his adopted persona of Luke the Drifter, a character who specialized in this type of moralistic mono- logue. The culmination of this style by Dylan would come on the longest song on *John Wesley Harding*, "The Ballad of Frankie Lee and Judas Priest," which even parodies the form with its use of a moralistic final verse.

When Dylan was singing his fair share of country and folk standards at these sessions, it was as if he was attempting to tap into some common constituency in American popular music. Thus he recorded Curtis Mayfield's spiritual "Peo- ple Get Ready"; country classics such as "I Don't Hurt Anymore," "Stones That You Throw," "Rock Salt and Nails" and "A Fool Such As I"; and traditional nuggets such as "Young but Daily Growin'," "Bonnie Ship the Diamond" and "The Hills of Mexico" (all three of which appear to have been recorded at the same session).

Not everything they ran through was recorded. And there are no recordings of Dylan, Robertson, Manuel, Hudson and Rick Danko working on the new songs they were writing, only attempted finished takes. The procedure was to work up an arrangement of a song, either an original or a cover, and, if they liked it, record it on a basic reel-to-reel using just three microphones.

Robbie Robertson: When we were inspired we'd go down to the basement and put something down on tape. Eventually it became quite a collection of songs that we had there. But it hadn't been recorded professionally, just on a little tape recorder.

Not all the songs were improvised or "covers" of other artists' material. The inspiration provided by the daily sessions was encouraging Dylan to work on new songs, and for the first time he seemed to be writing the words first and adding the music later, a technique that would carry over to the *John Wesley Harding* songs that fall. As a result, two of the best songs from the sessions were cowritten with members of the Hawks, "Tears of Rage" and "This Wheel's on Fire." In both cases he presented the typewritten lyrics, to Manuel and Danko respectively, to see if they could come up with some music.

Richard Manuel: He came down to the basement with a piece of typewritten paper . . . it was typed out—in line form—and he just said, "Have you got any music for this?" I had a couple of musical movements that fit . . . so I just elaborated a bit, because I wasn't sure what the lyrics meant. I couldn't run upstairs and say, "What's this mean, Bob: 'Now the heart is filled with gold as if it was a purse'?"

Rick Danko: We would come together every day and work and Dylan would come over. He gave me the typewritten lyrics to "[This] Wheel's on Fire." At that time I was teaching myself to play piano. Some music I had written on the piano the day before just seemed to fit with Dylan's lyrics. I worked on the phrasing and the melody. Then Dylan and I wrote the chorus together.

The *Basement Tapes* songs stand as some of Dylan's greatest achievements. Yet he had no idea what he wanted to do with them. He seemed to have no desire to release them himself, and the songs ended up being used as demos by a wealth of other artists, many already with a reputation for covering Dylan songs. In November 1967 Peter, Paul and Mary were the first act to chart with a *Basement Tapes* song, having released their version of "Too Much of Nothing" as a single. They were soon followed up the charts by Manfred Mann (with "The Mighty Quinn") and, in the U.K., Julie Driscoll, Brian Auger and the Trinity (with "This Wheel's on Fire"), while the Hawks, now known as the Band, featured a further three songs on their debut album, *Music from Big Pink*, and the Byrds included versions of "You Ain't Going Nowhere" (also a hit single) and "Nothing Was Delivered" on their superb foray into country-rock, *Sweetheart of the Rodeo.*

Bob Dylan: They were written vaguely for other people. . . . I don't remember anybody specifically those songs were ever written for. They must have been written at that time for the publishing company. . . . We must have recorded fifty songs at that place. At that time psychedelic rock was overtaking the universe and so we were singing these homespun ballads or whatever they were.
[1978]

When, after the release of the long-awaited *John Wesley Harding*, it became apparent that a whole stack of classic Dylan originals had been written and recorded in 1967 but remained unreleased, many fans began to search for a copy of the rumored tape that featured Dylan's own versions of all the songs that had been appearing on other artists' records. On June 22, 1968, the cover story of the newly formed *Rolling Stone* magazine was on "the missing Bob Dylan album," the fourteen-song acetate of these demos, which was now being written up as the missing link between *Blonde on Blonde* and *John Wesley Harding*. The story of rock bootlegging had begun.

15 1968 Drifters, Immigrants, Messengers and Saints

B y the time the Band began working on their own debut album in the fall of 1967, it had been eighteen months since the completion of *Blonde on Blonde*. In the meantime, the Beatles had recorded *Sgt. Pepper's Lonely Hearts Club Band*, a cornucopia of studio gimmicks obscuring a plethora of lightweight tunes that was a definite retrograde step from the inspired *Revolver*. Nevertheless, its so-called innovations caused a lemming-like rush of West Coast hippies intent on recording psychedelic versions of their most recent acid trip. Nineteen sixty-seven became the Summer of Love, and the media, always quick to recognize a bandwagon, responded with alacrity.

Dylan, though, knew that one didn't need to tune in and turn on to drop out. Indeed, only by turning off and tuning out had he found his own retreat. If there was much speculation at the time as to how Dylan would attempt to "top" *Sgt. Pepper*, Dylan himself was not interested in such an exercise. He was not unduly impressed by what he had heard coming from California or England.

Bob Dylan: I didn't know how to record the way other people were recording, and didn't want to. The Beatles had just released *Sgt. Pepper*, which I didn't like at all. . . . I thought that was a very indulgent album, though the songs on it were real good. I didn't think all that production was necessary, 'cause the Beatles had never done that before. [1978]

If Dylan had returned from the edge a little jaundiced in his worldview, he was still open to outside influences. In 1967 the Bengali Bauls came to the United States at the request of Albert Grossman and stayed on his estate in Woodstock, where they were introduced to Dylan. The Bauls were wandering minstrels who sang songs based on Baul tradition, dating back to the ninth or tenth century. Their songs, inspired in part by elements of Buddhism and Sufi Islam, had some similarities to Western popular song, including the use of a repetitive refrain after each verse. And the frequent theme of their poems and songs was the right of the individual to develop freely. Two of the Bauls, Purna and Lakhsman Das, are the figures on either side of Dylan on the cover of *John Wesley Harding*, the album he recorded that fall. It was an album that detailed the struggles of individuals to pursue their own destiny, often outside the restrictions of societal restraints. It was an album full of outlaws, drifters, immigrants, messengers and saints.

It was also an album full of religious imagery, its language reminiscent of the King James Bible, its characters seemingly lifted from the Old Testament but adrift in a land akin to some postlapsarian American frontier, on a border between past and present. Dylan's mother, Beattie Zimmerman, told Toby Thompson in 1968 that Dylan was increasingly delving into the Bible.

Beattie Zimmerman: In his house in Woodstock today, there's a huge Bible open on a stand in the middle of his study. Of all the books that crowd his house, overflow from his house, that Bible gets the most attention. He's continuously getting up and going over to refer to something.

On the *John Wesley Harding* album there are allusions to both the Old and New Testaments. In his study *The Bible in the Lyrics of Bob Dylan*, Bert Cartwright cites some sixty-one biblical allusions on the album.*

"All Along the Watchtower" features perhaps the most overt allusions to the Bible. The song's setting seems to be largely based on the section of Isaiah that

---

*The breakdown for each song is: "As I Went Out One Morning," one; "I Dreamed I Saw St. Augustine," three; "All Along the Watchtower," five; "The Ballad of Frankie Lee and Judas Priest," fifteen; "Drifter's Escape," four; "Dear Landlord," six; "I Am a Lonesome Hobo," five; "I Pity the Poor Immigrant," sixteen; "The Wicked Messenger," six.

deals with the fall of Babylon. Yet when the thief cries that "the hour is getting late" it seems apparent that this is the thief in the night foretold in Revelation, that is, Jesus Christ come again, for it is He who says in Revelation: "I will come on thee as a thief, and thou shalt not know what hour I will come upon thee."

Dylan would later say of *John Wesley Harding* that he was "dealing with the devil in a fearful way." It does seem as if he was not joking in 1976 when he told Neil Hickey of *TV Guide* that *John Wesley Harding* was "the first biblical rock album." None of this received much attention at the time of the album's release. Rather, it was the sound of the album and the directness of the imagery that surprised most commentators and fans.

The surreal symbolism of *Blonde on Blonde* had disappeared. Yet if there seemed to be little one could read into a song like "As I Went out One Morning," it, like most songs on the album, contained a symbolic figure who was not quite what he seemed (in this case Tom Paine). Here the character of Paine, like St. Augustine and John Wesley Harding in their songs, is slightly askew of the historical stereotype. Perhaps, as in "The Ballad of Frankie Lee and Judas Priest," Dylan was deliberately parodying those who looked for hidden meanings in his songs, as he most certainly was in the album's liner notes. According to Dylan, he was looking to strip bare his language. He discussed this approach with Ginsberg at the time.

Allen Ginsberg: In '68 he was talking poetics with me, telling me how he was writing shorter lines, with every line meaning something. He wasn't just making up a line to go with a rhyme anymore; each line had to advance the story, bring the song forward. And from that time came some of the stuff he did with the Band, like "I Shall Be Released," and some of his strong laconic ballads like "The Ballad of Frankie Lee and Judas Priest." There was to be no wasted language, no wasted breath. All the imagery was to be functional rather than ornamental.

Bob Dylan: What I'm trying to do now is not use too many words. There's no line that you can stick your finger through, there's no hole in any of the stanzas. There's no blank filler. Each line has something. [1968]

As with many of the *Basement Tapes* songs, Dylan wrote the words to all but two of the *John Wesley Harding* songs first. Presumably the two exceptions were the last two songs, which seem to have none of that "sense of fear," nor the biblical allusions.

Bob Dylan: There's only two songs on the album which came at the same time as the music. The rest of the songs were written out on paper, and I found the tunes for them later. I didn't do it before, and I haven't done it since. That might account for the specialness of that album. [1978]

The sound of the album was startling primarily because initially it was seen as a regressive step, more folk than rock, and had little in common with the more "contemporary" sounds being heard on albums by the Beatles, the Rolling Stones, Jefferson Airplane, the Doors or the Velvet Underground. After *Blonde on Blonde*, fans had expected more of the same. In fact, Dylan may have originally intended a quite different sound from the one he ended up with on *John Wesley Harding*.

Bob Dylan: I heard the sound that Gordon Lightfoot was getting, with Charlie McCoy and Kenny Buttrey. I'd used Charlie and Kenny both before, and I figured if he could get that sound, I could. But we couldn't get it. [1969]

After the final session for the album, in November 1967, he even considered embellishing the album by getting Robbie Robertson and perhaps Garth Hudson to overdub some guitar and organ over the basic tracks. But Robertson felt that the album sounded fine as it was, and anyway, the Hawks, now named the Band, were hard at work on their own album, having recently reunited with Levon Helm.

Robbie Robertson: As I recall, it was just on a kind of whim that Bob went down to Nashville. And there with just a couple of guys he put those songs down on tape. Then we did talk about doing some overdubbing on it, but I really liked it when I heard it and I couldn't really think right about overdubbing on it. So it ended up coming out the way he brought it back.

The recording and release of *John Wesley Harding* was a relatively painless affair. Having resolved his contractual difficulties with CBS and re-signed with the company in August 1967, Dylan was in the studio in October, and the album was completed in three sessions. Before completing the deal with CBS he and Grossman, dissatisfied with CBS's royalty scale and its failure to give Dylan the support an artist of his stature deserved, had agreed on terms with MGM. However, MGM was involved in a boardroom struggle at the time and board member Allen Klein in particular was keen to avoid signing Dylan, because of the seven-figure advance and 12-percent royalty Grossman was demanding.

When Clive Davis, head of CBS records, trying to keep Dylan at CBS, kindly furnished Klein with the *real* sales figures for Dylan's albums, Klein became even more opposed, and Grossman, realizing MGM was stalling, resumed negotiating with CBS and obtained an unheard of 10-percent royalty rate, but no advance. Thus MGM managed to lose one of the two most significant American acts in sixties rock music. The other, the Velvet Underground, MGM would abandon in 1969. Klein failed to appreciate that Dylan's low profile since July 1966 might have actually increased his salability. His next two albums would in fact generate greater initial sales than any of his previous albums.

The final session for *John Wesley Harding*, at which the bulk of the album was recorded, was on November 29, 1967. Within four weeks the album had been issued in the States, and, despite minimal publicity, shot to number two in the charts, sandwiched between the Beatles and the Rolling Stones.

Bob Dylan: I asked Columbia to release it with no publicity and no hype because this was the season of hype. [1985]

In retrospect, *John Wesley Harding* is one of Dylan's most enduring albums. When *Nashville Skyline* came out eighteen months later, many fans reexamined the earlier album and recognized its real quality. Fans would also note the way he had presaged his movement toward country music with the final two songs on *John Wesley Harding*, both of which featured the distinctive steel guitar of Peter Drake. If the remainder of the album had been so embellished, perhaps fans would have recognized the country tinges around the edges of the album's sound sooner than they did. As it is the dry, crisp sound remains unique, discernibly different from both the *Basement Tapes* songs, which in most cases were recorded without drums, and the syrupy *Nashville Skyline* material. What *John Wesley Harding* did share with the *Basement Tapes* was its moralistic tone. It was a remarkably prolific burst of creativity for Dylan to write an entire album within weeks of concluding the *Basement Tapes* sessions, particularly as he used none of the material already worked out.

At the end of 1967 Dylan must have been pleased with his way of life in Woodstock, both personally and artistically. Sara had given birth to a daughter that summer, named Anna. Dylan had also signed a lucrative contract with CBS and recorded and released his first album in two years, which had proved a major addition to his oeuvre.

In January 1968 he returned to live performance, even though it lasted less than fifteen minutes. In October 1967 Woody Guthrie had finally lost his fight against the hereditary disease that had slowly ravaged his body for more than ten years. When he heard about the death, Dylan phoned Harold Leventhal, Guthrie's longtime friend and manager, and said that if there was going to be a memorial show he wanted to be there.

Thus on January 20, 1968, he shared a bill at Carnegie Hall with singers such as Judy Collins, Tom Paxton and Guthrie's son Arlo, for the first Woody Guthrie Memorial Concert (a second was held on the West Coast in 1970). Dylan asked the Band, billed as the Crackers, to back him. Despite the fact that all acts played sets entirely composed of Guthrie songs, it was Dylan's presence that overshadowed the concert and attracted all the publicity. His first concert appearance in twenty months was more of an event than Guthrie's death, at least as far as the media were concerned. Perversely, the three songs he did perform—"Grand Coulee Dam," "Dear Mrs. Roosevelt" and "I Ain't Got No Home"—were hardly in the folk style that Guthrie had espoused and that all the other performers used that night. The sound the Crackers whacked out was more akin to rockabilly, and Dylan's singing was a crossbreeding of his *John Wesley Harding* tone, his 1969 "chewing the cud" voice and his early-sixties hollering.

Robbie Robertson: Everybody else was taking a different plane musically, you know it was a very folk-oriented show. But we just played what we were doing at the time. I can't help but think Woody Guthrie would have approved. I mean, if a song is going to live it must live in its contemporary surrounding. However, if the fans hoped that Dylan's appearance would whet his appetite for live performance again they were to be sorely disappointed. In his June 1968 interview for *Sing Out!*, Dylan made it clear that his touring days were over—at least for the moment.

Bob Dylan: When I was touring, it was my line of work, to go out there and deliver those songs. You must accept that in some way. There's very little you can do about it. The only other thing to do is not to do it. . . . It's pretty straining to do a show like that, plus a lot of really unhealthy situations rise up. . . . I did it, and I did it enough to know that there must be something else to do. [1968]

The Guthrie Memorial allowed the press their first real opportunity to view the new-look Dylan. Now bearded, he looked like a country squire who had accidentally wandered through a door marked "Stage." The new look accorded with his whole new manner. Since the accident he seemed to have mellowed out. Everybody who had contact with him in the two years following his accident commented on his new self. Bob Markel traveled to Woodstock in the winter of 1968 to see if he had made any decision about the publication of *Tarantula*.

Bob Markel: He was far more friendly, far less distracted. He was more grown up and professional, easier to be with. He said he didn't know if he wanted the book published at all. It wasn't something he wanted to improve; it didn't interest him anymore. He'd gone past it. He wasn't sure if he wanted it published as a "relic" or an unfinished work.

Others who spent time with Dylan in Woodstock in 1968 were less delighted by his demeanor. They thought him uncommunicative and out of touch with what was happening in the outside world. It was as if Dylan had actually absolved himself from a role in the world when recuperating from his accident.

George Harrison visited him in November 1968 and stayed a few days, even cowriting a song with him, "I'd Have You Anytime," though only after Dylan had requested he show him some chords, perhaps trying to develop his musical skills while in his self-imposed isolation. Possibly he was just anxious to share his music with somebody, now that the Band were rarely around.

George Harrison: He'd gone through his broken-neck period and was being very quiet, and he didn't have much confidence anyhow—that's the feeling I got with him in Woodstock. He hardly said a word for a couple of days.

Elliott Landy: He doesn't talk very much. He wants to hear. He needs people, to find out what's happening, you know? . . . The downside of it is that you can't really get a straight answer out of him sometimes.

In June 1968 Dylan told Happy Traum, who had moved to Woodstock the previous year, that perhaps he might do an interview for *Sing Out! Sing Out!* was experiencing considerable financial difficulties, and a Dylan interview would boost sales considerably. It would, after all, be his first major interview since the accident. Traum suggested John Cohen, a local musician and painter, to do the interview, and Dylan readily agreed. However, when it came to the interview his new mellow persona was in full evidence, and he seemed reluctant to express any opinions about the pressing political issues of the day. A second interview went the same way, despite Traum's intervention. Traum was extremely unhappy with his lack of commitment. The interview, when it was published, appeared to indicate a man who was unconcerned with anything outside Woodstock.

Happy Traum: He was totally not giving interviews. In fact, he was so changed by his accident that he had become religious; he had become a family man; he'd stopped smoking. You know, there'd been a total change in his personality. . . . Then one day he just said to me, "Why don't we do an interview," he just said that, "let's do an interview for *Sing Out!* . . . So I called John [Cohen] and he came up, stayed with me at my house, and we went out and saw Dylan. Through most of the interview I just sat and listened, I didn't say anything. I was letting John do it, because John is a very smart fellow, he has a very specific point of view. He's an artist, he's a photographer, as well as being a musician. Then about three quarters of the way through the interview— I believe it was two separate sittings—I began to feel that John was being too careful with Bob, he wasn't pushing him on anything. . . . He was intimidated by the fact that he was doing an interview with this man. But he was not pushing him, he was just too weak with him. And I felt that in order to be a good interview it needed some life, it needed somebody to stick something in there. . . . Now at this time—you've got to remember it was 1968—there was still a lot of talk about him leaving politics, about him not singing political songs anymore. He was writing only love songs and he had made some statements about how he had finished with politics and he wasn't interested, and all that kind of stuff. So I thought it was important to try to get some answers out of him, something of his ideas about politics, because people wanted to know that. . . . At the time the Vietnam War was on and we were upset about that, and I really wanted him to say something about that. I was trying to get Bob to make some definitive statement about where he stood. But he didn't say anything, he was just talking about this stonemason he knew.

Dylan himself refused to admit that he was retreating from the real world. He told reporter Hubert Saal that winter that he didn't think "living in the country is a retreat from anything. It's not as if I were getting ready to go out in a bouncing wave or anything like that. You have to be let alone to really accomplish anything."

Yet he had certainly cut himself off. Clive Davis at CBS was concerned that, without Grossman's input, Dylan might lose contact with CBS, forgetting his commitment to his record label and his public. Contact with him had become sporadic and was only achieved through an intermediary, Dylan's secretary, Naomi Saltzman.

Clive Davis: [Dylan and Grossman had] stopped working together. He did not have another manager; I had the feeling that he needed someone to bring him ideas, goad him a bit, make suggestions, offer help if he needed it. . . . I had to tread very softly. I began calling him. I could never reach him directly, for he guards his privacy very carefully. The technique was to call his secretary, Naomi, who would call him; then, if he chose to, he would call back.

Dylan's relations with Grossman had certainly cooled somewhat. Though Woodstock had been Grossman's home for far longer than it had been Dylan's, Dylan now kept his contact with Grossman to an absolute minimum. Indeed, speculation was rife that the song "Dear Landlord," his plea to some individual not to put a price on his soul, was about Grossman. Though he would later deny it, it certainly seems an appropriate address to a man who had pushed him so hard during that grueling world tour, and whose seven-year contract gave him huge cuts of all Dylan's earnings until it expired at the beginning of 1969.

Quite possibly Dylan was waiting for his legal commitment to Grossman to expire before entering the recording studio again.* Certainly at the end of 1968 he made moves to gain total control of his music publishing, forming his own company, Big Sky, to deal henceforth with his music. Dwarf Music, set up by Grossman and Dylan at the end of 1965, would no longer receive new compositions. However, all the evidence suggests he actually had very little to record.

Part of the problem for Dylan was Woodstock itself. As an artistic community for a hundred years, it did have a sense of retreat and otherworldliness about it. And, though this was exactly what he had required whenever he had retreated there during his New York days, and even more so as he recovered from his accident and discovered the joys of family life, by 1968 it was stifling his creative spirit.

Elliott Landy: Woodstock is a very womblike place. It's very special there. . . . It's filled with personal spiritual growth opportunity there . . . and people who go to Woodstock are transformed—people who live there, that is. And he is going through a transformation, I feel. . . . He was learning love and learning to feel love and express it and experience it in the family way. That's what *Nashville Skyline* was about—very introspective, very countrylike, very havenlike music.

Landy, a photographer, had moved to Woodstock himself and befriended all the musicians living in this artists' colony, people such as the Band, Dylan and Van Morrison. He was taking photos of all of them and becoming a regular provider of album covers. Landy visited Dylan on several occasions throughout 1968 and 1969, and he noticed that Dylan was working on a new interest that was perhaps distracting him from the serious business of writing songs: He was trying his hand at painting. Indeed, a typical Dylan painting graced the cover of the Band's debut album, *Music from Big Pink*.

Elliott Landy: His paintings I remember seeing a lot. I've seen the original *Big Pink* painting and it's incredible. It doesn't look so good on the album

---

*Marc Elliot in his woefully poor *Rockanomics* book manages to suggest that Dylan held back from writing songs until 1974 in order to avoid giving Grossman a share of his royalties.

cover. . . . His painting is really good and his drawings were like van Gogh. I mean, it's the same hand. He started painting when he was in Byrdcliffe. His neighbor was a painter and taught him how to use the tools of painting. That's what you do in Woodstock. . . . It's in the air.

Despite the success of *John Wesley Harding*, which remained on the *Billboard* charts throughout 1968, the year would be the first of Dylan's "lost" years. Though it seemed he had been in retreat since June 1966, 1967 had in fact been an extraordinarily creative period for him. Though the convenient myth persists that he was never the same after his accident, in no one year up to 1967 could he be said to have written as many masterful songs as he did in that year. As if operated by a tap, the songwriting stream was turned off in 1968. The only songs Dylan is known to have written in this year were "I Threw It All Away," "Lay Lady Lay"— which he wrote for the *Midnight Cowboy* movie but submitted too late—and a bridge in George Harrison's "I'd Have You Anytime." Whatever the quality of the former two songs, this was hardly prolific, especially by the standards he had previously maintained.

Bob Dylan: One day I was half-stepping, and the lights went out. And since that point, I more or less had amnesia. . . . It took me a long time to get to do consciously what I used to be able to do unconsciously. [1978]

When Dylan later talked about this "amnesia"—the period when he forgot how to create the way he always had—he was not referring to the period directly after the accident, but to a period that began in 1968. It was the first time he had been without his muse for more than a few months.

Bob Dylan: I . . . didn't sense the importance of that accident till at least a year after that. I realized [then] that it was a real accident. I mean, I thought that I was just gonna get up and go back to doing what I was doing before . . . but I couldn't do it anymore. [1969]

Bob Dylan: What I survived after that was even harder to survive than the motorcycle crash. That was just a physical crash, but sometimes there are things in life that you cannot see, that are harder to survive than something which you can pin down. [1978]

If he was looking for peace and quiet while he attempted to learn "to do consciously what I used to be able to do unconsciously," he was not getting a great deal of it in Woodstock. By the end of 1968 too many people had found out about his home in Byrdcliffe. He had, after all, been living there since before the accident, having purchased it in the summer of 1965 as a retreat from the city. It was a lovely old house built by one of Woodstock's founding fathers.

Elliott Landy: Everybody had rented beautiful, big, old wooden houses that are typical of Woodstock, or they lived on farms. Dylan's house in Woodstock, for example, had a huge living room with a high wood-paneled ceiling, all a little gloomy and spooky. Upstairs it looked like an old-fashioned hotel—long walkways with wooden floors and a red carpet, numberless children's and guest rooms. It was a so-called Byrdcliffe house, named after the man who built it. Byrdcliffe was a wealthy man who at the turn of the century had tried to found an artists' colony at Woodstock, and with his money had splendid and solid houses built.

At the beginning of 1969, Dylan moved his family to the southern part of Woodstock, purchasing a larger house previously owned by economist Walter Weyl. The Weyl place was considerably more private and far fewer people knew about it. Yet he would not even remain at his new home for the remainder of 1969. By September Dylan's Woodstock period was over.

16 | 1969: What's the Matter with Me?

In February 1969, Dylan flew to Nashville to record (or begin to record, depending on whom you believe) the follow-up to *John Wesley Harding*. It had been fifteen months since he had recorded that album, and he had not ventured into a recording studio or written more than a couple of songs in the interim.

Nashville Skyline confirmed the drought that fifteen months of silence had presaged. Though the album came quickly, this time it was a result more of the simplicity of the lyrics and downright obviousness of the arrangements than of any innate chemistry between Dylan and the musicians. Using Charlie McCoy,

Ken Buttrey and Pete Drake again may have helped the recording process, but the new songs hardly tested musicians of their quality.

Bob Dylan: We just take a song; I play it and everyone else just sort of fills in behind it. . . . At the same time you're doing that, there's someone in the control booth who's turning all those dials to where the proper sound is coming in. . . . [1969]

Norman Blake: He came in and Charlie McCoy was the session leader. Charlie was playing electric bass and he just kind of run them down in front of us with his guitar and harmonica and Charlie would take them down in the number system they use there in Nashville, the number changes, and Charlie would pass out numbered cards with the changes on them to all of us. As I recall, [with] a lot of those tunes, . . . seems like we got them pretty quick.

According to Dylan, he had not gone to Nashville with the intention of recording an entire album.

Bob Dylan: The first time I went into the studio I had, I think, four songs. I pulled that instrumental one out . . . then Johnny [Cash] came in and did a song with me. Then I wrote one in the motel . . . pretty soon the whole album started fillin' in together, and we had an album. I mean, we didn't go down with that in mind. [1969]

In fact to call songs like "Peggy Day" and "To Be Alone with You" fillers would be a considerable insult to so-called fillers on previous albums such as "On the Road Again" and "Leopard-skin Pill-box Hat." Despite padding out *Nashville Skyline* with an instrumental jam called "Nashville Skyline Rag," plus a rerecording of "Girl from the North Country" taken from two days of studio duets with Johnny Cash, the whole still failed to clock in at half an hour—short measure even if the twenty-seven minutes of music had been full of the inspiration evident on *John Wesley Harding*.

The aspect of the album that drew the most comment, though, was Dylan's voice. He had mysteriously developed a country twang, which he put down initially to giving up smoking, though family and friends from his youth soon pointed out that his new voice bore a remarkable similarity to the voice he used to sing when he played the Ten O'Clock Scholar and the Purple Onion in the winter and spring of 1960.

Bonnie Beecher: Do you know his voice on *Nashville Skyline*? . . . Well Dylan's early voice sounded like that. I was startled when I heard him again on

Nashville Skyline. He got this bronchial cough that lasted almost a year, and he wouldn't take care of it because he thought the rougher his voice sounded, the more [it was] like Woody Guthrie. I thought he had lost . . . that sweet voice altogether, until [*Nashville Skyline*].

The two sessions with Johnny Cash took place three days after the bona fide album sessions, and were intended to result in a separate Dylan/Cash album, but the results were pretty disastrous. Never the greatest harmony singer in the world, Dylan's duetting on this occasion was quite simply inept. The band plodded through the baker's dozen of country standards Dylan and Cash decided to do, collected their paychecks and hurried home. Perhaps the only notable aspect of the Dylan/Cash sessions was that they signaled an intent on Dylan's part to record an album of country standards to reinforce the change in direction evident on *Nashville Skyline*. Meanwhile, he was called upon to defend his new album to the two members of the press he deigned to talk to, Hubert Saal of *Newsweek* and Jann Wenner of *Rolling Stone*.

Bob Dylan: These are the type of songs that I always felt like writing when I've been alone to do so. The songs reflect more of the inner me than the songs of the past. They're more to my base than, say, *John Wesley Harding*. There I felt everyone expected me to be a poet so that's what I tried to be. . . . [My old] songs were all written in the New York atmosphere. I'd never have written any of them—or sung them the way I did—if I hadn't been sitting around listening to performers in New York cafés and the talk in all the dingy parlors. [1969]

In fact, Dylan was being surprisingly frank when he said the old songs reflected the "New York atmosphere" he had written them in. By default he seemed to be admitting that *Nashville Skyline*, in turn, reflected the "Woodstock atmosphere"—all of which suggested that his critical and creative faculties were rotting in upstate New York. If recuperating in Woodstock had probably saved his life, he was no longer finding the place the creative hive it had been in 1967. A large part of that decline must have been because of his lessening contact with the Band. Their influence helped him produce some of his greatest work in 1967.

By the end of 1968, the Band were on their own, hard at work on their masterful self-titled second album. It took Dylan some time to realize that he had overstayed his time in Woodstock, and even then his eventual departure was only dimly connected to a desire to locate his absent muse. He would later disavow *Nashville Skyline*, and on his cross-country tours of America in the seventies and eighties would almost entirely ignore its contents, save for an occasional "Lay Lady Lay."

Bob Dylan: On *Nashville Skyline* you had to read between the lines. I was trying to grasp [for] something that would lead me on to where I thought I should be, and it didn't go nowhere—it just went down, down, down. [1978]

Ironically *Nashville Skyline* proved to be one of Dylan's best-selling albums ever. This was primarily due to the success of the three singles issued from the album—particularly "Lay Lady Lay," which was his first top ten single since "Rainy Day Women." Both "I Threw It All Away," the first single from *Nashville Skyline*, and "Tonight I'll Be Staying Here with You" also reached the top hundred. Yet he provided virtually no input when it came to the choice of singles. He had never really been concerned with the singles market save for a brief period in 1965–66 that ended with the commercial failure of "One of Us Must Know."

Clive Davis: Our area of greatest difficulty was singles. Bob always said that he would leave the choice up to me—yet he was invariably surprised by my choices, and sometimes balked at them. He didn't think about singles, he said, and he didn't think AM radio was *that* important. None of his friends listened to it.

Whatever his reservations about Davis's selections, he stayed in the spotlight through 1969 mainly thanks to the release of the only three worthwhile songs on the album as singles, and to two important one-off performances that garnered him maximum publicity for minimum effort.

Performance number one was his first national TV appearance in more than four years, on "The Johnny Cash Show." Filmed in May 1969, its broadcast was designed to coincide with the album's climb up the charts. The show was recorded at the Grand Ole Opry in Nashville, and Dylan used the trip as an opportunity to spend a few days in a Nashville studio, working on his next project, an album of country standards in the style of the "new" Dylan, though this time without Cash's contribution.

Dylan's performance on the show was a little stilted. Included was a lightweight new ditty called "Living the Blues," which was due to be his next single until "Lay Lady Lay" was chosen instead. What was apparent to most of his long-standing friends was that he was terrified out of his wits. After all, this was his first TV appearance since he had achieved real mass success, and it was the public unveiling of his *Nashville Skyline* persona. The new Dylan was destined for another stormy reception.

Johnny Cash: I think Bob Dylan was scared. . . . When he went out to rehearse they had an old shack hanging from wires behind him to try to give it a backwoods look. He came offstage upset. He said, "I'm gonna be the laugh-ingstock of the business! My fans are gonna laugh in my face over that thing!" I said, "What would you like?" He said, "Have 'em get that out of the way. Just put me out there by myself."

Nashville Skyline's mixed reception had bought Dylan no real breathing space in which to work on something more ambitious. To many of his fans, *John Wesley Harding* was the solitary worthwhile product in three years and seemed poor return for their loyalty. After all, in the same period the Beatles had come up with *Sgt. Pepper, The White Album* and *Abbey Road* (and had recorded their own version of *The Basement Tapes, Let It Be*). The Stones, after a stormy 1967, had come up with *Beggars Banquet* and were hard at work on the equally impressive *Let It Bleed*.

If Dylan was considering a way to return to the public arena, an offer suddenly arrived that seemed to provide him with the perfect vehicle to see if the flame still burned. He had played no concerts since his fifteen-minute appear-ance at the Woody Guthrie Memorial Concert in January 1968. He was re-luctant to play in America because he felt there would be too much media attention, and no suitable venues sprung to mind.

Another problem was arising. A large pop festival was being planned for the mid-August weekend in Woodstock, and there was no way he wanted to be around when a hundred thousand children of the sixties started wandering through the brush trying to locate the home of their guru. He had to get out! Thus, when two English promoters suggested to Bert Block, his personal man-ager, that he play a festival on a small island just off the south coast of England, and that he and his family could travel first class on the *Queen Elizabeth II* and have a two-week vacation away from Woodstock, he became seriously inter-ested.

Ray Foulk: One thing I had discussed with Block was the way we could entice Dylan to do it. So we came up with the idea of making it a holiday for him and his family. We obtained a farmhouse in Bembridge which was suit-able. It had a swimming pool and a barn that had recently been converted which was suitable for rehearsing in. . . . We were offering Dylan a fortnight stay there, no expense spared, car with driver. Also we would have him come over on the QE2. The fee offered to Block was fifty thousand dollars.

The vacation would start on August 13, two days before half a million people descended on Max Yasgur's farm near Woodstock, and Dylan's entire family would accompany him on the QE2. Obviously he had to establish whether the Band would accompany him, though, as he had insisted that, as well as his own fifty-thousand dollar fee, the Band receive a further twenty thousand dollars, they were hardly likely to refuse. Dylan then decided to remind himself what playing to a large crowd was like, and became a surprise guest during the Band's set at the Mississippi River Festival in mid-July. Introduced as Elmer Johnson, he ran through four songs with the Band, to a rapturous reception.

Unfortunately, a slight mishap spoiled Dylan's plans. Boarding the QE2, his elder son, Jesse, temporarily lost consciousness after banging his head against a cabin door, and the ship's doctor refused to accept responsibility for the boy's ability to make the voyage. They had to disembark and take Jesse to a doctor in New York. So much for sailing to England!

When Dylan and Sara finally flew into Heathrow Airport, twelve days had elapsed and they were minus the children, who stayed at home in New York. Curiously, Sara looked extremely pregnant, though as far as is known the next Dylan child, Jacob, was not born until 1971. Shots of Sara backstage indicate an equally pregnant lady, so clearly the initial impression at Heathrow was not one of Dylan's little japes at the expense of the press. To confuse the issue further, Anthony Scaduto, in his biography, refers to a child of the Dylans' named Seth, though this was one of his brother's children.

On Dylan's arrival it became apparent that he had again seriously underestimated the international interest in his return to the stage. The British media were running stories every day about the crowds heading for the Isle of Wight, and began to talk of a British Woodstock. It was clear that he would have to make some concession to the press, and on the Wednesday before the festival he reluctantly held his first press conference since May 1966. The results were suitably farcical. He affected a country twang, and when asked about drugs responded, "I think everyone should lead their own lives, you know"; he informed the press, "I don't want to protest anymore"; and he disavowed his 1966 activities, saying, "That stuff was all for publicity. I don't do that kind of thing anymore." Meanwhile, Dylan and the Band got down to some serious rehearsing in the barn at Forelands Farm. Though they had briefly rehearsed in Woodstock at the end of July, three or four day's rehearsing on the Isle of Wight was required to whip the set into shape. As three of the Beatles arrived by helicopter for a game of tennis and a jam session on the Friday—day one of the Second Isle of Wight Festival—the island began filling up with mainlanders.

By the time Dylan took to the stage on Sunday night there were an estimated two hundred thousand fans awaiting his appearance. The size of the audience clearly unnerved him. Matters were not improved by a two-hour delay between Richie Havens's set and the Band's own set, as the press enclosure spilled over with a surfeit of journalists and hangers-on. The huge crowd became impatient.

The Band abbreviated their own set but when Dylan finally appeared and launched into "She Belongs to Me" it was past eleven, and he had been waiting to go on for more than two hours. The one-hour set he performed that night was not well received. On the first couple of songs his singing was understandably hesitant, and many fans, fed by tall stories planted in the press of a three-hour performance climaxing with an all-star jam, were bound to be unhappy. Throughout the show, Dylan stuck doggedly to his *Nashville Skyline* voice, and only on a raucous "Highway 61 Revisited" did some of the old fire return to his singing. His whole appearance drew unfavorable comments.

Levon Helm: I would've liked to have gotten carried away. I was ready, but I don't think everybody else was. . . . If things were like we hoped they would be, we were prepared to play for another fifteen minutes or so, just our part. And Bob had an extra list of songs with eight or ten different titles with question marks by them, that we would've went ahead and done, had it seemed like the thing to do. But it seemed like everybody was a little bit tired and the festival was three days old by then, and so if everybody else is ready to go home, let's all go.

Dylan himself seemed to leave the island with undue haste. Departing the following day, he was back in New York on Tuesday. On his return he informed waiting pressmen that he would not be returning to England: "They make too much of singers over there. Singers are front-page news." He said his original intention in playing the festival was to "get away from it all and give myself a chance to break back in."

His attempt to "get away from it all" had not been a great success. Neither had his return to live performance. CBS had recorded the show for a possible live album but, despite the fact that bootlegs of the show appeared before the end of the year, the project was shelved, though four "highlights" were later used on *Self Portrait*. The disappointing performance also seems to have ended any plans Dylan had to resume touring. In late June, Dylan had talked freely to Jann Wenner of *Rolling Stone* about going back on the road in the fall. If he had been testing the water at the Isle of Wight, he clearly decided to stay on the beach.

In fact, Dylan had been staying on the beach already. Woodstock was no longer a practical locale for him. Even his new house was becoming known to itinerant hippies on their pilgrimages to Woodstock, and it was no longer a creative environment.

Bob Dylan: Then came the big news about Woodstock, about musicians goin' up there, and it was like a wave of insanity breakin' loose around the house day and night. You'd come in the house and find people there, people comin' through the woods, at all hours of the day and night, knockin' at your door. It was really dark and depressing. And there was no way to respond to all this. . . . They kept comin'. We *had* to get out of there. This was just about the time of that Woodstock festival, which was the sum total of all this bullshit. . . . I couldn't get any space for myself and my family, and there was no help, nowhere. I got very resentful about the whole thing, and we got outta there. [1984]

As early as the spring of 1969 he had been looking to move on. When he was in Tennessee in May 1969 he considered purchasing a house there.

Bob Johnston: I took him around to see some places, but he was in such an uncommunicative mood.

Most of the summer, he avoided Woodstock. Apart from his trip to England, he spent a lot of time on Fire Island, an outpost of civilization off Long Island in New York. It was there that he seemed to have found a hideaway, and the picture he later painted of these times in the song "Sara" suggests an idyll. He even found a little time for music-making with a musicologist named David Amram.

David Amram: In the summer of 1969, I was about a quarter of a mile down the beach from where Bob Dylan and his family were staying, and I used to go by his place every day, bring my French horn and play.

But he knew that Fire Island was impractical as a new permanent home. The children were approaching school age. With the benefit of hindsight, his decision to return to New York may seem a little baffling, but it was in part intended as a return to the wellspring of his former creativity; it was also his and Sara's home turf, and it allowed the kids to attend local schools. The Woodstock festival signaled the death knell of the old Woodstock, the artists' colony, and in September 1969 he was back in the Village, having purchased a spacious town house on MacDougal Street.

17 | 1970: A Restless, Hungry Feeling

Having moved back to New York in September 1969, Dylan did not take long to regret his decision.

Bob Dylan: Lookin' back, it was really a stupid thing to do. But there was a house available on MacDougal Street, and I always remembered that as a nice place. So I just bought this house, sight unseen. But it wasn't the same when we got back. The Woodstock Nation had overtaken MacDougal Street also. There'd be crowds outside my house. [1984]

Bob Dylan: The worst times of my life were when I tried to find something in the past. Like when I went back to New York for the second time. I didn't know what to do. Everything had changed. [1989]

Inevitably the return to New York became common knowledge and even those who did not know Dylan's exact address would wander around the Village in the expectation of running into him. The most famous of these wandering devotees was A. J. Weberman, who had been writing a series of articles about him in underground publications such as the *East Village Other*. Except that Weberman was not really a fan of Dylan—or at least of the new Dylan. Indeed, he had convinced himself that it was his duty to make Dylan see the light, revert to his mid-sixties counterculture ways and give up producing capitalist shucks such as *Nashville Skyline*.

If *Nashville Skyline* had upset Weberman and his ilk, then they were in for a shock because the album that Dylan was working on throughout the latter part of 1969 and the early months of 1970 was not a return to form, but more a descent into parody. *Self Portrait*, a sprawling double album graced with a cover painting by Dylan, presumably a self-portrait, was issued, in June 1970. According to Dylan's later pronouncements about the album, the sense that he was parodying himself was absolutely deliberate, a concerted attempt to defuse the mythology that had begun to surround him.

Bob Dylan: That album was put out . . . [because] at that time . . . I didn't like the attention I was getting. I [had] never been a person that wanted attention. And at that time I was getting the wrong kind of attention, for doing things I'd never done. So we released that album to get people off my back. They would not like me anymore. That's . . . the reason that album was put out, so people would just at that time stop buying my records, and they did. [1981]

Bob Dylan: I said, "Well, fuck it. I wish these people would just forget about me. I wanna do something they can't possibly like, they can't relate to." . . . And then I did this portrait for the cover. I mean, there was no title for that album. . . . And I said, "Well, I'm gonna call this album *Self Portrait*." . . . And to me it was a joke. [1984]

Certainly the album contains considerable hints that Dylan had such a purpose in mind. The choice of songs from his Isle of Wight concert seems deliberately perverse. Of the four songs chosen, only "Minstrel Boy" seems remotely palatable, and perhaps that is only because there is no other version to compare it to. The Isle of Wight version of "Like a Rolling Stone," his most famous song, is certainly a joke. He forgets the words, strips the song of any feeling, and even the Band fails to inject any enthusiasm into the proceedings. "The Mighty Quinn" is equally disappointing, despite being the first official Dylan version of the most successful of the *Basement Tapes* "spin-off" songs (Manfred Mann's version had reached number one in the U.K. and number ten in the U.S.). "She Belongs to Me" sounds as though he is singing with a frog rammed down his throat but is perhaps in reality simply the sound of a very nervous man playing in front of two hundred thousand people after three years off the road.

The studio songs that make up the remainder of the album also seem to contain their fair share of in-jokes. The opening song, a Dylan original, features no Dylan vocal. Instead a chorus of female singers repeatedly sings, "How'm I s'pposed to get any ridin' [or is that 'writing'?] done?" Dylan's version of Paul Simon's "The Boxer" features two versions of himself taking Art Garfunkel and Paul Simon's parts. One version is the "old" Dylan, who had been considered by some to be the subject of the song—the whores on Seventh Avenue reportedly being CBS. The "new," smoother, richer tones of his *Nashville Skyline* voice sing the harmony vocal.

The album even features two versions of two of the songs, "Alberta" and "Little Sadie," performed in a ludicrously fast rag version and then as a more sympathetic, not to say sedate, ballad. Even the one new original Dylan lyric seems a parody—"Living the Blues" more than closely resembles Guy Mitchell's "Singing the Blues." On top of all these insults, real or imagined, there were the cover versions chosen to make up the bulk of the album. Six of the songs date from his *Nashville Skyline* period and feature the same style of crooning. More disconcertingly, these songs include an excruciating version of "Blue Moon," the syrupy "Take Me as I Am (or Let Me Go)" (presumably intended as an ironic choice) and "I Forgot More Than You'll Ever Know."

According to Charlie McCoy, many of the songs' backing tracks were recorded without Dylan even being in town, so unconcerned was he with obtaining takes he was entirely happy with.

Charlie McCoy: Dylan sent the tapes down with instructions that we were to just play over what he'd already recorded on it. . . . The tape was mostly other people's songs and it sounded like he was experimenting with them. The tempos didn't really hold together real well and he wasn't real steady with his guitar, either. . . . I assumed . . . it was just stuff he'd thrown together for the heck of it.

And yet . . . in order for Dylan to release an entire double album that said, "Fuck you," it would surely have had to consist wholly of instrumental riffs *à la* "Wigwam" and "Woogie Boogie," crooning covers such as "Blue Moon," butchery of his own masterpieces at the Isle of Wight and ludicrously unsuitable arrangements of perfectly good songs such as "The Boxer" and "In Search of Little Sadie." And *Self Portrait* does not. Parts of it seem simply, and quite acceptably, to be the work of a man who is going through a creative drought and has decided to record "covers" of some of his favorite songs. Certainly when he discussed the idea for the album with Clive Davis, that seemed to be the type of album he had in mind—not that even Dylan would go to the CBS Records president and say, "I have this great idea to issue an album which is one big 'Fuck you' to my audience and will hopefully alienate most of them so much they will not bother to buy my records in the future"!

Clive Davis: Bob asked my opinion of the album's concept early on. My objections wouldn't necessarily have stopped the album, but I knew he'd been having some difficulty coming up with his own material . . . so I encouraged him.

There are a couple of beautiful performances on the album. "Copper Kettle" in particular is one of the most exquisite recordings in his entire oeuvre. Other twenty-four-karat nuggets in this mountain of fool's gold include a restrained version of "It Hurts Me Too" and a lovely tribute to the Everly Brothers, "Let It Be Me." Even both "Albertas" and his version of Gordon Lightfoot's "Early Mornin' Rain" have something to commend them. Such performances confused listeners as to his real intentions, but at the same time they engendered hope that when his creative drought was ended he could still produce quality performances.

Not surprisingly, the album was panned on its release. The reviews were almost universally scathing, and included an extensive and famous review in *Rolling Stone* by Greil Marcus that began with the question on most people's minds when they first heard the album: "What is this shit?" (Dylan would later label Marcus's review "a piece of shit.") In the sprawling review, Marcus compared the album to the scattered collections that were making up bootlegs such as *Great White Wonder* and *Stealin'*. Ultimately, though, he wrote: "*Self Portrait* is a concept album from the cutting room floor. It has been constructed artfully, but as a coverup, not a revelation." For Marcus, the construction of the album made it clear that the album's effect was deliberate, and that made it doubly unpalatable.

Yet if producing nothing for what seemed an eternity, and then producing *Self Portrait*, seemed incontrovertible evidence of a creative drought, Dylan had a new album of original songs out within four months of *Self Portrait*'s release. Fans and critics alike concluded that the vituperative response to the double album had prompted him to scurry into the studio and record a "proper" album to appease them, and to convince the world that he still had something to say. As so often with Dylan, this feeling was primarily an illusion, a conjurer's trick.

Whether Dylan realized it at the time or not, and logic says he would have, it was inevitable that even a halfway respectable collection of original songs was bound to be greeted with undue fanfare, coming so swiftly on the heels of such an extravagant caricature of his former selves. Though he may have quickly realized that whatever his intentions with *Self Portrait*, it had failed; he had started work on *New Morning* three months before *Self Portrait* was released and, in all likelihood, did not consider *Self Portrait* anything more than a minor diversion from more serious fare. In fact, the *New Morning* album began with the last of the *Self Portrait* sessions: Dylan recorded "Went to See the Gypsy" at the same session in which he recorded "Woogie Boogie" and "In Search of Little Sadie."

Bob Dylan: We had a few of the tracks for *New Morning* before that *Self Portrait* LP came out. I didn't say, "Oh my God, they don't like this, let me do another one." It wasn't like that. It just happened coincidentally that one came out and then the other one did as soon as it did. The *Self Portrait* LP laid around for I think a year. We were working on *New Morning* when the *Self*

Portrait album got put together. Some of that stuff [on *Self Portrait*] was left over from *Nashville Skyline*. [1975]

An important point to consider is that, whatever disadvantages moving back to New York had brought with it, it did mean that Dylan was in close proximity to studios in the Village and to CBS's own studios uptown. Setting up sessions on a whim, at minimal notice, was considerably easier than when he was located in Woodstock. The move also suggests that he was serious about working at his music again. In the three years he had resided permanently in Woodstock he had spent a grand total of between eight and ten days in CBS's studios.

The final sessions for *Self Portrait* took up most of the winter of 1970, and work on *New Morning* started in earnest in May. Two days before May Day, George Harrison phoned Dylan, having arrived in New York the previous day, to arrange to meet that evening and discuss a joint recording session, scheduled for May 1. On April 30 they jammed informally at Dylan's apartment in preparation for the following day's session. The actual session was largely unproductive, despite using a stripped-down band featuring just Dylan, Harrison, Bob Johnston on keyboards, Charlie Daniels on bass and probably Billy Mundi on drums. The real problem was the lack of enough strong original songs to record. Most of the session was spent running through old Dylan originals such as "Song to Woody," "Mama You Bin on My Mind" and "Just Like Tom Thumb's Blues," almost as if he were still working on *Self Portrait*. Though at least three new originals were recorded—"If Not for You," "Working on a Guru" and an unknown song that according to *Rolling Stone* was about a father's wish to leave his son "air to breathe and water to wash in"—only "If Not for You" was under serious consideration for *New Morning*.

Nevertheless, Dylan persevered with work on a new album and later in May managed to record a further version of "If Not for You" (the official take) and another mellow original, "Time Passes Slowly," at a session featuring two former cohorts, Harvey Brooks on bass and Al Kooper on guitar.

Other sessions were also scheduled for May and June, one with Johnny Cash, one with Ringo Starr and one with the Byrds. The Byrds session did not take place because the band failed to appear. The session with Starr supposedly did take place but was later described as "not a success." With Dylan's return to New York, Bob Johnston's role as producer was discernibly devalued. Johnston was never the most technical producer, and in New York Dylan ignored the Nashville musicians Johnston favored and Al Kooper carried out many of the producer's duties. Johnston did not attend all the sessions. *New Morning* would be the end of Dylan and Johnston's association.

The problem was not really the recording of the songs, but the writing of them. Dylan was simply not coming up with enough good new songs. In the summer of 1970, he became involved with the production of a new "musical" called *Scratch* with the poet Archibald MacLeish. According to Dylan's *Biograph* notes, he played MacLeish and the producer three new songs—"New Morning," "Time Passes Slowly" and "Father of Night"—but they "didn't see eye to eye" on "Father of Night," "so I backed out of the production." In fact, according to a letter MacLeish wrote to his publisher in October of that year, the production was not meant to be a musical, but "a play with songs by Dylan." However, he "proved simply incapable of producing new songs, and things looked desperate until [we] decided about a month ago to use old songs of Dylan's."

Al Kooper: He was writing some songs for a stage play, a musical version of *The Devil and Daniel Webster*, so some of these songs were from there. That was pretty much the fulcrum for that album—"Well, I have these songs. Let's go in and cut these." That got him writing a little more. "Day of the Locusts" came from real life. And "Went to See the Gypsy." Same thing. It was just things that were going on in his life. It's like a diary.

Too late for MacLeish, Dylan produced half a dozen songs in the latter part of that summer. In June, he had received an honorary doctorate in music from Princeton University, which seems to have directly inspired "Day of the Locusts." As well as "New Morning" and the truly awful "Father of Night," he came up with a few of his best songs since his Woodstock heyday of 1967. "Sign on the Window," "The Man in Me" and "Winterlude" suggested a man at last finding a few shards of inspiration.

In August he assembled such notables as Al Kooper, Ron Cornelius, David Bromberg and Charlie Daniels for a full week of recording sessions in New York. If the official excuse for his "new" voice on *Nashville Skyline* was that he had given up cigarettes, the huskiness of his voice on the *New Morning* album would be attributed to a cold that he nursed throughout the entire week of sessions.

Ron Cornelius: Dylan had a pretty bad cold that week. You can hear it on one song, y'know, that bit about "Brighton girls are like the moon," where his voice really cracks up. But it sure suits the song. His piano playing's really weird; you fall over laughing the first time you see it, because his hands start at opposite ends of the keyboard and then sorta collide in the middle. He does that all the time, but the way he plays just knocks me out. . . . I asked him about "Went to See the Gypsy," and he told me that it was about going to see Elvis in Las Vegas. I really flashed on that!

In fact, the cracks around the edges on his vocals were most audible on two covers later released (as a B-side and on the shameful *Dylan* album, respectively)—a stunningly intense solo piano take of the traditional "Spanish Is the Loving Tongue" and a heartfelt "Can't Help Falling in Love." As in previous sessions, he and the band generally warmed up with "standards" like "Jamaica Farewell," "Mr. Bojangles" and "Big Yellow Taxi."

But if Dylan managed to complete the sessions for the album with relative ease, he seemed genuinely unsure of the worth of what he had recorded and how best to present the songs. His previous sureness deserted him at the production stage. Song selection and mixing became a tortuous affair. Al Kooper, his coproducer in all but name, was driven to distraction by Dylan's vacillating.

Al Kooper: When I finished that album I never wanted to speak to him again. . . . I was cheesed off at how difficult [the whole thing was]. . . . He just changed his mind every three seconds so I just ended up doing the work of three albums. . . . We'd get a side order and we'd go in and master it and he'd say, "No, no, no. I want to do this." And then, "No, let's go in and cut this." . . . When we finished that I was just furious with him. . . . There was another version of "Went to See the Gypsy" that was really good. . . . It was the first time I went in and had an arrangement idea for it and I said, "Let me go in and cut this track and then you can sing over it." So I cut this track and it was really good . . . it sounded like Cream. And he came in and pretended like he didn't understand where to sing on it, "Well, I can't sing to this track." But in fact he could have 'cause I took the meter from the original.

When *New Morning* was released in October it met with predictable euphoria. After the profound disappointments of *Nashville Skyline* and *Self Portrait*, it was clearly a step in the right direction. In *Rolling Stone* Ralph Gleason proved most enthusiastic—his rave review was headlined, "We've Got Dylan Back Again." It was perceived as a stamp of approval by a previously disillusioned fan. In retrospect, *New Morning* sounds patchy. There are songs of real beauty here, notably "If Not for You," the title track and "Sign on the Window"; songs of unfulfilled promise like "The Man in Me" and "One More Weekend"; and a not-so-healthy handful of real clunkers. At the time such songs as "Three Angels," "If Dogs Run Free" and "Father of Night" were seen as audacious attempts to work in new forms. Hindsight suggests that there is little on *Self Portrait* as excruciatingly bad as these three songs.

Nevertheless, Dylan must have been pleased with the reception of *New Morning*, and he was back in the top ten with an album of original songs. According to one report, Dylan even considered going back out on the road shortly after the album's release, going as far as rehearsing a small band featuring Al Kooper and Harvey Brooks. Apparently the results were disastrous, and he soon abandoned the idea.

He was still clearly unhappy with his decision to return to New York. As in his final days in Woodstock, he and his family regularly disappeared from New York for a week or two, presumably on vacations of various sorts. In the summer of 1970 Dylan allegedly went to Israel. In June, when he attended a postconcert party at the Fillmore East, he had apparently just returned from one of his little trips.

Joel Bernstein: After the last Crosby, Stills, Nash and Young show at the Fillmore East . . . Bill Graham threw a party for CSNY and the Who, who had just done *Tommy* at Carnegie Hall. . . . And Bob was there. . . . He said, "I just flew in from Venice for this." I didn't know whether he meant Venice, California, or Venice, Italy.

Sadly, the pressures, particularly from the absurd Dylan Liberation Front, Weberman's collection of misfits, would become particularly burdensome in the early months of 1971.

$\boxed{18}$ 1971–72: Smooth Like a Rhapsody

In no sense could 1971 be considered a "lost" year, as could 1968. For an artist who would issue only two singles of new material in this twelve-month period, Dylan maintained a surprisingly high profile. The reason for this goes back to a quote in the 1969 *Rolling Stone* interview about the period after the motorcycle accident: "I thought that I was just gonna get up and go back to doing what I was doing before . . . but I couldn't do it anymore."

Having learned that he could not just "get up and go back to doing what I was doing before," Dylan spent 1971 testing the water. Rather than attempting to force the pace, he tried different studios and different lineups at sessions in March, October and November. He tried another much-heralded "comeback" performance at a benefit concert in August, and he was the subject of a well-publicized biography published in the fall, written by ex–crime reporter Anthony Scaduto. All these various activities were seized upon by the media as examples of Dylan stirring again. In fact, at the end of the year Dylan concluded that the water was still a little too hot for his taste, and returned to lying on a bank of sand and watching the river flow.

In March he booked three days of sessions at a small studio in the Village, Blue Rock Studios, his first official sessions not held at a CBS studio. The sessions were to be produced by Leon Russell. It is unclear what the exact purpose of the sessions was. Only two originals were definitely recorded, "Watching the River Flow" and "When I Paint My Masterpiece," plus at least half a dozen covers, none of which ended up officially released. Clearly an album was not what Dylan had in mind—no further sessions were booked.

However, both original compositions were superior to anything he had recorded in the last three years—and both confronted head-on his continuing dearth of inspiration. "Watching the River Flow," a glorious honky-tonking three-minute roller-coaster ride, opens with a classic Dylan line, "What's the matter with me, I don't have much to say." The remainder of the song has him musing upon whether he wishes to be in the city or stay by this riverbank. The suggestion is that only in the city "with the one I love so close at hand," could the singer rediscover his muse, but the will seems to be lacking. "When I Paint My Masterpiece" is an even more overt admission that his muse has deserted him, and for the first time in song he confronts his own doubts as to whether he will ever paint his masterpiece. The song is set in Rome, a city where two millennia of culture surround the singer. He wanders the streets, looking for inspiration. Though he longs to return to "the land of Coca-Cola" (these lines were omitted from the released Dylan version), he heads for Brussels, but he cannot escape from his own notoriety.

Despite the quality of the song, "When I Paint My Masterpiece" would be first released by the Band, on their *Cahoots* album, and only later included as a "bonus" track on Dylan's second collection of greatest hits. "Watching the River Flow" was released as a single in June 1971 but failed to reach the top forty, despite being his first nonalbum single since "One of Us Must Know." By the time the single was released, he was abroad, enjoying a vacation in Israel with Sara.

On May 24, 1971, he was photographed by a UPI photographer at the Wailing Wall in Jerusalem. When the photographer realized he had captured Bob Dylan, né Robert Zimmerman, in the homeland of his forefathers on his thirtieth birthday, the photo was widely syndicated around the world. Rumors that Dylan was embracing the religion of his father, the religion he had rejected when leaving his fraternity house early in 1960, began to feature regularly in the press.

In fact, there was some basis for such speculation. The children had been brought up as Jews, and since his father's death in June 1968 Dylan had begun to explore his Jewish heritage.

Harold Leventhal: After his father died, Bob became quite conscious of his Jewishness. He was very excited about Israel when he got back and it was around that time he started talking with Rabbi Meir Kahane, who formed the Jewish Defense League.

Dylan himself would later attempt to play down the importance of his May 1971 visit, suggesting that he had just been "testing the water," as with his musical endeavors in 1971.

Bob Dylan: There was no great significance to that visit. But I'm interested in what and who a Jew is, I'm interested in the fact the Jews are Semites, like Babylonians, Hittites, Arabs, Syrians, Ethiopians. But a Jew is different because a lot of people hate Jews. [1976]

Yet while in Israel he did pursue the possibility of taking his family into a kibbutz for a year and, though he did not carry the project through, he did approach the Kibbutz Givat Haim.

Eve Brandstein: Dylan came to Kibbutz Givat Haim with an interest in bringing himself, Sara and the children to the kibbutz. The only thing was, he wanted to get a guest house, have the kids go each day to the kibbutz for experience, but that he and his wife would not have to work on the kibbutz. Rather, they'd stay in a guest house and pay for the stay and the keep of the children. He wanted to put some time in. . . . He was turned down. . . . He wanted special privileges and they were afraid that if word got out the kibbutz would be overrun.

Dylan continued to look for a new home, away from the pressures he was subjected to in New York. If he needed further evidence that life would continue to be difficult as long as he remained in New York, it came while he was in Israel. While he and Sara were at the Wailing Wall, A. J. Weberman was holding a birthday bash outside the Dylans' MacDougal Street town house. The birthday bash, like most of A. J.'s stunts, had a polemical purpose: A. J. addressed the small crowd assembled outside about Dylan's "CB" ("current bag," Weberman's slang expression referring to the "bag" Dylan was currently into).

At the beginning of January, Dylan had attempted to establish a dialogue with Weberman in an attempt to find out what his real motives were for his campaign against Dylan in the underground press. After talking to Weberman outside his house, he phoned him the following day and invited him to his Village studio to talk some more. After this informal discussion with Weberman, he was disconcerted to discover that A. J. intended to write an article for the *East Village Other* about their meeting, and requested the opportunity to see a draft of the intended article.

In a final telephone conversation on January 9, Dylan attempted to persuade Weberman not to publish his article, but without success. It was the last contact he had with Weberman until some time in 1972 when, after Weberman had promised to stop rummaging through Dylan's garbage searching for evidence of his drug habits, he returned to the MacDougal Street town house with a reporter in tow to hunt once more through the garbage as part of a feature on his new science, garbology. Sara came out of the house while this was going on and "freaked" at Weberman's reappearance. Later Dylan, having returned home to a presumably distraught Sara, went looking for Weberman.

A. J. Weberman: I was walking around with my head bowed down to my shoes, y'know. I was down on Elizabeth Street to get some Coca-Cola from the neighborhood store, when all of a sudden I felt this arm around my neck. I thought I was being mugged, y'know. I said, "Oh, God, what's happening here?" And I wrenched loose and I turned around and it was Bob Dylan. I said, "Hey, man, let's talk, man, what are you doing?" He started punching me, and I said, "Come on, stop! stop!" I thought, "Is this really happening to me? Could Bob Dylan be punching me out? My idol, the guy that wrote all the great poetry?" And a punch to my head convinced me it was. So then I thought maybe I'd wrestle him down, calm him down a little. But that didn't work out 'cause he had spirit on his side. He got me down on the sidewalk and started banging my head against the pavement. And then some hippies came along and broke it up.

Dylan's reaction was an indication that by the end of 1971 he had had enough of people imposing their own hang-ups on him and his family or attempting to hold him responsible for the failure of the liberal forces in America to get the U.S. out of an increasingly unpopular war. After all, he had not written a protest song in eight years.

At least not until November 1971. On November 3, Dylan wrote a straightforward elegy for George Jackson, the incarcerated black activist who had recently died in prison. The following day he hurriedly assembled a small band in Blue Rock Studios to record his new song as a single. He recorded two versions, a simple acoustic version and a "big band" version. Despite also recording another original song at the session, a lightweight country song called "Wallflower," he decided to put a version of "George Jackson" on both sides of his new single, presumably to ensure that radio stations could not get away with playing an innocuous B-side as the new Dylan single.

The speculation aroused by this sincere expression of grief at the death of a man he admired was remarkable. Those eager to take potshots at him questioned his motives for releasing the single, suggesting it was an attempt to get certain sections of his audience off his back. Despite the controversy, the single did not sell discernibly better than "Watching the River Flow."

Whatever Dylan's motives behind "George Jackson," it would appear that the recording of the single was his last attempt to "test the water." Perhaps he was disappointed by the sales, perhaps by the way his motives were questioned. Whatever the reason, it would be more than a year before he would once again enter a studio to record for CBS.

He did return to a studio only thirteen days later, to work on an entire album on which he provided the majority of the music but which would never be released. The album was intended as a collaboration between Allen Ginsberg and Bob Dylan. The idea seems to have originated at a poetry reading given by Ginsberg and Peter Orlovsky at the end of October.

Allen Ginsberg: That fall in New York Peter Orlovsky and I gave a poetry reading at NYU in Greenwich Village, and improvised for an hour on the theme "Why write poetry down on paper when you have to cut down trees to make poetry books?" . . . Unbeknownst to us, Bob Dylan was in the audience, in the rear with old musician fellow-actor companion David Amram.

Dylan was intrigued by the way Orlovsky and Ginsberg had improvised poetry on the spot. He had, after all, been interested in the results achievable by improvisation since at least 1965, and the lyrics to several of his classic songs from the peak years 1965–67 featured largely improvised sections. Ginsberg had set Dylan thinking: Perhaps he had been working too hard at creating new songs; perhaps he should see what happened if the sounds and the words just flowed naturally. That night he called Ginsberg, excited by this notion.

Allen Ginsberg: He called us up at our apartment in the Lower East Side, and said he liked the reading—so he came over the same evening and picked up a guitar that was around and began improvising. He started playing the blues and I started making up lyrics, just weird things that made him start giggling at first. Then Dylan said, "Why don't we go over to the studio and do this?" A week later we got a gang of musicians together, including some of the people who worked with him on his last album, and some musicians I'd worked with in movies, and a Buddhist cellist from San Francisco, and we improvised in the studio—a bunch of lyrics and music. . . . [On "September on] Jessore Road," I provided the chord changes, the mantra is traditional and Dylan provided the music on everything else. He'd just start strumming—da da da dum, chang chang—and I'd start babbling words.

The sessions, which lasted two days, took place on November 17 and 20. Ginsberg composed "September on Jessore Road" between sessions to give Dylan something a little more ambitious to work with.

Happy Traum: It was a very loose happening—as usual when Allen organizes something. We were laughing and falling all over the floor. [The poet Gregory] Corso was running across the studio like a neurotic, accompanied by a Tibetan female singer. The others were in a "state of transition" and walked around deliriously. Soon, only Allen, Bob and I were left. Then we recorded the music.

If the results were a little loose, Ginsberg and Dylan seemed happy enough with the sessions. Happy Traum fails to mention that his brother, Artie, David Amram and John Sholle all contributed, as did Peter Orlovsky. Pleased at the success of the idea, Ginsberg appeared with assorted friends (including Dylan) a couple of days after the final session, on a local half-hour public-television program called "Freetime" and performed much of the material they had recorded. Unfortunately, when Ginsberg attempted to get the album he had recorded with Dylan released, he found few interested parties. An entire album of improvised poetry, however distinguished the musical accompanists, was not considered a likely money-maker. Another major problem was some of the language used on the record, which was thought to lean toward the obscene, particularly "Jimmy Berman," Ginsberg's homosexual paean to a newsboy. Though John Lennon expressed an interest in releasing the album through Apple Records, as with most projects that involved his label it came to naught and it would be 1983 before even three songs from the sessions were finally officially released on a double-album compilation entitled *First Blues*. Dylan, though, continued to encourage Ginsberg to develop such musical and lyrical experiments, visiting him in January 1972 to hear several compositions and volunteering to appear on any further sessions that Ginsberg arranged.
    Happy Traum's involvement in the Dylan/Ginsberg sessions was not his first collaboration with Dylan that fall. In October, Dylan had asked him to help

rerecord a few of his old songs for a greatest hits compilation CBS had planned for that Christmas, lacking as it did any new Dylan product. The songs he had in mind were from *The Basement Tapes*, though he had largely rewritten "You Ain't Going Nowhere," and in such a way that the new version seemed to be a dig at Roger McGuinn, whose Byrds had had a hit with the song back in 1968. According to Traum, "Afterwards he told me that he felt stimulated to prove himself again."

Happy Traum: He knew that they had songs chosen out for this double album and there were some songs that he didn't agree with their choice. He felt there were some songs that he had written that had become hits of sorts for other people that he didn't actually perform himself and he wanted to fit those on the record as well. . . . So we just went in one afternoon and did it, it was just the two of us and the engineer and it was very simple. We cut about five songs and chose three on the spot and mixed them on the spot in the space of an afternoon. . . . Sometimes I wasn't even sure if it was a final take until we would just finish and Bob would say, "OK, let's go and mix it."

Despite his sporadic studio activities, there can be no doubt what was Dylan's most publicized activity of 1971—his first public appearance since the Isle of Wight. George Harrison organized two benefit concerts for Bangladesh, which was threatened by both civil war and drought; the concerts taking place on August 1, 1971, at Madison Square Garden. Both Harrison and Ringo Starr were scheduled to appear along with such luminaries as Eric Clapton and Ravi Shankar. Rumors soon began to circulate that at least one more Beatle would also turn up, and even that Dylan was considering appearing. Nothing was definitely confirmed as August 1 came around and, though Dylan had turned up for the soundcheck, even Harrison was not sure he would be there when the crunch came.

George Harrison: Right up to the moment he stepped on stage I wasn't sure if he was going to come on. So it was kind of nerve-racking. I had a little list on my guitar and I had a point after "Here Comes the Sun"—it just said, "Bob," with a question mark. So it got to that point, I turned around to see if Bob was there, to see if he was going to come on. Because the night before when we went to Madison Square Garden [to soundcheck] he freaked out, he saw all these cameras and microphones and this huge place. He was saying, "Hey, man, this isn't my scene, I can't make this." . . . I was just tired of trying to organize the whole thing, and he was saying, "Got to get back to Long Island, got a lot of business." So on stage I just looked around to see if there was any indication if Bob was going to come on or not, and he was all ready, he was so nervous, he had his harmonica on and his guitar in his hand and he was walking right on stage, like it was now or never.

The real surprise, though, was not Dylan's appearance but the songs he chose to perform. All the songs were from his early and mid-sixties albums, though he had rehearsed a version of "If Not for You." Among the five songs he performed at both the afternoon and evening shows were "A Hard Rain's a-Gonna Fall" and "Blowin' in the Wind."

Phil Spector: When he broke into "Blowin' in the Wind," it was a great surprise. We didn't expect him to do it. . . . [At the first meeting with Harrison,] George said to Bob, "Do you think you could sing. . . . 'Blowin' in the Wind'? The audience would just love it." . . . And Bob looked at him: "You interested in 'Blowin' in the Wind'? . . . Are you gonna sing 'I Want to Hold Your Hand'?"

The response to Dylan's set was tumultuous, and even the press responded enthusiastically, particularly delighted that he was singing in his good old nasal style and had abandoned the syrupy *Nashville Skyline* voice. In fact, in Dylan's evening set, which made up side five of the three-album boxed set of the shows, his singing sounds thin and pinched, as if he did indeed have some kind of adenoidal complaint. But the concerts kept him aware of public demand for his return to the stage and he obviously enjoyed the response, commenting later, "That was a good feeling, being onstage there."

The two concerts for Bangladesh were Dylan's only live appearances in 1971, though he appeared after midnight at the Band's New Year's Eve 1971–72 show at the Academy of Music in New York, where he performed four songs with them (three of which were postaccident compositions), as if hinting that 1972 might be the year he resumed regular live appearances.

In fact, despite Dylan's guest appearance with the Band, 1972 would be the second great lost year of his career. Until the fall of the year, he kept an exceptionally low profile. If he had been looking for the pressures in New York to ease, then the considerable reduction in Weberman's activities only partially helped. Dylan was still looking to get out of New York. Indeed, part of the reason he had such a low public profile in 1972 was that he spent so little time there.

Between January and June 1972 there is no evidence that he was in New York at all. Comments by Dylan in 1985 indicate that he was far, far away from the East Coast, on the arid plains of Arizona, where he owned a ranch. According to Dylan, it was here that he wrote one of his most enduring songs, "Forever Young," for his young son, Jacob, born the previous year. Yet if he thought he had managed to get away from it all in Arizona he was mistaken, for whenever he turned on the radio he was reminded of his songs, not by any of his own tunes the stations might be playing, but by a Neil Young song called "Heart of Gold," which was riding high on the charts that year.

Bob Dylan: I was living in Phoenix, Arizona, and the big song at the time was "Heart of Gold." I used to hate it when it came on the radio. I always liked Neil Young, but it bothered me every time I listened to "Heart of Gold." . . . I'd say, "Shit, that's me. If it sounds like me, it should as well be me." There I was, stuck on the desert someplace, having to cool it out for a while. New York was a heavy place. Woodstock was worse, people living in trees outside my house, fans trying to batter down my door, cars following me up dark mountain roads. I needed to lay back for a while, forget about things, myself included, and I'd get so far away and turn on the radio and there I am, but it's not me. [1985]

Neil Young's song haunted the airwaves through February, March and April. By May, Dylan was coming up for air, and was sighted in Los Angeles attending a Joe Cocker recording session. He was ready to return to New York, albeit reluctantly. After these months of crashing silence he restricted his "public" appearances that summer to nonrecording activities like attending Mick Jagger's twenty-ninth birthday celebration and shows by Elvis Presley and the Grateful Dead, and turning up in Toronto in July for the Mariposa Festival, to enjoy sets by David Bromberg, Gordon Lightfoot and Bukka White. He apparently considered performing himself, but the organizers feared that there would be bedlam if he did, and dissuaded him. However, he made a brief guest appearance at the beginning of September, when he appeared at the Bitter End in New York to see John Prine perform.

John Prine: I gave Dylan one of the first pressings of [my first] record. Two weeks later I played my first gig ever outside of Chicago. I was playing with David Bromberg and Steve Burgh and Goodman, but I needed a harmonica player. I asked if there was anyone around. Now, this is only my second night, and Dylan comes up. He had brought a harmonica and learned the words to all the choruses of my songs. I introduced Dylan and about two people were clapping. No one believed it. They thought Dylan was either dead or on Mount Fuji.

Dylan had already recorded (at the "George Jackson" session) one of the songs he accompanied Prine on that night, "Donald and Lydia." Prine was considered part of that early seventies tribe, the New Dylans. Like Loudon

Wainwright III, he was foolishly marketed under this banner. The following year a new talent from New Jersey, Bruce Springsteen, would be the last of this breed of New Dylans, and would go on to become as famous as Dylan himself.

During the latter months of 1972, Dylan oversaw the completion of his second book. *Tarantula* had finally been officially sanctioned for release in November 1970, though it drew few favorable reviews. He now planned to collect all his lyrics and poems in a book to be entitled *Words*. At some stage, though, he decided to illustrate a few of the songs with his own line drawings, and the title became *Writings and Drawings*. The book appeared in June 1973, though the last songs to be included, with perhaps a hint of irony, were "Watching the River Flow" and "When I Paint My Masterpiece." Dylan's role in the book's production should not be underestimated and, unlike the later *Lyrics*, *Writings and Drawings* shows signs of real care and attention, as publisher Robert Gottlieb observed in 1973.

Robert Gottlieb: At the time that this came to me as a publishing project the manuscript was complete. Bob demanded, and had every right to have, complete artistic control over his book. No editorial changes were made in the text. . . . Bob was involved in all its aspects and phases. . . . I know it wasn't a rushed, overnight piece of hysteria because too many books happen that way and I can recognize the signs. There was nothing sloppy or careless or rushed or hysterical about this. It seemed to me very carefully worked, and I imagine over quite a period of time.

The disconcerting aspect of this beautiful-looking book was the air of finality that hung over it. It almost seemed as if he were saying, "Well, here it is. Don't expect any more." In hindsight it seems that perhaps he was really saying, "This is my past. I have dispensed with it, and thus cleared the decks for the future." Yet at the time of the book's release it had been nearly three years since he had issued his last official studio album, and the imminent release of the soundtrack to *Pat Garret & Billy the Kid* was not suggestive of a major creative renaissance.

When the book was opened there seemed further evidence of a lack of current inspiration, for on the inside of both front and back covers were two pages of what looked like drafts of songs, and they seemed to be contemporary with the final stages of the book's composition. If "Bowling Alley Blues" and "Field Mouse from Nebraska" were indeed representative of his current output, it was clear why there had been no Dylan album since *New Morning*. As always, though, there were hints of his playfulness and delight in illusion. At the bottom of the front cover was an interesting piece of advice—"Sing something safe"—and a question, one he needed to come to terms with: "Is it right to think about what [one] can do or is it right to think about what one has done?"

As a step in the right direction, he made guest appearances on two albums recorded at the end of September and beginning of October at Atlantic Recording Studio in New York. The more important of the two was a Doug Sahm album. Dylan sat in for two weeks of sessions, playing keyboards and guitar and even providing backing vocals on a version of his own "Wallflower" and the well-known "Blues Stay Away from Me." Though Dylan later denigrated his contribution to the album, it represented an important opportunity to play music with other quality musicians, something he had been denying himself recently.

Bob Dylan: I just went to see [Sahm]. . . . We went out to Jerry Wexler's house. . . . I don't recall why he wanted me on that album. . . . I was just playing a Telecaster guitar and he was playing all the fills anyway. [1978]

He also recorded with Steve Goodman and popped in on the sessions for Bette Midler's album that month,* as well as attending one of Loudon Wainwright's shows at Max's Kansas City in New York. Maybe his mind was once again turning to what he could do rather than what he had done.

---

* Both Goodman and Midler were Atlantic acts, as was Doug Sahm. Given Dylan's role in arranging a one-album deal with Atlantic for Barry Goldberg at the beginning of 1973 it seems likely that Dylan was considering signing with Atlantic now that his contract with CBS had expired.

19 | 1972–73: Alias What?

*P*at Garret & Billy the Kid, the Sam Peckinpah film that landed Dylan in Durango for three hellish months at the end of 1972 and into 1973, is generally considered to be a minor episode in his life. In fact, the filming proved to be the necessary jolt to get him to write again and abandon New York for new pastures.

It has always been something of a mystery how Dylan ended up in a Western by the notoriously eccentric Peckinpah. He had been out of circulation for some time—in terms of popular perception he had never really returned from the accident—and talk about him appearing in movies, prevalent in 1965–66, had long subsided. However, the writer of the screenplay for *Pat Garret & Billy the Kid*, Rudy Wurlitzer, was not only a novelist in his own right, but a friend of Dylan's. It was Wurlitzer who approached him, originally hoping to persuade him to provide the film's musical sound track.

Bob Dylan: Rudy needed a song for the script. I wasn't doing anything. Rudy sent the script, and I read it and liked it and we got together and he needed a title song. And then I saw *The Wild Bunch* and *Straw Dogs* and [*The Ballad of*] *Cable Hogue* and liked them. The best one is *Ride the High Country*. Sam's really . . . the last of a dying breed. They don't hire people like that to make movies anymore. So I wrote that song ["Billy"] real quick. [1973]

"Billy" proved once again Dylan's mastery of the ballad form. Though a conventional ballad, it manages to convey a sense of inevitability about Billy's fate, while portraying a certain heroic quality to the figure. Having written "Billy," Dylan began to consider the possibility of playing a small role in the movie, an idea already mooted to him by Wurlitzer. He was still eager to escape New York. His three-year sojourn there had been unproductive, and several weeks in Durango would allow him to savor at first hand the Mexican culture he professed to love.

Bob Dylan: I'd gotten my family out of New York, that was the important thing. There was a lot of pressure back there. [1985]

At the tail end of November he went down to Durango with his wife to meet the fabled Peckinpah and play him the songs he had written for the movie. Peckinpah was genuinely unaware of Dylan's status, and required some coaxing from Wurlitzer as well as Kris Kristofferson and James Coburn—who were playing the title roles in the film—even to approach Dylan.

James Coburn: Rudy was a friend of Bob's, and he'd written this song about Billy. . . . Sam says, "Who's Bob Dylan? Oh yeah, the kids used to listen to his stuff. I was kinda thinkin' of that guy Roger whatsisname, 'King of the Road' guy, to do it." And we all said, "What!! You gotta see Dylan." He said, "OK, bring Dylan down." And Dylan had been in hiding—meditating or something—since his motorcycle accident and he came down with his tall Indian hat and his little mustache. Very strange cat. . . . Wonderful guy. He was like quicksilver. You could never put your finger on Bobby. . . . So the night we were over at Sam's house and we were all drinking tequila and carrying on and halfway through 'tween dinner, Sam says, "OK, kid, let's see what you got. You bring your guitar with you?" They went in this little alcove. Sam had a rocking chair. Bobby sat down on a stool in front of this rocking chair. There was just the two of them in there. . . . And Bobby played three or four tunes. And Sam came out with his handkerchief in his eye, "Goddamn, kid! Who the hell is he? Who is that kid? Sign him up!" He was very moved.

If Peckinpah's meeting with Dylan convinced him that here was an ideal choice to write the film's musical sound track, Wurlitzer felt he had a tailor-made role for Dylan to play in the film, one Wurlitzer could readily expand to a role worthy of Dylan's stature. The character he had in mind was as enigmatic and elusive as Dylan himself. His name was Alias. Dylan has been responsible over the intervening years for giving the impression that Alias was an invented character who was introduced into this border wasteland simply to provide him with a role in the film.

Bob Dylan: I don't know who I played. I tried to play whoever it was in the story, but I guess it's a known fact that there was nobody in that story that was the character I played. [1974]

In fact, Alias was a real historical character, mentioned by Garrett himself in his own account of Billy's life, and the character was present right from the beginning of the project, appearing in Wurlitzer's original version of the script.

He was not only a member of Billy's gang, but he could be considered Billy's right-hand man, as hinted by his riding alongside Billy during the turkey-chase sequence. If anything, Alias's role in the film was reduced in importance after Dylan's adoption of the character. According to Wurlitzer, this was Dylan's own intention. According to Kristofferson, it was because Peckinpah's problems with the film studio meant that Dylan's role remained undefined.

Kris Kristofferson: Unfortunately, Sam was going through so much shit with MGM that he was never able to sit down and figure out what Dylan was in the movie. . . . Bob kept sayin' to me, "Well, at least you're in the script."

Certainly the stuttering character Wurlitzer had created in the original script was soon gone. Not only did Alias's stutter vanish, possibly because it required a degree of acting technique beyond Dylan's range, but he only joined Billy's gang after witnessing his escape from Lincoln. Whatever the reason for the change in the character of Alias, Dylan soon found that instead of the planned respite from troubles in New York, he had placed himself in another very difficult situation—in relation not just to Peckinpah and the film but also to his family, whom he had brought down to Durango with him.

Bob Dylan: My wife got fed up almost immediately. She'd say to me, "What the hell are we doing here?" [1985]

Peckinpah had been delighted with Dylan's songs for the movie and had offered him a role in the film without really being aware of who he was, and what he was not. He was not an actor. He was a legend. Only as shooting started did Peckinpah become aware of this status, and realize here was a spirit very different from his own.

Rudy Wurlitzer: The really interesting thing [is] what's going on between Peckinpah and Dylan. Sam is really Western, like an outlaw, looking to the wide-open spaces, and he didn't know about Dylan before. Dylan . . . brings a different point of view, especially to a Western. The part is small, but it's important in a funny sort of way. Do the two of them have any common ground to meet on?

Dylan was by no means Peckinpah's only headache. His whole relationship with MGM, the studio financing the film, was fragmenting with every day of shooting. The underlying tension affected everyone. A major disaster had wiped out two weeks of filming, and the film's producer, Gordon Carroll, soon became Peckinpah's adversary as the director fought to retain artistic control of the film.

James Coburn: Somebody dropped the main camera and for a while we had focusing problems—the left and right of the screen were fine, but the bottom wasn't in focus. We needed to reshoot when we finally got the camera fixed but the studio said no.

According to the studio, the focus problems were unimportant and few would be unhappy with the footage. Peckinpah wanted to reshoot all the problem footage. MGM was not prepared to extend the budget or shooting schedule to accommodate the necessary delay such reshooting would cause.

Gordon Dawson: Sam would tell me to set up a scene. Carroll would veto it because it wasn't authorized. Then there'd be a race to see if I could get a wrap before they could rip it out.

The conflict soon affected Peckinpah—considered an eccentric character at the best of times—and his behavior became progressively more unstable. Dylan probably felt that the role of Alias was not high on Peckinpah's list of priorities in such a situation.

Bob Dylan: That was Peckinpah's kingdom, and he was sort of a madman. He kept saying, "It's my movie, my movie." [1986]

Dylan, like his fellow actors, admired Peckinpah and naturally sided with the creative artist in his struggle with the powers that be. Peckinpah's problems confirmed in Dylan a long-held suspicion that artistic concerns were anathema to big-business interests, and helped shape his own jaundiced view of major film studios, an attitude that would later manifest itself in the way he set about releasing and distributing *Renaldo and Clara*.

Bob Dylan: I learned by working in *Pat Garrett* that there is no way you can make a really creative movie in Hollywood. . . . You have to have your own crew and your own people to make a movie your own way. [1978]

Dylan was cast adrift by Peckinpah's problems, and became even more diffident than usual when in company. The press, who had started coming down to Durango to see the elusive Dylan, who had last appeared "in public" back in 1971, found him uncommunicative. It wasn't only with journalists that he was subdued.

Kris Kristofferson: He's writing really dynamite songs but I never know where his head's at. There are times when it can really be upsetting when somebody doesn't talk. Hell, he doesn't even talk to his old lady sometimes for weeks . . . according to her.

Sara was not enjoying her time in Durango any more than her husband was, and during a Christmas break she managed to convince Dylan to fly over to England to spend a week with George and Patti Harrison. Though this break temporarily restored their spirits, there were a further four weeks of filming awaiting him on their return—along with the actual recording of a sound-track album, Dylan's first studio work in over a year.

Kris Kristofferson: He had a hell of a hard time down there, man. I admire him for sticking it out.

As Super Bowl weekend approached, Dylan arranged to fly to Mexico City, where CBS had a studio, to record the song "Billy" and some incidental music. By this point, it was not only he who wanted a respite from Durango. On the plane out of Durango were the film's two stars, its writer and assorted wives and girlfriends.

Rudy Wurlitzer: Sam knows he's losing to Dylan. He's giving a screening of [his most recent film] *The Getaway* in town tonight, but everybody wants to go to Mexico City with Dylan for his recording session because that's heavier. Sam'll be counting heads at that screening, and he also just called a six thirty rehearsal for Monday morning because he knows we won't be back till after eight. But I don't care, man. I've got to get away from here for a while.

Unfortunately, when Dylan arrived at the CBS studio in Mexico City, he discovered that for once his chaotic recording techniques were not going to work. His attempts to record a couple of songs with Mexican trumpeters did not meet with success, and his undisciplined approach to recording infuriated the other musicians.

Kris Kristofferson: I flew my band down figuring they would love to pick with Bob Dylan. Because of the Mexican musicians' union, they had to have one Mexican musician for every American musician on the session. Bob doesn't speak Spanish so I asked him if he wanted me to talk to the trumpet players. I figured he wanted border trumpets. So I went over to talk to them and he said something real curt like, "You can do that on your own song!" That really pissed me off, so I left him alone. . . . I didn't understand what he was goin'

through. I didn't really understand how he records. My band would come up
to me and say he was barely showing them something, they would almost learn
it, and he'd move on to the next one. And they were trying to be so perfect for
Dylan! But he wanted their first impressions. He's like a certain kind of painter.
But I didn't understand that at all. I thought he was just fuckin' with my band.

None of the repeated takes of "Billy" satisfied Dylan so he began to pare the
sound down until, having dispensed with first trumpets, then drums, then organ
and electric guitar, he finally cut a take of the song accompanied by just Terry
Paul on bass—a sound he would later adopt for much of *Blood on the Tracks*.
At four in the morning he finally concluded the session and prepared to go back
to the hotel for some sleep. Apart from the final take of "Billy" (later issued as
"Billy 4") and a brief instrumental called "Billy Surrenders," thirty seconds of
which was used in the movie, there were no usable takes from the all-night
session. Even the other vocal track, "Goodbye Holly," ended up on the cutting-
room floor. He would have to record most of the sound track in California at
the end of shooting.

The prospect of even more work on the film cannot have pleased Dylan,
though he seems to have responded without vociferous complaint or wild tantrums. However, his delight in the little games he had played in his medicine
days once again came to the fore.

Kris Kristofferson: This one scene, Sam wanted him to come riding up to me,
and as usual, it wasn't in the script. So they put Bobby on a horse and told him
what they wanted. Now it's hard for Bobby to hit his marks in a scene with his
own feet 'cause he doesn't think like that. But he's supposed to come through
these sheep to where I'm standin', and old Sam says, "OK, Bobby, you just come
straight by the camera here." Well, Bobby went into a gallop, man, scaring
sheep, horses, cameramen and everybody. And I was laughin' so hard I was in
tears. So was Sam. And old Sam says, "No, Bobby, I really didn't mean that."
The strange thing is, I don't know whether Bobby did that on purpose or not.

The disappointing results from the Mexico City recording session required a
rethink regarding the film's musical sound track. Perhaps the intuitive nature of
Dylan's art required a little professional guidance. So Jerry Fielding, an experienced hand at scoring movies, was brought in to "supervise" Dylan's music
sound track. Sadly, Fielding considered Dylan an amateur who had written "a
lot of nonsense which is strictly for teenyboppers," an attitude that, though
probably not expressed directly to Dylan, was readily apparent. Nevertheless,
Dylan seems to have done his best to comply with Fielding's recommendations.
According to Fielding, his own idea was to have "Dylan sing a relevant verse"

of the song "Billy," as it fit the story at roughly nine separate points throughout the picture."* Dylan's other lyrical contribution to the sound track, "Goodbye Holly," had been dropped, and it was decided another song was required, this time to represent the death not of Holly but of Sheriff Baker. When Fielding heard the song Dylan had promptly provided to replace Holly's lament, he was not impressed.

Jerry Fielding: I set up two dubbing sessions, Dylan had this song ["Billy"] he'd written for which he had a limitless number of verses that he would sing in random order. . . . So I had to tape Dylan's song, because he had nothing written down, and have it transcribed. Dylan never understood what I wanted. At the same time I asked that he write at least one other piece of music because you cannot possibly hope to deal with an entire picture on the basis of that one ballad. So he finally brought to the dubbing session another piece of music— "Knock-knock-knockin' on heaven's door." Everybody loved it. It was shit. That was the end for me.

The egregious Fielding was and is in a very small minority in not recognizing "Knockin' on Heaven's Door" as one of Dylan's most evocative songs. With its plaintive gospel feel, the song made no attempt to glamorize the bloody tapestry of death that suffuses the film. It provided the film with a theme tune, just as "Billy" gave it a running narrative to counterpoint the action. It also gave Dylan a much-needed hit single.

With shooting finally completed in February, and editing of this complex and at times confused narrative due to commence immediately, Dylan and his family headed for California. His professional concern was the completion of the film sound track, further recordings for which were to take place in California at Burbank Studios; his personal concern was to ensure that one of his children, who had become ill during filming in Durango, received the best treatment. Los Angeles was as good a place as any to obtain the necessary medical supervision—and at least it wasn't New York.

The sessions at Burbank Studios went very well. Dylan was working with experienced session musicians able to adapt easily to his individual approach to recording: drummer Jim Keltner, guitarist Bruce Langhorne, Terry Paul—who was retained from Kristofferson's band—and even Roger McGuinn all lent a hand. If producer Gordon Carroll had not formed the best of working relationships with Peckinpah, he seems to have been able to deal with Dylan's temperament far better. The most complex piece of music—and perhaps the most

---

* Though the idea was adopted, it was modified so that "Billy" appeared in partial form at just four points.

successful instrumental in *Pat Garrett & Billy the Kid*—was "Final Theme," a haunting variant on "Billy," which provided the theme to Billy's death. With recorder, flute, harmonium, cellos, a three-piece ensemble of backing singers, three guitars and a rhythm section, it proved Dylan could indeed master some of the complexities of writing music for film scores.

Unfortunately, as a result of problems with the film's editing, much of the music Dylan recorded was used inappropriately and ineffectively. The final shooting script provided a story that, though Wurlitzer believed it had been "reduced to its most simplistic components," was a poignant commentary on the way two old friends confronted the demands of the New West. The film was released without several important scenes, including the opening sequence, in which Garrett is gunned down by Poe (the film was intended to be a flashback by Garrett at his death). Indeed, Poe's role was drastically cut, and the cuts altered the whole film. In the shooting script Garrett's reluctance to track down his old friend—he wanders in a convoluted, circular route around Fort Sumner knowing all along that Billy is there—eventually requires Poe to inform him where Billy can be found, in order to galvanize Garrett into providing the inevitable sacrifice. Other scenes cut include Poe's brutal beating of two old codgers in order to find out Billy's location; a vignette featuring Garrett and his wife, who informs him that she will leave him if he guns down the Kid; and an extended scene in which Peckinpah himself plays an undertaker building a child's coffin at Fort Sumner as Garrett rides in.

In the version cut by MGM after Peckinpah had produced a working version, these pivotal scenes vanished, the tempo of the film was irrevocably altered and the careful synchronizing of musical sound track to the appropriate scenes forgotten. All the leading players in the drama of making *Pat Garrett & Billy the Kid* were bitterly disappointed with the released version.

Bob Dylan: Sam himself just didn't have final control and that was the problem. I saw it in a movie house one cut away from his and I could tell that it had been chopped to pieces. Someone other than Sam had taken a knife to some valuable scenes that were in it. The music seemed to be scattered and used in every other place but the scenes in which we did it for. Except for "Heaven's Door," I can't say as though I recognized anything I'd done [as] . . . being in the place I'd done it for. [1985]

It was not only Peckinpah who became disillusioned with Hollywood because of MGM's shoddy treatment of him. Dylan now viewed major Hollywood studios as pariahs that would never be allowed to get their hands on his own film, should he ever manage to get his vision onto celluloid. As late as 1986 he expressed his bitterness at what MGM had done to his sound track when talking with Richard Marquand, the next film director he would work with.

Richard Marquand: What hurt him was that they took his music and they relaid it, the studio did, behind Peckinpah's back, so that Bob would write a piece of music for a particular sequence, and then the studio afterward, in postproduction, reedited the whole thing and put that piece of music against another sequence and just completely screwed up what had been Bob's concept of the movie in conjunction, presumably, with the director.

In its edited form, the film was not well received. Dylan's role was considered minor for a star of his renown, and he rarely looked comfortable with his dialogue—though on film he still exuded the same indefinable presence shown in *Don't Look Back*.

Kris Kristofferson: I've seen prints, and he's got a presence on him like Charlie Chaplin. He's like a wild card that none of 'em knew they had. I think they just hired him for the name and all of a sudden you see him on screen and all eyes are on him. There's something about him that's magnetic. He doesn't even have to move. He's a natural.

The sound-track album was not well received either, and in a particularly scathing review in *Rolling Stone*, Jon Landau, using a variant on Greil Marcus's famous "What is this shit?" line, adopted the headline "Merely Awful" and proceeded to accuse Dylan of actually stage-managing his decline into irrelevance. The review incensed Dylan.

Bob Dylan: Landau's . . . got his head up his ass. He wrote that article from a very inexperienced and immature position. . . . He wasn't connecting it to the film. He's into rock and roll, man, the way it was in the fifties . . . [but] Landau I had already crossed off as someone who just didn't understand. [1975]

Of course, part of Landau's and others' disappointment was because of unreasonable expectations. Landau seemed angry that the album was merely a sound track—as if it should have been anything else. Tuned in to the sort of populist myths that promised the Great Comeback, at which point the artist returned once again as Americana Personified, Landau was angry at an artist who fitted into none of his preconceived role models for rock and roll stars.

If Landau didn't recognize a stirring in Dylan's soul, the public was more perceptive. The obvious single, "Knockin' on Heaven's Door," was his first top thirty single since "Lay Lady Lay," four years earlier. It also helped boost the film's flagging receipts. Yet despite the single's obvious commerciality, it almost wasn't released. There were problems with the album that were unrelated to poor reviews. CBS seemed determined to hijack Dylan's minirenaissance. Through David Braun, his lawyer, Dylan had been negotiating the terms of a new contract with Clive Davis at CBS, having also had discussions with Warner Bros. and perhaps Atlantic Records, and was led to believe he had reached an agreement with Davis.

Clive Davis: Early in 1973 I finally did conclude negotiations for a new contract with Bob. Basically, it was limited to a commitment for two more albums, plus the *Billy the Kid* sound-track album—there was no time period involved. . . . The guarantee was about four hundred thousand dollars per album. . . . Columbia [then] backed out of the deal after I left. Since the *Billy the Kid* movie had just been released, Braun screamed that the sound-track album commitment had to be honored; they couldn't go elsewhere in so short a time. So Columbia released it at the royalty rate agreed upon during my negotiations with Braun. . . . When the single broke out of the album, and clearly showed Dylan's continued fertility, Lieberson tried to resume negotiations.

Dylan became disgusted with CBS at this point, and in sacking Clive Davis—with whom Dylan had always had a healthy working relationship—they cannot have helped convince him to continue his association with the label. (Dylan would later be a character witness on Davis's behalf during some of the legal repercussions resulting from his sacking.) He decided to look elsewhere. In fact, his rejection of CBS was in part a rejection of New York. After a couple of pleasant months in California, he was seriously considering settling on the West Coast, and when he finally resolved upon a recording label for his new album, it would be with a West Coast label he would sign. After a brief season in hell (aka Durango), he could look forward to a California summer. Finally Dylan had come to believe that Jim Morrison was right—the West was indeed the best.

20 | 1973–74: Into the Flood

In April 1973 Dylan leased a property in Malibu. Back in December 1971 he had bought a modest property on the Malibu coastline from a sportswriter. However, despite the fact that he had also bought some adjoining land, the original house needed extending if it was to accommodate the entire Dylan clan. His leasing of 21336 Pacific Coast Highway was therefore presumably a temporary measure. He certainly seemed intent on remaining in Malibu, even though he informed a reporter during the January 1974 tour that, "We're just there temporarily. It was cold in New York and we didn't want to go back there after Mexico."

Dylan was enjoying his summer in Malibu. He was hanging out with old friends such as Roger McGuinn and Barry Goldberg, and he was writing songs and making music again.

Roger McGuinn: [I'd] been hanging out a lot with Bob in Malibu, playing basketball and stuff. One day, he was sitting on my couch and we were trying to write a song together and I asked him if he had anything and he said he had one that he started but he was probably gonna use it himself and he started playing "Never Say Goodbye." He hadn't written all the verses yet, but he had the tune.

Barry Goldberg: I left a message with his service that if he ever wanted to jam to call me. He called me that same day and said he was coming over. That night he showed up ready to play and we played in my living room for eight or nine hours, everything from "Pledging My Love" by Johnny Ace to "Watching the River Flow." . . . It was so good he came back the next night.

Dylan was having fun, and his wife was equally pleased to be away from New York. Everybody seemed far more relaxed in California. However, one of the most important factors in his decision to move permanently to Malibu seems to have been Robbie Robertson and the Band's own decision to resettle there. They too had finally tired of Woodstock. Indeed, like Dylan, Robertson was currently suffering something of a creative drought, and had been since the completion of the Band's 1971 album *Cahoots*.

Robbie Robertson: For a year or two I was planning on going to Malibu; I was ready to leave Woodstock. When I went out there [Dylan and I] picked up on our talks and at this point it was more advanced, and we were coming out with a more positive attitude.

The talks were about the possibility of Dylan and the Band playing some gigs together—going back on the road. If Robertson had tired of life in upstate New York, Dylan also seemed to have a restless, hungry feeling again. In June he recorded three songs for a possible album, "Forever Young," "Never Say Good-bye" and the then-unreleased "Nobody 'Cept You." A sense of release seemed to follow from the completion of *Pat Garrett & Billy the Kid*, and it was galvanizing Dylan into seriously considering touring for the first time in nearly eight years. Robertson sounded out the other members of the Band, the only group Dylan could feel comfortable touring with, and they now joined Robertson in Malibu.

Robbie Robertson: We'd been talking about a tour for years. All of a sudden it seemed to really make sense. It was a good idea, a kind of step into the past. . . . The other guys in the band came out and we went right to work. We started rehearsing anyway so we thought we'd do the *Planet Waves* album and get back to rehearsing, and that's exactly what we did.

In the summer of 1973, Dylan found himself at the Band's new ranch studio in Malibu, Shangri-La Studios, working up a repertoire of some eighty songs for an as-yet-undefined series of dates.

Robbie Robertson: We sat down and played for four hours and ran over an incredible number of tunes. Just instantly. We would request tunes. Bob would ask us to play certain tunes of ours, and then we would do the same, then we'd think of some that we would particularly like to do.

The late summer of 1973 was a buzz of activity. Dylan had finally decided to leave CBS and duly signed a one-album deal with David Geffen's fledgling Asylum label.

Bob Dylan: It was long overdue. Just a feeling it was time to go on. . . . Suspected [CBS] were doing more talk than action. Just released 'em and that's all. Got a feeling they didn't care whether I stayed there or not. [1974]

If Dylan had tired of CBS, Geffen seemed enthusiastic, supportive of his decision to tour and on good terms with Bill Graham, the ideal promoter to arrange this "comeback" tour.

If Dylan was to go back on the road again, corporate wisdom said that he needed a new product to promote. This was certainly true in Dylan's case, as he needed to prove that his decision to tour again was part of a creative renaissance, not merely an attempt to cash in on an already burgeoning sixties nostalgia. As it happens, he was eager to produce his first album of new songs in three years, and set to work on putting together enough material to record.

Surprisingly, given Dylan's determination to leave New York, and his failure to find it conducive to songwriting after his return from Woodstock, it was to New York he flew in October to compose some new songs for the sessions, scheduled for November. He returned to California two and a half weeks later with a dozen songs he was happy with. It was almost like the old days: an album session was imminent, so dash off a few songs to put with those he had written since the last album.

On November 2, Dylan and the Band assembled in the Village Recorder Studio A in Los Angeles to begin recording the as-yet-untitled *Planet Waves*. It was the first (and last) time that he recorded a studio album with his most famous and regular backing band, though only Helm had not previously recorded with him at the December 1965/January 1966 sessions and/or the 1967 *Basement Tapes* sessions, so everyone else knew exactly what to expect. In fact, on day one Levon Helm was not in attendance. They came in that Friday just "to get set up and to get a feel for the studio," as engineer Rob Fraboni later observed, but still managed to lay down a cut of "Never Say Goodbye," a song Dylan had introduced the Band to that summer.

The sessions started in earnest on the following Monday, and the bulk of the album came very quickly and with a minimum of fuss in just three days, though "Wedding Song" was recorded the following Saturday, the first day set aside for mixing the album.

Rob Fraboni: They cut three or four things for the album on Monday. . . . Then on Tuesday they cut about four more things, and we used about three of them. We took two days off. Then they came in Friday and we cut the balance of the album that day. . . . Then we were assembling on Saturday, the next day . . . around noon, Bob said, "I've got a song I want to record later," and I said fine. He said, "I'm not ready right now. I'll tell you when." We were doing

what we were doing, and all of a sudden he came up and said, "Let's record."
So he went out into the studio, and that was "Wedding Song." . . . Usually he
wouldn't sing unless we were recording. That's the way he was. You couldn't
get him to go out and just sing, unless he was running something down with the
Band . . . [but this time] he asked, "Is the tape rolling? Why don't you just roll
it." So I did, and he started singing, and there was no way in the world that I
could have stopped him to say, "Go back to the top." It was such an intense
performance. If you listen to the record, you can hear noises from the buttons
on his jacket. But he didn't seem to care. . . . I mentioned recutting it to
eliminate the button sounds at one point, and Bob said, "Well, maybe."

Robertson, for one, was surprised how easily the album came. "It was over
before we realized we'd started."

How happy Sara Dylan was at her husband's decision to resume touring we
do not know. The new songs clearly suggested that Dylan was psychologically
preparing himself to confront his public for the first time since she picked up the
pieces after the motorcycle accident. On "Tough Mama" he again seemed to be
cavorting with his muse, and in the final verse addressing his audience, asking
them not to expect too much, because he would not be "hauling any of my
lambs through the marketplace anymore."

However, the song that came in for the most intense speculation, particularly
from those seeking to connect Dylan's art with his life, was "Wedding Song."
"Wedding Song" is the final song on *Planet Waves*. It begins with the narrator
attempting to convince his subject that he loves her "more than life itself," after
which he talks about her giving him babies and saving his life. Suddenly there
seems to be a very direct connection to Dylan's own life and his own wife. This
becomes disconcerting when, in the following verse, he tells her, "we can't
regain what went down in the flood," perhaps a suggestion that they should give
up looking for a new Eden. With the sixth verse we finally come to the crux of
the song. The singer is saying that he does not wish "to remake the world at
large," because he loves her "more than all of that." Yet why does he protest his
good intentions unless there is some doubt—in her mind at least—as to whether
he intends "to remake the world"? It is plausible to see the main theme of
"Wedding Song" as an attempt to reconcile his wife with the new Dylan ("I love
you more than ever now that the past is gone"), to try to ask her to accept his
decision to go out in the world again, because it does not mean in any way that
he loves her less or that he will not return to her and the kids very soon.

If Dylan seemed concerned to exorcise "Wedding Song" on the first take, the
most possessed vocal of the album would be reserved for the last song to be
recorded—"Dirge." He had in fact recorded this song at one of the three
sessions from which the bulk of the album came, with a simple acoustic guitar

accompaniment. However, while he, Fraboni and Robbie Robertson listened to the playbacks, he decided he wanted to rerecord the song.

Rob Fraboni: We had mixed about two or three songs. . . . Bob went out and played the piano while we were mixing. All of a sudden, he came in and said, "I'd like to try 'Dirge' on the piano." We had recorded a version with only acoustic guitar and vocal a few days earlier . . . we put up a tape and he said to Robbie, "Maybe you could play guitar on this." They did it once, Bob playing piano and singing and Robbie playing acoustic guitar. The second time was the take.

The take of "Dirge" on the album is an astonishing catharsis of years of seething resentment, seemingly directed at an ex-lover but surely one of that small body of songs in his oeuvre directed as much at his audience as at some disembodied ex-lover (along with "It Ain't Me Babe," "What Was It You Wanted" and so on). Though the imagery is not as finely honed as what he would later manage on *Blood on the Tracks*, "Dirge" came in for much praise at the time of the album's release.

The album itself seemed to pass most critics by in the euphoria of the 1974 tour. Indeed, it sold disappointingly, despite shooting to number one on the basis of advanced orders, Dylan's first number-one album in the U.S. As the tour faded from memory a few critics began to question the worth of *Planet Waves*. Surprisingly, several thought it a disappointment after the "promise" of *New Morning*, despite the patent superiority of *Planet Waves* to that motley collection of half-formed ideas. The sheer quality of the playing by the Band and Dylan's return to the use of strong melodic lines in his songs for the first time since *John Wesley Harding* were barely commented on. The directness of his lyrics again came in for most of the criticism, apparently because again they contained none of the surreal flights of imagination found on *Blonde on Blonde*.

Robbie Robertson: *Planet Waves* was as good as we could make it in the situation . . . he really didn't have a bag of songs there so it was just a last-minute thing. . . . Under those circumstances, I thought it was extraordinary. . . . But it wasn't an appropriate Bob Dylan album, that's what the problem was, and it wasn't superunusual, so it got a different kind of credit. People put so much weight on the words that it really limited that album, all those songs . . . [were] as simple as he's ever done and people just thought it wasn't a real effort.

The album was slightly delayed by Dylan's decision to change the album title at the last minute from *Ceremonies of the Horsemen* to *Planet Waves*. This meant that instead of being released as the tour began, and benefiting from the full six-week span that Dylan and the Band remained on the road, it did not come out until two weeks into the tour. This could have been a commercial disaster. If his "comeback" had been a major disappointment, the album would have bombed and Geffen would have been in financial difficulty. At least a pretour release would have enabled a healthy number of units to be shifted on the hype, before any disappointment set in.

It is difficult now to conceive of the degree of risk that Dylan was taking by touring with the Band in 1974. The tour had attracted unparalleled media interest, and demand exceeded even the most optimistic expectations. According to Graham, there were twelve million applicants for the 658,000 tickets, a phenomenal response, particularly for an artist who had not issued an album of new songs in over three years and had never had a number-one single or album in the U.S.

Bob Dylan: It wasn't a tour where a bunch of guys get together and say, "Let's go out and play." There was a great demand for that tour and it had been building up, so we went out and did it. You know we were playin' at that point three, four nights at Madison Square Garden and three, four nights at the Boston Garden but what justified that? We hadn't made any records. When we were playin' out there earlier in the era we weren't drawing crowds like that. [1989]

Dylan had committed himself to a forty-date tour in twenty-one cities, playing mostly arenas. This was very different from his original conception of hitting maybe a dozen cities, playing the larger theaters. This was testing the water by jumping in headfirst. A syndicated article by Lynn Van Matre, voicing the fears of many, was published the week he opened in Chicago:

Lynn Van Matre: Dylan will always sell no matter what he does—or doesn't—have to say, or how he says it. The memories are there, and it is the memories and the mystique that spurred millions of ticket requests on this long-awaited tour. What sort of musical [sic] Dylan takes to the stage remains to be seen and heard, but the concerts promise to be of as much interest as sociological events as musical ones. There is always something fascinating about watching a performer try to live up to his legend and emerge stronger than his mystique. There is generally something depressing about it as well. . . . Whether or not the clock of Dylan's creativity has ticked out all this time is the question.

On January 3, 1974, Dylan and the Band opened the tour at Chicago Stadium in front of 18,500 fans. Despite the fact that they were playing well away from the West and East Coasts, every major daily or weekly publication in America and Europe seemed to have sent a representative. Dylan opened the show with an unfamiliar rollicking blues, the 1963 composition "Hero Blues," which, despite having been especially rewritten for this tour, was dropped after the first two shows. At least its new lyrics announced that the singer was "walking down the highway just as fast as I can go."

The two-hour show, which featured two brief sets by the Band, one solo set by Dylan, and an hour of rousing anthems by them together, was enthusiastically received by the press, even if there were signs of road rust and the pacing of the show required a little tightening up. Dylan sounded in good voice, even if he did seem prone to shouting his way through a few songs. The acoustic set in particular was very effective. Dylan was cheered at every stop on the tour when he sang the line "Even the president of the United States sometimes must have to stand naked" during "It's Alright, Ma." As the newspapers were daily filled with reports of the Watergate scandal, clearly incriminating the president of the United States, Richard Nixon, it seemed that even Dylan's ten-year-old songs were still politically relevant.

Ironically, the hysteria and hype surrounding the tour seemed to grow as the quality of the performances diminished. After the first few shows in Chicago, Philadelphia and Toronto, Dylan's penchant for shouting his way through the bulk of the electric sets started to become more and more pronounced. Though the acoustic sets continued to have moments of greatness, they, too, often seemed unduly hurried, as if he just wanted to get them over with. Songs like "Just Like a Woman" became stripped of emotion and sounded harsh and unfeeling. It became apparent that he was pushing himself through the tour, almost willing himself to complete it. In 1978 he admitted he "hated every moment" of the tour, and in 1980 he compared the tour with Presley's fall from grace when he returned to the stage in 1969.

Bob Dylan: From the first moment I walked on stage at the opening concert, I knew that going through with the tour would be the hardest thing I had ever done. . . . The problem was that everyone had his own idea of what the tour was about. Everybody had a piece of the action. The publicity people. The promoters. I had no control over what was going on. [1978]

Bob Dylan: When [Elvis] did "That's All Right, Mama" in 1955, it was sensitivity and power. In 1969, it was just full-out power. There was nothing other than just force behind that. I've fallen into that trap, too. Take the 1974 tour. It's a very fine line you have to walk to stay in touch with something once you've created it. . . . Either it holds up for you or it doesn't. [1980]

Of course, the demand for the tour was such that it was inevitable that the concerts would be recorded for a possible live album. Even before the tour the decision to release a live album seems to have been taken. In Lynn Van Matre's article she noted, "The tour concerts are also to be recorded on the label, with a live album slated for release later in 1974." This was Dylan's first tour since the advent of bootlegging, and, as the reluctant father of the bootleg industry, he could be assured that the bootleggers would be out in force. Sure enough, fourteen bootleg albums, culled from eleven gigs, resulted from this tour. If an official album would not quell the demand from obsessive collectors, it would satiate most fans' desire for a memento.

As such, Dylan's first official live album was sure to be a big seller, and involve minimal cost. Unfortunately, all but one of the songs that constitute *Before the Flood* were from the final three shows at the huge Inglewood Forum, just outside Los Angeles. By this point he was singing with "just full-out power," as if really unable to embrace these old songs himself. At times he seemed to be rolling the words around in his mouth then spitting them out, like a wine connoisseur. This was not a successful approach. Clearly by this point he just wanted to get back to Malibu.

Yet if Dylan "hated every moment," the Band were clearly enjoying the experience somewhat more than in 1966. Indeed the rich, warm tones of Garth Hudson's keyboards and Robbie Robertson's sensitive guitar fills compensated a great deal for Dylan's overly raucous vocals.

Robbie Robertson: We enjoyed playing with him; there was no ego consciousness at all. This was a Dylan/Band tour. We got accepted very well. Ten years ago [*sic*] we were just some musicians working with Bob Dylan, but this time we were more than a backing band.

If Sara was concerned that Dylan would rekindle his taste for the road on this tour, she must have been a mightily relieved wife when she met him in Los Angeles for those final shows. Joining him for a final posttour party at the Forum Club on the evening of the fourteenth, she also accompanied him to the Beverly Wilshire Hotel for a more intimate gathering early the next morning with the members of the Band and their families. Dylan had returned to the fold. For a while.

21 | 1974–75: From Renaissance to Reformation

Dylan remains a master of illusion. Subsequent actions often belie what seems self-evident at the time. Thus Steven Goldberg, in 1970, could write in the *Saturday Review*, "There will be no more bitterness, no more intellectualization, no more explanation. There will be only Dylan's existence and the joyous songs which flow naturally from it." Goldberg mistook, as have many before and after him, Dylan pulling over at the roadside for the "finishing end," viewing him as an artist in final stasis, not temporarily at rest.

Planet Waves and the 1974 tour seemed to be some kind of return to form. Only with the release of *Blood on the Tracks*—the true unveiling of a masterpiece—would many fans recognize the lesser stature of *New Morning* and *Planet Waves*, and the lack of finesse evidenced by Dylan on the 1974 tour. To those close to him, the conclusion of the 1974 tour must have seemed like the end to a period of frenetic activity. In fact, it was only the beginning. If throughout the remainder of that winter Dylan seemed content to remain in Malibu, with spring came a reawakening of his search for new artistic frontiers.

While Rob Fraboni and Phil Ramone edited the tapes accumulated in New York, Seattle, Oakland and Los Angeles into a double album of the tour, and while David Geffen attempted to remind Dylan of his moral obligation to release the live album of the tour he had helped set up on his label, Asylum, Dylan headed for New York.

Disappointed by the sales of *Planet Waves*, which had sold something like six hundred thousand units, a fact he found hard to equate with twelve million ticket applications, Dylan was already looking to move on. Geffen, who had perceived his relationship with Dylan as being a long-standing one, stood to look ridiculous in the press if he failed even to secure the album of the tour. After considering marketing the album himself, Dylan did give *Before the Flood* to Asylum, but it now seemed he was ready to resume his association with Columbia.

In the meantime, Dylan returned to school. He had arrived in New York at the end of April and was soon seen scouting around the Village again, trying to sense what scene, if any, still existed. After all, even during the "amnesia" he had maintained a rapacious interest in what was happening in the music scene; he was particularly interested in the singer-songwriters who had emerged from behind his own shadow. The first act he caught that spring was Buffy Sainte-Marie, who was performing at the Bottom Line. A couple of days later he ran into Phil Ochs, who was desperately trying to arrange a benefit for the recently ousted communist forces in Chile at the Felt Forum, but had so far failed to attract the sort of name required to sell out such a large venue. Dylan was the best possible answer to his prayers. After an Ochs hard sell about the plight of the Chileans, and given his currently open schedule, Dylan agreed to appear at the benefit, scheduled for three days hence.

Unfortunately, he arrived for the show well ahead of time, and passed the hours by drinking wine and chatting with old friends like Dave Van Ronk, Pete Seeger and Arlo Guthrie. By the time he took the stage for his brief fifteen-minute set he was virtually legless, and the performance remains probably the most excruciating of all his many guest appearances, challenged only by his equally drunken contribution to Levon Helm and Rick Danko's Lone Star Café appearance in February 1983.

At about the same time as his well-publicized appearance at the Friends of Chile benefit, Dylan looked up an art teacher named Norman Raeben, who had been recommended by some friends in California. Raeben proved to be the man who would teach him to "do consciously what I used to do unconsciously."

Bob Dylan: [Some friends] were talking about truth and love and beauty and all these words I had heard for years and they had 'em all defined. . . . I asked them, "Where do you come up with all those definitions?" and they told me about this teacher. I made a point to look him up the next time I was in New York, which was in the spring of 1974. And I just dropped [in] to see him one day and I wound up staying there for two months. . . . Five days a week I used to go up there and I'd just think about it the other two days of the week. I used to be up there from eight o'clock to four. That's all I did for two months. He was a painter. . . . He came to this country in 1930 and he made his living boxing. He's a big guy. And then he started making his living painting portraits, but in the thirties in France he roomed with Soutine, the painter. He knew people like

Modigliani intimately. . . . Anyway, he didn't teach you how to paint so much. He didn't teach you how to draw. He didn't teach you any of these things. He taught you [about] putting your head and your mind and your eye together—to make you get down visually something which is actual. . . . He looked into you and told you what you were. . . . My mind and my hand and my eye were not connected up. I had a lot of fantasy dreams. He doesn't respect fantasy. He respects only imagination. . . . In this class there would be people like old ladies—rich old ladies from Florida—standing next to an off-duty policeman standing next to a bus driver, a lawyer. Just all kinds. Some art student who had been kicked out of every art university. Young girls who worshiped him. . . . Needless to say, it changed me. I went home after that and my wife never did understand me ever since that day. That's when our marriage started breaking up. She never knew what I was talking about, what I was thinking about, and I couldn't possibly explain it. [1978]

Though Norman Raeben had never in fact "roomed with Soutine" or known artists like Modigliani intimately, he put Dylan in touch with his creative self in a way that had been absent for at least six years. Dylan attended Raeben's classes throughout May, June and at least part of July. Raeben treated him as just another student. As an ex-student of Raeben said during a special on Dylan broadcast in 1986 on New York radio station WBAI, "Norman Raeben . . . used to call everybody an idiot because they couldn't see the nose on their face. They couldn't understand that it was a shadow and a light put together. . . . He called Dylan an idiot all the time, and Dylan stayed for about six months and took off and never said a word to any of us and just left. But he took a lot from Norman."

Dylan talked at great length about his time with Raeben in 1978, after his divorce from Sara and the failure of *Renaldo and Clara*, a film that used many of the ideas he learned from Raeben. He recognized his time with Raeben as a turning point in his career.

Bob Dylan: It locked me into the present time more than anything else I ever did. . . . I was constantly being intermingled with myself, and all the different selves that were in there, until this one left, then that one left, and I finally got down to the one that I was familiar with. [1978]

At this point he began writing songs that would make up the *Blood on the Tracks* album. Throughout the summer he applied the techniques he had learned from Raeben, which were primarily intended for use in painting, to writing new songs. The results were truly remarkable.

Bob Dylan: [Norman Raeben] taught me how to see . . . in a way that allowed me to do consciously what I unconsciously felt. And I didn't know how to pull it off. I wasn't sure it could be done in songs because I'd never written a song like that. But when I started doing it, the first album I made was *Blood on the Tracks*. Everybody agrees that that was pretty different, and what's different about it is there's a code in the lyrics and also there's no sense of time. [1978]

Dylan has generally avoided talking about his songs, except in essentially abstract terms. Yet the songs he was now writing were so strange, so unlike anything he had done before, that he was required to analyze the process that was taking place. Talking about the songs he released on *Blood on the Tracks*, he has repeatedly referred to the way that he dealt with the nature of time on that album. It seems as if he were trying to encapsulate past, present and future into each audio painting. "Tangled Up in Blue" in particular would take an entire full-length movie to disentangle visually, and even then the results would be unsatisfactory when compared with the five-minute song.

Bob Dylan: "Tangled Up in Blue" . . . was another one of those things where I was trying to do something that I didn't think had ever been done before. In terms of trying to tell a story and be a present character in it without being some kind of fake, sappy attempted tearjerker. I was trying to be somebody in the present time while conjuring up a lot of past images. I was trying to do it in a conscious way. I used to be able to do it in an unconscious way, but I just wasn't into it that way anymore. . . . See, what I was trying to do had nothing to do with the characters or what was going on. I was trying to do something that I don't know if I was prepared to do. I wanted to defy time, so that the story took place in the present and the past at the same time. When you look at a painting, you can see any part of it or see all of it together. I wanted that song to be like a painting. [1985]

But the power of the *Blood on the Tracks* songs was not merely the result of the new techniques he had developed under Raeben's tutoring, but of the pain and sorrow, passion and bitterness he was feeling, which he so faithfully communicated in his new lyrics and the performances in the studio.

Dylan's marriage was in trouble and it is this which remains the underlying concern of *Blood on the Tracks*.

When *Blood on the Tracks* was released in January 1975, Dylan found he was once again the subject of intense speculation, particularly about the state of his marriage. He responded predictably by denying any notion that the songs on the album were *about* him and any problems he might or might not be having with his wife. Such defensiveness, while wholly understandable, was nothing more than a classic Dylan smoke screen.

Bob Dylan: A lot of people thought . . . that album, *Blood on the Tracks*, pertained to me. . . . [1985]

Bob Dylan: "You're a Big Girl Now," well, I read this was supposed to be about my wife. . . . I don't write confessional songs. [1985]

But he could not escape such speculation once he committed himself to making such a public declaration of the pain the separation from his wife was causing him. He told Mary Travers in March 1975 that he found it hard to understand how people could enjoy hearing that type of pain. The overwhelming specter of his loss hangs over the album, however metaphorically or literally he dealt with it in specific songs. On one of the songs that did not make the album, entitled "Call Letter Blues," (now released on The Bootleg Series vols. 1–3) the children are crying for their mother and the narrator has to explain that their mother has gone on a trip. This is too close to real life for the listener to ignore the biographical connection.

Of course, the sophistication of *Blood on the Tracks* is markedly superior to the juvenile angst he had displayed on *Another Side*, his last "confessional" album, recorded ten years before. *Blood on the Tracks* is the album of a mature man coming to terms with his life. It is an album haunted by recollections— "ancient footsteps are everywhere." When he later described "Tangled Up in Blue" as "a song it took me ten years to live and two years to write," he is perhaps suggesting not only that it deals with a quest for a woman, but also that it was an attempt to come to terms with all the water that had passed under the bridge in the sixties. For the first time he was confronting that decade as a survivor, reminiscing about a time when there was "revolution in the air," and yet suggesting that then, as now, his concerns lay elsewhere. And indeed at the end of the song there can be no doubt he is a survivor, "still on the road," just as at the end of the album, though life may be sad, it may even be "a bust," "all ya can do is do what you must."

The choice of "Buckets of Rain" as the final track on the album seems to hint of reconciliation, or a desire for reconciliation. If the album had ended with "Up to Me," though "Up to Me" may be a superior song, and though it would have been a most poignant conclusion to an album haunted by the past, the tone would have been very different. Dylan clearly did not want the album to end with that final verse followed by his sorrowful harmonica refrain: "And if we never meet again, baby, remember me. . . ."

Of course, there is an air of self-delusion about many of the songs on *Blood on the Tracks*. The male narrator on "Idiot Wind" and "If You See Her, Say Hello" comes across as the wronged party. Hints of conciliation are offered with magnanimity. The central male figures in "Tangled Up in Blue" and "Lily, Rosemary and the Jack of Hearts" are of heroic proportions. The Jack of Hearts is a figure who wins hearts readily and whose outlaw life-style embodies freedom from responsibility. After Rosemary kills Big Jim to save the Jack of Hearts, he leaves behind the consequences of these events, free to rob and roam. The narrator in "Tangled Up in Blue," though less cavalier, is no less heroic, devoting his life to some form of romantic quest, ever "keepin' on," ever searching.

The reality is less palatable. Dylan had come to New York in April 1974, without his wife. How long he had originally intended to stay there is not known. However, he appears to have stayed for three solid months, regularly attending Raeben's classes, all the time separated from Sara. Inevitably this led to press speculation. A syndicated report in July suggested he had been dating Lorey Sebastian, John Sebastian's ex-wife, though she quickly refuted such allegations. However, he was certainly spending a lot of his time with Ellen Bernstein, a CBS A&R executive, and according to Joel Bernstein she was the subject of at least one song on *Blood on the Tracks*, "You're Gonna Make Me Lonesome When You Go." Though Dylan hints at the infidelity and promiscuity of the woman or women who populate the songs on *Blood on the Tracks* (writing in the original version of "If You See Her, Say Hello,": "If you're making love to her . . ."), it would seem his own personal infidelity was the major source of strife in his relations with his wife at this point.

Complications compounded when Dylan returned to the record label Ellen Bernstein worked for, signing again with CBS on August 2, 1974, at the Century Plaza Hotel in Los Angeles. After the commercial success of "Knockin' on Heaven's Door," the huge demand for the 1974 tour and the number-one album *Planet Waves*, CBS seemed to have belatedly realized its mistake in letting Dylan go. Negotiations had begun again early in spring and at one point it seemed that CBS might even secure the live album of the 1974 tour. Though David Geffen finally secured the rights for that album, Dylan had clearly decided that, having increased the demand for his own product, he could now benefit from the sort of commercial muscle only a company the size of CBS could offer.

He may also have been eager to ensure that CBS issued no more product like *Dylan*, its November 1973 "revenge" album, composed wholly of covers recorded by him as warm-ups at the *Self Portrait* and *New Morning* sessions. Ironically, CBS may have decided to release that album rather than more obvious (and aesthetically satisfying) unreleased recordings such as the legendary Albert Hall 1966 show because it felt that a large number of potential buyers would already own the bootleg version of the latter. Of more interest now was a new product. After all, Dylan was very eager to record his new songs.

Bob Dylan: I had a few weeks in the summer when I wrote the songs for *Blood on the Tracks* and then I recorded them. [1985]

When he returned to Los Angeles in August 1974 he had just come from a vacation with his children in Minnesota, where he had spent some time on his farm with relatives and old friends. While in Minneapolis he played Stephen Stills and Tim Drummond at least half a dozen of his new songs and sounded out their opinions. His jam session at the St. Paul Hilton Hotel was the first evidence that he had enough songs to record a new album and, according to Tim Drummond, the new songs were of a very high quality.

Tim Drummond: Dylan's got an album. It's great . . . it's gutsy, bluesy, so authentic. I heard eight or nine new songs and it's the first time I've sat in a room and liked everything I heard.

Though Dylan had returned to Los Angeles in August, he was not looking to stay around. He soon returned to New York, making plans to record his second studio album in a year. After three years without really writing songs, they seemed to be pouring out of him again. As he considered whom to enlist to help him record them, Dylan thought of some of the musicians who had helped him construct his mid-sixties masterpieces. His first selection for a possible guitarist was Michael Bloomfield. He had not seen Bloomfield since the Woody Guthrie Memorial Concert in January 1968. However, he decided to go over to Bloomfield's and play him his new songs, just as back in June 1965 he had brought Bloomfield up to Woodstock so he could teach him "Like a Rolling Stone." This time the results were less successful. Dylan seemed wound up and overly tense. Bloomfield was made to feel somewhat uncomfortable.

Michael Bloomfield: He came over and there was a whole lot of secrecy involved, there couldn't be anybody in the house. I wanted to tape the songs so I could learn them so I wouldn't fuck 'em up at the sessions . . . and he had this horrible look on his face like I was trying to put out a bootleg album or something. . . . He started playing the goddamn songs from *Blood on the Tracks* and I couldn't play, I couldn't follow them. . . . There was this frozen guy there. It was very disconcerting. . . . He took out his guitar, he tuned to open D tuning and he started playing the songs nonstop! And he just played them all and I just sort of picked along with it. . . . He was singing the whole thing and

I was saying, "No, man, don't sing the whole thing, just sing one chorus and if it's not gonna change let me write it down so I can play with you." And he didn't. He just kept on playing. He just did one after another and I got lost. They all began to sound the same to me, they were all in the same key, they were all long. It was one of the strangest experiences of my life. . . . He was sort of pissed that I didn't pick it up. . . . I just felt this big wall, this enormous barrier that was so tangible that there was no way you could say, "Hey, man, how are you? You getting much pussy? Drinking a lot still? How are your kids?"

As usual, Dylan's approach to recording proved disconcerting to many musicians, even those who knew his working practices. He decided not to use Bloomfield, though what alternatives he had in mind remained unclear. He booked CBS's A&R Studio in New York—it was the studio where he used to record in the sixties, but it was scorned by most modern recording acts—yet he appeared to have no specific backing musicians in mind. Possibly his initial intention was to record acoustically and have some embellishments overdubbed later. Yet he told John Hammond, his old mentor, who popped in on the first day of the sessions to welcome him back to the fold, that this was not the case. More likely is that all along he wanted *Blood on the Tracks* to be an understated album like *John Wesley Harding*, and therefore he intended to use minimal backing.

John Hammond: Bob said to me, "I want to lay down a whole bunch of tracks. I don't want to overdub. I want it easy and natural." And that's what the whole album's about. Bobby went right back the way he was in the early days and it works.

When he entered the studio that first September afternoon, he began recording solo while his office attempted to track down the renowned guitar and banjo player, Eric Weissberg, whom Dylan wanted to use, perhaps because he believed Weissberg would provide the type of accompaniment Happy Traum gave on the October 1971 *Greatest Hits Vol. II* session. Weissberg himself was not informed what instruments to bring along to the studio and arrived there at six in the evening no wiser as to what Dylan might have in mind. When Weissberg asked Dylan whether he wanted him to ask his band, Deliverance, to come to the studio, he said, "Sure, bring the whole band over."

When recording started, Dylan again proved difficult to follow. Just as Bloomfield had struggled to learn the new songs, so Weissberg, an equally respected musician, found Dylan's way of recording bizarre and unsatisfactory. The most disconcerting thing of all was that he appeared to be playing everything in open tuning, just as he had with Bloomfield, presumably not explaining to Weissberg what key he was tuned to, making it almost impossible to follow him.

Eric Weissberg: It was weird. You couldn't really watch his fingers 'cause he was playing in a tuning arrangement I had never seen before. If it was anybody else I would have walked out. He put us at a real disadvantage. If it hadn't been that we liked the songs and it was Bob, it would have been a drag. His talent overcomes a lot of stuff.

However, Charlie Brown, who played guitar at that first session, seemed delighted with Dylan's approach and reveled in the spontaneity of the session.

Charlie Brown: He seemed to be having a good time. His whole concept of making an album seemed to be go ahead and play it and whichever way it comes out, well, that's the way it is. It's what happens at the moment. He didn't want to do a lot of takes, and I don't blame him 'cause some of the songs are so long. We'd just watch his hands and pray we had the right changes.

The only song that definitely resulted from the first session was "Meet Me in the Morning," which featured some blistering blues guitar—one assumes courtesy of Brown. When Dylan later attempted to rerecord this song in Minneapolis the results were so patently inferior to the original version that he stuck with this recording, the only song on the album to feature Weissberg and Deliverance.

Despite attempting several other songs with Weissberg and his band, Dylan clearly felt that the session was not a great success. Though Weissberg was an original choice of his, the following day he was phoned and told that neither he nor the band would be required for the remaining sessions. Dylan seemed to have decided to revert to the more subdued sound he had originally intended, and he asked that only Deliverance bassist Tony Brown return for subsequent sessions, on which Dylan was supplemented by just bass, organ (provided by Paul Griffin) and, where appropriate, steel guitar (Buddy Cage).

Cage had been suggested by Ellen Bernstein, who turned up at the sessions. His country-tinged guitar playing on the New Riders of the Purple Sage's version of "You Angel You" had particularly impressed Dylan. Bernstein was delighted at the restrained sound of the album.

Joel Bernstein: As it happened, I knew Ellen Bernstein—no relation—who was the Columbia A&R representative, very intelligent, smart woman, and she was thrilled that Bob had recorded the album acoustic. . . . She was shocked when she heard that Bob's brother had said he should rerecord

it all with a band. She thought it was a bad idea, but of course he did
recut it.

Dylan completed *Blood on the Tracks* in three September sessions, and
CBS initially planned to issue it before Christmas 1974, making it his third
album of 1974. However, when Dylan heard a test pressing, he decided he
wanted to rerecord some of the tracks. Returning to Minneapolis for Christmas, he played the album to his brother, David, who suggested he recut some
songs in Minneapolis with some local musicians. David had good contacts
among the Minneapolis music community and soon assembled a motley ensemble of local talent. Over two sessions, on December 27 and 30, Dylan
proceeded to recut six of the songs that had been recorded in New York,
completing the album for February release.

Unfortunately, not only did Dylan rerecord the songs, he also rewrote
them. The Minneapolis versions of "Idiot Wind," "Tangled Up in Blue" and
"If You See Her, Say Hello" all featured different lyrics. In the case of "Idiot
Wind," only the first verse remained largely intact, and the new version was
less personal, more ambiguous. Though the Minneapolis version may have
had more sound, it had less passion. The understated delivery of the New
York version had seemed actually to add to the venom of the words. "If You
See Her, Say Hello" had only minor rewrites but one change—"If you're
making love to her" becoming "If you get close to her"—was a step back from
the intimacy and hint of real hurt in the original. The worst new version was
"You're a Big Girl Now," though in this case it was not because he rewrote
the song, it was just the considerable dilution of the sense of pain the New
York version betrayed. The naked sorrow of the original take was now masked
in a swirl of sound.

Though the cuts of "Lily, Rosemary and the Jack of Hearts" and "Tangled
Up in Blue" from Minneapolis probably have the edge on the New York takes,
it is difficult not to conclude that Dylan "copped out" by issuing the new
versions of the songs, compromising his art to tone down his previously naked
pain; that, three months after the original sessions, he decided he had laid
himself a little too much on the line on the original recordings.

Despite, or maybe because of, his decision to tamper with the original album
(which was rapidly bootlegged), *Blood on the Tracks* was greeted by press and
fans alike as the album they had been waiting seven years for. Though there
were a couple of dissenting voices, the majority of the U.K. and U.S. music
press loved the record. Jonathan Cott in *Rolling Stone* spent two pages on his
view of Dylan "standing naked." Michael Gray, in the English monthly *Let It
Rock*, wrote a, for him, surprisingly perceptive review that attempted to come to
terms with the historic importance of the album:

Michael Gray: I don't know how, but some adjustment in our consciousness must now follow from the fact that it is Bob Dylan who has produced, in *Blood on the Tracks*, the most strikingly intelligent album of the seventies. That seems to me to change everything. It transforms our perception of Dylan—no longer the major artist of the sixties whose decline from the end of that decade froze seminal work like *Blonde on Blonde* into a historic religious object. . . . Instead Dylan has legitimized his claim to a creative prowess as vital now as then—a power not, after all, bounded by the one decade he so much affected.

The fans seemed to agree. *Blood on the Tracks* became Dylan's second consecutive studio album to reach number one in the United States. The issue Gray raised in his review would become a central one in the succeeding years—whether *Blood on the Tracks* did indeed legitimize "his claim to a creative prowess as vital now as then." *Blood on the Tracks* is the central point of Dylan's career. With this album Dylan moved the posts. Instead of having to stand against *Blonde on Blonde*, as had all the albums from *John Wesley Harding* to *Planet Waves*, his subsequent albums have been up against *Blood on the Tracks*. The renaissance also, of course, allowed critics to talk about a new decline, as he was bound to "let them down" again.

But *Blood on the Tracks* is more than just an affirmation of his genius. For here Dylan had released an album at least the equal of his masterpieces from the mid-sixties. No other artist in white rock and roll can be said to have done that. When individuals or bands hit their stride and begin producing their "classic" albums, it becomes a self-fulfilling prophecy that they had better exploit the streak of genius while they can because they will never recapture it. The Rolling Stones would never top the four albums from *Beggars Banquet* through *Exile on Main Street;* neither Lennon nor McCartney would come close to the quality of *Revolver, The White Album* or *Abbey Road;* David Bowie would never match his early seventies trilogy; Bruce Springsteen would never again reach the heights of *Born to Run* and *Darkness on the Edge of Town.* And so on.

Only Dylan, whose mid-sixties oeuvre was itself more daunting than any of the above, succeeded in producing an album that demonstrated his genius nearly ten years after it was thought to be gone. And he did it by reinventing his whole approach to language. Gone were the surrealistic turns of phrase on *Blonde on Blonde,* gone was the swirl of sound that surrounded those mystical words. In their place was a uniformity of mood, coherence of sound, and an unmistakable maturity to the voice—as if he had had to make *Nashville Skyline, Self Portrait* and *New Morning* just so that he could assimilate those aspects of his voice into a stronger whole. He had never sung better.

Then, hard on the heels of the critical and commercial acceptance of *Blood on the Tracks*, Dylan decided to release *The Basement Tapes*. It was the ideal time to confront those songs from happier times. After *Blood on the Tracks*, no sensible critic could write the review that undoubtedly would have been written six months earlier, that *The Basement Tapes* was a final reminder of Dylan's lost genius. It also provided further proof that he lost none of his creative drive when he fell off that damned bike!

It was, in fact, Robbie Robertson rather than Dylan who was the prime mover in the project. Indeed, there were suggestions in the press that the album was being released to shore up the Band's depleted funds, which had fallen to a low after two years of relative inactivity and their commercial decline following *Cahoots*. It was Robertson who compiled the songs for the double album, which included eight songs that the Band had recorded in that famous basement and that they had originally intended for their first album. All these songs were subsequently replaced by superior material on *Music from Big Pink*, which may explain why, in subsequent conversation, Robertson seemed slightly defensive about the motives for releasing this album.

Robbie Robertson: It wasn't put out to combat anything. All of a sudden it seemed like a good idea. . . . It just popped up one day. We thought we'd see what we had. I started going through the stuff and sorting it out, trying to make it stand up for a record that wasn't recorded professionally. I also tried to include some things that people haven't heard before, if possible. . . . I just wanted to document a period rather than let them rot away on the shelves somewhere. It was an unusual time which caused all those songs to be written and it was better it be put on disk in some way than be lost in an attic.

In fact, the album that Robertson compiled from these tapes was a poor document of those heady days in Woodstock. Whatever his reasons for conjoining the Band material with the Dylan material, they do not mesh comfortably together. This is hardly surprising, given that the Band songs were recorded after Levon Helm rejoined the Band at the end of the summer, and so were not really the product of the same sessions as the work with Dylan. Second, though undoubtedly interesting, the Band material had not been released because the recordings for *Music from Big Pink* were generally superior. The Dylan material was unreleased for different reasons, unrelated to the merits of the songs, many of which stand alongside anything the man has done in thirty years of music-making.

Robertson also betrayed poor judgment in his selections. Though he dug up the lovely "Goin' to Acapulco," never previously bootlegged, he chose to leave off "Sign on the Cross," "I'm Not There (1956)," "I Shall Be Released," "Quinn the Eskimo" and "All You Have to Do Is Dream," songs of real inspiration. He also selected inferior versions of "Tears of Rage" and "Too Much of Nothing," both songs available in superior form on the widely boot-legged fourteen-song Dwarf Music acetate of *Basement Tapes* recordings. Though it shows commendable modesty on Robertson's part to omit his beautiful solos on "I Shall Be Released," "All You Have to Do Is Dream" and the alternate "Tears of Rage," the results were a real disservice to Dylan. The omissions preclude any real appreciation of the full scale of his songwriting triumphs that summer.

The final stages of the album's release seemed to have occurred without Dylan's input. In April 1975, when talking to Mary Travers on her West Coast radio show, he told her that the basement tapes were going to be released "in their entirety." By the time the finished product reached the presses, he was in France.

Though there seems to have been some form of reconciliation between Dylan and Sara that winter, he made the trip to France alone. Sara had been very visibly in his company at a show in San Francisco in March: She was photographed with him backstage at the SNACK (Students Need Athletic and Cultural Kicks) benefit in Golden Gate Park, prior to his half-hour appearance with Neil Young and assorted members of the Band in a communal performance of personal favorites for a huge fifty-thousand-plus crowd. The informality of the performance, with Dylan sharing vocal duties with Neil Young, Levon Helm and Rick Danko, and the atmosphere of the event—designed to raise funds to make up a cut in the schools' leisure and sports budget—would be closely mirrored by the later Rolling Thunder Revue.

Despite Sara's public return to Dylan's side, all was clearly not well. She had apparently been due to accompany him to France that April, but did not. While in France he stayed in regular contact with Sara, but she refrained from joining him. He evidently experienced a terrible sense of loneliness throughout his stay there. He stayed with painter David Oppenheim, who had painted the mural that graced the rear cover of later copies of *Blood on the Tracks* (the first pressing contained liner notes by American journalist Peter Hamill), and he seems to have continued to compensate for his loneliness with the occasional liaison.

David Oppenheim: At that time I had just built myself a house in Savoy. . . . He arrived at two in the morning. We stayed together for two months. . . . Two of us together here alone. To see this bloke completely despairing, isolated, lost—I didn't want to be like him. . . . He was having problems with his wife. She was supposed to have come with him but she hadn't arrived. He phoned her every day. . . . We lived an adventurous life. No complications. We screwed women, we drank, we ate. . . . Pathetic and superb at the same time, Dylan is a bloke who invents everything. He's the most egotistical person I know. That's what makes him an incredible person, his amazing self-confidence. . . . When I got him to understand that he was completely mad, he would grow pale in the face, and that made me feel good because I identified with the person that I thought he was in those moments of inner understanding. . . . This bloke who talked of nothing but love was very, very much on his own.

The word portrait Oppenheim paints is a harrowing one. Yet Dylan had recently enjoyed a creative peak, and it was probably this that brought out that occasionally dormant "amazing self-confidence." He was not about to abandon his muse again, whatever the cost. The one song he definitely wrote during his six-week stay in France was "One More Cup of Coffee." It came about as a result of attending a large Gypsy festival. It was Dylan's thirty-fourth birthday when he turned up at the event. Though "One More Cup of Coffee" is written from the viewpoint of someone seduced by one of the daughters of the king of the Gypsies, it was the king of the Gypsies himself who seems to have originally fascinated Dylan.

Bob Dylan: I . . . went to see the king of the Gypsies in southern France. This guy had twelve wives and a hundred children. He was in the antique business and had a junkyard, but he'd had a heart attack before I'd come to see him. All his wives and children had left. . . . After he dies they'll all come back. They smell death and they leave. [1977]

As May turned to June, he realized that the time had come to return home and face his responsibilities as a husband and an artist. As a husband he clearly needed to work at mending some of the damage caused by the events of the previous year. As an artist he needed to get back to performing. If *Blood on the Tracks* proved he could still cut it in the cold isolation of a studio, he had yet to prove that his renaissance extended to the medium he had previously been the consummate artist in—performing live. As Dylan said when he talked to Larry Sloman later in the year, it was an awareness that came upon him while musing in southern France.

Bob Dylan: I was just sitting in a field overlooking some vineyards, the sky was pink, the sun was going down, and the moon was sapphire, and I recall getting a ride into town with a man with a donkey cart and I was sitting on this donkey cart, bouncing around on the road there, and that's when it flashed on me that I was gonna go back to America and get serious and do what it is that

I do, because by that time people didn't know what it was I did. . . . Only the people that see our show know what it is that I do, the rest of the people just have to imagine it. [1975]

22 1975: From the Bottom Line to the Bitter End

On June 26, 1975, the *Basement Tapes* album was released, some eight years after the sessions that produced it. Dylan could now afford such a reminder of his so-called heyday. By this point he was back in New York. The word was on the wire.

New York once again was the center of a happening scene, though the focal point was not in the Village but in a seedy little dive on the Bowery known as CBGB. There bands such as the Ramones, Blondie and Television had been playing for almost a year, slowly establishing reputations. Television, along with New York poetess Patti Smith, had graduated to more esteemed establishments such as Max's Kansas City and the Bottom Line. In their wake followed the likes of Talking Heads, Pere Ubu and Richard Hell and the Voidoids.

If the Village was less a center for New York's new musical explosion, it still had an active club scene—Gerdes' was not the old Gerdes', but Mike Porco was still in charge. The Bitter End was now the Other End, and remained a popular venue for Dylan's contemporaries. The Bottom Line was a showcase venue for promising new acts and established artists who still sought a little contact with their audience. In August it would be the venue for ten of the most famous performances of the seventies, when Bruce Springsteen became "the main contender" with ten sets in five nights. There were lines around the block every day.

Having recharged his batteries in France, Dylan knew he had to take advantage of the momentum created by *Blood on the Tracks*. California had never really set his "creative juices-a-flowin". It was in New York that he had written all the songs that established his reputation, and it was to New York he had returned to reestablish that reputation with *Blood on the Tracks*. In the summer of 1975 he was on a scouting mission: He was looking for a new sound. Driving around the Village at the end of June, he ran across an exotic-looking violinist by the name of Scarlet Rivera. He invited her to his rehearsal studio to run through some songs. Perhaps he had a violin sound in mind for the next album.

Rivera spent the afternoon playing her electric violin along to some new songs from Dylan's pen, and he realized fairly promptly that he had found the first piece in his new jigsaw puzzle. There was a mantralike quality to the sound of Rivera's violin playing, and though she was not technically superb, there was an obvious chemistry between her and Dylan.

Scarlet Rivera: [I] played all afternoon with him on songs that I could never have possibly heard before at his studio in the Village. And he played them on guitar. I'm sure [he] consciously didn't play anything that he had recorded before so I couldn't have a head start on knowing how it sounded or how to play it. There was a little half smile after playing a few songs. . . . "One More Cup of Coffee" was one of the first songs we did that afternoon. . . . [We did] "Mozambique," "Isis." Then he moved to piano and tried some of the same songs in different keys. And so it progressed. Then by late, late afternoon we left there and he said he wanted to take me to a club to see a friend and that turned into his sitting in with Muddy Waters. . . . After that show that was my moment of acceptance fully and, having passed the final test—and part of the test is a certain chemistry, a certain recognition, a certain indefinable something was part of it—we went to [legendary blues singer] Victoria Spivey's house that very night. I think it was [in] Queens or Brooklyn. The entire Muddy Waters band went and Bob and I spent many more hours jamming, talking to her, listening to old records. He was really excited by the whole evening.

Dylan had been down to see Muddy Waters perform at the Bottom Line a few days earlier, but his surprise appearance with Scarlet Rivera on June 30 was the start of a hectic two weeks when he would be seen in Village clubs and bars almost every night, sometimes sitting in with old friends, sometimes just enjoying the show. It was the highest profile he had maintained in years. *The Village Voice* and *Rolling Stone* soon ran stories about his reemergence.

Meanwhile, Dylan was looking for other components for the sound he had in mind. Jack Elliott provided the next, a bassist by the name of Rob Stoner, who had his own band, Rockin' Robin and the Rebels. He backed Elliott on occasions, and was in the Village most nights when Dylan was hanging out. Stoner had already met Dylan back in 1971 in San Francisco while playing for the Greenbriar Boys, and they had hung out together in Los Angeles in 1973. Dylan knew his sound, and respected his knowledge of rockabilly.

Rob Stoner: I already knew him. . . . He ran into me at that Other End scene in '75 . . . he was back in New York and *Blood on the Tracks* was a success at the time. It was a very heady period for him. He was really reestablishing himself there.

Though Stoner did not audition in the way that Rivera had, he would get the call when the time came to go into the studio. Dylan sat in on performances by Bobby Neuwirth and Jack Elliott, and even went to the Bottom Line again—the Other End was a more regular choice, as it had an annex to which he and his retinue could escape if the scene became a little too heavy—to see New York's first female New Dylan: Patti Smith.

Smith was on the verge of recording her first album for Arista, perhaps the most remarkable debut album of the seventies, *Horses*. Her uninhibited performances, which combined frenetic rock and roll with long between-song raps and smatterings of her poetry, fascinated Dylan (who subsequently offered Patti a place on the Rolling Thunder Revue, though she refused to tour without her own band). Smith's shows at the Bottom Line were landmark performances— her first shows with a drummer in the band. Dylan was loose enough after seeing Patti perform to allow them to be photographed together.

Patti Smith: He started hanging out more—he liked the fact that he could be in a club and people didn't maul him to death, because there were a lot of things happening at that time. And we were all hanging out there, and it was really great 'cause we'd all get drunk and stuff and be falling around. People just started turning up in the Village. It happened very fast. Jack Elliott was around—everybody was around. Then one night, Bob started going up on stage, jamming with these people. I saw him start getting attracted to certain people, Rob Stoner, Bobby Neuwirth—it was great to see him and Bob back together, because he really brings out the worst in Dylan, which is what we usually love the best. And he was working out this Rolling Thunder thing—he was thinking about improvisation, about extending himself language-wise. In the talks that we had there was something that he admired about me that was difficult to comprehend then, but that's what we were talking about . . . when he started getting Rolling Thunder together.

Patti included two major improvisational pieces in her performances at this time—"Land" and "Birdland." She referred to them as "fields." "Land" in particular would develop each night as the feeling took Patti, the story of Johnny never being resolved. Dylan himself was working on a song that, like "Land" was a surreal travelogue driven by a slow piano riff. It was called "Isis." At this point it was, according to Jacques Levy, "almost a dirge, slow, unlike anything I'd ever heard before, slow, obviously setting you up for a long story."

If Dylan had a sound in mind, what he did not yet have was an album's worth of songs. There was "One More Cup of Coffee" from his days in France, and during his first week of club-hopping he had written a remarkable new song called "Abandoned Love," which he had premiered at the Other End in a brief guest spot during a Jack Elliott gig. However, "Abandoned Love" mined the same vein he had explored on *Blood on the Tracks* and, however brilliant he was in excavating such riches, he was not one to repeat himself. Apart from these two songs, all he had were scraps and half-formed ideas.

Fortunately, one of the individuals he met at the Other End was Jacques Levy, a songwriter then best known for his collaborations with Roger McGuinn on such songs as "Chestnut Mare," though he had also directed the risqué play *Oh! Calcutta!* Levy lived nearby and, since the subject of a possible songwriting collaboration had come up during their discussions at the Other End, Dylan went up to his loft and played him some of the fragments of songs he was working on. Virtually the first thing Levy heard was the original version of "Isis." Levy made some suggestions and suddenly Dylan started finding a thread to tie the song together.

Jacques Levy: We were just sitting, just talking . . . and then he went to the piano, sat down, and he started to play "Isis." But it was a very different style of "Isis" than you hear now. . . . So the two of us started working on that together. I started writing words, then he would say, "Well, no, how about this, what about that?" a totally cooperative venture. It was just extraordinary. . . . What happened was that we finished "Isis" that one night, up all night till the next morning. [It was] not the final version, we redid some stuff, but the basic story was there and I would write this stuff down and then type it up and we would go over the stuff. And we went down to the Other End and Bob read the lyrics to a bunch of people sitting around the bar, just read them, and everybody responded to the thing.

The way that Dylan described their initial collaboration was typically less direct, but indicates the value of Levy in their collaboration.

Bob Dylan: I had bits and pieces of some songs I was working on and I played them for him on the piano, and asked him if they meant anything to him, and he took it someplace else, and then I took it someplace else, then he went further, then I went further, and it wound up that we had this song ["Isis"] which was out there. [1975]

Dylan had discovered a companion to accompany him down a new path. If *Blood on the Tracks* had been the product of him "learning to do consciously what he used to do unconsciously," then Jacques Levy's very deliberate and conscientious approach seems to have naturally complemented his more inspirational but less disciplined way of working. Since Dylan appeared to want to write story songs again—but story songs that, though no less cinematic than "Tangled Up in Blue," advanced the story more directly and with fewer dramatic lurches in time and space—Levy was an ideal collaborator. Under Levy's influence, he even rewrote "Simple Twist of Fate" so that it was more linear in the telling of its tale (he performed this new version on a TV tribute to John Hammond in September 1975). He had never really collaborated before (in the case of songs such as "Ballad of Easy Rider" and "I'd Have You Anytime" he merely wrote a verse or a bridge for someone else). It was a new and exhilarating experience to have such measured but immediate feedback as Levy provided.

Roger McGuinn: Bob had never seen a thesaurus before, nor a rhyming dictionary. Imagine all the songs that Bob has written without a rhyming dictionary. When he saw one it blew him out. . . . He's going, "What! Think of all the time I could have saved." He didn't even know they existed.

Though Dylan and Levy now started seeing if they could repeat the "Isis" experiment on a daily basis, the next major song that they wrote together was again composed on the spur of the moment, a few days later, after a dinner they both attended given by two friends of ex–New York gangster Joey Gallo. On record the ballad "Joey" would clock in at eleven minutes.

Bob Dylan: I was leaving town and Jacques says he was going up to some place to have supper and I was invited to come if I felt like it and I was hungry so I went with him and it was up to Marty and Jerry Orbach's place and as soon as I walked in the door, Marty was talking about Joey. She was a good friend of Joey's. They were real tight. I just listened for a few hours, they were talking about this guy and I remember Joey. At that time, I wasn't involved in anything that he was involved in, but he left a certain impression on me. I never considered him a gangster. I always thought of him as some kind of hero in some kind of way. An underdog fighting against the elements. He retained a certain amount of his freedom and he went out the way he had to. But she laid all these facts out and it was like listening to a story about Billy the Kid so we went ahead and wrote that up in one night. [1975]

At this point Gallo was in the news: The paperback edition of Donald God-dard's biography of him had been published in June. Dylan, on the release of *Desire*, would come in for some considerable criticism for his song, which appeared to glorify a vicious hoodlum. Lester Bangs wrote a lengthy and de-tailed attack upon the historical veracity of the song in *Creem* magazine, under the title "Dylan's Dalliance with Mafia Chic." Dylan later defended the song as a valid re-creation of the traditional ballad form, which had often eulogized outlaws of the Old West. And in 1987 he even started performing it in concert. Along with "One More Cup of Coffee" it is the only song from *Desire* to appear in his shows in recent years.

Bob Dylan: I always grew up admiring those heroes . . . Robin Hood, Jesse James . . . those guys who kicked against oppression and had high moral stan-dards. . . . It amazes me I would write a song about Joey Gallo . . . [but] I feel that if I didn't, who would? But that's an old tradition. I think I picked that up from the folk tradition. . . . I used to sing a lot of those songs and it just kinda carried over. [1981]

Dylan was getting such a buzz from the new songs, he could not resist going out and performing them. Both "Isis" and "Joey" were premiered to a lucky few at the Other End during Bobby Neuwirth's one-week residency there. Neuwirth had been hanging out with Dylan throughout his two weeks of Village club-hopping. The more famous Bobby had even got up on stage and sung a duet with his old sidekick. However, the late nights and drunken revelries were not conducive to the writing of new songs.

Jacques Levy: What was happening was that we were going out and hanging out late at night and were getting together the next afternoon and there were lots and lots of distractions. So we said, "Let's get out of here," and suddenly it became serious that we were really going to do some serious work together, so we went out to a place out in the Hamptons. Nobody was around, and the two of us were just there for three weeks [sic] together, that summer. We had already written a couple of songs so there was a feeling of confidence that we both had that we could really do it.

In the seclusion of East Hampton, they wrote fourteen songs together in less than two weeks, including two complex travelogues, "Black Diamond Bay" and "Romance in Durango." "Durango" was the more conventional tale: an outlaw and his lover on the run, in an exotic Mexican landscape. "Black Diamond Bay" related, via a highly convoluted rhyme scheme, the destruction of a tiny island as if observed from a hotel on the island itself, before pulling back to reveal a man watching a news report about an earthquake that left behind just a Panama hat and a pair of shoes.

Also probably completed in East Hampton was the lengthy ballad that opens the *Desire* album. The song "Hurricane" took eight minutes to detail the unjust imprisonment of boxer Rubin "Hurricane" Carter back in 1967. Dylan had already visited Carter in Rahway Prison in Trenton, New Jersey, upon returning from France, and he had read Carter's autobiography, *The Sixteenth Round*.

Hurricane Carter: When I wrote the book *The Sixteenth Round*, I sent a copy to Bob Dylan, because of his prior commitment to the [civil rights] struggle. I sent a copy to him hoping that somehow I could influence him to come and see me. So I could talk to him. . . . So when he got the book and read it he came. And we sat and talked for many, many hours. And I recognized the fact that here was a brother.

Having met the man, Dylan decided that the same pen that had detailed the fates of Hattie Carroll, Emmett Till, Medgar Evers and George Jackson should turn to Carter's aid. Unfortunately, he was not really sure how to put across the story. After all, "George Jackson" had been a simple gut reaction to the death of a man he respected, and it had been twelve years since he wrote the last of his "topical" songs.

Bob Dylan: The first time I saw him, I left knowing one thing . . . I realized that the man's philosophy and my philosophy were running on the same road, and you don't meet too many people like that. . . . I took notes because I wasn't aware of all the facts, and I thought that maybe some time I could condense it all down and put it into a song. [1975]

Knowing Dylan's love of movies, Levy wisely suggested a cinematic approach, similar to that used in "Lily, Rosemary and the Jack of Hearts."

Jacques Levy: Bob wasn't sure that he could write a song . . . he was just filled with all these feelings about Hurricane. He couldn't make the first step. I think the first step was putting the song in a total storytelling mode. I don't remember whose idea it was to do that. But really, the beginning of the song is like stage directions, like what you would read in a script: "Pistol shots ring out in a barroom night. . . . Here comes the story of the Hurricane." Boom! Titles. You know, Bob loves movies, and he can write these movies that take place in eight to ten minutes yet seem as full or fuller than regular movies.

Writing "Hurricane" also gave Dylan a cause to champion. After writing his best love songs in years the previous summer, he was now writing his best story songs in nigh on a decade.

When they returned to New York, Dylan immediately set about putting together a set of musicians to record the songs that he and Levy had written. He had already attempted recording a couple of the songs with Dave Mason's band before his departure from New York, but now he decided to start afresh.

After the success of his return to Columbia's New York studios the previous September, Dylan, not surprisingly, opted to return there. He also chose to use an in-house producer, Don DeVito, though DeVito's role was more akin to engineer than producer. As ever, it was really Dylan who made the decisions at his recording sessions.

The initial concept for the album's sound was a little grandiose. Dylan had enlisted the entire eight-piece English pub-rock band Kokomo, Eric Clapton, and pop singer Yvonne Elliman, violinist Scarlet Rivera, country singer Emmylou Harris—presumably recruited on the basis of her work with the late Gram Parsons—plus assorted trumpeters, saxophonists and mandolin players. The first couple of sessions were disastrous.

Neil Hubbard: The sessions were all pretty chaotic. There were far too many musicians there—five guitarists, including me and Eric Clapton, played on the "Hurricane" set. And there was no one in overall control. No producer or anything.

Eric Clapton was having a hard time figuring out what exactly Dylan had in mind, and soon departed, though not before giving his opinion that some slimming down was in order.

Eric Clapton: He was trying to find a situation, you see, where he could make music with new people. He was just driving around picking musicians up and bringing them back to the sessions. It ended up with like twenty-four musicians in the studio all playing these incredibly incongruous instruments—accordion, violin—and it didn't really work. He was after a large sound, but the songs were so personal that he wasn't comfortable with all the people around. But anyway, we did take[s] on about twelve songs. He even wrote one on the spot all in one night. It was very hard to keep up with him. . . . I had to get out in the fresh air, 'cause it was madness in there.

Scarlet Rivera, the linchpin of the whole sound, was also having a hard time of it. They were her first-ever studio sessions and she had expected a somewhat more intimate setup.

AMPERSAND'S

SEPTEMBER/OCTOBER 1988

& ENTERTAINMENT GUIDE &

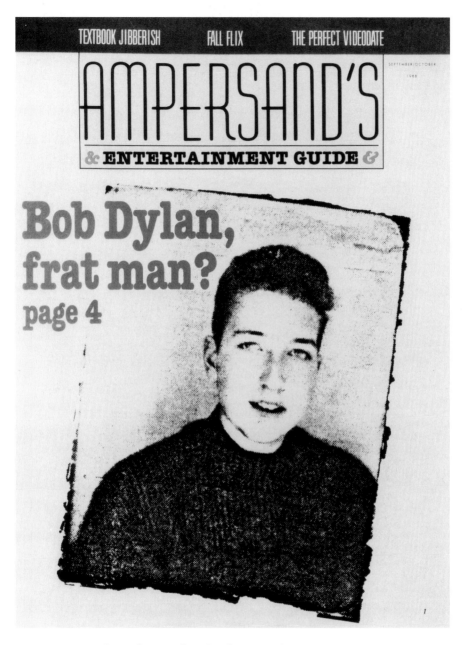

Bob Dylan, frat man?
page 4

A photo of Dylan from his fraternity days at the University of Minnesota, Fall 1959.

At the Singer's Club, London, December 22, 1962, his first trip to England. (Collections; Brian Shuel)

BELOW—*Backstage at the Town Hall, New York City, April 12, 1963, the night of his first major concert.* (Waterman/ Michael Ochs Archives)

Greenwich Village, 1963. Dylan lived there from 1961 to 1964, before fleeing to Woodstock, New York. (Pictorial Press)

Princeton University, March 1965, a stop on Dylan's final American acoustic tour. (Ken Regan/London Features)

ABOVE—*Howard Alk films Dylan at his London press conference, May 3, 1966.* (Tony Gale/Pictorial Press)

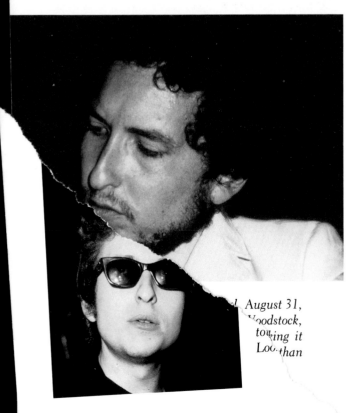

August 31,
oodstock,
touring it
Loo than

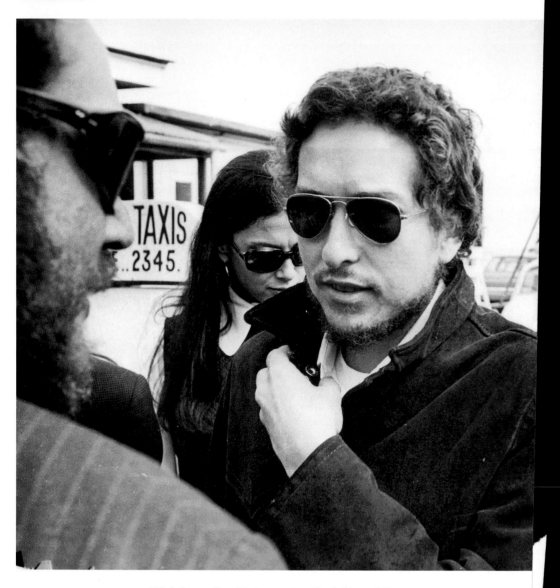

With journalist Al Aronowitz (far left) and Sara, on the Isle of Wight, August 31, 1969. (Dennis Grice)

On the set of the film Pat Garrett & Billy the Kid, *November 1972.* (Rex Features)

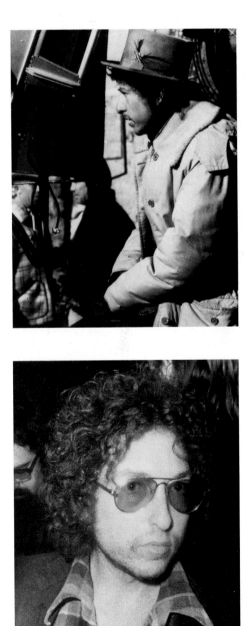

At the Bottom Line, New York, watching Little Feat perform, September 18, 1974. (Bob Gruen)

A rare photo of Dylan with Sara in public, during their reconciliation in 1975. (Rex Features)

With Joan Baez on the first Rolling
Thunder Revue, November 1975. (Bob
Gruen)

RIGHT—*Rolling Thunder Revue,
November 1975.* (Ken Regan/London
Features)

Sara Dylan leaves court, accompanied by lawyer Marvin Mitchelson, 1977. (Rex Features)

BELOW—*With Joan Baez, filming the Midnight Special TV show at Clearwater, Florida, April 22, 1976. The show never got off the ground.* (Ken Regan/London Features)

With French journalist Philippe Adler in London, June 16, 1978, on his return to Europe after nine years. (Jean-Pierre Couderc/Camera Press)

Dylan leaves court, 1977. (Rex Features)

*Onstage for the first "gospel show" at the Warfield Theatre
in San Francisco, November 1979.* (Nancy Cleveland)

LEFT—*A portrait, 1983.* (Lynn Goldsmith/Rex Features)

CENTER, LEFT—*At a dinner honoring him with the ASCAP Founders Award, March 31, 1986.* (Camera Press)

With Tom Petty at the Westwood One press conference in Los Angeles, April 10, 1986, his first meeting with the U.S. press since 1965. (London Features International)

LEFT—*Dylan outside the National Theatre, London, August 17, 1986, before beginning the filming of* Hearts of Fire. (Pictorial Press)

The death-mask look, Dylan's response to critics who had written about his unhealthy appearance, Frankfurt, September 28, 1987. (Georg Stein)

Dylan, Commandeur des Arts et des Lettres, a special award given by the French minister of culture, January 30, 1990. (Topham Picture Source)

Scarlet Rivera: They were very big sessions. It was a big surprise having worked so intimately. It was all a very big shock to me. . . .

The members of Kokomo, in particular, were unsuited to the type of approach Dylan usually adopted in the studio—the "tape it and run" method. They were used to working on songs meticulously for take after take until they got the music just the way they liked it. Spontaneity and freshness were not major factors at Kokomo sessions.

Mel Collins: Dylan . . . was pretty out of it. He came into the studio, played the songs through a couple of times and then expected everyone to provide some suitable backing material. I mean, he came up to me and this other guy who was playing trumpet—who I'd never met before—with a few ideas for one song but that was all.

DeVito and/or Dylan finally decided they needed a helping hand, a new perspective, in order to get these songs down while they still meant something to Dylan. It was to Rob Stoner, the Village perennial, that they decided to turn.

Rob Stoner: He was trying to get what became the *Desire* album together at CBS Studios on Fifty-second Street. . . . Don DeVito took me aside one night when Dylan had come down to hear some band I was backing up. I think it was Ramblin' Jack. He said, "Bob's been recording uptown. I want you to come up to the session tomorrow night and tell me what you think." . . . So next night I was up there and I was listening to it and they were doing the same songs that him and Levy had cowritten, that were gonna be the *Desire* album, but they weren't having any success. They were trying to do a superstar session thing: they had Dave Mason, they had this band Kokomo, Clapton was up there. A lot of people. But it was just too much of a hanging-out scene. In fact, they had to empty out an adjacent studio to put [on] a . . . buffet for all these overflow people—everybody was bringing their friends, "Hey, you wanna see me record with Bob Dylan?" . . . And DeVito came to me at the end of the night, when all these musicians had gone home, and asked me what I thought of it and I told him that I thought it was not a likely way to get a productive project out of Bob Dylan, that it was too crowded, it was too confusing, it was inefficient. Bob's music really is dependent on catching a moment—they're like snapshots, Polaroids. . . . The first take is gonna be better even if it's got some wrong notes or something. . . . These guys from Kokomo, I think they were the main culprits, 'cause they were really into this very slick, professional [sound] . . . it became their record because they kept doing takes so they would get their parts together and by that time Bob's bored. Bob doesn't want to do a song more than twice and I don't blame him. . . . So DeVito asked me what I would suggest. I said, "Why don't you come in with a tiny band and like nobody, no girl-friends, no wives, no nothing? Just the smallest possible band you can get—bass player, drummer and anybody else you wanna keep around."

As it happened, Kokomo already had impending commitments, and so did not attend any further sessions. Dylan, eager to adopt Stoner's suggestion, now needed a drummer. After failing to get hold of Kenneth Buttrey, a stalwart of previous Dylan sessions, he took Stoner's advice and asked him to bring his buddy Howie Wyeth along to the following night's session. With just Scarlet Rivera, Emmylou Harris, Rob Stoner and Howie Wyeth, Dylan would com-plete the album.

Bob Dylan: We tried it with a lot of different people in the studio, a lot of different types of sound, and I even had backup singers on that album for two or three days, a lot of percussion, a lot of going on. But as it got down, I got more irritated with all this sound going on and eventually just settled on bass, drums and violin. [1978]

Emmylou Harris had also been having a hard time at the sessions, not because of the big band setup, but rather because of Dylan's idiosyncratic phrasing. Reading off lyric sheets and with no opportunity for rehearsal, Em-mylou found the whole experience of recording with Dylan bewildering.

Emmylou Harris: I'd never heard the songs before and we did most of them in one or two takes. There were no tapes—we sang live. His phrasing changes a lot, but Gram did that a lot, too. Gram and I had the same feeling for phrasing, but I watched him all the time, so I did just the same thing with Dylan. I just watched his mouth and watched what he was saying. That's where all that humming comes from. You can hear me humming on some of those tracks. . . . It does take me a while to work out harmony parts and Dylan works very fast. I'm more of a perfectionist. I would have liked more time. There were times when I didn't even know I was supposed to come in and had to jump fast. But I later realized that you just don't overdub on a Dylan album. He's not that kind of artist. I asked to come and fix my parts and he said sure but I didn't have the time, and I really didn't think he'd use any of it.

By the time they had stripped down to the four-piece lineup, Emmylou had had a few days to come to terms with Dylan's unorthodox recording techniques. It was Howie Wyeth who was in at the deep end when they reconvened at Columbia Studios on July 30, 1975. The session did not start well for him.

Howie Wyeth: Emmylou and Bob had their own little table. It was like they were in a little French restaurant or something . . . the rest of us were all over here. It was like a separate scene. Bob would start a tune. He wouldn't tell us the names of the tunes. The first song we did—this is the gospel truth, man, I don't think people believe me—the first song we started to do, I had just barely met him. We started the song and I think they were recording it, we played the song and we sort of fumbled the ending. And I asked Bob—y'know, he said, "OK, we're gonna do that again"—and I said, "Bob," are we gonna end this or is it gonna fade?" And he went into such a lengthy explanation, he went on and on, that everybody got so confused, it ended up we didn't even do the song [again]. He said, "Let's not even do it." And Stoner said, "Don't ask him anything. Just play." He gave such a complicated answer. All I wanted to know was, Are we gonna stop or fade? Nobody knew what the hell he was talkin' about so he just said, "We better do something else." And we never played the song again.

If this was an inauspicious start, the remainder of the session was revelatory. Next up, they attempted "Isis," and right away Dylan and the band struck a groove. Not since the days of *Bringing It All Back Home* had he hit such a creative groove and managed to maintain it throughout an entire session.

Rob Stoner: Right away that [first] version of "Isis" was a take. Because it was a small group, there was no confusion. . . . Right after we finished "Isis," Bob came over to me and said, "Your drummer's great, it sounds great," and we all felt great because it was intimate. It had the sound that you can hear on *Desire*, just a bunch of people playing in a room with no overdubs, all live, happening right before your ears, and we could get that first-take spontaneity because we didn't have to keep going over and over things to show them to all these musicians who were faking it. . . . So we just listened to that take of "Isis," we just went back into the studio and started running through tunes, bam, bam, bam, just getting every complete take, every complete tune was a take . . . just like that. We were so hot we did "Rita Mae," which wasn't on the record, "One More Cup of Coffee," "Joey," "Mozambique," "Hurricane," "Oh, Sister," "Black Diamond Bay," we did them all that night. . . . I think we were still doing takes as late as five and six A.M. that morning, and we hung out listening to the playbacks until we had to go out to the street to move our cars at eight so they wouldn't get towed away.

Howie Wyeth: We had a lot of ESP that night. Even in "Joey" there was a place where I thought the song was ending and I drop out for a second and it wasn't the end but it worked great.

Though they had been working for less than a week in the studio, the relief was enormous. As they filed out of the session there was almost universal euphoria. Dylan and DeVito in particular had seen a great weight lifting from their shoulders as the evening progressed.

Howie Wyeth: I remember they drove me down here afterward and Bob and DeVito each had cars and they were like bumping each other, playing bumper cars, I mean I thought we were gonna die. They dropped me off about eight blocks from here. I walked back in the middle of the street 'cause I thought something was gonna fall on me. I thought those guys were gonna kill each other cause as they dropped me off they were stopped at a light and Bob was pushing DeVito on through the light. There were no cars around.

Though Stoner was equally pleased with the night's results, Emmylou Harris, from whom he hitched a ride remained less euphoric. If she had been almost hoping that the sessions might be aborted, it was now clear that Dylan had damn near recorded an entire album in one night. If a juggernaut had plowed into him while he played bumper cars, CBS now had fifty-two minutes of top-notch Dylan for his mourning fans.

Rob Stoner: She was a trooper [but] she was really bummed out at the end of that night. She was saying, "Oh, I can't believe this. Hope they don't put it out." He was so fucking loose.

The following night the euphoria had tempered a little. Dylan had spent the day in court, appearing as a character witness on behalf of ex–CBS president Clive Davis, and was understandably exhausted. Accompanying him to the studio was his wife, Sara, and her presence inspired him to attempt a take of a song he had written on his own during his time with Levy at East Hampton earlier in the month. "Sara" seemed self-evidently an honest and open paean to his wife, portrayed here as his eternal muse. However, there are doubts about the literalness of the song as certain lines seem patently untrue—such as his famous one about writing "Sad Eyed Lady of the Lowlands" in the Chelsea Hotel (it is fairly well documented that he wrote it in Nashville), having just taken some kind of cure (for what?—it would be another six months before he attempted to rid himself of his drug habits).

Ever perverse, Dylan then went on to record "Abandoned Love," a song about the rejection of an imperious woman whose ensnaring ways have haunted the singer for too long. Though rewritten and considerably less intense than at its premiere at the Other End earlier in the month, the song was hardly a tactful selection to perform before his recently reconciled spouse. Though it is a fine if decidedly loose performance, perhaps the lack of any hint of reconciliation in the song meant it was never in serious contention for inclusion on an album on which the outlaws end up imprisoned ("Hurricane"), gunned down ("Romance in Durango") or imprisoned and gunned down ("Joey"), but on which songs about women appear conciliatory ("Isis," "Sara," "Oh, Sister"). Despite the failure of the session on July 31, "Sara" completed the album—or at least it seemed so at the time.

Howie Wyeth: He was so bummed out . . . the night we played "Sara" and "Abandoned Love" and a bunch of other stuff. We thought everything sucked at that point and then Bob said, "OK, the next day we're gonna come in, we're gonna play everything and decide what makes it and what doesn't make it."

The following day Dylan, DeVito and the band all listened to playbacks of the songs recorded with both the stripped-down ensemble and the big band. "Romance in Durango" was the only big-band recording to make it to vinyl. In fact, the stripped-down band never recorded it. Apart from "Sara," the remaining songs on *Desire* were drawn from that one remarkable session on the thirtieth. *Desire* was now a reality. Dylan had recorded a follow-up, and a strong one, to *Blood on the Tracks* within seven months of concluding the sessions for that album.

With the album completed, Dylan and Sara traveled to their farm in Minnesota for a month's vacation, which they concluded by attending the marriage of his cousin, Linda Goldfine, at the Temple Israel Camp in Minneapolis. Stoner, Rivera and Wyeth had gone back to their regular gigs in the Village, expecting a check in the mail, but not a phone call from Dylan. Then, less than a week after he returned from Minneapolis, Dylan called them all. He wanted the three of them to accompany him to Chicago to perform three songs for a tribute to John Hammond that was being filmed by PBS for airing in the New Year.

Scarlet Rivera: We had less than twenty-four hours' notice. It was basically the night before that we got the call to be in Chicago the next day. . . . Our rehearsal basically took place in the dressing room, talking over the songs and what key they would be in and just mental refreshers. . . . We ran over [the new] "Simple Twist of Fate" in the dressing room.

At this point it became apparent to the trio that they had a gig. Dylan considered them to be his new band, and perhaps even had in mind touring with them. In fact, he had been talking with friends about a low-key tour since those humid July nights at the Other End. At that time, a Columbia sales representative indicated to *Rolling Stone* that Dylan had such an idea already in mind.

Columbia sales representative: You get the feeling he really digs being back in New York. He's looking into doing a show on Broadway, maybe a play. And he's looking closely at TV, maybe a special. But most of all, after these nights down here at the Other End, he'd like to tour small clubs like this. There has been some talk of getting a van and driving around the country, dropping in, unannounced like tonight, playing a couple of nights and moving on. Nobody would know he was there until he showed up, so there wouldn't be a crowd scene. And nobody would know where he would strike next.

In fact, the idea of a touring revue had not started at the Other End. It was an old Dylan dream. He had told Phil Ochs that he would love to play a tour of small clubs "and give the money away" when they were hanging out together after the Friends of Chile benefit. In 1972, according to Maria Muldaur, Dylan had said to her, "Wouldn't it be great if we got a train and put a revue together that would travel across the country?" He had even discussed the idea with Robbie Robertson back in the sixties.

Robbie Robertson: This thing has been a thing that Bob's been talking about for years. I'm sure he would have liked to have taken it all the way and done it by train. He's always wanted to have that kind of Gypsy caravan situation happening where it was loose and different people could get up and do different things at different times and nothing would be out of place.

After the filming in Chicago, Dylan returned not to New York but to his home in Malibu. But he was back in New York in the middle of October, moving into the Gramercy Park Hotel, while rehearsal time was booked at Studio Instrument Rentals. Ever secretive, only at this point did he assemble a touring band around the nucleus that had completed the *Desire* album (though Emmylou Harris was busy promoting her own album, *Luxury Liner*).

Rob Stoner: [We] start rehearsing up at S.I.R. in midtown there, Fifty-fourth Street. We're rehearsing for like a day or two—it's not really so much a rehearsal as like a jam, tryin' to sort it out. Meanwhile, all these people who eventually became the revue started dropping in. Baez was showing up. McGuinn was there. They were all there. We had no idea what the purpose for these jams was except we were being invited to jam. I think the only people who were being paid were the group that was already working for Bob—namely

Scarlet, myself and Howie. So we're up there jamming and it turns out what we're really doing is rehearsing.

As the sessions progressed, the band became considerably less stripped down than the one that had recorded the album. Four multitalented instrumentalists were drafted in from Los Angeles: Luther Rix, Steven Soles, T-Bone Burnett and the angel-faced David Mansfield. Mick Ronson, David Bowie's ex–lead guitarist, was also brought in. He seemed an incongruous choice, though Dylan had kept him in mind since hanging out with ex-Mott the Hoople band leader Ian Hunter and Ronson during the July late-night sessions at the Other End. Of course, the idea of a revue format for the shows required other headline acts as well as Dylan. In what was seen as a repaying of some old debts, he recruited Roger McGuinn, Jack Elliott and Bobby Neuwirth, who had all been in on the initial discussions back in July. Neuwirth was an obvious host for the show. Dylan also asked Joan Baez. Dylan/Baez— a bill with true nostalgia appeal!

Lou Kemp: Bob called Joan up and invited her just the week prior to leaving New York for the Cape. . . . We'd go out at night and run into people and we'd just invite them to come with us. We started out with a relatively small group of musicians and support people and we ended up with a caravan.

On October 22, Dylan turned up at the Other End to watch David Blue perform. He was with Ronee Blakley, a talented actress who had made quite an impression in Robert Altman's three-hour cult classic, *Nashville*. A powerful singer in her nonacting time, Blakley joined Dylan onstage for a few duets at the end of Blue's show. Dylan had found another member for the revue. Blakley could also be deployed in the film he intended to shoot on the tour.

Meanwhile, though, he was required back in the studio. The version of "Hurricane" recorded at the *Desire* sessions had become a source of concern to CBS lawyers. It was felt that a couple of the lines could lead to litigation, particularly the reference to Bello and Bradley "robbing the bodies." The song would have to be rerecorded.* By now, Dylan was deeply involved with rehearsing for the tour.

Rob Stoner: The first or second day all these suits from CBS come in and they're all talking about this "Hurricane" controversy, saying, "Look, the band is here. You got these guys sitting here right now. Let's go across town and do another version of it now so at least we got an alternate one." So that's what it

---

* Ironically they were sued anyway, by Patty Valentine, who lost her suit in 1979.

was. They interrupted this rehearsal/jam thing to go across town and just do this quickie thing that they put on the *Desire* album—they just slapped it on to appease the legal problems.

On October 24, Dylan returned to the CBS studios along with Stoner, Rivera, Wyeth, Luther Rix, Steven Soles and Ronee Blakley to rerecord a song he had got right the first time. Warming up with such old nuggets as "Sitting on Top of the World" and "That's All Right, Mama," he attempted to get the song down quickly. However, the chemistry was not right.

Howie Wyeth: We ended up doing it after we'd been rehearsing for about fourteen hours and they said, "OK, now we're gonna go and record." Everybody was burnt. It was not the right night to record. Everybody was drinking. Ronee was starting to ad-lib more and more. At first I think she hit an ad-lib that worked. Then of course everyone went, "Yeah," which we shouldn't have 'cause then she started ad-libbing. I think she was juiced.

Never one to enjoy repeated takes, Dylan was required to attempt eleven of them. He kept stumbling over the rewritten words, and by five in the morning he had had enough.

Larry Sloman: After the tenth take [*sic*] Don [DeVito] says, "Do you wanna hear it?" and Bob just put his coat on and says, "Man, I don't know. You mix it. You let me know which one you pick out."

Dylan just wanted the song out. In the end DeVito had to edit two of the takes together. Dylan's mind had not been on recording. The album was a thing of the past. What mattered now was the tour. He was going on the road with a package tour he had put together himself, billed as the Rolling Thunder Revue. First stop would be Plymouth, Massachusetts, the place where the first Pilgrims landed, an appropriate start to a bicentennial tour. In Plymouth Dylan discussed his return to performance with Allen Ginsberg, who would be the official bard for the revue.

Bob Dylan: I've been up the mountain and I had a choice. Should I come down? So I came down. God said, "OK, you've been up on the mountain, now you go down. You're on your own, free. Check in later, but now you're on your own." [1975]

He had indeed been in the wilderness. It was now time to go back out in the wind.

23 | 1975: You Come On to Me Like Rolling Thunder

The New York rehearsals had gone well. To celebrate the beginning of a great adventure, Dylan and the revue turned up at Gerdes' Folk City for a last New York City jam session on October 26. The following day they headed for Falmouth, Massachusetts, and two days of final rehearsals. The show that had been put together was not intended to be a standard rock and roll performance. Dylan asked Jacques Levy, with his theater experience, to put together a format for the show so that it could be carefully choreographed for maximum effect. The format, like that of Dylan's 1966 shows, was to be rigorously defined; set variations were to be few.

Jacques Levy: Bob said, "Can you figure out a way of doing it—a presentation? What would it be like?" So I sat down and I did something not unlike the kind of work I had to do in *Oh! Calcutta!*: to figure out what goes first and what follows what—the batting order. I knew we were talking about a big show—four hours or more. So I wrote up a thing like that and I left open spots so there could be guests and shifts. It wasn't really a rigid thing at all, the key point [was] how exactly we'd get to the point where Bob came on, and when to play the new material. We rehearsed the show in New York for almost two weeks. Again we had this enormous pile of material, and it had to be arranged and worked out and staged. And the idea was that it should not look staged. We didn't want it to be a flash show, because that didn't fit anybody's style. The thing was to make it appear like it was a spontaneous evening . . . like a traveling vaudeville show or a traveling circus. . . . There was almost a hootenanny feel. . . . There was [to be] no tuning up between songs, there were no pauses. Big chunks of the show were the same every night.

If song selection was intended to remain fairly constant for each show, actual performances of the songs would vary considerably. Dylan had always looked to change the way a song could be performed from night to night, keeping the experience fresh for him and the listener.

Mick Ronson: He used to come on one night and play real fast. Then next night he'd play the same songs real show. Either he was doing it on purpose or . . . I reckon he had a bad memory . . . 'cause he was all over the place some nights. He'd just wander off somewhere, expecting us to follow him. Come to think of it, he had problems knowing what key he was playing in. We'd just have to look at him all the time 'cause otherwise he'd have finished one song and be into another. There were nights when—if you weren't looking—you'd find yourself still playing when the song was over. . . . He really forced you to look at him, what with him being a bit shaky on his timings, key, changes and all, he didn't know what he was doing half the time. . . . Plus he never played anything the same way twice.

Though Rob Stoner agrees with Ronson that Dylan would "never play anything the same way twice," he adamantly disagrees with Ronson's assessment that it was his poor memory and musicianship that caused this. According to Stoner, the changes of key and tempo were absolutely deliberate, and specifically designed to keep the musicians on their toes. Most of the musicians who have worked with Dylan in performance seem to share this view.

Rob Stoner: For instance, "Isis"—we did a reggae version, we did funk versions, we did the waltzy one, we did the fast metal version. That's one tune that comes to mind, but Bob was really into that. . . . That's why he does that. He's not doing that to be a prick. He's doing that to keep himself from getting bored . . . anybody who's gonna complain about that shit shouldn't be on his bus! That's the gig!

The Rolling Thunder Revue attracted considerable interest from the media for a variety of reasons, most of them unrelated to the merits of the shows. There was the veil of secrecy that surrounded the location of the revue at any given point; the advocating of Hurricane Carter's cause; the new material that Dylan was premiering; the fact that he was playing his first tour since *Blood on the Tracks*; the stated intention to play smaller venues, primarily theaters; and the inclusion of Joan Baez on the same bill as Dylan for the first time in ten years. Any of these factors alone would have guaranteed media interest. Together they were a potent brew.

The three days at the Seacrest Motel in Falmouth before the tour acclimatized the crew to being out on the road, and allowed the musicians to begin to feel like a creative unit and to socialize together. This was not viable in New York, where each had his own circle and many had homes to return to after rehearsals.

In Falmouth, Dylan also began to work seriously on the film he intended to make on this tour. Back in 1968 he had told John Cohen that if he and Howard Alk had the opportunity to reshoot the type of footage they composed "Eat the Document" from, then "we could really make a wonderful film." They had not given up on the idea. In October 1975, Alk picked up the phone at his home in Montreal to hear a voice say, "Bob wants to know if you're ready." Dylan had begun filming some scenes in New York: David Blue telling stories about the early sixties in Greenwich Village while playing pinball; Dylan's surprise appearance at Mike Porco's birthday party at Gerdes'; a meeting between Dylan and Walter Yetnikoff, the president of CBS record division, to discuss the release of the "Hurricane" single. But it was in Falmouth that he started filming in earnest.

According to Mel Howard, who was the man in charge of Film Crew A, the film did not, in fact, start to come together until some way into the tour. The majority of the footage shot early on he disliked, saying "the stuff was home movies," the same accusation D. A. Pennebaker had made about some of the scenes in "Eat the Document."

Mel Howard: A lot of stuff that we were shooting in New York and at the beginning was stuff that was conversational and worse than that. . . . To take that opportunity [to film Dylan] and just parade him around as though he were some lame dick and everybody's gonna freak out over him and we can take funny movies of girls giggling, that to me was lame and a drag. . . . I thought the stuff was home movies, and I really disliked it.

Besides bringing in Howard Alk as coeditor, Dylan had also recruited Sam Shepard to write some scenes for the movie. At the time Shepard was a promising New York playwright, but he had yet to establish a firm reputation. Possibly Bobby Neuwirth suggested Shepard. They had both been friends of Patti Smith's in the early seventies and knew each other. Or possibly even Smith herself, who cowrote the play *Cowboy Mouth* with Shepard, mentioned him. Whatever, Shepard was summoned from California to New York, and he arrived during final rehearsals. His first meeting with Dylan was not auspicious. Dylan's first words to him were, "We don't have to make any connections. None of this has to connect."

Shepard soon discovered he meant the scenes in the film. Dylan asked him whether he had seen Marcel Carné's *Children of Paradise* or François Truffaut's

Shoot the Piano Player, adding that those were the types of films he had in mind. *Shoot the Piano Player* was a rather ironic choice on Dylan's part, since it is a film about an ambitious girlfriend's attempts to get an antihero to resume his once-prominent concert career. This would appear to be the reverse of Dylan's own circumstances. Sara Dylan would join the revue during November, but she stayed detached from the camaraderie of the musicians and crew.

Shepard, in fact, soon found his supposed role to be largely redundant. Even before they left Plymouth, it became apparent that the film would be largely, indeed primarily, improvised, and that there was little need for a scriptwriter. As Shepard himself later wrote in his *Rolling Thunder Logbook*, a fragmented chronicle of the revue, by November they had "abandoned the idea of developing a polished screenplay or even a scenario-type shooting script, since it's obvious that these musicians are not going to be knocking themselves out memorizing lines in their spare time. . . . So we've veered onto the idea of improvised scenes around loose situations." In the end, Shepard found himself sitting in on scenes in the film, his only real role in the revue.

Bob Dylan: *Renaldo and Clara* was originally intended as a more structured film. I hired playwright Sam Shepard to provide dialogue but we didn't use much of his stuff because of a conflict in ideas. [1978]

From Plymouth onward the film took its own course, not charted by Dylan, but sailing from rock to rock. The amount of direction provided to his actors was minimal. Certainly the other members of the revue were not at all sure what he had in mind. Joan Baez told Nat Hentoff, who was covering a story for *Rolling Stone*, that "the movie needs a director. The sense I get of it so far is that the movie is a giant mess of a home movie." She would later write a far more damning appraisal of the way the movie was shot in her autobiography, *And a Voice to Sing With*.

Joan Baez: One day I was trudging around in the snow on a farm in Canada with Dylan, doing a "scene." . . . Naturally, I was playing a Mexican whore—the Rolling Thunder women all played whores. The scene opened with Bob shoving me through the snow toward a shack. In fact there was neither a plot nor a script so the characters "developed" as we went along. . . . It was a cold day, and I wondered what I was doing in this monumentally silly project, and if Dylan was taking it seriously. Sam Shepard was there, supposedly directing it, or writing it, but it was never written, and barely directed. Bob would stand in back of the camera and chuckle to himself and get everyone to run around and act out his mind movies. The filming happened in gleeful little happenings, enacting whatever dream Dylan had had in the night.

Dylan himself observed at the time of the film's release that some of the members of the revue had not been particularly eager to enter into the spirit of the movie. When Scarlet Rivera says, "Nobody's behavior was monitored or really worked out," she saw that as a positive aspect of the filming. Others, and this presumably included Baez, despite her major part in the film, considered the lack of structure to be a hindrance.

Bob Dylan: There was a lot of chaos while we were making the film. A lot of good scenes didn't happen because we had already finished improvising them by the time the cameras were ready to film. You can't recapture stuff like that. There was a lot of conflict during filming. We had people who didn't understand what we were doing because we didn't have a script. Some who didn't understand were willing to go along with us anyway. Others weren't and that hurt us, and hurt the film. [1978]

However, some sense of coherence, some themes pertinent to the Rolling Thunder Revue experience, began to emerge as the revue weaved its way through Massachusetts, Rhode Island, Vermont, New Hampshire, Connecticut, upstate New York, Massachusetts again, Maine, Quebec and Ontario. In particular, certain revue figures on the fringe of the music were providing real input into the film. Larry Sloman was scouting for potential scenes after nearly every show; Sam Shepard was providing input, though on a wider basis than originally envisaged, and devised several scenes, including one between an alchemist and an emperor, which featured Dylan and Ginsberg; and Ginsberg seemed excited by the whole bicentennial idea, seeing the revue as a reclaiming of American heritage.

Mel Howard: Allen saw Dylan rightly connected to the whole tradition of the beat generation and through that to the earlier poets, Poe, the whole sense of the American vagabond. So Allen was keen to add that element too.

Gradually, indeed haphazardly, the themes of the movie began to come together. When Howard talked to Larry Sloman on the flight from Montreal to New York at the end of the tour, he felt that the footage necessary to construct a great movie had been filmed, and that the central story that had emerged was one that involved Dylan, Sara and Baez in some kind of ménage à trois, though like the critics who later savaged *Renaldo and Clara*, Howard found it difficult to perceive Dylan, Sara and Baez as playing the characters they were assuming rather than themselves. It was an important distinction. If Dylan had succeeded in shooting enough footage to put his vision onto celluloid, the movie Howard talked to Sloman about would only partially mirror *Renaldo and Clara* in its final form.

Mel Howard: There were all these themes running through it. Ginsberg had the idea of Dylan as an alchemist, rediscovering America, then [there are] the women, Sara is very much into Robert Graves and his notion of the muse . . . that's probably a big part of their relationship. . . . So there was this scene in Niagara Falls where Sara played this kind of witch goddess creature and she set tasks for him to fulfill, and nothing was ever good enough and that was the constant prod to keep him going. So we had a whole subplot, all of the women in the film, black magic and white magic, and the different powers of women and men and the focus of all of this was Dylan himself. . . . We started to use some of the songs as mythological characters, with horses in Quebec and escape scenes, all sorts of zany high jinks, but the thing that started to evolve as a general theme was Dylan, Sara and Joan. And Sara and Joan as opposing forces, in different mythological guises, Joan as a certain kind of energy, Sara as a different kind of energy, and Dylan in between, being attracted to both. . . . I guess in the last two weeks [of the tour] . . . the tour took hold enough so Dylan was sufficiently secure and the film just possessed him and it took him over. . . . But I'm afraid how the film is gonna turn out. . . . I think it's important to push Dylan in some way to make the film that's there.

Echoing Baez, Sara Dylan's own comment about the film was "After all that talk about goddesses, we wound up being whores," a reference to the bordello scene in which Sara and Baez reminisce about past loves and David Mansfield is brought in by Allen Ginsberg for his initiation. Dylan later claimed the scene was meant to represent Diamond Hell.

What the film did give Sara was a function on the tour apart from being Dylan's wife. She was clearly ambivalent about even being on the tour, but presumably felt obliged to support the husband with whom she had recently been reconciled. She informed revue chronicler Larry Sloman:

Sara Dylan: I really can't take the traveling. And I have no real function here. Back home I have the kids, and other things, but there's really nothing for me to do here.

It is important to remember that making the film was part of the motivation for Dylan to go back on the road. The film he was making during November 1975, whatever its final structure would be, was clearly not the sort for which he could readily raise finance. He used his own money to finance the filming, or, perhaps more accurately, the money from touring.

Bob Dylan: My lawyer used to tell me there was a future in movies. So I said, "What kind of future?" He said, "Well, if you can come up with a script, an outline and get money from a big distributor." But I knew I couldn't work that way. I can't betray my vision on a little piece of paper in hopes of getting some money from somebody. In the final analysis, it turned out that I had to make the movie all by myself, with people who would work with me, who trusted me. I went on the road in '76 to make money for this movie. [1978]

For this reason, and because of the expense of taking on the road such a large group of talented musicians, often headliners in their own right, it was inevitable that the revue would have to play some large gigs. This aspect came in for considerable criticism from the media. Shows at the Civic Center in Providence, the Veterans Memorial Coliseum in New Haven, the Maple Leaf Gardens in Toronto and the Forum in Montreal were considered to be against the original spirit of the revue, as supposedly suggested by Dylan. Dylan was thus being forced to defend a position he had never advocated in the first place. The suggestion that he had said that the revue would only play small theaters had taken root. Yet he had always known that he would have to play certain larger shows to defray expenses. As he told Larry Sloman during the tour:

Bob Dylan: We're gonna go any place we can. But we also have a lot of expenses to meet. I mean, we're not gonna go out and play living rooms, you know. It's not a nightclub show. . . . But we are gonna play small theaters and we have played theaters and we're going to continue to play theaters. [1975]

The Rolling Thunder Revue shows themselves were remarkable. They still stand as the most innovative shows of Dylan's career in a musical sense. Mansfield's steel guitar, Ronson's glam-rock lead guitar and Rivera's electric violin combined to give the ensemble a unique sound, locked in as they were with a tight rhythm section (Wyeth and Stoner) and some occasional percussion (Luther Rix). Dylan was also singing with a precision even he rarely displayed, snapping and stretching words to cajole every nuance of meaning from each line. The new songs in particular seemed to bring out an extra degree of vocal commitment from him. Every night he performed six of the songs that later appeared on *Desire*—"Romance in Durango" and "Isis" closed the first half, while "Oh, Sister," "Hurricane," "One More Cup of Coffee" and "Sara" made up the bulk of the concluding electric set.

Every night he also sang one, two, then three acoustic songs; and a five- or six-song set with Joan Baez. Once again the press had an opportunity to ring out the old clichés—The King and Queen of Folk Sing Together Again! Dylan would mercilessly play Baez up, leaning into her face and the microphone when she least expected it, stretching the notes to see who could hold them longer and informing her they were going to do "The Times They Are a-Changin' " and then singing "I Dreamed I Saw St. Augustine." Through it all Baez managed to retain her usual I'm-going-along-with-this manner and piercing voice; she even appeared in whiteface at one show to duet with Dylan, and dressed up as Dylan for the final benefit show, while he introduced her as Bob Dylan. According to one Rolling Thunder musician, Baez even managed to score one over Dylan during the tour:"Joan and Bob are doing a duet. . . . She's really moving. I mean dancing. She starts doing the Charleston and the audience is digging it and we're digging it. Dylan, though, he's plunking his guitar, moving his eyes around quick, like he does, looking at Joanie, looking at us, looking at the audience. Like, 'What the hell is she doing that's going over so damn big?' It's over, and Joan walks offstage, grinning, sees a friend in the wings, and says to him, 'You won't be hearing that number again from this little old duo on this tour.' "

Actually, the story does not accord with the usual set pattern, which had Baez remaining onstage at the end of their joint set. Next to singing with Baez again, Dylan drew the most comments for the whiteface he donned at most shows. At a couple of the shows he even came on stage wearing a plastic mask, which he tossed aside when required to play harmonica on the second song, "It Ain't Me Babe." No one seemed sure what the reason for the look was, and one person shouted to him at the Lowell, Massachusetts, show, asking why he appeared so.

Scarlet Rivera: There was a point where a heckler in the audience . . . said, like, "Why are you wearing the mask? What is it all about?" And I think his response was, "The meaning is in the words." . . . 'Cause it made him angry for that moment. I guess because he wanted to be understood.

In the film of the tour all the footage was drawn from shows at which Dylan donned his whiteface, and in talking about *Renaldo and Clara* he mentioned masks and the search for identity as integral to the film's unique symbolism. It is tempting to see the whiteface as essentially connected with the making of the film. But perhaps the best clue to his motives lies in a comment he made to Sloman during one of their interviews on the 1975 tour.

Bob Dylan: Ever see those Italian troupes that go around in Italy? Those Italian street theaters? Commedia dell'arte. Well, this is just an extension of that, only musically. [1975]

In the commedia dell'arte the majority of the players wore masks. The nature of the commedia dell'arte has been described by novelist Anne Rice thus: "Each actor had his role for life, and . . . they did not use memorized words, but improvised everything on the stage. You knew your name, your character, and you understood him and made him speak and act as you thought he should. That was the genius of it."

And that was perhaps the link between the revue and the movie. The players, both onstage and in the film, were living out their roles to their logical conclusions. The musicians stuck to the same core material, yet every night the show was different, spontaneous and of the moment. The movie tried to capture that sense as well, though less successfully than the music. Every musician speaking of the 1975 tour talks of an atmosphere unique to the revue, of a sense of freedom to express oneself fully, almost a belief that they could redefine themselves.

Scarlet Rivera: I felt this incredible freedom to express or to represent whatever feeling, whatever thought, whatever symbolism and actually carry it out.

The 1975 Rolling Thunder Revue wound to an end with a benefit show for Hurricane Carter at Madison Square Garden in New York. They had played to an unsympathetic, largely black audience at the Clinton Correctional Institute for Women the previous day, a show intended as part of the publicity drive to free Carter, who was temporarily imprisoned there. At the Garden Dylan and the revue delivered a steaming four-hour show to an ecstatic audience. Even Nik Cohn, a critic renowned for his antipathy toward Dylan, found positive aspects in the performance. It was a triumphant end to the tour, and in stark contrast to the end of Dylan's 1974 tour twenty-two months earlier. Or his 1976 tour six months later.

$\boxed{24}$ 1976: Hard Reign or Last Waltz?

Nineteen seventy-five was perhaps the most triumphant year of Dylan's career, both artistically and commercially. The release of *Blood on the Tracks* and the recording of *Desire* proved that his creative genius was in full flow for the first time in eight years. His commercial stock had never been higher. He had concluded perhaps the finest tour of his career, and in the meantime finally filmed enough footage to put his vision on celluloid. It even seemed as if by the end of the year he had succeeded in being reconciled with his recently estranged wife. She had, after all, been a regular fixture on the latter part of the 1975 revue.

Nineteen seventy-six should have been equally triumphant. His long-awaited follow-up to *Blood on the Tracks*, *Desire*, which had been so prominently featured in the 1975 shows, was released in January. Plans were afoot for a second Rolling Thunder tour, and there was that mass of celluloid waiting to be knitted together into something resembling a coherent film. In the interim NBC was interested in filming the revue for a one-hour in-concert edition of the "Midnight Special" series.

And yet 1976 came to represent something of a lost opportunity. Dylan avoided the recording studio, and so his momentum as a recording artist was lost. By the time he released the follow-up to *Desire* thirty months had elapsed and his commercial stock was in discernible decline, while the 1976 revue failed to recapture the previous year's spirit.

The year started promisingly enough. *Desire* was released on January 16 and within three weeks was number one on both sides of the Atlantic—the one and only such occurrence in Dylan's career. The revue also reassembled in Santa Monica to rehearse for a one-off benefit show, a second Night of the Hurricane, originally scheduled to be held at the Louisiana Superdome but soon moved to Houston.

The show proved an absolute disaster. Flying the entire revue out to Los Angeles to rehearse for just one show was an expensive exercise in itself. The new venue, the Astrodome, was an acoustical nightmare and, at seventy thousand capacity, it seemed unlikely that it would be filled by Texas bottoms. Stevie Wonder and Stephen Stills both volunteered to appear at the show—and then both brought their own bands with them.

Howie Wyeth: It was just too much. That show went on forever. And the air—you couldn't breathe. There was just too much. The show was like twenty-four hours long, everybody did too much, everybody did too many songs and there were too many stars there. . . . All these guys brought their own bands. They weren't doing it the way we'd been doing it. . . . We lost the whole togetherness thing.

Even the Hollywood starlets got in on the act, swelling the size of the Revue, and the band itself sounded underrehearsed and ramshackle, and the sound bounced around the cavernous Dome like a ricocheting bullet in a tin barrel.

Rob Stoner: I was surprised he did it again after that one. Whoa, that was nightmarish, that one. Could have been Bob Dylan's worst gig of his entire career, that one—but he meant well. That was the hanger-on junket. All these Hollywood people were just tagging along with Bob Dylan. We chartered our own plane.

If the sense of intimacy was gone, so now was any pretense of marital fidelity on Dylan's part. Sally Kirkland, an up-and-coming American actress, was at this point his "motion of the moment," to use Stoner's descriptive phrase. If Houston did not start 1976's touring activities auspiciously, the trail of concert disasters, sexual infidelities and economic problems would not end there. The financial result of Night of the Hurricane II, which grossed some half a million dollars, was a mere fifty thousand dollars net for Carter's defense coffers. Dylan himself returned to Malibu for a rethink, after a few days in Texas hanging out with Doug Sahm and Joni Mitchell.

In March, Rubin Carter was finally granted a retrial. Dylan had performed his last live version of "Hurricane," despite the fact that Carter was found guilty on two more occasions before finally being freed in 1985. With the arrangements for a spring tour of the southern states in the formative stages, and with no intentions to record himself, Dylan started turning up at sessions for Eric Clapton's new album, which was being recorded down the road at the Band's Shangri-La Studios. He seemed at ease here. There were no pressures. He did not have to go home; and musicians such as Clapton and Ron Wood were always good for a jam or two. Disinclined to save any new songs for himself, he even gave Clapton and Wood a song apiece. "Sign Language," featuring a Dylan/Clapton duet, appeared on Clapton's No Reason to Cry; "Seven Days," which he donated to Ron Wood, has the singer waiting for his true love to return, insisting that he has been good while waiting. Obviously this was not one of Dylan's more literal songs.

Ron Wood: One night I was up on Sunset in Hollywood and I happened to ring Shangri-La [Studios] and said, "Anything happening up there tonight?" And they said, "Nothing, other than Bob Dylan's here playing." I went, "What?!" They said, "Yeah. Bob's here. Playing bass. On one of your songs." I said, "Don't let him leave!" . . . Anyway, this session went on for a couple of days solid. There was a point where we stopped the master tape and just ran a two-track. That's where I got "Seven Days" from. . . . He made this tent up from the clothes on my bed. He made off with my sheets and pillows and everything. At the sessions we very rarely got the chance to have a break and crash . . . one night I went to creep off to my room and there were no bed-clothes at all, and the window was wide open, and I looked out and I could see this tent in the distance, right in the middle of this big field. And Bob had made off with this girl, but she was in a plaster cast—her leg and her arms in plaster! That was quite funny. It was like *Invasion of the Zombies*.

Clearly, restlessness was an important factor for Dylan when he arranged to reassemble the revue at a large Florida hotel at the beginning of April. If he had no desire to return to the studio and was reluctant to stay at home, he hoped a reassembled revue would revive the magical spirit created throughout the New England tour the previous fall.

Rob Stoner: It was an attempt to recapture that Rolling Thunder thing. 'Cause what we did . . . the first time was we all holed up in a hotel and rehearsed in the ballroom and it worked that time. But here everybody was too far from home. There was a problem with the water down there, too.

The rehearsals had barely started when word came through that Phil Ochs, in a manic-depressive state, had hanged himself in New York. Ochs had desperately wanted to be a part of the revue, though Dylan knew that he had become too unstable to take along on a lengthy tour. Despite his minimal contact with Ochs in the previous ten years, Dylan took the death badly. Perhaps he recalled how he had learned of Richard Fariña's and Paul Clayton's deaths during that manic 1966 world tour.

Scarlet Rivera: I was sitting at the table when he got the word about that [suicide]. And he was really upset and angry that he had done that to himself. . . . It was a combination of real sadness and anger. A couple of days went by when he was missing. I think he took the news very, very hard. . . . Before he came back to the rehearsals he wanted to clear his mind.

Dylan's mood did not substantially improve after his two days of solitude, and the rehearsals became tortured affairs. Dylan, on the occasions when he deigned to turn up, failed to communicate with the band, and his melancholy affected the whole homesick revue: "A month and a half of this, and the boss won't talk to anyone," said Rob Stoner, who did his best to keep the band in a good groove, but everyone was bummed out.

Joel Bernstein: The rehearsals were in the Starlight Room of the Bellevue Biltmore Hotel in Clearwater and they went on for some time before the tour. It was somewhat strange. Bob would show up late for rehearsals, he wouldn't talk to the band, he'd just start a song. I never liked Rob Stoner's playing very much but I have to give him credit. He really understood, could follow Bob by looking at his foot, following his heel, listening for the first note and then he'd get a feel for the key, and the rest of the band took their cue from him. Bob spoke very little—he wasn't talking to me for a while—and it seemed a very strange way to proceed with rehearsals. . . . And the rehearsals went on for quite some time. The first rehearsals were in the poolhouse, and that proved to be too small, so after a day or two we moved into the ballroom, which of course they had to pay more money for. Usually rehearsals began around noon and Bob wouldn't show up until two or so and not say anything, just pick up a guitar and play a song. My impressions were that he was either angry about something or that the whole thing was getting old for him. It was just a mood he was in.

Dylan's mood did not discernibly lighten once the tour started. At the first show, in Lakeland, Florida, he introduced a very different set from the one he had performed a mere five months earlier. He opened with two acoustic songs, and the choice of material was perhaps indicative of the mood he was in. Gone were the vignettes-in-song of *Desire*. At the first couple of shows "Mozambique" was the solitary inclusion from the album that had just spent five weeks at number one. Dylan replaced "Sara" with "Idiot Wind," a brutal substitution.

Indeed, *Blood on the Tracks* seemed generally restored to favor for this tour. Rather than the solitary acoustic versions of "Tangled Up in Blue" or "Simple Twist of Fate" that he performed in 1975, he chose to sing most of the album at some point on the tour. "Tangled Up in Blue" was given a grinding stop-start arrangement late in the tour. "Shelter from the Storm" and "Idiot Wind" became savage denunciations. "You're Gonna Make Me Lonesome When You Go" was given an easy, almost fatalistic vocal over a wistful country arrangement.

But the most startling inclusion from *Blood on the Tracks* was an acoustic version of "If You See Her, Say Hello," performed as song number two at the opening show, and wholly rewritten. In the new version, the singer is haunted by the lady, but he hates her power over him, and he hates himself for allowing her such power (almost a continuation of "Dirge"). His tone starts as dismissive, he becomes threatening toward her new lover ("If you make love to her / Watch it from the rear") and finally he admits to his own doubts about having the strength to reject her should she return: "I know that she'll be back some day / Of that there is no doubt / And when that moment comes / Dear Lord, give me the strength to keep her out."

A rewritten "Going Going Gone" also suggested a man who was getting used to "sleeping in the dust." In fact, Dylan now seemed to be spending his time with a lot of unusual women. As so often in his life, his unhappiness seemed to have a direct effect upon his libido. And clearly he was looking as much for guidance as companionship. He later said he had had enough of "witchy women," but he was certainly having his fair share of mystics, seers and sages along for the ride through the southern states that spring.

Howie Wyeth: [There was] the tightrope walker. The girl from "The Dating Game." . . . She was a circus performer, she walked tightropes and stuff. She sort of seemed like a mystic but then we found out she also wrote a book about "The Dating Game." . . . There was a real tall chick that was also a magician that was with Bob, sort of off and on, and then there was this other chick . . . they were sort of both with Bob off and on. They were on the tour, they had their own room. They didn't do anything else. There was a faith healer too, though she was real innocent. She was really a nice lady from Vermont, into all sorts of weird foods. . . . My old lady at the time was an astrologer and she was on the tour and I know she'd been talking to Bob and there was a guy on the tour that was into pyramid power, a cat from England, and he looked like a pyramid.

If witchy women failed to improve his mood as the tour progressed through Florida and Louisiana, neither did the way the shows were going. There were major problems that had never occurred the previous year. Part of the difficulty was just the general mood; part was inexperience on the part of Dylan's management; part was the poor choice of the southern states in the first place.

Rob Stoner: Bob was going through a lot of personal changes. It was just shit, man. . . . I mean, "Idiot Wind" is a very angry song and it definitely reflects what must have been going on with him. I mean, he was really upset back then. . . . He was drinking a lot. Ronson was frozen out of the '76 tour. He was on the bus but they never let him play. [Dylan] had leaditis then. I don't know what the fuck came over him. . . . It was a big void in his life. The marriage was falling apart and this thing which had seemed so exciting and promising— Rolling Thunder—that wasn't [working] and he couldn't figure out why, I don't think. . . . It was like a midlife crisis. He was confused and he was searching. He tried a lot of chicks; he tried one chick; he tried [every] kind of chick.

If the show was reasonably well received by fans in Louisiana and Florida, Texas proved a complete wipeout. Ever since September 1965, when Dylan went to Dallas and Austin with his new rhythm and blues band, the Hawks, and had been enthusiastically welcomed by the locals, he had been under the illusion that Texas was a good place to play. In fact, the type of music most Texans preferred was a shade less sophisticated than that of Dylan and his band of East Coast folk-rockers.

This was a shame, as the April performances in Florida had been steadily improving. Indeed, when the band returned to Clearwater four days into the tour to film a concert for NBC the band really started to click.

Howie Wyeth: The rehearsals sucked in that place . . . it just wasn't happening. . . . Then we did the [Clearwater] concerts and they were filming it and it happened. That was the first day that the music started feeling right again. Bob did a really hip version of "Like a Rolling Stone." He did some tunes that he hadn't done at all.

Unfortunately, Dylan took a dislike to both the celluloid results achieved by Bert Sugarman's "Midnight Special" team and to Sugarman personally, at least according to Wyeth.

Howie Wyeth: Well, Bob got into a fight with [one of] the guys that were doing [the Clearwater special]. . . . He got into a big argument with the guy over the dinner table one night after we'd already done half of it. And then he said, "No! We're not doing it. Fuck it!" So he decided that wasn't the way we were going to do it and then they decided to record right at the end [of the tour].

By the time Dylan's own film crew came to shoot the penultimate show of the tour, at the end of May, the revue had passed through Texas, and the mood was very different from the mood at those Clearwater performances. Though the filming of the aborted TV show is crass and obvious (during the final chorus of "Just Like a Woman" the camera actually cuts from a woman to a girl in the audience), the second half of the show featured some terrific performances by Dylan and the band, as he produced a seething "Like a Rolling Stone," a delicate "Just Like a Woman" and a raucous rewrite of "Lay Lady Lay" that became the bawdiest moment of each and every one of the 1976 shows. No longer subtly coaxing the lady, Dylan now hollers: "Let's go upstairs / Let's take a chance / Who really cares?"

After two great sets in New Orleans (during which he performed the one and only live version of "Rita Mae," his "tribute" to writer Rita Mae Brown), and one in Baton Rouge at the beginning of May, the revue's first Texas date was back in Houston. It came after a four-day break, the result of the cancellation of a show at Lake Charles in western Louisiana, on May 6 because of poor ticket sales. The cancellation presaged a disastrous sortie through the second-largest state in the union. Less than five months after the catastrophe that was Night of the Hurricane II, the Rolling Thunder Revue failed even to sell out Houston's eleven-thousand-seat Hofheinz Pavilion, despite the late addition of Willie

Nelson to the bill. The auditorium was barely three quarters full, and the following day's show was canceled altogether.

Three days later, the revue's San Antonio gig was moved from the Hemisfair Arena to the somewhat smaller Municipal Auditorium. The next day two shows at Austin's Municipal Auditorium were combined into one, again because of poor ticket sales (reserved seating also became general admission and nine hundred fans were excluded from the show). Here was someone who two years ago had generated twelve million applications for tickets for his American tour and who, since then, had secured the only three American number-one albums of his career, yet he was failing to sell out small arenas in Texas. Ironically, the Austin show turned out to be one of the best dates of the tour.

Howie Wyeth: There was a whole bunch of hassles. The promoter didn't get along with the people out west. He was Jewish. I heard there was a whole bunch of stuff he just didn't know. He said the wrong things to the wrong people and they were prejudiced. . . . In Austin they booked us the same night as four other concerts and then they made all the kids stay out in the rain all night to get the good tickets and then they decided to make it general admission after these guys had waited to get tickets so they could be in the front row. Oh boy, were they pissed. They were ready to kill us. . . . The papers had been saying, "These guys are from the East. They came down here just to grab your money. They don't give a fuck about you." Neuwirth came out [at the start of the show] and said all that . . . but then once it was said and done, then it was great. "OK, let's have the concert!" And it really worked.

Even a show in Dallas on May 15 was canceled because of poor ticket sales, despite Dylan's high opinion of Dallas fans. Instead, the Dallas fans had to trundle out to the already arranged show in Fort Worth the following day, which remained on the schedule in preference to the Dallas date because there was a recording crew taping the show for a possible live album. Though the show seemed to go well and the sound was good, Dylan was clearly unhappy with the results, and only four tracks were subsequently used on the live album *Hard Rain*. The revue finally headed out of Texas, and at shows in Oklahoma City and Wichita, Kansas, Dylan experimented with the set in an attempt to keep from being bored. In Wichita, he even performed the first-ever live version of "One of Us Must Know," a twisted look at an ended relationship.

After Wichita, the revue headed into Colorado and friendlier territory. There they were informed that they had a weekend off in a well-appointed cabin-*cum*-hotel up in the mountains, where they could hang out and prepare for the Fort Collins show, a big show in an open-air stadium that was being filmed for

NBC TV and recorded for the live album. But even this seemingly innocent gesture on Dylan's part backfired, as it poured throughout the weekend.

Howie Wyeth: All of a sudden they said, "We got four days off before we do Fort Collins and the record." They said, "You're gonna love this. We got you in this dude ranch up in the mountains." And it was raining so you couldn't go riding and it was up in the mountains so you couldn't breathe. There was nothing to do. And we were all stuck up there. So after all this adrenaline it was like detoxing or withdrawal . . . for four days we had nothing to do. And it was raining. It was dreary.

Rob Stoner: Bob was really hitting the bottle that weekend. That was a terrible fuckin' weekend. There was a lot of stuff that makes *Hard Rain* an extraordinary snapshot—like a punk record or something. It's got such energy and such anger. . . . It was an outdoor stadium and it had rained for days before the gig. We had done this aborted Bert Sugarman special for NBC in Clearwater. I think the deal was that Bob had the right of refusal if he didn't like the videotape but the terms were that he had to make good on it at his expense, by doing his own thing to deliver to NBC. Therefore, Bob had to hire video, sound crew, twenty-four-track remote truck, all this extra stuff, and every day you have these people sitting around and they've all driven this shit from L.A.—which is the reason we did it in the West. So they could get a crew there from L.A., video and audio, which was a lot more expensive then than it is now, relatively speaking. . . . We were supposed to do the gig [on] two or three consecutive days—each time the rain date was supposed to be the next day—but it was pouring for days and days and meanwhile it's costing Bob a lot of bread. Everybody's holed up in this little hotel up in the mountains in the middle of nowhere, with nothing to do except get drunk. . . . Here's the last gig and it's taking forever to do it. The boss is getting in a progressively shittier mood. . . . Eventually they just decided to go and do it in the rain anyway. As it turns out the rain cleared up on the last fucking song—it was the first time that the sun had shone in a week.

Dylan's mood was not greatly improved by the surprise arrival of his wife, who had brought his kids and mother along with her, apparently intent on celebrating his thirty-fifth birthday. As Wyeth has observed:

Howie Wyeth: She showed up the day of *Hard Rain*. . . . But she didn't tell him and he had two of his girlfriends there. It was tense.

According to Baez, Sara just waited outside Dylan's room quietly, but in a seething rage, and eventually he emerged to face his comeuppance.

Joan Baez: Sara showed up late in the tour, wafting in from a plane looking like a madwoman, carrying baskets of wrinkled clothes, her hair wild and dark rings around her eyes. . . . Bob was ignoring her, and had picked up a local curly-headed Mopsy who perched on the piano during his rehearsals in a ballroom off the main hotel lobby. Sara appeared airily at the front door dressed in deerskin, wearing her emerald necklace and some oppressively strong and sweet oils. She greeted me with a reserved hello and talked distantly about nothing in particular, all the while eyeing the closed door to the ballroom.

Possibly Sara had arrived with the intention of confronting Dylan. If she had any idea of the life-style he had adopted on the tour, she was certainly entitled to confront him. Whatever her reasons, Dylan was not in a mood to listen as, according to both Stoner and Wyeth, Sara censured him in the parking lot, refusing to ignore his adulterous activities. Such personal trauma cannot have improved Dylan's mood as he prepared for the most important gig of 1976.

Finally, on May 23, the revue performed their penultimate show to a wet but surprisingly appreciative Fort Collins audience. And, perhaps not surprisingly, Dylan and the band responded with one of the best shows of the tour. The sense of desperation and frustration is there on the film and on the record. The performance may be ragged but there was real fire in it.

Rob Stoner: Everybody's soaked, the canopy's leaking, the musicians are getting shocks from the water on the stage. The instruments are going out of tune because of the humidity. It was awful. So everybody is playing and singing for their lives and that is the spirit that you hear on that record.

Scarlet Rivera: There was a lot of pressure on that day to get that filmed [and recorded]. . . . This was the last possible moment for this recording to be made and it was under the worst circumstances.

Can it be coincidence that Dylan sang perhaps the most rancorous version of "Idiot Wind" of the tour the night that Sara was there to watch him? On the final verse, in which the singer seems finally to accept the fact that he is as much an idiot as the subject of the song, Dylan rocked his head from side to side on the word *sorry*, clearly implying that he felt no such remorse. He had also added a new coda to "One Too Many Mornings": "I've no right to be here / And you've no right to stay / Until we're both one too many mornings / And a thousand miles away."

The Dylan singing on *Hard Rain* has never been more attuned to his performance art. The results may be harsh—as Stoner says, the album comes across as almost a punk record—but for sheer vitriol there can be few songs ever performed that stand up alongside "Idiot Wind" at Fort Collins. "Shelter from the Storm" also brought a demonic performance from a man seemingly prepared to face the consequences of his own actions. When he says one day he is bound to cross the line, you feel sure he means it.

The final Rolling Thunder show was in Salt Lake City. Playing in a half-empty seventeen-thousand-seat Salt Palace, the revue gave another great performance. They did not want the tour to just fade out. To make the show extra special, Dylan even pulled out "Gates of Eden" during his acoustic set, and sang "Lily, Rosemary and the Jack of Hearts" as a duet with Baez.

Joel Bernstein: Salt Lake City was the only show that I recall that Bob and Joan did "Lily, Rosemary and the Jack of Hearts" together. The song has something like eighteen verses, and Bob wrote the first lines down on the back of his hand, on his cuff, on his sleeve. . . . They did a very good version of it, really good. It was a very spirited show, perhaps because it was the last show. People knew that it wouldn't happen again.

If Dylan's public profile had been up front during the first half of 1976, he seemed to disappear off the face of the earth during the second half. In September NBC screened the one-hour *Hard Rain* TV film to disappointing ratings and unfavorable reviews. The album of the TV special clocked up healthy initial sales but rapidly dropped from the charts. A period of hibernation was approaching. Dylan and his old friend Howard Alk, with whom he coedited *Hard Rain*, had more pressing editing tasks to undertake.

In November, Dylan flew to San Francisco to appear at the Band's farewell concert. After sixteen years on the road (though their touring since 1966 could hardly be described as incessant), the Band had decided to call it quits. The concert was being filmed by Martin Scorsese, and Dylan performed four songs with his old backing band before leading everyone through an encore of "I Shall Be Released." He looked considerably less wired than at Fort Collins six months earlier. Indeed, he looked positively loose. Yet his strident performance contrasted markedly with the beautifully understated power of the Band. Still, he had done his duty. Now he had to return to Malibu to attend to his duties as a husband and father. Or not.

25 | 1977: Everything Went from Bad to Worse

Sara Dylan: "I can't go home without fear for my safety. I was in such fear of him that I locked doors in the home to protect myself from his violent outbursts and temper tantrums. . . . He has struck me in the face, injuring my jaw. . . . My five children are greatly disturbed by my husband's behavior and his bizarre life-style."

On the face of it, 1977 might seem like another of Dylan's "lost" years. He played no shows and recorded no albums. Yet in fact it was a year of considerable activity, both artistically and personally. Personally it was the year of his divorce, which would be only a prelude to his primary trauma, a lengthy and bitter custody struggle for his children. Artistically there were also problems with the editing of the film Dylan and Alk worked on throughout 1977, the four-hour *Renaldo and Clara*. At the end of the year, extensive and untogether tour rehearsals proved a further distraction, as reflected in Dylan's state of mind during an unparalleled series of press interviews he gave at the time to promote his new film at minimal expense.

It would appear that Dylan's adulterous behavior, which had been a constant backdrop to the 1976 Rolling Thunder tour, had not ceased by the beginning of 1977. Rather, it had become more blatant. According to a declaration by Sara Dylan's legal representative, released to the press in March 1977, "On February 13th of this year, she came down to breakfast and found Dylan, the children, and a woman named Malka at the breakfast table. She said that it was then that Dylan struck her on the face and ordered her to leave."

If the prospect of a very public and acrimonious divorce had tabloid hacks sharpening their pencils, on the day proceedings commenced in Sara's divorce suit a plea was made for the sealing of the documents relating to the court case. The *Los Angeles Times* noted: "Mrs. Dylan's attorney, Marvin Mitchelson, concurred in the request of Dylan's attorney, Marvin Burns [*sic*], to prevent disclosure of the marriage dissolution filed by Mrs. Dylan March 1st. Judge Raffedie additionally sealed other documents stipulating the assets of the Dylans, and ordered sealing of a response by Dylan yet to be filed."

The divorce thus proceeded in relative privacy, without, it would appear, any particular attempt by Dylan to be reconciled with Sara, and by June the divorce was final, though the judge announced he was "retaining jurisdiction of their communal property for future determination." The question of the custody of the children would not be settled for some time. Initially, Sara retained legal custody of the children. The situation became charged only when Sara decided to go to Hawaii to look for a new home for herself and the children. While in Hawaii, she left a woman named Farida McFree in charge of her home. McFree had originally been employed by Sara to help the children during the legal wrangles, using a technique called "art healing," which involved encouraging children to express themselves through art.

Farida McFree: Rosanna [Taplin, an actress] came to me and she said, "Farida, Sara is in such a bad way. Would you please help her with the children? You're doing art healing and the children really benefit by it." . . . So that's how I got involved with the children and I did art healing. . . . We'd work together on the same piece [of art].

At some point it became apparent that Sara and Farida were not getting along. Yet Sara needed someone to look after her house while she and the children were in Hawaii, and she had little recourse but to ask McFree.

Farida McFree: I started off with her, and then she really treated me very badly. I just said, "I'm here to help you, I'm not here to be abused. I don't think you need my services anymore." And she went to Hawaii. But she said, "Do me a favor: Just stay in the house, please. Do me this one favor because I really want someone in the house and I trust you."

While Sara was in Hawaii, McFree, who had met Dylan in 1975 at the wedding of Rosanna and Jonathan Taplin, awakened from an intense dream involving Dylan.

Farida McFree: I fell out of bed. I mean it was so intense, this loneliness, and I didn't understand it. Then that morning the next-door neighbor, [who] was a filmmaker, a very big one, called me and said, "Did you hear, Farida, that Bob got a divorce last night from Sara in Santa Monica?" And I said, "No, Sara's getting the divorce." And he said, "Uh-uh, he beat her to it." And then I had this pain again in my heart all day. I said, "I can't stand it." I picked up the phone and I said, "Bob, this is Farida. I work with Sara and the children. I'm the children's art teacher. Are you OK?" And he said, "No, I'm not OK." So I said I had this strong feeling that I should call you. And he said, "Isn't that nice?" And then he [asked me], "What are you doing right now?" I said, "Nothing." He said, "Why don't you come over? I really, really need to talk to someone." I said, "It's late. I don't really want to." 'Cause he was thirteen miles from the house that she had rented at the colony. So he said, "Well, I really need to talk to someone tonight," and I was a little afraid of him so I said, "I don't think so." He said, "I really do." So I said, "Oh, OK." . . . Anyhow, I go there and I was scared because there are all these bodyguards and it just seemed very scary, all these guys. So they let me in. It just seemed very spooky and then Bob came toward the light, and as I was driving slowly, he looked like he was crazed. And I got so scared. I said, "Oh my God, what am I doing here?" But he came to the car and he drove with me to the house and we just never stopped talking. . . . We just talked into the night. I don't think we stopped talking until four or five o'clock in the morning. He just poured and poured and poured out his heart and all these grievances that he was feeling, grief and everything else. So he never stopped talking. We talked right around the clock. And that's how [our affair] started.

Dylan's involvement with McFree was bound to make an already complex situation more difficult, and Sara's response was an understandable one. She had had to deal with so many women who had befriended her for the sole purpose of getting close to Dylan.

Farida McFree: When she came back I was already with him. I had moved into his house. It was fast with us. She was totally freaked out. And I said, "Bob, I don't know what's happening with us but I feel it's the wrong move. I don't think I should move." . . . But he insisted that I move in with him. And I said, "I think this is a bad move. She is going to misunderstand all this." So he said, "Well, is she your mother?" I said, "No, she's not my mother but I don't want to start any problems." 'Cause she had told me all these stories about all these women that would use her to get to him.

Like Sara, Dylan now wanted to get away from it all, so he decided to take a temporary rest from editing his film, which he had begun with Howard Alk. He, too, wished to take the children along. He also invited McFree, who had already established a rapport with the children through her art healing. His chosen locale was less exotic than Hawaii and more familiar to the children, a farm he owned in Laredo, Minnesota. At last, in the relative calm of a Minnesota summer, he began to write songs again. It had been two years since the burst of creativity that had produced *Desire*. Now he began writing perhaps the most complex and convoluted lyrics of his life. New songs such as "Changing of the Guards" read like poems that were later put to music, something he had not attempted since *John Wesley Harding*. These new songs would require a sophistication in their arrangement if the complex words were to rise above the sound that enfolded them.

Farida McFree: He started to write *Street-Legal* when we were together. He would show me some of the songs that he was writing. [It was] practically the entire album. . . . It started when we were on the farm. . . . He was very down. Don't forget, he was suffering when I met him. He was in a bad way. I brought him back to life. He was practically dead . . . this guy was shot emotionally and he had to get away from all the pressures in Malibu and the farm was really where he got back up on his feet again. But then that custody case was so vile and so treacherous. I mean, I kept running away 'cause I couldn't handle it. The kids were on the farm.

If Dylan was starting to get "back up on his feet again," there was one real moment of sadness for him during his time in Laredo. On August 16, 1977, at 3:30 P.M., Elvis Presley was pronounced dead at the Baptist Memorial Hospital in Memphis, Tennessee. Like the death of Phil Ochs in April 1976, the death of Elvis Presley made Dylan temporarily morose and difficult to communicate with.

Farida McFree: I was with him the night Presley died. It was in August. . . . He really took it very bad. He didn't speak for a couple of days. He was really grieving. He said that if it wasn't for him he would never have gotten started. That he opened the door.

Bob Dylan: I went over my whole life. I went over my whole childhood. I didn't talk to anyone for a week after Elvis died. If it wasn't for Elvis and Hank Williams, I couldn't be doing what I do today. [1978]

Dylan's time with the children had helped him to make an important decision: He was going to contest the custody of the children with Sara. He probably already knew that Sara had been considering the possibility of setting up home in Hawaii with the children, and was understandably reluctant to have them so inaccessible. Possibly he felt that he could set up a home with Farida, who had a good rapport with them. If so, such hopes were decidedly unrealistic. It was inevitable that Marvin Mitchelson, Sara's lawyer, would exploit the relationship with McFree to Sara's advantage.

Farida McFree: That's when he decided that he was going to keep the children. And then the custody case followed that immediately. . . . Right after the divorce, that was going to be decided and he felt that he wanted them and the children wanted to be with him, and that's when he decided to go to court and fight for them. And Marvin Mitchelson . . . used everything he could to win the case and Bob's lawyers knew that and warned Bob to get rid of me. They said, "Let her go. She shouldn't be around you 'cause you'll lose the case." And he just wouldn't. So I used to go into hiding when they came over. This was both on the farm and in Malibu. They knew I was on the farm and said, "Send her away. She's going to ruin the case—your just being with her. Mitchelson will use that." And he did.

Matters came to a head on September 2. Marvin Mitchelson, on behalf of Sara, asked the court to give her permission to move the children to Hawaii to live there with her. The original settlement had required that the children not be taken out of California without a court order or the other parent's written consent. Within four days Dylan's attorney, Robert Kaufman, filed papers alleging that Sara Dylan had violated the original court order by taking the children with her to Hawaii at the beginning of the summer. Dylan had previously chosen not to press the issue, but changed his mind on hearing of Sara's petition.

Dylan now asked that the court grant sole custody of the children to him after Sara's "direct violation of the court's order." Mitchelson repudiated the charges and insisted that the legal action Dylan had taken was "precipitous, hysterical and without foundation." Meanwhile, Sara had returned to Hawaii to finalize her attempts to set up home there, leaving the children in California.

At this point, according to press reports of a November custody hearing, Dylan took the opportunity provided by Sara's absence to take physical custody of the children. In a declaration to the court Mitchelson claimed that Dylan and Farida McFree were "attempting to brainwash the minor children and to deprive them and [Mrs. Dylan] of the natural love and companionship of each other." Dylan refrained from responding to the allegations at the November 3 hearing, though his attorney made it clear that he denied them.

A further hearing was set for December 1. In the interim Sara Dylan obtained physical custody of the children. In the case of Jesse, their eldest son, she managed this only after an interim hearing at which a Santa Monica court ordered Dylan to return him to Sara's custody. According to Mitchelson, Dylan had employed "bodyguards and armed guards."

The return of the children to Sara did not resolve the custody battle. Within days of the Santa Monica hearing, Sara was involved in assaulting a teacher at the children's school in Malibu. According to a syndicated report of the incident, Sara invaded a classroom, "flanked by three private detectives, chased the Dylan children through the school, frightening other students" and attacked teacher Rex Burke "when he asked to see the court order." The children "apparently resisted going with Mrs. Dylan." Sara was later fined for her assault on the teacher. Why Sara acted in this way is unknown, as she already had a court order giving her custody of all five children (including Maria, her daughter from a previous partner). According to Farida McFree, the "raid" could have been a life-threatening affair for her. For once, though, Farida was not with the children.

Farida McFree: She came in with two detectives, two burly guys, into this schoolhouse with guns. . . . I was always with the children and that was the first day that I wasn't and she went into the school system and they took the children by force. I think they didn't get Anna and Jesse. It was really a traumatic experience for them.

Though custody had been temporarily restored to Sara, a legal settlement had yet to be reached. When it was finally made, late in December, the conditions that Sara Dylan and Mitchelson imposed apparently included the complete exclusion of Farida McFree from the children's circle of influence. It would seem that Sara had never forgiven Farida for what she saw as her traitorous actions toward her, and Farida became the sacrifice required to resolve the custody battle.

Farida McFree: The upshot in our relationship was, when I came to New York, Mitchelson made [Dylan] sign a paper that he would never see me again. It was either me or the children . . . there was a lot of money involved too, and he didn't want that case to go on any longer. It was really painful. I don't know what all the details were but he told me that and I just knew it was the end for us. . . . He told me that Mitchelson made him sign a piece of paper that he would never see me again and then the case was settled. . . . If your children are at stake and your life is upside down, you're gonna sign that piece of paper. . . .

The exact details of the custody settlement are unknown, but it was at last resolved. When Dylan was giving a plethora of interviews in the first two months of 1978, he seemed to consider his relations with Sara irrevocably breached. Though they would later be reconciled, at least as parents of their children, he hinted to at least one reporter that the custody battle had taken a considerable toll.

Bob Dylan: No one in my family gets divorced. It's just unheard of, nobody does that. And so when I did get married I never conceived of getting divorced. I figured it would last forever. But it didn't, and now there's a marriage and there's a divorce. And the circumstances in my life have led to the divorce really being a divorce. . . . Most people don't really get divorced. They keep some contact, which is great for the kids. But in my case, I first got really married, and then got really divorced. [1978]

The custody battle took place against a backdrop of Dylan assembling his massive, sprawling opus *Renaldo and Clara* with Howard Alk. Inevitably, the inclusion of scenes with Sara and Dylan led to speculation that he was washing his dirty laundry in public. He denied all such intentions.

The footage had been filmed during a period of reconciliation for Dylan and Sara, and it was only the editing that took place during the divorce and custody struggle. The editing lasted through most of the winter, spring, late summer and early fall of 1977. Dylan and Alk soon realized they had a lot of footage to work with.

Howard Alk: We knew from the beginning that the film was going to be too long . . . [though] our final ratio of what was shot to what's in the final film is the standard documentary ratio of twenty to one. . . . Actual cutting took about six months. We began work on the film [in 1976] . . . but we were interrupted by the second leg of the tour and by the television show, so we were actually in the editing room for six months [in 1977].

Bob Dylan: I knew it was not going to be a short hour movie because we couldn't tell that story in an hour. Originally I couldn't see how we could do it under seven or eight hours. But we just subtracted songs and scenes and dialogue until we couldn't subtract any more. [1978]

Dylan realized that the length of the film would scare off just about all major studios. Though he approached at least one major studio before starting the editing, it was readily apparent that there would be no rapprochement between Dylan's ideas about the structure of the movie and its theme and the studio's desire for a movie that had a direct story line and traditional structure.

Bob Dylan: All the financiers wanted something more definite than an improvisational film with just an outline and based on death and rebirth. [1978]

When the movie was completed he again considered using the major studios to ensure that *Renaldo and Clara* received adequate distribution, despite his understandable aversion to dealing with studio moguls after the shameful way MGM had treated Sam Peckinpah over the filming and editing of *Pat Garrett & Billy the Kid*. With *Renaldo and Clara*, Dylan wanted to present a *fait accompli*.

Bob Dylan: We took the movie to one of the major studios. They treated us like dogs. As far as I can remember, they didn't want to see more than fifteen minutes of the film before they bought the picture. We felt it only proper they should see it all. Besides, a major studio would never release this as a four-hour movie. They thought it should run for one and a half hours and that it had to be all music. [1978]

The structure, symbolism and sheer length of the film inevitably meant that Dylan had to put up most of the money to distribute the film himself. Though the film would be attacked for its lack of cohesion, it was in fact structured very carefully and with a very specific approach in mind. Dylan talked at length to the press about the film's oblique symbolism, but it was its structuring that was the most innovative aspect of *Renaldo and Clara*.

Bob Dylan: People were told this, this, this—the rest of it is up to you, what you say in this scene is your business, but at the same time, beyond that, the only directions you have are: You're going to die in a year, or see your mother for the first time in twenty years. So far as instructions to actors go, less is more. [1977]

Bob Dylan: This was a movie done without a script. There were ideas from the beginning, but a lot of this film developed as we were doing it. Quite a bit was improvised, but only within certain rules. [1978]

The idea of structuring the film around improvised scenes was obviously preconceived. Only a general framework was provided by Dylan. According to the production notes that accompanied its release, there were four types of scene shot for the movie:

(i) Dylan would set up a scene for improvisation and let the actors work around a given concept. People such as Ronee Blakley, Ronnie Hawkins and Mick Ronson had great talent for expanding on Dylan's ideas, and they took off from these starting points and embellished them with their own contributions.

(ii) Dylan would give the cameraman an assignment to get a certain type of image, then he would let him go about his work.

(iii) After shooting proceeded and cast and crew had picked up on Dylan's *modus operandi*, the director opened the film up so that people could create their own types of drama. Characters had taken on lives of their own, and actors were given free rein to extend these lives out to their logical conclusions.

(iv) Documentary coverage had its place in *Renaldo and Clara*—when Dylan visited Jack Kerouac's grave in Lowell, Massachusetts, with Allen Ginsberg, or when he traveled to a CBS Records executive meeting in New York, the camera was present.

Once this mass of footage had been accrued, the film was constructed according to very rigorous criteria. The problems with its reception by the American media could perhaps have been alleviated if Dylan had been given a better chance to explain how it was constructed. As it was, few reporters were interested in the way he had spent a year of his life putting the film together. All they wanted to know was why Bob Dylan was played by someone else (Ronnie Hawkins) in the movie, and whether there was a literal connection between the film's ménage à trois of Renaldo, Clara and the Woman in White and Dylan, Sara and Baez in real life. Allen Ginsberg attempted to explain the way the film was built up, trying to dissuade people from approaching it as a conventional linear construct.

Allen Ginsberg: It's built in a very interesting way. You'd have to study it like *Finnegans Wake*, or Cézanne, to discern the texture, the composition of the tapestry. He shot about 110 hours of film, or more, and he looked at all the scenes. Then he put all the scenes on index cards, according to some preconceptions he had when he was directing the shooting. Namely, themes: God, rock and roll, art, poetry, marriage, women, sex, Bob Dylan, poets, death—maybe eighteen or twenty thematic preoccupations. Then he also put on index cards all the different characters, as well as the scenes. He also marked on index cards the dominant color—blue or red . . . and certain other images that go through the movie, like the rose and the hat, and Indians—American Indians—so that he finally had a cross-file of all that. And then he went through it all again and began composing it, thematically, weaving these specific compositional references in and out. So it's compositional, and the idea was not to have a plot, but to have a composition of those themes. So you notice the movie begins with a rose and a hat—masculine and feminine. The rose is like a "traveling vagina"—those are his words. The hat is masculine—crowns. The rose . . . travels from hand to hand. . . . It's a painter's film, and was composed like that. I've seen it about four times, and each time I see it, it becomes more logical—not rational, but logical.

Like Ginsberg, Dylan wanted to talk about the texture of the film. *Renaldo and Clara* to him was a further step in advancing the approach adopted on *Blood on the Tracks*, the one advocated by Norman Raeben, which Dylan sought to apply not just to painting but also to other artistic media.

Bob Dylan: The film is no puzzle, it's A-B-C-D, but the composition's like a game—the red flower, the hat, the red and blue themes. The interest is not in the literal plot but in the associated texture—colors, images, sounds. [1977]

Significantly, when talking about the film Dylan referred more often to painters than to filmmakers. To him *Renaldo and Clara* was a moving picture. He refused to admit to any real connection with America's populist film heritage.

Bob Dylan: I'm . . . doing this . . . to put forth a certain vision which I carry around and can't express on any other canvas. [1978]

He perceived his primary influences not as Ford, Huston and Hitchcock but Cézanne, Modigliani and Dalí. When talking to one reporter, he claimed, "In writings songs I've learned as much from Cézanne as I have from Woody Guthrie." The only film that he referred to as an influence was *Children of Paradise*, which he had previously mentioned as a signpost to both Sam Shepard and Allen Ginsberg.

Bob Dylan: Regardless of what it's about—*Renaldo and Clara*, a guy selling a horse, a guy singing on a stage or fighting with a man, whatever it is—we have stopped time in this movie. We've grasped that time. And we are the only ones. I've never seen a film except one other that has stopped time—*Les enfants du paradis*. [1977]

As he did when discussing the songs on *Blood on the Tracks*, Dylan talked a great deal about the nature of time in *Renaldo and Clara*. There does indeed seem to be no discernible chronology to the film. Everything happens at once; the history of the characters is given only by their actions and their conversation. Dylan made it clear that the film had to be perceived as a dream. In Renaldo's dream the identity of a given individual represents no more than some form of latent manifestation of his subconscious, symbolic rather than realistic. And this is the case throughout the film.

Bob Dylan: The man on the floor [at the end], who's obviously dreaming, no one asks him anything—but the whole movie was his dream. . . . Renaldo has faith in himself and his ability to dream, but the dream is sometimes so powerful it has the ability to wipe him out. Renaldo has no ordinary mind—he might not even have a soul. He may in actuality be Time itself, in his wildest moments. [1977]

The dream nature of the film allows for the distortion of identity. It was this factor that bemused so many critics. Of course, Dylan did not make it easy on them. Even when talking to Allen Ginsberg about the movie, he never resolved the question of whom Bob Dylan played.

Bob Dylan: Renaldo is everybody. . . . Renaldo is you, struggling within yourself, with the knowledge that you're locked within the chains of your own being. . . . He's Everyman in the movie, and he survives. He is a man contemplating the future. . . . At the opening of the movie he's in a mask you can see through—it's translucent. At the end he's seen putting on face paint. [1977]

Yet when he is seen putting face paint on, this does not necessarily mean he is about to become the man with the white-painted face. According to Dylan, this white-faced figure has no name—he is "the Chorus of the movie." He is the figure that Renaldo aspires to become, in his dreams.

Bob Dylan: The man in whiteface is what Renaldo cannot become at the moment. At the Indian party that isn't Renaldo, that is the man in whiteface. He represents the compelling figure of authority. [1977]

But the presence of Bob Dylan cannot fail to hang over the movie. It is, after all, billed at the beginning as "a film by Bob Dylan." He is referred to throughout the movie, notably when the Canadian Broadcasting Corporation reporter is waiting "breathlessly for Bob Dylan." He even gets Ronnie Hawkins, a rather grotesque figure, to play a character called Bob Dylan. It was this overwhelming presence that was seized upon by critics as evidence of a giant ego at work, and *Renaldo and Clara* was characterized by many as one massive exercise in narcissism. Dylan's conceit in using his own name was certainly deliberate:

Bob Dylan: Bob Dylan is being used here as a famous name, so we don't have to hire Marlon Brando! . . . Let's say that in real life Bob Dylan fixes his name on the public. He can retrieve that name at will. Anything else the public makes of it is its business. [1977]

If Dylan's intention was to require the audience to abandon their preconceptions of who Bob Dylan was, the ruse did not work. Bob Dylan proved too potent a symbol. He overshadows the movie. The implication that beneath the whiteface of Bob Dylan-as-Chorus lies Renaldo, the real self behind the mask, was too oblique for the filmgoing public.

Likewise, the identity of Clara was a further source of (deliberate) confusion. Sara Dylan plays Clara, but she also plays a whore stuck in Diamond Hell during the so-called bordello scenes. Meanwhile, Mrs. Dylan is played by the ravishing Ronee Blakley.

If the figure in Diamond Hell is Clara, she appears to be deep in conversation with the Woman in White (dressed in red), if that is whom Joan Baez is playing here. Logic says not. Yet Baez plays the Woman in White in the film. But so does Sara (or is that Clara?). It soon becomes apparent that Clara and the Woman in White are different aspects of the same symbolic figure.

Bob Dylan: Clara is the symbol of freedom in this movie. She's what attracts Renaldo at the present. Renaldo lives in a tomb, his only way out is to dream. . . . You know at the end of the movie he's about to or has broken out of that tomb . . . you feel that even though he may be under strenuous times, he might transcend them. . . . He's trying to break out of himself—not only that, he's trying to break out of himself by means of reason. . . . He's actually in the process of conquering his own soul. . . . [The end of the movie] is in fact the morning of Renaldo's life. He has ceased to be Renaldo. From that moment on he will become what he wishes to become. No more will he answer to Renaldo. . . . [The Woman in White] is the ghost of Death—Death's ghost. Renaldo rids himself of death when she leaves, and he goes on, alive, with his greasepaint. He's becoming the hero of his own dream. [1977]

Dylan has never stated that Clara and the Woman in White were intended as aspects of the Triple Goddess, Robert Graves's all-encompassing conception of the muse as Virgin/Lover/Hag, though he admitted to Jonathan Cott that the Death Mother is represented in the movie. However, it is difficult not to see the women in the film in these terms, particularly with the way he uses the primary colors white, red and black to represent the many women.

Clearly *Renaldo and Clara* remains Dylan's most deliberate exposition of himself as a conscious artist. In the many interviews he gave at the time about the film, of which his conversations with Ginsberg (from which the above quotes are drawn) are the most important, he seemed for the first time prepared to talk about his art in an authentic, expository way.

Bob Dylan: I am a conscious artist. . . . I had a teacher who was a conscious artist and he drilled it into me to be a conscious artist, so I became a conscious artist.

Again Dylan is referring to Norman Raeben, the painter who had helped him to learn the conscious approach that resulted in *Blood on the Tracks*. And in many ways *Renaldo and Clara* attempts to duplicate aspects of Dylan's writings on that album. On songs such as "Tangled Up in Blue" and "Lily, Rosemary and the Jack of Hearts," identity is often unresolved or opaque. In "Tangled Up in Blue" Dylan seems to meet his lost love in a topless bar, yet he does not recognize her. Later on he "lives with them on Montague Street," but who are they? Only hints are given. The Rimbaudian figure starts "dealing with slaves," but are this figure and the narrator one and the same (a common enough interpretation)? In "Lily, Rosemary and the Jack of Hearts," events are even vaguer. Who pulled the empty gun on whom, when "a cold revolver clicked"? Who is the man Lily "couldn't stand, who hounded her so much"? On celluloid such ambiguities of identity could have been clarified, shoved into the faces of the paying customers. Dylan, though, challenged such notions by constantly asking the viewers to question the identity of the people they saw on the screen.

The notion of time in *Blood on the Tracks* could be illusory. Dylan used a dream sequence as the basis for the song "Tangled Up in Blue"—"I was layin' in bed / Wonderin' if she'd changed at all." Yet the dream itself seems to be a flashback, the narrator reminiscing from "the side of the road" as he's "headin' for another joint." The time scale in the song is in no way linear. Rather the song is like a cutup of incidents involving the singer and a woman (or is it Woman?). The order is seemingly random, but the effect cumulative. In *Renaldo and Clara*, Dylan applies a very similar technique. The viewer is not sure how scenes relate to the primary struggle of Renaldo. Likewise, there is no linear chronology to the events in the movie. The narrator, played by David Blue, does not narrate the film. Like everyone else in the movie, he is a figment in Renaldo's dream.

Bob Dylan: David seems to know what's going on, but he's only existing in Renaldo's dream. He's the narrator who links the movie to generational history . . . he's a figment of Renaldo's imagination that attempts to reconcile the past that never was. [1977]

As in "Tangled Up in Blue," there is a strong journeying element to the movie. There is a constant procession of people coming and going, and the rose and hat become linking symbols.

Bob Dylan: In the symbol of the rose we see the vagina traveling around. You see it a lot. You could trace it every time it comes up. Go to the movie and pick up all the signs where the rose goes. First on the table in front of the truck driver, who's almost contemplating it; then Clara in one of her former selves—a manifestation of her as desperation—picks up the rose and then travels with it. It was nobody's rose. Clara picked it up and went off alone to the train station, where she sees and lures Renaldo for the first time. [1977]

Renaldo and Clara took all of Dylan's creative energies through most of 1976 and 1977 to complete. It was the most sustained and conscientious work that he had ever done, or would ever do. If in the recording studio he sought spontaneity, in the editing room progress was necessarily slow and required an immense amount of discipline from this die-hard maverick.

Having completed this monumental work—for the scale of the film is certainly impressive—Dylan did some market research. In October, Allen Ginsberg spent a week with him watching and discussing the movie, and Ginsberg, albeit not your average filmgoer, gave the film a thumbs-up. Ginsberg also recorded at least three interviewers with Dylan about *Renaldo and Clara*, intending to publish a brief study of the film. Two further major interviews were arranged in the fall of 1977, one with Ron Rosenbaum of *Playboy* magazine, the other with Jonathan Cott of *Rolling Stone*. Both were shown the movie, and Dylan went to great lengths to answer any questions that the film might have raised. Cott in particular seemed positive about the movie, though he did observe "How easy it is to mistake people in the film for one another," and he commented that "some people will obviously think that this film either broke up your marriage or is a kind of incantation to make your marriage come back together." This was only the beginning.

In early December, Dylan conducted his own preview for *Renaldo and Clara*. Stopping at a restaurant near Goldwyn Studios, where he had been completing the film, he invited some of the customers to a screening of the picture. The mixed response proved a fair barometer of the public's view of the film. Comments varied from "An avant-garde piece of work" through "It's Dylan. That's all that counts" to this complaint from a disgruntled attendee: "I'm a little upset. I missed Carl Perkins on the Johnny Cash Christmas TV special for this." To such people would he have to sell his movie.

In December 1977 Dylan was required to become adept at juggling time. Embroiled in the last stages of the custody battle, he also began to give his first interviews to promote the release of *Renaldo and Clara*. Meanwhile, he summoned Rob Stoner to bring a band to Los Angeles to start rehearsing for a Far East tour to which he had now committed himself.

Rob Stoner: I was really surprised when I got the call to do the '78 gig. Man, I thought the *Hard Rain* thing was the last I'd ever hear from Bob to work. . . . Then suddenly I get this call—I think Bob called me up personally. He called me up and asked me to bring Howie and a couple of other people to L.A. to just try some things out. . . . I brought a guy who used to play with Charlie "Bird" Parker, Walter Davis, Jr., on piano . . . and Otis Smith, a great percussionist and singer, a friend of Howie's and mine. No girls.

The band, though, seems to have initially taken a backseat, as Dylan dealt with his other distractions. After all, the Far East tour was two months away, and the film was due for its premiere in January. Dylan was largely absent from the initial rehearsals with the musicians Stoner had arrived with. Even when he made it to rehearsals his mind was not on playing, and the musicians were finding him difficult to communicate with.

Rob Stoner: I brought this weird band out with me and Bob kept us sitting around for a week or two. He just never showed up. Meanwhile, we have this rehearsal hall right down the street from where we're all staying. We're waiting for the guy to show up. Meanwhile, to pass the time and keep everybody together I was doing the surrogate singing—I was just singing the tunes that I thought everybody should know in case Bob does show up. And we keep waiting. And he drops in and he's distracted. Maybe he didn't like the band. He was really fucked up [mentally]. He was always bummed out. He was chain-smoking and he was really in a bad mood. He was short with people. It just wasn't working out.

As December turned into January, though, the other distractions became less important. The custody struggle was finally resolved, and the majority of the important interviews for the film were out of the way—reporters from *Rolling Stone, Playboy, The New York Times* and the *Los Angeles Times* had all come and gone. Meanwhile, he realized he had a month at best to put a band together and get them roadworthy.

Joel Bernstein: I wound up actually living [at Rundown Studios, Dylan's rehearsal studio] from about September 1977 until we left for the Japanese tour early the following year. Bob actually had a room too. I turned one of the offices into my bedroom and he had an office that was set up as a bedroom too. . . . There were auditions and rehearsals all the time. There were members of the band that he knew that he wanted, like Steven Soles and Rob Stoner, but he was looking for other players.

Dylan certainly had specific musicians in mind—Rob Stoner, Steven Soles, David Mansfield, Howie Wyeth—but he also wanted a saxophone player and some female vocalists. He had decided from the start that he would take a big band on the road. However, his approach to recruiting the singers seems to have been a shade unorthodox, having little to do with the sound of the backing singers.

Rob Stoner: He starts inviting all these chicks to come down and sing and I felt it was like: Is he doing these things to impress these girlfriends of his? 'Cause they weren't professional singers. I tell you, one of 'em was Katey Sagal from that show "Married with Children." She was down there for a couple of days. I mean, they were like actress-singers. Not like real singers. . . . The first time he shows up to do anything serious it's 'cause he's got these chicks around. Oh God, and we tried rehearsing with them. It was a revolving door. Eventually we settled on the three or four that ended up doing the tour—but they were pros. . . . When the chicks start showing up to rehearsals, then Bob starts to get interested in it. Suddenly he's in contact with me every day. He says, "Well, call Jesse Ed Davis. Have him come down and play." He tried to get Al Kooper, he couldn't make it. He had Barry Goldberg down there, Barry couldn't do it for another reason. We had Mickey Jones, the actor. . . . He was calling up people from like twenty years ago. It was like he was gonna have a reunion party and check everybody in L.A. out. I was having a good time doing this! Every day we were having a jam with people who Bob had called to show up. Some of them he'd say, "Call this guy and have him show up, call that guy and [have him] show up." And I'd do that. And there would also be people who he showed up with. And things went on like that for a couple of weeks and nothing was getting done, and there were gigs booked.

As Stoner implies, constructing the actual band Dylan finally ended up touring with became something of a rushed affair. Even the basic core of Rolling Thunder musicians were not as certain about doing the tour as Dylan perhaps thought they would be. In May 1977 he had signed to Jerry Weintraub's management company for personal representation, Weintraub effectively becoming his first manager since the days of Albert Grossman. Weintraub was known for middle-of-the-road acts such as Neil Diamond, and for his strictly moral views on sex, drugs and rock and roll. Touring Japan also presented serious problems for anyone who indulged in even a minor drug habit. Paul McCartney had only recently been busted there for possession of marijuana. Dylan found that Howie Wyeth was reluctant to play a country where even this mild drug could be in short supply.

Howie Wyeth: I went to L.A. on Christmas Eve. I showed up out there and they weren't ready yet and I tried to rehearse with them and then I heard that Bob had a new manager and that the guy said, "We're not gonna even have any grass on this tour." I think they were serious. They were going to Japan. I was thinkin', "Man, if they're not even gonna have grass I'm really gonna be in trouble, because really, on the previous tours there was a guy carrying duffel bags full of coke . . . and you could buy grams for twenty-five dollars and just get 'em written off to your per diem. . . . So I went out there and we tried to play and it didn't feel right and I was tryin' to kick too, 'cause I knew I couldn't get high once we'd left, so [with] the combination of all these things I could see the writing on the wall. I realized I was either gonna get busted or I'd end up being tortured to death. So I literally had to just tell Bob one night, "Bob, I can't do it." That was terrible. He had his own problems. He felt bad that I wasn't gonna do it and he called me up when I got back to New York and said, "Are you sure?"

Suddenly the axis of the band was undermined. Securing the right backup singers and horn players was not a big deal, but a drummer like Wyeth held the whole sound together. The first replacement for Howie Wyeth was ex-Wings drummer Denny Seiwell, but, though he jelled very well with Stoner and the rest of the band, visa problems prohibited him from getting the gig.

Joel Bernstein: He needed a drummer and he auditioned a number of drummers, maybe ten or a dozen. It was an interesting experience for me, watching all these different musicians trying to play Bob's songs. . . . Bob had settled on Denny Seiwell. He was very happy with his playing but it turned out that he couldn't be used because of the Wings bust in Sweden—he wouldn't have been allowed into Japan, much to Dylan's disappointment, and I'm sure his.

The drummer Dylan finally chose was detrimental to the sound of the band. Ian Wallace had played with King Crimson, and so had a pedigree, but he seemed unable to apply the same crisp dispatch as Wyeth, and his sense of time was occasionally wayward, speeding songs up unduly. Stoner did not enjoy playing with Wallace, and this would be a contributory factor in Stoner's premature departure at the end of the first leg of the world tour.

Rob Stoner: It was tough, everybody had to stop doing drugs. We had that guy from Wings. I can't remember half the people that showed up to that. . . . We had the guy from Derek and the Dominos, Jim Gordon, great drummer. Man, we had all kinds of drummers. But y'see, because we waited so long to make the final cuts in the band, the deadline was pressing and eventually we had to settle on somebody. And Wallace happened to be it. . . . The guy from Wings sounded great, man, but he had a visa problem 'cause he was with McCartney. Wallace was just convenient—he was Mr. Right for the night. It's just that the night was too fuckin' long. . . . So the band that ended up being that band was something that I had to do hastily because we had blown our time having all these jam reunion things. But Bob had no relationship with that band. He wasn't hanging out. . . . I had tried out a lot of people but because of this casual attitude until the last week, then everyone got scared. We had to get Steve Douglas, who costs a fuckin' fortune—he's one of the top sax men in Hollywood. . . . I was in L.A., don't forget—I don't know people in L.A., so I'm depending on recommendations from other people who are not people I really know. I had to come to the office early every day and be his secretary and then I had to go rehearse and then I'd finish rehearsing and there'd be like a hundred messages from musicians.

Stoner had arranged for Billy Cross, a lead guitarist from an old band of his, to fly in from Sweden to play. Dylan had settled on Steve Douglas to play sax. With these two final additions, the band was at last a unit—by the last week in January. For the two weeks before flying to Japan, Dylan and his new ensemble worked on the repertoire without distraction. *Renaldo and Clara* was finally out (though not for long), and Dylan was providing some real input into the arrangements.

According to Stoner, they had been working up arrangements just to make some songs different, and this was how they ended up with the Douglas/ Mansfield penny whistle/violin arrangement on some songs, and even a quasi-baroque version of "If You See Her, Say Hello" (which actually worked quite well). As Stoner notes, when they put these arrangements to Dylan, "Sometimes he'd like it and he'd use it and other times he'd say, 'Forget it.' " In an attempt to get the maximum out of the final two weeks of rehearsals, Dylan began having the sessions taped.

Joel Bernstein: The [rehearsal] recording[s were] specifically for him to listen back to, not for him to ever use, but to let the band hear how things were progressing, and for him to hear how arrangements were coming together. He was much more disciplined than . . . [on] the 1976 tour. Not only was everything taped but he would have the band stay over after rehearsals finished and he would have me play back particular performances of the best versions of each song that day that either I would pick or he would pick, and spend an hour, hour and a half, listening back to things. . . . Rehearsals would usually begin about one o'clock. . . . People would show up and have lunch and then we'd start around one and play until six. . . . The band got bigger as time went on, and once it was reasonably together he got them to play certain songs in different ways, in one key and then another key and then half-time, then country, then reggae, then rocked up. It was really an experimental thing. And then listening to those songs he would just pick one, say, "Yeah! That's the one!" And I would

inwardly groan and go, "Oh, no! Not the reggae one!" But he had his own idea
about what was the best one to do.

The tapes that exist from these final rehearsals suggest that, despite his lack-
adaisical approach to the earlier rehearsals, the band was sufficiently together to
tour. Indeed, it was clearly better rehearsed than the bands on some of Dylan's
subsequent tours. When a recording of a rehearsal from December 30, 1977, is
compared with one from exactly one month later, the sound is a world apart.
If the early rehearsal sounds like a jam session from a rather untogether Rolling
Thunder band with some female singers wailing along for good measure, by the
end of January the band had its own identity and some of the new arrangements
were worthwhile—even if the reggae-style versions of "Don't Think Twice" and
"Knockin' on Heaven's Door" smacked of different for different's sake. Still,
Dylan was going back on the road, away from Malibu, away from legal battles
and financial difficulties. Like a new musical, this show was opening well out
of town, and Dylan and the band could work on it away from the scrutiny of the
Western media. CBS-Sony in Japan had other ideas.

26 | 1978: Someone's Got It In for Me

W hen Dylan finally flew to Japan on February 16, 1978, he
was especially glad to leave behind the American press,
who had just given him the most intense critical roasting of his career. On
January 25 *Renaldo and Clara* had been premiered simultaneously in Los
Angeles and New York. The reviews were almost universally hostile, not to say
spiteful. In one astonishing attempt to assassinate the film's credibility, *The
Village Voice* sent no less than four reviewers to savage it. Farida McFree, who
was staying at Dylan's town house in New York recovering from the trauma of
the custody battle and the end of her relationship with Dylan, read the New
York reviews to him over the phone. His reaction suggests he had anticipated
that the film would not be accepted by the critics, though he seems to have
underestimated the amount of bile they would be sending in his general direction.

Farida McFree: I read the reviews to him over the phone and it was horrible, absolutely horrible what they said about him, especially in *The Village Voice*. One guy said they hated him and they wished he'd die. And I said, "Bob, they actually really wish you were dead," and he said, "It doesn't bother me." . . . It just rolled right off of him. And he said, "Farida, they say all kinds of things about me, so I've just learned to live with it." . . . My experience being around him [was that] people were so obsequious and therefore how could you trust anybody?

The New Yorker used Pauline Kael, who, fresh from trashing Orson Welles's reputation in her *Citizen Kane Book*, felt that a little more debunking of a genius was in order. Her view of Dylan was betrayed by statements such as "The Bob Dylan [his fans] responded to [in the sixties] was a put-on artist. He was derisive, and even sneering, but in the sixties that was felt to be a way of freaking out those who weren't worthy of being talked to straight. . . . In *Renaldo and Clara* his mocking spirit is just bad news." In fact, Kael's sour review was one of the least personalized assaults upon the movie. In most of the reviews there seemed to be a sense of personal grievance, as if the critics believed now that everything Dylan had produced to date was somehow a con—a put-on, as Kael would say. Dylan, not surprisingly, felt a need to defend himself and the movie.

Bob Dylan: Reading the reviews of the movie, I sensed a feeling of them wanting to crush things. Those reviews weren't about the movie. They were just an excuse to get at me for one reason or another. . . . I was disappointed that the critics couldn't get beyond the superficial elements. They thought the movie was all about Bob Dylan, Joan Baez and Sara Dylan . . . and [it] wasn't. [1978]

Despite his attempts to defend the movie in the press by committing himself to a further flurry of interviews at the beginning of February, the film sank without trace. It opened in only one more city, Minneapolis, and disappeared from American cinemas within weeks, never to reappear. A consortium later convinced Dylan to edit the movie down to two hours—their two-million-dollar offer for the edited version at least helped to reduce the film's financial deficit—and rereleased it to American cinemas. Dylan, mocking those who had savaged the film so mercilessly, gave the consortium a film that was all the critics had claimed the four-hour version to be, that is, an inchoate jumble of improvised scenes, edited in a seemingly random order with little evidence of a rationale. He included virtually all the concert footage featured in the original movie, presumably to appease the uncomprehending consortium. It was his final revenge on those responsible for the brutal reception given to *Renaldo and Clara*.

Ironically, when the four-hour version received its European premiere at Cannes in May it was enthusiastically received, and when it made its London debut in July it ran for three months and proved to be a regular favorite at repertory cinemas for the next few years. TV rights were later bought up in England, Germany and Sweden. Though reviews were still mixed, several European reviewers considered it an audacious work, and even those who were unhappy with it showed considerably more restraint than their American counterparts. The friendlier response to the film in Europe would mirror the more favorable reviews there of the 1978 concerts and the *Street-Legal* album, which between them would constitute a year of considerable artistic activity from Dylan.

To describe the reviews of the shows in the Far East and Europe as kinder is something of an understatement. They verged on the ecstatic. The new arrangements of a cross section of Dylan's finest songs were enthusiastically welcomed in Japan and Australia. Despite Stoner's distaste for the sound, which would be shared by American critics, the two-hour-plus shows seemed well thought out, and Dylan seemed genuinely communicative. The early shows were lacking in punch, and some of the more incongruous elements in the band, such as the flute and congas, seemed temporarily in the ascendant. But Cross's guitar playing and the saxophone playing of Douglas became more dominant as the tour progressed, and Dylan's voice became harder, more insistent. In Japan, though, he was still finding his feet, looking for a way to work this band into a cohesive unit.

Rob Stoner: He had in mind to do something like Elvis Presley, I think. That size band and the uniforms. Also, he wasn't very sure about it, which is why he opened way out of town. I mean, we didn't go anyplace close to Europe or England or America forever, man. . . . He was very insecure about it and I don't blame him. I think he knew subconsciously he was making a big mistake.

Unfortunately, Dylan once again picked the wrong end of the tour to record a live album. In 1974 and 1976 the earlier shows on the tour were certainly superior. In this case he would have been well advised to hold back until the European leg before recording an album. As it was, *Bob Dylan at Budokan*, the double album released in November 1978 in Japan and April 1979 in America and Europe, was intended only as a souvenir for the Japanese of the earlier shows, rather than the testament to a 115-date world tour it has become.

Bob Dylan: They twisted my arm to do a live album for Japan. It was the same band I used on *Street-Legal*, and we had just started findin' our way into things on that tour when they recorded it. I never meant for it to be any type of representation of my stuff or my band or my live show. [1984]

The scale of the band and the size of the arenas he was playing precluded Dylan from trying out new songs live, and there were few surprises after the first couple of dates, as the band settled into a standard format for the tour. The major set variation on the first leg of the tour was which of several blues standards he would open each show with. Over the course of the Far East tour fans heard Dylan's versions of Billy Lee Riley's "Repossession Blues" (a dig at those who sought to dub this the Alimony Tour), Ernest Lewis's "Lonesome Bedroom Blues," Tampa Red's "Love Her with a Feeling" and at one show Robert Johnson's "Steady Rollin' Man." In Europe and America, Tampa Red's "Love Crazy" and Willie Dixon's "I'm Ready" vied for inclusion with "Love Her with a Feeling."

On the Far East leg Dylan had no new album to promote—indeed, his last album was more than two years old—so there was a nagging sense that he was playing an oldies show, an impression partly confirmed by the Japanese promoter's insistence that he include certain songs in his set, a demand he would have resisted in previous years. But now Dylan's new manager, Jerry Weintraub, was attempting to instill the ethos of the professional entertainer in Dylan. Also, his serious financial difficulties, primarily the result of his messy and expensive divorce and the commercial failure of *Renaldo and Clara*, precluded him from aborting what would be a very profitable Far East tour.

Rob Stoner: That guy [Weintraub] accompanied us to Japan and he was like always around. Yeah, suddenly we were the Entertainer and it was a little too stodgy. I'll never forget one day [at rehearsals] a telegram arrived from the Japanese promoter and in it he had a manifest of the songs he expected Bob to do on this tour. In other words, he was a jukebox, he was playing requests. "We don't want you coming here and doing like your new experimental material or getting up there and jamming. It's not enough for people to be paying good yen to see Bob Dylan. They want to see Bob Dylan doing 'Blowin' in the Wind' " and like on and on—the most predictable greatest-hits ten songs you could name. . . . By then I might as well have been working in Wayne Newton's band or something.

If the press reacted well in the Far East, there was already dissension in the band. Dylan had become very close to one of the backing singers, Helena Springs, and this inevitably caused animosity and envy among some of the other members of the crew. Helena Springs had been recruited during the impressing-women-I-like phase of the rehearsals, and she had no experience singing in a band on this scale. Her lack of experience was frowned upon, but she was a fresh and vivacious personality, and the band benefited from her inclusion. Dylan tried to encourage her development as a singer, and even started teaching her to write songs. While in Brisbane in March, they worked up a few songs together.

Helena Springs: We were together in Brisbane one evening and he was playing on the guitar and we were just goofing around, laughing, and I said, "I can't really write." . . . He said, "Well, come on, I'll write something with you. We'll write something together." And I said, "OK." He said, "You start singing some stuff and I'll start playing." So he started strumming his guitar and I started to sing, just making up lyrics. And he'd make up stuff and that was when we got "If I Don't Be There by Morning" and "Walk Out in the Rain."

Dylan and Springs remained close for some time to come. They also wrote many songs together on the 1978 tour. Springs did not leave his employ until the winter of 1980, when, ironically, she was replaced by Carolyn Dennis, her fellow backing singer on the 1978 tour.

If certain members of the crew were unhappy with Springs' intimacy with Dylan they refrained from comment, in his earshot at least. However, by this time Rob Stoner was very unhappy, and Springs was not the source of his dissatisfaction. He did not feel that the 1978 band suited Dylan's music, and he was bored by the lack of spontaneity. He was also getting, because of his position as bandleader, all the complaints the musicians wanted to direct at Dylan. Even the way his coplayer in the rhythm section played was getting to him.

Rob Stoner: Ian Wallace, man, had a beat like a cop. . . . The drummer sounds like fuckin' sludge . . . when he was playing with Bob he couldn't swing from a rope. . . . I was not happy and Bob knew this and my not being happy meant that I was fucking every chick on the bus and I was getting a little wild myself. Fortunately, you can't get drugs in Australia and Japan as easily as you can places that you know [but] . . . I was drinking a lot.

When the Far East tour wound to an end on April 1 at the Sydney Fairgrounds, Stoner told Dylan he wanted out. Dylan, after spending a three-day vacation in New Zealand with Ra Aranga, a New Zealand princess he had met in Auckland earlier on the tour, returned to Los Angeles to find a new bass player and bandleader, and set about recording his first studio album in thirty months.

Dylan's choice for Stoner's replacement was not a cheap option. Jerry Scheff, like Steve Douglas, had made his reputation as part of Presley's touring band in the early seventies. With Scheff's recruitment it did seem as if Dylan really was intent on assuming Presley's mantle. Scheff was thrown in at the deep end as, within a week of joining the band, he was required to take part in the sessions for *Street-Legal*.

Dylan had very little time to record his new album. A European tour was scheduled to begin in June, and the members of the band were looking for a brief respite in the interim. Realistically, he only had something like two weeks to record the album. In order for the sessions to proceed as smoothly as possible, he decided to record with the touring band, which had worked on several of the scheduled songs during soundchecks and rehearsals, and were by now conversant with his idiosyncrasies. He also decided to use his own rehearsal studio, Rundown in Santa Monica, as the venue for the recording sessions, with the help of a mobile studio console. The album was recorded even more quickly than required.

Bob Dylan: It took us a week to make *Street-Legal*—we mixed it the following week and put it out the week after. If we hadn't done it that fast we wouldn't have made an album at all, because we were ready to go back on the road. [1978]

The outcome, however, was unsatisfactory. Dylan had always recorded "on the run" and the results were normally perfectly acceptable, if not always the best achievable. But this time he was using a large band, a band that required more than the basic sixteen-track setup that had been suitable for his purposes in the past. The sophistications of modern studio techniques had overtaken him, and *Street-Legal* would be the first of three albums that eventually would force him to reevaluate his entire approach to recording. Dylan himself soon admitted to a sense of disappointment with the results, though he would persevere with his time-tested approach for some time yet.

Bob Dylan: There were some problems with the record: I didn't want to do it there; couldn't find the right producer. But it was necessary to do it. So we just brought in the remote truck and cut it, went for a live sound. During that whole period we forgot about the shows. So they were a little stiff. [1978]

The sound on the album is thin yet muddy, a poor representation of a band that on a good day could produce a full and rich sound and sophisticated arrangements. Also, Dylan's vocals lacked the crisp clarity that he had achieved on *Blood on the Tracks* and *Desire*. The results, though well received in Europe during the euphoria of his tour there, were savaged in the American press. The critics had got their teeth into the impudent runt with his film and they were not going to let go just because he was doing what he did best, writing and recording new songs. Greil Marcus's ill-considered review in *Rolling Stone*, headlined

"Never So Utterly Fake," set the tone for the jaundiced U.S. press, which chose in the late seventies to forget survivors of the sixties like Dylan and Van Morrison, and to ignore or castigate innovators of the seventies like Patti Smith and Television, preferring instead the regressive "authenticity" of Bruce Springsteen or the mock-artistry of David Bowie. Dylan was in for a hard time in the second half of 1978.

June broke promisingly enough, with seven sold-out shows at the Universal Amphitheater in Los Angeles, intended to whip the band into shape for Dylan's first European tour in twelve years. When he arrived in London on June 13, it was the Isle of Wight mayhem all over again. The English press had hyped his six sellout dates at London's massive seventeen-thousand-seat Earls Court to such an extent that he must have been somewhat nervous about how the English would respond to his new arrangements, particularly in the light of the punk revolution that had transformed the English music scene beyond all recognition in the previous two years.

He need not have worried. One newspaper review, headlined "The Greatest Concert I Have Ever Seen," set the tone for most U.K. press reviews. The next issue of *Melody Maker* included an eight-page pullout that celebrated the engagement with four enthusiastic reviews of the London shows. From London, he headed for Rotterdam, where fifty-five thousand fans were waiting; then Dortmund, Berlin and Nuremberg, where he played to eighty thousand in the stadium where Hitler had held his rallies. Six shows in Paris were as triumphant as the London engagement, as were two shows in Göteborg, Sweden. He finally returned to England a month to the day after opening his European tour at Earls Court. This time he was concluding the tour with a massive open-air show at a disused airfield in the Surrey countryside, attended by an estimated two hundred thousand fans.

The Blackbushe show represented the high point of the 1978 world tour. Playing to his most devoted fans—the English—in his largest show since the Isle of Wight, Dylan performed for two and a half hours, singing ten songs not performed at the shows a month earlier, including six from the newly released *Street-Legal*. The fans loved it and accorded Dylan a rapturous reception.

Ironically, Dylan was not the only one to "clean up" on that hot summer day. Bootleggers had rapidly pressed an album from the last Earls Court show and were selling copies on the site. Later he expressed considerable anger at this new wave of illicit vinyl. Yet his failure to respond to the euphoria of the European tour by releasing an official live album meant inevitably that the bootleggers would create a product to meet the demand.

The European tour was extensively bootlegged: Twelve of the twenty-seven shows appeared, at least partially, on vinyl. Conversely, only two concerts were bootlegged from his somewhat lengthier sixty-five-date tour of America that fall, an indication of the demand in Europe for the 1978 Dylan and the lack of demand in America.

Dylan's fall tour of North America began in Augusta, Maine, on September 15, after two months off the road. The backdrop to the tour was not promising. Aside from the critical flak he had been subjected to in the U.S. press all year, *Street-Legal* had sold poorly. His three previous studio albums had all reached number one; *Street-Legal* failed even to reach the top ten. Meanwhile, the first single from the album, "Baby Stop Crying," which had been a smash hit in Europe, providing Dylan with his first top twenty single in the U.K. since "Knockin' on Heaven's Door," had failed even to make it onto *Billboard*'s Hot 100. If he was to remain a commercial force into the eighties, the 1978 U.S. tour would have to reaffirm his big-league status.

This was his first nationwide tour since that legendary 1974 tour, when twelve million people had scrambled for tickets to a mere forty shows. This time Dylan, though still playing the large arenas, would not even sell every show out, as the U.S. press suggested that the show was an indication of Dylan's desire to end his days playing Las Vegas, his big band belting out those classic tunes from his sixties heyday. He reacted with understandable anger.

Bob Dylan: The writers complain the show's disco or Las Vegas. I don't know how they came up with those theories. We never heard them when we played Australia or Japan or Europe. It's like someone made it up in one town and the writer in the next town read it. [1978]

Determined to disavow the notion that he was copying Presley or even Bruce Springsteen (whose 1978 tour was the biggest commercial and critical success of the year), and refuting the idea that he was deliberately playing the entertainer, he attempted to illustrate how every aspect of this band had been represented in his past work.

Bob Dylan: I don't know how radically different it is from things in the past, considering the elements that I have in this band I've . . . used before. I made an album called *New Morning* and we used singers on just about every track, so I've done that. As far as using the horn sound, I used the horn sound in Nashville on "Rainy Day Women" . . . there isn't really anything new, just a bunch of pieces put together. [1978]

In fact, there was one discernible similarity between Dylan's fall shows and the concurrent Springsteen tour: It represented the first time Dylan had ever prefaced songs with brief rap-stories, along the lines of the reminiscences and tall tales that often served as introductions to Springsteen's best-known songs.

The most peculiar of Dylan's raps was the one before "Señor." It may be tempting to read some kind of religious meaning into it in the light of subsequent events, particularly as it appeared in the shows sometime during November:

Bob Dylan: I was riding on a train one time through Mexico, traveling up north to San Diego, and I must have fell asleep on this train and I woke up and it was about midnight . . . and the train had stopped at a place called Monterrey. . . . This bunch of children were getting off the train, this family—there must have been about seventeen children and a mother and father and they were getting off the train. And at the time I was watching it all through the glass; it was dark outside so the whole side of the train was like a mirror. So I was watching it all happen and I saw this old man stumble up onto the train and he gets onto the car, and he was walking down and he took a seat right across the car from me. I felt a vibration in the air. . . . I turned to look at him and I could see he wasn't dressed in anything but a blanket; he was just wearing a blanket. He must have been a hundred fifty years old. I turned around to look at him and I could see both his eyes were burning out—they were on fire and there was smoke coming out of his nostrils. I said, "Well, this is the man I want to talk to."

The sound Dylan was presenting to the Americans was considerably harsher than what the Europeans had heard and loved. He was giving most songs a raucous, hollering delivery that sometimes stripped them of their sensitivity, notably "Tangled Up in Blue," whose torch-ballad arrangement had come in for such praise in Europe. But some songs really benefited from the treatment, notably the *Street-Legal* songs, which now really came into their own. New arrangements of songs such as "I Threw It All Away," "The Times They Are a-Changin' " and "Mr. Tambourine Man" were also more inventive than on the previous legs of the world tour.

Yet he was fighting a losing battle. Though the fans who saw the shows were as enthusiastic as ever, it seemed that his overwhelming self-confidence and unerring sense of timing was audibly draining from him with each successive performance. His best performances now seemed to be given to the empty arenas when he was soundchecking, as he would frequently work on new songs like "I Must Love You Too Much," "You Treat Me Like a Stepchild" and "This Way That Way" or run through favorite covers such as Lowell Fulson's "Reconsider Baby," Shel Silverstein's "Daddy's Little Girl" or Tampa Red's "But I Forgive You." The two-hour shows were wearing on his vocal cords, his temper and his spirits. He needed someone to pull back on the reins.

Part
3

Busy Being
Born Again . . .

27 | 1978–79: Pulling Back on the Reins

By mid-November 1978, Dylan was in a poor state of mind. He was forty dates into a tortuous sixty-five-date American tour—his first nationwide tour in four years—that had been lambasted by the U.S. press, and attendances at some of the shows had been disappointing. The cumulative effect upon him of the negative receptions for *Renaldo and Clara*, *Street-Legal* and now the American tour—in stark contrast with the rhapsodic response for both the album and tour in Europe—can only be surmised. After an impressive show in his hometown, Los Angeles, on November 15, he still had a month to go on the road. His next stop was in San Diego on the seventeenth, where something remarkable happened.

Bob Dylan: Toward the end of the show someone out in the crowd . . . knew I wasn't feeling too well. I think they could see that. And they threw a silver cross on the stage. Now, usually I don't pick things up in front of the stage. Once in a while I do. Sometimes I don't. But I looked down at that cross. I said, "I gotta pick that up." So I picked up the cross and I put it in my pocket. . . . And I brought it backstage and I brought it with me to the next town, which was out in Arizona. . . . I was feeling even worse than I'd felt when I was in San Diego. I said, "Well, I need something tonight." I didn't know what it was. I was used to all kinds of things. I said, "I need something tonight that I didn't have before." And I looked in my pocket and I had this cross. [1979]

Stuck in a Tucson hotel room, Dylan—in his own words—needed something that he did not have before. He later talked about what being "born again" meant to him. He seems to have experienced a literal vision of Christ, Lord of Lord, King of Kings. The state of mind Dylan was in clearly made him susceptible to such an experience. In the song lyrics on his next two albums he would refer again and again to a feeling that Jesus entering his life literally saved him from an early grave.

Bob Dylan: There was a presence in the room that couldn't have been anybody but Jesus. . . . I truly had a born-again experience, if you want to call it that. . . . Jesus put his hand on me. It was a physical thing. I felt it. I felt it all over me. I felt my whole body tremble. The glory of the Lord knocked me down and picked me up. [1980]

Bob Dylan: Jesus did appear to me as King of Kings, and Lord of Lords. . . . I believe every knee shall bow one day, and He did die on the cross for all mankind . . . they call it reborn . . . it changes everything. I mean, it's like waking one day and can you imagine being reborn, can you imagine turning into another person? It's pretty scary if you think about it. . . . It happens spiritually, it don't happen mentally. [1981]

On the road, "heading toward the sun," Dylan started to question his own moral values, though he still seemed uncertain how to interpret his vision. The meaning of his born-again experience temporarily eluded him. He turned to those in his band who had discovered peace with Christ, notably Helena Springs, the lady with whom he had been writing songs of betrayal and loneliness, songs such as "If I Don't Be There by Morning" and "Coming from the Heart," and who, of all the musicians, was closest to Dylan at this point.

Helena Springs: I think he was having some problems. . . . He called me and he asked me, and they were questions that no one could possibly help with. And I just said, "Don't you ever pray?" . . . And he said, "Pray?" Like that, you know. And he said, "Really?" And he asked me more questions. . . . He started inquiring. . . . He's a very inquisitive person—which is one good thing about searching for truth.

When Springs referred to Dylan "having some problems," it would appear that his soul-searching was primarily motivated by "woman trouble." Since his divorce, he had been involved with several women, notably Farida McFree, Springs herself and a black actress by the name of Mary Alice Artes, who receives an acknowledgment on *Street-Legal*. If the subject matter of the songs on that album was not related to his divorce from Sara, as Dylan repeatedly insisted it was not, then it clearly indicated that his problems with "witchy women" remained. In Dylan's 1979 composition "Trouble in Mind," Satan whispers to the singer that when he grows bored of Miss So-and-so he has "another woman for ya." If Dylan was on the run from the Triple Goddess, he would need the protection of a strong, patriarchal religion.

Bob Dylan: Beauty can be very, very deceiving and it's not always of God. Beauty appeals to our eyes. . . . The beauty of the sunset . . . that's God-given. [But] I spent a lot of time dealing with man-made beauty, so that sometimes the beauty of God's world has evaded me. [1981]

David Mansfield and Steven Soles, who had both been in Dylan's various touring bands since 1975, were committed born-again Christians, and both were subjected to his inquiries about the nature of their faith, as was ex–Rolling Thunder member T-Bone Burnett. One thing they said in particular struck a chord with Dylan, and reflected the toll the custody battle and his subsequent enforced separation from his children had taken on him.

Howie Wyeth: T-Bone [Burnett] read Bob that line in the Bible that says if you listen to astrologers and people who are into the black arts . . . your family will be taken from you. And he'd just lost the battle in court. . . . T-Bone told me that the thing that really nailed it was when he showed him in the Bible that quote.

Steven Soles: I kept telling him that I was so glad that I didn't have to place my faith in man any longer.

Dylan gave few clues to the thousands of fans he was playing to every night in the final four weeks of his yearlong world tour that he was reevaluating his moral code. A "small silver cross," though, clearly represented a new starting point. Six days after Tucson, Dylan was in Fort Worth playing the Convention Center. Onstage he was wearing a not-so-small metal cross around his neck. For a man raised a Jew this could not be a casual gesture. He also began to improvise a new line for the powerful, stripped-bare version of "Tangled Up in Blue" he was performing at the time. Rather than having the mysterious lady in the topless bar quoting an Italian poet from the fourteenth century, she was now quoting from the Bible, initially from the Gospel according to Matthew—the Gospel written to convince Jews that Jesus fulfilled the Old Testament prophecies regarding their Messiah. Gradually, though, the lines she quoted changed, until Dylan settled upon a verse from Jeremiah, the very verse he would quote on the inner sleeve of the *Saved* album: "Behold, the days come, saith the Lord, that I shall make a new covenant with the house of Israel, and with the house of Judah" (Jeremiah 31:31).

As he entered the final two weeks of the 115-date world tour, Dylan began to attack the shows with renewed vigor. The songs he had been writing on the American tour to date had titles like "(You Treat Me Like a) Stepchild" and "I Must Love You Too Much." He now began writing songs that addressed some of the more pressing issues that were whirling around in his head. At sound-checks he worked on a new song called "Slow Train." For the final show of the tour, in Miami, he introduced another new song, called "Do Right to Me Baby (Do unto Others)," the first song he had ever written wholly around a dictum from the Bible, and a New Testament Gospel at that: "All things, therefore, that you want men to do to you, you also must likewise do to them; this, in fact, is what the Law and the Prophets mean" (Matthew 7:12).

It was not only Dylan's fellow musicians who were steering him in this particular direction. His sometime girlfriend, Mary Alice Artes, had been brought up as a Christian, but her faith had faded. On returning to Malibu, he discovered she too was reevaluating her religious beliefs. Indeed, according to most reports, Artes had moved out on him after deciding to reembrace her founding faith. According to Ken Gulliksen, pastor of the Vineyard Fellowship in West Los Angeles, this was not quite the case. Rather, Artes attended a Vineyard Fellowship meeting in Tarzana, California.

Ken Gulliksen: At the end of the meeting she came up to me and said that she wanted to rededicate her life to the Lord. . . . That morning she did rededicate her life to the Lord. Then she revealed that she was Bob Dylan's girlfriend and asked if a couple of the pastors would come there and then and talk to Bob. And so Larry Myers and Paul Esmond went over to Bob's house and ministered to him. He responded by saying, Yes, he did in fact want Christ in his life. And he prayed that day and received the Lord.

Dylan was duly baptized at the home of Bill Dwyer, one of the pastors from the Vineyard Fellowship.

Before he embraced the uniquely Californian brand of Christianity advocated by the Vineyard Fellowship, Dylan could not be described as a fundamentalist. Indeed, he did not seem to have immediately considered his vision in Tucson to be a born-again experience. Only when the born-again creed was outlined for him did he recognize the nature of his vision—that this change was not merely a shift in his moral values but a total rebirth, an awakening from original sin.

Bob Dylan: Being born again is a hard thing. You ever seen a mother give birth to a child? Well, it's painful. We don't like to lose those old attitudes and hang-ups. Conversion takes time because you have to learn to crawl before you can walk. You have to learn to drink milk before you can eat meat. You're reborn, but like a baby. A baby doesn't know anything about this world and that's what it's like when you're reborn. You're a stranger. You have to learn all over again. [1980]

Bob Dylan: What they mean by saying that is that they're born again by the spirit from above. Born once is born with the spirit from below—when you're born, that's the spirit that you're born with. Born again is born with the spirit from above. That's a little different. [1981]

The first stage in having "to learn all over again" required him to go back to school. Dylan had never been the best of students when it came to formal learning, and when it was suggested that he undertake an intensive course in learning to walk in the spirit of the Lord, he was his usual recalcitrant self. The three-month course at the Vineyard School of Discipleship demanded regular attendance, four days a week, something he had not attempted since his time with Norman Raeben back in 1974.

Bob Dylan: At first I said, "There's no way I can devote three months to this [Bible course]. I've got to be back on the road soon." But I was sleeping one day and I just sat up in bed at seven in the morning and I was compelled to get dressed and drive over to the Bible school. . . . I didn't know myself if I could go for three months. But I did begin telling a few people after a couple of months and a lot of them got angry at me. [1980]

If the simple acceptance of Christ as his savior did not imbue Dylan with righteous fervor, the adoption of the Vineyard Church brand of Christianity transformed him into a Bible-thumping evangelist. The classes at the Vineyard School of Discipleship were held in a back room above a realtor's office in Reseda, California. They lasted from half past eight in the morning until noon, four days a week. The kinds of classes they were is best described by an anecdote recounted in *Stairway to Heaven*, a thorough survey of Christian rock music by David Seay and Mary Neely.

David Seay and Mary Neely: During class breaks, Dylan would often walk into the parking lot in back of the prefab building, dressed against the brisk morning air in a leather jacket and stocking cap, to smoke Marlboro cigarettes and talk with his girlfriend. . . . One morning a student stood to report a dream he had the night before. In the dream, the members of the class were gathered in an upper room, a beautiful cedar-paneled loft lit golden by sun pouring through a skylight. One corner of the room, the student said, had been left unfinished, exposing insulation padding, ducts and a tangle of dangerously frayed electric wiring. The hazardous wiring, it seemed, had to be pulled down before the room could be made safe for habitation. It was a difficult, dangerous job, and the dreamer was frightened, until an unidentified man assured him that only boldness was required. Encouraged, the dreamer thrust his hands into the wiring and pulled. It fell away, and through the hole in the roof, fresh, clean water began to flow. From his seat in the corner of the room, Dylan's eyes were bright. He was nodding and smiling as a moment of unmistakable recognition passed between the student and the star. . . . Bob Dylan's interpretation of his classmate's dream of the upper room was the simple one. Old things are passed away, and all things are made new. Old circuits must be stripped for the cleansing water to flow.

According to Ken Gulliksen, the course taught Dylan all about his basic responsibilities as a Christian, about the message of Jesus and about spreading the Gospel.

Ken Gulliksen: Bob went through our school of discipleship . . . for three and a half months. He was faithful there every day, learning the Word, growing in the Lord. That's basically what happened. It was an intensive course studying about the life of Jesus, principles of discipleship, the Sermon on the Mount, what it is to be a believer, how to grow, how to share. It was very practical, but at the same time a good solid Bible study overview type of ministry.

The important phrases here are "principles of discipleship" and "how to share." The later controversy surrounding Dylan's conversion might have been somewhat more muted if it were not for the evangelism present in the songs on *Slow Train Coming* and *Saved*. Many fans could probably have tolerated a Dylan who felt that Christ was the savior. It was less palatable for him to suggest that there was a clear dividing line between the saved and the damned.

Bob Dylan: That [born-again period] was all part of my experience. It had to happen. When I get involved in something, I get totally involved. I don't just play around on the fringes. [1983]

The *Chambers Dictionary* definition of *evangelical* reads as follows: "Of the school that insists especially on the total depravity of unregenerate human nature, the justification of the sinner by faith alone, the free offer of the Gospel to all, and the plenary inspiration and exclusive authority of the Bible." These were exactly the beliefs Dylan was learning. He was taught to conceive of man as born into a state of sin, that the Gospels represented not only figurative but also literal truth and that the Devil was at work every minute of every day, insidiously undermining man's morals.

Bob Dylan: You would think the enemy is someone you can strike at and that would solve the problem, but the real enemy is the Devil. That's the real enemy, but he tends to shade himself and hide himself and put it into people's minds that he's really not there and he's really not so bad, and that he's got a lot of good things to offer too. . . . What Jesus does for an ignorant man like myself is to make the qualities and characteristics of God more believable to me, 'cause I can't beat the Devil. Only God can. . . . Satan's working everywhere. You're faced with him constantly. If you can't see him he's inside you making you feel a certain way. He's feeding you envy and jealousy. [1981]

The message conveyed by the fellowship was not merely evangelical, it was imminently apocalyptic. Indeed the key word here is *imminent*. The end of the world was not merely nigh, it was NIGH, with a capital double-underlined N!

Bob Dylan: What I learned in Bible school was just . . . an extension of the same thing I believed in all along, but just couldn't verbalize or articulate. Whether you want to believe Jesus Christ is the Messiah is irrevelant, but whether you're aware of the messianic complex, that's all that's important. . . . People who believe in the coming of the Messiah live their lives right now as if He was here. That's my idea of it, anyway. I know people are going to say to themselves, "What the fuck is this guy talking about?" but it's all there in black and white, the written and unwritten Word. I don't have to defend this. The Scriptures back me up. [1985]

If the classes taught Dylan about the infallibility of the Gospels, they were also providing a good grounding for the works and teachings of one Hal Lindsey, who, according to writer Steve Turner, was once a leading member of the Vineyard Church. Lindsey's book *The Late Great Planet Earth* became Dylan's second Bible and added an apocalyptic edge to his worldview.

If his doomsday poems had always displayed a keen sense of the apocalyptic, he had rarely drawn from a wholly "black"or cataclysmic apocalyptic tradition (the only examples that spring to mind are "I'd Hate to Be You on That Dreadful Day," "All Along the Watchtower" and "Changing of the Guards"). Rather, he had preferred to use the red, or revolutionary, tradition (as in "Ain't Gonna Grieve," and "The Times They Are a-Changin' ") or the green or pastoral tradition (as in "Chimes of Freedom," "When the Ship Comes In" and "Gates of Eden").*

---

*My terminology here is largely derived from Joseph Campbell's important essay "Bob Dylan and the Pastoral Apocalypse" in *Journal of Popular Culture*, 1975.

The black apocalyptic tradition, to quote Campbell, "finds expression in the Old Testament prophets—Isaiah, Jeremiah, Ezekiel—and in the New Testament, Revelation of St. John the Divine." It was specifically Revelation on which Hal Lindsey based his concept that the events predicted there were taking place in the second half of the twentieth century. Little versed in the historical background required to refute Lindsey's dubious tenets, Dylan was an ideal disciple for Lindsey's rhetoric.

According to Lindsey, current world events had been foretold in the apocalyptic tracts of the Bible. Lindsey's basic premise in *The Late Great Planet Earth* is that the events revealed to St. John the Divine in Revelation directly parallel twentieth-century history, starting with the reestablishment of the Jews' homeland, Israel; Lindsey proceeds by identifying Russia as Magog and Iran as Gog—the confederation responsible for the instigation of the Battle of Armageddon. It seems inconceivable that a man as innately skeptical as Dylan could so wholeheartedly embrace Lindsey's interpretations. Yet there can be no question that in 1979—and for some time to come—he believed that the end was indeed at hand. A lengthy rap from one of his fall 1979 shows illustrates the unequivocal nature of his beliefs at this time.

Bob Dylan: You know we're living in the end times. I don't think there's anybody . . . who doesn't feel that in their heart. The Scriptures say, "In the last days, perilous times shall be at hand. Men shall become lovers of their own selves. Blasphemous, heavy and high-minded." Now, I don't know who you're gonna vote for, but none of those people is gonna straighten out what's happening in the world today. But what's happening in it right now? Take a look at the Middle East. We're heading for a war. That's right. They're heading for a war. There's gonna be a war over there. I'd say maybe five years, maybe ten years, could be fifteen years. . . . I told you the times they are a-changin' and they did. I said the answer was blowin' in the wind and it was. I'm telling you now Jesus is coming back, and He is! And there is no other way of salvation. . . . There's only one way to believe, there's only one way—the Truth and the Life. It took me a long time to figure that out before it did come to me, and I hope it doesn't take you that long. But Jesus is coming back to set up His kingdom in Jerusalem for a thousand years. [1979]

Aside from songs like "Precious Angel," "When You Gonna Wake Up" and "When He Returns"—all subsequently included on *Slow Train Coming*, and all of which drew heavily and directly upon the Book Of Revelation—Dylan also wrote at this time a song called at this time "Ye Shall Be Changed" (now issued on the Bootleg Series) perhaps the most extreme of all his songs from this period. "Ye Shall Be Changed" was based on chapter 11 of Lindsey's *The Late*

Great Planet Earth. In this chapter Lindsey interprets a passage from 1 Corinthians (15:52), "In the twinkling of an eye, at the last trumpet . . . we shall be changed," to mean that "when God has the last trumpet blow it means He will move out all Christians—and at this point we shall be changed" into essence. Only at this point will the Battle of Armageddon be fought.

Lindsey takes a classic premillennialist position—that Christ will return before the thousand-year rule and defeat evil. The alternative view adopted by the postmillennialists—that Christ will return only after the Christians have established a thousand-year rule by "their own efforts"—is subjected to considerable scorn by Lindsey. The gradual transformation into a truly Christian kingdom on earth was never likely to appeal to the author of "The Times They Are a-Changin' " and "When the Ship Comes In," songs steeped in the apocalyptic fervor rediscovered on *Slow Train Coming.* For in the early months of 1979 Dylan was writing his most "political" album in sixteen years. This time, though, it was the politics of the millennium.

Indeed, a positive aspect of Dylan's spiritual quest was that he was once again writing songs at a prolific pace. Just as his classes with Raeben soon resulted in the *Blood on the Tracks* material, the intense tutorship from the Vineyard Fellowship provided the necessary inspiration for a number of remarkable new songs. During the three months of classes at the School of Discipleship, he wrote at least a dozen songs later recorded for *Slow Train Coming.* Of course, the Vineyard Fellowship was careful to ensure that such an important public figure was seen to be unequivocally adopting their creed.

Ken Gulliksen: He shared his music with Larry Myers, one of the pastors who had originally ministered to him. I freed Larry to go with Bob as much as possible. Bob asked him to come with the band on the road, so that Larry would be there to lead them in prayer and Bible study, and to minister to him personally. He and Bob became very close and trusted each other. Larry was often the sounding-board for Bob to share his lyrics.

28 | 1979: On the Holy Slow Train

W hen Dylan feels he has something important to say, he seems to approach recording with considerably more discipline than on those occasions when he just feels it is time to record another album. The album he planned to record in the spring of 1979 was bound to be controversial, irrespective of what care he took with it. The more palatable the sound of the album, though, the easier it would be to assimilate the message contained within it.

The essential ingredient in previous successful formulas had been the guitarist. On previous landmark recordings Dylan's selections had been inspired. This time his choice was ingenious. On March 29, 1979, he attended the final show of a successful engagement at the Roxy in Los Angeles by the British group Dire Straits. In their homeland they were regarded by the music press as a band who would have sought to join the finishing school for pub-rockers but had arrived too late, and were certainly too twee to pass the new-wave entrance exam.

In America in 1979, when the average journalist's conception of punk rock was Elvis Costello, the pleasant melodic sensibilities in the Straits' tunes, and their easy assimilation into the uniquely West Coast concept of AOR (adult-oriented rock), meant they were embraced with considerable enthusiasm. Guitarist and songwriter Mark Knopfler's distinctive instrumental flourishes defined mellifluous. If Dylan had a bitter pill for his audience to swallow, a spoonful of Knopfler's sugar would help the medicine go down. After the Roxy show, he approached Knopfler about playing on his next album. Knopfler agreed.

Though Dylan had succeeded in recording albums such as *Highway 61 Revisited, Blonde on Blonde, John Wesley Harding* and *Desire* with the producer serving as little more than a well-paid engineer, by 1979 he needed help to get his vision onto vinyl. The complexities of recording a big band sound had eluded him on *Desire* and *Street-Legal*. Determined to persevere with female singers and even horns, he required an experienced hand at the helm. He already had someone in mind.

Back in December 1977 he had dropped in on an Etta James session at Cherokee Studios. While there he had taken the opportunity to play some new tunes at the piano for James and her producer, Jerry Wexler. One eyewitness to the session later suggested that the songs Dylan had played were in fact "pieces of his new [1979] songs."

It was suggested in the press at the time that Wexler would produce Dylan's next album. After all, they had worked together—as coproducers—on Barry Goldberg's debut album back in 1973, and Dylan was a great admirer of Wexler's previous work as the prime exponent of the Muscle Shoals sound, a soulful amalgam of horns and a tight rhythm section, originated at Memphis's Muscle Shoals Studio and seemingly the exclusive property of Wexler's Atlantic acts in the sixties.

Dylan's next album was, of course, *Street-Legal*, which was recorded with barely a pause, or due notice, in one week in April 1978. Yet the idea of working with Wexler remained, and after the commercial failure of *Street-Legal*, using a producer who could provide his own creative input became imperative. Wexler's background in gospel and soul made him an ideal collaborator in producing the most unequivocally Christian album a white rock musician had produced since the times when repentant rock and rollers came out of the fifties, bottle in hand, in search of some solid ground to stand upon.

The sessions duly commenced on May 1. Wexler had suggested that Barry Beckett play keyboards. Beckett could also provide charts of individual parts for Knopfler and the rhythm section. He would later receive a coproducer's credit for the album. On drums was Pick Withers from Dire Straits, and on bass Tim Drummond, to whom in a St. Paul room back in 1974 Dylan had played the songs later included on *Blood on the Tracks*, and who was now a member of Ry Cooder's touring band. The horn section came courtesy of Muscle Shoals Studio. Two of the three female vocalists, Helena Springs, inevitably, and Carolyn Dennis, were the sole survivors of Dylan's 1978 band.

There were equally few survivors among the songs he had been writing on the European and American tours that summer and fall. The only song recorded at these sessions from those shows was "Do Right to Me Baby," which had been premiered at the final 1978 show in Miami, "in the theater of divine comedy." Another song he had been working on in December, called "Slow Train," would be the 1979 album's title track, though the lyrics were wholly rewritten during his period at the School of Discipleship.

The songs recorded at these historic May sessions fell neatly into two distinct categories: those that testified to Dylan's personal redemption, such as "I Believe in You," "Precious Angel," "Gonna Change My Way of Thinking" and "Trouble in Mind," and those that admonished the unrepentant and foretold their imminent damnation if they refused to embrace his message of salvation. The latter formed by far the bulk of the songs recorded, and spanned the full gamut of browbeating, from the gentle cajoling of "Do Right to Me Baby" to the out-and-out menace of "When You Gonna Wake Up" and "Slow Train."

For nonbelievers such as Pick Withers, Mark Knopfler and Tim Drummond, Dylan's unrelenting evangelism proved initially disorienting. As Withers has observed, "Things were a little strained the first day we went in the studio." Knopfler had already been forewarned about the nature of the material when Dylan had played him his new songs before the sessions, just as he had with Bloomfield before *Highway 61 Revisited* and *Blood on the Tracks.*

Mark Knopfler: Bob and I ran down a lot of those songs beforehand. And they might be in a very different form when he's just hittin' the piano and maybe I'd make suggestions about the tempo or whatever. Or I'd say, "What about a twelve-string?" . . . Each song has its own secret and needs teasing out.

Yet Knopfler phoned his manager, Ed Bicknell, during the sessions and remarked on how the Bible-thumping nature of the material had required him to make some conscious adjustments.

Mark Knopfler: The first night was pretty awful—it just didn't happen—but once we got into it, it was good. But all these songs are about God!

Even Wexler himself, who had worked with such singers as Aretha Franklin, Otis Redding and Ray Charles, all of whom had been raised within the gospel tradition, was a little taken aback by Dylan's stance—particularly when Dylan decided to work on his producer's beliefs during the sessions.

Jerry Wexler: I had no idea he was on this born-again Christian trip until he started to evangelize me. I said, "Bob, you're dealing with a sixty-two-year-old confirmed Jewish atheist. I'm hopeless. Let's just make an album."

According to a later statement by Dylan, he had not originally intended to record the *Slow Train Coming* material himself. He realized that the songs were extremely controversial, and knew that performing them himself would only lead to further furor. If the songs on *John Wesley Harding* had dealt with "the Devil in a fearful way," then *Slow Train Coming* was its bastard son.

Bob Dylan: The songs that I wrote for the *Slow Train* album [frightened me]. . . . I didn't plan to write them, but I wrote them anyway. I didn't like writing them, I didn't want to write them. . . . But I found myself writing these songs and after I had a certain amount of them I thought I didn't want to sing them, so I had a girl sing them for me . . . a girl I was singing with at the time, Carolyn Dennis. . . . I [would give] them all to her and [have] her record them, and not even put my name on them. I wanted the songs out but I didn't want to do it because I knew that it wouldn't be perceived in that way. It would just mean more pressure. I just did not want that at that time. [1984]

Though Dylan had clearly abandoned the notion of Carolyn Dennis recording the *Slow Train Coming* songs when he approached Knopfler at the conclusion of Dire Strait's U.S. tour, he originally intended to conclude the album with the female singers performing his most apocalyptic vision to date, "When He Returns." When he talked about the new songs frightening him, he must have had "When He Returns" in mind. He was initially reluctant to give the song his own voice.

He had, at least temporarily, abandoned his usual practice of recording songs without running through them in order that the musicians could pick the basic structures up. Thus the sessions progressed smoothly and the musicians blended together easily. The band's composition had proved perfect.

Jerry Wexler: Whatever we did was live. Bob might run it down on piano or guitar, just singing and playing the background until we had a rough shape in our minds, then the Muscle Shoals band would start to play it. As soon as it sounded right, Bob and the girls would start to sing. . . . [On] *Slow Train*, we furnished Bob with a band. It was something that we projected and thought might work.

Yet "When He Returns" required something different. Dylan recorded a demo vocal for the song, accompanied—apparently spontaneously—on the piano by Barry Beckett, in order that the singers could learn it. However, Beckett's remarkable, sparse accompaniment made him think again and, after practicing overnight, he sang a new, impassioned vocal over Beckett's original piano track, thus endowing the album with perhaps his strongest vocal since the exquisite "Visions of Johanna." He was right in his original thoughts— concluding the album with this stark, intensely foreboding song, which dealt so unequivocally with The End, was a terrifyingly audacious move, one that was bound to bring its own fair share of righteous anger down upon him.

With the album barely completed, the news of Dylan's conversion to Christianity began to filter through to the media. On May 22, he was required to give a pretrial deposition in Beverly Hills to answer a defamation-of-character suit by Patty Valentine regarding the song "Hurricane." Asked about his wealth, he replied, "You mean my treasure on earth?" Asked about specifics in the song he referred to the song's "fool" as being "whoever Satan gave power to" and "whoever was blind to the truth and was living by his own truth." Five days later *The Washington Post* reported his pretrial statements and noted that one Ken Gulliksen had revealed that Dylan had accepted Christ into his life and joined the Vineyard Christian Fellowship.

In June, Dylan provided Capital Radio in London with an acetate of "Precious Angel" in order that the song could be premiered on Roger Scott's afternoon show. Despite the unequivocal nature of the line about either having faith or "unbelief / And there ain't no neutral ground," the song did not fully convince his British followers of the truth of his conversion. By July, though, prerelease tapes of *Slow Train Coming* were being freely passed to the media, the intent presumably being to cushion the blow with a little forewarning, and were widely reviewed. The British music press responded with unmistakable glee to the opportunity of joining the U.S. media in taking potshots at Dylan's new creed. *New Musical Express* came up with the most original headline for its gossipy report on the conversion: "Dylan & God—It's Official."

Dylan presumably did not expect the album to be well received. Certainly the songs on *Slow Train Coming* contain their fair share of hints of already received ridicule and vilification at his embracing of Christianity, notably "Precious Angel" and "I Believe in You," in which the singer claims "they" want to drive him from their town because he believes in Him.

When the album was officially released on August 18, an important endorsement was received from a most surprising and welcome quarter, *Rolling Stone* magazine. *Rolling Stone* had not always been supportive of Dylan's activities in the seventies, and because it was the only major biweekly U.S. music journal its opinion carried unwarranted weight with American consumers. Editor Jann Wenner gave *Slow Train Coming* a two-page review in which he affirmed that in his opinion it was Dylan's finest work since *The Basement Tapes.* He concluded the review with words of unstinting praise:

Jann Wenner: Musically, this is probably Dylan's finest record, a rare coming together of inspiration, desire and talent that completely fuses strength, vision and art. Bob Dylan is the greatest singer of our times. No one is better. No one, in objective fact, is even very close. His versatility and vocal skills are unmatched. His resonance and feeling are beyond those of any of his contemporaries. More than his ability with words, and more than his insight, his voice is God's greatest gift to him.

Dylan found that the care he had taken with the album's sound was reaping rewards. Despite preferring "Gotta Serve Somebody" to the more instantly palatable "Precious Angel" as the first single release from *Slow Train Coming*, he was back on the singles chart before the album was even released. "Gotta Serve Somebody" provided him with his first top thirty single in six years. Though it did not make number one, *Slow Train Coming* was a surprise commercial success, indeed Dylan's second-best-selling album, outselling both *Blood on the Tracks* and *Blonde on Blonde*. Its twenty-six weeks on the chart again proved his remarkable durability when it seemed that his commercial standing had reached an all-time low. Possibly he also benefited from a recent spate of newly Christianized rock artists whose own albums had presaged his. Both Van Morrison's *Into the Music* and Patti Smith's *Wave* had preceded *Slow Train Coming*, and though both were less overt testaments to newfound beliefs, they suggested that rock and roll and religion could be appropriate bedfellows.

Meanwhile, Dylan was pressing on. By the time *Slow Train Coming* had entered the charts in early September, he had begun rehearsals for a fall tour that would take his new message into the theaters. Even as apologists prepared their texts suggesting that *Slow Train Coming* merely represented another phase in his chameleon career, and would quickly fade, he was hard at work on even more songs of faith and salvation. Wrapping his words in palatable sounds was not meant to obscure the import of the message.

Bob Dylan: I follow God, so if my followers are following me, indirectly they're gonna be following God too, because I don't sing any song which hasn't been given to me by the Lord to sing. [1979]

As Gulliksen has observed, at this stage Dylan was sharing his music with pastor Larry Myers, who "was often the backboard for Bob to share the lyrics." What he needed to decide before he went on the road was: Did he intend to perform any of the songs he had written before being born again? Despite Myers assuring him that his old songs were not "anti-God," and ever delighting in upsetting preconceptions, Dylan decided he had already spent the previous year touting around new versions of his old songs. The time had come to perform something wholly different.

Bob Dylan: In 1979 . . . we started out with a different show. We didn't play any song you'd ever heard before. Played a completely different show, with no song that anybody had ever heard. I thought that was interesting, you know. . . . I had never heard of . . . anybody who'd recorded songs for twenty years and then one day just didn't play any of 'em again, just played nothing but new songs. . . . I got a kick out of that. [1981]

Having envisaged such a format, he could hardly go out on the road and perform only the songs from *Slow Train Coming* and a couple of outtakes. He needed new material, particularly as at this stage his faith was changing with each passing day. The songs he wrote that summer and early fall were less self-evidently apocalyptic, concentrating more on affirming his own personal sense of gratitude at his redemption. "What Can I Do for You?," "Covenant Woman," "Saving Grace," "Saved" and "Pressing On" were songs about the joy of salvation, rather than the fear of hellfire that had fueled *Slow Train Coming*.

Initially, the rehearsals were fairly grandiose affairs. Despite the more stringent economics affecting a theater tour as opposed to an arena tour, Dylan seemed intent on having as large a band as in 1978. He soon realized the impracticality of this.

Dave Kelly: There was an intensive period of rehearsals before [the tour began]. There was more than the band then. . . . They started with a five- or four-piece horn section as well—Jim Horn, a well-known horn player, and some of the more famous L.A. session men. They were supposed to go with the horns on one side and the girls on the other. He had percussionists. Russ Baboo, the Jamaican guy . . . [David] Lindley made two solo albums with Baboo, having brought him from Jamaica to America. He also introduced him to Dylan. He did all sorts of weird things. Playing saucepan lids and things. He's a real percussionist. . . . About a week [*sic*] before we went on the road . . . he said, "What do you think, the horns or the girls?" I was totally flabbergasted! He said, "We can't really have both financially. It's just ridiculous." . . . I didn't know what to say . . . the horns were not doing a lot. The next day I came in and there were no horn players.

The rehearsals acted as a further spur to Dylan's muse. Having made the decision to perform only new songs, he entered rehearsals with only "Saving Grace" definitely composed.

Dave Kelly: He did write an awful lot of stuff [during rehearsals]. . . . There must have been twenty songs that he pulled from to do that tour, and they probably had forty. It was like nearly every day he'd come up with two or three new songs.

Dylan was not pausing to take stock after a successful album. He was already thinking about his next record. According to Kelly, his personal assistant at this time, Jerry Wexler was regularly in attendance at the rehearsals, making suggestions for the arrangements of the new songs. Dylan envisaged working with Wexler again on his next Christian album, which was likely to be more of a hit-and-run affair, slotted in during a respite from the tour, which would begin in the fall of 1979 and continue through the summer of 1980. Any album would have to be recorded much as *Street-Legal* had been. However, this time the musicians would be fully conversant with the material, since they were playing the songs night after night onstage.

As a final warm-up before the tour, Dylan and his slimmed-down touring band flew to New York in mid-October to perform three of the songs from *Slow Train Coming* on the popular late-night comedy show "Saturday Night Live." His performance was rather intense for such light fare, and he seemed at pains not to crack anything that might pass for a smile. If on his last national TV appearance, the John Hammond tribute, he had been positively loose, it seemed he had reverted to his previous demeanor when performing on this most popular of media—out-and-out terror. At least the performance suggested that no one looking for an evening of light entertainment need attend his forthcoming shows, scheduled for November and early December in the American West.

29 | 1979–80: Middle of the Road, East Coast Bondage

On November 1, 1979, Dylan played his first show since his conversion, at an intimate two-thousand-seat theater in one of the seedier parts of San Francisco. He had originally been booked into the Warfield Theater for seven dates, but exceptional demand led to the scheduling of a further seven shows. For six months he would tour the U.S. with his new show. And new it was. He had abandoned all the songs he had exhumed the previous year. The message he delivered that first and every subsequent night on his gospel tour was uncompromising.

The evening opened with his three female backing singers performing six gospel songs, concluding with the traditional "This Train (Is Bound for Glory)." The tone did not change perceptibly when Dylan took to the stage. He launched straight into "Gotta Serve Somebody," and followed it with six more songs from his new album, all without a single spoken comment. Finally a song was introduced that was not on the new album. "Covenant Woman" was a beautiful tribute to the woman who had led him to the Lord. It was the first song of the night to be fully convincing, Dylan having seemed tense throughout the first seven songs. After a brief interlude while one of the backup singers sang another spiritual, he returned and ran through the two songs he had yet to perform from *Slow Train Coming*.

By now it was clear that there would be no concessions to the audience, no memorable anthems. After "Do Right to Me" the set became distinctly unfamiliar. The remaining five songs of the main set were all new, with titles such as "Hanging On to a Solid Rock Made Before the Foundation of the World" and "When They Came for Him in the Garden." There could be no doubting the message being reiterated in each song. Despite some sections of the audience being less than enthusiastic about what they heard, Dylan and the band returned for an encore and after running through the traditional "Blessed Is the Name," Dylan walked to the piano, where, unaccompanied by the band, he began to sing "Pressing On." After one verse he got up from the piano, walked to the front of the stage and, with no guitar between him and the audience, picked up the mike and sang the remainder of the song.

Unfortunately, the two most important local reviewers, Philip Elwood of the *Examiner* (Headline: "Born-Again Dylan Bombs!") and Joel Selvin of the *Chronicle* (Headline: "Bob Dylan's God-Awful Gospel!"), were obstinately unimpressed by even this touching instance. If Elwood considered the show "a pretty grueling experience," it was Selvin's review that was most widely syndicated and that caused the most damage. The conclusion ran: "Dylan is no longer asking hard questions and raising an angry fist. Instead, he has opted for the soothing soporific which the simple 'truths' his brand of Christianity provides."

Yet perhaps the most damaging part of Selvin's review was the statement that "Catcalls and boos echoed throughout the ornate hall." These catcalls and boos remain wholly inaudible on the audience recordings of this, and subsequent, Warfield shows. Other journalists were more fanciful still. Michael Goldberg claimed that "only four or five hundred remained" for the encore, suggesting that the theater was only a quarter full at the end of the show. In fact, the Warfield audiences were generally responsive to the naked intensity of Dylan's performances. The reviews clearly upset Dylan. On the second and the third he bought copies of the *Examiner* and *Chronicle*, respectively.

Dave Kelly: Next morning we would go to this little restaurant next to the gig and he'd buy all the papers and we'd read the reviews, and you would not believe that these people were at the show. . . . I mean, yeah, there were some people that walked out, but they were small by comparison with people that were there.

Dylan continued to resent the inaccuracies and untruths in these reviews for some time to come. Talking at the conclusion of his evangelical tour, he admitted that the message element in his new songs had been unrelenting, but was mystified by the attacks on the music and the musicians.

Bob Dylan: All my stuff at that time was influenced or written right off the Gospel but that was no reason to say it wasn't a musical show. [1980]

In fact, he had assembled a band that was an imaginative blend of the soulful (Spooner Oldham), the rock-solid (Tim Drummond and Jim Keltner), the melodic guitarist (Fred Tackett) and the technically superb keyboardist (Willie Smith). Of course, the American press had been down on him for at least the past two years. The problem would remain throughout a further two years of touring with this band. Dylan gave his view on the critical response in a 1984 interview:

Bob Dylan: The reception's always good. . . . The problem is media problems. For some reason, the media reportage of the shows I've done has never been entirely accurate since 1978. . . . They say, "It was all gospel, oh, the crowd booed and walked out." This wasn't true. Maybe three or four people walked out. [1984]

Dylan had other problems at these shows, caused by those around him who sought to ensure that he remained an important example, and enthusiastic advocate, of the Vineyard Fellowship's particular brand of evangelism. Sometimes he felt that he was being hemmed in.

Helena Springs: I remember a lot of people [backstage at the Warfield Theater] were from the Vineyard in Los Angeles. . . . I remember a lot of them pressuring him about a lot of things. . . . Like if he'd drink some wine . . . they were not allowing him to live. They were just being too much of a headache. And I remember one time he said to me, "God, it's awfully tight, it's so tight, you know." And I thought and said, "Yeah, it seems like you gotta get out from under it a bit." And I felt a lot of pressure from those people. . . . Also, he found a lot of hypocrisy from those people. . . . They were saying one thing and doing another. He mentioned that to me too.

Dylan commented, albeit obliquely, on the hypocrisy he came across from professed Christians, during one of the later gospel shows.

Bob Dylan: I know a lot of country-and-western people do that. They sing, very often, "You can put your shoes under my bed anytime." And then they turn around and sing, "Oh Lord, just a closer walk with thee." Well, I can't do that. That's right, you cannot serve two masters. You gotta hate one and love the other one. You can't drink out of two cups. [1980]

This seems a somewhat paradoxical comment in view of Dylan's own continuing relationships with women. He seems to have remained intimate with Helena Springs throughout the first leg of the tour, before a furious row occurred between them and, after two years together, she quit the tour.

Dave Kelly: At the end of the first tour [Dylan and Helena] had a big row and he told her to leave. They were pretty close. . . . I remember her throwing things around the room and Bob standing there. But it didn't work out.

What exactly had happened to his "covenant woman," Mary Alice Artes, remains unclear. According to a report in *Rolling Stone*, Dylan purchased a twenty-five-thousand-dollar engagement ring in Seattle, Washington, in January 1980—by which time Springs had left the tour. Clydie King, with whom he was involved throughout most of the early eighties, did not join his band until a month later, before the recording of *Saved*. The intended recipient of the ring remains unknown, though before the year was out he would write his masterful "The Groom's Still Waiting at the Altar."

If Dylan's performance on November 1 had been somewhat hesitant, a further thirteen dates at the same small theater gave him plenty of opportunity to work on the new songs and to grow comfortable with playing live again. The show had obviously been rigidly structured, and the set remained constant night after night. However, his demeanor did not. Starting in the second week at the Warfield, he became positively verbose between songs. His between-song raps were really an extension of his reason for touring in the first place. If the dictionary definition of *to evangelize* is "to make acquainted with the Gospel . . . to preach the Gospel from place to place," that is exactly what he was doing. Talking to the crowd also allowed him to gauge the responses more accurately than just belting through a seventeen-song set. Thus one night he informed the audience:

Bob Dylan: Satan is called the god of this world. Anyone here who knows that? That's right—he's called the god of this world, and prince of the power of the air. [Someone shouts: "He sucks!"] That's right! He does! But anyhow, we know he's been defeated at the cross. I'm curious to know how many of you all know that? [1979]

In 1985 Dylan talked about the element of self-righteousness in these shows. He made it clear that evangelizing was the primary motive behind the entire tour.

Bob Dylan: Self-righteousness would be just to repeat what you know has been written down in Scripture some place else. It's not like you're trying to convince anybody of anything. You're just saying what the original rule is, and it's just coming through you. But if someone else can get past you saying it and just hear what the message is, well, then it's not coming from you but through you. And I don't see anything wrong in that. [1985]

Despite the amount of ridicule he was subjected to, it would appear that Dylan himself does not consider this period as an embarrassing episode in his career. It was something he felt he had to do, almost as if the tour itself answered the question he asked in the penultimate song of the main set, "What Can I Do for You?"

Bob Dylan: I was saying stuff I figured people needed to know. I thought I was giving people an idea of what was behind the songs. [1980]

He was certainly willing to give some fairly extreme and eschatologically unsound sermons. Of the Warfield shows, the final one on the sixteenth, apart from being one of his two or three finest performances, featured his most talkative self to date. As usual, it was before "Slow Train" and "Solid Rock" that his sermonizing came. Before "Slow Train" he gave the bare bones of a rap that would expand to epic proportions as the tour progressed:

Bob Dylan: You know, we read in the newspaper every day what a horrible situation this world is in. Now, God chooses to do these things in this world to confound the wise. Anyway, we know this world's gonna be destroyed; we know that. Christ will set up His kingdom in Jerusalem for a thousand years, where the lion will lie down with the lamb. Have you heard that before? I'm just curious to know, how many people believe that? All right. This is called "Slow Train Coming." It's been coming a long time and it's picking up speed. [1979]

If Dylan had gradually won over most of the attending San Franciscans, it seemed those in attendance at his next four shows needed little convincing.

Two days on from the Warfield, he returned to Santa Monica for shows at the Civic Auditorium, his first concerts there in nearly fifteen years. The shows were benefits for World Vision, a nondenominational Christian charity. This plus the fact that this was home territory for the Vineyard Fellowship had a positive effect upon both Dylan and the band. In fact, on the first night, when Dylan asked the audience how many knew that Satan had been defeated at the cross, the response was ecstatic. Dylan was clearly delighted, affirming, "Awwright! At least we're not alone." The following three shows were *tours de force*. He was singing with a passion that only a newborn burning conviction could induce. His apocalyptic sermons were becoming more and more imbued with the same fiery fervor. The second night his pre–"Solid Rock" rap was his most lengthy pronouncement to date:

Bob Dylan: You wanna know something, we're not worried at all that even though it is the last of the end times, because we see all these hostages being taken here and drugs being outlawed there. All these sad stories that are floating around. We're not worried about any of that—we don't care about the atom bomb, any of that, 'cause we know this world is going to be destroyed and Christ will set up His kingdom in Jerusalem for a thousand years, where the lion will lie down with the lamb. Y'know, the lion will eat straw that day. Also, if a man doesn't live to a hundred years old, he will be called accursed. That's interesting, isn't it? And we don't mind. We know that's coming, and if any man have not the spirit of Christ in him, he is a slave to bondage. I know you're all into bondage, so you need something just a little bit tough to hang on to. This song's called "Hanging On to a Solid Rock Made Before the Foundation of the World." And if you don't have that to hang on to, you better look into it. [1979]

The nights in Santa Monica were the culmination of eighteen increasingly impressive shows. The new songs had come into their own, and could be perceived as heartfelt testaments of faith, an advance upon the more overtly sermonizing songs on *Slow Train Coming*. However, it would be some time before he would play to such friendly crowds again. As he and the band headed for Arizona, they were unaware of the uproar awaiting them. Dylan was booked for two shows in Tempe, his first shows away from the coast. He would be playing primarily to the students of Arizona State University. The students were not at all tolerant of his new stance.

Dave Kelly: In Arizona he had to talk. I don't think they were walking out but they were definitely heckling. They were insisting on the old songs. . . . At the first one I thought he was going to put his guitar down and leave, but he stayed and talked to them.

The first night the audience refused to sit still, shouting between songs until Dylan asked his lighting crew to "turn the light on them down there." As the heckling continued he began to sermonize, but this time without the gentle coaxing tone adopted in San Francisco and Santa Monica.

Bob Dylan: In San Francisco—we opened there about a month ago—about three or four people walked out because they didn't get the message. But we're still here. Don't you walk out before you hear the message through. Anyway, "The lamb of God which taketh away the sins of the world"—I wonder how many of you people understand that. I'm curious to know how many of you understand. [1979]

The response was more shouting, and, as the second half progressed, the heckling started up again. If the hecklers found his songs unpalatable, though, they liked what he had to say even less:

Bob Dylan: The world as we know it now is being destroyed. Sorry, but it's the truth. In a short time—I don't know, in three years, maybe five years, could be ten years, I don't know—there's gonna be a war. It's gonna be called the War of Armageddon. . . . As sure as you're standing there, it's gonna happen. [1979]

If the first night in Tempe had been an unhappy experience for Dylan, matters only grew worse with the second show, when he met the most hostile audience of this entire tour. Indeed, the heckling of the 1966 fans pales in comparison to the uniform hostility he met in Tempe. The result was Dylan openly haranguing the crowd. Not waiting until "Slow Train," he gave his first sermon, which lasted five solid minutes, after his second song. It was delivered against repeated shouts of "Rock and roll!" until finally he spat words of damnation at the nonbelievers.

Bob Dylan: Hmmm. Pretty rude bunch tonight, huh? You all know how to be real rude! You know about the spirit of the Antichrist? Does anyone here know about that? Ah, the spirit of the Antichrist is loose right now. Let me give you an example. [He begins to tell a story about a guru spraying his disciples with a fire extinguisher, at which point someone loudly shouts, "Rock and roll."] . . . If you want rock and roll, you go down and rock and roll. You can go and see Kiss and you can rock and roll all the way down to the pit. . . . [He continues the story, while members of the audience continue to shout, "Rock and roll."] You *still* wanna rock and roll? I'll tell you what the two kinds of people are. Don't matter how much money you got, there's only two kinds of people: There's saved people and there's lost people. Yeah. Remember that I told you that. You may never see me again. You may not see me, but sometime down the line you remember you heard it here, that Jesus is Lord. Every knee shall bow! [1979]

This was not the end of his battle with the Tempe crowd. His pre–"Solid Rock" rap took another five minutes and again emphasized the imminence of the end. It concluded with a direct retelling of Hal Lindsey's Armageddon scenario.

Bob Dylan: Russia will come down and attack in the Middle East. China's got an army of two million people—they're gonna come down in the Middle East. There's gonna be a war called the Battle of Armageddon which is like something you never even dreamed about. And Christ will set up His kingdom and He'll rule it from Jerusalem. I know, far out as that may seem, this is what the Bible says. [Somebody shouts, "Everybody must get stoned!"] . . . I'll tell you about getting stoned—what do you want to know about getting stoned? What you're gonna need is something strong to hang on to. You got drugs to hold on to now. You might have a job to hold on to now. But you're gonna need something very solid to hang on to when these days come. Let me tell you one more thing: When Jesus spoke His parables, He spoke them to people . . . everybody could hear the parables. Some people heard them and understood them, some didn't. He said the same thing to everybody. Do you understand? He didn't try to hide it. He just said it. Those that believed it believed it and understood it. Those that didn't didn't. . . . You talk to your teachers about what I said. I'm sure you're paying a lot of money for your education, so you'd better get one. [1979]

The first night in Tempe, he had not played a second encore. Tonight, for the only time on the tour, he refused to play any encore at all. Instead, before the final song, "In the Garden," he preached one last message.

Bob Dylan: Remember what I said if you ever hear some other time that there is a truth, a life and a way. You may not get it now, it may not be next week or so, not the next year or so, but you remember the next time it happens. [1979]

At a show in Toronto the following April, which he was having filmed for possible release, he talked at length about his sermonizing at the second Tempe show in particular, and at these shows in general. Though the Toronto audience was reasonably tolerant of Dylan's new set, he soon worked himself into another frenzy.

Bob Dylan: Actually, I wanna tell you a story. We were playin' about four months ago some place that was a college or a campus. I forget exactly where. Arizona I think it was. Anyway, I read the Bible a lot; it just happens I do. It says things in the Bible that I didn't really learn until recently, and I really mentioned these because there are higher learning people there, preaching their philosophy. So people can study all the different philosophies, of Plato and, uh, who else? Who? Well, I definitely recall reading Nietzsche and those people like that. Anyways, in the Bible it tells a specific thing in the Book of Revelations that just applies to these times. . . . [Dylan explains Lindsey's contention that the biblical Gog and Magog are actually Russia and Iran.] So anyway, I was telling this story to these people. I shouldn't have been telling it to them. I just got carried away. I mentioned it to them and then I watched, and [I said] Russia was going to come down and attack in the Middle East. It says this in the Bible. And I been reading all kinds of books my whole life—magazines, books, whatever I could lay my hands on, anyway—and I never found any truth in any of it, if you wanna know the truth. But I said, "This country is gonna come down and attack." And all these people—there must've been fifty thousand . . . maybe it wasn't fifty thousand, five thousand maybe . . . they all booed. Everybody just booed; and it was the whole auditorium of people. . . . And a month later Russia moved her troops into, I think, Afghanistan. And the whole situation changed, you know. I'm not saying this to tell you they were wrong and I was right, or anything like that. These things that it mentions in the Bible I'm gonna pay mighty close attention to . . . been a lot of previews of what Antichrist could be like. . . . You need something strong to hang on to. It was manifested in the flesh! Testified in the spirit! Received by angels! Preached out in the world! [1980]

This was not his only account of the Tempe experience. Even six years later, when talking about the gospel tour to Cameron Crowe for the booklet enclosed with the *Biograph* album, Dylan commented on the college kids, and there can be no doubt which particular shows he was recalling.

Bob Dylan: We'd play the so-called colleges, where my so-called fans were. And all hell would break loose "Take off that dress," "We want rock and roll," lots of other things I don't even want to repeat, just really filthy mouth stuff. [1985]

The remaining shows on the first leg of the gospel tour, which concluded with two shows back in Arizona, at Tucson on December 8 and 9, were less eventful. Still, before his two shows in Tucson, Dylan agreed to a telephone interview on the local radio station KMGX to respond to a press release from the

Tucson chapter of the American Atheists Association stating that they planned
to leaflet his two Tucson concerts. Throughout the brief interview he remained
quite restrained, agreeing that religion was "just another form of bondage,"
though a necessary one.

Bob Dylan: Religion is another form of bondage which man invents to get
himself to God. But that's why Christ came. Christ didn't preach religion. He
preached the truth, the way and the life. [1979]

He also made it clear that he believed in the literal truth of the Scriptures,
that he considered them to be divinely inspired.

Bob Dylan: My ideology now would be coming out of the Scripture. Y'see,
I didn't invent these things—these things have just been shown to me. I'll stand
on that faith—that they are true. I believe they're true. I know they're true.
[1979]

His "preaching the Gospel from place to place" began again in January with
shows in Oregon. The show remained the same, though Helena Springs had
departed from the tour. For the monthlong winter leg, Dylan restrained himself
from preaching much between songs, though occasionally he made brief asides
about the reception, at one show sarcastically observing, "Well, the hits just
keep a-comin'," and in Nebraska suggesting that potential hecklers leave right
away.

Bob Dylan: Shan't be hearing any old songs tonight, so anyone who wants
to leave better leave right now. Might be somebody outside who wants the seat.
[1980]

At the final two winter shows, in Charleston, West Virginia, he introduced
a new song, which seemed a continuation of his between-song raps. Called
"Are You Ready," it was a catalog of questions about what you should be ready
for, notably Armageddon.

Within a week of the Charleston shows, Dylan and his touring band were
ensconced in Muscle Shoals Studio to record the songs they had now been
performing for three months. The intention was to get the new songs on tape
quickly, so that the new album could be released in time for the continuation
of the gospel tour later that spring. This should have been relatively easy, as
everyone knew the songs. Jerry Wexler was again filling the producer's chair.

Jerry Wexler: The arrangements were built in, because the band had been playing the songs live. Most of the licks are their own licks, which they perfected on the road, as opposed to the Dire Straits confections on the last album, which were all done in the studio. This one was like when Ray Charles used to call me up and say, "Hey, pardner, I'm coming in in three weeks, let's do a record."

Certainly the songs came easily enough. The bulk of the album was recorded in a mere four days, with two songs then recut the following day. The sessions were over by February 19.

Jerry Wexler: On the fifth day . . . we reexamined everything we'd done and wound up recutting . . . "Covenant Woman" and "Saved." . . . It was pretty much Bob's instinct to redo them. . . . We did a little touching up. In five days it was ready for mixing.

Yet the album was massively flawed. In the cold isolation of the studio, the band seemed to be going through the motions and Dylan's singing lacked the attention to detail he had brought to the live performances. Evidence of lack of care in producing the songs in the studio lies strewn across the album.* "Solid Rock" is devoid of the insistent tension that its rumbling bass riff had previously given it; in "What Can I Do for You?" the "I'm sure to make it through" had become "I sure did make it through," a line totally out of accord with the humility of the remainder of the song; in "Covenant Woman" Dylan had rewritten another line, preferring to commend his precious angel for knowing "those most secret things of me," rather than the original "the invisible things of Him." The most successful song on the album was "Pressing On," which required a wholly different arrangement on record from that used in performance. Dylan attacked the song with considerably more vigor than the other tracks.

Dave Kelly: They were all dissatisfied with the album. He wanted to redo it but there was no time. . . . He was contemplating issuing a live record. . . . It occurred to him to record the shows, but the record company were not interested. They wouldn't put any money into it.

Ironically, a mere eight days after the final session, Dylan and the band delivered a definitive rendering of another song they had been regurgitating in concert nightly over the last three months. The song was "Gotta Serve Some-

---

* For a more extensive commentary on the *Saved* album, readers are referred to Paul Williams's *What Happened—One Year Later* pamphlet.

body." The occasion was the annual Grammy awards ceremony. Nominated for best vocal performance for his single of the song, Dylan proceeded to deliver a vocal considerably superior to the official version he had been nominated for. He impressed a nationwide prime-time TV audience and collected the award.

Saved was beyond redemption. Though Dylan seems to have seriously considered issuing the songs in the form of a live album, even recording two shows in Toronto in April at his own expense using a twenty-four-track mobile studio, CBS dissuaded him, thus negating all the good work achieved by the surprise commercial success of *Slow Train Coming*.* When Dylan approved a garishly arrogant jacket, which seemed to suggest that only the chosen few should buy the record, it was inevitable that sales would not repeat those of his previous album. Not released until a month after the conclusion of his spring tour, the album failed even to make the top twenty. Dylan remained philosophical about the failure, though he was not to know that his last top ten album of the eighties (save for the Traveling Wilburys) had left the charts a week after his acceptance of the Grammy award.

Bob Dylan: *Slow Train* was a big album. *Saved* didn't have those kinda numbers but to me it was just as big an album. I'm fortunate that I'm in a position to release an album like *Saved* with a major record company so that it will be available to the people who would like to buy it. [1981]

In mid-April he resumed his touring activities in Canada, aiming to spend a month working his way across to and down the East Coast. He had written three new songs for this leg of the tour, none of which suggested any lessening of his evangelistic fervor: "Ain't Gonna Go to Hell (for Anybody)," the somewhat strange "Coverdown Breakthrough" and "I Will Love Him."

On night one he half-jokingly asked the audience, "I know you're gonna read in the newspapers tomorrow that everybody walked out, but will you tell them the truth now?" In fact, the Canadian journalists were considerably kinder than their California equivalents, and his four shows in Toronto and four in Montreal went well.

If there were now fewer apocalyptic sermons, Dylan did not stop attempting to evangelize. The main subject matter at the East Coast shows was the Devil and his demons. The two shows in Hartford, Connecticut, saw a more talkative Dylan than at any show since Tempe. On the first night he seemed to sense a degree of hostility and asked, before the fourth song:

---

* Dylan still put together a live album entitled *Solid Rock* to be issued after *Saved*. It was an amalgam of songs from both gospel albums, and again CBS would not release it.

Bob Dylan: Anybody left yet? They tell me everybody leaves at these shows. I don't know—it's kinda hard to see out there. Middle of the road, East Coast bondage. But God's waiting to set you free. I know you don't hear much about God these days. We're gonna talk about Him all night. We're not gonna be talking about no mysticism, no meditation, none of them Eastern religions. We're just gonna be talking about Jesus. Demons don't like that name. I'll tell you right now, if you got demons inside you they're not gonna like it. [1980]

The following night the crowd was more evenly divided between believers and nonbelievers, and though Dylan seemed in a considerably better mood he still preached extensively to the crowd. Before "Coverdown Breakthrough" he tried an alternate version of his demons rap.

Bob Dylan: I know the modern trend. It's not fashionable to think about heaven and hell. I know that. But God doesn't have to be in fashion because He's always fashionable. But it's hard not to go to hell, you know. There's so many distractions, so many influences; you start walking right 'n' pretty soon there's somebody out there gonna drag you down. As soon as you get rid of the Enemy outside, the Enemy comes inside. He got all kinds of ways. The Bible says, "Resist the Devil and the Devil will flee." You got to stand to resist him. How we got to stand? Anybody know how to stand? How do we stand? Anybody know how? [There was a muted response.] We gotta stay here and play another night. [1980]

The final four shows of what proved to be the final leg of his gospel tour were away from the East Coast, in Ohio. At both Akron shows he found a surprisingly friendly crowd, leading him to observe, in his introduction of singer Regina McCreary, "Seems like I don't have to tell you about Jesus—seems like you know all about Him."

On both nights the Akron fans were rewarded with a third encore. In Dayton, the locale of his final gig, the audience was also suitably appreciative, yet Dylan talked little between songs. After the show, though, he was extremely talkative, giving his first major interview of 1980 to young Australian journalist Karen Hughes. Hughes had conducted her first ever interview back in April 1978 in Sydney, and Dylan was the subject. Having hooked up with him again at Hartford, she found him in considerably better shape than he had been in 1978. He talked about his continuing faith, and exactly what he meant by Christianity.

Bob Dylan: Christianity is making Christ the Lord of your life. You're talking about your life now, you're not talking about just part of it, you're not talking about a certain hour every day. You're talking about making Christ the lord and master of your life, the king of your life. And you're also talking about Christ,

the resurrected Christ; you're not talking about some dead man who had a
bunch of good ideas and was nailed to a tree. [1980]

30   1980–82:   In the Summertime

When Dylan concluded his spring 1980 tour in Dayton,
Ohio, he envisaged only a temporary hiatus, fully intend-
ing to return to the road that summer after the release of the *Saved* album. A
major heat wave sweeping the North American continent preempted his plans,
leaving him with several months to work on new songs.

The new songs abandoned the evangelism present on *Slow Train Coming*
and *Saved*, though the apocalyptic conceits remained. In the summertime he
wrote four of his finest songs of the eighties, though only one of these would be
included on his next album. The two that had the closest links with the songs
on *Saved* were "Every Grain of Sand" and "Yonder Comes Sin." The seven-
verse "Yonder Comes Sin," though not specifically exhorting repentance, provided an extensive catalog of the "total depravity of unregenerate human
nature," both throughout history and during these end times.

Another song dealing with depravity in the context of the Second Coming
was "Ain't Gonna Go to Hell." Though the song was performed as a straightforward Bible-thumping brandishment of threats during the spring East Coast
tour, Dylan wholly rewrote it before his brief fall tour. The message remained
the same, but the imagery was more Dylanesque, less evidently biblical. Thus,
the glorious image of the woman in a cold black dress "walking away with your
legs spread apart" was a typically Delta blues–drenched line.

The other overtly Christian song that he wrote that summer was his most
sublime song from this intensely creative period. "Every Grain of Sand" was the
summation of his attempts to express what the promise of redemption meant to
him personally. One of his most intensely personal songs, it also remains one
of his most universal. Dealing with "the time of my confession," the song was
perhaps also the real conclusion of his evangelical period as a songwriter.

Though several songs he subsequently wrote for his next album, *Shot of Love*, dealt with living dead men and the property of Jesus, they did so in a worldly manner. The ethereal fragility of "Every Grain of Sand" was not attempted again.

Surprisingly, the other songs he wrote that summer, either on his farm in Minneapolis or while sailing around the Caribbean, dealt more with his perennially troubled relations with women than with the higher calling. Two of these songs could be considered soul partners, dealing with, if not the same relationship, then markedly similar ones, and both are set within a familiar landscape of imminent apocalypse. In "Caribbean Wind" the story has as its backdrop messengers "bringing evil reports of rioting armies and time that is short." It seems that this time the "distant ship of liberty" was not coming in but sailing away, as the singer attempted to resolve whether he should stay with the mysterious lady from Haiti, "fair brown and intense." By the time he decided, she had left.

Bob Dylan: I started it in St. Vincent when I woke up from a strange dream in the hot sun. . . . I was thinking about living with somebody for all the wrong reasons. [1985]

"Caribbean Wind" was the first of a number of songs that he wrote while sailing the Caribbean in his newly constructed schooner. A sense of the power of nature returned to his songwriting. Interestingly, "distant ships" make a reappearance in "Jokerman" written two years later in the Caribbean, on this occasion "sailing into the mist," possibly never to return.

Bob Dylan: I'm usually either [in New York] or on the West Coast or down in the Caribbean. Me and another guy have a boat down there. "Jokerman" kinda came to me in the islands. It's very mystical. The shapes there, and shadows, seem to be so ancient. The song was sorta inspired by these spirits they call jumbis. [1984]

Like the other songs written in the summer of 1980, Dylan recorded "Caribbean Wind" using a mobile studio, presumably located in Minneapolis. However, the original version has never emerged, and when the song was recorded for *Shot of Love* (this take appears on *Biograph*) it was wholly rewritten, losing much of its drama along the way. Asked why he left the song off *Shot of Love*, Dylan later admitted:

Bob Dylan: We left [it] off the album [because it was] quite different from anything I wrote. . . . The way the storyline changes from third person to first person and that person becomes you, then these people are there and they're not

there. And then the time goes way back and then it's brought up to the present.
I thought it was really effective. [1981]

The companion piece to "Caribbean Wind" was entitled "The Groom's Still
Waiting at the Altar." It was also largely rewritten in the spring of 1981 and
recorded for, but originally omitted from, *Shot of Love.** In the rewritten
version Dylan included references to "cities on fire," the killing of nuns and
"fighting on the border." The sense of doom surrounding the original version
was less overt but was still a constant undercurrent. Claudette, the lady in this
song, seems to be toying with the singer's affections, and finally leaves him for
parts unknown. She could be on the notorious Fanning Street immortalized by
Leadbelly, she could be "in the mountains or prairies," or even be running a
brothel somewhere down in South America. The singer insists with each chorus
of the first version that he will forget her, setting his "affections on things
above," letting "nothing get in the way of that love."

"Caribbean Wind" and "The Groom's Still Waiting at the Altar" are important songs in Dylan's oeuvre, particularly as their synthesis of apocalyptic conceits and his familiar theme of disaffected love was more familiar terrain to his
fans than anything explored on his previous two albums, suggesting that he was
at last learning to assimilate rather than ignore his pre-born-again work. That
the songs reflected Dylan's own problems with women, given past history,
seems extremely likely. Helena Springs had left his employ that winter, and
Mary Alice Artes, the black actress supposedly most directly responsible for his
conversion, was now on the East Coast, according to pastor Ken Gulliksen.

The two songs presaged a move away from a purely evangelical format in
both his recordings and his performances. Both were worked on at October
rehearsals at the familiar Rundown Studios, as part of preparations for a
nineteen-date tour of the Northwest, starting with a further twelve shows at the
Warfield Theater in San Francisco. The shows were billed as a retrospective,
and radio ads for the show included rehearsal versions of such songs as "Blowin'
in the Wind" and "Gotta Serve Somebody" in the background. Dylan even
gave two radio interviews during the Warfield engagement, during which he
insisted, "This is a stage show we're doing, it's not a salvation ceremony." He
also hinted that the next album would be something of a departure from *Saved*.

Bob Dylan: You can't record every album and have it be a *Saved*-type album
because you just don't get that many kinda songs all in a row like that. So I'm
sure there'll be a difference. [1980]

---

*It was added to the album before reissue on Nice Prince Vinyl and CD.

Yet on the first night at the Warfield, a year and a week after his 1979 debut there, the show opened with an identical six-song set from the backup singers, and Dylan then appeared on stage singing "Gotta Serve Somebody" and "I Believe In You." Indeed, only five songs—"Like a Rolling Stone," "Girl from the North Country," "Just Like a Woman," "Señor" and "Blowin' in the Wind"—were performed from his pre-born-again albums, though he did duet with Clydie King on the old Dion classic "Abraham, Martin and John." Still, with only one encore and a Dylan set that lasted well under ninety minutes, he had some very dissatisfied customers that first night.

Dylan's exact intentions in embarking on this brief tour were not clear. It promoted no product, and did not precede a major U.S. or European tour. Presumably he intended to work up a new set as the tour progressed, rather than present the finished article as in 1979. Predictably, the first night was lambasted by the same syndicated columnists who had attacked the previous year's shows with such relish. Dylan himself commented on these critics when thanking Bill Graham, the promoter, at the final 1980 Warfield show: "Last year we came in here with the show and the newspapers they distorted it and slandered it and lied about it—whatever they did, that's enough for most promoters in the business to cancel out the rest of the shows." Graham in 1980, as in 1979, kept faith with Dylan and was duly rewarded.

After that first night the late 1980 tour became Dylan's most consistently inventive. The shows just got better and better with every performance. The arrangements of such old chestnuts as "To Ramona," "Señor" and "Girl from the North Country" were inspirational. The introduction of new songs such as "The Groom's Still Waiting at the Altar," "Caribbean Wind," "City of Gold" and "Let's Keep It Between Us" provided a rare opportunity for fans to hear songs Dylan had not even recorded for CBS, affirming the "new Dylan" on display at these shows. Dylan even sang rewritten versions of "Ain't Gonna Go to Hell" and "Simple Twist of Fate," the latter now featuring this glorious passage: "With the neon burning dim / He looked at her and she looked at him / With that look that can manipulate / Brought on by a simple twist of fate."

He also introduced some superb and surprising covers into the set: a contemporary Christian ballad called "Rise Again," Shel Silverstein's "Couple More Years," Dave Mason's "We Just Disagree," the traditional "Mary from the Wild Moor" and an absolute knock-'em-dead version of Little Willie John's "Fever." As if such delights were not enough, night after night he brought on special guests to help out on a few songs. Carlos Santana helped out on November 13, on November 15 Michael Bloomfield reproduced the ringing guitar riffs he had immortalized on the original "Like a Rolling Stone" (sadly, his last live performance) and even Jerry Garcia seemed comfortable playing along on November 16. Maria Muldaur contributed a song on the nineteenth, and finally, at the concluding Warfield show on the twenty-second, Roger McGuinn joined Dylan for two songs they could both feel familiar with, "Mr. Tambourine Man" (complete with a Byrdslike intro) and "Knocking on Heaven's Door." While Dylan's singing was as impassioned as during the previous year's shows, the band seemed more comfortable with the material, guitarist Fred Tackett in particular coming into his own.

As the shows progressed, Dylan grew positively talkative, though he resisted the temptation to preach. On the sixteenth he prefaced "Just Like a Woman" with a story about a beautiful transvestite approaching him as a woman and then an hour later as a man; on the eighteenth he told a lengthy and bizarre story about being stranded in an underwater cave during one of his stays with Joan Baez in Carmel; on the twenty-second he told the audience improbably about his first experience of live rhythm and blues at the age of twelve in a bingo parlor in Detroit; on the twenty-sixth he told a story about a couple of newlyweds accidentally stumbling onto his hotel balcony the previous night; and on December 3 he dedicated "Señor" to a lady in the audience named Victoria, whom he had met in 1972 in Durango. Some raps became nightly occurrences, such as his introduction of "Mary from the Wild Moor" with, "People always talk about old songs. This is a *real* old song." He also couldn't resist making a few digs at the press, correcting one reviewer who claimed he performed "Maggie's Farm" the previous night, and dedicating one song to Greil Marcus, "one of the top rock and roll critics of the era—whatever that is!" He made a subtle point about the way the media had portrayed him in the past year during his introduction to the one and only live version of "Caribbean Wind":

Bob Dylan: The first person I ever heard of play[ing] a twelve-string guitar was named Leadbelly. . . . He was a prisoner in [a] Texas state prison . . . and he was recorded by a man named Alan Lomax. . . . Anyway, he got Leadbelly out and brought him up to New York and he made a lot of records there. At first he was just doing prison songs and stuff like that . . . until he'd been out of prison some time and decided to do children's songs. People said, "Oh, what, has Leadbelly changed?" Some people liked the older ones, others liked the newer ones. But he didn't change—he was the same man. [1980]

Reacting to the failure of *Saved*, he refrained from taking his band into the studio to record his next album straight after the tour. Rather he took a three-month breather in the winter of 1981 to work on further songs. The sad result of this breather was that the bulk of the songs written in the summer of 1980 were excluded from his 1981 album, *Shot of Love*, which instead featured its share of inferior, lightweight tunes presumably dating from the winter.

"Caribbean Wind" and "Groom's Still Waiting" were both recorded for *Shot of Love* but ended up excluded. (Years later, CBS would add "Groom's Still Waiting" to copies of the album.) Another classic Dylan composition recorded at the sessions was about a witchy woman manipulating the singer, against a backdrop of marching men "trying to take heaven by force." This time the woman's name was Angelina, though she was clearly a close relative of Claudette and the lady from Haiti. The exclusion of three songs of real quality might suggest that Dylan had written even finer material that winter, but this was not the case. Though "Shot of Love," "Dead Man, Dead Man," "Property of Jesus" and "In the Summertime" warranted inclusion alongside such works, his ill-considered tribute to Lenny Bruce, the lightweight "Heart of Mine" and the unexciting "Trouble" were several notches down from them.

After Dylan spent a couple of days in late March trying to produce results at Muscle Shoals, the sessions were moved to Clover Studios in Los Angeles, where the bulk of the album was completed (save for "Shot of Love," which was the result of preliminary work at Rundown Studios). Though he relied primarily on his touring band, Dylan did bring in guitarists Steve Ripley and Danny Kortchmar, organist Benmont Tench of Tom Petty's Heartbreakers, and Steve Douglas from his 1978 band to provide saxophone on a few songs. For Tench, who had no experience of Dylan in the studio, it proved a disorienting experience.

Benmont Tench: The first day I worked with him, he didn't say a word the whole session, and I didn't know anybody at the session. [But] at the end of the day, when I was leaving, he said, "Can you come back tomorrow?"

Aside from these musicians, Dylan continued to embellish just about every song with a wailing chorus of female vocalists, his fourth consecutive album to feature such a distraction. On this occasion they were his touring singers, and the chorus still featured Carolyn Dennis, the only survivor from 1978, plus Clydie King, a large, effusive lady with a pair of lungs that could put out a forest fire. King had joined Dylan's band before the *Saved* album sessions, replacing Helena Springs. She also appears to have quickly replaced Springs in his affections. When Dylan indulged in a hotel jam session with Mark Knopfler during Dire Straits's October 1980 tour, it was King who remained on his arm throughout the night. When Ron Wood arrived at the final session for the *Shot of Love* album, which featured a different lineup including Ringo Starr and Donald "Duck" Dunn, he found Dylan and King on the best of terms.

Ron Wood: Bob was with Clydie King then. He used to go to her for solace all the time. She was great with him, but they were like chalk and cheese. Two [more] different people you couldn't hope to meet—her a black, outrageous, hamburger-eating soul singer, and Bob all quiet and white, nibbling off the side of her hamburger. I always remember him trying to share her hamburger, and she was bossing him around and stuff. He needed it at the time.

In 1982 Dylan and King spent much of their time together and even recorded an album of duets, though it remains unreleased and unheard, Dylan later claiming this was because "it doesn't fall into any category that the record company knows how to deal with." Clearly he was having major problems with CBS after two commercially unsuccessful albums. The Dylan-King relationship lasted into 1983, when King duetted on a couple of the songs recorded at the *Infidels* sessions, though they appear to have parted company shortly after the completion of that album.

Shot of Love was completed by the middle of May, though there was no prospect of it being released in time for his summer '81 European tour. Dylan himself has always had something of a soft spot for his 1981 album, describing it in 1983 as his personal favorite. As late as 1989 he was still performing "Dead Man, Dead Man," "Trouble," "Heart of Mine," "Lenny Bruce" and "Every Grain of Sand" in his concert sets, when his other eighties albums received scant attention indeed. However, the album was considered by the public the third in his religious trilogy, and, though relatively successful in Europe in the wake of his tour there, was his first studio album since *Another Side* to fail to make *Billboard*'s top thirty.

Bob Dylan: The record had something that could have been made in the forties or maybe the fifties . . . there was a cross element of songs on it . . . the critics . . . all they talked about was Jesus this and Jesus that, like it was some kind of Methodist record. [1985]

After four warm-up gigs in the Midwest and Maryland, Dylan was still committed to the road and undertook two tours in 1981, both twenty-seven shows, one in Europe in the summer, the other in the States in the fall. They were markedly different affairs. The European shows were almost universally impressive and included eight shows in England, where he had been so well received in 1978. The American shows were lackluster affairs: The sound was a mush of drums and guitars and Dylan's singing lacked any real variety, as each song was delivered in the same high-pitched whine.

The contrast escaped the media, and the European shows were not well received. Critics viewed even the modified show that was now being presented as overly religious in content, preferring to ignore the extra commitment Dylan seemed to bring to his gospel material. The American press, on the other hand, after reports of grueling evangelist sets the previous year, were relieved at how much pregospel material he was playing. He also seemed to be deliberately avoiding the areas where he had met the most media resistance in the recent past: the West Coast, Arizona and Texas (save for one show in Houston, Texas).

Part of the reaction in the European media was because of the contrast between the new shows and his 1978 "experiment," which had been so well received there. The new shows, as orthodox rock concerts, were attacked for lacking audacity and originality. Dylan was also a victim of the Bruce Springsteen Effect: Springsteen had delayed his first major European tour that spring, and ended up leaving England less than three weeks before the Dylan shows, so his much-hyped 1981 tour was a fresh experience to contrast with Dylan's considerably more demanding show. Springsteen benefited from the fact that European critics had no benchmark to compare his 1981 shows against. (It had been six years since a somewhat less famous Springsteen played four European shows.) Thus, an endless procession of critics lived out a new version of "The Emperor's New Clothes," none prepared to admit to being anything other than overwhelmed by his performances.

Dylan sprang surprises with every line he sang, twisting words and phrases, wringing meaning from each tapestry of song he wove. Though his new, highly mannered vocal delivery was initially disorienting, repeated performances suggested he had found a voice that, in the words of *New Musical Express* editor Neil Spencer, "was quite astonishing, clearly superior to all his many past styles; from all of which he borrows for the present." Though not required to defend his new show to Spencer, Dylan had this to say:

Bob Dylan: I feel very strongly about this show. I feel it has something to offer. No one else does this show, not Bruce Springsteen or anyone. [1981]

Sadly, it seemed that Dylan had stretched even the most flexible vocal cords in rock and roll too far. At two shows in Birmingham, two days after the end of his six nights at London's cavernous Earls Court, he sounded as if he was in physical pain onstage, and on the first night he cut short his set. Though a respite before he played mainland Europe repaired some of the damage and allowed Dylan to impress audiences throughout the few remaining European shows, when he returned to the American stage three months later he sounded as if he was unwilling or unable to provide any of the legendary vocal gymnastics of yore.

He had also added a second drummer on this U.S. tour, a baffling decision, coming after the addition of an equally unnecessary second guitarist, Steve Ripley, on the European tour. If any drummer in modern rock music does not require assistance, it is Jim Keltner. For the first part of the tour the second drummer was in fact a roadie, Arthur Rosato. Though the more impressive Bruce Gary was brought in as a replacement for the last ten shows, the rationale behind the use of two drummers was still not readily apparent.

Also lost was the sympathetic Willie Smith on keyboards, whose departure seems to have been something of a surprise. His replacement, the versatile Al Kooper, was given only a few days' notice and then on the tour was largely restricted to providing his trademark organ sound. Inevitably, the recruitment of Kooper was seen as a concession to "greatest hits"–loving fans, and indeed "I Want You" received its first live outing in three years, while both "A Hard Rain's a-Gonna Fall" and "Señor" were also restored to favor.

Al Kooper: I was asking him to do that because we were together so why not play the songs that we used to play because we were together and it wasn't a common occurrence. . . . So I'd say, "Let's play 'I Want You.' " . . . 'Cause I think when it started it was almost totally Christian and when it was over it was almost totally greatest hits. . . . The shows were long. We did like two-and-a-half, three-hour shows. It was brutal. One of the first nights we played "Like a Rolling Stone" so slow it must have taken him twenty minutes to go through the whole song. So after the show I put my arm around him and said, "You can't play 'Like a Rolling Stone' that slow, or if you do, let's do it really slower and then we won't have to do any more songs." . . . By the end of the tour the old Bob was back.

But the band's chemistry had been irrevocably altered. They had played so majestically on every tour since November 1979. Now they sounded as though they were going through the motions. The twenty-seven American shows, which spanned the latter part of October and most of November, concluded in America's favorite resort state, Florida. It was time for Dylan to take a vacation. After all, he had been on the road for the last four years. It would be two and a half years before his next tour.

Nineteen eighty-two was Dylan's third "lost" year since 1961. As in 1968 and 1972, he made no officially released recordings, nor did he play any shows save for a single ten-minute guest appearance (with Joan Baez during the Peace Sunday benefit show at Pasadena in June).

After spending much of the summer of 1982 attending gigs with his eldest son, Jesse, in Minneapolis, taking in shows by the Clash, Elvis Costello and the Attractions, X, the Stray Cats and Squeeze, all new-wave bands that were idols of young Jesse, Dylan's thoughts turned to the question of a new album. In December 1982 he approached Frank Zappa with a view to his producing it. Though Zappa considered the idea interesting, nothing came of their discussions. By January 1983 other "name" producers were being considered, including Elvis Costello and David Bowie.

Yet unlike the two previous "lost" years, 1982 was not without its recording activity. Dylan made several recordings with Clydie King at Gold Star Studios in Los Angeles, and at least four songs were copyrighted (and therefore presumably recorded) in the spring, though only "You Changed My Life" had any real merit. Its lyrics implied a worrying degree of self-doubt about his constancy to his newly found faith.

Indeed, at the same time Dylan was recording songs of doubt, the media began to speculate about an element of backsliding in his much-vaunted Christian beliefs. In a syndicated article published in March 1982, an alleged "source close to" Dylan was quoted as suggesting that Dylan had reverted to the religion of his forefathers, and that, "In a sense, he never left his Judaism. My interpretation is that the New Testament and Jesus were a message he thought he got, but that he was still testing." Who the source was remains unknown, but Dylan typically remained silent in response to such speculation, though voices refuting such stories attempted to be heard.

The speculation became more acute as Dylan was photographed at the bar mitzvah of one of his sons in Jerusalem in September wearing a yarmulke. The photos were widely published. Then, early in 1983, came reports that he had been spending considerable time with members of a sect of Hasidic Jews called the Lubavitchers, and even that he had recorded an album of Hasidic songs. While fans speculated upon what Dylan's new album might have in store, the Vineyard Fellowship and the Lubavitchers set about attempting to interpret Dylan's actions in diametrically opposed manners.

Paul Esmond: I don't think he ever left his Jewish roots. I think he is one of those fortunate ones who realized that Judaism and Christianity can work very well together, because Christ is just [Jesus the Messiah]. And so he doesn't have any problems about putting on a yarmulke and going to a bar mitzvah, because he can respect that.

Rabbi Kasriel Kastel: He's been going in and out of a lot of things, trying to find himself. And we've just been making ourselves available. As far as we're concerned, he was a confused Jew. We feel he's coming back.

The release of *Infidels* did not abate the speculation. Indeed the lack of overtly evangelistic lyrics only fueled the skepticism of those who doubted the strength of Dylan's beliefs, despite the fact that, as Bert Cartwright has written, "There is no song without direct allusion to the Bible." However, only two songs draw heavily upon New Testament works, "Jokerman" and "Man of Peace," songs that both seemed to enmesh the narrator in a battle with false prophets who assume attributes of Christ with evil intent. Thus "Man of Peace" was based upon the dictum "even Satan disguises himself as an angel of light" (2 Corinthians 11:14).

Both songs contain allusions to the Book of Revelation, suggesting an abiding belief in the imminent apocalypse. In an interview published in July of 1983, conducted at the mixing sessions for *Infidels*, Dylan clearly seemed to be suggesting that, after years of being acclaimed a prophet, he was finally prophesying, only to be misunderstood and reviled:

Bob Dylan: Roots, man—we're talking about Jewish roots, you want to know more? Check on Elijah the prophet. He could make rain. Isaiah the prophet, even Jeremiah, see if their brethren didn't want to bust their brains for telling it right like it is, yeah—these are my roots, I suppose. Am I looking for them? . . . I ain't looking for them in synagogues with six-pointed Egyptian stars shining down from every window, I can tell you that much. [1983]

Despite that final sentence, the extensive references to Old Testament prophets in this interview (with Martin Keller) and the preponderance of allusions to Old Testament works on *Infidels* were cited as evidence of Dylan's reversion to Judaism. Despite all the evidence to the contrary on the album and Dylan's unequivocal statement in a *Rolling Stone* interview in March 1984 that he believed in the Book of Revelation, in which Christ returns to judge humanity, the media painted *Infidels* as an album from a lamb returned to the fold.

On the 1984 European tour Dylan seemed to make no effort to reaffirm his beliefs overtly. No songs from *Saved* were performed and only one from *Slow Train Coming*—"When You Gonna Wake Up"—and though the song was wholly rewritten, the new words were so garbled it was impossible to discern them. Likewise, *Shot of Love's* only contributions to the tour set were "Every Grain of Sand," with its almost pantheistic tones, and the unreligious "Heart of Mine." It seems likely that Dylan was genuinely concerned that an overly religious tone to the shows would have disastrous commercial consequences on his first-ever stadium tour. Yet in interview after interview on the tour he referred to his abiding faith in the prophecies foretold in Revelation.

Toward the end of 1984 two Christian writers published books attempting to prove that Dylan's spiritual journey was still on that slow train, and that it was picking up speed. Bert Cartwright's important *The Bible in the Lyrics of Bob Dylan* attempted to evaluate Dylan's use of biblical references in all his work to date, but the book received little distribution. Don Williams published a book entitled *The Man, the Music, the Message*, which received much wider dissemination and was considerably more polemical. However, it was clear that, despite his enduring beliefs, Dylan had spent much of 1982 reevaluating those beliefs and that with the release of *Infidels* his evangelical phase was over. From now on, fellow believers would have to read between the lines.

31 | 1983: Songs of Experience

Nineteen eighty-three could, and should, have been the year of Dylan's second major creative renaissance. The songs he recorded for the album *Infidels* that year were the strongest since the songs from *Blood on the Tracks* nine years earlier. The fact that Dylan issued a bastardized version of the album and then failed to promote the record with a tour or even a spate of interviews, but preferred to spend his time jamming with local musicians in the privacy of his Malibu residence, meant that he reversed neither his commercial nor his critical decline.

When Dylan entered Power Station Studios New York on April 11 to begin recording his follow-up to *Shot of Love*, he knew the importance of these sessions. It had been two years since *Shot of Love*, which—like *Saved*—had been disastrous commercially. Since *Shot of Love*, MTV, a cable station that supplied a perennial diet of promotional videos, brief "newsy" items on the day's pop stars and the occasional half-hour "in-concert" special, had come to prominence. No longer were the kids listening to their radios for the latest "fave rave." They wanted an image *and* the music, all wrapped into one. Two years after *Shot of Love*, there were abundant stories in the press that Dylan had abandoned Christianity. A Dylan returned to secular values or even the faith of his father was certainly news. After all, the stories implied that Dylan had seen the error of his ways in having advocated a born-again creed.

It is easy to say that Dylan plows his own furrow and if the world catches up all well and good, but he has always thrown in a sweetener to make each dramatic change more palatable: On *Bringing It All Back Home* the second side gave the folkies some solace, on *Slow Train Coming* he used Knopfler's sinewy sounds and Wexler's superlative production to give fans his best-sounding album in years.

For 1983, Dylan again turned to Knopfler. Since the recording of *Slow Train Coming*, Dire Straits had become one of the most successful acts of the early eighties. Using Mark Knopfler would in itself attract sales and press coverage, though Dylan's main motive for recruiting Knopfler was his need for a coproducer. He wanted to produce the album himself, but technology had passed him by. He needed an artist who felt at home in the modern recording studio— hence the approaches to such names as David Bowie and Frank Zappa. Knopfler was the best choice he could have made. They had worked together. Knopfler knew it was better to coax Dylan than command him and his own ego was likely to be considerably less of a problem than some of the names previously considered. Knopfler was also a highly distinctive guitarist.

Bob Dylan: Mark . . . encouraged me to go to the studio when I didn't feel like it, when I'd rather have been someplace else. . . . As far as guitar playing goes, he never steps all over with fancy licks. [1983]

Dylan had had no touring band for eighteen months, and was required to start from scratch. Mark Knopfler's syrupy tones on guitar required a harder, bluesier second guitarist to compensate and provide the cutting edge needed on the record. Dylan's choice was Mick Taylor, who had apprenticed with John Mayall's Bluesbreakers in the sixties before spending six years with the Rolling Stones.

Dylan's choice of rhythm section was also inspired. His most successful recordings and performances had always been founded on a dynamite rhythm section that "grounded" the sound while he extemporized, whether it was Ken Buttrey and Charlie McCoy, Howie Wyeth and Rob Stoner or Jim Keltner and Tim Drummond. Sly Dunbar and Robbie Shakespeare were already well established in their own field, and they were able to provide Dylan with a sound that was contemporary without adopting the whomp-synth-whomp approach so prevalent in the music then assailing the airwaves. The final member of the band was Knopfler's suggestion, his fellow Dire Straits member Alan Clark, who would play keyboards.

Mark Knopfler: Bob decided on the whole band, although I did suggest that Alan [Clark] be there. . . . And I suggested the engineer, Neil Dorfsman. . . . We were like a three-man team at that point. Sly Dunbar and Robbie Shakespeare were Bob's ideas, as well as Mick Taylor. I suggested Billy Gibbons, but I don't think Bob had heard of ZZ Top.

Predictably, recording with digital technology at a top modern studio, like the Record Plant, was not going to dissuade Dylan from recording live with the band, nor from avoiding multiple takes. As throughout his career, he winged it and the band was required to wing it too.

Alan Clark: He doesn't play anything more than once. If you can get him to play it twice, you're doing well. Three times is *really* pushing it. We used to just sit at our instruments . . . and Bob would wander in, sit down, put his headphones on and struggle with his guitar strap for a couple of minutes, light a cigarette and then stub the cigarette out, take his guitar off, take his headphones off and walk across to the organ where I was sitting and write down about . . . half a dozen lines of the next tune in tiny, meticulous handwriting. It was quite interesting! And he'd sort of wander back over, maybe forget to put the headphones on and start playing the track. Just like that! If you weren't sitting there—if you had to go to the bog or something—he just started, y'know. It was amazing. And that's the way the album went.

The advantage now was that if anyone did blow an otherwise fine take, the technology enabled that particular part to be overdubbed without in any way impairing the rest of the performance. This meant that the songs could be got down relatively easily, leaving Dylan time to experiment with the words or the arrangement.

Mark Knopfler: I remember some things worked really well. If you get the chance to get the band sorted out you can get it really fast. I remember "License to Kill" was the first take, for instance.

A remarkable recording exists of Dylan and the band working on "Sweetheart Like You," which gives the best idea of what working with him in the studio is really like. As the tape starts, Dylan and the band are running through a verse of the song. It is clear that the arrangement is pretty much in place, but he has only a skeleton of the words. As in so many sessions before, he chooses to work on the song in the studio, filling in loose lines and gaps while he can hear the song taking shape. Thus, as a second take starts up he cuts it dead after one line—" 'The boss ain't here / he gone north, he gone north' . . . no, wait a sec. That ain't right." He sings to himself, " 'Well the boss ain't here." Oh, shit." He strums his guitar while tapping his foot to the rhythm of the song. "OK." Count in. " 'Well the boss ain't here / he gone north / I can't remember where / he caught the red-eye / it left on time / he's starting a graveyard up there.' " After the take Dylan says, "Let's try it again. I think it's getting closer. The bass part is getting right. It's got that feel, y'know." It is obvious as the tape runs out that Dylan is becoming bored and disenchanted with the way the song is developing and they will have to return to the song again, by which time he will have rewritten large chunks of it.

This process became a major factor during both the recording sessions and the subsequent mixing sessions. Whole verses were rewritten, dropped, resurrected in new form. The original version of "Union Sundown" featured a final verse that was a thinly veiled attack upon "a masked man in the White House" who if "he understands the shape of things to come" will be allowed to remain there until he dies. Another verse was also wholly rewritten. "Jokerman" and "Sweetheart Like You" were substantially altered during the mixing sessions. A fine verse on the original "Jokerman" about women sitting in a shack and sewing a shirt for the Jokerman because he cannot afford a store-bought shirt was lost. In the case of the marvelous "Someone's Got a Hold of My Heart," the rewriting process did not finish until 1985, when it was recorded for *Empire Burlesque* as "Tight Connection to My Heart."

If "Sweetheart Like You" had a fairly straightforward arrangement, other songs at the sessions went through various forms before Dylan was happy. "Blind Willie McTell," perhaps the strongest song recorded at these sessions, was attempted à la "Dirge," with just acoustic guitar and piano, as well as with the full band, and Dylan's powerful vocal was embellished with some gorgeous slide guitar. "Foot of Pride" was attempted bossa nova style, with backing singers, and eventually laid down as a grungy, riff-driven slab of primeval rock and roll.

The sessions did not always progress smoothly. It was widely reported in the press that Knopfler walked out of one session in disgust for reasons unknown. Thankfully, he did return and the sessions were completed by the beginning of May, in time for Knopfler and Clark to resume touring Germany with Dire Straits. Before leaving, though, Knopfler and Dylan compiled and mixed a rough version of the album they intended to release.

Mark Knopfler: I had to go on tour in Germany. . . . I had a bag at the studio and went to the airport from the studio having just finished recording pretty much the album. But then Bob went on and overdubbed certain things.

The album they put together was Dylan's finest albums in eight years. Though it contained two meritless tracks, "Neighborhood Bully" and "License to Kill," the remaining seven songs were all of a high caliber, and included four of Dylan's finest works of recent years, "I and I," "Jokerman," "Blind Willie McTell" and "Foot of Pride." It was an album that was bound to reestablish both his commercial standing and his critical credibility. Even with the omission of the superb "Someone's Got a Hold of My Heart," it was the album all Dylan fans were hoping for.

Sadly, it was not the album that Dylan chose to release. In the past he had always trusted his first instincts as the truest. On the only previous occasion he had rerecorded part of an album, *Blood on the Tracks*, he had produced mixed results.

If the recording of the *Infidels* material had been a collaboration between Dylan and Knopfler, Dylan's decision to rework the album allowed no input from his collaborator. Not surprisingly, Knopfler later disowned the album as released.

Mark Knopfler: Some of [*Infidels*] is like listening to roughs. Maybe Bob thought I'd rushed things because I was in a hurry to leave, but I offered to finish it after our tour. Instead, he got the engineer to do the final mix, and I must say that listening to it makes me wish I'd done it myself.

After a couple of weeks away from the material, Dylan had returned to Power Station studios to complete the mixing of the album. At this point he seems to have decided to reconstruct the album, even going as far as rerecording the vocal tracks for three of the songs.

Bob Dylan: Somehow, I figured I could always get away with just playing the songs live in the studio and leaving. It got to the point where I felt people expected that from me. But I decided [on *Infidels*] to take my time like other people do. [1983]

Though he had used overdubs in the past, there is no evidence that Dylan had ever redubbed a new vocal track over an existing backing track before. He had always preferred to retain the chemistry of a live take. With *Infidels*, he began to reconsider his view of recording technology. The opportunity to re-record vocal tracks was too great a temptation and, as with "Idiot Wind," "Tangled Up in Blue" and "If You See Her, Say Hello" on the released version of *Blood on the Tracks*, he rewrote parts of both "Jokerman" and "Sweetheart Like You." Ironically, though the "Jokerman" rewrites were an improvement, the vocal was not. The original vocal performance was a *tour de force*. The new "Jokerman" was less arresting, the vocals unsuccessfully vying with the band for attention.

Bob Dylan: Well, we didn't really approach it any differently than any other record. We put the tracks down and sang most of the stuff live. Only later when we had so much stuff, we recorded it over [again]. . . . I wanted to fill it up more. I've never wanted to do that with any other record. . . . Did you ever listen to an Eagles record? . . . Their songs are good, but every note is predictable, you know exactly what's gonna be before it's even there. And I started to sense some of that on *Infidels*, and I didn't like it, so we decided to redo some of the vocals. . . . [But] that record's not an overly produced record. [1984]

The prime disaster, though, was Dylan's decision to restructure the entire album. If the album had been released as it was—even with the new vocals—it would have been well received. However, he decided to delete "Blind Willie McTell" and "Foot of Pride" from the album and replace them with a reworked version of "Union Sundown." It was as if he had taken "Visions of Johanna" and "Stuck Inside of Mobile" off *Blonde on Blonde* and replaced them with "If You Gotta Go, Go Now." The album tilted off its axis. It had previously been able to support "Neighborhood Bully" and "License to Kill." The change made *Infidels* a pale reflection of its former self. Few would ever hear the outtakes that proved his muse had been working overtime, even if his critical faculties were not.

The remixing also meant that the album was not released until November, a full six months after the sessions, when Dylan's mind had long passed on to his next project. Yet if his perspective on his own songs had never been poorer, there was no doubt that he was writing songs of true quality, as indeed he had been back in 1979–80, when *Saved* and *Shot of Love* provided equally minimal evidence of a creative renaissance. *Infidels* seemed to reinforce the false impression of Dylan's well having run dry.

Larry Sloman: When he was finishing up *Infidels*, one night we were leaving the studio, he was talking about the next album. This one was barely even mixed, and already he was talking about getting in the studio to do another album . . . that means his creative juices are cooking!

If Dylan didn't actually hot-foot it back into the studio after completing *Infidels*, he seemed to be compensating for his lack of touring by jamming with as many people as he could. In February he had turned up at the Lone Star Café to jam with Levon Helm and Rick Danko, though the results were a little loose; he was even rumored to have recorded an album of Hasidic songs (taken as further evidence of his reversion from Christianity to orthodox Judaism); and in the fall he recorded a series of demos at informal sessions at his house in Malibu. It is not known what songs resulted from these sessions, but they clearly followed well-established patterns, with Dylan requiring the musicians to respond as best they could, refusing to provide guidance himself. Two of those who regularly attended these sessions were Charlie Sexton and Charlie Quintana.

Charlie Quintana: I got word that maybe I could come over and jam once in a while. Bob was really cool about it. Either he'd call or somebody else would, and they'd say, "Come over!" Or, "Bring another guitar player!" So I would take other musicians down there. . . . I'd just go down there, sit and wait, and he'd just come in and we'd start playing. He'd start tinkering, then I'd jump in, the other guitar player, and we'd go on for five minutes, or for forty-five minutes, and then he'd stop. . . . I took a lot of local musicians from Los Angeles. . . . My impression of what was going down there is that he was trying to get back into playing, that he just wanted some guys, low-key, to jam. And that's what we did. We didn't sit around and talk a lot. He came in, we played, we had some coffee, we played again. He'd say, "All right, that's it," and he'd split, walk out.

Charlie Sexton: He'd just pick up his guitar and start singing and playing without any introduction or explanation—no keys, no chords, nothing! And my job was to figure out all the charts and produce it on the spot. We must have cut about nine or ten songs. I'd keep asking him, "Is this one yours?" and he'd just mumble in that gravelly voice, "Nah, it's from the Civil War."

Dylan was still reluctant to return to touring, and he was not granting interviews, save for one with Robert Hilburn of the *Los Angeles Times*, in which he barely mentioned the new album. Yet the release of *Infidels* required some promotion. "Sweetheart Like You" had been released as a single before the album and became his first top-sixty single since "Gotta Serve Somebody." It was the logical choice for a video. But he was reluctant to involve himself with the medium without having specific ideas in mind. Three songs had been filmed in the studio during the *Infidels* sessions for possible use as promo videos, but the footage was never used. Dylan himself wanted to produce a video of "Neighborhood Bully," but it was a poor choice for a single—particularly with its Zionist slant—and his own ideas for the video were typically vague.

Bob Dylan: I'm not quite sure I know what a video is except that the market for video is new, but the form has always been there. Yeah, [some people see the promotional film made in 1965 for] "Subterranean Homesick Blues" as a video. I don't know if it was a video. We didn't think of it as a video at the time, we just needed a piece of film to go at the beginning of a movie. . . . We wanted to do "Neighborhood Bully," but tryin' to explain it to somebody what you see and drawin' up storyboards; I haven't really found anybody that really thinks a certain way that needs to be [done], like the German filmmakers, the English filmmakers. In the States there aren't people like that. They just don't exist. . . . I visualized "Neighborhood Bully" . . . there were certain segments which I just wrote down one night which I thought would look great on film and it would be like a Fassbinder movie. [1984]

Despite Dylan's disavowal, "Subterranean Homesick Blues" had been adopted as an early example of the promo video, and was considered an inspired example of the genre. Perhaps not surprisingly, he was expected to produce something other than a standard promotional video. Yet, with the rejection of his idea for "Neighborhood Bully" he was uncooperative, and unwilling to provide any creative input into one for "Sweetheart Like You." Mark Robinson, the video director, seemed equally short of ideas.

Mark Robinson: We were . . . about to do a simple club scene where one woman's face was every woman's face, and we had thirty extras . . . lined up ready to shoot. But while we were setting up the club with upturned chairs on tabletops, there was someone sweeping up the cigarette butts. . . . I went to Bob and suggested we take an old lady and have her sweeping up, with it all coming from her point of view.

The "Sweetheart Like You" video may have got Dylan onto MTV but it did nothing to persuade younger music fans to investigate this guy who looked like a rabbi and evidently one whose barber had a sense of humor. Nevertheless, *Infidels*, having garnered good reviews on its release in November, was a consistent seller in the weeks before Christmas, and proved to be Dylan's only top twenty album of the eighties (excluding the first Traveling Wilburys album). It stayed on the charts until April 1984. As a result, CBS was eager for him to produce another video to promote the album and the February single release of "Jokerman," a strange choice for a single given its oblique content and six-minute length.

Dylan recruited two old friends from his Rolling Thunder days to codirect the video, Larry Sloman and George Lois. However, when he turned up at their initial meeting he still had his heart set on making the "Neighborhood Bully" video, and again he lacked enthusiasm for the "Jokerman" project.

Larry Sloman: Dylan walked into that [video] meeting with the intention of doing a video for "Neighborhood Bully." . . . But Lois had each lyric from "Jokerman" blown up and tacked to the wall in the conference room and underneath each line was the corresponding visual image we had selected. Now the big pitch. . . . Lois began his lecture: "Now, when you say 'You were born with a snake in both of your fists,' that's the Minoan snake goddess from Crete, circa 1500 B.C. Case closed. That's what you meant, right, Bob?" Dylan managed something between a shrug and a nod.

Sloman and Lois's video of "Jokerman" was based upon a remarkable idea—combining Dylan's lyrics, which were featured at the bottom of the screen, with visual images that complemented them. It meant they only needed to film Dylan for the refrain, though even this proved difficult enough—Dylan was reluctant to be filmed close up and perpetually squinted at the camera lights.

The results, though they still failed to impress Dylan, were able to convey a sense of the song's significance.

Whatever his reservations, Dylan clearly recognized the growing value of this new medium. The promo video was not going to reduce in importance, particularly for an artist with only a marginal profile on top forty radio in America. Throughout 1984 and 1985 he harangued journalists about the insidious influence of the video. It remains a medium he has never really mastered, despite having one of the most cinematic imaginations of any songwriter today. Indeed, in 1975 he intended to make a film of "Lily, Rosemary and the Jack of Hearts" with Jonathan Taplin. In 1986 a film could have been made of the epic "Brownsville Girl." The essential problem is that the scale of Dylan's storytelling songs is such that they can never be contained in three minutes of celluloid and Dylan has preferred to refrain from solidifying images intended to be left to each listener's imagination. However, in March 1984, the same month that Lois and Sloman finished the "Jokerman" video, Dylan went on national TV and proved once again that, filmed in performance, there was still no one who could exude the same swaggering authority and charismatic fury. He also reminded himself that he could trust his performing instincts considerably more than his recording instincts.

32 | 1984: Still Life and Real Live

By spring 1984, Dylan had been off the road for thirty months, by far his longest break since he resumed touring in 1974. In the interim, he had produced his strongest and most commercial album since *Slow Train Coming*, though *Infidels* was already old hat to Dylan, even if the album was still selling healthily and CBS was still eager to promote it.

David Letterman had been trying to get Dylan to appear on his popular "Late Night with David Letterman" TV program for some time. In March 1984 Dylan finally said yes, though he would not be interviewed and he would supply his own band (it being usual to perform with Letterman's in-house band). He then asked Charlie Quintana to put a band together, though the purpose was not made immediately apparent.

Charlie Quintana: Originally it was all very vague. There was talk of going to Hawaii and doing a show there for his label or something, and then it fell through. And then the Letterman show came out of nowhere really. I think it was about a week's notice. . . . It didn't really matter whether it was a week or a month because we didn't know what we were going to play until about a minute before we went on the air!

The band Quintana recruited consisted of two fellow members of L.A.'s burgeoning postpunk scene, Justin Jesting on guitar and Tony Marisco on bass. This was Dylan's first real dalliance with third-generation American rock and rollers. If his inexperienced new cohorts expected guidance from the man, they did not know Dylan. Flying to New York, they rehearsed for what they now knew to be a major national TV appearance the day before Letterman's show. The rehearsals followed the familiar Dylan pattern.

Charlie Quintana: We rehearsed at the TV soundcheck and we'd rehearsed the night before, but the night before we went through fifty fucking songs we didn't know! At the soundcheck they sealed off the studio and all the NBC brass was there 'cause it's Bob, and we'd never start "One-two-three." He'd just start strumming and we'd just jump in and follow it. And it would end the same way—he'd just stop playing. There was none of this "Da-da-da-da, boom boom!" to end a song, none of that! And it was five minutes before we were supposed to go on and I'm asking Bill Graham, saying, "Jesus Christ, we're shitting bricks over here! Can you please go in and ask Bob what songs we're gonna do?" And he'd come back and say, "He's not sure yet." And we're going, "Oh, shit! We only learned a hundred fifty songs!"

In fact, the TV soundcheck formed the basis for their three-song performance, Dylan and the band having run through two tunes from *Infidels*— "License to Kill" and "Jokerman"—and a version of Roy Head's "Treat Her Right." The difference in performance between soundcheck and TV appearance, though, was night and day. At the last minute Dylan decided to open with a cover of Sonny Boy Williamson's "Don't Start Me Talking" (instead of "Treat Her Right"), a song Quintana does not think was even rehearsed. Fortunately, a band of postpunk L.A. musicians could hardly fail to be conversant with a somewhat different version of the song, recorded in the early seventies by punk's godfathers, the New York Dolls. Dylan's vocal may have been a nod to Williamson, but the band played pure Dolls! And it worked. Dylan blew an impressive harp solo and the whole thing was the freshest and most intense performance he had ever given on national TV. "License to Kill" was equally astonishing, with Dylan wailing away on harmonica again and reveling in the sledgehammer sound of that Marisco-Quintana rhythm section. "Jokerman," the final song, was abbreviated to three verses but still raged with an incandescent passion, until he picked up his harp for one final blow and realized it was in the wrong key. While technicians fumbled around looking for the correct harmonica the band played on. And on.

Charlie Quintana: Maybe if we had rehearsed a song from beginning to end, it would have fallen apart. But because we were used to not knowing what was happening, when he was fumbling around for the harmonica I was just able to keep on tapping it out—a couple of verses, a chorus. It seemed like ten years! The cameraman got so bored he actually did a close-up of me.

Dylan finally blew in with a terrific harp solo and finished to a rousing reception from the stunned studio audience. Letterman asked if perhaps they could make it every Thursday and Dylan finally cracked a grin. But he knew that he had delivered a definitive TV performance. Indeed, any viewers who raced out to buy *Infidels* on the strength of this set must have been mighty disappointed when they heard the leaden, soulless version of "License to Kill" that was included on the album.

The appearance seems to have stirred Dylan's desire to perform again, and he was soon framing plans with Bill Graham for a South American tour with an as-yet-unspecified band. He had never played South America, and had had a hankering to play there for some time. He had no recording sessions scheduled and his thoughts turned to recruiting a new touring band. His previous touring bands had been relatively extravagant affairs. This time he wanted to stick to a fairly basic setup—organ, guitar, bass, drums.

Given the success of his brief association with Quintana's ensemble, they would have seemed a logical starting point. However, it seems that only Quintana was ever a serious candidate for the gig. Indeed, after playing regularly at Malibu, where Dylan conducted his informal auditions for the band, Quintana was not notified until the last minute that he would not be on the summer tour. Colin Allen had been preferred.

Charlie Quintana: I remember it was about a week before the tour started, and I was calling two or three times a day, asking whether or not I was going. They'd say, "We're not sure yet. Call back in an hour." This happened for a fucking week. I didn't sleep for a week. I really wanted to do it.

Perhaps the essence of any great band Dylan has ever played with has been the rhythm section. He has certainly been extremely fortunate to have played with combinations such as Rick Danko and Mickey Jones (or Levon Helm), Rob Stoner and Howie Wyeth, and Tim Drummond and Jim Keltner. Indeed, Sly Dunbar and Robbie Shakespeare, who had done such a sterling job on *Infidels*, had expressed an interest in touring with Dylan.

His selections in 1984 showed none of his previous unerring judgment when it came to musicians. Perhaps, as in 1978, when Ian Wallace played the sticks, there was just not enough time to work at finding a worthwhile rhythm section. Which still does not explain Dylan's baffling decision to prefer the wholly unknown and unimpressive Colin Allen to the supremely rhythmic Quintana.

The likely explanation is that Dylan once again left a great deal of the decision-making to his appointed bandleader, in this case Mick Taylor. Colin Allen was a friend of Taylor's, they had worked together in the past and he was auditioned at Taylor's suggestion. If it was Taylor who convinced Dylan to prefer Allen to Quintana, he did him a great disservice. Aside from the profound difference in rhythmic sense, Quintana was used to Dylan's idiosyncrasies. Allen was not, and he had barely a week of serious rehearsing to learn them.

Allen was not the only unfortunate choice, though the other selections, if not ideal, were more than competent. However, after the decision was made not to use Marisco it was somewhat surprising that Dylan and/or Taylor should then select an equally inexperienced (if promising) L.A. bassist by the name of Greg Sutton.

Greg Sutton: Mick Taylor liked the way I played, so [Dylan] told me about a week before the tour began that I had the gig! He was very mysterious about it. . . . The same was true with [keyboard player] Ian MacLagan. He told Ian MacLagan about three days before the tour.

Dylan had initially wanted Benmont Tench of Tom Petty's Heartbreakers to play keyboards on the tour. Tench would have been an excellent choice. He had worked on the *Shot of Love* album and, as he later proved in 1987, had a natural sense of dynamics in his playing and was not afraid to wing it with Dylan. Unfortunately, he could not spare the time to play the tour.

Colin Allen: Benmont couldn't do it—he would've been perfect, the best choice—'cause he was involved with Petty and they were going to do some recordings. . . . So I said, "What about Nicky Hopkins? . . . And so he came up. But he was really . . . a piano player. He was saying to me on the phone, "Get Bob to get a grand piano in to rehearse on." . . . So he came up with this manager guy, and maybe it was all a bit too much for Bob. But anyway, then we got Ian MacLagan. . . . Ian finally got the word only a couple of days before we actually left Bob's estate and went to the Beverly Theater in Beverly Hills to rehearse in a theater situation for about five days.

Ian MacLagan had a good pedigree, notably from his time in the Faces, though again he was a Mick Taylor selection rather than a Dylan one. As Sutton and Allen have indicated, MacLagan did not get the call until a week before the tour. By now, the location had changed dramatically: South America had fallen through, so, since Dylan had put a band together, Europe was the only feasible location for a tour at such short notice.

Bob Dylan: I wanted to do a South American tour. It was just not feasible at this time so I took this tour. . . . There's no particular reason for it. . . . I specifically wanted to do a South American tour. . . . At the last moment I had sort of set my mind mentally to do something so I did this 'cause the other one didn't come off. [1984]

Serious rehearsals started at the Beverly Theater in Los Angeles barely a week before the first show was booked for Verona, Italy. The rehearsals were frankly awful. The band sounded as though they were playing underneath fifty pounds of porridge, and Dylan's singing sounded devoid of passion. The choice of material they rehearsed was also predictable. Never before had Dylan toured without an album in the can or new material to premiere. Yet *Infidels* was a year old as far as he was concerned. Only some four songs from his "new" album were even rehearsed. Likewise, Dylan's seventies oeuvre was largely ignored as he constructed his first oldies show. Even 1978 had featured a cross section of his career, and the songs had been spruced up with new arrangements. In 1984 Dylan had a much more basic sound to work with, and a rhythm section best utilized by sticking to basics.

Four or five days' rehearsals was clearly nowhere near enough time to get the band into shape, particularly as Dylan wanted the band to work on a few new songs he had written, which had titles such as "Angel of Rain," "Dirty Lie" and "Enough Is Enough," or middle-of-the-road oldies such as "Always on My Mind," rather than work on arranging his older songs, the songs his fans would be expecting.

Flying into Italy, Dylan knew he would have to rehearse further with the band. A rehearsal on May 27, the day before his first Italian concert, saw him continue to treat the rehearsals as extended jam sessions. On the afternoon of May 28 he ran through the basic set with his band before the ancient portals of the Arena di Verona were opened to eager Italian fans about to get their first glimpse of Bob Dylan in concert. The evening's show started disastrously.

Dylan seemed reluctant to give the band any guidance about when to end songs, and without any obvious direction from Taylor either, the songs spluttered to their conclusions. The first half was as ramshackle as any performance he had ever given.

Though the band sounded a little more together during their second set, Dylan must have been seriously worried about them. Taylor was a poor choice for leader, and seemed determined to prove his undoubted pedigree as a guitarist by playing extended and indulgent solos during songs that did not require such embellishment.

Surprisingly, though, within a week after the tour beginning, the band began to shape up. In part this was because Dylan seemed to realize that he had better stamp his authority on the proceedings before everything collapsed around his ears. By the time they reached Rotterdam, seven days after that first Verona show, he was at last singing with a little of the old fire and was brimming with ideas, to the extent that he set about rewriting two of his greatest songs, "Tangled Up in Blue" and "Simple Twist of Fate."

Bob Dylan: There's a version [of "Tangled Up in Blue"] we used to do on stage with just electric guitar and a saxophone—keeping the same lyrics, thinking that maybe if I did that to it it would bring it out in an emotional way. But it didn't hold up very well that way. So I changed the lyrics, to bring it up to date. But I didn't change it 'cause I was singing it one night and thought, "Oh, I'm bored with the old words." The old ones were never quite filled in. I rewrote it in a hotel room somewhere. I think it was in Amsterdam. . . . When I sang it the next night I knew it was right. [1985]

"Tangled Up in Blue" rapidly became a nightly highlight for the fans. At the first few performances the crowd hung on every word, waiting to see where the story led. The end of the song was an audacious inversion of the original narrator's intent. In 1974, the singer was "still on the road, heading for another joint," for that is where he felt the subject of his quest lay. In 1984, the singer was "still walking towards the sun, trying to stay out of the joints." The joints were now distractions along the way and he had to avoid them as he headed toward the light of knowledge. It also seemed a subtle admission that he was still walking in the spirit of the Son. "Simple Twist of Fate," unlike "Tangled Up in Blue," was performed with the full band, and MacLagan started to come into his own with some effective organ playing. The new version was an imaginative reworking, a little more surreal than the original.

As the first set settled into a rigid seven-song pattern nightly, the band started to sound a lot more comfortable, and both Sutton and Allen started to play with something approaching competency. Sutton soon realized Dylan enjoyed his little game of changing keys.

Greg Sutton: Bob was saying, "What key are we in now?" 'Cause he started "Maggie's Farm" wrong and he asked me, "What key are we in?" I said, "Bob, we're in G, the key you started it in." And he says, "Well, can you go back to the right key?" I said, "Whatever you say, Bob."

Allen also began to understand the boss a little better in Rome when he asked him about those song endings, which earlier had been so disastrous and even by midtour were on occasions shaky. Dylan was his usual helpful self.

Colin Allen: One day we were sitting in this hotel in Rome, the Lord Byron Hotel. . . . We were sitting outside, and Bob was there, and I said, "Hey, Bob, you know when you look at me at the end of a song, what's the story? Do you want me to end the song immediately, as soon as possible, or wait till the sequence goes?" He said, "Well, I just figure we've done enough with the songs and that we should finish them when we felt comfortable."

The 1984 tour established a fairly standard pattern for subsequent Dylan tours. It was his first nostalgia tour, and subsequent tours would all rely heavily on his more famous sixties material, generally at the expense of his no less impressive seventies and eighties oeuvre. Subsequent tours also generally discounted contemporary product, with only a small sampling from the previous album, generally a year old by the time he hit the road. From this point on he favored a basic guitar/organ/bass/drums or even a guitar/bass/drums setup. Though he would again use female backing vocalists in 1986–87, Dylan mainly relied on his own vocals to get him through the later eighties. Meanwhile, the voice has deteriorated. In 1984 Dylan rarely chose to go for the notes he had attempted on his previous European tour, but at least when he did he could still hit them. By his next European visit, in the fall of 1987, he knew there was little point in trying to hit some of those notes—even if he could still hold his breath three times as long as Caruso.

This decision by Dylan to adopt a more nostalgic, perhaps to be fair a more conciliatory, approach—most of the crowds did genuinely seem to want to hear tired retreads of "All Along the Watchtower"—inevitably and justifiably led to some critical flak during the 1984 tour. The sizes of the venues Dylan played—large arenas or stadiums—required that he maintain some kind of high profile with the press simply in order to sell tickets. After all, his "special guests," the wearisome Santana, were hardly major crowd-pullers in 1984. In France he actually agreed to his first televised interview in nineteen years to help sell tickets for the Paris, Grenoble and Nantes shows. All along he was asked: Are your songs relevant today? Do you still have a role to play in modern music? At press conferences in Verona and Hamburg he was surly, uncommunicative, indeed downright rude. As the tour progressed and he felt more confident about the worth of what he was peddling this time around, he became more talkative, more prepared to defend himself.

Bob Dylan: For me, none of the songs I've written has really dated. They capture something I've never been able to improve on, whatever their statement is. . . . People say they're "nostalgia," but I don't know what that means, really. A *Tale of Two Cities* was written a hundred years ago; is that nostalgic? This term *nostalgic*, it's just another way people have of dealing with you and putting you some place they think they understand. It's just another label. [1984]

A month to the day after that disastrous first Verona show, Dylan arrived in Barcelona for his second-ever Spanish show (the first had been in Madrid two days earlier). His performance in Barcelona proved that he was still the consummate performer. The band, if lacking invention, had at least become tight and professional, and Dylan sang like a bird, albeit one with a touch of laryngitis. The final song of a two-and-a-half-hour set, "Blowin' in the Wind," found Dylan actually cajoling the huge stadium crowd into chorus after chorus of the song—"Once more"; "Just once more"—before delivering an impassioned last verse that expressed more sense of the song's meaning than had any version he had sung in the last twenty-two years.

Playing to stadium crowds of between thirty and a hundred thousand, Dylan then weaved his way through Nantes, Paris, Grenoble, Newcastle, London and finally Dublin. Though the last two shows—which constitute the bulk of the disappointing live album *Real Live*—were a little slick and lacking in passion, they were well received and Dylan had, by July 8, completed his one and only stadium tour without in any way diminishing his reputation as a charismatic performer. Considering the huge, roofless barns he was playing, the wasted rehearsals and the disappointing choice of rhythm section, this was certainly far more than any unfortunate member of the Verona crowd six weeks earlier would have expected.

33 | 1984–85: Burlesques and Benefits

Perhaps the buzz of being on the road again was what was necessary to get Dylan writing once more. He had two or three nearly finished songs he had tried out at the rehearsals in May, though only "Enough Is Enough" became a feature of the tour, and his writing on the tour had not been confined to rewriting of earlier classics. Within two weeks of the tour's end he was back in the studio working on a new album.

It had been fourteen months since the *Infidels* sessions, and a strong album might indicate a mid-eighties revival to parallel his mid-seventies surge of creativity. The summer sessions were not confined to one studio or one burst of activity. Over July and August, Dylan worked at Intergalactic Studios, Delta Studios and even returned to the Record Plant. Rather than forming a nucleus of musicians to record a new album with, he tried out different combinations, in search of a new sound. This time he had decided to produce the sessions himself, though one session at the Power Station featured "Miami" Steve Van Zandt, Bruce Springsteen's ex-guitarist, a noted producer in his own right. The only known result from this session with Van Zandt was a stunning new composition called "When the Night Comes Falling from the Sky," a seven-minute apocalyptic vision that first simmers and then burns with an unrestrained Dylan vocal, ably supported by some fine keyboards by Roy Bittan and exemplary guitar work from Van Zandt. This recording would never be used.

A session at Intergalactic was less successful, even though Dylan had brought old friend Ron Wood along to help out and provide moral support. He had temporarily recruited Al Green's usual band of shit-hot Memphis musicians. Unfortunately, they were not used to the idiosyncratic approach Dylan took, particularly when he not only refused to sing any song the same way twice but kept changing the keys on them.

Ron Wood: [There was one session], it was at Intergalactic, the old Hit Factory, in New York, with the Al Green band. All these guys from Memphis couldn't understand Bob's chord sequences. Every time he started off a new song, he'd start in a new key, or if we were doing the same song over and over, every time it would be in a different key. Now I can go along with that with Bob, but the band was totally confused, and one by one they left the studio.

Apart from recording a straightforward shot of rhythm and blues called "Honey Wait" and a run-through of the old chestnut "Mountain of Love," the session seems to have been without result. Sessions at Delta Sound studios were more successful, with Ron Wood again providing a helping hand, along with Anton Fig and John Paris as the rhythm section. "Clean Cut Kid," originally an outtake from *Infidels*, was successfully recorded, as were two new songs, the funky "Driftin' Too Far from Shore," which later ended up on *Knocked Out Loaded*, and an insidious blues number called "Who Loves You More." However, Dylan still seemed uncomfortable with the technology available to him in digital thirty-two-track studios. Talking at the end of July in a radio interview, he revealed he was still a Luddite at heart.

Bob Dylan: We were recording something the other night and we were gonna put some handclaps on it. And the guy sitting behind the board, he was saying, "Well, do you guys wanna go out there and actually clap? I got a machine right here that can do that." . . . We went out and clapped instead. . . . But that's just a small example of how everything is just machine orientated. [1984]

Unfortunately, once again Dylan's lack of discipline in failing to stamp his personal artistic authority on his songs let him down. The superb original version of "When the Night Comes Falling from the Sky," which was as good as anything he had recorded in the last decade, ended up unused. At the end of the sessions at Delta, which had proved the most productive of the summer, Ron Wood looked on with astonishment as he allowed the engineers to mix the material without his own input. In the case of "Driftin' Too Far from Shore" this meant that, when the song came to be used for *Knocked Out Loaded*, the entire drum track had to be rerecorded.

Ron Wood: When we'd go in at . . . Delta for a playback, every time he'd have the same attitude. The weak side of him would come out. They'd say, "Hey, Bob, we don't need this," and he'd say, "Oh. OK." And they'd make a mix to their ears, and he'd just stand outside and let them do it. And I'd be saying, "Hey! You can't let these guys . . . Look! They've left off the background vocals!" or "What about the drums?!" But there would be something going on in the back of his head which didn't allow him to interfere. And yet if he'd have gone into the control room with the dominance that he had while we were cutting the stuff, it could have been mind-bending.

Still, the burst of new songs, even if only "When the Night Comes Falling from the Sky" had any claims to major status, suggested that the new album could be an important work, despite Dylan's failure to capitalize on the quality of his songwriting on his last three albums. Meanwhile, he was keeping tabs on a buoyant American postpunk scene, which was producing quality "cow-punk" bands such as Lone Justice, Jason and the Scorchers and Green on Red, along with more sixties-sounding bands such as R.E.M. and Rain Parade. Indeed, his current girlfriend, Carole Childs, an executive for Geffen Records, who seemed to have replaced Clydie King in his affections, had been responsible for signing up the most exciting of all the new bands, Lone Justice, and convinced Dylan to give them one of his new songs, a fairly lightweight number called "Go 'Way Little Boy." Since Lone Justice were also recording in New York that summer— toiling over their long-awaited debut album with producer Jimmy Iovine— Dylan turned up at the sessions to give them the song in person, accompanied by Ron Wood.

Maria McKee: Carole Childs . . . was the woman who originally signed me to Geffen Records. She's very close to Dylan—very, very close—and she brought him to a gig or something. . . . She said, "Why don't you write Maria a song?" He said, "OK." . . . He came down to the studio when we were recording our first album and taught us the song. And he stayed around. He brought Ron Wood with him and they played on it. . . . We ended up working on it a very long time because he didn't like the way I sang it . . . until I sang it like him! It got to the point where finally I just did my best Bob Dylan imitation—and he said, "Ah, now you're doin' some *real singing!*"

Like most of the material recorded by Dylan himself in New York during July, "Go 'Way Little Boy" did not end up included on the album it was intended for (it was later issued as a bonus track on a Lone Justice twelve-inch single).

By November 1984, Dylan's new album still required a cogent identity. Despite numerous recording sessions, enough normally to produce an entire album, Dylan had very little that he could be happy with. There were new sessions in Los Angeles which he again decided to produce himself, relying on house engineers to get the actual recordings down. However, he now had some further important compositions to add to "When the Night Comes Falling from the Sky."

One of the first songs recorded was "Something's Burning Baby," an ominous tune set to a slow march beat, seemingly an outlandish tangent to his "Ain't Gonna Go to Hell (for Anybody)" theme. Dylan reworked the lyrics several times before settling on the final released version. The constantly changing words and his idiosyncratic singing certainly proved difficult for second vocalist Madelyn Quebec, who was expected to sing live with him.

Ira Ingber: ["Something's Burning Baby"] is a very weird song. And Maddy did not know the words when they did the vocal, 'cause I watched her trying to follow him. She was trying to sing harmonies with him live, which is tough because Bob doesn't necessarily know where he's going.

Even more impressive was a song that Dylan had cowritten that fall with Sam Shepard, the playwright originally recruited in 1975 to work on *Renaldo and Clara*. The song was a twelve-minute epic based on a Gregory Peck film, *The Gunfighter*, and was called "New Danville Girl" (after a Woody Guthrie song, "Danville Girl"). The idea arose when Dylan and Shepard decided to write a song along the lines of Lou Reed's "Doin' the Things That We Want To," which was about attending one of Shepard's plays. In "New Danville Girl," the singer seems to identify with the murderer of Peck's gunfighter character. The cinematic sweep of the singer's narrative about his travels through Texas, with and without his Danville girl, makes the song Dylan's most epic since the comparable "Lily, Rosemary and the Jack of Hearts." Like the earlier song, it lent itself naturally to being visualized on celluloid. Indeed, according to Shepard the song was written with such an intention in mind.

Sam Shepard: It has to do with a guy standing on line and waiting to see an old Gregory Peck movie that he can't quite remember—only pieces of it, and then this whole memory thing happens, unfolding before his very eyes. He starts speaking internally to a woman . . . reliving the whole journey they'd gone on. . . . We spent two days writing the lyrics—Bob had previously composed the melody line, which was already down on tape. . . . At one point he talked about making a video out of it.

The sessions at Cherokee Studios, where "New Danville Girl" and "Something's Burning, Baby" were recorded, featured some young L.A. musicians who had been rehearsing with Dylan at his Malibu home. Among them were Ira Ingber and Vince Melamed, who had been in a local band together, and Don Heffington, the then drummer with Lone Justice. According to Ingber, it was Heffington who made "New Danville Girl" a much less daunting listening experience with his inspired timing and sense of the drama of the song.

Ira Ingber: Don [Heffington] really wrote "Brownsville Girl's" music, because as the drummer he played it with such dynamics that he actually created a song, because it's the same four chords that go over and over again, but the way Don played the drums would accentuate the choruses and come down for the verses.

Yet "New Danville Girl" did not make it onto *Empire Burlesque*. Like the equally impressive 1984 version of "When the Night Comes Falling from the Sky," it was passed over to allow such fluff as "Never Gonna Be the Same Again" and "Emotionally Yours" to fill up the grooves. The inexplicable omission of "New Danville Girl," like the removal of "Blind Willie McTell" and "Foot of Pride" from *Infidels*, gravely impaired the quality of an album that should have been a welcome continuation of the promise even the released *Infidels* managed to display. There seemed to be a deliberate perversity to Dylan's decision. The song's eventual inclusion, under the new title "Brownsville Girl," on *Knocked Out Loaded*, meant that the song's quality went largely ignored, surrounded as it was by the obvious "filler" that constituted the remainder of that album.

Ira Ingber: When we first recorded ["Danville Girl"], we . . . made a cassette. And he took it out and started playing it. He came back the next day we were working and said, "Yeah, a lot of people like this thing." And then he didn't do anything with it. It's like he was doing it to spite people who were all liking it and he just held on to it. He should have put it on *Empire Burlesque*, but he reworked it.

Thus, at the end of 1984, after six months of earnest work on the follow-up to *Infidels*, Dylan had recorded only two tracks that would eventually appear on *Empire Burlesque*. It seemed as if this new approach to recording was providing him with too many choices, too much opportunity to work on more and more material at his leisure.

When *Empire Burlesque* was finally released in June 1985, Dylan talked at length about his new approach to his work. He had spent three solid months working on *Infidels*. The work load was more evenly spread on *Empire Burlesque*, but it still represented an unprecedented expenditure of time on his part.

Bob Dylan: When I'm making a record I'll need some songs, and I'll start digging through my pockets and drawers trying to find these songs. Then I'll bring one out and I've never sung it before, sometimes I can't even remember the melody to it, and I'll get it in. Sometimes great things happen, sometimes not-so-great things happen. But regardless of what happens, when I do it in the studio it's the first time I've ever done it. I'm pretty much unfamiliar with it. In the past what's come out is what I've usually stuck with, whether it really knocked me out or not. For no apparent reason I've stuck with it, just from lack of commitment to taking the trouble to really get it right. I didn't want to record that way anymore. Now I'm recording more than I used to record. About two years ago I decided to get serious about it and just record. . . . What I do now is just record all the time. Sometimes nothing comes out and other times I get a lot of stuff that I keep. I recorded [*Empire Burlesque*] for a long time. I just put down the songs that I felt as I wanted to put them down. Then I'd listen and decide if I liked them. And if I didn't like them I'd either rerecord them or change something about them. [1985]

Further sessions at Cherokee Studios in Los Angeles and Power Station Studios in New York through the winter of 1985 provided most of the *Empire Burlesque* album. When he chose to "rerecord [songs] or change something about them," the results were fairly disastrous. One of the songs rerecorded in New York was "When the Night Comes Falling from the Sky," which acquired a whomping synthesizer/horn track that only served to obscure a less-than-impressive new Dylan vocal.

In New York that winter he also chose to rework an *Infidels* outtake, "Someone's Got a Hold of My Heart." The many new lines in every single case were inferior to the original and the dreadful use of his backing singers, the Queens of Rhythm, produced a disco-funk feel that destroyed the essence of a once-great song. The result, which would open *Empire Burlesque* as "Tight Connection to My Heart," proved a taste of things to come.

The remainder of the winter 1984–85 cuts were largely mawkish ballads that would not have been out of place on *Nashville Skyline*, and they suggested that any creative renaissance was receding fast. "Seeing the Real You at Last" seems like a cutup of half-remembered lines from Hollywood B movies, and indeed contains many allusions to Humphrey Bogart movies, *Shane, Bronco Billy* and even a "Star Trek" episode. The final song for the album was recorded acoustically during preliminary mixing, as "Wedding Song" had been on *Planet Waves*. "Dark Eyes," though, is a hollow shell compared with "Wedding Song." Dylan sounds as if he were the worse for drink when he recorded the track. When trying to perform his one and only live version of the song, in Sydney in February 1986, he could no longer play the ridiculous, droning melody and wisely abandoned the attempt. Yet with "Dark Eyes" he felt that he had completed the album and that he could now turn it over to someone else for mixing.

Bob Dylan: I'm the final judge of what goes on and off my records. This last record I just did, *Empire Burlesque,* there were nine songs I knew belonged on it, and I needed a tenth. I had about four songs, and one of those was going to be the tenth song. I finally figured out that the tenth song needed to be acoustic, so I just wrote it. I wrote it because none of the other songs fit that spot, that certain place. [1985]

By the beginning of March Dylan had accumulated an innocuous enough collection of new songs—only "Something's Burning, Baby" and "When the Night Comes Falling from the Sky" having any real substance to them—to put together a pleasant enough new album, an adequate holding exercise until he could weld his critical faculties to his wanton creative spirit. But, having produced the sessions himself, he decided he needed a helping hand to mix the album, and he hired one producer who proved too meticulous for his tastes before settling on the inappropriate Arthur Baker.

Bob Dylan: [The other producer] listened to the songs too much. I could see him thinking too much, y'know; and then I saw him once and when he was mixing he would have rolls of paper writing notes. I didn't want that. So Arthur just listened to the stuff and said, "Yeah." And he fixed it up a lot. I listened to the sound of the previous record I made and the last one and it does sound better. [1985]

Though Dylan has proved skillful at presenting the illusion that he is concerned only with satisfying himself artistically, in 1985, as in 1983 or 1979 or 1970, he wanted his new album to be commercial and contemporary. Baker was the in-vogue producer whose work with Bruce Springsteen, New Order and assorted funk exponents had given him some kind of pedigree. Unfortunately, his idea of remixing was to place several extraneous layers of noise over perfectly acceptable basic tracks, cluttering up the sound and hiding what was in fact a conventional rock album behind the facade of eighties-style whomping drums and glistening synths. Though Baker gave the songs a unity of sound, it was not Dylan's sound. It seemed as if Dylan himself lacked the will to complete the album and passed it to an unsympathetic soul just to get it out.

Bob Dylan: I'm not too experienced at having records sound good. I don't know how to go about doing that, though I thought I got pretty close last time with Arthur Baker. . . . I just went out and recorded a bunch of stuff all over the place and then when it was time to put this record together I brought it all to him and he made it sound like a record. [1985]

Ron Wood referred to Dylan's inability or unwillingness to impose his authority when mixing the July 1984 material. A similar syndrome now entirely neutered what had started out as a promising follow-up to *Infidels*. Though *Empire Burlesque* was greeted reasonably favorably by the music press, its shallowness could not disguise for long a man treading water. Yet it would be four years before he again summoned up the effort to put in the requisite discipline required to record another album of wholly original material.

Empire Burlesque was the end of Dylan's grand experiment in the modern studios of North America, which had all but kept him off the road for four years. Surprisingly, Dylan agreed to promote this album—unlike *Infidels*—with a flurry of interviews, promotional videos and TV appearances, as if feeling the need to reverse his commercial decline but unwilling to readopt the punishing life-style of the road.

Returning to the States from a brief trip to Russia in early August, where he had been invited to perform at a Moscow poetry festival by Russian poet Yevgeny Yevtushenko and had traveled on to Odessa to visit the homeland of his ancestors, Dylan began an unprecedented bout of interviews intended to promote the new album, though *Empire Burlesque* was already descending the charts after a disappointing peak at number thirty-three, making the publicity a little belated.

Dylan was already beyond any real interest in his last album, and the August and September interviews became more an attempt to confront his own past. With a five-album boxed retrospective set and a revised edition of *Writings and Drawings* that would cover all his albums through *Empire Burlesque* both planned for the fall, it seemed now was a time for summarizing and appraising the past. By far the best of these interviews was a remarkably in-depth series by Scott Cohen intended for a front-cover story in *Spin*, the new rival to *Rolling Stone*. Cohen managed to convince Dylan to answer his first questionnaire in twenty years. The categories included Three Authors I'd Read Anything By (Dylan's list was Tacitus, Chekhov and Tolstoy) and Questions You Can't Answer. In the latter category Dylan came up with: "How does it feel to be a legend? How does it feel to have influenced a bunch of people? What did you change your name to? Are you somebody? Where's your music taking you? Did you write that song for me? Did you know Nixon?"

In August, Dylan also completed two promotional videos for *Empire Burlesque*, a further belated attempt to promote the album. The first attempt to film a promo video for *Empire Burlesque* had been something of a failure. Having selected "Tight Connection to My Heart" as the first single, Dylan asked Paul Schrader to film the video of the song. Schrader, a noted film director, had just completed his Japanese epic *Mishima*, which had greatly impressed Dylan. Though Schrader agreed to the assignment, he required the video to be filmed in Japan. Dylan traveled to Tokyo in April to spend two days filming. The results were most disappointing, a story video of no fixed abode. Both Schrader and Dylan would dismiss the video, Schrader claiming that it "was a little piece of eye-candy I shot in Tokyo. . . . It means as little as it looks like it means." Dylan was equally disappointed, apportioning a large part of the blame to Schrader. At a press conference in Sydney the following February, he observed:

Bob Dylan: I thought that I might be able to make a video with the man who made the movies and pull it off, but I was wrong. [1986]

Schrader had previously said that Dylan remained uncommunicative throughout the preshoot meeting and the two days of shooting, offering few ideas of his own. Nevertheless, Dylan did not abandon his idea of shooting a video that had something of the look of *Mishima*. Unfortunately, his reasons for wanting to shoot two videos in August in black and white was never relayed from "executive producer" Dave Stewart [of the Eurythmics], in whom Dylan confided, to the actual video directors, Markus Innocenti and Eddie Arno.

Markus Innocenti and Eddio Arno: We were simply told by Dave that black and white was required. We weren't told why. In fact, we wished that Dylan had talked directly to us earlier, because we learned that Dylan wanted it to look like an old Japanese movie, and we could have filmed it differently. When we saw Paul Schrader's *Mishima* we understood why Dylan wanted it. If you ever watch that movie, look out for the black-and-white sequences. It would be interesting to put Dylan's music over the images—there would be something extraordinary, quite beyond what a music video can do. We could really understand why Dylan wanted Schrader for "Tight Connection to My Heart," but once the project had not lived up to his expectations it is reasonable to think that he wanted to try again [to] get the wonderful beauty and stillness that black-and-white can achieve.

The two videos to be shot on August 22 and 23 in Los Angeles were the A and B sides of the second *Empire Burlesque* single "When the Night Comes Falling from the Sky" and "Emotionally Yours." This time Dylan wanted a performance-type video like "Sweetheart Like You," and a little-used church on Sunset Boulevard was the locale suggested. Dylan actually had a tenuous thread in mind to link the two videos: An ex-girlfriend would be in the audience during the performance of "When the Night Comes Falling from the Sky," and he would later reminisce about her in "Emotionally Yours."

Markus Innocenti and Eddie Arno: Dylan is having an affair with a new girl. Dressed in buckskin, she goes with him to the gig, where the band play "When the Night Comes Falling." Unknown to Dylan, a former lover—also an attractive brunet dressed in buckskin—has seen Dylan on the way to the gig. She comes to watch the performance but the memories are too much and she has to leave, close to tears. She wanders off down Hollywood Boulevard without approaching him again. This is where "When the Night Comes Falling" ends and "Emotionally Yours" begins. But Dylan has carried a torch for this buckskin-clad, dark-eyed beauty—why else would his new girlfriend be such a replica of the first? After the gig Dylan is left alone in the hall. Playing an acoustic guitar, his memories go back to his original buckskin girl. With regret, he remembers the moment when he told her the relationship was over.

Dylan wanted the group in the video to look as if it was the kind of "band of gypsies" he still liked.

Markus Innocenti and Eddie Arno: Dylan and Dave wanted "When the Night Comes Falling" to have a "band of gypsies" atmosphere. For example, on the bus there was Dylan's buckskin girl; Dave's girlfriend, Clare, playing a journalist; a host of celebrated musicians; and one of the waiters from the Talesai restaurant in the role of Dylan's manager. It was very loose and chaotic. Dylan also wanted a juggler at the concert. The juggler was another chaotic/ symbolic element who was to be standing in the wings as the band played. We decided to edit him out—it looked too contrived for our taste.

Unfortunately, the results were once more disappointing, suggesting again that Dylan was still unable to understand the video medium. The film-video conversion was poorly executed and the black-and-white film looked washy when broadcast, with none of the clarity and stillness Dylan was looking for. At Stewart's behest, several negative flashes intended to resemble the white light of nuclear blasts were inserted into "When the Night Comes Falling from the Sky"; they gave a false ring to the video and detracted from the sketchy story line. Also, the broadcast of the videos separately and several weeks apart meant that any continuity between the two was lost on a jaundiced MTV audience. One positive result, though, came through Dylan's insistence that all the instruments used in the shoot be real, so that the participants could jam between takes, to alleviate the inevitable boredom.

Markus Innocenti and Eddie Arno: He jammed extensively with the band, mostly twelve-bar blues, though he didn't sing. He was more interested in riffing or taking solos on guitar.

Playing to the handful of extras who had responded to a local radio ad wanting help in filming a Dylan video—no one believed the request was genuine until Dave Stewart went on the air himself—Dylan seemed again to be enjoying the idea of playing live, even if it was only jamming. He later told Mikal Gilmore of the *Los Angeles Herald-Examiner*:

Bob Dylan: [Dave Stewart] put together a great band for this lip-sync video and set us up with equipment on this little stage in a church somewhere in West L.A. So between all the time they took setting up camera shots and lights and all that stuff, we could just play live for this little crowd that had gathered there. I can't even express how good that felt—in fact, I was trying to remember the last time I'd felt that kind of direct connection. [1985]

Ironically, despite *Empire Burlesque*'s many flaws, the failure of the promo videos to incite any real interest and Dylan's disinclination to return to the road, 1985 was a year in which his public profile was at its highest since 1979. Largely this was because it was the year that American pop music decided to develop a conscience. The "We Are the World" single, recorded in January 1985, and the huge Live Aid benefit shows in London and Philadelphia in July, both designed to provide funds to aid starving Ethiopians, inevitably involved Dylan, whose profile as the conscience of pop music was perhaps somewhat more long-standing than those of Simple Minds and U2. Though he remained unconvinced of the merits of "We Are the World," he recognized a worthy cause. And the author of a song about grain elevators bursting while people were starving could hardly refuse to participate.

Bob Dylan: People buying a song and the money going to starving people in Africa . . . is a worthwhile idea but I wasn't so convinced about the message of the song. To tell you the truth, I don't think people can save themselves. [1985]

"We Are the World" reminded the American public that Dylan was still alive and kicking, but Live Aid quickly undid a lot of the good publicity. Though many of the reasons behind his disastrous appearance at Live Aid, in front of an estimated two billion viewers, lay outside his control, it was perceived at the time as evidence that Dylan could not even sing his old songs with any conviction, let alone write new songs of quality and perform them.

Though what happened on stage was largely out of Dylan's hands, the decision not to play solo, nor with Tom Petty's Heartbreakers, as had been suggested, but to perform accompanied by Ron Wood and Keith Richards, was certainly his. And it proved an unfortunate one. Matters started propitiously enough. Dylan was unsure what to do at Live Aid and mentioned his predicament at Ron Wood's New York apartment.

Ron Wood: Bob says, "I'm playing in Philadelphia the day after tomorrow." I didn't even know about Live Aid. He says, "It's a big charity thing." He says, "Bill Graham's got a band for me and I have to go along with it." Then he says, "Do you think that maybe you and me could play together sometime?" I said, "Sure. Let's do the gig on Saturday." He said, "Really?" I said, "Yeah. You don't necessarily have to go along with Bill Graham." And I said, "Keith would love to do it too." So I rang Keith up again and I said, "Get over here because Bob wants us to do Live Aid with him." He said, "You'd better not be lying, Woody." . . . Some of the rehearsal tapes from my basement in New York are incredible. We were playing in there for a couple of days. We were playing in the upstairs dining room just before we left for Philadelphia and it was brilliant. When we got to the stadium he was saying, "I wonder what Bill Graham wants me to do?" We were going, "Do what you want to do, Bob!" But he was saying, "Bill might make me do this." Very odd. He wanted to be bossed around again. Even going up the ramps—we'd decided what songs we were going to play and he turns and says, "Hey! Maybe I should do 'All I Really Want to Do'!" We were going, "Aargh! Oh my God!"

When Dylan went on stage he discovered that he could not hear a thing. The stage monitors had been switched off and there were assorted would-be singers practicing their grand moment, singing the "We Are the World" finale behind the curtain at the back of him.

Bob Dylan: They screwed around with us. We didn't even have any monitors out there. When they threw in the grand finale at the last moment they took all the settings off and set the stage up for the thirty people who were standing behind the curtain. We couldn't even hear our own voices, and when you can't hear, you can't play; you don't have any timing. It's like proceeding on radar. [1985]

Also, Keith Richards seemed to be on some other planet that was not as yet receiving this global broadcast. Dylan started with "Hollis Brown," but was having genuine problems pitching his voice without monitors and with the racket coming from behind. By "When the Ship Comes In" his voice was all over the place, and "Blowin' in the Wind" was sung hurriedly and without meaning. Dylan just wanted to get off stage, and Ron Wood seemed anxious to join him.

Ron Wood: We came off looking like real idiots.

Live Aid did have one silver lining. After "Ballad of Hollis Brown" Dylan asked the millions watching to remember those in their own country who were starving and struggling because of economic events that were beyond their control. In particular, he asked that we remember the plight of the American farmers. Though his comments struck an oddly inappropriate, not to say discordant, note among all the self-congratulatory back-patting that had gone on all day, Willie Nelson took them as his cue to organize a further event in September to publicize the plight of American farmers. Farm Aid would signal Dylan's return to peak performing powers.

34 1985–86: Junco and His Partners in Crime

It was inevitable that Dylan would appear at Farm Aid. Having been responsible for the genesis of the idea with his comments at Live Aid, he could hardly refuse Willie Nelson when the call came. Since the conclusion of the benefit was scheduled to be broadcast on national primetime TV live on Saturday, September 22, it also gave him an opportunity to reaffirm his credibility as a live performer after the Live Aid debacle.

This time he decided to follow Bill Graham's original suggestion for Live Aid and ask Tom Petty and the Heartbreakers if they would like to provide him with the necessary backing. He had already used most of the Heartbreakers on *Shot of Love* and *Empire Burlesque*, which featured organist Benmont Tench, guitarist Mike Campbell and bassist Howie Epstein. The Heartbreakers were scheduled to perform their own set at the benefit, so it was unlikely to be an imposition to back Dylan as well.

Tom Petty: He just phoned up after Live Aid—it was for the Farm Aid thing. He didn't want to try an acoustic set with no soundcheck again. And I said, "Come on down and we'll try it out." And he did, and we had a marvelous time. We played for hours, all week long.

Dylan and the band began rehearsing a week before Farm Aid, on a sound-stage at Universal Studios in Hollywood. The Heartbreakers seemed prepared to play just about any kind of song. Dylan was in his element. They tried every genre from Hank Williams through Spector, Motown, blues and Tin Pan Alley. Very little time was spent working on Dylan's own songs. Yet there was clearly a chemistry between him and the Heartbreakers, and everyone seemed to be reveling in the experience of playing whatever they felt like playing.

Benmont Tench: He knows a million songs, old Delta blues songs and stuff like that. Well, they sound like they may be Delta blues songs. Sometimes I'm not sure if they're blues songs or a new arrangement of "It's Alright, Ma."

On the final day of rehearsals a crew arrived to film a brief excerpt for a profile of Dylan scheduled to be broadcast on the "20/20" TV program. He looked comfortable, chatting between takes with the female vocalists he had brought in to augment the Heartbreakers, and even improvising a version of "Forever Young" for the TV cameras.

On the night before Farm Aid, Dylan and the band ran through a half-hour soundcheck, determined to avoid a repeat of Live Aid. Even here they sounded tight and revved up to play. The performance the following day was a revelation. Though Dylan had given some impressive performances on the 1984 European tour, it had been four years since his triumphant 1981 European tour, and after the disappointing American tour of that year and the only sporadically impressive '84 tour, little was expected from him.

Yet from the first song at Farm Aid, Dylan was magnificent. The band also played with a fire lacking at recent Heartbreakers shows. After ripping through "Clean Cut Kid" and a semioriginal reworking of an old blues theme, "Shake," Dylan quieted things down with a surprisingly effective "I'll Remember You," during which he duetted with poor Madelyn Quebec, who bravely wrestled with his vocal idiosyncrasies. "Trust Yourself" had him punching the air with the exhilaration of it all, then a heartbreaking rendition of "That Lucky Old Sun" led into the appropriate "Maggie's Farm." Dylan's timing and intonation had never been more impressive.

Though only three and a half of the six songs were broadcast on national TV, the sheer verve of the performance and the joy of a man back onstage with a great band were evident for all to see. Farm Aid proved the perfect antidote to Live Aid. It also represented the culmination of a period when Dylan was rarely out of the news. With three videos receiving regular rotation on MTV, two live broadcasts in just over two months on national TV, a fifteen-minute profile on the popular "20/20" TV show and interviews syndicated that fall by the *Los Angeles Times* and the *Los Angeles Herald-Examiner*, plus the front cover of the

December issue of *Spin* and further interviews with *Rolling Stone* and *Time*, he had never had such a high media profile.

In November a five-album boxed retrospective, featuring a dozen rare cuts to entice the collectors, provided a bewildering summary of the most important oeuvre in rock music. Dylan himself was not unduly impressed by the project, which had been compiled by Jeff Rosen, an employee of his current music publishing company, Special Rider. The set was entitled *Biograph*.

Bob Dylan: There's some stuff that hasn't been heard before, but most of my stuff has already been bootlegged, so to anybody in the know, there's nothing on it they haven't heard before. . . . All it is, really, is repackaging, and it'll just cost a lot of money. About the only thing that makes it special is Cameron's book. [1985]

"Cameron's book" was a lavish thirty-two-page album-size résumé of Dylan's career, freely composed from a series of anecdotes provided by Dylan to Cameron Crowe. Allowed the opportunity to comment on his own history, he talked effusively about matters that he most delighted in, or that had most upset or angered him. Also, following in the tradition of Neil Young's 1978 retrospective set, *Decade*, he provided brief (and some not-so-brief) commentaries on the songs chosen for the five-album set, which proved occasionally illuminating.

The combination of Dylan's high profile, the impressive look of the set, and its motley assortment of favorites and unreleased gems proved surprisingly popular in America, where *Biograph* became only the second ever such boxed set to receive a gold record (the other being the posthumous eight-album *Elvis Aron Presley* collection), and the first to reach as high as thirty-three on the *Billboard* charts. *Biograph* would spawn a plethora of imitations. In the age of eighty-minute CDs, record companies now realize the potential of such retrospectives, and, with rock music well into its fourth decade, many sixties artists warrant such collections.

Biograph was not the only résumé of his career Dylan provided at this time. As well as the interviews he was freely giving, in which he seemed happy to talk about all aspects of his career, November also saw the publication of *Lyrics*, which provided the lyrics to all of Dylan's published songs up to and including *Empire Burlesque*. Though *Lyrics* was something of a disappointment, in that Dylan refrained from including many of the songs he had left off of his post-*Desire* albums—songs of the quality of "Blind Willie McTell," "New Danville Girl" and "Angelina"—the book was well produced and sold well.

Also in November, Dylan began rehearsing with the Heartbreakers and working on his follow-up to *Empire Burlesque*. Clearly Farm Aid had been a necessary fillip to getting him active again. The studio sessions he undertook in

November were in fact conducted in London, his first English sessions in twenty years. At the behest of Dave Stewart of the Eurythmics, he traveled there to record for four days at Stewart's own studio in Crouch End. However, he had few new lyrics, and the sessions were primarily used to provide backing tracks, of which supposedly some twenty were recorded, two of which were excerpted on the BBCs "Whistle Test" TV program. Only one of the tracks from these sessions was later included on *Knocked Out Loaded*.

Preliminary rehearsals in early November confirmed Dylan and the Heartbreakers' interest in continuing their association. Now that he had the itch to perform again, plans were made for a Far East tour in the winter of 1986, his first Far East tour in eight years, and, if the gigs went well, a summer U.S. tour was also likely. Rehearsals for the tour were quite extensive, taking up most of December and January. The precedent set by the Farm Aid rehearsals was upheld, as Dylan and the band again worked up reams of covers, including several songs more associated with crooners than with the croaky cords of Dylan: "This Was My Love" (made famous by Sinatra), "We Three" (an old Ink Spots chestnut) and "All My Tomorrows" (another Sinatra song).

Though these diversions helped maintain Dylan's interest in the extensive pretour rehearsals, they were again leading him away from the matter at hand— to work up a professional set of primarily Dylan originals that would constitute a two-hour show for the Japanese and Australasians. When Dylan and the band arrived in Auckland, New Zealand, on February 3, 1986, a further rehearsal was in order and, the night before opening at the open-air Wellington Athletic Park on the fifth, they ran through a three-and-a-quarter-hour soundcheck-*cum*-rehearsal. The volume of the soundcheck and the open-air stadium's proximity to local residences led to many complaints to the police, and the opening concert was under serious threat of cancellation.

Ironically, after probably more rehearsals than for any previous tour, the first shows in Wellington and Auckland were both scrappy affairs, with little evidence of two months' rehearsing. Petty was quoted as saying, "What we've done is take the rehearsals on the stage." If not the literal truth, Petty's comments were not far off. Apart from including such obscure covers as Ricky Nelson's "Lonesome Town," Warren Smith's "Uranium Rock," Hank Snow's "I'm Movin' On" and John Hiatt and Ry Cooder's "Across the Borderline," each Australasian show featured an opening blues jam and a Dylan/Petty duet on the country nugget "I Forgot More (Than You'll Ever Know)." Throughout the tour Dylan continued to pull his usual set of surprises on the band, though the Heartbreakers were more adept than most at dealing with them.

Mike Campbell: There's a lot of room for free playing in his songs, which makes everything pretty spontaneous. It's just never the same—that's the only way I can describe it. During one show in Australia we were supposed to do "When the Night Comes Falling from the Sky," and he didn't feel like doing it. He turned around to me and said, "You know the chords for 'All Along the Watchtower,' don't you?" And we'd never rehearsed it. I said, "There's only three, right?" And he said, "Yeah, let's go!" You never know what's coming. There'll be different songs, or we'll do the same thing in different keys. It reminds me of a high school dance band. It's more polished maybe, but it has that looseness, that freshness, that chaos.

Perhaps Stan Lynch, the Heartbreakers drummer, came closest to unraveling the rationale behind Dylan's approach, which has remained consistent throughout twenty-five years of playing live with bands.

Stan Lynch: There's nothing tentative about Dylan onstage. I've seen gigs where the songs have ended in all the wrong places, where it's fallen apart, and it's almost as if, in some perverse way, he gets energy from that chaos.

The results, though, were considerably more hit-and-miss than Farm Aid had been. After the first show, Dylan seemed to have decided the pacing of the second half needed tightening up. The sad result was that three of his recent songs were dropped from the set—"Shot of Love," "Heart of Mine" and "Gotta Serve Somebody"—making the show considerably more weighted toward his older material, as in 1984. Dylan also was considerably less fired up than at Farm Aid, possibly burned out by the rehearsals. The Far East shows still had their moments, and Dylan was surprisingly talkative throughout, regularly quoting Tennessee Williams in a prologue to "Lenny Bruce":

Bob Dylan: Here's a song about recognition, or lack of recognition. Tennessee Williams, it was he who said: "I don't ask for your pity, just your understanding. Not even that, but just your recognition of me in you, and time, the enemy in us all." Tennessee Williams led a pretty drastic life. He died all by himself in a New York hotel room without a friend in the world. Another man died like that. . . . [1986]

He regularly prefaced "Ballad of a Thin Man" with a story about how he refused to answer questions at a press conference in England in 1965, insisting that a man's life speaks for itself; concluded "Rainy Day Women" by admitting it was a song that could be taken a couple of ways, as could a lot of his songs; and one night in Sydney introduced a one-off performance of "License to Kill" by stating that it was "a song about the space program" before dedicating the song to the seven people who had tragically been killed in an American rocket days earlier. If he seemed to be supporting the space program, he then added, "They had no business being up there in the first place . . . as if we haven't got enough problems down here on earth." Though the Sydney crowd roared their approval, it suggested he was considerably out of step with American public opinion. His most unequivocal statement, though, came before the final song of the main set, "In the Garden." Though the 1986 shows suggested he had successfully assimilated the religious songs into his repertoire—after the 1984 tour, when the religious songs were virtually ignored—he obviously wished to make it clear that his beliefs remained intact.

Bob Dylan: This last song now is all about my hero. Everybody's got a hero. Where I come from there's a lot of heroes. Plenty of them. John Wayne, Clark Gable, Richard Nixon, Ronald Reagan, Michael Jackson, Bruce Springsteen. They're all heroes to some people. Anyway, I don't care nothing about those people. I have my own hero. I'm going to sing about him right now. . . . When they came for him in the garden. . . [1986]

Dylan reinforced the message by using a version of this rap to open an hour-long cable TV special filmed at Sydney and broadcast on American TV in June. His talkativeness and the length of the shows suggest he remained in good humor throughout the monthlong tour, as does a TV interview he gave in Sydney and a well-publicized press conference, also in Sydney. He enjoyed the company of two special guests at different Sydney shows, Mark Knopfler and Stevie Nicks, and he returned the favor for Knopfler by joining Dire Straits for four songs in Melbourne. The final four shows in Japan also suggested that Dylan and the Heartbreakers were increasingly comfortable with each other and that a U.S. tour would make sense.

With a nice three-month gap in Dylan's schedule, CBS succeeded in convincing Dylan of the importance of having a product available for such a major tour—his first U.S. tour in five years and with the Heartbreakers, a highly popular outfit in their own right. Early in April he set about recording a new album at a small studio in the beautiful Topanga Canyon, conveniently located between Malibu and L.A. His initial intention was to get an album down quickly and with a minimum of fuss, as in the old days. Gone was the will to toil over the finished product evidenced on his two previous albums.

Ira Ingber: He did some stuff with Petty that was done somewhere else in the Valley, but we did pretty much a monthlong run. He said, "Can we do it in a week?" I said, "I don't think we can do it in a week." He just wanted a band to play and to sing, but then we got into the recording world, which is a different mentality. He realized he was into this thing a little deeper than he initially thought.

The various ensembles that came and went during his monthlong stint at Skyline Studios would take an entire book to catalog as Dylan looked to produce the necessary chemistry with assorted West Coast musicians. Charlie Quintana was asked to turn up one day with two guitarists he knew, but the results were unimpressive.

Charlie Quintana: There was . . . a studio session, proper full-blown re- cording studio at Skyline in Topanga Canyon. I took these two guys, one an incredible bass player and an incredible guitar player, both extremely good technically. I said, "When we get there and start playing, just follow me. Just follow me. Rule number one." . . . I'd already played with Bob for three months, so I knew more or less the way the routine was. But when we got to the session, these guys both wanted to get the gig so desperately bad and they were just so in awe of Bob that they rushed the whole fucking thing. . . . In the middle of it all I took 'em to the bathroom and said, "What the fuck are you guys doing? I told you, watch me!" But it went over their heads.

Ira Ingber, who had done sterling work on "Something's Burning, Baby" and "New Danville Girl," was asked to work out an arrangement of an old Ray Charles song, but when it came to recording the song, Dylan seemed unable or unwilling to stick with it.

Ira Ingber: He wanted me to do an arrangement for him of "Come Rain or Come Shine," the Ray Charles tune. It's a beautiful song and he gave me the record. We took down the chords, brought in the band and tried playing it. It's a fairly complicated song and he wanted me to show him how to play it. . . . I showed him, but there's some really weird chords because it's an orchestra arrangement, not piano or guitar. The chords more or less reflect the complex- ity, and Bob couldn't play those chords too well because they're not even guitar-player chords, they're orchestral chords, and he got kinda discouraged by that.

According to Mikal Gilmore, who attended several of the sessions for a cover story for *Rolling Stone*, the early sessions also featured the Tex-Mex band Los Lobos, T-Bone Burnett, Al Kooper and Steve Douglas, though only Douglas would make a major contribution to the finished album. Kooper became rap- idly disenchanted with the whole ambience of the sessions and Dylan's ap- proach to the recording and, after doing his best to provide input, gave it up as a bad lot. He believes, however, that there was much of worth recorded at these early sessions.

Al Kooper: I didn't care for the drive. I didn't care for the engineer or the studio too much either. There was enough stuff cut on *Knocked Out Loaded* to have put out a great album. There was some really wonderful things cut at those sessions, but I don't think we'll ever hear 'em. . . . I was really frustrated because then I was involved in a way that I get involved and I made suggestions and all that and then I just sort of fucked off. And then I heard that record, and the only thing was "Brownsville Girl." There was more stuff as exciting as that was.

According to Gilmore, Dylan recorded some twenty songs of "R & B, Chicago-steeped blues, rambunctious gospel and raw-toned hillbilly forms." Yet *Knocked Out Loaded* provides precious little evidence of these recordings. Only the opening track, Junior Parker's "You Wanna Ramble," falls into any of the above categories.

Though Kooper suggests there was quality original material recorded, the inescapable problem was simply that Dylan was proving incapable of writing new songs of sufficient quality to merit release. Generally in the past the prospect of imminent recording commitments proved a fillip to his writing, but this time little of worth came about. Taking a brief respite to work with the Heartbreakers at a nearby studio in Van Nuys, he attempted to produce some new songs with them.

Tom Petty: I had booked some time at Sound City for something Dylan wanted to do—he was makin' a record. Then it turned out he wasn't gonna be ready at that time.

Petty and the band got on with recording their own album, managing just one track with Dylan, "Got My Mind Made Up," though Dylan also contributed to a Petty song called "Jammin' Me." Clearly even working with a band he felt comfortable with was not producing results. The final evidence of his writer's block came when he returned to Topanga Canyon and decided to abandon most of his previous work and to produce a potpourri collection of half-finished songs and outtakes from earlier sessions.

Mikal Gilmore: Somewhere along the line he has decided to put aside most of the rock and roll tracks he had been working on in Topanga . . . [instead] assembling the album from various sessions that have accrued over the last year. "It's all sorts of stuff," he says. "It doesn't really have a theme or a purpose."

Whatever the flaws evident on his albums of the previous decade, all had maintained a certain integrity. *Knocked Out Loaded* sounds like Dylan's first "bootleg" album since *Self Portrait*, another album with an identity crisis. Of the eight basic tracks, one came from the sessions with the Heartbreakers at Sound City, one from the November 1985 London sessions, three from the *Empire Burlesque* sessions and the remaining three from the Topanga Canyon sessions—all of which were covers. The final few sessions at Skyline were taken up with reworking the 1984–85 outtakes. "Maybe Someday" was given new words, as was "Driftin' Too Far from Shore" and "Under My Spell." More importantly, Dylan decided to rework "New Danville Girl," now retitled "Brownsville Girl." Using the basic backing track from November 1984, he changed several lines, added an overzealous wailing chorus courtesy of the omnipresent Queens of Rhythm, a trumpet and Steve Douglas's saxophone plus an impressive new Dylan vocal.

Dave Garfield: ["Brownsville Girl"] was one of the ones he would stop in the middle of things, sit down for fifteen minutes or so right here in the lounge and start penning some new lyrics.

"Brownsville Girl" saved *Knocked Out Loaded* from total disposability, but it also highlighted the dearth of comparable material now coming from Dylan's pen. Despite the fact that the album sounded lovely, its lapses of taste (children and steel drums were used on "They Killed Him" and "Precious Memories"), abbreviated length (a total of thirty-five minutes) and perhaps the most gaudy of all his album covers quickly destined the record for the cutout bins.

Knocked Out Loaded continued the steady commercial decline since *Infidels*, failing to even make the top fifty, despite its release at a time when Dylan was making a very successful tour of the U.S. The fans preferred to spend their money on concert tickets. Dylan himself seemed equally unconvinced of the album's merits, refusing to play any of its songs throughout a two-month-long tour, save for "Got My Mind Made Up" on the opening night and a chorus of "Brownsville Girl" at the final show.

On June 6 Dylan and the Heartbreakers warmed up for their U.S. jaunt with a three-song set at an Amnesty International benefit at the Forum in Inglewood, California. Dylan chose the appropriate "License to Kill" and his new single, "Band of the Hand," recorded with the Heartbreakers back in February but omitted from *Knocked Out Loaded*. Both songs' portrayals of a world run by the mad and the corrupt were apposite to the cause of political prisoners. The concluding "Shake a Hand" was less relevant, though it featured an outrageously loose Dylan vocal. All in all, the Amnesty show was a very positive omen for the forthcoming tour.

Sadly, the 1986 U.S. tour acted out in reverse the progress of the 1984 tour: It started with impressive shows on the West Coast but rapidly ran out of steam and spluttered to a conclusion two months later back at Inglewood's Forum. Dylan seemed to be coasting through most of the songs and there were few highlights. Dylan also adopted his "arena voice," more shouting than singing, so in evidence in 1974, 1978 and 1984. The torpor seemed to affect even the Heartbreakers, who, on their home turf, were given a larger part of the show but whose eight songs defined the meaning of the phrase "going through the motions."

At the age of forty-five, Dylan was clearly not able to give his all throughout two-hour shows, but seemed determined to defy time by pushing himself through them rather than performing a briefer but more cogent set. The tour was well received, though more for the selection of old favorites performed than for the way they were actually sung. The summer U.S. tour was a disappointing conclusion to twelve months of considerable activity, which had failed to produce much of enduring worth save for the single performance at Farm Aid. Yet when compared with the next twelve months, the period from September 1985 through August 1986 would later seem like an oasis of creative genius.

35 1986–87: Down Among the Deadheads

Typically, Dylan reserved his best performance in six months for a sound check. In early August, singing with verve and commitment and backed by the Heartbreakers, he ran through Hank Williams's "Thank God" for a Lubavitchers' telethon intended to raise funds for an anti-drug program. It was not broadcast until September, by which time he was in England.

He had decided it was time to make his return to celluloid. He had talked to Dave Stewart about wanting to make his own film when shooting the two *Empire Burlesque* videos in August 1985, and when interviewed during filming in England in September 1986, he admitted to an abiding interest in making his own film.

Bob Dylan: I do have plans to make a movie. . . . It's a complicated story about a piano player who gets into trouble because of a good buddy of his, and then he winds up doing some book work for a woman whose husband has disappeared, marries her, then falls in love with his daughter. And the other guy finally shows up again and the movie comes to a screeching halt. [1986]

This was not exactly the elemental film he had discussed with Stewart, but clearly *Renaldo and Clara* had not satisfied his filmic impulses. As part of the process of feeling his way back into moviemaking he had agreed, before the summer tour, to star in a movie to be directed by *Jagged Edge* director Richard Marquand. It was called *Hearts of Fire*.

Richard Marquand: I discovered that he's always been interested in film—I mean not only the Peckinpah film but his own film; that it's always something that has intrigued him, and now at this stage of his life, forty-six, forty-seven, he's thinking, "Well, let's really try it out, let's see if I'm any good."

The story line featured him as Billy Parker, a disillusioned ex–rock and roll star who takes an aspiring singer with him to England. There she meets James Colt, a contemporary rock star played by Rupert Everett, who shares with Parker a mystifying lust for the distinctly asexual leading lady, played by Fiona Flanagan.

Portraying Dylan as an aging and somewhat cynical rock and roll star who threw his hand in at the height of his fame and retired to the backwoods to raise chickens was playing on popular perceptions of Dylan. However, his character's added dimension in the screenplay—the fact that he was also a Jesse James–type outlaw figure who enjoyed robbing tollbooths, Burger Kings and even concert halls—was cut from the final film.

The rather predictable shooting script required that the Fiona Flanagan character exude enough charisma and sensuality to ensnare two very jaundiced rock and rollers, while also impressing a modern rock audience. In fact, Flanagan exuded the sensuality of Kleenex and the charisma of a parrot, and inevitably the film was a commercial and critical disaster. Ironically, Dylan, despite insisting that there were "a hundred guys I know who could have played this role," was one of the few highlights of the movie. Though he was still unable to mime to a prerecorded track and he struggled to memorize his words, on screen he did exude a kind of stiff charisma, as the film's line producer observed:

Iain Smith: In *Hearts of Fire* I think he's arguably the best thing in the film. It's not because he's a great actor, it's because Richard has worked very hard to bring out, by cutting and editing Bob's material, what is in the man, which is his natural charisma. . . . He's funny and quirky and strange and you watch him on the screen and you think, "Well, he's not acting . . . , but, and it's a bit odd, he's very very watchable." You just want to watch him. And it's a totally undefinable quality.

A premonition of the likely reception for the movie came at a hastily arranged press conference on Dylan's arrival in England for the start of filming. Despite his insistence that he was only interested in making the movie, the journalists expressed no interest in his costars or director, and doggedly pursued him to answer the one question that burned in all their minds: What the hell was a poet and songwriter like Dylan doing in tripe like this?

The one revealing reply from Dylan came when he was asked about the half-dozen songs he had supposedly written for the movie. Admitting that he had not yet written them, he stated he would be writing them during filming. In fact the sound-track sessions were due to commence in just ten days. However, his writer's block had not let up. Ten days later all he had come up with was two execrable efforts "Had a Dream About You, Baby" and "Night After Night." At least two further songs were required for the movie, so he drew from other writers, singing John Hiatt's "The Usual" with some panache, as well as a pleasant enough acoustic version of Shel Silverstein's "Couple More Years," a song that summed up the theme of the movie far more concisely and artistically than the ninety minutes of squandered celluloid that made up *Hearts of Fire*. When in "Couple More Years," he sang, "It ain't that I'm wiser / It's just that I spent more time with my back to the wall" it perhaps defined the experience of making the movie.

Ironically, Dylan did make one of his more notable film appearances while on the *Hearts of Fire* set. The highly respected team from the BBC TV series "Omnibus" was intent on making a fifty-minute documentary about him, entitled "Getting to Dylan." Marquand, as a former "Omnibus" director himself, provided what help he could, but as Dylan flew out of England for Ontario at the beginning of October, the filmmakers had so far failed to ensnare their prey.

Richard Marquand: They didn't know quite what they were going to do, but they knew that this was a chance to maybe find some sort of framework to do a film on Bob—the framework of the making of the movie. Bob, in the end, opened up to them quite a lot.

It took a further two weeks of filming in Hamilton, Ontario, before Dylan finally consented to a filmed interview with "Omnibus" director Christopher Sykes. When he did, the twenty-five-minute interview, which was the centerpiece of the "Getting to Dylan" documentary, proved to be a remarkable exchange. It may not have been Sykes's intention to produce a fifty-minute update on *Don't Look Back*, yet that is the way "Getting to Dylan" comes across. It was as if Sykes had been intent on saying, "Well, let us see what happened to that man."

In 1986 Dylan was twenty-one years older than he had been in *Don't Look Back*, the film of the 1965 English tour that perpetually froze him in monochrome hipness. In the first flush of fame he had parried every question, every expectation, with lightning wit. He was the very prototype of supercool. The lines, whether scourging self-analysis ("You're gonna die. . . . You do your work in the face of that") or half-whispered dismissals ("Oh, you're one of those. I understand now"), defined a Dylan persona for, if not all time, some considerable time.

In 1986, Dylan was again in England to make a movie, though this time there was no tour to punctuate the nights. In "Getting to Dylan," we see him pursued by BBC cameras, a mystified *Hearts of Fire* film crew and of course his fans. The one-to-one interview in "Getting to Dylan," like Horace Judson's in *Don't Look Back*, is the climax of the film. Are we finally going to see a glimpse of the private Dylan? Can the public image be reconciled with the private man? Though there is not the brutal intensity of the earlier interview, Dylan insists at the outset that if the interviewer is looking for revelation "it just ain't gonna come." Yet he proceeds to show a man with few secrets to conceal.

Bob Dylan: Fame, everybody just kind of copes with it a different way. But nobody seems to think it's really what they were after. . . . It's like, say you're passing a little pub or an inn, and you look through the window and you see all the people eating and talking and carrying on, you can watch outside the window and you can see them all be very real with each other. As real as they're gonna be, because when you walk into the room it's over. You won't see them being real anymore. [1986]

In 1965 Dylan's screening system had been brutal arrogance—the best form of defense is attack—and there were precious few instances of chinks in the armor. In 1986 the armor had become more of a burden than those it was designed to safeguard against. His response to his iconography now suggested a dramatic isolation from the outside world. By his own admission, he saw only rare glimpses outside the walls he had constructed back in the mid-sixties to safeguard his privacy.

Bob Dylan: I don't know what people think of me. I only know about what record companies say . . . and managers and people like that. People who want you to do things . . . I only hear about that stuff. [1986]

"Getting to Dylan" remains the essential filmed portrait of Dylan in the eighties, an important adjunct to *Don't Look Back*, "Eat the Document" and *Renaldo and Clara*, the three previous films to deal with the Dylan myth.

Hearts of Fire took a year to be released in England, after which it lasted barely three weeks in general release before disappearing from the cinemas; within eighteen months it was released on video, to universal apathy. The film's financiers, Lorimar Pictures, decided to cut their losses and abandoned a U.S. cinema release, which would have required considerable publicity and attendant costs. The film had to wait until the spring of 1990 for commercial video release in the U.S. It seemed that Dylan was not destined to be a successful actor.

With a new film career stillborn, Dylan reverted to the album/tour syndrome that had dominated his life in the late seventies and early eighties and which had recommenced at Farm Aid.

Perhaps surprisingly, given the dearth of new songs from his pen, Dylan was back in the studio in April 1987 recording his follow-up to *Knocked Out Loaded*. If *Knocked Out Loaded* had been the most disappointing album of (mostly) original Dylan material since *Nashville Skyline*, it seems Dylan had decided to reinforce further that sense of history being replayed by recording his second version of *Self Portrait*. He had mentioned the idea of recording an album essentially composed of covers several times during his extensive bout of interviews at the time of *Biograph*, and had specifically suggested to one journalist that he was intent on doing "an album of standards," which he would try to record with the producer Richard Perry. Though nothing came of this, he continued to reiterate his interest in the project when talking to Cameron Crowe for the notes accompanying *Biograph*.

Bob Dylan: I'd like to do a concept album . . . or an album of cover songs but I don't know if the people would let me get away with that . . . "A Million Miles from Nowhere," "I (Who Have Nothing)," "All My Tomorrows," "I'm in the Mood for Love," "More Than You Know," "It's a Sin to Tell a Lie." . . . [1985]

When Dave Alvin (of the Blasters and later X) was asked to appear at a recording session for the new album, he was told Dylan was working on *Self Portrait Volume Two*. There was nothing artistically unsound about Dylan attempting an album of covers. He had made the occasional cover a regular feature of his shows since 1975, and they had often been highlights. Indeed, the more Tin Pan Alley form of song had held an increasing fascination for Dylan throughout the mid-eighties. This perhaps explains his own attempts at replicating the genre with the likes of "I'll Remember You" and "Emotionally

Yours." In his interview with Mikal Gilmore in late September 1985 he had expressed his admiration for the crooners of the forties and fifties:

Bob Dylan: Sinatra, Peggy Lee, yeah, I love all these people, but I tell you who I've really been listening to a lot lately—in fact, I'm thinking about recording one of his earlier songs—is Bing Crosby. I don't think you can find better phrasing anywhere. [1985]

During the *Infidels* sessions he had recorded Sinatra's "This Was My Love"; in rehearsals for the 1984 tour he had tried out versions of the perennial standards "Always on My Mind" and the Ink Spots' "To Each His Own"; in rehearsals and on the 1986 tour he performed Sinatra's "This Was My Love" again, as well as "All My Tomorrows" and the Ink Spots' "We Three." And a month before the start of his spring 1987 recording sessions, he performed an acoustic version of "Soon," a George Gershwin composition best known in Ella Fitzgerald's version, at a New York gala to commemorate the fiftieth anniversary of Gershwin's death.

Yet when the time came to start work on the new album, Dylan produced another collection of songs that lacked any sense of purpose. The songs recorded for the album varied from mawkish ballads such as "When Did You Leave Heaven?" and "Important Words," through the sort of stomping blues favored in the 1978 shows ("Let's Stick Together," "Sally Sue Brown," "Got Love If You Want It"), and, more successfully, traditional country standards, "Rank Strangers to Me" and "Ninety Miles an Hour," and the traditional folk of "Shenandoah." As if this potpourri were not enough, Dylan insisted on recording two songs he had cowritten with Grateful Dead lyricist Robert Hunter, which even the Dead had refrained from using themselves. Dylan was prepared to defend his decision to record an album of unoriginal material, but was not called upon to explain the sheer lack of thematic coherence in the collection. *

Bob Dylan: There's no rule that claims that anyone must write their own songs. And I do. I write a lot of songs. But so what, you know? You could take another song somebody else has written and you can make it yours. I'm not saying I made a definitive version of anything with this last record, but I liked the songs. Every so often you've gotta sing songs that're out there. . . . Writing is such an isolated thing. You're in such an isolated frame of mind. You have to get into or be in that place. In the old days, I could get to it real quick. I can't get to it like that no more. [1988]

---

*Van Morrison was also in the midst of recording an entire album of covers at the time, *Irish Heartbeat,* but the coherence of his collection of Irish folk songs actually garnered his best reviews and sales in years.

That final sentence—"I can't get to it like that no more"—made clear the trouble he was having writing new songs. Of course, part of the problem was his constant desire to reinvent himself. However well he could conjure up his many past selves in concert, he knew that presenting a counterfeit "new Dylan" (that is, deliberately trying to sound like a previous self) on vinyl had been unsuccessful on the two albums on which he had seemed to flirt with such a notion, *New Morning* and *Street-Legal*. When working with the somewhat less talented Bono, at the time of the sessions for the album *Down in the Groove*, he made a halfhearted attempt at jointly composing some songs with him.

Bono: He's very hung up on actually being Bob Dylan. He feels he's trapped in his past and, in a way, he is. I mean, no one asks Smokey Robinson to write a new "Tracks of My Tears" every album, y'know. But, like, we were trading lines and verses off the top of our heads and Dylan comes out with this absolute classic: "I was listenin' to the Neville Brothers, it was a quarter of eight / I had an appointment with destiny, but I knew she'd come late / She tricked me, she addicted me, she turned me on the head / Now I can't sleep with these secrets, that leave me cold and alone in my bed." Then he goes, "Nah, cancel that." Can you believe it? He thought it was too close to what people expect of Bob Dylan.

If Dylan was looking for talented individuals to exchange ideas with as he had with Robbie Robertson in 1966, Jacques Levy in 1975 and Sam Shepard in 1984, then turning to Carole Bayer Sager (with whom he had written "Under My Spell," which appeared on *Knocked Out Loaded*), Robert Hunter and Bono suggested an element of desperation. Originality was hardly a byword with Bono, one of rock music's more prolific magpies.

It was 1988 before *Down in the Groove* was released. As with his previous eighties albums, he could not resist tampering with it at the last minute, to its detriment. Even though it was barely thirty-two minutes long and featured only two songs even cowritten by Dylan, it had some sort of cogent sound despite its disparate sources, the up-tempo songs maintaining a momentum right up until the penultimate song.

Although the album was originally intended to feature his impressive version of John Hiatt's "The Usual," the one redeeming tune from the *Hearts of Fire* sound track, and his pleasant if workmanlike reworking of "Got Love If You Want It," at the last minute Dylan decided to cut these two tracks, restructure the running order, and replace them with a turgid outtake from *Infidels*, "Death Is Not the End," perhaps the only song from those sessions that had *nothing* to recommend it, and a remixed but still abysmal "Had a Dream about You, Baby." Any charm his *Self Portrait II* had was lost with the changes, which postdated CBS's release of promotional cassettes of the new album. If *Self Portrait* had not been a wholly successful "Fuck you" to his audience, Dylan's standing was now at such a low ebb that *Down in the Groove* drew none of the controversy *Self Portrait* had generated. It was simply ignored. The maverick was in a land of rank strangers.

Between recording and releasing his worst album, Dylan conducted the most profoundly dull tour of his career. Fortunately, his joint tour with the Grateful Dead spanned a mere six shows. Even when his previous tours had been disappointing, moments of real fire had occurred: He occasionally spat his words with real venom or caressed his more lilting melodies. The Grateful Dead, though, played at one tempo, and that was dead slow.

Dylan's association with the Dead went back to July 1972, when he attended a show in New Jersey and was rumored to be considering recording with them (indeed, the existence of a finished Dylan/Dead album was rumored for many years). In 1980, Jerry Garcia had joined Dylan at one of his ground-breaking November shows at San Francisco's Warfield Theater and provided some suitable guitar embellishments. Then in early July 1986 Dylan and the Heartbreakers doubled up with the Dead for three stadium shows, and Dylan joined the Dead for a couple of songs during two of their sets. The desecration of the previously sacrosanct "Desolation Row" and "It's All Over Now, Baby Blue" by the band's crude insensitivity should have provided Dylan with ample warning to steer clear of future associations. Yet the idea of a brief Dylan/Dead tour was resurrected later in the year.

Jerry Garcia: When he was playing with Tom Petty, we did a few shows with him and Tom Petty and us and when we were doing it we said, "Hey, Bob, you wanna sing a song or two with us?" He said, "Yeah, sure. That'd be fun." So he agreed and did it a couple of times. And it was fun. We always loved his music—we still do. It was one of those things we'd always thought, "Wow, that'd be far out." Bob Dylan and the Grateful Dead. So we hit on him later in the year and we talked about it and he said yeah. And he came around for two or three weeks and we rehearsed stuff, and tried stuff out, and played through things and goofed around and hung around a lot, and we ended up doing it.

Dylan first admitted to a serious interest in the idea when he popped in on the Dead as they rehearsed and recorded at San Rafael Stadium in January 1987. By March the tour was being finalized, and he was forced to consider rehearsing with his third touring band in three years. The rehearsals in San Rafael that March did not go well.

Bob Weir: He was difficult to work with inasmuch as he wouldn't want to rehearse a song more than two times, three at the most. And so we rehearsed maybe a hundred songs two or three times. . . . This is sorta a standard critique of the way he works.

Though Dylan had long delighted in using rehearsals as extended jam sessions, and though he could be sure that the Dead were conversant with many of his songs from their own performances, at these rehearsals he seemed barely interested in working up a song, and did not trouble even to sing from a songbook to ensure that he got the words right. Songs fizzled out rather than ended. Despite the unfamiliarity of working with the Dead, he refused to restrict himself to a couple of dozen songs from which he could choose fourteen or fifteen each night. Instead, as Weir says, they gave cursory run-throughs to at least fifty songs, including such off-the-wall selections as the 1963 unreleased composition "Walkin' Down the Line," Ian and Sylvia's "The French Girl" and even Paul Simon's "The Boy in the Bubble." Dylan seemed most comfortable when jamming on traditional standards such as "John Hardy" and "Roll in My Sweet Baby's Arms," rather than working up new arrangements of his own best-known songs.

The actual shows were all held in July 1987, in baking hot stadiums spanning both coasts and to crowds primarily composed of Deadheads, the Dead's own superavid army of obsessives in search of their own or someone else's lost youth. Responding to the self-evident and the superficial, they rousingly applauded anthems such as "Rainy Day Women" and "Knockin' on Heaven's Door," while Dylan's more audacious works passed them by. For whatever the dubious merits of the actual performances, he was introducing some astonishing songs into his repertoire for the first time ever. Songs such as "Queen Jane Approximately," "The Ballad of Frankie Lee and Judas Priest" and "The Wicked Messenger" all received first-ever live outings, though they received little recognition from the audiences.

Dylan seemed to have forgotten this brief but embarrassing minitour when, in the winter of 1989, nearly two years after the shows, he decided to approve the release of a live album from this absolute nadir of his career as a performing artist. Even the members of the Dead seemed surprised at the notion of releasing such a memento as *Dylan & the Dead*, though they also countenanced its release.

Jerry Garcia: We had this funny experience when we were working on [the *Dylan & the Dead* album]. We went over to his house in Malibu which is . . . out in the country somewhere . . . and he has these huge dogs which are like mastiffs, about seven of 'em. And so we drive up and these dogs surround the car and Dylan's kinda rattling around in the house, this rambling structure, and he takes us into this room that's kinda baronial—y'know, big fireplace and wooden paneling and steep roof. And on the table is about a thirty-nine-dollar ghetto blaster and he's got the cassette and he sticks it in there and says, "Don't you think the voice is mixed a little loud in that one?" So we just sat and listened to it on this funky little thing and he'd say, "I think there ought to be a little more bass."

Mickey Hart: We were trying to back up a singer on songs that no one knew. It was not our finest hour, nor his. I don't know why it was even made into a record.

Happily, by the time the *Dylan & the Dead* album was released, Dylan himself had once again proved he was a consummate live performer, even in his late forties, and had released his most successful recording project of the eighties (with a little help from his friends). The renaissance began within six weeks of the Dylan/Dead debacle.

36 1987–88: Temples in Flames, Wilburys on the Run

Bruce Springsteen: Dylan was a revolutionary. Bob freed your mind the way Elvis freed your body. He showed us that just because the music was innately physical did not mean it was anti-intellectual. He had the vision and the talent to make a pop song that contained the whole world. He invented a new way a pop singer could sound, broke through the limitations of what a recording artist could achieve and changed the face of rock and roll forever. Without Bob, the Beatles wouldn't have made *Sgt. Pepper,* the Beach Boys wouldn't have made *Pet Sounds,* the Sex Pistols wouldn't have made "God Save the Queen," U2 wouldn't have done "Pride (in the Name of Love)," Marvin Gaye wouldn't have done "What's Going On," the Count Five would not have done "Psychotic Reaction," Grandmaster Flash might not have done "The Message" and there never would have been a group named the Electric Prunes. To this day, wherever great rock music is being made, there is the shadow of Bob Dylan. Bob's own modern work has gone unjustly underappreciated because it's had to stand in that shadow. If there was a young guy out there writing the *Empire Burlesque* album, writing "Every Grain of Sand," they'd be calling him the new Bob Dylan. . . . So I'm just here tonight to say thanks, to say that I wouldn't be here without you, to say that there isn't a soul in this room who does not owe you his thanks.

Thus did Bruce Springsteen induct Bob Dylan into the Rock and Roll Hall of Fame on January 20, 1988. If the eighties had brought Dylan precious little recognition for his current work, it seemed he could not escape receiving awards for his past achievements. In March 1982 he had been inducted into the Songwriters Hall of Fame. In November 1985 he was the subject of a tribute at the Whitney Museum in New York, attended by many of those who owed him their thanks: names such as David Bowie, Neil Young, Pete Townshend as well as those who had derived less benefit from his work, such as Billy Joel and Dave Stewart. In March 1986 he received a Founders Award from the American Society of Composers, Authors and Publishers. And now the Rock and Roll Hall of Fame. Dylan himself seemed surprisingly impressed by the honor.

Bob Dylan: It was a great honor to be included, but more important was the recognition of Leadbelly and Woody, seeing them get the respect they deserve. [1988]

But though Springsteen recognized some quality in his more recent work, *Empire Burlesque, Knocked Out Loaded* and the not-yet-released *Down in the Groove* were hardly works of genius, and Dylan's last three American tours, in 1981, 1986 and 1987, had been progressively more disappointing. Ironically, in the same period Dylan had conducted three European tours that, though erratic, had all contained flashes of the old consummate performer.

His last European tour, three months earlier, was just thirty dates, and had not received a good press. In the U.S. the only report came from his opening show in Tel Aviv, his first show ever in Israel, where the circumstances—two shows commuted at the last minute to one that attracted a Saturday night crowd of young Israeli drunks who heckled the support acts—obscured what was in fact an audacious performance. He was backed again by the Heartbreakers, who were at last given their own set, and who welcomed the opportunity to play a major tour in Europe, where their work was considerably less well known than in the States.

This renewed association with the Heartbreakers was much more successful than the previous year's tours, primarily because Dylan approached the shows differently himself. Gone were the relatively uniform sets of the 1986 U.S. tour, as were uniform arrangements. The sets were astonishingly varied and thankfully abbreviated. Playing between seventy and seventy-five minutes most nights, Dylan was actually on the first encore of his third show before he repeated a single song from the two previous shows.

The brevity of the sets and of the tour itself meant that Dylan's voice remained in good shape throughout, and the lack of an acoustic set enabled the shows to be paced more consistently. When Petty talked about taking the rehearsals on stage, this tour was what he might have had in mind. Both set list and song order changed every night. Dylan sometimes decided to lead into a song himself with a harmonica break; sometimes it would be left to Benmont Tench or Mike Campbell. Likewise, endings were extended or abbreviated as the whim took him, and the Heartbreakers, at last put through their paces, responded magnificently, Campbell proving as inventive and sympathetic a guitarist as had ever augmented Dylan. If the female backup singers were still a trifle overbearing, and the sheer variety of numbers performed meant Dylan stumbled over a few lines, it was clear that he was conducting his finest tour in six years.

Benmont Tench: He's been great to play with. Great fun as well, mostly because you can never let your mind drift. He'll give the most familiar song an odd twist—a change of rhythm or a peculiar delivery. Playing with Bob Dylan certainly gives you a good kick up the ass. . . . One night he'll do something like he'll say—onstage—"Right, we'll begin with 'Forever Young,' " and the Heartbreakers have maybe played the song once before. Then he'll say, "And Benmont, you start it off."

The English and European press did not agree. While in 1978 they had been so supportive when Dylan was at his most audacious, in 1987 they seemed solely concerned with how he looked (old) and how brief his set was. Presumably they would have preferred tired retreads of "Masters of War," "Ballad of a Thin Man" and "Just Like a Woman" night after night, as long as the set clocked in at an extra thirty minutes. What really seems to have upset the press was his newfound taciturnity. Throughout the tour he refrained from making comments between songs, and he granted no interviews apart from two in Israel to American journalists.

Even if the European press did not recognize the change, the tour was the first sign that Dylan was emerging from a period when even his performance art was seemingly in terminal decline. The next matter was to record some new songs to reaffirm his status as a songwriter. Yet CBS had still not released the excruciating *Down in the Groove.* Its 1988 release confirmed the media's view of Dylan's poor standing.

If by the winter of 1987–88 Dylan had recognized the futility of trying to force himself to write new songs, some old friends provided him with the necessary impetus to return to writing. With another summer U.S. tour scheduled to start in June, he was called up one day in April by George Harrison, who required a studio at short notice to record a bonus track for a European twelve-inch single, and wondered if he could use Dylan's garage studio in Malibu.

George Harrison: Warners needed a third song to put on a twelve-inch single. I didn't have another song. I didn't have an extended version, so I just said to Jeff [Lynne]—I was in Los Angeles and he was producing Roy Orbison . . . "I'm just going to have to write a song tomorrow and just do it." I was just kind of thinking of "Instant Karma"—that way. And I said, "Where can we get a studio?" And he said, "Well, maybe Bob, 'cause he's got this little studio in his garage." . . . We just went back to his house, phoned up Bob; he said, "Sure, come on over." Tom Petty had my guitar and I went to pick it up; he said, "Oh, I was wondering what I was going to do tomorrow!" And Roy Orbison said, "Give us a call tomorrow if you're going to do anything—I'd love to come along."

Thus did Tom Petty, George Harrison, Jeff Lynne and Roy Orbison assemble at Dylan's Malibu home to record a hastily written Harrison song called "Handle with Care." With no engineers or extraneous studio personnel present, the session turned into a spontaneous songwriting session.

Tom Petty: We were a very self-contained group. We had one roadie and five Wilburys, and that was it. The funniest thing was I remember the first track we did—out in Bob Dylan's garage—and we didn't have a roadie. . . . And you could see us all digging through boxes to find a cable and a cord. "Well, there used to be one over here. Goddamn, I need new batteries for this." . . . It was refreshing.

Roy Orbison: We were at Bob's house working on "Handle with Care" and we needed a couple of lines and Bob and Tom wandered in and just threw in the lines we needed.

The participants realized that a good time was being had by all and, with a gap in all five schedules, their thoughts turned to the notion of perhaps recording more material. They had christened themselves the Traveling Wilburys, a name that reflected the good humor and refreshing lack of ego-massaging in the partnership. When Warner Bros. recognized the quality of "Handle with Care," a Traveling Wilburys album became inevitable.

Roy Orbison: George took the record to his record company and they said, "This is much too good for a B side. We're not sure what to do with this." And then we had the idea of putting together the album. We had all enjoyed it so much; it was so relaxed, there was no ego involved and there was some sort of chemistry. So we'd go to Bob's house and we'd just sit outside and there'd be a barbecue and we'd all just bring guitars and everyone would be throwing something in here and something in there, and then we'd just go to the garage, the studio, and put it down. Some days we'd finish just one song, sometimes two or three. We put down all the tracks, writing and singing and everything, in about ten or twelve days.

The actual sessions for the album, as opposed to "Handle with Care," took place in early May, a month after the initial session. They wrote songs and then recorded them, just as Dylan and the Band had in 1967. The informality and camaraderie were bound to appeal to Dylan, the one Wilbury who had pressing commitments that spring.

George Harrison: It was just a question of timing, 'cause Bob had to go on the road at the end of May, and this is like early April when we did "Handle with Care," so he said, "Well, I got a bit of time at the beginning of May," so we just said, "OK, we'll meet on—I think it was the seventh of May or something, and we had nine or ten days that we knew we could get Bob for, and everybody else was relatively free, so we just said, "Let's do it!" We said, "We'll write a tune a day and do it that way."

The lack of time was, in fact, a major advantage. It meant that Dylan's fellow Wilburys had to rely on the same precepts that had surrounded all his best studio work—spontaneity and first instincts.

Jeff Lynne: That's why the songs are so good and fresh—because they hadn't been second-guessed and dissected and replaced. It's so tempting to add stuff to a song when you've got unlimited time.

The songs came with remarkable ease. Though each song had one or two major composers, each member contributed ideas about the melody, the words or the arrangements. The first song they recorded at the *bona fide* Wilburys sessions was "Dirty World," a typical Dylan pastiche in the tradition of "Leopard-skin Pill-box Hat" and "Rita Mae."

George Harrison: Bob's very funny—I mean, a lot of people take him seriously and yet if you know Dylan and his songs, he's such a joker really. And Jeff just sat down and said, "OK, what are we gonna do?" And Bob said, "Let's do one like Prince!" . . . And he just started banging away—"Love your sexy body. . . ."

Though "Dirty World" needed a little rewriting after the initial take, it never seemed the most faithful Prince pastiche. What it did was reflect the joyful ease involved in these collaborations.

Bob Dylan: It wasn't that difficult to make that record. There weren't really a lot of heavy decisions that went into it. Cooperation is great on something like that because you never get stuck. [1989]

Dylan was the main author of two more songs on the album, though it was later emphasized that the whole album was a cooperative venture and, though Harrison and Dylan were the main songwriters, the royalties were divided equally. Of the other two songs on which he sang lead vocals, "Tweeter and the Monkey Man" came in for most comment. With its repeated allusions to Springsteen song titles and its New Jersey setting, he seemed to be showing he could lampoon Springsteen at least as successfully as Bruce himself. "Tweeter and the Monkey Man" was the highlight of the album, and was the first suggestion that Dylan's unique turns of phrase could still be put to good use in the late eighties.

George Harrison: "Tweeter and the Monkey Man" was Tom Petty and Bob sitting in the kitchen. Jeff and I were there too, but they were talking about all this stuff which didn't make sense to me—Americana kind of stuff. And we got a tape cassette and put it on and transcribed everything they were saying and wrote it down. And then Bob sort of changed it. . . . He had one take warming himself up and then he did it for real on take two; the rest of us had more time but Bob had to go on the road and we knew he couldn't do any more vocals again, so we had to get his vocals immediately. On take two he sang that "Tweeter and the Monkey Man" right through.

By the time the Wilburys' album was released in October, Dylan had completed his five-month-long tour of the U.S., his most impressive and well-received American tour since the heyday of the Rolling Thunder Revue. The press loved the unrelenting pace and stripped-down sound of Dylan's new three-piece combo. The media seemed to be turning in his favor once again. The Wilburys' album, with its superstar session tag, was expected to sell well, but exceeded all expectations, staying on the American album charts for more than forty weeks. It was Dylan's first platinum album of the eighties, his only double-platinum album ever, and one of the great commercial successes of 1989. Though in part a considerable testament to George Harrison's and Roy Orbison's enduring appeal, it confirmed that Dylan himself could still be a highly commercial artist. The good-time feel of the sessions comes over on vinyl, the eclecticism of the musicians makes it a delightfully varied listening experience and, though there is precious little soul-searching going on, the album features some of Harrison and Dylan's best songs in years.

There was plenty of soul-searching evident on Dylan's next album. Promoting the Wilburys' album with assorted radio interviews, Harrison informed the world that the experience of recording the album had given Dylan the bug to write again, and that his new songs were very strong. If the eighties had been largely disappointing from the viewpoint of Dylan's official vinyl output, a strong album in 1989 might still confirm Dylan's own enduring appeal. Paul Simon's shallow *Graceland* had proved that a contemporary-sounding album with a strong melodic sense and the right promotion could provide renewed commercial status.

Dylan's first problem in preparing the groundwork for a return to form was his choice of producer. The last producer he had worked with had been the in-vogue man of the moment, Arthur Baker, and the "contemporary" sound he gave him sounded utterly fake. Baker's successor as producer of the moment, Mitchell Froom, had provided some keyboards during the remixing of the atrocious "Had a Dream about You, Baby" at the beginning of 1988, though thankfully Dylan decided to steer clear of a man who on the evidence of his albums with Richard Thompson and Maria McKee believes bass to be some form of fish.

On the face of it, his final selection was no more inspiring. Daniel Lanois had been responsible for recent works by U2, as well as both Peter Gabriel's and Robbie Robertson's long-awaited 1986 and 1987 solo albums. Both Robertson's and Gabriel's albums were major disappointments from artists responsible for a couple of the seventies' finest albums. In both cases the sound of the albums was ultracontemporary, but inappropriate.

Dylan first met Lanois when he decided to show up during sessions for a Neville Brothers album that Lanois was producing in New Orleans. The meeting occurred at the time of Dylan's September 1988 show there—the final show of his summer U.S. tour. The Neville Brothers were intending to include two songs from the *Times They Are a-Changin'* album, "Hollis Brown" and "With God on Our Side," to which they had added an extra verse about Vietnam. Dylan liked the informality of recording with a portable studio in an old colonial house in Louisiana, and the sound Lanois was getting on what would become the *Yellow Moon* album. Indeed, he was so impressed by the new version of "With God on Our Side" that he added the new verse in subsequent live performances.

Daniel Lanois: He just sat there and thought that "God on Our Side" was one of the best records he'd ever heard. . . . He just kept saying, "That's a great record." Kept repeating it over and over again. From Bob that's a big compliment.

Bob Dylan: Bono had heard a few of [my new] songs and suggested that Daniel could really record them right. Daniel came to see me when we were playing in New Orleans last year and . . . we hit it off. He had an understanding of what my music was all about. It's very hard to find a producer that can play. . . . It was thrilling to run into Daniel because he's a competent musician and he knows how to record with modern facilities. For me, that was lacking in the past. [1989]

The songs that Dylan brought to New Orleans six months later were certainly very different from the Wilburys' material. Though they trod familiar Dylan territory with their portrayals of a world on the brink of doom with only outlaws and saints remaining true to themselves, there were also songs of scourging self-analysis, notably "What Good Am I?," a surprisingly frank look at his own moral worth.

Bob Dylan: Most of [the songs on *Oh Mercy*] are stream-of-consciousness songs, the kind that come to you in the middle of the night, when you just want to go back to bed. [1989]

Talking about *Oh Mercy* at the time of the album's release, Dylan admitted that before writing the songs he had had to make a conscious decision to try to put together an album of original material, recognizing that the will might no longer be there.

Bob Dylan: Some people quit making records. They just don't care about it anymore. As long as they have their live stage show together, they don't need records. It was getting to that point for me. It was either come up with a bunch of songs that were original and pay attention to them or get some other real good songwriters to write me some songs. . . . Everybody works in the shadow of what they've previously done. But you have to overcome that. [1989]

In his own case that "shadow of what [he'd] previously done" was considerably more daunting than for any contemporary. The sessions began in New Orleans in late March and took up most of April, lasting some six weeks. Lanois had rented a large house on Soniat Street, where he set up his portable Studio on the Move. He had decided to create a mood conducive to the subterranean feel Dylan was looking for on the album.

Daniel Lanois: We found an empty turn-of-the-century apartment building—a five-story building, a fantastic place . . . it had a bordello-ish overtone. We essentially turned the control room into a swamp . . . we had moss all over the place and stuffed animals and alligator heads.

Despite spending six weeks recording and making preliminary mixes, and with only fourteen or fifteen songs he wanted to try to record, Dylan was still determined to record the songs in the usual fashion—with a minimum of fuss.

Daniel Lanois: Bob likes to get something quickly if possible in the name of spontaneity. On this record . . . some things came quick and we grabbed them that way. And then we spent a lot of time on detail. Some of the vocals we worked on quite a bit and the lyrics were changed and we chipped away at them.

Inevitably it was the process of reworking and recutting alternate versions of the songs that used up much of the time. The vocal tracks in particular were given considerable attention. Dylan seemed intent on a smoky, rumbling resonance—almost a cross between Leonard Cohen and Tom Waits.

Daniel Lanois: We put in a lot of care with the vocals and the sounds. On the Dylan record there's not really the obvious presence of synthesizers, just straight-ahead drums and bass and guitars, yet there's this blazing strangeness about it.

The bulk of the album was recorded with the same basic collection of local New Orleans musicians who had worked on the Neville Brothers' album. Lanois himself contributed musically to all but one of the album's songs, providing Dobro, guitar, lap steel guitar, and even omnichord. Engineer Malcolm Burn was also required to turn his hand to tambourine, keyboards and bass in order to capture moments of inspiration from Dylan. Local musicians Willie Green and Tony Hall provided a reliable rhythm section. The ease with which such talented players could be called up at minimal notice delighted Dylan, who had grown tired of the notice that L.A. musicians required.

Bob Dylan: Daniel just allowed the record to take place any old time, day or night. You don't have to walk through secretaries, pinball machines and managers and hangers-on in the lobby and parking lots and elevators and arctic temperatures. You need help to make a record, in all the directions that go into making a record. Some people expect me to bring in a Bob Dylan song, sing it and then they record it. Other people don't work that way—there's more feedback. [1989]

Though Dylan showed remarkable discipline throughout the weeks of work, as the sessions progressed Lanois's role became more and more that of keeping Dylan motivated and committed to producing a great album, not half a great album. With Dylan's low boredom threshold, this required Lanois to develop skills as a taskmaster and diplomat.

Daniel Lanois: With all records there comes a time when people get a little bit lazy, because it's a tiring and unnatural process. At that lull it's very important to take command and turn that . . . valley into a mountain; whatever it takes to reach that mountain is what you have to do at that point to turn the record into a great record. There came a time with Bob Dylan when I felt he fell into old habits—"Get somebody else to play on it," he'd say, or "Just hire somebody," when really he should have been playing the parts. And I made it clear to him that we weren't going to fly anybody in and we weren't going to have session players play these parts. The parts would be played by the people in the room—by himself, by myself, by the engineer, Malcolm Burn, by the neighborhood guys that we'd chosen to be on the record. It was not going to be a studio record. He was going to play the parts and if they were a little sloppy they would be accepted that way.

Though most of the press comments about *Oh Mercy* on its release in September 1989 were about the sound of the album, it was also remarked that rock music's foremost lyric writer had rediscovered his previous flair for words. Though his usual inability to be critical of his own lyrics meant that the album featured two poor lyrics, "Disease of Conceit" and "Where Teardrops Fall," the ominous "Man in the Long Black Coat," the resigned "Most of the Time" and the simply beautiful "Shooting Star" revealed lyric writing as incisive, audacious and acutely human as the best of his previous work.

Daniel Lanois: Bob Dylan is a very committed lyricist. He would walk into the studio and put his head into the pages of words that he had and not let up until it was done. It was quite fascinating to see the transformation that some of the songs made. They would begin as one story and at the end of the night they would be something else. One of my favorites is "Man in the Long Black Coat," which was written in the studio and recorded in one take.

The release of *Oh Mercy* capped a year when several of the previous decade's survivors had come back with their best work of the eighties: Neil Young with *Freedom*, Pere Ubu with *Cloudland* and Lou Reed with *New York* were the other outstanding examples. Though *Oh Mercy* failed to make the top twenty even after enthusiastic reviews, inclusion in *Rolling Stone's* Hundred Best Albums of the Eighties, two years of successful touring and the massive commercial success of the Wilburys, it at least proved to be his most consistent seller since *Infidels*, the album that both inspirationally and thematically it seemed most closely linked to. Sharing *Infidels'* sense of imminent apocalypse, and its patchy but occasionally dazzling brilliance, *Oh Mercy* suggested there was considerably more life in this sixties survivor than in the trio of fellow sixties renegades, the Stones, the Who and Paul McCartney, who all made the circuit of American arenas and stadiums that summer, playing to huge numbers of fans, old and new, all in search of a past.

Within a month of the release of *Oh Mercy*, Dylan played a twenty-seven-hundred-seat theater in New York, while on the same night on the outskirts of the city the Rolling Stones played to seventy thousand worshiping fans. The difference was, here was an artist trying to confront his past glories, not merely to regurgitate them.

37 | 1989–90: Lord Have Mercy!

Bob Dylan: People can learn everything about me through my songs, if they know where to look. They can juxtapose them with certain other songs and draw a clear picture. [1990]

In the eighties, as throughout most of his career, it was Dylan's songs that best illustrated his state of mind. The albums since *Saved* certainly confirm the impression that Dylan's troubled relationships with his ladyloves became less important as his apocalyptic conceit wholly colored his work. Yet his most successful work in the last decade has generally been a result of the fusion of that "black" conceit with his love-ballad strain. Thus "Shot of Love," "The Groom's Still Waiting at the Altar," "Caribbean Wind" and "Angelina" all tap into this combined theme.

At the time of writing those songs, in 1980–81, Dylan was emerging out of his evangelist phase and the end of intense relationships with Mary Alice Artes and Helena Springs, and it seemed a natural enough process to fuse the two. Since the *Infidels* album, recorded at a time when his three-year relationship with Clydie King was coming to an end, he has been less willing to unite the two forms, though "Sweetheart Like You" on *Infidels*, "When the Night Comes Falling from the Sky" and "Something's Burning, Baby" on *Empire Burlesque* and "Shooting Star" on *Oh Mercy* have all broached both concerns.

However, Dylan's overriding concern has remained the end times. Whereas there seemed to be a refreshing strain of universal redemption creeping into Dylan's work with songs such as "Every Grain of Sand" and "In the Summertime" (with its "flood that set everybody free") on the *Shot of Love* album, Dylan has steadfastly stuck to the black apocalyptic tradition in his post–*Shot of Love* work. Songs such as "Jokerman," "When the Night Comes Falling from the Sky," "Band of the Hand" and "Ring Them Bells" are littered with allusions to the finishing end. Some of his bleakest work has gone unreleased or ignored. The sublime "Blind Willie McTell" is a valedictory to a world teetering on the brink. "Something's Burning, Baby" is a song overcome by the fumes of hell.

Though Dylan's three pre–*Oh Mercy* works all concluded with songs that seemed to detail a personal desperation ("Dark Eyes," "Under My Spell" and "Rank Strangers to Me"), his two most recent works combine such personal despair with a more macrocosmic disintegration. The bleakness of *Oh Mercy* has not in anyway dissipated on Dylan's most recent album, *Under the Red Sky*, despite its raunchy sound. On "God Knows" Dylan reminds us that the next flood will not be water but fire, and the finale, "Cat's in the Well," concludes with a prayer for safekeeping of the near and dear in the troubled times that will be imminently upon us all. May the Lord indeed have mercy on us all!

Dylan's two most recent albums seem the logical culmination of a worldview adopted first on *Slow Train Coming*. Since 1979, Dylan has pursued a solitary path. In the seventies his primary artistic struggle was "to learn to do consciously what I used to do unconsciously," and his thematic quandary was the power of Woman: "Dylan has always believed, not unreasonably, in the power of Woman. When he finally lost faith in the ability of women to save him (and he seems to have explored the matter very thoroughly, in and out of marriage, in the years 1974 through '78), his need for an alternative grew very great indeed, and he found what people in our culture most often find in the same circumstances: the uncritical hospitality of Jesus Christ."

So wrote Paul Williams, perhaps the most perceptive of all Dylan commentators, in his contemporary study of Dylan's conversion, *What Happened?* If Williams is correct, then Dylan's conversion was—largely if not wholly—an attempt at immunizing himself against the power of Woman, an admission that he had indeed "lost faith in the ability of women to save him." If so, then it seems that Dylan's failure to maintain a permanent relationship throughout the last decade is as much the result of that "loss of faith" as an inability to find "the right woman."

There are many clues that support this supposition. In 1984 Dylan rewrote what may well be his most perfect love song, "Tangled Up in Blue." In the new version, the singer is no longer searching relentlessly for the object of his desires; instead he describes the woman/women in the song as distractions who have waylaid him in his real quest, walking toward the sun/Son. In January 1990, during his mammoth four-hour show in New Haven, Dylan introduced "Lay Lady Lay" as a song from his romantic period, further noting that romance used to be important to him but not anymore. Of course, there is a tongue firmly in his cheek here, yet the truth is that he could never write such a straightforward song of desire anymore.

Since *Shot of Love* Dylan's love songs have tended to be the more wistful kind, almost remembrances of things past. Though "In the Summertime," "I and I," "I'll Remember You," "Shooting Star" and "Born in Time" all cover familiar terrain, the listener cannot ascertain whether events in the songs date from the recent or the not-so-recent past. All have a dreamlike quality to them.

As Dylan has removed himself from the power of Woman, so he has emphasized the more judgmental and patriarchal aspects of his faith. In 1985 Allen Ginsberg talked about Dylan's faith in these terms.

Allen Ginsberg: It might have been expected that he'd evolve out of [the born-again period and embrace] something closer to his natural Judaism, which he has. . . . He hasn't been a born-again Christian for a long time now. People still think he is and five years ago he changed. In the conversation we had a couple of weeks ago there was a great deal of judgmental Jehovaic . . . a figure of judgmental hyperrationality. There's this judgmental Jehovaic theism in his recent work, and he said: "Allen, do you have a quarrel with God?" And I said: "I've never met the man." And he said: "Then you have a quarrel with God." And I said: "Well, I didn't start anything!" So he still has a fixed notion of divinity.

Though Dylan's apocalyptic conceit has driven most of his finest postconversion songs, his millennial fervor now seems out of step with his audience's view of world affairs. In the sixties the process of change was so imbued with the overthrow of existing structures that Dylan's anthems of doom were freely adopted. In the eighties there has been a sense of a man out of time in all of Dylan's work, compounded initially by his unpopular evangelism and lately by his reactionary distaste for such products of man's "progress" as the space program, television, videos and synthetic music. Thus his songs seem imbued with a sense of isolation.

The isolation also seems to have been personal. In his postaccident career there have only been three periods when Dylan has combined frequent studio activity with prodigious bouts of touring: November 1973 to December 1975, February 1978 to November 1981 and May 1988 to the present. All have coincided with periods of turmoil in Dylan's personal life, almost as if the road became an easy escape from issues he must face head-on in life away from the road. During his recent burst of activity Dylan has recorded two albums with the Wilburys and two original albums, *Oh Mercy* and *Under the Red Sky*, and played over three hundred shows on his Never-Ending Tour.

If there had been a considerable gap between his previous album of original material and *Oh Mercy*, the successor followed with unexpected, and perhaps undue, haste. Like 1989, the early months of 1990 were primarily taken up with writing and recording a new album. In 1990, however, Dylan actually sandwiched shows between sessions, though the follow-up to *Oh Mercy* took up considerably less studio time than its predecessor. The album was composed from just five sessions. There was a session in January and four sessions in early April, featuring such luminaries as NRBQ—with whom Dylan recorded three songs, none of which ended up on *Under the Red Sky* despite being "real strong," according to Don Was—Bruce Hornsby, Elton John, George Harrison and Slash from Guns n' Roses.

There was much speculation about Dylan's motives for using such "names" to play on his new album. Several writers implied that it was a ruse to encourage the consumers to buy the album. In fact, the deal that Dylan had struck with his producers, Don and David Was, was that he would not show Don and Dave his new songs until they recorded them, and they would select the musicians:

Don Was: The personnel for the first session was Stevie Ray and Jimmy Vaughan; David Lindley; our keyboard player from Was (Not Was), Jaimie Muhoberac; Kenny Aranoff. I played bass and Bob was set up at the piano. And he walked in and Stevie walked up to him. I don't think they'd ever met before and he said, "Hi, Stevie Ray Vaughan." But Stevie didn't have his hat on and Bob [was] just like, "Yeah, sure," and kept going. He didn't believe it, he thought it was like an assistant engineer, and then he saw Jimmy and he flipped. . . . And then he saw Lindley. Then he realized it was Stevie Ray and he went back and he was like very warm and very excited about having Stevie Ray on the record.

Dylan's choice for producers boded well for the album. Don and David Was may have achieved fame primarily for their work with black artists, but their Detroit background made them as prone to the influences of the MC5 and the Stooges as to more soulful sounds. Like Daniel Lanois, both Don and David Was were musicians in their own right (indeed, Don would contribute bass guitar on six of the tracks on the album).

It was that first session, on or around January 6, 1990, that really made *Under the Red Sky*. Dylan had played Don Was a demo of one song he had tried at the *Oh Mercy* sessions but could not get quite right. "God Knows" would have fit quite nicely in the middle of side two of *Oh Mercy*, with its sense of the inherent fragility of man's tenure here on earth. It still proved to be mighty problematic.

Don Was: We rehearsed it a few times before [we recorded it but] that was one that we had difficulty with. The other ones we cut that day were "Handy Dandy," "Cat's in the Well" and one other one. It was originally called "Hat Pin"—"10,000 Men." . . . They went much smoother than "God Knows."

The first session resulted in all but one of the five tracks on side two of *Under the Red Sky*. At this point Dylan seems to have realized another quality album was within his grasp. He had nearly half the album already in the can in just one session, and all the songs had an intriguing feel, even if the words on "10,000 Men" seemed a little half formed. Dylan could always redub a vocal track for that one. He also had "Born in Time," another of his wistful ballads, already written and it would be a perfect respite from the tales of the end times already recorded for the album.

The first public intimation of what the new album would actually sound like came from a most unexpected quarter, a promotional CD release of "Most of the Time." In late March, Dylan recorded a live version of the *Oh Mercy* song in a rehearsal studio in Culver City, California, with David Lindley on guitar, Randy Jackson on bass and Kenny Aranoff on drums. The intention was to produce a video to promote *Oh Mercy* further. The video was shot by Dylan's eldest son, Jesse, who had attended film school in New York. The best take was included as a bonus track on the promo CD, credited as produced by Don Was. Dylan's voice was very hoarse, but the track had a thudding resonance the more sedate original lacked. It was a promising preview to the new album.

Indeed, the video shoot was a dry run for the pukka sessions booked to commence directly afterward. Dylan intended to complete the album using a basic line-up of Lindley on guitar, Aranoff on drums and either Don Was or Randy Jackson on bass. One session involved them all and resulted in "2 × 2" and "Wiggle Wiggle." A further session with Jackson and Aranoff, supplemented by Bruce Hornsby and Robben Ford, produced "Born in Time" and "T.V. Talkin' Song." The last of the sessions, featuring just Aranoff, Don Was on bass and Al Kooper, making his first studio recordings with Dylan since the dispiriting *Knocked Out Loaded* debacle, provided the last two tracks required. In three sessions the basic tracks for the six remaining songs that would make up *Under the Red Sky* had been completed. The songs recorded with NRBQ at a separate session remained on the cutting-room floor.

If the laying down of basic tracks had been achieved in a mere five sessions, Al Kooper has intimated that a lot of studio time was spent overdubbing (Kooper himself overdubbed on three songs, only one of which appears on *Under the Red Sky*, "Handy Dandy") and mixing. As with *Oh Mercy*, Dylan spent considerable time working on his vocals.

Al Kooper: On some record I think he learned what the pros were [of overdubbing] and now, Don tells me, he works for hours on vocals getting it just the way he wants it. . . . I think that's positive, not negative.

The completed *Under the Red Sky* was in CBS's hands before Dylan began his 1990 summer tour in Montreal on May 29. It was an album that had a unity of sound and a sense of purpose. The rough edges had not been honed down but rather preserved, and the suitably raunchy backing evoked memories of side three of *Blonde on Blonde*, crossed, it seemed, with the sound Dylan had been trying to achieve on *Down in the Groove*.

Yet *Under the Red Sky* was destined for a bumpy ride on its release. The reality is that Dylan did not really have songs for the second half of the album to match the five songs he had ready in January ("Born in Time" was already written though not actually recorded until April). The remaining songs included two badly in need of tunes, "Unbelievable" and "T.V. Talkin' Song"; one that had been "written by numbers," "2 × 2"; one that was an all-too-brief adaptation of an old rock and roll song, "Wiggle Wiggle"; and finally the title track, "Under the Red Sky," which came in for the most scathing criticism of all. Attacked as trite and nonsensical, the song's use of the nursery-song form to tell a Grimm parable seemed to pass most reviewers by. It was the one song that Dylan discussed with Don Was:

Don Was: That's the only time I really ever asked him about a lyric and he told me about it. He said, "It's about my hometown." . . . It's such a great little fable. These people who have all this opportunity and everything and they choose to be led around by a blind horse and they squander it. It's beautiful and it was so simple and he just sang it one time through and it was perfect.

Though the majority of the songs were attacked for being superficial fodder after the murky magnificence of *Oh Mercy*, the new lyrics only seem to reaffirm Dylan's view of a world gone badly awry. Indeed, *Under the Red Sky* further develops the bleak worldview in evidence on every album from *Slow Train Coming* through to the present release. Despite the levity of "Wiggle Wiggle," the remainder of the album is a catalog of heroes and villains from the end times.

Through the mid-eighties, as he wrestled with his own creativity and indeed his performance art, Dylan seemed to make little attempt to seek a rapprochement with his audience. The previous chapters of this book have detailed that struggle to come to terms with modern technology, with the new limits age has imposed on his singing voice and with his second great creative drought. With *Oh Mercy* he banished the doubts and wrapped the songs in an alluringly subterranean sound that garnered good reviews and sales. If the Dylan on *Under the Red Sky* once again offended his critics, he showed he still had the ability to conjure up profoundly disturbing images and wrap them up in a cogent sound spanning the entire era of rock and roll. The album's stripped-down, guitars-blazing sound also tips its hat to the sound Dylan and his band have been touting around the world these last three years. On the road again, Dylan had attempted to span the years and rebuild the bridge between his audience and his art.

38 | 1988–90: The Never-Ending Tour

Since 1975 the primary arena for Dylan's art has been the stage, not the studio. After his halfhearted return to the stage in 1974, the Rolling Thunder Revue was a triumphant return to form. It affirmed, not only to the press and the fans but to Dylan himself, that he could still cut it, up there where it mattered.

Nineteen seventy-five was also the year when Dylan seems to have realized that technology had passed him by. No longer did he feel comfortable in the studio. No one, it seemed—at least among his contemporaries—went into the studio and recorded an album in three days. No one except Dylan, who recorded the bulk of *Planet Waves* at three sessions, *Blood on the Tracks* at three (plus a further two when he rerecorded half the album) and all but two tracks on *Desire* in one session.

From then on, Dylan has increasingly struggled to get his vision onto vinyl. The results have only been sporadically satisfying, though anyone but Dylan would be proud of a post-*Blood* legacy that includes *Desire, Slow Train Coming, Infidels* and *Oh Mercy*. Most of the time he has committed his artistic energies to something far more instant.

Bob Dylan: What I do is more of an immediate thing: You stand up on stage and sing—you get it back immediately. It's not like writing a book or even making a record. . . . What I do is so immediate it changes the nature, the concept, of art to me. [1981]

Since 1978 he has talked repeatedly about the nature of live performance, but journalists have continued to judge him by his official output. The maverick, though, has denigrated videos as synthetic and producers as exponents of the artificial, and has dismissed musicians who cannot reproduce their work in concert as charlatans. Dylan has cast himself in the mold of the ol' blues musicians. Like Cisco Houston, he can see himself on the road until the doctor finally says his time is up—only then will he head for that California sun one last time.

If the struggle to reconcile the desire to perform with the inspiration to write has not been an easy one, it would appear that after *Infidels* and *Empire Burlesque* Dylan gave up attempting to come to terms with technology. Since February 1986 he has recommitted himself to the road—as he did from 1978 through 1981. Two major tours in 1986 and two tours in 1987 gave him the bug to perform again.

The Heartbreakers, though, could never commit themselves to the type of relentless touring Dylan had in mind. A touring band remained an intractable problem for him. In 1975 he had assembled the first of his rolling revues—a tour that would never end, a free-rolling express through the heartland of America. The idea of the revue went back many years, according to close friends such as Robbie Robertson and Bobby Neuwirth, and it didn't die in 1976. In 1979 Dylan embarked on another kind of medicine show. Preaching the Gospel from place to place, only months after completing a 115-date world tour, he again committed himself to the road, this time the one that "leads to Calvary." By the time that spurt of fervor had died down and his three-year-old touring group been disbanded, Dylan seemed, for the first time in six years, weary of the road and reluctant to live that life. A brief twenty-seven-date tour of Europe in the summer of 1984 proved the only break in his temporary abandonment of the stage, up until February 1986, and the first of three tours with the Heartbreakers in two years.

On June 7, 1988, Dylan embarked on his second major tour of the States in two years. However, it was a very different tour from the True Confessions Tour of 1986. Bob Dylan and the Heartbreakers were no more, so an arena tour on the scale of 1986 was out of the question. Dylan's commercial stock was at an all-time low. *Down in the Groove*, coming hard on the heels of *Knocked Out Loaded*, was his worst-received album since *Self Portrait*. The tour itself did not start auspiciously. His sixty-five-minute opening show was not well received. Far worse was the second show, two days later, in Sacramento, when he departed after twelve songs and less than an hour on stage, refusing even an encore. Most fans assumed that it was simply the end of the first half of the show and had to be told that the show had ended. The scathing reception from the California press the following day made Dylan realize he could not get away with such stunts and still hope to have an audience into the nineties. Thankfully, the band soon kicked into gear and Dylan began to enjoy himself.

The band Dylan toured with in 1988 was as stripped down as stripped down can be. On lead guitar was "Saturday Night Live" bandleader G. E. Smith. The rhythm section was composed of two relatively unknown New York musicians, Christopher Parker on drums and Kenny Aaronson on bass. The considerably better known Marshall Crenshaw had been selected as the original bassist but was finally deemed unsuitable.

Kenny Aaronson: They had him playing six-string bass. Six-string bass and Marshall Crenshaw means to me he was probably playing one of those old DanElectro six-string basses that they used to double the upright with in Nashville for more distinction. The six-string bassist would play with a pick. . . . Now, that's not really the kind of a bass that's gonna give you real low end. It's more of a midrange instrument. . . . Apparently he wasn't really playing as a bass player, more like he was just like floating. . . . They would try different amps to get him to be louder but it's just his touch and this particular instrument so I think they just figured it wasn't working out.

The rehearsals in May were even more basic than previous affairs. With no keyboards or female vocalists to work into the arrangements, Dylan was free to go where he pleased. Even before the tour had started, Dylan and the band had worked up a huge repertoire of something like seventy songs, though "worked up" is probably something of a euphemism.

Certainly for Aaronson, thrown in at the deep end, it was a daunting experience. Like others before him, he was given less than a week to master an entire repertoire, and Dylan would never work a song to death in rehearsal. Indeed, he gave some songs only the most cursory of run-throughs.

Bob Dylan: Rehearsing for me and my band might, in order to rehearse a song, only consist of knowing the title and what key to play it in. If we can do that, that's rehearsing. [1989]

Kenny Aaronson: I got this other call from someone who represented him saying, "Can you come down to rehearsal tomorrow? He wants you there tomorrow." . . . Bob didn't show up that day. I just played with the band. . . . So I came down a second day and Bob showed up for that day and then we started playing. They didn't even tell me if I had the gig. They just had me playing for days and I was learning fifteen to twenty tunes a day. Next thing I know, a couple of days before the tour starts they finally say, "Oh, yeah, you got the gig." . . . I rehearsed for five days and I left for the West Coast. . . . I learned sixty tunes in five days.

This was not the end of Aaronson's, or drummer Parker's, education in Dylan's repertoire. Throughout the tour he added to the repertoire as the fancy took him. In some cases he introduced a song into the set partway through the tour, and the song worked so well that it remained in the set, with something else going at its expense. Most, though, did not reappear except on rare occasions.

Kenny Aaronson: On the road every so often . . . before the show G. E. [Smith] would come back and go, "Fellows, Bob wants us to do this tune and here's how it goes." And G. E. would show it to me and Chris Parker right before the show.

If Dylan had rehearsed loosely before, if he had introduced one-off songs into the set before, and if he had varied the set from night to night before, never had he done it on the scale of 1988. Playing sets of, on average, fourteen or fifteen songs, he compiled a staggering repertoire of more than ninety songs in the space of three months on the road. The pace of the shows was unrelenting, save for a three- or four-song acoustic set at the midpoint of the seventy-minute shows.

Ironically, given his commercial status by 1988 and the complaints made in Europe the previous year about the short sets, the vast majority of reviewers loved the shows. They said that Dylan had not shown such energy and verve in many a moon, and that his stripped-down trio of rockers were breathing fresh air into his music. Certainly the variety of songs in the repertoire was remarkable—Dylan played more songs in the 1988 tour's seventy-one shows than on the entire 115-date world tour of 1978, when he was playing shows of virtually twice the length.

Every show opened with a shocking blast from the past, the amphetamine rush of "Subterranean Homesick Blues"; this was the first time the song had ever been performed in concert. The opening volley indicated the shape of things to come, as Dylan stuck fairly doggedly to his sixties repertoire. His work in the seventies and eighties was almost totally ignored save for a regular work-out on one of three songs from *Blood on the Tracks*, "Shelter from the Storm," "Tangled Up in Blue" or "You're a Big Girl Now"; a fairly consistent "In the Garden"; and the soon-statutory "Silvio" from *Down in the Groove*. Other gems from Dylan's more recent work, such as "Forever Young," "One More Cup of Coffee," "Gotta Serve Somebody," "Every Grain of Sand" or "I'll Remember You," were rare events indeed.

Ironically, Dylan reserved his best vocal performances each night for the one or two covers he was including. In most cases these covers formed part of the acoustic set. Dylan showed his roots with gorgeous renditions of folk songs such as "Barbara Allen," "Trail of the Buffalo," "Wagoner's Lad," "Lakes of Pont-chartrain," "The Two Brothers," "Eileen Aroon" and "Man of Constant Sorrow," or country standards such as "Rank Strangers to Me" and "Give My Love to Rose." Some surprising one-off covers did occasionally crop up in the electric sets, sometimes in hometowns of the song's writers: "Nadine" in Chuck Berry's St. Louis and "Halleluiah" in Leonard Cohen's Montreal.

The tour crisscrossed the North American continent twice, starting in California in June, working across the Midwest to the East Coast, then across Canada, back down to California, up through the Northwest, then back down the East Coast as far as Florida in late September. As if this were not enough, after a three-week break Dylan played two shows in Philadelphia, then four in mid-October at New York's Radio City Music Hall. It was a remarkable stint of touring for a forty-seven-year-old man. He was committing himself totally to his performance art again, and the 1988 tour was just the beginning of what Dylan himself later christened the Never-Ending Tour.

Bob Dylan: It's all the same tour. The Never-Ending Tour. . . . It works out better for me that way. You can pick and choose better when you're just out there all the time and your show is already set up. You know, you just don't have to start it up and end it. It's better just to keep it out there with breaks . . . extended breaks. [1989]

Within seven months of completing his 1988 tour, Dylan was back on the road with the same band and a tour schedule designed to surpass even that marathon. Starting in May, the tour began in Europe with twenty-one shows scheduled through June. A further fifty-one in the States took in July, August and the beginning of September. He then embarked on a further twenty-seven shows in the U.S. in October and November, making it ninety-nine shows in 1989. Along with the winter 1990 shows, he totaled 114 shows in less than nine months, an even more arduous itinerary than in 1978, when Dylan was eleven years younger.

The differences between the latter 1988 and latter 1989 shows were like night and day. Two more contrasting tours featuring such a stripped-down line-up would be difficult to imagine. Though the first couple of shows of each tour were fairly disastrous, in 1988 the quality of the performances peaked in mid-tour and tailed off dramatically after a mid-August eleven-day break. In contrast, the 1989 shows were increasingly impressive, as Dylan seemed to draw renewed strength from each performance, though he sorely needed his mid-September break to recharge his batteries.

The quality of Dylan's singing varied considerably between these tours. Since his 1981 European tour, a fairly steady decline in the quality of his singing in live performance, checked only in his 1987 shows with the Heartbreakers, had been readily discernible. Perhaps this is not surprising given the punishment he inflicted on his singing voice through the seventies and the eighties, and the lack of care he has taken of it. Though some less discerning critics have dismissed Dylan's singing or, worse still, apologized for it, explaining that he does not need a great voice to get what he is saying across, throughout most of his career he has been the master of inflection, the overseer of the most flexible vocal cords in contemporary popular music. In the eighties, and Dylan's forties, the punishment took its toll. Without reasonable time to repair the damage inflicted with each successive tour, Dylan's voice is no longer the flexible tool it once was.

In 1988 Dylan, seemingly unwilling to accept the passage of time, refused to adapt his voice to bring out the best it was still capable of, and roared through songs, trying to bend and twist the words in that age-old way and going for notes that used to bring gasps of astonishment but now only brought sighs of disappointment. However, his innate sense of timing still existed, and a growling rumble had developed in his voice that was at times most effective. In 1988, though, it was generally used only during the acoustic sets, when he was not raging against the roaring glory around him. The electric sets tended to be brutal affairs. On the bittersweet *Blood on the Tracks* songs the snappy delivery and ill-considered wails often detracted from the power of the words. Only on "You're a Big Girl Now," in which Dylan adopted a clipped, reggaefied inflection, could the new style of singing be considered successful.

In 1988 the acoustic sets were the highlights of the shows night in, night out. Despite a tendency to indulge in unnecessary instrumental doodling with G. E. Smith, who played second guitar on these sets throughout the tour, and his decision not to use his harmonica to add variety to the sound, his singing was often marvelously expressive, his choice of covers adventurous and the performances full of conviction.

So to 1989 and the Never-Ending Tour Mark II. The rehearsals for the tour suggested that this would be very different. Dylan seemed confident playing with the band, having broken them in in 1988, and began to experiment with a lot of unusual covers during rehearsals—though, surprisingly, they worked on none of the songs he had just recorded in New Orleans.

Christopher Parker: Among the stranger things we did [at rehearsals] were "I Can See for Miles," the Who tune; "You Keep Me Hangin' On," the Vanilla Fudge version, slow version; "Where or When" by Rodgers and Hart, we've done that a lot of times now . . . "Mystery Train," that's Junior Parker; something called "12-Volt Waltz," that was pretty neat; "Sweet Dreams of You," Patsy Cline; "Walking After Midnight"; "Little Queen of Spades," I think that's Robert Johnson; "Poison Ivy"; "The Blue Ridge Mountains"; "High School Hop" [*sic*], Jerry Lee Lewis; "Mountain of Love," Johnny Rivers; "Ring of Fire"; "Give My Love to Rose"; "Love's Made a Fool of You," Buddy Holly; "God

Only Knows," the Beach Boys, we do that every set, so that's probably gonna be in there. . . . Sometimes G. E. and I request something, like "Tears of Rage." I requested "When I Paint My Masterpiece," and he got out the lyric book and sang the lyrics, and to watch him singing, it was like rediscovering the songs for himself.

In 1988, most of the covers had come during the acoustic sets (only seven of the twenty-three covers performed were with the band). Though the fans did not get to hear all the songs listed above, Dylan performed something like forty covers on his massive 1989 stint, the vast majority with the band. At least one member of the band, bassist Kenny Aaronson, found it a little hard going.

Kenny Aaronson: The second time around this past year when I was rehearsing for the European tour . . . he was pulling out tunes that I'd never heard, and I was having a hard time there for a while. I mean, I was like making notes, constantly making notes and writing out charts and going home with tapes that the sound man would give me.

Aware that he would be treading familiar terrain for much of the 1989 tour, Dylan even considered ways of making the sound a little different from the previous year's shows. According to Aaronson, he thought of touring with some of the local New Orleans musicians he had worked with in March and April. Having decided to stick with the tried and tested, he brought in an extra musician to add some variety to the sound. Sadly, she did not last out the rehearsals.

Kenny Aaronson: He even had at one point this girl called Mindy—I forget her last name but she's the girl in Billy Joel's new band—playing guitar and she plays fiddle and I guess G. E. knew her so Bob was looking for something possibly to add to the band, so for a few days we were rehearsing with her. And he would just pull out all these songs she could just play fiddle on.

However, there was another change, less welcome, that also threatened to make the 1989 tour very different from the previous one—Dylan's mood. In 1988 he seemed delighted to be playing with a tight, kick-ass band, and after the first two shows he seemed totally into the performance each night. The musicians found him reasonably outgoing, at least for a man as intensely private as Dylan can be, and there was a definite camaraderie evident at the shows.

If the songs he had recorded in New Orleans in spring 1989 were anything to go by, in 1989 he was a different person. Gone was the light whimsy of the songs on the Wilburys' album. Every song on *Oh Mercy* suggested a mightily

troubled man. His songs of personal relationships were sad and resigned, hinting of the irreconcilable ("Most of the Time," "What Good Am I?," "What
Was It You Wanted"); his songs on wider themes were suffused once again with
the apocalyptic ("Ring Them Bells," "Everything Is Broken"). Each side of the
album ends with the resigned narrator stuck in a holocaust of terrifying
proportions—"the water is high," "tree trunks uprooted," "the last fire truck
from hell goes rollin' by." The mood seemed to carry over into rehearsals.

Kenny Aaronson: I found during rehearsals the second time around that he
was a lot more distant. . . . He seemed a bit more distracted. I'm sure that's one
of the many moods of Bob Dylan. . . . I found rehearsals with him the second
time around in 1989 very, very vague. . . . Like he'll just play something and
play something and you kinda don't know what he wants you to do, and then
you mess around and he'll never really tell you much. I mean, in rehearsals he
hardly said a word or even hardly looked at me at all for [the] two, three weeks
I rehearsed with him in '89.

Dylan's mood did not improve when he was informed just before flying to
Europe that Aaronson would be unable to complete the European leg of the
tour, as he had been diagnosed as having skin cancer. An immediate operation
would probably be successful but it meant he would have to leave the tour
within a week of its start.

Two shows in Sweden opened Dylan's 1989 sortie through Europe, where
just twenty-one shows were planned—the tour would scarcely touch base with
many centers of support. As in 1988, the opening shows were more than a little
disappointing. Opening in Stockholm with "Subterranean Homesick Blues,"
he performed just one song new to hard-core fans, an old Eddy Arnold tune,
"You Don't Know Me." Worse still, he seemed bored with the performance—a
rare occurrence at the first gig of a tour—and he performed the entire show with
an anorak hood over his head, obscuring all but part of his face. Throughout the
first week, during shows in Malmö, Stockholm and Helsinki and the first show
in Dublin, Dylan continued to perform with hood up, a peaked hat peeking out
from underneath, and with the lights very dim. It was not a promising start.

However, at that first of two shows in Dublin, though he still remained
hooded, he at least started to suggest he was approaching his songs with some
commitment. A lengthy show by Never-Ending Tour standards, it crept over
the ninety-minute mark. It also featured a seemingly impromptu electric version of "The Water Is Wide," a beautiful traditional song he had last performed
with Joan Baez on the first Rolling Thunder tour.

The tide had turned. The following night the hood was gone, and Dylan
brought out U2's Bono for a rabble-rousing encore. On to Scotland and En-

gland, where the shows were full of a pugnacious energy and Dylan's voice seemed to be in good shape for the first time on the tour. The London show was Kenny Aaronson's final show. A substitute named Tony Garnier had flown into Dublin the previous weekend, rehearsed with the band that Saturday and played the first Dublin gig, at which Dylan started to unwind, typically playing the most interesting and perverse set of the tour to date while a new man fumbled through the changes.

Unperturbed by Garnier's lack of rehearsal, Dylan began to pepper show after show with previously unperformed covers, from Hank Williams's "House of Gold" through Sonny Knight's "Confidential to Me" and Townes Van Zandt's "Poncho and Lefty" to Thomas A. Dorsey's "(There'll Be) Peace in the Valley," a song perhaps most associated with Elvis Presley. If Garnier felt he was in at the deep end in Europe, matters became no easier back in the United States. At the first three shows, Dylan drew out Van Morrison's "One Irish Rover," Glen Glenn's "Everybody's Moving," Gordon Lightfoot's "Early Mornin' Rain," and from his own back catalog "I Believe in You," "Gotta Serve Somebody," "Pledging My Time," "Driftin' Too Far from Shore," "I Dreamed I Saw St. Augustine" and "Just Like Tom Thumb's Blues."

The most encouraging aspect of these shows was that Dylan was singing once again with his previously keen precision, his delivery rarely forced or hurried. He seemed more willing to caress the words he had written, as he had been doing the previous year during the acoustic sets. The covers he was playing were often spectacular. On the summer jaunt through the States, he sang superb versions of two Van Morrison songs, "And It Stoned Me" and "One Irish Rover," the former of which Dylan had largely rewritten.* Equally impressive and surprising were versions of Don Gibson's "I'd Be a Legend in My Time," Steve Earle's "Nothing but You" and Jimmy Cliff's "The Harder They Come."

The 1989 tour also proved a delight because of Dylan's decision to bring the harmonica back to center stage. Even today, his picking up the mouth harp brings whoops of excitement from his fans, and in 1989, though occasionally wayward and even sometimes in the wrong key, most often Dylan's harmonica playing gave a new dimension to the band's sound.

The one disappointing event that summer was Dylan's decision not to bring the now fully fit and ready for action Kenny Aaronson back into the band. Though Garnier had performed perfectly adequately, his bass playing lacked the rib-thudding resonance of Aaronson's, and Aaronson was a more colorful con-

---

*Morrison and Dylan had spent some time together on the European tour, culminating, in Athens, with Morrison coming out during Dylan's encore to perform "Crazy Love" and "And It Stoned Me" and Dylan and Morrison singing together on the hill overlooking the Acropolis for an as-yet-unseen BBC documentary on Morrison.

tributor to the band. According to Aaronson, there had never been any question that Garnier was anything but a substitute while he was treated. He thus headed to Jones Beach, near New York City, on July 23, three weeks into Dylan's nine-week trek through the U.S., to say hi to him and inform him he was ready to return. However, Dylan had clearly decided he could get along without him.

Kenny Aaronson: That was a weird day for me, man. . . . I got there and every guy in the crew came up to me and hugged me and in my ear whispered, "When you comin' back, man? We miss you." And I said, "Well, I came to talk to Bob." About half an hour, forty minutes before the show Bob's manager came up to me and said, "Bob wants to know if you wanna come up and play some tunes." I said, "Sure." Then about five minutes before the show Bob called me into the dressing room just to have a chat. He just wanted to talk I guess, and see how I was doing. I was all focused on wanting to come back to work. So we talked for a little while and then I said, "Well, do I look like I'm a sick guy? I'm ready to come back to work." And he started giving me this beating-around-the-bush kinda thing, "Well, I wanna get out of this area and get up back out there and think about it and I'm not sure if I wanna change the band right now." Just gave me all this shit. Basically I got the vibe, y'know. . . . He actually said to me, "I don't give a shit who plays bass."

Inevitably, as the tour progressed through the southern states in late August, three months after the performances in Sweden, the shows began to become workmanlike. Dylan had never toured this long without a break, and in previous instances, during the late seventies and eighties, his voice had begun to show signs of real wear if he played more than thirty shows without a break. Though he was still managing to put real enthusiasm into his shows in early August, the voice was already badly tattered, and the band sounded a little burned out.

Dylan did his best to make these shows sound fresh, introducing new slow, taunting arrangements of some of his 1965 classics—"Positively 4th Street," "Queen Jane Approximately" and "It Takes a Lot to Laugh." He also began to embellish more and more songs with the piping whine of his harmonica. The shows were now stretching beyond ninety minutes night after night, though the number of songs generally remained around the sixteen to seventeen mark established at the later European shows. However, by the time he arrived in California the shows were not impressive. The two shows at the Greek Theater in Los Angeles concluded three months' solid touring, and the choice of material was unadventurous save for a spirited if unsuccessful opener on the first night, an electric "Visions of Johanna." Three days before, in San Diego,

Dylan had seemed to confirm worst predictions by performing an entire show of songs recorded between 1961 and 1967.

Perhaps the Never-Ending Tour, after many glorious moments, had finally run its course. After all, the Rolling Thunder band lasted two tours; the 1978 band 115 shows; the evangelist-trilogy band from November '79 to November '81; the Heartbreakers a Far East, an American and a European tour. Though tickets had gone on sale for further shows in October, starting with a four-day residency at the wonderfully intimate twenty-seven-hundred-seat Beacon Theatre in New York, perhaps this would be the finale for the Never-Ending Tour. After all, Dylan had generally only previously performed when he had something new to say. If the Never-Ending Tour was to continue he needed to find that something new.

On October 10, 1989, Dylan was back on the road. A month's respite was all that separated his seventy-one-date summer 1989 tour from his monthlong fall tour. In the interim, though, CBS had finally released his last album of the eighties, which was his first album of wholly original compositions in four years—*Oh Mercy*. It turned out to be his most critically acclaimed album of the eighties, even warranting inclusion in *Rolling Stone*'s year-end selection of Albums of the Eighties (Dylan's only other inclusion being the Wilburys' album).

October 10 was opening night in a four-date residency at the Beacon Theater. Although Dylan had played seventy-one shows since recording *Oh Mercy*, the summer tour had been singularly bereft of new Dylan songs. He had also paid scant attention to his eighties work, to the extent that he had dropped "Silvio" and "Driftin' Too Far from Shore," the only two regulars in the 1988 sets that were drawn from his two previous studio albums. Despite the undoubted energy and commitment he had displayed through the tour, there was an unfailing sense that Dylan was trucking around with an oldies show.

With the release of *Oh Mercy*, Dylan could now reevaluate what exactly he wanted to say in his concerts. The fall shows needed to combine the best aspects of the Never-Ending Tour to date—a tight band, interesting sets, inventive singing and harp playing from Dylan—with a more contemporary song selection designed to illustrate the fact that here was a still-vital artist.

The indications were that Dylan was aware of this. Despite the fact that the band now sounded as smooth as a well-oiled engine, he booked three days of rehearsals in New York before the Beacon shows, suggesting that he intended to work some *Oh Mercy* songs into the set. The opening charge at the Beacon was a decent blast from the recent past: "Seeing the Real You at Last" seguing into a heartfelt "What Good Am I?" and a rambling "Dead Man, Dead Man." An opening trio of eighties cuts seemed an invigorating statement of intent, particularly as this pattern remained for all the Beacon shows. The third night even saw the welcome introduction of "Man of Peace" from *Infidels* into the first set. With two cuts from *Oh Mercy*, "Most of the Time" and "Everything Is Broken," saved for the second half of the show, it seemed the most satisfying cross section of Dylan songs in concert for eight years.

The eighties songs were not the only surprises at the Beacon shows. If Dylan's voice in the summer 1989 shows represented a quantum leap over the 1988 vocals, the fall voice was a further leap back to former glories. It actually seemed as if, after a wasted decade, he had heeded the obvious and obtained some vocal training to teach him how best to use his forty-eight-year-old vocal cords. The version of "Queen Jane Approximately" at the third Beacon show proved even such hallowed territory as a *Highway 61 Revisited* cut could be redefined and surpassed. The electric "My Back Pages" was treated to the vocal it had deserved back in 1988. The vehemence of "Positively 4th Street" was tinged with an underlying sorrow, as Dylan tightly wound the words round a beautiful, brooding arrangement. The harmonica playing remained erratic but also occasionally dazzlingly brilliant.

Ironically, given the remarkable stamina and consistency maintained throughout most of the summer, the fall tour peaked early and declined rapidly into "more of the same." Within ten days of the first Beacon show the best dates were over and gone. A show in Poughkeepsie, New York, provided the early peak: Dylan performed two songs standing up at the piano, one of which was a unique live "Ring Them Bells," part of an exhausting hundred-minute set of sustained peaks. Subsequently the *Oh Mercy* songs were all shunted together in an overlong second band set and the more sensitive material became overly strident. The other eighties songs, so welcome at the Beacon, soon disappeared from view.

Yet Dylan himself seemed unaware of any loss of momentum. Within two months of concluding his fall tour in Miami, he was playing his first show of 1990. On January 12, as a warm-up for two stadium shows in Brazil and ten shows in Paris and London, he played his first show as a nightclub headliner in more than twenty-five years, at the seven-hundred-capacity Toad's Place in New Haven. This in itself would have been remarkable. That this forty-eight-year-old man then stayed on stage for longer than any concert Springsteen, the king of marathon performances, has ever given makes his Toad's performance the definitive testament to his enduring love for performing. Starting at a quarter to nine, with a cover of Joe South's "Walk a Mile in My Shoes," Dylan finally left the Toad's stage at twenty minutes past two in the morning, after playing four sets interspersed by three breaks of just twenty-five minutes each, having played some fifty songs in total, only eight of which were derived from his supposed halcyon days of 1963–66. He sang seventies songs he had rarely performed, such as "One More Cup of Coffee," "Joey," previously unaired eighties songs such as "Tight Connection to My Heart," "Political World" and "What Was It You Wanted," plus a total of no less than eighteen covers, including such off-the-wall choices as Springsteen's "Dancing in the Dark," Kris Kristofferson's "Help Me Make It Through the Night" and, the fifties-style "Wiggle Wiggle." He was even relatively talkative, jokingly referring to "Man of Peace" as from his religious period and "Lay Lady Lay" as from his romantic period, and responding to requests. His performance of "Joey" came after he initially insisted it was too long and after he reminded the requester this was the fifth such request he was playing for him.

Two further warm-up shows at colleges on the East Coast, though somewhat shorter, continued to feature a Dylan experimenting with the format of his shows. At Penn State he wholly abandoned his acoustic set and played a hundred-minute set with the band. Though the acoustic set was restored to favor at Princeton, it came after just one electric number. The reports of these shows suggested Dylan was back to his Beacon best in time for his ten dates in Paris and London, and sure enough the spirit of adventure prevailed at these shows too. In a mere ten shows, he performed some seventy-eight songs. From *Oh Mercy*, only "Shooting Star" and "Ring Them Bells" remained unperformed that winter, while lovers of the traditional were treated to acoustic versions of "Barbara Allen," "Man of Constant Sorrow" and "Dark as a Dungeon," and electrifying reworkings of "Pretty Peggy-O" and "Hang Me O Hang Me," a song that, prior to Toad's, he had last performed back in 1963 for the BBC production of "Madhouse on Castle Street." Though the European fans still welcomed the inevitable greatest hits, the greatest cheers seemed to be reserved for the *Oh Mercy* songs. The English press for once sensed the fervor that greeted his revival, and responded with their best concert reviews for Dylan in twelve years.

If the European shows seemed the logical culmination of the Never-Ending Tour, Dylan refused to see it that way. Once again summer shows were scheduled in North America and Europe, though the schedule was considerably less hectic than in 1988 and 1989—a mere sixteen dates in Canada and the Midwest, nine dates in Europe and a further twenty-two dates in the States represented the sum total of his spring and summer activities. The early shows, though, affirmed that as Dylan's grasp of his own inimitable performing abilities was gradually being restored to him, his perspective on his own career was rapidly deteriorating.

Dylan's motives for this brief summer jaunt remain unclear. The early shows featured some unique moments and several encouraging signs. His singing remained impressive and his harmonica playing was consistent and often spellbinding. In midconcert the acoustic slot had given way to a semiacoustic set, with Dylan and Smith remaining on acoustic guitars, Garnier reverting to stand-up bass and Parker playing with brushes or keeping a simple beat on high hat and bass drum.

The most welcome change, though, was in Dylan's demeanor. At the final Beacon show in October 1989 he had astonished fans by diving into the audience during the last encore. In Miami, at the penultimate fall show, he was seen grinning his way through an acoustic "Tangled Up in Blue" while a lady from the audience climbed onto the stage and began stripping. At the shows at London's Hammersmith Odeon he actually mumbled the occasional one-liner to the audience, informing them that "Watching the River Flow" was a new arrangement of "Subterranean Homesick Blues" and so forth. By the fourth of his North American shows in early June, he was being positively gregarious and seemed to be genuinely enjoying his time onstage, even responding to requests. On one occasion he was in the middle of the introduction to "It's All Over Now, Baby Blue" when a request for "Tomorrow Is a Long Time" caused him to stop and observe, "It sure is. Awfully long," before switching to the requested tune.

Yet the summer shows were a disappointment after the fall 1989 and winter 1990 shows. They suggested that Dylan had returned to perceiving himself as an oldies act again. The preponderance of sixties "hits" was overwhelming. Two or three songs from *Oh Mercy* were all fans could expect at each show, and the songs from such remarkable albums as *Planet Waves, Desire, Street-Legal, Shot of Love*, and *Infidels* were all wholly ignored.

So why has Dylan so little faith in his own later material and his ability to put these songs across? His feelings about his greatest hits have always been ambiguous. There is a common story that Paul Simon once complained to Dylan that his fans always seemed to want to hear him perform "Homeward Bound," "The Sounds of Silence," and so on. Dylan supposedly replied that if he went to a Paul Simon concert those would be the songs he would like to hear. Yet Dylan himself has not always seen fit to dish out his own hits. In 1975 the Rolling Thunder set concentrated on the as-yet-unreleased *Desire* songs. In 1976 the choice of old songs seemed deliberately perverse. In 1979–80 the old songs were wholly excluded, and even when reintroduced in late 1980 were outnumbered by covers and as-yet-unreleased songs. In 1981 the old songs were often tossed away with nary a thought, Dylan reserving an extra vocal commitment for his newer material. Yet still the fans bayed for the oldies.

Since 1984 Dylan has not been quite so tenacious in his resistance to the audience's preconceptions. Though he began each of his mid-eighties tours (1984, 1986, 1987) with reasonably audacious sets, within two or three shows he had revised the sets to the detriment of the more recent songs. In 1984 the shambolic first show in Verona featured versions of "When You Gonna Wake Up," "Heart of Mine" and "Man of Peace," all of which were rare events

indeed at later shows. In 1986 a similarly ramshackle opening show inWelling-
ton featured "Gotta Serve Somebody," "Shot of Love" and "Heart of Mine," all
of which were quickly dropped.

The 1987 European tour featured a more adventurous Dylan; he was widely
castigated for this adventurousness. At the first show in Tel Aviv he played a
lovely cross section of his work—five of the seventeen songs were from the
seventies, four songs were from the eighties and there was one traditional cover.
The response was such that Dylan was required to defend himself in print,
insisting to Robert Hilburn of the *Los Angeles Times*, before his show in Jerusalem:

Bob Dylan: You don't want to just get up there and start guessing with the
people what they want. For one thing, no one agrees on that. The songs a few
people want to hear may not mean anything to a whole lot of others, and you
can't let the audience start controlling the show or you're going to end up on a
sinking ship. You've got to stay in control, or you might as well go hole up in
Las Vegas somewhere because you're not being true to the music anymore . . .
you're being true to something else that doesn't really mean anything except
some applause.

Nevertheless the show in Jerusalem saw restored to favor the irksome likes of
"The Times They Are a-Changin'," "Like a Rolling Stone," "Rainy Day
Women" and "Ballad of a Thin Man." At the final seven shows of the European tour, in England, he seemed to parody himself deliberately by opening
with "The Times" or "Blowin' in the Wind" followed by "Maggie's Farm" and
"Like a Rolling Stone," and methodically stripped each song of every ounce of
meaning. If such disrespect worried new Dylan concertgoers, he then turned up
the heat with sets of remarkable intensity. The press was too busy emphasizing
Dylan's "death mask" look and his between-song taciturnity to notice the gesture.

When the Never-Ending Tour started, Dylan seemed more willing to reach
a rapprochement with those fans there to hear "the hits." Yet after "I'll Remember You" at the fourth show, he retorted, "I don't think that's an obscure
song. Do you think that's an obscure song? I don't think so," incensed by a
review of the previous show, where again he had been attacked for his bold song
selections.

Since the mid-seventies Dylan has constantly had to balance the wishes of
the members of the audiences who are there for a night out, who know him
mainly by reputation and from inferior cover versions by other artists and
perhaps the odd compilation album once left behind at an all-night party, with
his own artistic integrity. With his low commercial stock and the sheer need to

fill seats in three years of summer gigs with the same trio, Dylan no longer seems sure of his instincts. Outside the presumably hip havens of the West and East Coasts, London and Paris, he seems unwilling to take risks on the Midwest picnic circuit. This is reflected in his unwillingness to perform new, as-yet-unreleased songs in his sets.

The summer 1990 shows reverted to the 1988 pattern, and Dylan is again perceived as an artist trading on his past, no matter how convincingly he may interpret his sixties material. This seems somewhat incongruous given that in the fall of 1989 and the winter of 1990 he had so convincingly championed his recent work, notably from the impressive *Oh Mercy*. He did this at a time when the survivors of perhaps the three most important British bands of the sixties—the Who, the Rolling Stones, and, from the Beatles, Paul McCartney and Ringo Starr—were all traveling around the world with shows sold on the back of a nascent nostalgia. Dylan's performances remained a refreshing alternative.

The way that Dylan approaches his oeuvre has generally belied nostalgia. At his best, when the songs are transformed in arrangement and/or delivery, they resonate with new meaning. Yet the simple gesture of playing "Like a Rolling Stone" or "I Shall Be Released" remains an all-too-easy option to incite the crowd and reduce his performances to rock and roll spectacles, no more valid and considerably less profitable than the 1989 Stones extravaganza.

That Dylan was still capable of his best in 1990 was proved in Paris and London, at the earlier of the summer shows in Canada and at the five shows at the Beacon Theatre in October. Despite such welcome exceptions, by October not only had Dylan's commitment to performance dimmed somewhat, but so had the patience of his right-hand man through the entire Never-Ending Tour. The October shows in New York were G. E. Smith's final stand, despite the fact that a further twenty G. E.–less dates had already been slotted into the fall 1990 itinerary.

At the August and September shows guitarists had been auditioning for G. E.'s place in the band onstage, playing alongside G. E. as Dylan churned out predictable greatest-hits sets. None of the four aspiring incumbents seemed adequate to the task of compensating for the loss of a man whom Dylan seems to have considered no more than a hired hand—and whom Dylan has repeatedly ignored when making studio recordings—but who, as every witness to the shows they played together realizes, was the mainspring of the band, a flexible, responsive bandleader who had saved Dylan from many a scrape in midconcert. G. E.'s gradual disillusionment with the tour after the euphoria of the London shows was probably a major factor in the decline evident in recent months. Without G. E. the band has become rudderless, adrift night after night, presumably with little faith in Captain Bob's ability to steer them through.

Dylan's shoddy treatment of Smith, though G. E. is less evidently bitter than

Kenny Aaronson, closely mirrors his treatment of the ex-bassist. Taken together with stories of Dylan's reasons for rejecting the two most suitable candidates for G. E.'s place in the band, Miles Joseph and Steve Bruton, on the grounds that Joseph asked him for an autograph and Bruton had too many hardware guitar effects, hardly inspires confidence in Dylan's ability to command loyalty and respect from the next ensemble he seeks to create.

Gone are the days when musicians played with Dylan for the experience of playing with the great man. Playing with Dylan has become just another gig. After all, since 1987 Dylan has not reserved his gruff, taciturn exterior for just the fans and media. Band members rarely see the man except onstage, and most signals to the band were relayed through G. E. before his departure.

The worry that Dylan is showing signs of paranoia has for many colored an appreciation of the achievements of the Never-Ending Tour. It would be no exaggeration to say that Dylan and G. E. Smith have literally redefined the meaning of live rock and roll performance in an era when the pomp of the spectacle has all too often drawn attention away from the essence of the rock and roll experience—live music played and sung with a commitment to the genre. Yet Dylan's increasingly bizarre demeanor as the Never-Ending Tour has progressed suggests that he is now only playing lip service to the audience he seemed so keen to seek a rapprochement with back in 1988.

39 | 1990: The Finishing End?

In 1973 Dylan insisted, in the song "Dirge," that he was not one of those that worshiped loneliness. Yet neither *Oh Mercy* nor *Under the Red Sky* sounds like the work of a man reveling in the joys of human companionship. Since Dylan broke up with Clydie King in 1983, only two women have definitely been contenders for any kind of serious relationship with him. Undoubtedly the most enduring of his postdivorce girlfriends has been Carole Childs. A respected A&R executive at Atlantic Records, Childs has been a recurring factor in Dylan's life since 1984. She has been portrayed as "long-suffering and intense." Dylan has evidently taken a great deal of notice of Childs's opinions: He offered her protégés Lone Justice one of his unreleased songs back in 1984, and he even heeded her advice on choosing a producer for his 1990 album.

Don Was: She'd played our stuff for him and made him aware of it, talked about us . . . and then six months later I got a call from Carole saying, "Bob would like to know if you're interested in doing a track [with him]." And that was "God Knows."

Far more blatant in advertising her relationship with Dylan has been American actress Sally Kirkland, who since 1989 has rarely given a TV or newspaper interview without detailing at length her "long-standing" love affair with Dylan. She has implied on American TV that Dylan is a voracious lover. Inevitably she has also suggested that he has written some of his recent songs with her in mind.

Sally Kirkland: He is often away on the road and I am away working, but we keep in touch through his songs and my poems. In . . . "Everything Is Broken," he wrote the lines for me "Every time you leave / and go off some place / things go to pieces in my face."

Kirkland had originally been involved with Dylan at the time of the second benefit for Hurricane Carter in January 1976. Their affair was short-lived (though she was photographed on his arm in March 1977 at the time Sara was filing for divorce). They renewed their friendship in the late eighties. Yet Kirkland is no constant companion. Like Childs, she seems bound to Dylan by occasional mutual gaps in their schedules.

Nor are Childs and Kirkland the only women to have flitted in and out of his life in the last few years. Apart from his many women friends who are indeed friends—and Dylan has always seemed more able to maintain an ongoing dialogue with women than men—he has continued to indulge his love for women on a random basis. As someone recently put it in an article on Dylan's recent life-style, "There are a lot of different women he sees, from all different walks of life. But they all tend to have one thing in common. They're invariably all very weird or very intense." Which closely accords with descriptions of the women whom revue members recall surrounding him on that 1976 caravan through the southern states.

What none of these relationships have succeeded in doing is keeping Dylan at home to enjoy the delights of the hearth, rather than playing the perpetual troubadour moving on from town to town. Save possibly for Clydie King, none of his postdivorce girlfriends seems to have managed to sublimate his restless, hungry feelings, and despite regular contact with his children and ex-wife—there was even speculation in the press in 1983 that he and Sara were on the verge of remarrying again—Dylan remains a solitary figure.

Of course, he has never had a problem being by himself. For much of his youth in Hibbing he kept to himself, and he has rarely revealed his inner thoughts and feelings except in song, even to friends and lovers. Now that he has closed himself off from much of the real world—perhaps the only feasible solution to the incursions and impositions made upon him by outsiders—only his close relationships with friends and lovers allow him to maintain contact with a degree of normality.

Indeed, several friends have confirmed that in a one-to-one situation or as part of a small group of confidants Dylan remains the same person he has been throughout his creative years, a painfully shy but wry and witty man who genuinely craves sincere input and expression. Certainly Dylan values the long-standing friendships he has managed to maintain in the goldfish-bowl-like existence he has been forced to lead for most of his life. Friends and fellow musicians all speak of Dylan's desire to maintain at least sporadic contact with those he has known along the way.

However, Dylan has become increasingly wary of strangers, and new faces are very rarely allowed to peer inside the inner circle. His notorious unpredictability also instills a fear in many of the people that work for him. This is perhaps exemplified by the fact that his own musicians and road crew are afraid to ask for something as mundane as a dub of a soundboard tape of a show—Dylan's paranoia about bootlegging is long-standing—preferring to ask the perennial audience tapers who remorselessly pursue the man for dubs of their recordings.

A friend of Dylan's recently insisted that he is not "a control freak," constantly seeking to control the dissemination of his output, yet in the notes for *Biograph* he described bootleggers as "outrageous . . . you're just sitting and strumming in a motel . . . the phone is tapped . . . and then it appears on a bootleg record. With a cover that's got a picture of you that was taken from underneath your bed." When asked for an autograph by a fan who had been caught videotaping a show he replied that he did not give autographs to thieves. The more meticulously thorough his fans who seek to document his performances become, the more Dylan seems to resent their enterprise rather than embrace them as the Grateful Dead have, even though in the Walkman era efforts to restrict such attempts remain utterly futile.

If Dylan's reputation as a live performer and recording artist has once again been in the ascendant since 1988—harsh reviews for *Under the Red Sky* notwithstanding—stories of his eccentricities have become more and more prevalent. Even in 1986 he still seemed able to confront his detractors with razor wit while maintaining a refreshingly down-to-earth approach to his own fame. Since 1987, though, he has adopted a bizarre Howard-Hughes-of-rock-and-roll persona, at variance with less eccentric contemporaries such as Paul McCartney and Mick Jagger.

It may seem curious to call Dylan a Hugheslike figure given the amount of touring, and therefore the number of very public apperances, he has undertaken in the last five years. Yet even in concert his recalcitrance has led to bizarre rituals. Since 1987, when the European press delighted in reproducing photos of Dylan's "death mask" look on his European tour, he has consistently refused to allow photo passes at concerts and has hounded any illicit photographers. Indeed, at a show in Toronto in June 1990 he requested that anyone in the audience who saw someone next to him taking photos restrain the offender. When Kenny Aaronson asked for a photo of the 1988 band in rehearsal, he had to swear he would allow no one to take copies. Dylan recently commented in an interview:

Bob Dylan: It rubs me the wrong way, a camera. It doesn't matter who it is, someone in my own family could be pointing a camera around. It's a frightening feeling. . . . Cameras make ghosts out of people. [1990]

Dylan has always remained ambivalent about photos of himself. He has previously enjoyed photo sessions at which he could provide his own creative input. Yet they are rare events indeed these days. Recently he has made photographing him in concert extra difficult by shrouding himself in darkness for most of each show. During two shows in Greece in June 1989 he insisted that the lights be turned down for the conclusion of his main sets, even barking out a command midsong, and the encores were played out virtually in total darkness. Earlier on that European tour he had appeared onstage for the first four shows wearing a hood over his head and a cap underneath, and he retained this ludicrous attire throughout these shows. Though the 1990 shows have been considerably better lit than the two previous summers' shows, Dylan's own features still remain largely shadowed by overhead and back lighting, particularly because he now generally wears hats onstage.

His Hooded Man persona would be outlandish enough if adopted solely onstage, but now he seems to have made the cape/cap look his public image, along with a pair of shades that shut him off completely from those around him. This look could hardly have been chosen for reasons of inconspicuousness. Sitting in a deserted New York bar on a humid October evening with one's hood up is not the sort of appearance that discourages a second glance. As if this were not strange enough, he apparently turned up at sessions for *Under the Red Sky* and the second Wilburys' album similarly attired, sitting in the recording studio with his hood up and cap on. Quite what he fears friends such as George Harrison and Tom Petty might see, one can only guess.

Slash: Even when he was talking to me [at the *Under the Red Sky* sessions], all I could see behind all those fuckin' hoods and the shades was his nose and, like, his upper lip.

The decision to rehire Victor Maimudes as his personal assistant for the Never-Ending Tour, after a major disagreement with his longtime assistant Gary Shafner during the previous European tour, confirms an unwillingness on Dylan's part to allow new faces into his camp. Members of the crew, and indeed members of the band, now rarely see him except onstage. He travels on his own bus, separate from the band, and often stays at different hotels. He rarely appears at soundchecks, is often absent at rehearsals and even avoids studio sessions when overdubs or mixing are the major activities. He out-and-out refuses requests for autographs from fans who run across him in his travels, and in one instance before a recent show in New York he was seen running the couple of yards from his limo to the stage door to avoid two bemused middle-aged English fans standing five yards back from his car.

It should be no surprise that Dylan betrays the occasional sign of paranoia. After all, he has been subjected to an incalculable degree of adulation from fans who have been "bothered"—to use Dylan's own word—by the words to his songs. An indication of these pressures and Dylan's intense concern about them formed the basis of a declaration to the courts by his lawyer, David Braun, in March 1977, requesting that the records of his divorce case be sealed:

David Braun: When people know where he is, his garbage is sifted and examined regularly; groups appear in front of his house on his birthday. Fans constantly tried to reach him to talk to him, to touch him and to see him. Recently, the sheriff had to be called to remove a girl from the driveway of his home; afterwards she sprayed black paint all over his windows. A disturbed person has been trying to reach Mr. Dylan through me and is threatening to harm himself if he is unsuccessful. As a result of this and much, much more, Mr. Dylan has been required to engage twenty-four-hour guards about his property to prevent trespassing and to protect the privacy of himself and his family. . . . In my twenty-two years' experience of representing famous personages no other personality has attracted such attention, nor created such a demand for information about his personal affairs.

The irony is that whatever commercial success Dylan has enjoyed (and certainly his sales do not start to compare with his fellow sixties' "icons," the

Beatles and the Rolling Stones), and whatever degree of adulation has been expended on other rock and roll stars, it is perhaps only Dylan who has been perceived as a seer, even a messiah. That Dylan should thus shrink from the expectations of his audience is perhaps not surprising. Indeed it almost represents a modus operandi for much of his work.

It is understandable that thirty years of dealing with the media have made him reluctant to grant interviews. Yet when promoting *Oh Mercy* he was so tight-lipped during an interview for a two-hour syndicated radio special that the producers had to use chunks of a 1981 interview with Dave Herman, and had to interview people who had worked with him, in order to come up with enough material. An equally taciturn Dylan was the subject of a major feature in *Q*, yet he repeatedly put off giving the interview necessary for the feature and finally gave a string of one-line replies to the questions asked. In order to promote *Oh Mercy*, CBS was required to produce its own composite video for "Everything Is Broken" from existing footage, without any input from Dylan at all. When he finally got around to producing a video himself, of "Most of the Time," Dylan recorded a live version of the song wholly different in sound and performance from the album version. Produced by Don Was, the new version of "Most of the Time" seemed more a foretaste of the new album than a promotional item for *Oh Mercy*.

Of course, Dylan's whole career has been driven by acts of perversity. The only thing predictable about Dylan is that he will be unpredictable. Still, his recent eccentricities must give cause for concern. The triumph of his career has been the way he has constantly inverted, desecrated or just downright stomped upon audience expectations, and yet his artistry has survived each chameleon twist.

But perversity in his art does not presuppose a man careering out of control. His recent eccentricities do. Such peculiar practices have inevitably led to rumors of a resumption of drug-taking by Dylan, though save for his abiding penchant for alcohol no concrete evidence has ever been provided of a drug habit in the eighties. John Bauldie commented in *The Telegraph*, in response to such speculation, that "occasional rantings from the stage in 1986 were possibly the products of his medicinal consumption of rather rough American whisky-like cough linctus. Snufflings on the *Hearts of Fire* set we can put down to the inclement British weather, and the stumblings around on stage in 1987 surely were evidence of a most uncomfortable back problem." Certainly Dylan's wildly varying demeanor onstage from concert to concert suggests that his drinking habits are not always under tight rein.

About the future for Dylan the artist, a degree of optimism seems warranted. Many great artists have produced their finest works when no longer sprightly youths, and there is no reason to assume that he is no longer capable of producing work as remarkable as *Blood on the Tracks* or *Blonde on Blonde*. As he observed in an interview for *USA Today* at the time of the release of *Oh Mercy*:

Bob Dylan: An easy way out would be to say, "Yeah, it's all behind me, that's it and there's no more." But you want to say there might be a small chance that something up there will surpass whatever you did. Everybody works in the shadow of what they've previously done. But you have to overcome that. [1989]

Certainly his latter work will not have the impact his sixties work had on that generation. The work must now stand alone. Yet the fact that Dylan remains a frequently inspirational artist thirty years after his Minneapolis apprenticeship—only he could have written "God Knows" or "Man in the Long Black Coat"—suggests that the flame still burns. He seems to have emerged from his second great creative drought, which engulfed him between 1985 and 1988, a trough as daunting as the more famous drought between 1968 and 1972. That he completed a new—if only sporadically impressive—album less than nine months after the release of *Oh Mercy* suggests that the faucet is flowing again. Already Dylan has sustained his creativity far longer and with more impressive peaks than any of his sixties contemporaries. I doubt that we have heard the last great Bob Dylan song.

For the man born Robert Zimmerman, who is only Bob Dylan when he has to be, the future seems less rosy. Though *Oh Mercy* suggests that he continues to draw solace from his enduring beliefs, the oppressiveness of the lyrics and his current offstage demeanor reminds me of that sad quote from Suze Rotolo about the twenty-five-year-old Dylan:

Suze Rotolo: People live with hope for green trees and beautiful flowers, but Dylan seems to lack that sort of simple hope—at least he did from 1964 to 1966. This darkness wasn't new to me. It became stronger as the years passed by.

Sara seemed to rescue him from that darkness temporarily, and then his faith initially seemed to provide renewed light, but as the eighties progressed his faith seemed only to reinforce him in his view of a world gone mad. Whether the darkness will continue to grow, and how the artist in him will deal with it if it does, is perhaps the most pressing question as Dylan approaches fifty. His work and life will continue to fascinate and intrigue, and like an artistic Rorschach test he will continue to mean different things to each and every fan. And though the worn lines and scruffy beard suggests he is unlikely to stay forever young, long may he endeavor to paint his masterpiece.

Notes

PART ONE. Busy Being Born . . .

Chapter 1.   1941–59: In My Younger Days

The Dylan quotes in this chapter are derived from his December 1963 Message to the Emergency Civil Liberties Committee; two raps he gave at concerts at the Warfield Theater, San Francisco, on November 11, 1980; and interviews conducted by Philippe Adler (*L'Expresse*, July 3, 1978), Chris Welles (*Life*, April 10, 1964), Barbara Kerr (*Toronto Sun*, March 26–29; 1978), Scott Cohen (*Spin*, December 1985), Les Crane (his TV show, February 17, 1965), Martin Bronstein (Canadian Broadcasting Company radio, February 20, 1966), Sam Shepard (*Esquire*, July 1987), Bert Kleinman and Artie Mogull (Westwood One radio broadcast, November 25, 1984), Bob Aschenmacher (*Duluth News-Tribune and Herald*, June 29, 1986), Paul J. Robbins (*Los Angeles Free Press*, September 17 and 24, 1965) and Nat Hentoff (his October 1965 interview, transcribed as the *Whaaat!* booklet).

Quotes from Bill Marinac, Val Peterson, Georgie Haben, Steve Friedman and Bobby Vee were all derived from a major profile on Dylan's youth in the *Duluth News-Tribune and Herald*, published on June 29, 1986. Further comments by Bobby Vee were taken from a BBC radio interview broadcast on June 4, 1976. Beattie Zimmerman's observation was derived from Larry Sloman's *On the Road with Bob Dylan* (Bantam Books, 1978). Echo Helstrom's comments are drawn largely from *Positively Main Street* by Toby Thompson (Coward-McCann, 1971) and from Anthony Scaduto's Dylan biography (Grosset & Dunlap, 1971). Bonnie Beecher's comments come from an interview by Marcus Whitman, published in *Telegraph* 36.

Dylan's youth has been dealt with in detail by Robert Shelton in his Dylan biography, *No Direction Home* (William Morrow, 1986). Anthony Scaduto's biography, and Bob Spitz's *Dylan: A Biography* (McGraw-Hill, 1989) also have useful sections on Dylan's Hibbing youth. Also worthy of investigation are Dylan's own free-form poems, which provide impressionistic recollections of his youth, notably "My Life in a Stolen Moment," his notes to *Joan Baez in Concert 2* and the second part of the "11 Outlined Epitaphs." All of these are readily available in Dylan's *Lyrics* (Knopf, 1985).

Chapter 2.   1960: SAMmy Bound for Glory

The Dylan quotes in this chapter are derived from a poem that forms part of the Margolis and Moss manuscripts, published in *Telegraph* 35, and interviews conducted by Bob Coburn

("Rockline" radio show, June 17, 1985), Barbara Kerr (*Toronto Sun*, March 26–29, 1978), Ron Rosenbaum (*Playboy*, January 1978), Cameron Crowe (*Biograph*), John Cohen and Happy Traum (*Sing Out!*, October 1968) and Izzy Young (*Other Scenes*, December 1968).

The quotes from Bonnie Beecher are derived from an interview conducted by Markus Wittman, and published in *Telegraph* 36. Comments by Dave Whitaker are derived from an interview by Stephen Pickering, published in *Telegraph* 26. Terri Wallace's comments are derived from an interview conducted by her sister Karen Moynihan and transcribed by Chris Cooper for *Freewheelin'* fanzine. Ellen Baker's and Maurice Zimmerman's observations have been drawn from Toby Thompson's *Positively Main Street* (Coward-McCann, 1971). Judy Rubin's and Stanley Gottlieb's quotes are from Bob Spitz's biography (McGraw-Hill, 1989). Harvey Abrams's quote is from Robert Shelton's *No Direction Home* (William Morrow, 1986). Kevin Krown's quote is from Anthony Scaduto's biography (Grosset & Dunlap, 1971). Bill Marinac's comment is from the *Duluth News-Tribune and Herald*, June 29, 1986. Marshall Brickman's comment is from Robbie Woliver's *Bringing It All Back Home* (Pantheon, 1986).

Also highly useful in helping formulate my ideas about this crucial period of Dylan's development was the second chapter of Paul Williams's *Performing Artist* (Underwood-Miller, 1990).

Chapter 3.   1961: Hard Times in New York Town

The Dylan quotes in this chapter are derived from a transcript of his acceptance speech for the Rock and Roll Hall of Fame on January 20, 1988, and interviews conducted by Billy James (a transcript of the November 1961 interview), Martha Quinn (MTV, July 7, 1984), Bert Kleinman and Artie Mogull (Westwood One radio broadcast, November 25, 1984), Pete Oppel (*Dallas Morning News*, November 18–23, 1978), Dan Meer ("Close Up" radio show, October 30, 1989) and Gil Turner (*Sing Out!*, October 1962).

Quotes by Izzy Young are derived from an interview by Jorgen Lindstrom, Ake Johnson, and Arne Hartelius. Liam Clancy's comment is from an interview by Patrick Humphries published in *Telegraph* 18. Happy Traum's comment is from an interview by Jacques Van Son. Pete Seeger's is from an interview conducted by myself. J. R. Goddard's observation is from *The Village Voice*, April 26, 1962. Paul Davies's and Mark Spoelstra's comments are from Bob Spitz's biography (McGraw-Hill, 1989). Pete Stampfel's is from *Zigzag* 26. Jack Nissenson's is from the Montreal *Gazette*, January 12, 1974. Terri Thal's is from Robbie Woliver's *Bringing It All Back Home* (Pantheon, 1986). Eric von Schmidt's are from his own *Baby, Let Me Follow You Down*, written with Jim Rooney (Anchor Books, 1979), and Anthony Scaduto's biography (Grosset & Dunlap, 1971). Robert Shelton's comment is from a May 1966 issue of *Record Mirror*. Carolyn Hester's is from an interview in *Goldmine*, January 26, 1990. John Hammond's comments derive from an interview in *Fusion*, October 31, 1969.

Of general use in putting this chapter together have been Robbie Woliver's *Bringing It All Back Home* and Eric von Schmidt and Jim Rooney's *Baby, Let Me Follow You Down*. But by far the most detailed study of Dylan's early months in New York is John Bauldie's two-part essay in *Telegraph* 24 and 25, entitled "Hard Times in New York Town."

Chapter 4.   1962–63: I Am My Words

The Dylan quotes in this chapter are derived from interviews conducted by Bert Kleinman and Artie Mogull (Westwood One radio broadcast, November 25, 1984), Henrietta Yurchenco (*Sound and Fury*, April 1966), Pete Seeger (transcript of May 1962 WBAI radio show), Gil Turner (*Sing Out!*, October 1962), Nat Hentoff (the original galleys for the liner notes to *The Freewheelin' Bob Dylan*, published in *Telegraph* 8), Studs Terkel ("Wax Museum" radio show, April 26, 1963) and Kurt Loder (*Rolling Stone*, June 26, 1984).

Quotes by Anthea Joseph and Pete Seeger are derived from an interview conducted by myself. Izzy Young's comments are from an interview by Jorgen Lindstrom, Ake Johnson, and Arne Hartelius. D. A. Pennebaker's are from an interview by John Bauldie (*Telegraph* 26). Martin Carthy's are from an interview on Radio Merseyside, June 18, 1983. Ron Gould's and Jim McLean's comments are from interviews by Brian Wells and Val Lawlan respectively. John Hammond's quotes are from an interview in *Fusion*, October 31, 1969. Peter Yarrow's are from the July 1987 edition of *Musician* magazine. Eve MacKenzie's observation is drawn from Scaduto's biography (Grosset & Dunlap, 1971).

Of general use in constructing the difficult chronology of Dylan's first trip to London has been the Lawlans' essay on this visit in their *Steppin' Out* pamphlet. For a detailed discussion of Dylan's involvement with *Broadside*, readers are referred to the essay by David Pichaske and myself in *Telegraph* 20.

Chapter 5. 1963: From Town Hall to Carnegie Hall

Dylan's quotes in this chapter are derived from a prose poem published in the 1963 Newport Folk Festival program, entitled "To Dave Glover"; a statement he gave to *The Village Voice*, published on May 16, 1963; and interviews conducted by Anthony Scaduto for his biography in 1971, by Mary Merryfield (*Chicago Tribune*, November 21, 1965), by Jack Smith (*National Guardian*, August 22, 1963) and by an unknown interviewer for the *New York Post* (January 12, 1965).

Suze Rotolo's comments come from Robbie Woliver's *Bringing It All Back Home* (Pantheon, 1986). Tom Wilson's observations are from interviews in *Melody Maker* (January 31, 1976) and *Fusion* (October 31, 1969). Michael Bloomfield's are from a radio interview given in 1979 (transcribed in the *Friends and Other Strangers* booklet). Joan Baez's are from her autobiography *And a Voice to Sing With* (Summit Books, 1987). Beattie Zimmerman's are from Larry Sloman's *On the Road with Bob Dylan* (Bantam Books, 1978).

Chapter 6. 1963: Troubled and I Don't Know Why

Dylan's prose poems quoted in this chapter are derived from excerpts from the Margolis and Moss manuscripts published in *Telegraph* 35 and Isis 30/31; his liner notes to Peter, Paul and Mary's *In the Wind* album; his program notes for the 1963 Newport Folk Festival, entitled "To Dave Glover"; his December 1963 Message to the Emergency Civil Liberties Committee; and his open letter to *Broadside* magazine, published in the January 14, 1964, issue. The quotes by Dylan have been derived from interviews conducted by Nat Hentoff (*The New Yorker*, October 24, 1964), Jenny De Yong and Peter Roche (*Darts*, May 1965), Studs Terkel ("Wax Museum" radio show, April 26, 1963), Scott Cohen (*Spin*, December 1985) and an unknown interviewer for *Gargoyle* magazine (February 1964).

Joan Baez's quote is derived from Anthony Scaduto's biography (Grosset & Dunlap, 1971). For full details of those prose poems omitted from *Lyrics*, readers should refer to my article "*Lyrics*: A Version Short of the Definitive" in the *All Across the Telegraph* anthology (Sidgwick & Jackson, 1987).

Chapter 7. 1964: On the Heels of Rimbaud

Dylan's quotes in this chapter are from excerpts of a letter he wrote to Ralph J. Gleason, reproduced in *This Week* magazine, November 22, 1964; and from interviews conducted by Klas Burling (Swedish public radio, April 29, 1966), Bill Flannagan (*Written in My Soul*, Contemporary, 1986), Nat Hentoff (*The New Yorker*, October 24, 1964), Pete Oppel (*Dallas Morning News*, November 18–23, 1978) and Jenny De Yong and Peter Roche (*Darts*, May 1965).

Quotes by Anthea Joseph are derived from an interview conducted by myself. Suze Rotolo's comments have been drawn from *Rock Wives* by Victoria Balfour (Beech Tree, 1986). Eric Burdon's comments are derived from an uncredited article reproduced in *Endless Road* 5. Barry Kornfeld's quote comes from Bob Spitz's biography (McGraw-Hill, 1989). John Cooke's is from *Baby, Let Me Follow You Down* by Eric von Schmidt and Jim Rooney (Anchor Books, 1979).

Both Scaduto and Shelton have dealt with the February 1964 trek around America at considerable length, though Shelton's chronology is for once the more accurate, while Bob Spitz deals with Dylan's breakup with Suze Rotolo in graphic detail.

Chapter 8.   1964–65: The Ghost of Electricity

Dylan's quote in this chapter is derived from a transcript of the September 1965 Beverly Hills Hotel press conference.

Joan Baez's comments are derived from her autobiography *And a Voice to Sing With* (Summit Books, 1987).

Daniel Kramer's quotes are from his photo book on Dylan (Castle Books, 1967). Bob Blackamar's comment is from a letter published in the March 1965 issue of *Sing Out!* magazine. Bobby Neuwirth's is from Eric von Schmidt and Jim Rooney's *Baby, Let Me Follow You Down* (Anchor Books, 1979).

Kramer's brief text in his photo book provides useful background for this period of Dylan's growth. For a detailed study of Dylan's performance at the 1964 Newport Folk Festival and the response thereto, readers are referred to Bill Allison's essay on the subject in *Telegraph* 9.

Chapter 9.   1965: Over Your Shoulder

Dylan's quotes in this chapter are derived from interviews conducted by Ron Rosenbaum (*Playboy*, January 1978) and Jenny De Yong and Peter Roche (*Darts*, May 1965).

Quotes by D. A. Pennebaker are derived from an interview by John Bauldie, published in *Telegraph* 26. Comments by Anthea Joseph are from an interview conducted by myself. Eric Clapton's are from an interview by Roger Gibbons, published in *Telegraph* 29. Hughie Flint's are from *Telegraph* 36. Terry Ellis's are from an interview by Adrian Deevoy published in *Telegraph* 31. Dana Gillespie's comments are from her story in *News of the World*, August 31, 1980, and an interview by Spencer Leigh published in the *British Blues Review*, February 1990. John Lennon's comment has been taken from *Playboy: The Interviews*. Marianne Faithfull's are derived from a May 1965 edition of *Record Mirror*.

The most useful sources for Dylan's 1965 English tour are the film *Don't Look Back*, which is commercially available as a home video, and the privately published pamphlet *The Circus Is in Town*, written by Chris Cooper and Keith Marsh.

Chapter 10.   1964–65: A Book of Words

Dylan's quotes in this chapter are derived from four letters written to Tami Dean in 1964 and published in *Telegraph* 16; a letter written to Lawrence Ferlinghetti in April 1964 and published in *Telegraph* 36; and interviews conducted by Jann Wenner (*Rolling Stone*, November 29, 1969); Studs Terkel ("Wax Museum" radio show, April 26, 1963), Max Jones (*Melody Maker*, May 23, 1964), Paul J. Robbins (*Los Angeles Free Press*, September 17 and 24, 1965), Allen Stone (WDTM radio, October 24, 1965) and interviews conducted by Nat Hentoff for *Playboy* magazine (March 1966).

Bob Markel's quotes are derived from Michael Gross's *Bob Dylan: An Illustrated History* (Elm Tree, 1978).

Though there is little of worth that has been written about *Tarantula*, Gabrielle Goodchild's "A Web Untangled" in the *Conclusions on the Wall* anthology (Thin Man, 1980) is perhaps the best of a bad bunch.

Notes

445

Chapter 11. 1965: I Accept Chaos

Dylan's quotes in this chapter are derived from a transcript of his December 3, 1965, San Francisco press conference and from interviews conducted by Martin Bronstein (Canadian Broadcasting Company radio, February 20, 1966), Nat Hentoff (his October 1965 interview transcribed as the *Whaaat!* booklet, and *Playboy*, March 1966), Nora Ephron and Susan Edmiston (*Bob Dylan: A Retrospective*, edited by Craig McGregor, William Morrow, 1972) and Jules Siegel (*Saturday Evening Post*, July 30, 1966).

Quotes by Joe Boyd are derived from an interview by Jonathan Morley, published in *Telegraph* 31. Comments by Al Kooper and Pete Seeger are from interviews conducted by myself; the Al Kooper interview was published in *Telegraph* 37. Michael Bloomfield's comments are primarily drawn from Larry Sloman's *On the Road with Bob Dylan* (Bantam Books, 1978), as well as a 1979 radio interview. Maria Muldaur's comments are from Eric von Schmidt and Jim Rooney's *Baby, Let Me Follow You Down* (Anchor Books, 1979). Charlie McCoy's are from an interview in the October 1966 issue of *Hit Parader*.

The 1965 Newport Folk Festival is one of the most written-about concerts in rock's brief history. Bob Spitz devotes a considerable number of pages to one of the most inaccurate accounts of the events that weekend. Considerably more useful are the sections in Eric von Schmidt and Jim Rooney's *Baby, Let Me Follow You Down* (Anchor Books, 1979) and Al Kooper's *Backstage Passes* (Stein & Day, 1971), which also includes a lot of background information on the *Highway 61 Revisited* sessions. Details about these sessions were also provided by Tony Glover for Glen Dundas's privately published *Tangled Up in Tapes Revisited*.

Chapter 12. 1965–66: Just Like a Freeze Out

Dylan's quotes in this chapter are derived from transcripts of press conferences in Beverly Hills, Los Angeles, and Adelaide, Australia, in September and December 1965 and April 1966; and from interviews conducted by Margaret Steen (*Toronto Weekly*, January 29, 1966), Barbara Kerr (*Toronto Sun*, March 26–29, 1978), Nat Hentoff (his October 1965 interview, transcribed as the *Whaaat!* booklet, and *Playboy*, March 1966) and Ron Rosenbaum (*Playboy*, January 1978).

Quotes by Al Kooper are derived from an interview conducted by myself, published in *Telegraph* 37. Gerard Malanga's comments are from an interview by John Bauldie, published in *Telegraph* 35. Robbie Robertson's comments are derived from an interview in the January 1967 *Hit Parader*, Larry Sloman's interview in *On the Road with Bob Dylan* (Bantam Books, 1978) and Rob Bowman's notes for the Band's *To Kingdom Come* double-CD set. Allen Ginsberg's comments come from Ralph Gleason's essay "Children's Crusade" in the March 1966 edition of *Ramparts* and from an interview in *Melody Maker*, March 18, 1972. Nat Hentoff's come from an interview by Brian Stibal in *Zimmerman Blues #6*. Michael Bloomfield's are from Larry Sloman's *On the Road with Bob Dylan* (Bantam Books, 1978). Phil Ochs's is from his 1968 *Broadside Interview* album. Paul Morrissey's is from Jean Stein's *Edie* (Knopf, 1982). Sally Grossman's is from the July 1987 edition of *Musician* magazine. Levon Helm's is from the August 1984 edition of *Modern Drummer*. Pete Rowan's is from a July 1966 edition of *The Journal of Country Music*. Charlie McCoy's is from *Hit Parader*, October 1966.

Chapter 13. 1966: A Curious Way to Make a Living

Dylan's quotes in this chapter are derived from interviews conducted by John Rockwell (*New York Times*, January 7, 1974), Anthony Scaduto (Grosset & Dunlap, 1971) and Craig McGregor (*Sydney Morning Herald*, March 18, 1978).

Quotes by D. A. Pennebaker are from an interview by Shelly Livson, published in

Telegraph 16. Comments by Anthea Joseph are derived from an interview by myself. Robbie Robertson's comments are from an interview in *New Musical Express*, June 17, 1978, and the notes accompanying the *Biograph* and *To Kingdom Come* sets. The French reporter's are from an article in *Salut les copains* in June 1966. Rosemary Gerrette's are from a similar piece in the *Canberra Times*, May 7, 1966. Adrian Rawlins's comments are drawn from the relevant chapter in John Bauldie's study of the 1966 world tour, *Ghost of Electricity*. Suze Rotolo's comment is from Shelton's biography, *No Direction Home* (William Morrow, 1986). Phil Ochs's comments are from an interview in *Broadside* magazine in October 1965.

The best general source for information on the 1966 tour remains John Bauldie's privately published *Ghost of Electricity*. For a detailed study of the recordings available from this historic tour, readers may wish to consult my article in *Telegraph* 25.

PART TWO.   Learning to Do Consciously . . .

Chapter 14.   1966–67: Evening Things Up

Dylan's quotes in this chapter are derived from interviews conducted by Sam Shepard (*Esquire*, July 1987), Barbara Kerr (*Toronto Sun*, March 26–29, 1978), Kurt Loder (*Rolling Stone*, June 26, 1984), Ben Fong-Torres (*Knockin' on Dylan's Door*, Straight Arrow, 1974), Michael Iachetta (New York *Daily News*, May 8, 1987), Ron Rosenbaum (*Playboy*, January 1978), John Cohen and Happy Traum (*Sing Out!*, October 1968) and Pete Oppel (*Dallas Morning News*, November 18–23, 1978).

Quotes by D. A. Pennebaker are derived from an interview by Shelly Livson, published in *Telegraph* 16. Robbie Robertson's comments are from Larry Sloman's *On the Road with Bob Dylan* (Bantam Books, 1978), a 1970 Dutch radio interview on VPRO and a 1978 Australian radio interview on Radio 2JJ. Richard Manuel's and Rick Danko's comments are drawn from a March 1985 edition of the *Woodstock Times*. Garth Hudson's are derived from the July 1987 *Musician*. Al Aronowitz's are from his article "A Family Album," published in volume 1 of *The Age of Rock* (Vintage Books, 1969). Bob Markel's are from his introduction to the American edition of *Tarantula* (Macmillan, 1970). Allen Ginsberg's are from Barry Miles's biography of Ginsberg (Simon and Schuster, 1989).

The most comprehensive account of Dylan's Woodstock retreat is John Bauldie's in *Telegraph* 20, a highly edited version of which appears in the *All Across the Telegraph* anthology (Sidgwick & Jackson, 1988). For full details of the machinations surrounding Dylan's signing with MGM and his return to CBS, readers should seek out Clive Davis's autobiography, *Clive: Inside the Record Business* (William Morrow, 1974).

Chapter 15.   1968: Drifters, Immigrants, Messengers and Saints

Dylan's quotes in this chapter are derived from Barry Miles's biography of Allen Ginsberg (Simon and Schuster, 1989) and from interviews conducted by Marc Rowland (U.S. radio, September 23, 1978), Jann Wenner (*Rolling Stone*, November 29, 1969), Cameron Crowe (*Biograph*), John Cohen and Happy Traum (*Sing Out!*, October 1968), Jonathan Cott (*Rolling Stone*, November 16, 1978) and Matt Damsker (*Circus Weekly*, December 19, 1978).

Quotes by Elliott Landy are from an interview conducted by Paul Williams, published in *Telegraph* 30. Happy Traum's comments come from an interview by Jacques Van Son, published in *Changin'* 10. Robbie Robertson's are from a 1978 Australian radio interview on Radio 2JJ. Beattie Zimmerman's is from Toby Thompson's *Positively Main Street* (Coward-McCann, 1971). Allen Ginsberg's is from *Rolling Stone*, January 15, 1976. Bob Markel's comment is from Michael Gross's *Bob Dylan: An Illustrated History* (Elm Tree, 1978). George Harrison's is from his book of songs and anecdotes, *I Me Mine* (Simon and Schuster,

1981). Clive Davis's is from his autobiography, *Clive: Inside the Record Business* (William Morrow, 1974).

Bert Cartwright's book *The Bible in the Lyrics of Bob Dylan*, published in 1985 as part of the Wanted Man Study Series, remains an invaluable guide to Dylan's increasing use of biblical imagery in his work.

Chapter 16. 1969: What's the Matter with Me?

Dylan's quotes in this chapter are derived from interviews conducted by Jann Wenner (*Rolling Stone*, November 29, 1969), Hubert Saal (*Newsweek*, April 4, 1969), Jonathan Cott (*Rolling Stone*, November 16, 1978) and Kurt Loder (*Rolling Stone*, June 26, 1984).

Quotes by Ray Foulk are derived from an interview by Chris Hockenhull, published in *4th Time Around #3*. Norman Blake's comment comes from an interview by Pete Tesoro in *Look Back #12*. David Amram's is from *Rolling Stone* magazine. Levon Helm's is from a September 1969 BBC radio interview. Johnny Cash's is from the May 1988 edition of *Musician* magazine. Bob Johnston's comment is from Spitz's biography (McGraw-Hill, 1989). Clive Davis's is from his autobiography, *Clive: Inside the Record Business* (William Morrow, 1974).

The third issue of the Dylan fanzine *4th Time Around* was entirely devoted to the Isle of Wight Festival and covers the background to the festival in considerable detail.

Chapter 17. 1970: A Restless, Hungry Feeling

Dylan's quotes in this chapter are derived from a transcript of the Travemunde press conference on February 13, 1981, and interviews conducted by Kurt Loder (*Rolling Stone*, June 26, 1984), Larry Sloman (*On the Road with Bob Dylan*, Bantam Books, 1978) and an unknown interviewer (*El Diario Vasco*, June 18, 1989).

Quotes by Al Kooper are from an interview conducted by myself, published in *Telegraph* 37. Joel Bernstein's comments are from an interview by John Bauldie, published in *Telegraph* 35. Ron Cornelius's are from a 1971 edition of *Melody Maker*. Clive Davis's are from his autobiography, *Clive: Inside the Record Business* (William Morrow, 1974). Charlie McCoy's comment is from Spitz's biography (McGraw-Hill, 1989).

Chapter 18. 1971–72: Smooth Like a Rhapsody

Dylan's quotes in this chapter are derived from interviews conducted by Neil Hickey (*TV Guide*, September 11, 1976), Scott Cohen (*Spin*, December 1985) and Pete Oppel (*Dallas Morning News*, November 18–23, 1978).

Quotes by Happy Traum are derived from an interview by Jacques Van Son (*Changin'* 10) and from *Melody Maker*, July 29, 1972. Allen Ginsberg's comments are from his introduction to his *First Blues* (Full Court Press, 1975) and from an interview in *Melody Maker*, March 18, 1972. Harold Leventhal's comment is from Miles's *Bob Dylan* (Big O, 1978). Eve Brandstein's is from Michael Gross's *Bob Dylan: An Illustrated History* (Elm Tree, 1978). A. J. Weberman's is from the Alex Bennet radio show, January 28, 1974. George Harrison's is from a BBC Radio One interview in 1976. Phil Spector's is from *Rolling Stone*, March 2, 1972. John Prine's is from the *Illinois Entertainer*, November 1981. Bob Gottlieb's is from *Crawdaddy*, September 1973.

Chapter 19. 1972–73: Alias What?

Dylan's quotes in this chapter are derived from interviews conducted by Chet Flippo (*Rolling Stone*, March 15, 1973), Cameron Crowe (*Biograph*), Ben Fong-Torres (*Knockin' on Dylan's Door*, Straight Arrow, 1974), Donald Chase (San Francisco *Chronicle*, November 23,

1986), an unknown interviewer (*Photoplay*, September 1978) and Larry Sloman (*On the Road with Bob Dylan*, Bantam Books, 1978).

Quotes by Kris Kristofferson are derived from Bill Flannagan's *Written in My Soul* (Contemporary, 1986); the March 15, 1973, and February 23, 1978, editions of *Rolling Stone*; and *Peckinpah: A Portrait in Montage* by Garner Simmons (University of Texas Press, 1982). James Coburn's comments come from an interview on a Los Angeles cable TV station in 1988 and the London *Evening Standard*, August 31, 1989. Rudy Wurlitzer's comments are from *Melody Maker*, February 3, 1978, and *Rolling Stone*, March 15, 1973. Gordon Dawson's is from the London *Evening Standard*, August 31, 1989. Clive Davis's is from his autobiography, *Clive: Inside the Record Business* (William Morrow, 1974).

Chapter 20.   1973–74: Into the Flood

Dylan's quotes in this chapter are derived from interviews conducted by Ben Fong-Torres (*Knockin' on Dylan's Door*, Straight Arrow, 1974), Dan Meer ("Close Up" radio show, October 30, 1989), Robert Hilburn (*Los Angeles Times*, November 23, 1980) and Barbara Kerr (*Toronto Sun*, March 26–29, 1978).

Quotes by Robbie Robertson are derived from *Knockin' on Dylan's Door*, the March 1976 issue of *Crawdaddy* and Larry Sloman's *On the Road with Bob Dylan* (Bantam Books, 1978). Rob Fraboni's comments come from *Recording Engineer–Producer*, March/April 1974. Barry Goldberg's is from *Crawdaddy*, July 1974. Roger McGuinn's is from *On the Road with Bob Dylan*.

Rolling Stone's Knockin' on Dylan's Door collects together all the magazine's coverage of the 1974 tour along with other press reports and is well worth seeking out. Stephen Pickering's *Approximately* (McKay, 1975) also covers the entire tour and is beautifully illustrated, though the text is largely unreadable.

Chapter 21.   1974–75: From Renaissance to Reformation

Dylan's quotes in this chapter are derived from interviews conducted by Pete Oppel (*Dallas Morning News*, November 18–23, 1978), Karen Hughes (*Rock Express* 1), Jonathan Cott (*Rolling Stone*, January 26, 1978, and November 16, 1978), Bill Flannagan (*Written in My Soul*, Contemporary, 1986), Cameron Crowe (*Biograph*) and Larry Sloman (*On the Road with Bob Dylan*, Bantam Books, 1978).

Quotes by John Hammond, Eric Weissberg and Charlie Brown are derived from *Rolling Stone's* feature on the recording of *Blood on the Tracks* in its November 21, 1974, edition. The comment by the student of Norman Raeben is from a WBAI radio special on Dylan on May 23, 1986. Tim Drummond's is from *Rolling Stone*, August 29, 1974. Michael Bloomfield's is from Larry Sloman's *On the Road with Bob Dylan*. Joel Bernstein's is from an interview by John Bauldie in *Telegraph* 35. Robbie Robertson's is from *Crawdaddy*, March 1976. David Oppenheim's is from an English translation of his "I Could Have Kidnapped Bob Dylan" article, published in *4th Time Around* 1.

As is presumably evident, I have relied heavily on Bert Cartwright's ground-breaking articles in *Telegraph* 23 and 26, in which he dealt at length with Dylan's time in Norman Raeben's class and its effect upon him.

Chapter 22.   1975: From the Bottom Line to the Bitter End

Dylan's quotes in this chapter are derived from Barry Miles's biography of Allen Ginsberg (Simon and Schuster, 1989) and from interviews conducted by Larry Sloman (*On the Road with Bob Dylan*, Bantam Books, 1978), Dave Herman (transcribed from the *London Interview* promotional album) and Lynne Allen (*Trouser Press*, June 1979).

Quotes by Scarlet Rivera, Howie Wyeth and Rob Stoner are derived from interviews by myself, save for one quote by Stoner, which comes from Larry Sloman's *On the Road with Bob Dylan*. Comments by Jacques Levy and Robbie Robertson are also derived from *On the Road with Bob Dylan*. Patti Smith's comments are from an interview by Miles, published in *Telegraph* 32. Quotes from Rubin Carter and Lou Kemp come from the 1976 "Rock Around the World" radio show. Comments by Neil Hubbard and Mel Collins are from a 1975 issue of *Liquorice* magazine. Roger McGuinn's comment is from a 1976 TV interview. Eric Clapton's is from *Rolling Stone*, November 20, 1975. Emmylou Harris's comments have been taken from a composite feature on the *Desire* sessions in *Occasionally* 5. The CBS rep's quote comes from a feature in *Rolling Stone*, August 28, 1975. Larry Sloman's is from an interview in *4th Time Around* 2.

Chapter 23. 1975: You Come On to Me Like Rolling Thunder

Dylan's quotes in this chapter are derived from interviews conducted by an unknown interviewer (*Photoplay*, May 1978), Ron Rosenbaum (*Playboy*, January 1978) and Larry Sloman (*On the Road with Bob Dylan*, Bantam Books, 1978).

Quotes by Mel Howard and Sara Dylan are derived from Larry Sloman's *On the Road with Bob Dylan*. Comments by Rob Stoner and Scarlet Rivera are from interviews conducted by myself. Joan Baez's comments are from her autobiography *And a Voice to Sing With* (Summit Books, 1987). Jacques Levy's are from *Rolling Stone*, April 7, 1977. Mick Ronson's are from *New Musical Express*, December 15, 1979. The uncredited tour musician's observation comes from a feature in *Rolling Stone*, January 15, 1976.

As a chronicle of the 1975 Rolling Thunder Revue, Larry Sloman's *On the Road with Bob Dylan* cannot be commended highly enough, though copies are extremely hard to locate. Also useful is Sam Shepard's *Rolling Thunder Logbook* (Penguin, 1978).

Chapter 24. 1976: Hard Reign or Last Waltz?

Quotes by Rob Stoner, Howie Wyeth and Scarlet Rivera are from interviews conducted by myself. Quotes by Ron Wood and Joel Bernstein are from interviews conducted by John Bauldie, published in *Telegraph* 33 and 35 respectively. Joan Baez's comments are from her autobiography *And a Voice to Sing With* (Summit Books, 1987).

Chapter 25. 1977: Everything Went from Bad to Worse

Dylan's quotes in this chapter are derived from interviews by Robert Shelton (*Melody Maker*, June 24, 1978), Barbara Kerr (*Toronto Sun*, March 26–29, 1978), Mary Campbell (*Houston Post*, February 12, 1978), John Austin (source unknown), interviewer unknown (*Photoplay*, September 1978), John Rockwell (*New York Times*, January 8, 1978) and Allen Ginsberg (*Telegraph* 33).

Quotes by Sara Dylan are taken from a press release based on her declaration to the court in March 1977. Quotes by Farida McFree, Rob Stoner and Howie Wyeth are from interviews conducted by myself. Howard Alk's quote is from an interview in *Take One* magazine in March 1978. Allen Ginsberg's comments are derived from a transcript by John Hinchey of a discussion with students at Swarthmore College, Swarthmore, Pennsylvania, in November 1978. Joel Bernstein's are from an interview by John Bauldie published in *Telegraph* 35.

Putting together the story of the divorce and custody battle in this chapter has been possible thanks to the detailed coverage provided in the *Los Angeles Times*.

Chapter 26. 1978: Someone's Got It In for Me

Dylan's quotes in this chapter are derived from a concert rap given at a show in Nashville on December 2, 1978, and from interviews conducted by Robert Hilburn (*Los Angeles Times*, May 28, 1978, and November 12, 1978), Kurt Loder (*Rolling Stone*, June 26, 1984),

Jonathan Cott (*Rolling Stone*, November 16, 1978), John Mankiewicz (*Sound*, November 12, 1978) and Marc Rowland (U.S. radio, September 23, 1978).

Quotes by Rob Stoner and Farida McFree are derived from interviews by myself. Comments by Helena Springs are from an interview by Chris Cooper, published in *Endless Road* 7.

PART THREE.   Busy Being Born Again . . .

Chapter 27.   1978–79: Pulling Back on the Reins

Dylan's quotes in this chapter are derived from raps given in concerts at the Golden Hall, San Diego, November 27, 1979, and the Convention Center, Albuquerque, December 5, 1979; a transcript of the Travemunde press conference on July 13, 1981; and interviews conducted by Robert Hilburn (*Los Angeles Times*, November 23, 1980, and October 30, 1983), Dave Herman (transcribed from the *London Interview* promotional album), Karen Hughes (*Dominion*, August 2, 1980), Neil Spencer (*New Musical Express*, August 15, 1981) and Scott Cohen (*Spin*, December 1985).

Quotes by Ken Gulliksen are derived from an interview in the November 1980 issue of *Buzz*. Howie Wyeth's comments are from an interview by myself. Helena Springs's are from an interview by Chris Cooper published in *Endless Road* 7. Steven Soles's are from *New Musical Express*, September 8, 1979. Also quoted is an excerpt from David Seay and Mary Neely's *Stairway to Heaven* (Ballantine Books, 1986).

Worthy of further reading are Bert Cartwright's commendable *The Bible in the Lyrics of Bob Dylan* in the Wanted Man Study Series (1985), Hal Lindsey and C. C. Carlson's *The Late Great Planet Earth* (Zondervan, 1970) and Joseph Campbell's "Bob Dylan and the Pastoral Apocalypse" in *Journal of Popular Culture*, 1975, from which I have purloined much of my terminology. Also essential to an understanding of this crucial period is Paul Williams's excellent *What Happened?* (and/Entwistle Books, 1980).

Chapter 28.   1979: On the Holy Slow Train

Dylan's quotes in this chapter are derived from a transcript of the Travemunde press conference, July 13, 1981, and from interviews conducted by Bono (*Hot Press*, August 24, 1984) and Bruce Heiman (KMGX radio, December 7, 1979).

Quotes by Dave Kelly are derived from an interview by Chris Cooper published in *Freewheelin'* magazine. Jerry Wexler's comments are from *Rolling Stone*, November 27, 1980. Mark Knopfler's comments have been drawn from the "What About a Farfisa?" article in the Lawlans' privately published *Steppin' Out* pamphlet.

Chapter 29.   1979–80: Middle of the Road, East Coast Bondage

Dylan's quotes in this chapter are derived from raps given in concerts at the Stanley Theater, Pittsburgh, May 15, 1980; the Civic Auditorium, Santa Monica, November 19, 1979; the Warfield Theater, San Francisco, November 16, 1979; the Gammage Theater, Tempe, November 25 and 26, 1979; the Massey Hall, Toronto, April 20, 1980; the Orpheum Theater, Omaha, January 25, 1980; and the Bushnell Memorial Center, Hartford, on May 7 and 8, 1980—as well as interviews conducted by Paul Vincent (*Endless Road* 2), Martha Quinn (MTV, July 7, 1984), Scott Cohen (*Spin*, December 1985), Robert Hilburn (*Los Angeles Times*, November 23, 1980), Cameron Crowe (*Biograph*), Bruce Heiman (KMGX, December 7, 1979), Dave Herman (transcript from the *London Interview* promotional album) and Karen Hughes (*Dominion*, August 2, 1980).

Quotes by Helena Springs and Dave Kelly are from interviews conducted by Chris Cooper, published in *Endless Road* and *Freewheelin'* respectively. Jerry Wexler's comments are from *Rolling Stone*, November 27, 1980.

The bulk of this chapter has been condensed from my considerably more detailed survey of Dylan's gospel tour, published as the three-part "Saved!" feature in *Telegraph* 28–30. All the transcribed raps from those articles have also been published in the U.S. in the Handyman Books pocket-book series.

Chapter 30. 1980–82: In the Summertime

Dylan's quotes in this chapter are derived from a rap given in concert at the Warfield Theater, San Francisco, on November 12, 1980, and from interviews conducted by Cameron Crowe (*Biograph*), Kurt Loder (*Rolling Stone*, June 26, 1984), Neil Spencer (*New Musical Express*, August 15, 1981), Paul Vincent (*Endless Road* 2), and Martin Keller (*New Musical Express*, August 6, 1983).

Quotes by Ron Wood are derived from an interview by John Bauldie, published in *Telegraph* 33. Al Kooper's comments are from an interview conducted by myself, published in *Telegraph* 37. Benmont Tench's comments are from the *Chicago Sun-Times*, January 26, 1986. Paul Esmond's and Rabbi Kasriel Kastel's comments are from *Christianity Today* in 1983.

Readers are again referred to Bert Cartwright's *The Bible in the Lyrics of Bob Dylan* (Wanted Man Study Series, 1985). Paul Williams's *What Happened? One Year Later* pamphlet (Hobo Press, 1981) provides a thorough overview of the 1980 Warfield engagement.

Chapter 31. 1983: Songs of Experience

Dylan's quotes in this chapter are derived from interviews conducted by Martin Keller (*New Musical Express*, August 6, 1983), Robert Hilburn (*Los Angeles Times*, October 30, 1983), and Martha Quinn (MTV, July 7, 1984).

Quotes by Mark Knopfler and Alan Clark are drawn from the article "What About a Farfisa?" in the Lawlans' privately published *Steppin' Out* pamphlet. Larry Sloman's comments are from an interview in *4th Time Around* 2 and from a 1984 edition of *Music Video*. Mark Robinson's comments are from an article on Dylan's early videos in *Telegraph* 16. Charlie Sexton's are derived from the newsletter *The Wicked Messenger*. Charlie Quintana's are from an interview by John Bauldie in *Telegraph* 37.

Chapter 32. 1984: Still Life and Real Live

Dylan's quotes in this chapter are derived from interviews conducted by Martha Quinn (MTV, July 7, 1984), Bill Flannagan (*Written in My Soul*, Contemporary, 1986), and Mick Brown (London *Sunday Times*, July 1, 1984).

Quotes by Charlie Quintana are taken from an interview by John Bauldie published in *Telegraph* 37. Comments by Greg Sutton are from an interview by Thomas Lasarzik published in *Telegraph* 27. Colin Allen's are from an interview by Jorgen Lindstrom published in *Telegraph* 28.

Chapter 33. 1984–85: Burlesques and Benefits

Dylan's quotes in this chapter are derived from a transcript of his Sydney press conference, February 10, 1986, and interviews conducted by Bert Kleinman and Artie Mogull (Westwood One radio broadcast, November 25, 1984), Bill Flannagan (*Written in My Soul*, Contemporary, 1986), Denise Worrell (*Icons*, Atlantic Monthly Press, 1989), Toby Creswell (*Australian Rolling Stone*, January 16, 1986), Scott Cohen (*Interview*, February 1986), Mikal Gilmore (*Los Angeles Herald Examiner*, October 13, 1985), Bob Brown, ("20/20" TV show, October 20, 1985) and Robert Hilburn (*Los Angeles Times*, November 17, 1985).

Quotes by Markus Innocenti and Eddie Arno, and by Ira Ingber, are from interviews conducted by myself, published in *Telegraph* 34 and 27 respectively. Comments by Ron Wood are from an interview by John Bauldie published in *Telegraph* 33. Maria McKee's are from an interview by Thomas Lasarzik published in *Telegraph* 27. Sam Shepard's are from a December 1985 issue of *Rolling Stone*.

Chapter 34. 1985–86: Junco and His Partners in Crime

Dylan's quotes in this chapter are derived from raps given in concert at the Gymnasium, Nagoya, Japan, March 8, 1986, and from an interview conducted by Mikal Gilmore (*Los Angeles Herald-Examiner*, October 13, 1985).

Quotes by Ira Ingber, Dave Garfield and Al Kooper are from interviews conducted by myself, published in *Telegraph* 27 and 37. Charlie Quintana's comments are from an interview by John Bauldie in *Telegraph* 37. Mikal Gilmore's comments are from his feature in *Rolling Stone*, July 17 and 31, 1986. Comments by Mike Campbell and Stan Lynch are taken from *Telegraph* 25, with additional comments by Tom Petty from a 1988 edition of *The Leeds*.

Chapter 35. 1986–87: Down Among the Deadheads

Dylan's quotes in this chapter are derived from interviews conducted by Christopher Sykes (*Telegraph* 30 and a transcript of *Getting to Dylan*, September 18, 1987), Cameron Crowe (*Biograph*), Mikal Gilmore (*Los Angeles Herald-Examiner*, October 13, 1985) and Kathryn Baker (*Stars and Stripes*, September 7, 1988).

Quotes by Iain Smith and Richard Marquand are from interviews conducted by John Bauldie and published in *Telegraph* 28. Bono's comments are from *New Musical Express*, December 19 and 26, 1987. Jerry Garcia's comments are from the "Close Up" radio show, October 30, 1989, and *Melody Maker*, May 13, 1989. Bob Weir's are from the "Close Up" radio show, October 30, 1989. Mickey Hart's are from *Melody Maker*, May 13, 1989.

Chapter 36. 1987–88: Temples in Flames, Wilburys on the Run

Dylan's quotes in this chapter are derived from interviews conducted by Dan Meer ("Close Up" radio show, October 30, 1989) and Edna Gundersen (*USA Today*, September 21, 1989).

Bruce Springsteen's quote is a partial transcription of the speech he gave at the Rock and Roll Hall of Fame induction ceremony on January 20, 1988. Daniel Lanois's quotes are derived from *New Musical Express*, October 7, 1989; the "Close Up" radio show, October 30, 1989; *Request*, October 1989; the "Stereo Sequence" radio show, September 1989; and an interview with Mark Cooper (published in *Telegraph* 34).

Two publications dealt exclusively with the 1987 European tour, one a photo-documentary by Georg Stein simply entitled *Temples in Flames* and the other a pamphlet by John Lindley on the seven English shows, entitled *Seven Days*, which sought to provide an antidote to the uncomprehending media reviews.

Chapter 37. 1989–90: Lord Have Mercy!

Dylan's comment in this chapter is derived from an interview with Edna Gundersen (*USA Today*, September 14, 1990).

Don Was's quotes are from an interview by Reid Kopel and Al Kooper's are from an interview by myself, both first published in *Telegraph* 37. Allen Ginsberg's comments are from an interview by Wes Stace published in *Telegraph* 20.

Chapter 38. 1988–90: The Never-Ending Tour

Dylan's quotes in this chapter are derived from interviews by Neil Spencer (*New Musical Express*, August 15, 1981), Dan Meer ("Close Up" radio show, October 30, 1989), Adrian Deevoy (*Q*, December 1989) and Robert Hilburn (*Los Angeles Times*, September 7, 1987).

Quotes by Kenny Aaronson are derived from an interview by myself published in *Telegraph* 36. Christopher Parker's comments are taken from *Telegraph* 33.

Chapter 39. 1990: The Finishing End?

Dylan's quotes in this chapter are derived from interviews by Edna Gundersen (*USA Today*, September 21, 1989, and September 14, 1990).

The quote from Suze Rotolo derives from *No Direction Home* by Robert Shelton (William Morrow, 1986). The quote from Slash comes from an article in *Vox* 1. The Sally Kirkland quote is from the London *Daily Mail*, November 13, 1989. David Braun's declaration is drawn from a deposition to the courts, dated March 1, 1977.

Dramatis Personae

This dramatis personae provides a brief checklist of the individuals who are quoted in the main text of *Behind the Shades*, and a short summary of their involvement with Dylan. The aim is to describe their credentials as authorities on aspects of Dylan's career. It is not to provide résumés of the individuals, however distinguished they may be, as this lies outside the scope of this book.

Kenny Aaronson: Bassist on the entire 1988 tour and six of the first seven 1989 shows, after which he was replaced by Tony Garnier.

Harvey Abrams: Fellow student at the University of Minneapolis in 1960, as well as regular drinking companion and fellow folksinger.

Howard Alk: Co-owner of a Chicago club, the Bear; cameraman on both the 1965 and 1966 English tours; and coeditor (with Dylan) of "Eat the Document" and *Renaldo and Clara*. Alk also filmed several concerts on the 1981 tour. He died in January 1982.

Colin Allen: Drummer on the 1984 European tour.

David Amram: French horn player and ethnomusicologist who became friendly with Dylan while staying on Fire Island in the summer of 1969.

Eddie Arno: Codirector (with Markus Innocenti) of the promo videos for "When the Night Comes Falling from the Sky" and "Emotionally Yours."

Al Aronowitz: New York journalist and supporter of Dylan; he introduced him to the Beatles in 1964, coauthored an article with him in 1965 and remained in contact throughout Dylan's Woodstock period.

Joan Baez: The Queen of Folk in the early sixties, she began a sporadic affair with Dylan in spring 1963, which lasted until his May 1965 English tour. They were reunited on the 1975–76 Rolling Thunder Revue and sang together subsequently in 1982 and 1984.

Ellen Baker: A girlfriend in Minneapolis in 1960 whose father's impressive folk-music collection provided Dylan with a regular source of reference.

Bonnie Beecher: Purportedly the "real" Girl from the North Country, she first met Dylan in 1959 and they remained close throughout his days in Minneapolis. After he left for New York in December 1960 they remained in regular touch throughout Dylan's rise to fame.

Joel Bernstein: Guitar technician on the 1976 Rolling Thunder tour and during the rehearsals for the 1978 tour.

Bob Blackamar: Interviewed Dylan before a show in San Diego in December 1964.

Norman Blake: Guitarist on the sessions for *Nashville Skyline* and the Nashville sessions for *Self Portrait*.

Michael Bloomfield: First met Dylan in Chicago in April 1963. The lead guitarist on the *Highway 61 Revisited* album and at the 1965 Newport Folk Festival appearance, he subsequently jammed with Dylan prior to the *Blood on the Tracks* sessions and made a guest appearance at a November 1980 show, his final live performance. He died in February 1981.

Bono: Lead singer of the Irish stadium-rock combo U2, he interviewed Dylan in 1984 and they subsequently collaborated on a couple of songs, one of which appeared on U2's *Rattle and Hum* collection.

Joe Boyd: One of the behind-the-scene principals responsible for organizing the 1965 Newport Folk Festival; later established himself as a highly acclaimed record producer.

Eve Brandstein: Member of the Kibbutz Givat Haim in May 1971, when Dylan was looking into the possibility of joining the kibbutz with his family.

David Braun: Dylan's lawyer.

Marshall Brickman: Was at school in Madison, Wisconsin, rooming with Eric Weissberg, when Dylan passed through on his way to New York in January 1961.

Charlie Brown: Member of Eric Weissberg's Deliverance, he played on the first couple of sessions for *Blood on the Tracks* in New York.

Eric Burdon: Lead singer of the Animals, the English rhythm and blues outfit responsible for "rocking up" "House of the Rising Sun." He met Dylan in the winter of 1965 in New York.

Mike Campbell: Lead guitarist of Tom Petty and the Heartbreakers. As well as touring with Dylan through 1986–87, he recorded with him on *Empire Burlesque* and *Knocked Out Loaded*.

Rubin "Hurricane" Carter: Unjustly imprisoned black middleweight boxer whose cause Dylan championed in his 1975 single "Hurricane"; he was not set free until 1986.

Martin Carthy: Respected English folksinger who befriended Dylan on his first visit to London in December 1962.

Johnny Cash: Important champion of Dylan's cause during his early days at CBS, Cash performed one duet with Dylan on his *Nashville Skyline* album, part of an entire unreleased album of Dylan/Cash duets. Dylan subsequently guested on Cash's TV show in May 1969.

Liam Clancy: Member of the esteemed Clancy Brothers, who were one of the most popular bands on the early-sixties Greenwich Village scene.

Eric Clapton: Originally recorded with Dylan at an unproductive session in London in May 1965. He subsequently worked in the studio with him in 1975 (for Dylan's album *Desire*), 1976 (for his own album *No Reason to Cry*) and 1986 (for the film *Hearts of Fire*), and guested at Dylan shows in 1978 and 1984.

Alan Clark: Dire Straits keyboardist who worked on the *Infidels* album and one song on *Empire Burlesque*.

James Coburn: Actor who portrayed Pat Garrett in Sam Peckinpah's *Pat Garrett & Billy the Kid*.

Mel Collins: Saxophonist for the British pub-rock combo Kokomo who played on the first couple of sessions for the *Desire* album.

John Cooke: Photo-chronicler of the early-sixties Boston folk scene.

Ron Cornelius: Guitarist at the *New Morning* sessions.

Rick Danko: Bass player with the Hawks, aka the Band, who recorded with Dylan in December 1965, January 1966, 1967 and November 1973 and toured with him in 1965–66 and 1974. He also played one-off concerts with Dylan in 1968, 1969 (twice), 1972 and 1976 (all with the Band) and in 1983 (with Levon Helm).

Paul Davies: A Minneapolis student during Dylan's time there.

Clive Davis: President of the CBS record division throughout the late sixties and early seventies; until he was fired in May 1973, he was Dylan's most regular contact with Columbia.

Gordon Dawson: Associate producer of *Pat Garrett & Billy the Kid.*

Tim Drummond: Bassist in Dylan's touring band from 1979 through 1981, he also played with him at the SNACK benefit in 1975 and on the sessions for *Saved* and *Shot of Love.*

Sara Dylan: Née Shirley Noznisky, she first met Dylan through their mutual friend Sally Grossman in 1964. They were married in November 1965 and divorced in 1977, though they have remained in regular contact since.

Terry Ellis: The "science student" who is given such a hard time in *Don't Look Back,* he went on to cofound Chrysalis Records.

Paul Esmond: One of the pastors of the Vineyard Fellowship who attended Dylan at the time of his conversion to the born-again creed in 1979. They remained in contact into the early eighties.

Marianne Faithfull: English *chanteuse* who frequented Dylan's Savoy Hotel suite during his May 1965 English tour.

Jerry Fielding: Brought in to supervise the scoring of the music for *Pat Garrett & Billy the Kid.*

Hughie Flint: The drummer for John Mayall's Bluesbreakers in 1965, when he played at a recording session with Dylan. He subsequently cofounded McGuinness-Flint, who recorded an entire album of (then) unreleased Bob Dylan songs, *Lo & Behold.*

Ray Foulk: Co-organizer of the 1969 Isle of Wight Festival.

Rob Fraboni: Recording engineer on the *Planet Waves* sessions, he also cosupervised the mixing of the *Before the Flood* live album.

Steve Friedman: Fellow camper of Camp Herzl and a teenage traveling companion of Robert Zimmerman's.

Jerry Garcia: Guitarist in the Grateful Dead, he played with Dylan in 1980, 1986, 1987 and 1989.

Dave Garfield: Assistant engineer on the *Knocked Out Loaded* sessions.

Rosemary Gerrette: Australian actress-*cum*-journalist who spent some time with Dylan at the end of his April 1966 Australian tour.

Dana Gillespie: English model/singer whom Dylan befriended on his 1965 English tour.

Mikal Gilmore: Los Angeles journalist who interviewed Dylan in the fall of 1985 and subsequently attended many of the sessions for the *Knocked Out Loaded* album.

Allen Ginsberg: Perhaps the most noted American poet of the beat generation, he first met Dylan in December 1963 and they have remained friends ever since; they recorded together in 1971 and 1982. He was also a member of the 1975–76 Rolling Thunder Revue.

Dave "Tony" Glover: Respected folk musician on the 1960 Minneapolis scene who was an important influence on Dylan in his later months there. They remained in regular contact through Dylan's days in Greenwich Village, and he conducted an unpublished interview in 1971.

J. R. Goddard: Writer for *The Village Voice* who reviewed Dylan's first album and with whom Dylan concocted a fake press conference in 1965.

Barry Goldberg: As a friend of Michael Bloomfield, he was recruited to play piano at the notorious 1965 Newport Folk Festival performance. Dylan subsequently coproduced his first solo album in 1973.

Robert Gottlieb: Chief editor at Alfred Knopf, responsible for overseeing publication of Dylan's collection, *Writings and Drawings*.

Ron Gould: English folksinger who was a habitué of the London folk scene during Dylan's time there in December 1962 and January 1963.

Sally Grossman: Wife of Albert Grossman and long-standing friend of Sara Dylan. She is the lady languorously stretched out on the cover of *Bringing It All Back Home*.

Ken Gulliksen: A pastor at the Vineyard Fellowship whose born-again creed was introduced to Dylan in 1979.

George Haben: Classmate of the young Robert Zimmerman at Hibbing High School.

John Hammond: Legendary producer who signed Dylan to CBS and produced his first two albums before being ousted at Albert Grossman's behest. He died in July 1987.

Emmylou Harris: After her sterling work with Gram Parsons, she was recruited to sing harmony with Dylan on the *Desire* album, which proved a fortuitous break in her own career.

George Harrison: The Beatle who maintained the most regular and lasting contact with Dylan; they worked together in 1970 and cofounded the Traveling Wilburys in 1988.

Mickey Hart: Drummer/percussionist in the Grateful Dead.

Levon Helm: Member of Dylan's first "electric" band, with whom he played at Forest Hills and Hollywood Bowl; then, reunited with the Hawks, later known as the Band, he toured with Dylan through November 1965. Helm then left the Hawks, only rejoining them after the 1967 *Basement Tapes* sessions. Helm subsequently gigged with Dylan in 1968, 1969, 1972, 1974 and 1983 and worked on the 1973 *Planet Waves* sessions.

Echo Helstrom: Robert Zimmerman's girlfriend from the fall of 1957 to the fall of 1958, she subsequently suggested she was the subject of "Girl from the North Country."

Nat Hentoff: Jazz and folk critic who was an important champion of Dylan's music in the early sixties and who conducted several important interviews with him between 1963 and 1966, including the *Playboy* interview.

Carolyn Hester: Richard Fariña's first wife, she befriended Dylan in August 1961 and invited him to play on her debut album for CBS, the occasion of his first meeting with John Hammond.

Leroy Hoikkala: Drummer in Robert Zimmerman's Hibbing combo, the Golden Chords.

Mel Howard: Associate producer of *Renaldo and Clara.*

Neil Hubbard: Guitarist for the British pub-rock combo Kokomo who played on the first couple of sessions for the *Desire* album.

Garth Hudson: Organist in the Hawks, aka the Band, with whom Dylan toured in 1965–66 and 1974, he also performed with them in 1968, 1969, 1972 and 1976, and recorded *The Basement Tapes* and *Planet Waves* with them in 1967 and 1973, respectively.

Ira Ingber: Guitarist on several Los Angeles sessions for both *Empire Burlesque* and *Knocked Out Loaded.*

Markus Innocenti: Codirector with Eddie Arno of the promotional videos for "When the Night Comes Falling" and "Emotionally Yours."

Bob Johnston: Producer of *Highway 61 Revisited, Blonde on Blonde, John Wesley Harding, Nashville Skyline* and *Self Portrait* and coproducer of *New Morning.*

Anthea Joseph: As coorganizer of London's Troubadour folk club, she befriended Dylan on his first visit in December 1962 and they have regularly renewed their friendship on his subsequent visits to the U.K.

Rabbi Kasriel Kastel: A member of the Lubavitchers, a Hasidic sect, and organizer of the Brooklyn Lubavitch center where Dylan apparently "studied" in 1983.

Dave Kelly: Dylan's personal assistant from the summer of 1979 through the winter of 1980, as well as a noted blues musician himself.

Lou Kemp: Fellow camper of Camp Herzl between 1956 and 1958; subsequently organized the two Rolling Thunder tours of 1975 and 1976.

Sally Kirkland: American actress first involved with Dylan in 1976; she has renewed her association in the last couple of years.

Mark Knopfler: Guitarist on the 1979 *Slow Train Coming* sessions and guitarist/coproducer on the 1983 *Infidels* album. He made a guest appearance at a Dylan show in Sydney in 1986.

Al Kooper: Organist/guitarist who worked on *Highway 61 Revisited, Blonde on Blonde, New Morning, Empire Burlesque, Knocked Out Loaded* and *Under the Red Sky.* He also played with Dylan at Newport, Forest Hills and the Hollywood Bowl in 1965 and toured with him in 1981.

Barry Kornfeld: Folksinger on the early-sixties Greenwich Village scene.

Daniel Kramer: Could be considered Dylan's "official" photographer between the fall of 1964 and August 1965. He attended the *Bringing It All Back Home* sessions and took the photos used on the album jacket. He subsequently published a book of his photos of Dylan.

Arthur Kretchmer: A member of the Greenwich Village scene and a magazine editor.

Kris Kristofferson: Actor/singer-songwriter who played the role of Billy the Kid in Sam Peckinpah's *Pat Garrett & Billy the Kid.*

Kevin Krown: An itinerant folksinger in Denver in the summer of 1960, when he first met Dylan. He provided Dylan with accommodation in Chicago in December of that year, when Dylan was on his way to New York.

Elliott Landy: Woodstock resident and noted photographer who photographed Dylan on several occasions during his Woodstock residency in the late sixties, including the cover for *Nashville Skyline.*

Daniel Lanois: Achieved a reputation by producing Peter Gabriel, U2, Robbie Robertson and the Neville Brothers before working on Dylan's *Oh Mercy* album in March and April 1989.

John Lennon: Spent some time with Dylan during both of his mid-sixties U.K. tours, as well as during the Beatles' own American tours in 1964 and 1965. He was assassinated in December 1980.

Harold Leventhal: Manager of Woody Guthrie and Pete Seeger, and organizer of the first Guthrie Memorial Concert in January 1968.

Jacques Levy: Dylan's collaborator on the lyrics for the *Desire* album. He also contributed to the genesis and structure of the 1975 Rolling Thunder Revue.

Stan Lynch: Drummer in Tom Petty and the Heartbreakers, with whom he backed Dylan in concert from September 1985 to October 1987.

Jeff Lynne: Cofounder and coproducer of the Traveling Wilburys.

Charlie McCoy: After playing guitar on "Desolation Row" in New York, he worked with Dylan on *Blonde on Blonde, John Wesley Harding, Nashville Skyline* and *Self Portrait,* playing both bass and lead guitar.

Farida McFree: Having been the art teacher for Dylan's children, she had an intense affair with Dylan against the backdrop of his custody battle for the children.

Roger McGuinn: Despite his leadership of seminal folk-rockers the Byrds, he did not record with Dylan until the fall of 1972. Subsequently played on the *Pat Garrett & Billy the Kid* soundtrack album, was a member of the Rolling Thunder Revue in 1975 and 1976, and guested with Dylan in 1980, 1987, and 1990.

Maria McKee: Immensely talented but wayward leader of the now-defunct Lone Justice, with whom she recorded one of Dylan's compositions, donated by the man himself.

Eve MacKenzie: Wife of Mac MacKenzie; they both befriended Dylan on his arrival in New York in 1961 and provided him with an occasional bed when required.

Jim McLean: Folksinger on the London scene in the winter of 1962–63, during which Dylan made the rounds of the London folk clubs.

Bill Marinac: Member of Robert Zimmerman's Hibbing combo, the Shadow Blasters, he also jammed with the young Robert on occasions after the band disbanded.

Bob Markel: Editor at Macmillan who supervised the eventual publication of *Tarantula* in all its stages from 1964 to 1970.

Richard Marquand: Director of *Hearts of Fire*; he died shortly after the film's release in 1987.

Gerard Melanga: Photographer/filmmaker who made a brief celluloid study of Dylan at Andy Warhol's Factory in 1965.

Paul Morrissey: Filmmaker and noted member of Andy Warhol's mid-sixties Factory coterie.

Maria Muldaur: Grew up in Greenwich Village and was a popular figure on the Village scene in the early sixties, when she played in two jug bands and as part of a duo with husband Geoff.

Bobby Neuwirth: First met Dylan at the Indian Neck Festival in May 1961. He subsequently became Dylan's regular sidekick on his mid-sixties tours. They were reunited on the Rolling Thunder Revues of 1975 and 1976.

Jack Nissenson: Early admirer of Dylan who had the foresight to record his performance at the Finjan Club, Montreal, in July 1962.

Phil Ochs: Prolific topical songwriter on the Village scene in 1963–64, he was viewed as a natural heir when Dylan abandoned the genre, but he never achieved any substantial commercial success. He had a falling-out with Dylan in November 1965 but later managed to cajole him into appearing at the Friends of Chile benefit in May 1974. He committed suicide in April 1976.

David Oppenheim: After he had painted the mural used on the back cover of *Blood on the Tracks,* Dylan stayed with him in the south of France for six weeks in spring 1975.

Roy Orbison: Sang on the 1988 Traveling Wilburys album. He died shortly after the album's release in 1989.

Christopher Parker: Drummer in Dylan's touring band from 1988 through 1990.

Don Pennebaker: Director of *Don't Look Back,* the *cinéma vérité* study of Dylan on his 1965 English tour, he was also used by Dylan to shoot footage for a scheduled one-hour documentary on Dylan's 1966 European tour, later shown as "Eat the Document."

Val Petersen: Robert Zimmerman's music teacher at Hibbing High School.

Tom Petty: Leader of the Heartbreakers, with whom he accompanied Dylan at Farm Aid in 1985, on Far East and U.S. tours in 1986 and on a European tour in 1987. In 1988 he cofounded the massively successful Traveling Wilburys.

John Prine: American singer-songwriter whose 1971 debut attracted the "New Dylan" tag, and who in September 1972 had Dylan as a guest at one of his shows in New York.

Charlie Quintana: Los Angeles drummer who originally appeared in Dylan's "Sweetheart Like You" video before jamming with him at his home in Malibu and putting together a band for his appearance on David Letterman's show in March 1984.

Adrian Rawlins: Australian journalist who was temporarily welcomed into Dylan's inner coterie during his April 1966 visit to Australia.

Scarlet Rivera: Previously unknown violinist discovered by Dylan on the streets of Greenwich Village in June 1975; her sound made a significant contribution on the *Desire* album and Rolling Thunder tours of 1975 and 1976.

Robbie Robertson: Played on all but two of Dylan's live performances between Forest Hills in August 1965 and the final show of the 1974 Dylan/Band tour. He also made sterling contributions as a guitarist on *Blonde on Blonde, The Basement Tapes* and *Planet Waves.* They last played together at the Band's Last Waltz farewell concert in November 1976.

Mark Robinson: Director of the promotional video for "Sweetheart Like You."

Mick Ronson: A surprise inclusion as lead guitarist on the Rolling Thunder tours in 1975 and 1976, considering his background as David Bowie's right-hand man and bandleader during the heights of glam rock.

Suze Rotolo: Dylan's steady girlfriend from July 1961 through March 1964. Her six-month sojourn in Italy in 1962 and their eventual break-up in 1964 inspired some of Dylan's most beautiful love songs.

Pete Rowan: Was in attendance at the *Blonde on Blonde* sessions in March 1966. He later founded the band Earth Opera.

Judy Rubin: Early girlfriend of Dylan's (she first met him at summer camp), and later a fellow student at the University of Minnesota.

Pete Seeger: Highly esteemed folksinger who first befriended Dylan in the early months of 1962 and continued to champion him as a songwriter of note until 1965, when Dylan's performance at the Newport Folk Festival annoyed him.

Charlie Sexton: Respected musician in his own right, he recorded a series of demos with Dylan in the fall of 1983.

Robert Shelton: As the folk critic of *The New York Times*, he came across Dylan in the summer of 1961. His glowing review that September gave Dylan his first major break, and they remained in sporadic contact through the years. In 1986 he published his own biography of the man, which concentrated largely on the Greenwich Village years.

Sam Shepard: Playwright commissioned by Dylan to write a screenplay for a film to be shot during the 1975 Rolling Thunder Revue tour. Though the script idea was later dropped, Shepard contributed his ideas and acting to the film *Renaldo and Clara* and documented the tour in his *Rolling Thunder Logbook*. He subsequently collaborated with Dylan on the 1984 song "New Danville Girl" and on a June 1987 feature for *Esquire* magazine.

Slash: Guitarist in the American hard-rock band, Guns 'n' Roses who played guitar on the opening track of Dylan's 1990 album, *Under the Red Sky*.

Larry Sloman: Unofficial chronicler of the 1975 Rolling Thunder Revue, his work was published as the magnificent *On the Road with Bob Dylan*. In 1984 he coproduced the promotional video of Dylan's "Jokerman."

Iain Smith: Line producer of the film *Hearts of Fire*.

Patti Smith: Seventies New York poet and rock and roll star, considered by some a female Dylan, she hung out with Dylan during the summer of 1975 and was invited to join the Rolling Thunder Revue.

Steven Soles: Multifaceted West Coast musician originally recruited for the Rolling Thunder Revues; he subsequently played on the 1978 world tour. A devout Christian, he proved supportive of Dylan's own religious conversion in 1979.

Phil Spector: Notoriously eccentric producer whose only work involving Dylan has been the 1971 Concert for Bangladesh project and Leonard Cohen's 1977 album, *Death of a Ladies' Man*.

Mark Spoelstra: Fellow folksinger and regular sidekick of Dylan's during his early days in Greenwich Village.

Helena Springs: Remained very close to Dylan throughout her time as a backing singer in his touring bands in 1978 and 1979, cowriting several songs with him during their time together.

Bruce Springsteen: Last of the New Dylans, so touted in 1973, he finally met Dylan in 1975, and inducted him into the Rock and Roll Hall of Fame in 1988. They finally played together at a Tom Petty and the Heartbreakers gig in March 1990.

Pete Stampfel: Arrived in Greenwich Village at about the same time as Dylan and after playing around the Village as a solo artist cofounded the Holy Modal Rounders in 1963.

Rob Stoner: Bassist and unofficial bandleader on both Rolling Thunder tours, Stoner was also largely responsible for putting together the 1978 tour band, though he quit after the Far East leg of the world tour.

Greg Sutton: Bassist on the 1984 European tour.

Benmont Tench: Keyboardist in Tom Petty and the Heartbreakers, Tench first worked with Dylan on the 1981 *Shot of Love* album and subsequently on the 1985 sessions for *Empire Burlesque* before touring with him through 1986 and 1987.

Terri Thal: In 1961 was Dylan's part-time manager and enthusiastic supporter, as was her boyfriend (later her husband), Dave Van Ronk.

Happy Traum: Member of the early-sixties Village folk scene. He recorded with Dylan in 1963, 1970 and 1971, and arranged and coconducted the 1968 *Sing Out!* interview.

Bobby Vee: Rock-and-roll singer from Fargo, North Dakota, with whom a young Robert Zimmerman played two shows as pianist before Vee dropped him.

Eric von Schmidt: Cambridge folksinger who first met and befriended Dylan in Boston in June 1961. They renewed their friendship when both were in London in January 1963.

Terri Wallace: Early fan of Dylan in his Minneapolis days; her sister, Karen Moynihan, made the first extant recording of Dylan at her apartment.

Don Was: The coproducer (with his partner, David Was) of Dylan's 1990 album, *Under the Red Sky.*

A. J. Weberman: In the late sixties and early seventies was the self-proclaimed world's leading Dylanologist who, after three years of self-publicity, finally met Dylan in January 1971.

Bob Weir: Guitarist/vocalist in the Grateful Dead.

Eric Weissberg: Banjo player and guitarist who first met Dylan in Madison in January 1961 and later played on the initial New York session for the *Blood on the Tracks* album.

Jerry Wexler: Producer who defined the Atlantic Records sound in the sixties; he co-produced Barry Goldberg's debut album in 1973 with Dylan, and produced Dylan's albums *Slow Train Coming* (1979) and *Saved* (1980).

Dave Whitaker: Dylan's mentor during his Minneapolis days; he helped acquaint Dylan with both traditional music and contemporary literature.

Ron Wood: First worked with Dylan in 1976 on Eric Clapton's *No Reason to Cry* album. They subsequently worked together during the summer of 1984 on the early sessions for the *Empire Burlesque* album; and on the 1986 *Hearts of Fire* recordings. He also guested at Dylan shows in 1985, 1986 and 1987.

Rudy Wurlitzer: Wrote the screenplay for the film *Pat Garrett & Billy the Kid*; his friendship with Dylan was a major factor in Dylan's involvement with the film.

Howie Wyeth: The drummer (and occasional pianist) on both Rolling Thunder tours and the *Desire* album. He rehearsed for, but withdrew before, the 1978 tour.

Peter Yarrow: One third of Albert Grossman's other major act in the early sixties, Peter, Paul and Mary. It was his cabin in Woodstock to which Dylan sometimes retired in 1963 and 1964.

Izzy Young: Owner of the Folklore Center in New York, a regular hangout for all the Village regulars in the early sixties. Young also arranged Dylan's first concert, at Carnegie Recital Hall, in November 1961.

Beattie Zimmerman: Mother of Bob Dylan *né* Robert Allen Zimmerman.

Maurice Zimmerman: Bob Dylan's uncle.

A Selected Bibliography

This is a bibliography of the sources that have been most useful in the composition of this book. For a more complete bibliography readers are referred to my chronology of Dylan's career, *Stolen Moments* (Wanted Man/Music Sales, 1988; a revised edition, *Dylan Day by Day*, is due for publication in December 1991).

Baez, Joan, *And a Voice to Sing With* (Summit Books, 1987).

Balfour, Victoria, *Rock Wives* (Beech Tree, 1986).

Bauldie, John, *The Ghost of Electricity* (privately published).

Bauldie, John, and Gray, Michael (eds.), *All Across the Telegraph* (Sidgwick & Jackson, 1987).

Bauldie, John (ed.), *Wanted Man: In Search of Bob Dylan* (Black Spring Press, 1990).

Cartwright, Bert, *The Bible in the Lyrics of Bob Dylan* (Wanted Man Study Series, 1985).

Cooper, Chris, and Marsh, Keith, *The Circus Is in Town* (privately published).

Davis, Clive, *Clive: Inside the Record Business* (William Morrow, 1974).

Dylan, Bob, *Tarantula* (Macmillan, 1970).

Dylan, Bob, *Lyrics* (Alfred A. Knopf, 1985).

Flannagan, Bill, *Written in My Soul* (Contemporary, 1986).

Fong-Torres, Ben, *Knockin' on Dylan's Door* (Straight Arrow, 1974).

Ginsberg, Allen, *First Blues* (Full Court Press, 1975).

Gross, Michael, *Bob Dylan: An Illustrated History* (Elm Tree, 1978).

Kooper, Al, *Backstage Passes* (Stein & Day, 1971).

Kramer, Daniel, *Bob Dylan* (Castle Books, 1967).

Lawlan and Lawlan, *Steppin' Out* (privately published).

Lindley, John, *Seven Days* (privately published).

Lindsey, Hal, and Carlson, C. C., *The Late Great Planet Earth* (Zondervan, 1970).

McGregor, Craig (ed.), *Bob Dylan: A Retrospective* (William Morrow, 1972). An excellent anthology recently republished as *Early Years: A Retrospective* (DeCapo, 1990).

Miles, Barry, *Ginsberg: A Biography* (Simon and Schuster, 1989).

Scaduto, Anthony, *Bob Dylan* (Grosset & Dunlap, 1971).

Seay, Davin, and Neely, Mary, *Stairway to Heaven* (Ballantine, 1986).

Shelton, Robert, *No Direction Home* (William Morrow, 1986).

Shepard, Sam, *Rolling Thunder Logbook* (Penguin, 1978).

Simmons, Garner, *Peckinpah: A Portrait*

in Montage (University of Texas Press, 1982).

Sloman, Larry, *On the Road with Bob Dylan* (Bantam Books, 1978).

Spitz, Bob, *Dylan: A Biography* (McGraw-Hill, 1989).

Thompson, Toby, *Positively Main Street* (Coward-McCann, 1971).

von Schmidt, Eric, and Rooney, Jim, *Baby, Let Me Follow You Down* (Anchor Books, 1979).

Webster, Patrick, *Friends and Other Strangers* (private publication).

Williams, Paul, *Dylan: What Happened?* (and/Entwistle books, 1980).

Williams, Paul, *What Happened? One Year Later* (Hobo Press, 1981).

Williams, Paul, *Performing Artist* (Underwood-Miller, 1990).

Woliver, Robbie, *Bringing It All Back Home* (Pantheon, 1986).

Worrell, Denise, *Icons* (Atlantic Monthly Press, 1989).

Reference Sources

Bauldie, John (ed.), *Telegraph*, nos. 1–37.

Dundas, Glen, *Tangled Up in Tapes* (privately published, 1990).

Heylin, Clinton, *Stolen Moments* (Wanted Man/Music Sales, 1988).

Krogsgaard, Michael, *Master of the Tracks* (SSRR, 1988).

Interviews with Bob Dylan Used in This Book

Adler, Philippe, *L'Expresse*, July 3, 1978.

Allen, Lynne, *Trouser Press*, June 1979.

Aschenmacher, Bob, *Duluth News-Tribune and Herald*, June 29, 1986.

Austin, John, source unknown.

Baker, Kathryn, *Stars and Stripes*, September 7, 1988.

Burling, Klas, Swedish public radio, April 29, 1966.

Bronstein, Martin, Canadian Broadcasting Company radio, February 20, 1966.

Brown, Bob, "20/20" TV show, October 20, 1985.

Brown, Mick, London *Sunday Times*, July 1, 1984.

Campbell, Mary, *Houston Post*, February 12, 1978.

Chase, Donald, San Francisco *Chronicle*, November 23, 1986.

Coburn, Bob, "Rockline" radio show, June 17, 1985.

Cohen, John, and Traum, Happy, *Sing Out!*, October 1968.

Cohen, Scott, *Spin*, December 1985.

Cohen, Scott, *Interview*, February 1986.

Cott, Jonathan, *Rolling Stone*, January 26, 1978.

Cott, Jonathan, *Rolling Stone*, November 16, 1978.

Crane, Les, transcript of his TV show on February 17, 1965.

Creswell, Toby, *Australian Rolling Stone*, January 16, 1986.

Crowe, Cameron, *Biograph*.

Damsker, Matt, *Circus Weekly*, December 19, 1978.

Deevoy, Adrian, *Q*, December 1989.

De Yong, Jenny, and Roche, Peter, *Darts*, May 1965.

Ephron, Nora, and Susan Edmiston, *Bob Dylan: A Retrospective*, Craig McGregor, editor (see above).

Flannagan, Bill, *Written in My Soul* (see above).

Flippo, Chet, *Rolling Stone*, March 15, 1973.

Fong-Torres, Ben, *Knockin' on Dylan's Door* (see above).

Gilmore, Mikal, *Los Angeles Herald Examiner*, October 13, 1985.

Ginsberg, Allen, *Telegraph* 33.

Gundersen, Edna, *USA Today*, September 21, 1989.

Gundersen, Edna, *USA Today*, September 14, 1990.

Heiman, Bruce, KMGX radio, December 7, 1979.

Hentoff, Nat, the original galleys for the liner notes to *The Freewheelin' Bob Dylan*, galleys published in *Telegraph* #8.

Hentoff, Nat, *The New Yorker*, October 24, 1964.

Hentoff, Nat, his extensive October 1965 *Playboy* interview, published as the booklet *Whaaat!*

Hentoff, Nat, *Playboy*, March 1966.
Herman, Dave, transcript from the *London Interview* promotional album.
Hickey, Neil, *TV Guide*, September 11, 1976.
Hilburn, Robert, *Los Angeles Times*, May 28, 1978.
Hilburn, Robert, *Los Angeles Times*, November 12, 1978.
Hilburn, Robert, *Los Angeles Times*, November 23, 1980.
Hilburn, Robert, *Los Angeles Times*, October 30, 1983.
Hilburn, Robert, *Los Angeles Times*, November 17, 1985.
Hilburn, Robert, *Los Angeles Times*, September 7, 1987.
Hughes, Karen, *Rock Express* 1.
Hughes, Karen, *Dominion*, August 2, 1980.
Iachetta, Michael, New York *Daily News*, May 8, 1967.
James, Billy, transcript of the November 1961 interview.
Jones, Max, *Melody Maker*, May 23, 1964.
Keller, Martin, *New Musical Express*, August 6, 1983.
Kerr, Barbara, *Toronto Sun*, March 26–29, 1978.
Kleinman, Bert, and Mogull, Artie, Westwood One radio broadcast, November 25, 1984.
Loder, Kurt, *Rolling Stone*, June 26, 1984.
Mankiewicz, John, *Sound*, November 12, 1978.
McGregor, Craig, *Sydney Morning Herald*, March 18, 1978.
Meer, Dan, "Close Up" radio show, October 30, 1989.
Merryfield, Mary, *Chicago Tribune*, November 21, 1965.
Oppel, Pete, *Dallas Morning News*, November 18–23, 1978.
Quinn, Martha, MTV, July 7, 1984.
Robbins, Paul J., *Los Angeles Free Press*, September 17 and 24, 1965.
Rockwell, John, *The New York Times*, January 7, 1974.
Rosenbaum, Ron, *Playboy*, January 1978.
Rowland, Marc, U.S. radio, September 23, 1978.
Saal, Hubert, *Newsweek*, April 4, 1969.
Scaduto, Anthony, *Bob Dylan* (see above).

Seeger, Pete, transcript of unbroadcast May 1962 WBAI radio show.
Shelton, Robert, *Melody Maker*, June 24, 1978.
Shepard, Sam, *Esquire*, July 1987.
Siegel, Jules, *Saturday Evening Post*, July 30, 1966.
Sloman, Larry, *On the Road with Bob Dylan* (see above).
Smith, Jack, *National Guardian*, August 22, 1963.
Spencer, Neil, *New Musical Express*, August 15, 1981.
Steen, Margaret, *Toronto Weekly*, January 29, 1966.
Stone, Allen, WDTM radio, October 24, 1965.
Sykes, Christopher, *Getting to Dylan*, September 18, 1987.
Sykes, Christopher, tour program, 1989.
Terkel, Studs, "Wax Museum" radio show, April 26, 1963.
Turner, Gil, *Sing Out!*, October 1962.
Vincent, Paul, *Endless Road* 2.
Vox, Bono, *Hot Press*, August 24, 1984.
Welles, Chris, *Life*, April 10, 1964.
Wenner, Jann, *Rolling Stone*, November 29, 1969.
Worrell, Denise, *Icons* (see above).
Young, Izzy, *Other Scenes*, December 1968.
Yurchenco, Henrietta, *Sound and Fury*, April 1966.
Unknown interviewer for *El Diario Vasco*, June 18, 1989.
Unknown interviewer for *Gargoyle* magazine, February 1964.
Unknown interviewer for the *New York Post*, January 12, 1965.
Unknown interview for *Photoplay*, May 1978.

Transcripts of Dylan Press Conferences Used in This Book

Beverly Hills Hotel press conference, September 4, 1965.
San Francisco press conference, December 3, 1965.
Adelaide press conference, April 21, 1966.
Travemunde press conference, July 13, 1981.
Sydney press conference, February 10, 1986.

A Bob Dylan Sessionography
1961–90

This sessionography aims to detail the products of Dylan's official studio sessions. It is not intended to include his appearances as a guest musician, except when he has been both performer and composer. The resultant official albums and singles are listed (album titles are in italics), followed by known outtakes and alternate takes. Asterisked items are not currently in circulation among the Dylan collecting fraternity. All titles that appear solely in lowercase refer to recordings that have already been listed as part of a prior release (full-fledged official releases are here considered prior to promotional or limited releases). Only those singles that feature previously unavailable material are included in the discography, and all singles are U.S. releases unless so indicated. Compilation albums, which CBS seems inordinately fond of, are also featured only when they contain material new to vinyl.

For a considerably more detailed chronology of Dylan's studio activities readers are referred to my chronology of his career, *Stolen Moments* (Wanted Man/Music Sales, 1988; a revised edition, *Dylan Day by Day*, is due for publication December 1991). Finally, please note there is a degree of speculation involved in the compilation of this discography. Generally reliable it is. Gospel it is not.

1. CBS Studios, New York, November 20 and 22, 1961

Bob Dylan: You're No Good. Talkin' New York. In My Time of Dyin'. Man of Constant Sorrow. Fixin' to Die. Pretty Peggy-O. Highway 51. Gospel Plow. Baby, Let Me Follow You Down. House of the Risin' Sun. Freight Train Blues. Song to Woody. See That My Grave Is Kept Clean.

The Bootleg Series Vols. 1–3:   He Was a Friend of Mine. Man on the Street. House Carpenter.

Outtakes: Connecticut Cowboy (spoken introduction to You're No Good). Ramblin' Blues.*

Note: A mono copy of this album is essential. The acute stereo of the vinyl and CD releases makes them unlistenable.

2. CBS Studios, New York, April 25, July 9, October 26–27, November 13–15 and December 6, 1962, and April 24, 1963

The Freewheelin' Bob Dylan: Blowin' in the Wind. Girl from the North Country. Masters of War. Down the Highway. Bob Dylan's Blues. A Hard Rain's a-Gonna Fall. Don't Think Twice, It's All Right. Bob Dylan's Dream. Oxford Town. Talking World War III Blues. Corrina, Corrina. Honey, Just Allow Me One More Chance. I Shall Be Free.

Single: Mixed Up Confusion/Corrina, Corrina (alternate take).

Biograph: Babe, I'm in the Mood for You. Mixed Up Confusion (alternate take).

The Bootleg Series Vols. 1–3:   Ramblin' Gamblin' Willie. Talkin' Hava Negeilah Blues. Worried Blues. Talkin' Bear Mountain Picnic Massacre Blues. Let Me Die in My Footsteps. Quit Your Lowdown Ways. Kingsport Town.

The Freewheelin' Bob Dylan, earlier version: Talkin' John Birch Society Blues. Rocks and Gravel. Let Me Die in My Footsteps. Ramblin' Gamblin' Willie.

Outtakes: Baby, Please Don't Go. Milk Cow Blues (two takes). Wichita Blues (two takes). The Death of Emmett Till. Babe, I'm in the Mood for You. Corrina, Corrina (acoustic). Rocks and Gravel (acoustic). Going to New Orleans. Sally Gal. That's All Right, Mama (two takes). Mixed Up Confusion (two takes). Whatcha Gonna Do? Ballad of Hollis Brown. Hero Blues.* (I Heard That) Lonesome Whistle.

Note: The earlier version of **Freewheelin'** is extremely rare and much in demand. Again, a mono vinyl copy is preferable to the stereo version.

3. "The Broadside Sessions," Sis Cunningham's Apartment, New York, November 1962; January 19 and 24, 1963; February and March 1963

Broadside Ballads Vol. 1:   Talkin' Devil. Only a Hobo. John Brown. Let Me Die in My Footsteps.†

Broadside Reunion: I'd Hate to Be You on That Dreadful Day. Train a-Travelin'.

Outtakes: Oxford Town. Paths of Victory. Walkin' Down the Line. Playboys and Playgirls. Farewell. Masters of War. I Shall Be Free. Cuban Missile Crisis.

---

†Happy Traum on vocals, Dylan on harmonica.

4.   "The Witmark Demos," New York, June, November and
     December 1962; March, April, May, August, September and
     December 1963; January and June 1964

The Bootleg Series Vols. 1–3:   Walkin' Down the Line. When the Ship Comes In. The
Times They Are a-Changin'.

Warner Bros. demo album: Long Ago, Far Away. The Death of Emmett Till. Babe, I'm
in the Mood for You. I'd Hate to Be You on That Dreadful Day. I Shall Be Free. Ain't
Gonna Grieve. Only a Hobo. John Brown. I'll Keep It with Mine.

Outtakes: Blowin' in the Wind. Tomorrow Is a Long Time. Guess I'm Doing Fine.
Ballad of Hollis Brown. A Hard Rain's a-Gonna Fall. Let Me Die in My Footsteps. Quit
Your Lowdown Ways. Long Time Gone. Don't Think Twice, It's All Right. Oxford Town.
Masters of War. Talkin' John Birch Paranoid Blues. All Over You. Bound to Lose, Bound
to Win. Bob Dylan's Dream. Bob Dylan's Blues. Boots of Spanish Leather. Girl from the
North Country. Seven Curses. Hero Blues. Gypsy Lou. Whatcha Gonna Do? Paths of
Victory. Baby, Let Me Follow You Down. Mr. Tambourine Man. Mama, You Bin on My
Mind. Farewell.

5.   CBS Studios, New York, August 6, 7, and 12 and October 23, 24,
     and 31, 1963.

The Times They Are a-Changin':   The Times They Are a-Changin'. Ballad of Hollis
Brown. With God on Our Side. One Too Many Mornings. North Country Blues. Only a
Pawn in Their Game. Boots of Spanish Leather. When the Ship Comes In. The Lonesome
Death of Hattie Carroll. Restless Farewell.

Biograph: Percy's Song. Lay Down Your Weary Tune.

The Bootleg Series Vols. 1–3:   Suzy. Kentucky Moonshiner. Only a Hobo. Seven
Curses. Eternal Circle. Walls of Redwing. Paths of Victory.

Outtakes: Percy's Song. Hero Blues. California. Eternal Circle.

Note: Again a mono vinyl copy is preferable to the stereo LP. Suzy is also known by the
titles Mexican Rag and The Cough Song.

6.   CBS Studios, New York, June 9, 1964.

Another Side of Bob Dylan: All I Really Want To Do. Black Crow Blues. Spanish
Harlem Incident. Chimes of Freedom. I Shall Be Free No. 10. To Ramona. Motorpsycho
Nitemare. My Back Pages. I Don't Believe You. Ballad in Plain D. It Ain't Me, Babe.

The Bootleg Series Vols. 1–3:   Mama, You Bin on My Mind.

Outtakes: Denise Denise. Farewell. East Laredo Blues. Bob Dylan's New Orleans Rag.
That's All Right, Mama. Sally Free and Easy. Mr. Tambourine Man.*

Note: Again a mono vinyl copy is preferable to the stereo CD.

7. CBS Studios, New York, January 14–15, 1965.

Bringing It All Back Home: Subterranean Homesick Blues. She Belongs to Me. Maggie's Farm. Love Minus Zero/No Limit. Outlaw Blues. On the Road Again. Bob Dylan's 115th Dream. Mr. Tambourine Man. Gates of Eden. It's Alright, Ma (I'm Only Bleeding). It's All Over Now, Baby Blue.

Single: If You Gotta Go, Go Now/To Ramona (CBS Benelux)

Biograph: I'll Keep It with Mine.

The Bootleg Series Vols. 1–3: If You Gotta Go, Go Now. Subterranean Homesick Blues (acoustic). Farewell Angelina.

Outtakes: She Belongs to Me. Love Minus Zero/No Limit. I'll Keep It with Mine (instrumental). Mr. Tambourine Man.* It's All Over Now, Baby Blue.

8. CBS Studios, New York, June 15 and 16, July 29 and 30 and August 2 and 4, 1965

Highway 61 Revisited: Like a Rolling Stone. Tombstome Blues. It Takes a Lot to Laugh, It Takes a Train to Cry. From a Buick 6. Ballad of a Thin Man. Queen Jane Approximately. Highway 61 Revisited. Just Like Tom Thumb's Blues. Desolation Row.

Highway 61 Revisited, earlier version: From a Buick 6 (alternate take).

Singles: Can You Please Crawl Out Your Window?/From a Buick 6. Positively 4th Street/From a Buick 6.

Biograph: Jet Pilot. Positively 4th Street.

The Bootleg Series Vols. 1–3: Sitting on a Barbed Wire Fence. It Takes a Lot to Laugh, It Takes a Train to Cry. Like a Rolling Stone.

Outtakes: Can You Please Crawl Out Your Window? Sitting on a Barbed Wire Fence. Phantom Engineer. Desolation Row (with bass and electric guitar). Highway 61 Revisited.* Tombstone Blues.* Positively 4th Street.*

Note: Some early copies of the Positively 4th Street single were mispressings that featured the *Highway 61* outtake of Can You Please Crawl Out Your Window? Likewise, some early copies of the album featured the first take of From a Buick 6 rather than the superior take found on all subsequent pressings. Phantom Engineer is the fast version of It Takes a Lot to Laugh, It Takes a Train to Cry.

9. CBS Studios, New York, October 20, 1965, and January 21, 24 and 25, 1966; Sunset Studios, Los Angeles, November 30 and December 1, 1965; CBS Studios, Nashville, February 14–17 and March 8–9, 1966.

Blonde on Blonde: Rainy Day Women #12 & 35. Pledging My Time. Visions of Johanna. One of Us Know (Sooner or Later). I Want You. Stuck Inside of Mobile with the Memphis Blues Again. Leopard-skin Pill-box Hat. Just Like a Woman. Most Likely You Go Your Way and I'll Go Mine. Temporary Like Achilles. Absolutely Sweet Marie. 4th Time Around. Obviously 5 Believers. Sad Eyed Lady of the Lowlands.

Single: Can You Please Crawl Out Your Window?/Highway 61 Revisited.

Biograph: I Wanna Be Your Lover. Can You Please Crawl Out Your Window?

The Bootleg Series Vols. 1–3: Medicine Sunday. She's Your Lover Now. I'll Keep It with Mine.

Outtakes: Freeze Out (two takes). I Wanna Be Your Lover. Can You Please Crawl Out Your Window? Number One. Leopard-skin Pill-box Hat. She's Your Lover Now.

Note: Freeze Out was retitled Visions of Johanna after the two unreleased versions were recorded. An original stereo vinyl copy (preferably the Japanese edition, which remains in print) is aurally superior to the CD.

10. "Big Pink," West Saugerties, New York, June–October 1967

The Basement Tapes: Odds and Ends. Million Dollar Bash. Goin' to Acapulco. Lo and Behold! Clothes Line Saga. Apple Suckling Tree. Please, Mrs. Henry. Tears of Rage. Too Much of Nothing. Yea! Heavy and a Bottle of Bread. Crash on the Levee (Down in the Flood). Tiny Montgomery. You Ain't Goin' Nowhere. Nothing Was Delivered. Open the Door, Homer. This Wheel's on Fire.

Biograph: The Mighty Quinn (Quinn the Eskimo).

The Bootleg Series Vols. 1–3: Santa Fe. *dwarf music acetate:* I Shall Be Released. Too Much of Nothing (alternate take). Tears of Rage (alternate take). The Mighty Quinn (Quinn the Eskimo).

Outtakes: Apple Suckling Tree. I'm Not There (1956). Get Your Rocks Off. Tears of Rage. The Mighty Quinn (Quinn the Eskimo). Open the Door, Homer (two takes). Nothing Was Delivered. Sign on the Cross. Lock Your Door. Baby, Won't You Be My Baby. Try Me, Little Girl. I Can't Make It Alone. Don't You Try Me Now. Young but Daily Growin'. Bonnie Ship the Diamond. The Hills of Mexico. Down on Me. One for the Road. I'm Alright. One Single River. People Get Ready. I Don't Hurt Anymore. (Be Careful of the) Stones That You Throw. One Man's Loss. All You Have to Do Is Dream (two takes). Baby Ain't That Fine. Rock Salt and Nails. A Fool Such as I. Gonna Get You Now. Bourbon Street.* Wild Wolf.* All American Boy.* Silent Weekend.*

Note: The original music publisher's acetate of these demos featured two songs omitted from the official album, as well as two alternate takes of songs featured on the album. The official album has been mixed into mono from the original stereo tapes.

11. CBS Studios, Nashville, October 17 and November 6 and 29, 1967.

John Wesley Harding: John Wesley Harding. As I Went Out One Morning. I Dreamed I Saw St. Augustine. All Along the Watchtower. The Ballad of Frankie Lee and Judas Priest. Drifter's Escape. Dear Landlord. I Am a Lonesome Hobo. I Pity the Poor Immigrant. The Wicked Messenger. Down Along the Cover. I'll Be Your Baby Tonight.

12. CBS Studios, Nashville, February 13, 14 and 17, 1969

Nashville Skyline: Girl from the North Country (with Johnny Cash). Nashville Skyline Rag. To Be Alone with You. I Threw It All Away. Peggy Day. Lay Lady Lay. One More Night. Tell Me That It Isn't True. Country Pie. Tonight I'll Be Staying Here with You.

Outtake: One Too Many Mornings (with Johnny Cash).

13.   CBS Studios, Nashville, February 18, 1969, with Johnny Cash

The Dylan/Cash Album (unreleased);   One Too Many Mornings. Good Ol' Mountain Dew. I Still Miss Someone. Careless Love. Matchbox. That's All Right, Mama. Big River. I Walk the Line. You Are My Sunshine. Guess Things Happen That Way. Just a Closer Walk with Thee. Blues Yodel #1. Blues Yodel #5. Ring of Fire. Understand Your Man.* Wanted Man.*

14.   CBS Studios, Nashville, May 1969, and CBS Studios, New York, February to March 3, 1970

Self Portrait: All the Tired Horses. Alberta #1. I Forgot More Than You'll Ever Know. Days of 49. Early Mornin' Rain. In Search of Little Sadie. Let It Be Me. Little Sadie. Woogie Boogie. Belle Isle. Living the Blues. Copper Kettle. Gotta Travel On. Blue Moon. The Boxer. Take Me as I Am (or Let Me Go). Take a Message to Mary. It Hurts Me Too. Wigwam. Alberta #2.

Dylan: Lily of the West. Sarah Jane. A Fool Such as I. Spanish Is the Loving Tongue.

New Morning: Went to See the Gypsy.

Outtakes: Folsom Prison Blues. Ring of Fire. Thirsty Boots.* Pretty Sara.* Sittin' on the Dock of the Bay.* Universal Soldier.* (When a Man's) Out of a Job).* These Working Hands.* Spanish Eyes.*

Note: *Self Portrait* also features four songs from Dylan's appearance at the Isle of Wight festival on August 31, 1969.

15.   CBS Studios, New York, May 1, June and August 1970

New Morning: If Not for You. Day of the Locusts. Time Passes Slowly. Winterlude. If Dogs Run Free. New Morning. Sign on the Window. One More Weekend. The Man in Me. Three Angels. Father of Night.

Single: Watching the River Flow/Spanish Is the Loving Tongue.

Dylan: Can't Help Falling in Love. Mr. Bojangles. Mary Ann. Big Yellow Taxi.

The Bootleg Series Vols. 1–3:   If Not For You.

Outtakes: Song to Woody. Mama, You Bin on My Mind. Don't Think Twice, It's All Right. Yesterday. Just Like Tom Thumb's Blues. Da Doo Ron Ron. One Too Many Mornings. Working on the Guru. Jamaica Farewell.* Alligator Man.* Running.* Tomorrow Is a Long Time.* Went to See the Gypsy.*

16.   Blue Rock Studios, New York, March 16–18, 1971

Single: Watching the River Flow/Spanish Is the Loving Tongue.

Bob Dylan's Greatest Hits, Vol. II: When I Paint My Masterpiece. Watching the River Flow.

Outtakes: Spanish Harlem.* That Lucky Ol' Sun.* Alabama Bound.* Blood Red River.* Rock of Ages.*

17. CBS Studios, New York, October 1971, with Happy Traum

Bob Dylan's Greatest Hits, Vol. II: You Ain't Goin' Nowhere. I Shall Be Released. Down in the Flood.

Outtakes: You Ain't Goin' Nowhere. Only a Hobo.*

18. Blue Rock Studios, New York, November 4, 1971

Single: George Jackson (big band version)/George Jackson (solo).

The Bootleg Series Vols. 1–3: Wallflower.

Outtakes: Donald and Lydia.*

19. The Record Plant, New York, November 17 and 20, 1971, with Allen Ginsberg

First Blues: Vomit Express. Going to San Diego. September on Jessore Road.

Disconnected: Jimmy Berman.

Outtakes: Om My Soul Shalom. Nurse's Song. Many Loves. Rashupate Rayham. Spring.* A Dream.*

20. Atlantic Recording Studios, New York, October 1972, with Doug Sahm

Doug Sahm and Band: Wallflower.

Outtakes: Just Like Tom Thumb's Blues.*

21. CBS Discos Studios, Mexico City, January 20, 1973, and Burbank Studios, Burbank, California, February 1973.

Pat Garrett & Billy the Kid: Main Title Theme (Billy). Cantina Theme (Workin' for the Law). Billy 1. Bunkhouse Theme. River Theme. Turkey Chase. Knockin' on Heaven's Door. Final Theme. Billy 4. Billy 7.

Film sound-track takes: Billy Surrenders. Knockin' on Heaven's Door. Final Theme. Cantina Theme. Billy. Billy.†

Outtakes: Billy (instrumental). Billy (four takes). Under Turkey (two takes). Billy Surrenders. And He Killed Me Too (two takes). Goodbye Holly. Peco's Blues (two takes). Knockin' on Heaven's Door.* Knockin' on Heaven's Door (instrumental).* Final Theme.* Billy 7 (two takes).* Rock Me Mama.* Amarillo.* Billy Ride.*

Note: The takes used for the film do not correspond to the takes used for the album in most cases. Alternate takes are indicated accordingly.

22. Ram's Horn Offices, June 1973

Biograph: Forever Young.

Outtakes: Nobody 'Cept You.* Never Say Goodbye.*

---

†A "new" version of Billy concludes the recut version of the film released in 1988.

23. Village Recorder Studios, Los Angeles, November 2, 5, 6, 9 and 10, 1973

Planet Waves: On a Night Like This. Going, Going, Gone. Tough Mama. Hazel. Something There Is About You. Forever Young (two versions). Dirge. You Angel You. Never Say Goodbye. Wedding Song.

The Bootleg Series Vols. 1–3: Nobody 'Cept You.

Outtakes: Forever Young (two takes).* Crosswind Jamboree (instrumental).* Dirge.*

24. CBS Studios, New York, September 16, 17 and 23–25, 1974; Sound 80 Studios, Minneapolis, December 27 and 30, 1974

Blood on the Tracks: Tangled Up in Blue. Simple Twist of Fate. You're a Big Girl Now. Idiot Wind. Meet Me in the Morning. Lily, Rosemary and the Jack of Hearts. If You See Her, Say Hello. Shelter from the Storm. Buckets of Rain.

Biograph: You're a Big Girl Now. Up to Me.

The Bootleg Series Vols. 1–3: If You See Her, Say Hello. Idiot Wind. Tangled Up in Blue. You're Gonna Make Me Lonesome When You Go. Call Letter Blues.

Blood on the Tracks, **earlier version:** Tangled Up in Blue. Idiot Wind. Lily, Rosemary and the Jack of Hearts. If You See Her, Say Hello.

Outtake: Meet Me in the Morning (Minneapolis version).* You're Gonna Make Me Lonesome When You Go.*

Note: Test pressings were made (and circulated) of the original version of *Blood on the Tracks,* which was entirely derived from the New York sessions. Dylan then decided to rerecord six of the songs in Minneapolis. The bulk of the alternate versions from the earlier version of the album have now been included on *Biograph* and *The Bootleg Series.*

25. CBS Studios, New York, July 28–31 and October 24, 1975

Desire: Hurricane. Isis. Mozambique. One More Cup of Coffee. Oh, Sister. Joey. Romance in Durango. Black Diamond Bay. Sara.

Single: Stuck Inside of Mobile with the Memphis Blues Again/Rita Mae.

Biograph: Abandoned Love.

The Bootleg Series Vols. 1–3: Catfish. Golden Loom.

Outtakes: Hurricane.* Isis.* Mozambique.* One More Cup of Coffee.* Oh, Sister.* Joey.* Black Diamond Bay.* Wiretappin'.* Money Blues.* (All the preceding songs are big band versions from July 28 and 29, 1975.) Hurricane. Jimmy Brown the Newsboy.* Sitting on Top of the World.* That's All Right, Mama.* Ride 'Em, Jewboy.* I'm Dreaming Tonight of Blue Eyes.* I Still Miss Someone.* Simple Twist of Fate.*

Note: Prior to the formal sessions for *Desire* there was also apparently a session with the Dave Mason Band, at which four songs were recorded.

26. Studio Instrument Rentals Studio and Secret Sound Studio, New York, October 1975

Four Songs from **Renaldo and Clara***:*   People Get Ready.

Songs for the New Depression: Buckets of Rain (with Bette Midler).

Outtakes: Buckets of Rain (with Bette Midler).

27. Shangri-La Studios, Malibu, March 1976, with Eric Clapton

No Reason to Cry: Sign Language.

28. Rundown Studios, Santa Monica, April 1978.

Street-Legal: Changing of the Guards. New Pony. No Time to Think. Baby, Stop Crying. Is Your Love in Vain? Señor (Tales of Yankee Power). True Love Tends to Forget. We Better Talk This Over. Where Are You Tonight? (Journey Through Dark Heat).

Outtake: New Pony (unedited version).*

29. Muscle Shoals Sound Studio, Sheffield, Alabama, May 1–11, 1979

Slow Train Coming: Gotta Serve Somebody. Precious Angel. I Believe in You. Slow Train. Gonna Change My Way of Thinking. Do Right to Me, Baby (Do unto Others). When You Gonna Wake Up. Man Gave Names to All the Animals. When He Returns.

Single: Gotta Serve Somebody/Trouble in Mind.

The Bootleg Series Vols. 1–3:   Ye Shall Be Changed.

Outtakes: When He Returns.* Trouble in Mind (unedited version). No Man Righteous (No Not One).*

30. Muscle Shoals Sound Studio, Sheffield, Alabama, February 15–19, 1980.

Saved: A Satisfied Mind. Saved. Covenant Woman. What Can I Do For You? Solid Rock. Pressing On. In the Garden. Saving Grace. Are You Ready?

Outtakes: Covenant Woman.* Saved.*

31. Home-Studio Demo, Laredo, Minnesota, Summer 1980

The Bootleg Series Vols. 1–3:   Every Grain of Sand.

32.   Clover Recorders Studio and Peacock Studios, Los Angeles, April 7–May 11, 1981

Shot of Love: Shot of Love. Heart of Mine. Property of Jesus. Lenny Bruce. Watered-Down Love. Dead Man, Dead Man. In the Summertime. Trouble. Every Grain of Sand.

Singles: Heart of Mine/The Groom's Still Waiting at the Altar. Heart of Mine/Let It Be Me (U.K.).

Biograph: Caribbean Wind. The Groom's Still Waiting at the Altar.

The Bootleg Series Vols. 1–3:   Angelina. Need a Woman. You Changed My Life.

Outtakes: Heart of Mine. Watered-Down Love (unedited version). Mystery Train. Fur Slippers.* Don't Ever Take Yourself Away.*

Note: The Nice Price reissue of *Shot of Love* and the subsequent CD release include The Groom's Still Waiting at the Altar as track number six.

33.   Power Station Studios, New York, April 11–May 8, 1983

Infidels: Jokerman. Sweetheart Like You. Neighborhood Bully. License to Kill. Man of Peace. Union Sundown. I and I. Don't Fall Apart on Me Tonight.

Single: Union Sundown/Angel Flying Too Close to the Ground.

Down in the Groove: Death Is Not the End.

The Bootleg Series Vols. 1–3:   Blind Willie McTell. Foot of Pride. Someone's Got a Hold of My Heart. Tell Me. Lord Protect My Child.

Outtakes: Jokerman. Sweetheart Like You (multiple takes). Don't Fall Apart on Me Tonight. Blind Willie McTell (full band version). Foot of Pride.* Someone's Got a Hold of My Heart. Clean Cut Kid. Julius and Ethel. This Was My Love. Green, Green Grass of Home.* Sultans of Swing.*

34.   Delta Studios, New York, July 1984; Power Station Studios and Intergalactic Studios, New York, August 1984; Cherokee Studios, Los Angeles, November 1984–January 1985; Power Station Studios, New York, February–March 1985

Empire Burlesque: Tight Connection to My Heart (Has Anybody Seen My Love) Seeing the Real You at Last. I'll Remember You. Clean Cut Kid. Never Gonna Be the Same Again. Trust Yourself. Emotionally Yours. When the Night Comes Falling from the Sky. Something's Burning, Baby. Dark Eyes.

Knocked Out Loaded: Driftin' Too Far from Shore. Maybe Someday. Brownsville Girl. (Backing tracks only.)

The Bootleg Series Vols. 1–3:   When the Night Comes Falling from the Sky.

Outtakes: Wolf. Who Loves You More. Groovin' at Delta. Straight A's in Love. Clean Cut Kid. The Very Thought of You. Driftin' Too Far from Shore. Go 'Way Little Boy. New Danville Girl. Something's Burning, Baby. Seeing the Real You at Last (unedited version). Waiting to Get Beat. Honey, Wait. Mountain of Love.*

Note   The backing tracks for three songs on *Knocked Out Loaded* originate from these sessions.

35.   Church Studios, London, November 19–22, 1985; Skyline Studios, Topanga Canyon, California, April and May 1986; Sound City Studios, Van Nuys, California, May 1986

Knocked Out Loaded: You Wanna Ramble. They Killed Him. Driftin' Too Far from Shore (overdubs). Precious Memories. Maybe Someday (overdubs). Brownsville Girl (overdubs). Got My Mind Made Up. Under Your Spell.

Outtakes: London Instrumental. Come Rain or Come Shine.*

Note: The three songs from the *Empire Burlesque* sessions feature new Dylan vocals, backing vocals and some instrumentals overdubs.

36.   Festival Recording Studio, Sydney, Australia, February 8–9, 1986

Single: Band of the Hand (It's Helltime Man)/non-Dylan B side.

37.   Townhouse Studio, London, August 27–28, 1986

Hearts of Fire: The Usual. Had a Dream About You, Baby. Night after Night.

Down in the Groove: Had a Dream About You, Baby (alternate mix).

Film sound-track takes: The Usual. Had a Dream About You, Baby. Couple More Years.

38.   Sunset Sound Studios, Los Angeles, April 24–May 1987

Down in the Groove: Let's Stick Together. When Did You Leave Heaven? Sally Sue Brown. Ugliest Girl in the World. Silvio. Ninety Miles an Hour (Down a Dead End Street). Shenandoah. Rank Strangers to Me.

Down in the Groove, **earlier version:**   Got Love If You Want It. The Usual.

Outtake: Important Words.

Note: The earlier version of *Down in the Groove* was mistakenly released in Argentina and features the two songs listed above instead of Had a Dream About You, Baby and Death Is Not the End.

39.   Garage Studio, Malibu, early April and May 7–16, 1988, with the Traveling Wilburys

Volume One: Dirty World. Congratulations. Margarita. Tweeter and the Monkey Man.

Working takes: Congratulations. Dirty World.

Note: Only songs featuring lead vocals by Dylan are cited here. The working takes, which appear on a bootleg album entitled *Volume II*, are very close to the finished version used on the album.

40.   Studio on the Move, New Orleans, March–April 1989

Oh Mercy: Political World. Where Teardrops Fall. Everything Is Broken. Ring Them Bells. Man in the Long Black Coat. Most of the Time. What Good Am I? Disease of Conceit. What Was It You Wanted. Shooting Star.

The Bootleg Series Vols. 1–3:   Series of Dreams.

Outtake: God Knows.*

41.   Bellmont Mall Studio, Brown County, Indiana, November 20, 1989

Flashback—The Soundtrack: People Get Ready.

42.   Culver City, Oceanway, Record Plant and the Complex, Los Angeles, and Sorcerer Sound, New York, January 6 and March 1990

Under the Red Sky: Wiggle Wiggle. Under the Red Sky. Unbelievable. Born in Time. T.V. Talkin' Song. 10,000 Men. 2 × 2. God Knows. Handy Dandy. Cat's in the Well.

Most of the Time CD: Most of the Time (video).

Outtake: Some Enchanted Evening (with NRBQ).*

Note: The promotional CD for the Most of the Time video features the March 1990 version of the song, recorded with the *Under the Red Sky* musicians.

43.   Mobile Studio, Los Angeles, April 1990, and Friar Park, Henley-on-Thames, England, July 1990, with the Traveling Wilburys

Vol. 3:   She's My Baby. Inside Out. If You Belonged to Me. The Devil's Been Busy. Seven Deadly Sins. Where Were You Last Night? New Blue Moon. Wilbury Twist.

Single: Nobody's Child/non-Wilburys B side.

Working takes: If You Belonged to Me. She's My Baby (complete Dylan vocal). The Devil's Been Busy. Inside Out. Where Were You Last Night? Seven Deadly Sins.* New Blue Moon.* Wilbury Twist.*

Note: Only songs featuring lead vocals by Dylan are cited here. The working takes are close to the finished versions used on the album.

INDEX